Paris

THE ROUGH GUIDE

There are over sixty Rough Guide titles covering
destinations from Amsterdam to Zimbabwe & Botswana

Forthcoming titles include
Goa • Hawaii • London • Moscow • Romania • Singapore

Rough Guide Reference Series
Classical Music • World Music

Rough Guide Phrasebooks
Czech • French • German • Greek • Italian • Spanish

Rough Guide Credits

Text Editor:	Graham Parker
Series Editor:	Mark Ellingham
Editorial:	Martin Dunford, Jonathan Buckley, Jules Brown, Samantha Cook, Jo Mead, Alison Cowan, Amanda Tomlin
Production:	Susanne Hillen, Andy Hilliard, Melissa Flack, Alan Spicer, Judy Pang, Link Hall, Nicola Williamson
Finance:	John Fisher, Celia Crowley, Simon Carloss
Publicity:	Richard Trillo (UK), Jean-Marie Kelly (US)
Administration:	Tania Hummel

Acknowledgements

We'd like to thank all the readers who have helped us revise and update the guide by sending information, comments and criticisms: Sophie Aldred, Eilis Boland, Harry and Jo Bond, Marie-Christine Bourgeois, S. Bradburry, Tim Burford, Simon Carter and Dawn Judge, Kristi Chavane de Dalmassy, Tony Clarke, Bob Dellavalle, Juliet Donnelly, Jim Dominy, M.F. du Bois, Pascal Fautrat, Robin Futoran, Charlie Gibbs, Kay Hatfield, C. Hutt, Simon Jones, Richard Keen, Jane Kingsbury, David Lacaillade, Sarah Lamb, Victoria Lee, Michel Mendjel, Allan Morris, Hannah Murdoch, David Parkin, Mike and Monica Pennington, Amy Purdom, Chris Relton, Oliver Rowe, Greg Sandell, Jennifer Sanderson, Jonathan Sheldrake, James A. Sinclair, Paul Stainforth, A.M. Teasdale, Valerie Vastine Orbell, Roland White, Mrs J. Whitlow, Claire Williams, Ken Williamson, Jean Williamson, Stephen Wilson, Vicky Wright.

Many thanks also to Oristelle Bonis, Hélène Rouch, José Lavezzi, Sina, Jacqueline Alencourt, Peter Polish, Ozi Osmond, Claudiu and Isabel Lavezzi, Beth Preston and Jo Wallis for helping research this edition; and to Mike Power for permission to reprint extracts from the Richard Rogers interview in *New Times*, and Andy Morgan for music shop research from *Folk Roots* magazine.

The publishers and authors have done their best to ensure the accuracy and currency of all information in *The Rough Guide to Paris*; however, they can accept no responsibility for any loss, injury, or inconvenience sustained by any traveller as a result of information or advice contained in the guide.

This edition published in 1995 by Rough Guides Ltd, 1 Mercer Street, London WC2H 9QJ.

Distributed by the Penguin Group:

Penguin Books Ltd, 27 Wrights Lane, London W8 5TZ.

Penguin Books USA Inc, 375 Hudson Street, New York 10014, USA.

Penguin Books Australia Ltd, 487 Maroondah Highway, PO Box 257, Ringwood, Victoria 3134, Australia.

Penguin Books Canada Ltd, 10 Alcorn Avenue, Toronto, Ontario, Canada M4V 1E4.

Penguin Books (NZ) Ltd, 182–190 Wairau Road, Auckland 10, New Zealand.

Previous editions published in the US and Canada as *The Real Guide Paris*.

Printed in the United Kingdom by Cox & Wyman Ltd (Reading).

Typography and **original design** by Jonathan Dear and The Crowd Roars.

Illustrations throughout by Edward Briant.

British Library Cataloguing in Publication Data

A catalogue record for this book is available from the British Library.

ISBN 1-85828-125-3

Paris

THE ROUGH GUIDE

Written and researched by
Kate Baillie and Tim Salmon

With additional research by
Sharon Clay

THE ROUGH GUIDES

The Contents

List of Maps

Help Us Update

We've gone to a lot of effort to ensure that this new edition of *The Rough Guide to Paris* is up-to-date and accurate. However, Paris information changes fast: new bars and clubs appear and disappear, museums alter their displays and opening hours, restaurants and hotels change prices and standards. If you feel there are places we've under-praised or overrated, omitted or ought to omit, please let us know. All suggestions, comments or corrections are much appreciated and we'll send a copy of the next edition (or any other Rough Guide if you prefer) for the best letters.

Please mark letters "Rough Guide Paris Update" and send to:

The Rough Guides, 1 Mercer Street, London WC2H 9QJ, or

The Rough Guides, 375 Hudson Street, 4th Floor, New York NY 10014.

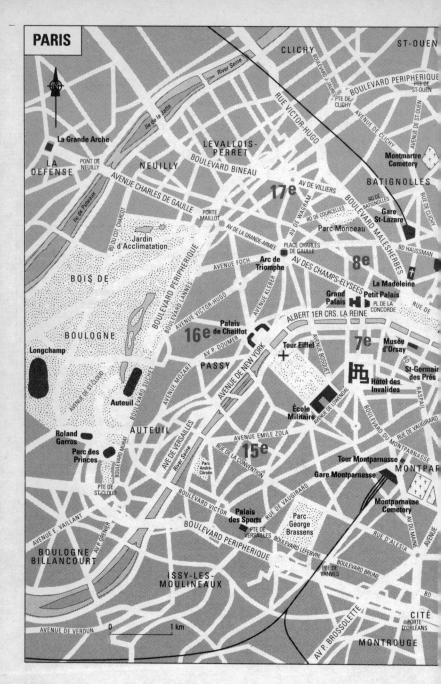

PARIS

CLICHY · ST-OUEN

River Seine

BOULEVARD PERIPHERIQUE · PTE DE ST-OUEN

PTE DE CLICHY

La Grande Arche

LEVALLOIS-PERRET

Montmartre Cemetery

BATIGNOLLES

LA DEFENSE · PONT DE NEUILLY · NEUILLY · BOULEVARD BINEAU

AVENUE CHARLES DE GAULLE

AV DE VILLIERS

17e

BD DE COURCELLES

BD DE BATIGNOLLES

Gare St-Lazare

RUE DE CLICHY

PORTE MAILLOT

AV DE WAGRAM

Parc Monceau

BD HAUSSMAN

Jardin d'Acclimatation

AV DE LA GRANDE-ARMEE

PLACE CHARLES DE GAULLE

8e

La Madeleine

BOULEVARD MALESHERBES

BOIS DE

AVENUE FOCH · Arc de Triomphe

AV DES CHAMPS-ELYSEES

Grand Palais · Petit Palais

PL DE LA CONCORDE

RUE DE

BOULEVARD PERIPHERIQUE · BOULEVARD LANNES · BOULEVARD SUCHET

AVENUE VICTOR-HUGO

ALBERT 1ER CRS. LA REINE

BOULOGNE

Palais de Chaillot

16e

AV P. DOUMER

Tour Eiffel

Musée d'Orsay

7e

Longchamp

AVENUE MOZART

PASSY

AVENUE DE NEW YORK

AVENUE BOSQUET

St-Germain des Prés

Hôtel des Invalides

RASPAIL

Auteuil

AVENUE DE ST-CLOUD

École Militaire

AVENUE DE LOWENDAL

AUTEUIL

AVENUE EMILE ZOLA

RUE DE VAUGIRARD

BOULEVARD DU MONTPARNASSE

Roland Garros

Parc des Princes

BOULEVARD MURAT

River Seine

RUE DE LA CONVENTION

15e

Tour Montparnasse

Gare Montparnasse

MONTPAR

PTE DE ST-CLOUD

AVE DE VERSAILLES

Parc André-Citroën

Montparnasse Cemetery

AVENUE E. VAILLANT

BOULEVARD VICTOR

Palais des Sports

RUE DE VAUGIRARD

Parc George Brassens

RUE D'ALESIA

AV DU MAINE

AV P. GRENIER

PTE DE VERSAILLES

BOULEVARD LEFEBVRE

AVENUE

BOULOGNE BILLANCOURT

BOULEVARD PERIPHERIQUE

BOULEVARD BRUNE

BD

ISSY-LES-MOULINEAUX

PTE DE VANVES

CITÉ PORTE D'ORLÉANS

AVENUE DE VERDUN

0 ___ 1 km

AV P. BROSSOLETTE

MONTROUGE

Introduction

Romantic . . . glamorous . . . innovative . . . when it comes to summing up Paris, there is no escaping the clichés. More dreamy-eyed, wistful songs have been penned over the years about France's capital than anywhere else on the globe, and it's little wonder: what city experiences could be more seductive than sitting in the gardens of Notre-Dame beneath the drifting cherry blossom, strolling the riverside *quais* on a summer evening as dusk thickens under the lime trees, sipping coffee and cognac in the early hours while someone plays the blues, or exploring the ancient narrow lanes and cobbled alleyways of the Latin Quarter or Montmartre? Paris seems to have no problem living up to its postcard images and movie myths.

Nor does it falter on its reputation as a great creative hive of intellectual and artistic stimulation. The new national library – open to all – sums up a cultural attitude that both proclaims Parisian self-confessed cleverness and invites you to share in it. And it is only the latest in a line of grand and often ground-breaking modern buildings – the Pompidou Centre, the Arab World Institute – that assert modern architecture and design.

But the greatest work of art has to be the city itself. Paris has been very fortunate throughout its history: saved from Hitler's intended destruction, spared the ravages of floods or fires, the centre of the city has been developed purposefully to reflect the ever-present power of the French state. And it does so with tremendous pomp and magnificence and with a sense of continuity and homogeneity, however great the changes and the contrasts with what went before – sweeping avenues, esplanades and bridges link monuments that span centuries, and the evolution of the Louvre from fortress to glass pyramid has somehow managed to maintain a sense of unity. Time has acted as judge as buildings once swathed in controversy – the Eiffel Tower, Sacré-Cœur, the Pompidou Centre, the glass pyramid – have blended into the overall artistic backdrop and often become symbols of the city; the new Opéra-Bastille is the latest in a long line of ridiculed candidates awaiting assimilation.

Two thousand years of shaping and reshaping has resulted in monumental buildings and public spaces although the city itself remains on a very human scale, with exquisite, secretive little nooks tucked away from the *grands boulevards* and very definite little communities revolving around games of *boules*, the local *boulangerie*, *charcuterie* and café.

The Parisians are probably the most maligned people of Europe. Their aloofness, indifference and superiority are renowned. But so is their swiftness to enter a quarrel in the street, the habit of falling to their knees on the pavement to coo over a fluffy miniature dog, their ineffable elegance and sexiness, and their attachment to fashion: outsiders may dismiss it all as posing or attention-seeking, but to a Parisian it's simply a matter of playing a part in the great game of keeping up appearances.

Accustomed to being at the centre of the nation's life, admired, envied and imitated by half the world, Parisians naturally think of themselves as superior beings. But don't be put off by that arrogance and self-absorption; firstly, there is entertainment in it, and, secondly, courtesy and humour lurk not far below the surface. Neither should you be intimidated by the city's reputation for sophistication. Certainly there are expensive pleasures on offer, but you can enjoy Paris without them. The city is so beautiful and its street life so animated and varied that one of the greatest joys of a visit is simply to browse along with eyes and ears at the café-*pâtisserie* level of existence.

One of the most important strands in the kaleidoscopic pattern of the city's life is its **ethnic diversity**. Long a haven and a magnet for foreign refugees and artists, Paris in this century has sheltered aspiring politicians, deposed leaders, dissidents, exiled freedom fighters and members of warring factions from every corner of the globe. It has welcomed black musicians denied civil rights in the United States and others from Africa and Latin America. Writers escaping censorship or just disillusionment in their own countries have flocked to the city.

Some highlights

Paris is a city of great **art** and of dazzling contemporary **architecture**. The general backdrop of the streets is predominantly Neoclassical, the result of nineteenth-century development. But each period since has added, more or less discreetly, novel examples of its own styles – with **Auguste Perret**, **Le Corbusier**, **Mallet-Stevens** and **Gustave Eiffel** among the early twentieth-century innovators. In the last two decades, the architectural additions have been on a dramatic scale, producing new and major landmarks, and recasting down-at-heel districts into important centres of cultural and consumer life. **Beaubourg (the Pompidou Centre)**, **La Villette**, **La Grande Arche**, the **Bastille Opéra**, the **Louvre pyramid**, the **Institut du Monde**

Arabe and the new **national library** have all expanded the dimensions of the city, pointing it determinedly towards the future as well as enhancing the monuments of the past.

The **museums and galleries** of Paris are among the finest in western Europe, and, with the tradition of state cultural endowment very much alive, certainly the best displayed. The art of conversion – the **Musée d'Orsay** from a train station, the **Cité des Sciences** from abbatoirs, and spacious well-lit exhibition spaces from mansions and palaces – has given the great collections unparalleled locations. The Impressionists at the **Musée d'Orsay**, the **Orangerie** and **Marmottan**; the moderns at **Beaubourg** and the **Palais de Tokyo**; the ancients in the **Louvre**; **Picasso** and **Rodin** with their own individual museums: all these deservedly entice art-lovers from around the world. In addition, there's the contemporary scene in the **commercial galleries** that fill the Marais, St-Germain, the Bastille and the area round the Champs-Élysées, and an ever-expanding range of museums devoted to other areas of human endeavour – science, history, decoration and performance art.

As for more hedonistic pleasures, few cities can compete with the thousand and one **cafés**, **bars** and **restaurants** – ultra-modern and designer-signed, palatial, traditional and scruffy (and for every pocket) – that line each Parisian street and boulevard. The restaurant choice is not just French, but includes a tempting range of cuisines and social cultures that draws from every ethnic origin represented among the city's millions.

Where **entertainment** is concerned, the city's strong points are movies and music. Paris is the **cinema** capital of Europe, and the **music** on offer encompasses excellent jazz, top-quality classical, avant-garde experimental, international rock, West African *soukous* and French Caribbean *zouk*, Algerian *raï*, and traditional *chansons*. If you want to hear world dance rhythms, Parisian clubs are exciting grounds to discover.

In the final two chapters of this book, we've described an assortment of excursions **beyond the city**. The region surrounding the capital, known as the Île de France, contains cathedral and châteaux that bear comparison with anything in Paris itself – **Chartres**, **Versailles**, and **Fontainebleau**, for example. It also boasts what can only be seen as a very *un*-French "attraction" – **Disneyland Paris**, which is covered in a separate chapter of this guide.

When to go

When to visit Paris is largely a question of personal taste. The city has a more reliable **climate** than Britain, with uninterrupted stretches of sun (and rain) all year round. However, while it maintains a vaguely southern feel for anyone crossing the English Channel, Mediterranean it is not. Winter temperatures drop well below freezing, with sometimes biting winds. If you're lucky, spring and autumn will be mild and sunny – in summer it can reach the 30s°C (80s°F).

In terms of pure aesthetics, winter sun is the city's most flattering light, when the pale shades of the older buildings become luminescent without any glare, and the lack of trees and greenery is barely relevant. By contrast, Paris in high summer can be choking, with the fumes of congested traffic becoming trapped within the high narrow streets, and the reflected light in the city's open spaces too blinding to enjoy.

If you visit during the **French summer holidays**, from July 15 to the end of August, you will find that large numbers of Parisians have fled the city. It's quieter then, but a lot of shops and restaurants will be closed. There is, too, the **commercial calendar** to consider – fashion shows, trade fairs, etc. Paris hoteliers warn against September and October, and **finding a room** even at the best of times can be problematic. Given the choice, early spring, autumn if you book ahead, or the midwinter months are most rewarding.

Part 1

The Basics

Getting There from Britain

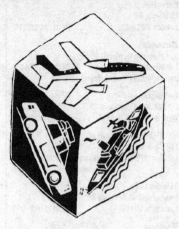

The quickest way of reaching Paris from Britain is, of course, by air, though it is rivalled closely by the Channel Tunnel London–Paris rail link that makes the 340 kilometre journey in just three hours, but is costly with it. The standard rail- or road-and-sea routes are significantly more affordable, but can be uncomfortable and tiring. Furthermore, if you're just going for a short break, the journey time of up to nine hours can drastically eat into the time you have to spend in Paris itself.

By Air

Deals on flights to Paris change all the time. To find the best ones, you should shop around, ideally a month or so before you plan to leave. Students and anyone under 26 can take advantage of a range of special discount fares from London to Paris. Promising sources for checking the possibilities include the classified travel sections in the quality Sunday newspapers and, if you're in London, *Time Out* and *TNT*, the free listings magazine available outside many tube and *British Rail* stations.

General Deals From London

The cheaper choices boil down to either a charter, a Bargain Saver (on *British Midland*) or Apex

(on *British Airways* and *Air France* as well as *British Midland*) scheduled ticket, or – often cheapest – a flight with an airline that makes a stop in Paris en route to more distant destinations (typically *Malaysia Airlines* or *Pakistan International Airlines*).

Charters are in theory supposed only to be sold in conjunction with accommodation. It is, of course, possible just to buy the air ticket, though doing so is generally a matter of luck, scrounging for whatever seats remain . . . often at the last moment. *Nouvelles Frontières* (see box on p5) sell scheduled flights to Paris for £79 return, but on limited dates. Otherwise they offer daily *British Airways* flights out of Heathrow and Gatwick to Paris; current prices start at £84 return.

British Airways, *Air France* and *British Midland* **Apex** tickets must be reserved two weeks in advance, and you must stay one Saturday night. Your return date has to be fixed when purchasing, and no subsequent changes are allowed. Current cost is £108 return, £120 at weekends. *British Midland* Bargain Savers for mid-week travel can be bought at any time and cost £81 return; once more you have to stay one Saturday night. Their ordinary availability tickets start from £159 return, £197 if you don't want to stay Saturday night. *British Airways* ordinary rates start from £155 return, while *Air France* have late availability offers, like the *Discover France* ticket costing £155 and again requiring a Saturday night stay. Discount agent *Masterfare* (☎0171/ 259 2000) has prices starting at £75 return with *British Midland*, with a Saturday night included in your stay.

Bargains with **long-haul airlines** are harder to predict. Like charters, availability can be chancy, but a good travel agent should usually find you something to Paris. The drawback is that there is generally only one flight each week, on variable days, though there's no maximum stay and you're allowed to make changes if necessary.

Finally, if you're based in central London and wish to get to Paris with the minimum of hassle, you can fly from **London City Airport** with *Air France* (3 flights daily Mon–Fri, 1 on Sun; from

Air, Rail and Bus Travel addresses

Air France
177 Piccadilly
London W1V OLX ☎ 0181/742 6600

Brit Air
239 Longbridge House
Gatwick Airport
West Sussex
Crawley RH6 0NP ☎ 01293/502044

British Airways
156 Regent St
London W1R 5TA ☎ 0181/897 4000

British Midland
Donington Hall
Castle Donington
Derby DE4 2SB ☎ 0171/589 5599
or ☎ 01345/554554

British Rail
Victoria Station
European Rail Enquiries: ☎ 0171/834 2345

Eurolines, National Express
Victoria Coach Station
164–172 Buckingham Palace Rd
London SW1W 97P ☎ 0171/730 0202

and 23 Crawley Rd, Luton
Beds LU1 1HX ☎ 01582/404511

Eurostar
19 Worple Rd
London SW19 4JS ☎ 01233/617575

Eurotrain
52 Grosvenor Gardens
London SW1W 0AG ☎ 0171/730 3402
and regional Campus Travel *offices.*

Le Shuttle
PO Box 300, Crawley
West Sussex RH10 2YW ☎ 01303/271100

SNCF (French Railways)
179 Piccadilly
London W1V 0VA enquiries ☎ 01891/515 477
bookings ☎ 01345/300 003

Thomas Cook
Head office: 45 Berkeley St
London W1A 1EB ☎ 0171/499 4000

Wasteels
Platform 2
Victoria Station
London SW1V 1JT ☎ 0171/834 7066

Note that addresses and telephone numbers may not be in the same location:
some airlines and agents use a single telephone-sales number for several offices.
Note also that 0891 numbers are premium rate and charge around 49p per minute before 6pm,
39p after.

£199 return). Check-in time has been cut to a minimum and tickets can be collected at the check-in desk. Shuttle buses for the airport leave from Liverpool Street station (£3; 30min) and from Canary Wharf (£1; 5–10min).

General Deals Outside London

As often as not, whether you live in Birmingham or Newcastle, Manchester or Aberdeen, you will find it pays to go to London and then fly on to Paris from there. Scheduled direct flights from British regional airports are very expensive. Charters do exist, though availability is a big problem and prices are unfavourable in relation to London flights, even taking into account the cost of coach or rail travel to London. What is worth considering, however, is a **package deal**, which often offers exceptional bargain travel – even if you go it alone on the actual holiday. See the box on p.6 for further details.

Student/Youth Flights

STA Travel (see box) offers flights to various cities for which any person under 26, and any student under 32, is eligible. Current return price to Paris (Charles de Gaulle) is £84. *Campus Travel* student/youth charter returns to Paris also start at £84. *Air UK* offers seven daily return flights to Paris for £87.

Special-deal **flight passes** within France with various airlines exist for students, and if you plan to travel elsewhere in France, it's worth enquiring about these from *STA* or *Campus Travel.*

By Train

The Channel Tunnel has slashed travelling time by train from London to Paris and has also led to special cut-rate deals on train and ferry or hovercraft fares via Calais, Boulogne or Dieppe.

The **Channel Tunnel** operates high-speed trains from London Waterloo via Folkestone and

Calais to Paris Gare du Nord in just over three hours. *Le Shuttle* service runs 40 high-speed passenger trains a day, and at peak times services operate every fifteen minutes, making advance reservations unnecessary; during the quietest times of the night, services still run hourly. Tickets are available at the terminal toll booths, or in advance from travel agents and *Le Shuttle*'s customer services department at £95 return, booked 14 days in advance (☎01303/271100).

Alternatively, catch one of the many trains from London Victoria which connect with cross-Channel ferries or hovercraft, with onward services on the other side. On the shortest and most economical Channel crossings the choice is between **train and hovercraft**, on which the total journey time from London to Paris is six hours, or **train and ferry**, taking seven or eight hours. Fare

options include special deals on *Eurotrain* (for anyone under 26) and senior citizen reductions for those over 65. If you plan to take in Paris as part of a longer trip you might also consider an *InterRail* or *Euro Domino Pass* (see p.7).

The **hovercraft** crossing links Dover with Boulogne. Services are frequent (up to twenty a day in peak season) and tie in well with the trains. By **train and ordinary ferry**, the cheapest crossing is currently Newhaven–Dieppe; best deals are on the conveniently scheduled (though slightly slower) night trains. Students and anyone under 26 can buy heavily discounted *BIJ* tickets from *Eurotrain* outlets (see opposite) and most student travel agents; these cost £49 return (departing Tues–Thurs), any other day £70 return, £47 one way; or with *Hoverspeed* (1hr 30min faster), whose prices are £55 return Tues–Thurs, any other day £74 return.

Addresses of Specialist Agencies for Independent Travel

Campus Travel
52 Grosvenor Gardens
London SW1W 0AG — ☎0171/730 8832

541 Bristol Rd, Bournbrook
Selly Oak, Birmingham B29 6AU
☎0121/414 1848

39 Queens Rd
Bristol BS8 1QE — ☎0117/929 2494

5 Emmanuel St
Cambridge CB1 1NE — ☎01223/324283

53 Forrest Rd
Edinburgh EH1 2QP — ☎0131/225 6111

13 High St
Oxford OX1 4DB — ☎01865/242067
Also at YHA shops and university campuses.

Council Travel
28a Poland St
London W1V 3DB — ☎0171/287 3337
Eight offices in France.

Masterfare
269 Old Brompton Rd
London SW5 9JA — ☎0171/259 2000
Discount agent with competitive deals.

Nouvelles Frontières
11 Blenheim St
London W1Y 9LE — ☎0171/629 7772
French agency.

STA Travel
86 Old Brompton Rd
London SW7 3LH

and 117 Euston Rd
London NW1 2SX — tele-sales ☎0171/937 9921

75 Deansgate
Manchester M3 2BW — tele-sales ☎0161/834 0668

88 Vicar Lane
Leeds LS1 7JH

25 Queens Rd
Bristol BS8 1QE

38 Sidney St
Cambridge CB2 3HX — tele-sales ☎01223/66966

36 George St
Oxford OX1 2AQ

Strathclyde University
90 John St
Glasgow G1 1JH
Also on various university campuses.

South Coast Student Travel
61 Ditchling Rd
Brighton BN1 4SD — ☎01273/570226
Plenty to offer non-students as well.

Trailfinders
42–50 Earls Court Rd
London W8 6EJ — ☎0171/937 5400

Note that addresses and telephone numbers may not be in the same location: some airlines and agents use a single telephone-sales number for several offices.

Packages From Regional Britain

The following is a selection from the wide range of companies selling travel plus accommodation packages to Paris from outside London, either on direct regional charter flights, or including the fare to the capital to catch a flight from London in the overall price, or offering special deals on ferry crossings. More complete lists are available from the *French Government Tourist Office*, 178 Piccadilly, London W1V OAL (☎0171/491 7622).

Allez France
27 West Street, Storrington
West Sussex RH20 4DZ ☎01903/742345
Paris accommodation packages from all major British airports – Manchester, Birmingham, Glasgow and Edinburgh, as well as Stanstead, Heathrow and Gatwick. Flights and two nights accommodation from Stanstead £129; more expensive from regional airports than from Gatwick or Heathrow.

British Airways Holidays
Pacific House
Hazelwick Ave
Crawley RH10 1PN ☎01293/615 353
City Breaks flights from a number of regional airports, and package deals from around £149 for a flight and two nights in Paris.

Brittany Ferries
The Brittany Centre
Wharf Road
Portsmouth PO2 8RU ☎01705/751833
Short breaks in Paris for 3, 6 or 10 days, including ferry crossing with car in peak season: 4 nights £183, 2 nights £113.

Gîtes de France
178 Piccadilly
London W1V 9DB ☎0171/493 3480
Houses, cottages and chalets in the Île-de-France region, mostly about half an hour from Paris by train. One week minimum Sat to Sat or Tues to Tues from £195 per person, inclusive of car ferry crossing.

Kirker European Holidays
3 New Concordia Wharf
Mill Street
London SE1 2BB ☎0171/231 3333
Departures from most regional airports. Two nights in a two-star hotel, travelling by coach, from £117.

Paris Travel Service
Bridge House, Ware
Herts SG12 9DF ☎01920/467 467
Very wide range of packages from £105 (Paris Rail Express) for rail and Sealink ferry with basic accommodation, to two nights in three-star accommodation flying from Heathrow from £186. Good for regional flights (Aberdeen, Birmingham, East Midlands, Edinburgh, Glasgow, Leeds/Bradford, Manchester, Humberside, Exeter, Bournemouth, Newcastle, Cardiff, Belfast, Bristol, Southampton), and rail deals via London from anywhere in Britain.

Sally Holidays
92–96 Lind Rd
Sutton SH1 4PL ☎0181/395 3030
Ferry for car and two adults plus two-star hotel accommodation from £84 per person first night (£27 each subsequent night) in central Paris.

Time Off Ltd
Chester Close
Chester St
London SW1X 7BQ ☎0171/235 8070
Short breaks to Paris by air, coach and rail (including Orient Express packages). Two nights in a one-star hotel, travelling by coach, from £121; self-drive packages from £100.

Travelscene Ltd
11–15 St Ann's Road, Harrow
Middlesex HA1 1AS ☎0181/427 4445
Short breaks in all grades of accommodation, by air, rail, or coach. Two nights in a one-star hotel by coach from £99, and £78 self-drive. Two- and three-centre breaks with Amsterdam and Brussels.

Venice Simplon-Orient-Express
Sea Containers House
20 Upper Ground
London SE1 9PF ☎0171/928 6000
From £555 for two nights, flying to Paris, returning in day-car accommodation on the Orient Express.

VFB Holidays; French Weekenders
Normandy House, High Street
Cheltenham GL50 3HW ☎01242/580187
Flights from regional destinations including Newcastle, Aberdeen and Belfast. Two nights hotel accommodation plus flight from Gatwick from £181, or £129 by ferry and car.

Agencies for Train Travel in London

Eurotrain/London Student Travel,
52 Grosvenor Gardens, SW1W 0AG
☎0171/730 3402

British Rail, International Rail Centre, Victoria
Station, SW1V 1JU   ☎0171/834 2345

For **timetable information**, it's best to
approach *British Rail,* either at Victoria or at
your nearest major station.

The *Paris Explorer* option, on which you can
travel to and from your destination via different
routes (with stopovers), is £100 via Dieppe; £95
via Calais. *British Rail's* cheapest five-day return
fare is £57 via Dieppe; cheapest two-month
return is £78 via Dieppe.

Rail Passes

If you plan to use the rail network to visit other
regions of France, you might consider buying a
France Vacances or *Euro Domino* pass.

The **Euro Domino** pass, available from the
International Rail Centre at London Victoria, or the
SNCF in France, offers unlimited rail travel through
France for any three (£108), five (£150) or ten
(£222) days within a calendar month; passengers
under 26 pay £87, £123 and £183 respectively.
The pass also entitles you to fifty percent reduc-
tions on rail/ferry links to France.

The *InterRail* pass, offering one month's
unlimited use of all European train services for
£249 to anyone under 26 who has been resident in Europe for at least six months, is available from *British Rail* and some travel agents,
including branches of *Campus Travel* and *STA
Travel.* Cheaper new *InterRail* passes have also
been introduced which cover one, two or three
"zones". France is within the zone including
Belgium, the Netherlands and Luxembourg; a 15-
day pass to travel this area is £179.

By Bus

At the time of writing, the bus companies have
no plans to usee the Channel Tunnel, so the
choice remains between **bus and hovercraft,**
and **bus and ordinary ferry**. Prices are very much
lower than for trains, especially by hovercraft.

The **Hoverspeed City Sprint** bus service
leaves in the morning from London's Victoria
Coach Station, catches the hovercraft from Dover

to Calais, and arrives in Paris between eight and
nine hours after setting off. There are two
coaches per day in winter, four in summer. The
regular adult return is £55, and there's a student
discount of £3. Tickets can be purchased through
any local agent; for details call *Hoverspeed* on
☎01304/240241.

The main company for the bus/ordinary ferry
combination is *Eurolines,* 52 Grosvenor Gardens,
Victoria, London SW1W 0AN (☎0171/730 8235).
They run overnight as well as daytime buses,
both taking roughly nine hours, at a regular adult
return fare of £55.

By Car and Channel Tunnel

The most convenient way of taking your car
across to France is to **drive** down to the Channel
Tunnel, load your car onto the train shuttle, and
be whisked under the Channel in 35 minutes,
ready for a leisurely drive through northern
France to Paris.

The Channel Tunnel entrance is off the M20
at Junction 11A, just outside of Folkestone, and
Le Shuttle services operate round the clock, 365
days a year. Because of the frequency of the
service, you don't have to buy a ticket in
advance; just arrive and wait to board one of the
four trains an hour during peak time, with a
promised loading time of just ten minutes. While
you're inside the carriages, you can get out of
your car to stretch your legs during the
35-minute crossing.

Tickets are available through *Le Shuttle*
Customer Service Centre (☎01303/271100) or
from your local travel agent, and fares are per
carload: one-way £110–155, return £220–310.

By Car and Ferry/Hovercraft

Cheaper cross-Channel options are the **conventional ferry or hovercraft** links between Dover
and Calais or Boulogne, Folkestone and
Boulogne, and Ramsgate and Dunkerque. If your
starting point is significantly further west than
London, it may well be worth heading direct to
one of the south coast ports and catching one of
the ferries to Normandy or Brittany – Newhaven
to Dieppe; Portsmouth, Southampton, Weymouth
or Poole to Le Havre, Caen, Cherbourg and St-
Malo; and Plymouth to Roscoff.

Ferry prices vary according to the season and,
for motorists, the size of car; details of routes,
companies and fares are given on p.7.

1995 FERRY ROUTES AND PRICES

Note: return prices are substantially cheaper but generally need to be booked in advance.

	Operator	Crossing Time	Frequency	One-way Fares Small car 2 adults	Foot passenger
BRITTANY					
Poole–St Malo	*Brittany Ferries*	8hr	3–4 wkly	£104–248	£24–50
Portsmouth–St-Malo	*Brittany Ferries*	8hr 45min	Mar–Nov 1 nightly	£84–248	£20–50
Plymouth–Roscoff	*Brittany Ferries*	6hr	Feb–Dec 3–17 wkly	£82–242	£26–48
NORMANDY					
Southampton–Cherbourg	*Stena Sealink*	6–10 hr	1–2 daily	£61–176	£12–27
Portsmouth–Cherbourg	*P&O European Ferries*	4hr 45min	1–3 daily	£54–185	£19–49
Poole–Cherbourg	*Brittany Ferries*	4hr 15min	Feb–Dec 1–2 daily	£72–200	£16–38
Portsmouth–Caen	*Brittany Ferries*	6hr	3 daily	£78–212	£18–42
Portsmouth–Le Havre	*P&O European Ferries*	5hr 45min	2–3 daily	£84–185	£21–36
Newhaven–Dieppe	*Stena Sealink*	4hr	4 daily	£70–186	£22–26
PAS-DE-CALAIS					
Folkestone–Boulogne	*Hoverspeed‡*	55 min	3–4 daily	£103–153	£22–44
Dover–Calais	*Stena Sealink*	1hr 30min	25 daily	£114–168	£26
Dover–Calais	*P&O European Ferries*	1hr 15min	20–25 daily	£57–147	£25
Dover–Calais	*Hoverspeed‡‡*	35min	20–24 daily	£129–196	£25–50
Ramsgate–Dunkerque	*Sally Ferries*	2hr 30min	5 daily all year	£63–147	£22

Special Offers
Brittany Ferries and *Stena Sealink* – 3, 5 and 10-day returns; discounts for regular users who own a property abroad.
Sally Line, Hoverspeed and *P&O European Ferries* – 3 and 5-day returns.

Addresses in Britain

Brittany Ferries
Wharf Rd, Portsmouth PO2 8RU ☎01705/827701

Millbay Docks, Plymouth PL1 3EW
☎01752/221321

Poole ☎01202/666466

Hoverspeed
Maybrook House, Queens Gardens,
Dover CT17 9UQ ☎0304/240202
‡*Seacat high-speed catamaran.*
‡‡*Hovercraft and Seacat.*

P&O European Ferries
Channel House, Channel View Rd,
Dover CT17 9TJ ☎01304/203388

Continental Ferry Port, Mile End,
Portsmouth PO2 8QW ☎01705/827677

London ☎0181/575 8555

Sally Line
Argyle Centre, York St, Ramsgate,
Kent CT11 9DS ☎01843/595522

81 Piccadilly, London W1V 9HF
☎0181/858 1127

Stena Sealink Line
Charter House, Park St, Ashford,
Kent TN24 8EX ☎01233/647047

24-hr information, Dover ☎01304/240028

You can either contact the companies direct to reserve space in advance (essential at peak season if you're driving), or any competent travel agent in Britain or France can do it for you.

Hitching

Hitching from Calais or Boulogne towards Paris is notoriously difficult. If you can possibly afford one of the cheaper bus or train tickets, you'll save yourself a lot of trouble. If not, get friendly with drivers on the boat over and try to get a promise of a lift before docking. Dieppe is not that much easier to hitch out of. It's a long way to hitch to Paris from the ports in Normandy or Brittany, but actually getting the lifts could well be easier.

Coming back, it may well be worth contacting the ride-share organization *Allostop*, 84 Passage Brady, 75010 Paris (☎ 47.70.02.01; Mon–Fri 9am–7.30pm, Sat 9am–1pm & 2–6pm), which matches riders with drivers for 65F for one journey, 200F for eight journeys, plus shared expenses of 16 centimes per kilometre.

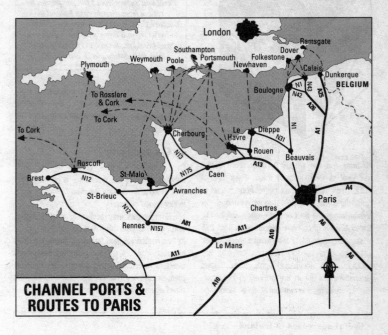

CHANNEL PORTS & ROUTES TO PARIS

Getting There from Ireland

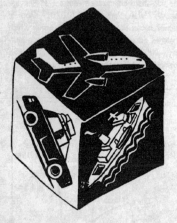

Packages From Ireland

Irish Ferries
2–4 Merrion Row
Dublin 2   ☎01/6610511

*Paris Rail Savers from £169 per person for
return from anywhere in Ireland to
Rosslare/Cork, and return between Le Havre/
Cherbourg and Paris, plus two nights bed
and breakfast. Return to Paris from any
Irish Rail station via Le Havre £119.*

Air Inter and *Aer Lingus* fly direct from Dublin and Cork to Paris, with a return Apex fare of £182. There are no direct flights from Belfast to Paris, and a routing through London or Amsterdam is the best option – often airlines like *British Airways* often have special deals from £75 or so; otherwise, the *Paris Travel Service*, based just outside of London (see box on p.6), has package deals including flights from Belfast. Alternatives via Britain are unlikely to be attractive, considering the additional time factor and

the cost of a flight from Ireland to Britain. For up-to-date details on the situation, try contacting *USIT*, specialists in student/youth travel (see the box below).

By Car and Ferry

The cheapest way of getting to France – although far from the quickest – is by **ferry** from Cork or Rosslare outside Wexford to various ports in Normandy or Brittany.

Ferry prices vary according to the season and, for motorists, the size of car; details of routes, companies and fares are given in the box opposite. You can either contact the companies direct to reserve space in advance (essential at peak season if you're driving), or any competent travel agent at home or France can do it for you.

Useful addresses in Ireland

AIRLINES
Aer Lingus
42 Grafton St, Dublin   ☎01/637 0011
46 Castle St, Belfast   ☎0800/626747

Air Inter
29–30 Dawson St, Dublin   ☎01/677 8899

British Airways
60 Dawson St, Dublin   ☎0800/626747
9 Fountain Centre, College St, Belfast
                                 ☎0232/245 151

AGENTS AND OPERATORS
Joe Walsh Tours
8–11 Baggot St, Dublin   ☎01/678 9555

31 Castle St, Belfast   ☎0232/241144
Discount flight agent.

Thomas Cook
118 Grafton St, Dublin   ☎01/677 1721)
11 Donegal Place, Belfast   ☎0232/240 833
*Mainstream package holiday and flight agent,
with occasional discount offers.*

USIT
O'Connell Bridge
19/21 Aston Quay, Dublin   ☎01/778 117
10–11 Market Parade, Cork   ☎021/270 900
31a Queen St, Belfast   ☎0232/242 562
Student and youth specialists.

1995 FERRY ROUTES AND PRICES

Note: return prices are substantially cheaper but generally need to be booked in advance.

	Operator	Crossing Time	Frequency	One-way Fares	
				Small car 2 adults (£IR)	Foot passenger (£IR)
Cork–Roscoff	*Brittany Ferries*	14hr	mid-March to Oct 1 1–2 wkly	£210–298	£60–82
Cork–St-Malo	*Brittany Ferries*	18hr	mid-May to Sept 1 wkly	£210–298	£60–82
Cork–Le Havre	*Irish Ferries*	21hr 30min	May–Sept 2 wkly	£210–275	£55–80
Cork–Cherbourg	*Irish Ferries*	17hr 30min	July–Sept 1 wkly	£210–275	£55–80
Rosslare–Cherbourg	*Irish Ferries*	18hr	1 wkly	£216–281	£61–86
Rosslare–Le Havre	*Irish Ferries*	22hr	2–3 wkly	£216–281	£61–86
Rosslare–Brest	*Irish Ferries*	15hr	May–Sept 1–2 wkly	£210–275	£55–80
Cork–Brest	*Irish Ferries*	15hr 30 min	June–July 2 wkly	£210–275	£55–80

Special Offers
Irish Ferries – 13-night excursion returns (10-night July & Aug).
Brittany Ferries – 3-, 7- and 11-day returns.

Irish Ferries
2–4 Merrion Row, Dublin 2 ☎ 01/661 0511
Cork ☎ 021/504333
Rosslare ☎ 053/33158

Brittany Ferries
42 Grand Parade, Cork ☎ 021/277801

Getting There from the US and Canada

Getting to Paris from the US or Canada is straightforward. The city is the only French transatlantic gateway and has direct flights from over thirty major North American cities. Nearly a dozen different scheduled airlines operate flights, making Paris one of the cheapest destinations in Europe – especially in these days of cut-throat inter-airline competition. In fact, only London can offer more discounted flights; and while a visit to England may appeal, the price difference is rarely sufficient to make a stopover in London a money-saving idea.

The cheapest way to take any of these scheduled flights is with a non-refundable **Apex** fare, which normally entails booking 21 days in advance of flying, travelling midweek, and staying for at least seven days. Apart from special offers, this is likely to be the best deal you'll get direct from an airline ticket counter.

The best guarantee of a cheap flight, however, is to contact a travel agent specializing in **discounted fares**. The travel sections of the *New York Times*, *Washington Post*, and *Los Angeles Times* advertise them. Restrictions on such tickets are often not all that stringent; you need not assume that youth or student fares are the best bargain, nor worry if you're not eligible for them. The independent travel specialists *STA Travel* and *Council Travel* are two of the most reliable agents,

but not surprisingly the French group **Nouvelles Frontières** has some good offers. These firms, together with several of the other larger agents, act as "consolidators" for particular airlines with which they maintain contracts to sell seats on specific terms, invariably below the airlines' own fares, though sometimes less conveniently.

Estimating the cost of **round-trip economy class fares** to Paris is tricky, especially as routes, carriers and the state of the market in general are changing all the time. The round-trip fares shown in the box below are a general guide to what you might expect to pay; startling variations are due to specific airlines engaging in price wars on specific routes. Fares are dependent on **season**, and are highest from around early June to the end of August, when everyone wants to travel; they drop during the "shoulder" seasons, September–October and April–May, and you'll get the best deals during the low season, November through March (excluding Christmas). Note that Friday, Saturday and Sunday travel tends to carry a premium. One-way fares are generally slightly

---

Sample Round-trip Fares to Paris
Typical lowest discounted fares in low season/high season, flying midweek.

Atlanta: $600/$670
Boston: $570/$680
Chicago: $590/$720
Cincinnati: $590/$730
Dallas: $660/$780
Houston: $640/$760
Los Angeles: $500/$720
Miami: $600/$700
Montréal: CDN$680/$820
New York: $400/$520
Raleigh-Durham: $600/$700
St Louis: $650/$780
San Francisco: $620/$840
Toronto: CDN$680/$820
Vancouver: CDN$800/$1000
Washington DC: $520/$670

more than half the round-trip. If you have a specific destination in mind in France outside Paris and you're in a hurry – and if you're prepared to pay extra – it's possible to be ticketed straight through to any of more than a dozen regional airports. Most of these entail connecting flights on *Air Inter*, *Air France*'s domestic arm, and require a change of planes in Paris (check to make sure there's no inconvenient transfer between Charles de Gaulle and Orly). Some sample round-trip add-on fares from Paris: Bordeaux $60; Brest $100; Grenoble $60; Lyon $60; Marseille $100; Nice $100; Strasbourg $60; Toulouse $100.

Charter flights (a flight chartered by a tour operator from an airline to ferry tourists) can be even cheaper than these prices for scheduled services. But while discounted scheduled services sometimes carry eligibility restrictions, charter flights hedge you in with restricted dates and major financial penalties if you cancel. They're worth considering if you're very organized and know exactly what you plan to do. Most agents sell them.

If you're prepared to travel light at short notice and for a short duration it might be worth getting a **courier flight**. *Now Voyager* (☎212/431 1616) arranges such flights to Europe from JFK, Newark, and Houston. Flights (from about $400 round trip) are issued on a first-come, first-served basis, and there's no guarantee that the Paris route will be available at the specific time you want.

Flights from the US

The most comprehensive range of flights from the US is offered by *Air France*, the French national carrier, which flies non-stop to Charles

---

Discount Agents, Consolidators and Travel Clubs in North America

Council Travel
Head Office, 205 E 42nd St, New York,
NY 10017   ☎800/743-1823
Nationwide US student travel organization with branches (among others) in San Francisco, Washington DC, Boston, Austin, Seattle, Chicago, Minneapolis.

Discount Travel International
Ives Bldg, 114 Forrest Ave, Suite 205,
Narberth, PA 19072   ☎800/334-9294
Discount travel club.

Encore Travel Club
4501 Forbes Blvd,
Lanham, MD 20706   ☎1-800/444-9800
Discount travel club.

Interworld Travel
800 Douglass Rd, Miami,
FL 33134   ☎305/443-4929
Consolidator.

Moment's Notice
425 Madison Ave,
New York, NY 10017   ☎212/486-0503
Discount travel club.

New Frontiers/Nouvelles Frontières
12 E 33rd St, New York, NY 10016
                            ☎800/366-6387

1001 Sherbrook East, Suite 720,
Montréal, H2L 1L3   ☎514/526-8444
French discount travel firm; also markets charters to Paris and Lyon. Other branches in LA, San Francisco and Québec City.

STA Travel
Main office: 48 East 11th St,
New York, NY 10003
         nationwide enquiries ☎800/777-0112
Worldwide specialist in independent travel with branches in the Los Angeles, San Francisco and Boston areas. Has French branches in Paris and Grenoble.

Travel Cuts
Main office: 187 College St,
Toronto, ON M5T 1P7   ☎416/979-2406
Canadian student travel organization with branches all over the country.

Travelers Advantage
3033 S Parker Rd, Suite 900,
Aurora,
CO 80014   ☎800/548-1116
Discount travel club.

Travac
Main office: 989 6th Ave,
New York NY 10018   ☎800/872-8800
Consolidator; branch in Orlando.

Unitravel
1177 N Warson Rd,
St Louis, MO 63132   ☎800/325-2222
Consolidator.

Worldwide Discount Travel Club
1674 Meridian Ave,
Miami Beach, FL 33139   ☎305/534-2082
Discount travel club.

---

de Gaulle airport from Anchorage, Boston, Chicago, Houston, Los Angeles, Miami, New York (JFK and Newark) and Washington DC – in most instances daily. *Air France* tends to be expensive, however.

The **major American competitors** tend to be cheaper, but offer fewer non-stop routes. *American* and *TWA* have the biggest range of "direct" routes. The former flies to Paris Orly non-stop from Chicago, Dallas, New York (JFK and Raleigh-Durham), or with a stop from LA (via Dallas), San Francisco (via Chicago) and San Diego (via JFK) and has good or guaranteed connections from 14 cities in the south and west. *TWA* flies non-stop to Paris Charles de Gaulle from Boston, New York, St Louis and Washington DC, and has one-stop flights from Chicago and LA and guaranteed connections (same flight number) from Atlanta, Kansas City, Portland, San Francisco and Seattle.

• *Delta* flies non-stop to Paris Orly from Atlanta and Cincinnatti with good or guaranteed connections from over a dozen southern and western cities.

• *United* flies daily non-stop to Paris Charles de Gaulle from Chicago and Washington DC.
• *Tower Air* has direct flights from New York to Paris.
• *US Air* features a direct Philadelphia–Paris routing.
• *Continental* flies daily non-stop from New York (Newark) to Paris Orly and also has direct flights (with a stop or same-number flight change) from Boston, Denver, Houston, LA and Washington.
• *Northwest* flies daily, direct LA–Detroit–Paris Charles de Gaulle.
• Lastly, there are twice-weekly direct flights (often cheap) with *PIA Pakistan International* from New York to Paris Orly.

Flights from Canada

The strong links between France and Québec's Francophone community ensure regular air services from Canada to Paris. The main route is Vancouver–Toronto–Montréal–Paris Charles de Gaulle. Most departures originate in Toronto, however, with *Air France* flying almost daily from

---

Airlines in North America

Only gateway cities are listed for each airline; other routings are always possible using connecting flights.

Air Canada (call ☎1-800/555-1212 for local toll-free number). Montréal, Toronto and Vancouver to Paris.

Air France (☎1-800/237-2747). New York, Washington, Miami, Montréal, Toronto, Chicago, Houston, San Francisco and Los Angeles to Paris; internal connections to many French cities.

American Airlines (☎1-800/433-7300). New York, Miami, Dallas-Fort Worth, Chicago and Raleigh-Durham to Paris.

British Airways (☎1-800/247-9297; in Canada ☎1-800/668-1080). Many North American cities to London, with connections to Paris and Nice.

Canadian Airlines (☎1-800/665-1177). Montréal, Toronto and Vancouver to Paris.

Continental Airlines (☎1-800/231-0856). Newark and Houston to Paris.

Delta Airlines (☎1-800/241-4141). Atlanta, Cincinnati and New York to Paris; New York to Nice.

Iceland Air (☎1-800/223-5500). New York, Baltimore and Orlando to Reykjavik and on to Paris.

KLM (☎1-800/374-7747). Many North American cities to Amsterdam, with connections to Paris, Lyon, Marseille and Nice.

Northwest Airlines (☎1-800/225-2525). Boston and Detroit to Paris.

PIA Pakistan International Airways (☎1-800/221-2552). New York to Paris.

Tower Air (☎1-800/221-2500). New York to Paris.

TWA (☎1-800/892-4141). New York, Boston, St. Louis and Washington to Paris.

United Airlines (☎1-800/538-2929). Washington, Chicago, Los Angeles and San Francisco to Paris.

US Air (☎1-800/428-4322). Philadelphia to Paris.

Virgin Atlantic Airways (☎800/862-8621). Flights to London from Newark, JFK, Boston, Miami and Orlando.

Toronto to Charles de Gaulle, either non-stop or via Montréal. *Air Canada* and *Canadian Airlines* fly direct to Paris from Toronto and Montréal, again pretty well daily, and *Canadian Airlines* flies in from Vancouver twice weekly to guarantee the connection to Paris.

Travel Cuts and *Nouvelles Frontières* are the most likely sources of good-value discounted seats; call for details as flights vary from season to season.

Flying via the UK

Although **flying to London** is usually the cheapest way of reaching Europe, price differences these days are minimal enough for there to be little point travelling to France via London unless you've specifically chosen to visit the UK as well. Having said that, you may well be able to pick up a flight to London at an advantageous rate.

In recent years, *Virgin Atlantic* has offered some of the best fares from New York and Newark; and has now added flights from Miami, Orlando and Boston to its schedules (all into London Gatwick). *British Airways* has entered the fray with a series of rival offers. In summer, the savings are bound to be less, but shop

around as there may yet be some European bargains. As well as from JFK and Newark, *British Airways* has regular non-stop flights from Philadelphia, Boston, San Francisco, and Los Angeles – and Detroit via Montréal.

Package Tours

Dozens of tour operators specialize in travel to Paris and the surrounding countryside. Many can put together very **flexible deals**, sometimes amounting to no more than a flight and accommodation; if you're planning to travel in moderate or luxury style, and especially if your trip is geared around special interests, such packages can work out cheaper than the same arrangements made on arrival. A tour is inevitably more confining than independent travel, but it can help you make the most of time if you're on a tight schedule; and if Paris is your first stop on a longer trip, a tour can ensure a worry-free first few days while you're finding your feet.

The accompanying box mentions a few of the possibilities, and a travel agent will be able to point out others (remember, bookings made through a travel agent cost no more than going through the tour operator).

Getting There from Australia and New Zealand

Most people travelling to Paris from Australia and New Zealand will choose to travel via London. There are, however, alternative stop-over points in Europe, and these are often available at economical fares. Whichever way you route, most airlines can add on a Paris leg to an Australia/New Zealand–Europe ticket.

From Australia

From Australia, fares to Paris vary according to the season and carrier. you choose to travel with. **Discount agents** should be able to get you a discount of at least ten percent off the following low-season published fares: *Garuda International* (via Bali, Jakarta, Singapore or Bangkok and Abu Dhabi, with two stopovers allowed each way),

A$1685 to Paris; *Air France, British Airways* (via London), *KLM* (via Amsterdam), *Lufthansa/Lauda* (via Frankfurt), *Alitalia/Qantas* (via Rome), *JAL* (overnight in Tokyo), A$2199; *Aeroflot* (via Moscow), A$1700; *Thai International* (via Bangkok), A$2055; *Malaysian Airlines* (via Kuala Lumpur), A$2099.

Airpasses, coupons, and discounts on further flights within Europe vary with airlines, but the basic rules are that they must be prebooked with the main ticket, are valid for three months, and are available only with a return fare with the one airline – for example, you have to fly to France with *British Airways* alone to be eligible for their airpass deals. *Air France* offers a **Euroflyer** for use in France and Europe at A$100 each flight; *British*

Specialist Agents

Australia

Flight Centres, Circular Quay, Sydney (☎ 02/241 2422); Bourke St, Melbourne (☎ 03/650 2899); plus other branches nationwide.

France Accommodation, 47, North Blackburn Square, Blackburn, Melbourne (☎ 03/877 6066).

France and Travel, 55 Hardware Street, Melbourne (☎ 03/670 7253).

France Unlimited, 232 Flinders Street, Melbourne (☎ 03/650 9892).

French and International Travel, 383 George Street, Sydney (☎ 02/299 8696).

French Bike Tours, 16 Goldsmith Street, Elwood, Melbourne (☎ 03/531 8787).

French Cottages and Travel, 674 High Street, East Kew, Melbourne (☎ 03/859 4944).

French Tourist Bureau, 12 Castlereagh Street, Sydney (☎ 02/231 5244).

French Travel Connection, 90 Mount Street, Sydney (☎ 02/956 5884).

Renault Eurodrive, cnr Jamieson and York streets, Sydney (☎ 02/299 3344); branches in other state capitals.

STA Travel, Australia: 732 Harris Street, Ultimo, Sydney (☎ 02/212 1255); 256 Flinders St, Melbourne (☎ 03/347 4711); other offices in Townsville and state capitals.

New Zealand

Budget Travel, PO Box 505, Auckland (☎ 09/309 4313).

Flight Centres, National Bank Towers, 205–225 Queen St, Auckland (☎ 09/309 6171); Shop 1M, National Mutual Arcade, 152 Hereford St, Christchurch (☎ 09 379 7145); 50-52 Willis St, Wellington (☎ 04 472 8101); other branches countrywide.

STA Travel, Traveller's Centre, 10 High St, Auckland (☎ 09/309 9995); 233 Cuba St, Wellington (☎ 04/385 0561); 223 High St, Christchurch (☎ 03/379 9098); other offices in Dunedin, Palmerston North and Hamilton.

Airways have a zone system: A$103 for each flight within France, A$133 each for single flights to and around Germany, Italy and Belgium. Both airlines also arrange **fly-drive packages**; check with an agent for current deals as prices are variable. *KLM*'s **Passport to Europe** uses coupons for single flights: three coupons for US$405, up to six for US$710; *Lufthansa* start at US$375 for three coupons, with extra flights US$105 each, to a maximum of nine.

From New Zealand

From New Zealand, best deals are (discounted): *Japanese Airlines* (NZ$2200, overnight stop in Tokyo), *Thai International* (NZ$2265, due to rise end of 1994), *Malaysian Airlines* (NZ$2295) and *Garuda* (NZ$2249). For **stopovers** in Europe, *British Airways* charge NZ$2399 via London; *Qantas/Alitalia* are slightly less at NZ$2295 via Rome and London. For **side trips** within Europe, *Qantas/Lufthansa* have a four-coupon deal on a six-month fare for NZ$2600.

Airline Addresses in Australia and New Zealand

Aeroflot, 388 George St, Sydney (☎02/233 7911).

Air France, 12 Castlereagh St, Sydney (☎02/233 3277); 57 Fort St, Auckland (☎09/303 1229).

Alitalia, Orient Overseas Building, 32 Bridge St, Sydney (☎02/247 1308); Floor 6, Trust Bank Building, 229 Queen St, Auckland (☎09/379 4457).

British Airways, 64 Castlereagh St, Sydney (☎02/258 3300); Dilworth Building, cnr Queen and Customs streets, Auckland (☎09/367 7500).

Garuda, 175 Clarence St, Sydney (☎02/334 9900); 120 Albert St, Auckland (☎09/366 1855).

JAL, Floor 14, IBM Centre, 201 Sussex St, Sydney (☎02/283 1111); Floor 12, Westpac Tower, 120 Albert St, Auckland (☎09/379 9906).

KLM, 5 Elizabeth St, Sydney (☎02/231 6333, 0800/222 747).

Lufthansa/Air Lauda, 143 Macquarie St, Sydney (☎02/367 3800); 109 Queen St, Auckland (☎09/303 1520).

MAS, 388 George St, Sydney (☎02/231 5066, 0800/269 998); Floor 12, Swanson Centre, 12–26 Swanson St, Auckland (☎09/373 2741).

Qantas, International Square, Jamison St, Sydney (☎02/957 0111, 236 3636); Qantas House, 154 Queen St, Auckland (☎09/303 2506).

Thai International, 75–77 Pitt St, Sydney (☎02/844 0999, 0800/422 020); Kensington Swan Building, 22 Fanshawe St, Auckland (☎09/377 0268).

Red Tape and Visas

Citizens of EU (European Union) countries, Canada, the United States, New Zealand, Finland, Norway and Sweden do not need any

sort of visa to enter France, and can stay for up to ninety days. The British Visitor's Passport and the Excursion Pass, both obtainable over the counter at post offices, can be used as well as ordinary passports. All other passport holders (including British Travel Document holders and Australians) must obtain a visa before arrival in France. Obtaining a visa from your nearest French consulate is fairly automatic, but check their hours before turning up, and leave plenty of time, since there are often queues (particularly in London in summer).

Three types of **visa** are currently issued: a transit visa, valid for two months; a short-stay (*court séjour*) visa, valid for ninety days after the date of issue, good for multiple entries; and a long-stay (*long séjour*) visa, which allows for multiple stays of ninety days over three years,

---

French Consulates Overseas

Australia
492 St Kilda Road, Melbourne   ☎ 03/820 0921

31 Market St, Sydney, NSW 2000   ☎ 02/261 5779

Canada
Embassy: 2 Elysee, Pl Bonaventure,
Montréal BP 202, QUE H5A 1B1
  ☎ 514/878 4381 to 87

Consulates: 1 place Ville Marie,
Bureau 22601 Montréal,
Québec H3B 4S3   ☎ 514/878 4381

1110 av des Laurentides,
Québec-H G1S 3C3   ☎ 418/688 0430

130 Bloor Street West, Suite 400,
Toronto, Ont M5S 1N5   ☎ 416/925 80441

1201-736 Granville St,
Vancouver – BC V6Z 1H9   ☎ 604/681 2301

Ireland
36 Ailesbury Road, Dublin 4   ☎ 01/694 777

Netherlands
Vijzelgracht 2, Amsterdam   ☎ 20/624 8346

New Zealand
1 Willeston St, PO Box 1695,
Wellington   ☎ 04/720200

Norway
Drammensveien 69, 0244 Oslo 2   ☎ 02/41820

Sweden
Narvavägen 28, Stockholm 115–23   ☎ 08/63685

UK
French Consulate General (Visas Section):
1 Cromwell Place, London SW7
  ☎ 0171/581 5292, fax 0171/838 2046

Also: 7–11 Randolph Crescent, Edinburgh
  ☎ 0131/225 7954, fax 0131/225 8975

USA
Embassy: 4101/Reservoir Rd NW,
Washington DC 20007   ☎ 202/944 6000

Consulates: 3 Commonwealth Ave,
Boston, MA 02116   ☎ 617/266 1680

737 North Michigan Ave, Olympia Centre,
Suite 2020, Chicago, Ill 60611   ☎ 312/787 5359

10990 Wilshire Boulevard, Suite 300,
Los Angeles, CA 90024   ☎ 310/479 4426

934 Fifth Ave, New York,
NY 10021   ☎ 212/606 3621

540 Bush St, San Francisco,
CA 94108   ☎ 415/397 4330

---

but which is issued only after an examination of an individual's circumstances. EU citizens (or other non-visa citizens) who **stay longer than three months** are officially supposed to apply for a *Carte de Séjour*, for which you'll have to show proof of income at least equal to the minimum wage. However, EU passports are rarely stamped, so there is no evidence of how long you've been in the country. If your passport does get stamped, you can cross the border – to Belgium or Germany, for example – and re-enter for another ninety days legitimately.

Health and Insurance

Citizens of all EU and Scandinavian countries are entitled to take advantage of French health services under the same terms as residents. You will need the correct documentation: form E111, available from post offices. North American and other non-EU citizens have to pay for most medical attention and are strongly advised to take out some form of travel insurance.

Under the French Social Security system every hospital visit, doctor's consultation and prescribed medicine incurs a charge (though in an emergency not up front). Although all employed French people are entitled to a refund of 75–80 percent of their medical and dental expenses, this can still leave a hefty shortfall, especially after a stay in hospital (accident victims even have to pay for the ambulance that takes them there).

Travel Insurance

Travel insurance policies generally allow one hundred percent reimbursement (minus the first £5 or so of every claim on medical bills), and also cover the cost of **repatriation**, which ordinary E111 cover does not.

Most British policies also cover **loss or theft** of luggage, tickets, money etc, but remember that claims can only be dealt with if a report (*un constat de vol*, in the event of theft) is made to the local police within 24 hours and a copy of the report sent with the claim. Insurance policies can be taken out on the spot at just about any British bank or travel agent. *ISIS*, originally designed for students but now available to all, is a particularly good one, obtainable at any of the student-youth companies detailed in the box on p.5.

Specific Problems

AIDS/HIV – see p.47.

Burns (adults)
Hôpital Saint-Antoine,
184 rue du Fbg-St-Antoine, 12ᵉ
(Mᵒ Faidherbe-Chaligny)   ☎ 49.28.20.00

Burns (children)
Children's Hospital (Hôpital Necker),
149–151 rue de Sèvres, 15ᵉ
(Mᵒ Duroc)   ☎ 42.73.80.00

Dog bites
Institut Pasteur, 211 rue de Vaugirard, 15ᵉ
(Mᵒ Pasteur/Volontaires)   ☎ 40.61.38.00

Drugs
Hôpital Marmottan,
19 rue d'Armaillé,
17ᵉ (Mᵒ Argentine)   ☎ 45.74.00.04

Poisoning
Hôpital Femand-Widal,
200 rue du Fbg-St-Denis, 10ᵉ
(Mᵒ Gare-du-Nord)   ☎ 40.37.04.04

Sexually transmitted diseases
Syphilis and gonorrhea are treated free by law.
Institut A-Fournier,
25 bd St-Jacques, 5ᵉ
(Mᵒ Glacière)   ☎ 40.78.26.00

Alternative Medicine

Association Française d'Acuponcture,
1bis Cité des Fleurs, 17ᵉ
(Mᵒ Brochant)   ☎ 42.29.63.63

Centre d'Homéopathie de Paris,
48 av Gabriel, 8ᵉ
(Mᵒ Champs-Elysées/Clemenceau) ☎ 45.55.12.15

Most pharmacies sell homeopathic medicines.

Emergency Medical Help

All **pharmacies** are equipped, and obliged, to give first aid on request – though they will make a charge. When closed, they all display – usually on the door – the address of the nearest open pharmacy, day or night.

Pharmacies open at night

Dhéry, 84 av des Champs-Elysées, 8e; ☎45.62.02.41 (M° George V): 24 hours.

Carigliogi, 10 bd Sébastopol, 4e; ☎42.72.03.23 (M° Châtelet): Mon–Sat 9am–midnight, Sun noon–midnight.

Opéra, 6 bd des Capucines, 9e; ☎42.65.88.29 (M° Opéra/Madeleine): Mon–Sat 8am–12.30am, Sun 5pm–1am.

Pharmacie d'Italie, 61 av d'Italie, 13e; ☎44.24.19.72 (M° Tolbiac): Mon–Sat 8am–midnight, Sun 9am–midnight.

Drugstore Saint-Germain, 149 bd St-Germain, 6e; ☎42.22.80.00 (M° St-Germain-des-Prés): Mon–Sat 9am–2am, Sun 8pm–2am.

La Nation, 13 pl de la Nation, 11e; ☎43.73.24.03 (M° Nation): Mon noon–midnight, Tues–Sat 8am–midnight, Sun 8pm–midnight.

Pharmacie Swann (Anglo-American pharmacy), 6 rue Castiglione, 1er; ☎42.60.72.96 (M° Tuileries): Mon–Sat 9am–7.30pm). Will translate English prescriptions and make up an equivalent medicine.

At night and on Sundays you can call the local police station (*commissariat de police*) for the address of the nearest open pharmacy or for a doctor on duty.

To trace someone who has been hospitalised, the number to ring is ☎42.77.11.22, 8.30am–5.30pm.

English-speaking hospitals

The American Hospital in Paris, 63 bd Victor-Hugo, Neuilly-sur-Seine (☎46.46.41.25.25; M° Anatole-France/Pont-de-Levallois).

The Hertford British Hospital, 3 rue Barbès, Levallois-Perret (☎46.39.22.22 ; M° Anatole-France).

Immediate Assistance Ambulances

Fire brigade (*with paramedical equipment*) ☎18 or *SAMU* ☎15 or ☎45.67.50.50

Fire ☎18

Nursing SOS Infirmière ☎43.43.25.45

Police/Rescue service ☎17

SOS Help
In English ☎47.23.80.80
(*crisis line/any problem: 3–11pm*).

In French (*24hr*) ☎46.08.52.77

The American Church ☎47.05.07.99
(*Help and counselling on all kinds of problems, Mon–Fri 9.30am–7pm, Sat 9.30am–1pm*).

Rape Crisis (SOS Viol) ☎05.05.95.95
(*free from anywhere in France*).

Doctors and dentists

SOS Médecins (*doctors*) *24hr* ☎47.07.77.77

SOS Dentistes *24hr* ☎43.37.51.00

Association pour les Urgences Médicales de Paris *24hr* ☎48.28.40.09

Urgences Dentaires
9 bd St-Marcel, 13e (M° St-Marcel)
☎47.07.44.44

Urgences psychiatres
(*psychiatrists*) ☎45.65.81.09

Non-EU members should make sure that they aren't already covered by existing policies before taking out travel insurance; Canadians, for example, are usually covered for medical expenses by their provincial health plans. North American travel policies do not insure against theft, except in the case of items in the possession of a responsible third party. Americans might, therefore, prefer to take out a British policy, or supplement existing cover.

Health

To find a **doctor**, stop at any *pharmacie* and ask for an address, or look under *Médecins Qualifiés* in the Yellow Pages of the Parisian phone directory. To qualify for Social Security refunds, make sure the doctor is a *médecin conventionné*. An average consultation fee would be between 100F and 150F. You will be given a *Feuille de Soins* (Statement of Treatment) for later documentation of insurance claims. Prescriptions should be taken to a *pharmacie*, which is also equipped – and obliged – to give first aid (for a fee). The medicines you buy will have little stickers (*vignettes*) attached to them, which you must remove and stick to your *Feuille de Soins*, together with the prescription itself.

Centre Médical Europe, 44 rue Amsterdam, 9ᵉ; ☎42.81.93.33 (Mᵒ Liège; Mon–Fri 8am–7pm, Sat 8am–6pm), has a variety of different practitioners charging low consultation fees.

Disabled Travellers

Paris has no special reputation for providing ease of access or facilities for disabled travellers, but information is readily available. The main tourist office in Paris has *Paris: Guide des Musées, Bibliothèques, Centres et Ateliers Culturels* and *Paris: Guide des Cinémas, Théâtres, Concerts* published by the *Fondation de France* in French only, detailing disabled access and facilities. There is also a booklet called *Touristes Quand Même*, which covers accommodation, transport, and particular aids such as buzzer signals on pedestrian crossings.

In Britain, both the *Holiday Care Service* and *RADAR* have some information about accessible **accommodation**; most of the cross-channel ferry companies offer good facilities, though up-to-date information about access is difficult to get hold of. As far as airlines go, *British Airways* has a better-than-average record for treatment of disabled passengers, and from North America, *Virgin* and *Air Canada* come out tops in terms of

disability awareness (and seating arrangements) and might be worth contacting first for any information they can provide.

The *French Government Tourist Office* in London has a free booklet on disabled access to hotels, called *Paris, Île de France: Hôtels et Residences de Tourisme*. For more information, plus first-hand accounts by disabled travellers to France, see the *Rough Guide* special *Able to Travel/Nothing Ventured*, and contact the organizations below.

Getting Around

If you are physically handicapped, taxis are obliged by law to carry you and to help you into the vehicle – also to carry your guide dog if you are blind. Specially adapted taxis are available on ☎48.37.85.85 or ☎47.08.93.50, but they need to be notified the day before. For travel on the **métro** or **RER**, the *RATP* offers accompanied jour-

---

Travel with a Disability: Useful Contacts

APF (*Association des Paralysés de France*)
22 rue Père-Guerain, 13ᵉ ☎44.16.83.83
A national organization with regional offices all over France which can provide useful information and lists of new and accessible accommodation. Their guide Où ferons-nous étape *is available at the office for 70F or by post to a French address for 100F.*

CNFLRH (*Comité National Français de Liaison pour la Réadaptation des Handicapés*)
38 bd Raspail, 75009 Paris ☎45.48.90.13
Information service for disabled travellers; details of accessible accommodation, holiday centres etc, and various useful guides.

Holiday Care Service
2 Old Bank Chambers, Station Rd,
Horley, Surrey RH6 9HW ☎0293/774535
Information on all aspects of travel.

Kéroul
4545 av Pierre de Coubertin, CP 1000,
Montréal, PQ H1V 3R2 ☎514/2523104
Specializes in travel for mobility-impaired people.

Mobility International USA
PO Box 3551, Eugene,
OR 97403 ☎503/343 1248
Information, access guides, tours and exchange programme.

RADAR (*The Royal Association for Disability and Rehabilitation*)
12 City Forum, 250 City Road,
London EC1V 8AF ☎0171/250 3222
Minicom ☎0171/637 5315
Information on all aspects of travelling with a disability.

Travel Information Center
Moss Rehabilitation Hospital,
1200 W Tabor Rd,
Philadelphia, PA 19141 ☎215/329 5715 x2233
Write for access information.

TRIPSCOPE
63 Esmond Rd,
London W4 1JE ☎0181/994 9294
Phone-in travel information and advice service.

neys for disabled people not in wheelchairs – *Voyage accompagné* – which operates (free) from 8am to 8pm. You have to book your minder on ☎46.70.88.74 a day in advance.

For **wheelchair users**, *RER* lines A and B are accessible, and there is an *RER* guide obtainable from *Régie Autonome des Transports Parisiens*, 53 quai des Grands-Augustins, 6e

(☎43.46.14.14), and for blind people a Braille métro map, obtainable from *L'Association Valentin Haüy*, 5 rue Duroc, 7e (☎47.34.07.90). **AIHROP** (weekdays 10am–3pm; ☎40.24.34.76) arranges transport to and from the airports and within the city.

Cars with hand controls can be rented from **ITS**, 11 bd Auguste-Blanqui, 13e (☎45.88.52.37).

Points of Arrival

Points of arrival in Paris are central – with the exception of the two main airports, Orly and Roissy-Charles de Gaulle, which are easily accessible from the centre by train, bus or taxi. The major bus station and all the main train stations lie on the fast and efficient métro network, making it easy to get to the centre.

By Air

The two main Paris **airports** dealing with international flights are Roissy-Charles de Gaulle (*BA* and *Air France*, as well as most transatlantic flights; flight information on ☎48.62.22.80, 24hr) and Orly Sud/Orly Ouest (flight information is on ☎49.75.15.15; 6am–midnight). Both of these have information desks that can provide maps and accommodation listings.

Roissy-Charles de Gaulle Airport

Roissy, to the northeast of the city, is connected with the centre by the following:
Roissy-Rail: a combination of airport bus and *RER ligne B* train to Gare du Nord and Châtelet (every 15min from 5am until 11.15pm), where you can transfer to the ordinary métro. Taking about 35 minutes, this is the quickest route and costs 35F.

The cheapest route is by **Roissy bus** (30F), connecting the airport with the Opéra-Garnier on the corner of rue Auber and rue Scribe, every 15 minutes from 6am to 11pm. Journey time is approximately 45 minutes.

Air France bus: this costs 48F, and departs every fifteen minutes from 5.45am to 11pm, terminating at Porte Maillot (métro) on the northwest edge of the city, stopping at avenue Carnot,

a hundred metres from the Arc de Triomphe. *Air France* buses also link with Montparnasse at 13 bd de Vaugirard every hour.

Taxis into central Paris cost from 170 to 260F, plus a small luggage supplement, and should take between 45 minutes and one hour.

Before leaving the airport, pick up a good free **map** of the city from the information desk.

Orly Airport

Orly, south of Paris, also has a bus-rail link. *Orly-Rail*, *RER ligne C* trains leave every fifteen minutes from 5.30am to 11.30pm for the Gare d'Austerlitz and other Left Bank stops which connect with the métro. *Orlyval* is a more expensive option of bus and *RER ligne B*. The journey takes around 30 minutes to Châtelet-les-Halles and costs 45F. There is also the *Orlybus* between the airport and Denfert-Rochereau *RER* station (27F). Alternatively, there are *Air France* **coaches** to Gare Montparnasse and Gare des Invalides in the 7e. Both services leave every ten or fifteen minutes from 6am to 11pm, and the journey time is about 35 minutes. A taxi will take about the same time, costing around 130F.

Other Airports

Paris' third airport, **Le Bourget**, is northeast of the centre and handles internal flights only. However, from time to time charter companies also operate services to Beauvais. This is a 70km bus journey from Paris, but all air tickets should include the price of the bus trip into the international coach terminal at Bagnolet.

By Train

Each of Paris' six mainline stations is equipped with cafés, restaurants, *tabacs*, banks, and *bureaux de change* (where you can expect lengthy waits in season), and they are all connected with the métro system.

The central phone number for information is ☎45.82.50.50, for reservations ☎45.65.60.60 and on Minitel 3615 SNCF, 8am–8pm.

The **Gare du Nord** (trains from Boulogne, Calais, the UK, Belgium, Holland, northern

Germany and Scandinavia; information on ☎42.80.03.03, reservations on ☎42.06.49.38) and **Gare de l'Est** (serving eastern France, southern Germany, Switzerland and Austria; information on ☎42.08.49.90, reservations on ☎42.06.49.38) are side by side in the northeast of the city, with the **Gare St-Lazare** (serving the UK, Dieppe and the Normandy coast; information on ☎43.38.52.29, and reservations on ☎43.87.91.70) a little to the west of them.

Still on the Right Bank but towards the southwest corner is the **Gare de Lyon**, for trains from the Alps, the south, Italy and Greece (information on ☎43.45.92.22, and reservations on ☎43.45.93.33); **Gare Montparnasse** is the terminus for Versailles, Chartres, Brittany, the Atlantic coast and *TGV* lines to southwest France (☎45.38.52.29); and **Gare d'Austerlitz** (☎45.84.14.18) for ordinary trains to southwest France, the Loire Valley, Spain and Portugal.

The central number for **all SNCF information** is ☎45.82.50.50.

By Bus

Almost all the **buses** coming into Paris – whether international or domestic – use the **main *gare routière*** at av du Général-du-Gaulle, Bagnolet; ☎49.72.51.51 (M° Gallieni); there's a métro station here for connections into the centre.

The main exception are *Citysprint* buses, which arrive at and depart from rue St-Quentin, around the corner from the Gare du Nord. Check-in for these services takes place at 135 rue Lafayette; ☎42.85.44.55 (M° Gare du Nord).

By Car

If you're **driving** in yourself, don't try to go straight across the city to your destination. Use the ring road – the ***boulevard périphérique*** – to get to the Porte nearest to your destination: it's much quicker, except at rush hour, and easier to find your way.

Once ensconced wherever you're staying, you'd be well advised to garage the car and use public transport. **Parking** is a major problem in the city centre.

Getting Around The City

Finding your way around is remarkably easy, for Paris proper, without its suburbs, is compact and relatively small, with a public transport system that is cheap, fast and meticulously signposted.

To help you get your bearings above ground, think of the Louvre as the **centre**. The Seine flows east to west, cutting the city in two. The Eiffel Tower is **west**, the white pimples of the Sacré-Cœur on top of the hill of Montmartre, **north**. These are the landmarks you most often catch glimpses of as you move about. The area north of the river is known as the **Right Bank** or *rive droite*; to the south is the **Left Bank** or *rive gauche*. Roughly speaking, west is smart and east is scruffy.

Chapter 1, *The Layout of the City*, provides a more detailed introduction to the topography and demography of Paris. See p.57.

Public Transport

The **métro**, combined with the *RER* express lines, is the simplest way of moving around. Trains run from 5.30am to 12.45am; *RER* trains stop at midnight. Stations (abbreviated: M° Concorde, etc) are far more frequent than on the London Underground. Free maps are available at most

> You'll find details of the various forms of help offered for **disabled travellers** on Paris' public transport on p.23.

stations. In addition, every station has a big plan of the network outside the entrance and several inside.

The métro lines are colour-coded and numbered; the *RER* lines are designated by letters. However, within the system you find your way around by following the signs saying *Direction Porte Dauphine, Direction Gallieni* etc; the lines are designated by the the name of the station at the end of the line in the direction in which you are travelling. For instance, if you're travelling from Montparnasse to Châtelet, you follow the sign, *Direction Porte de Clignancourt*; from Gare d'Austerlitz to Grenelle you follow *Direction Boulogne Pont-de-St-Cloud*. The numerous interchanges (*correspondances*) make it possible to travel all over the city in a more or less straight line.

For the latest in subway technology, use the express stations' **computerized routefinders**: at a touch of the button they'll give you four alternative routes to your selected destination, on foot or by public transport. In 1996, the first section – Madeleine to Tolbiac – of the new *Météor* line linking Gennevilliers and the Cité Universitaire via the new national library may be open.

Don't, however, use the métro to the exclusion of **buses**. They are not difficult and of course you see much more. There are free **route maps** available at métro stations, bus terminals and the tourist office. Ask for the *Grand Plan de Paris* which has the best bus map, as well as

> ### The Homeless
>
> There are at least 40,000 **homeless people** in Paris, about a quarter of whom are aged 15–25 and female. Unemployment is at around 12 percent. For the long-term unemployed and those who have never worked, benefits are very minimal. As a result, large numbers of people are forced to beg in the streets and, especially, on the métro.
>
> Some of the homeless (*les sans-logement*) make a bit of money by selling a trio of magazines – *Macadam Journal* (10F of which 6F goes to the seller), *Le Réverbère* (10F) and *Faim de Siècle* (12F of which sellers keep 6.50F). All three are well worth reading.

métro and *RER*. Every bus stop displays the numbers of the buses which stop there, a map showing all the stops on the route, and the times of the first and last buses. If that is not enough, each bus has a map of its own route inside and have a recorded announcement for each approaching stop. Generally speaking, they start around 6.30am and begin their last run around 9pm.

Night buses (*Noctambus*) run on ten routes from place du Châtelet near the Hôtel de Ville every half-hour between 1am and 5am. There is a reduced service on Sunday. Further information is on the *RATP* transport board (*Régie Autonome des Transports Parisiens*), 53ter quai des Grands-Augustins, 6ᵉ (☎43.46.14.14). The *RATP* also runs numerous excursions, including to quite far-flung places, much more cheaply than the commercial operators; their brochure is available at all train and some métro stations.

The **same tickets** are valid for bus, métro and, within the city and immediate suburbs, the *RER* express rail lines, which also extend far out into the Île de France. Long bus journeys can require two tickets; ask the driver, if in doubt.

For a short stay in the city, tickets can be bought in *carnets* of ten from any station or *tabac* – currently 39F, as opposed to 6.50F for a single ticket. There is also a *"Formule 1"* day pass (27F for the city, 85F to include outer suburbs and airports). Don't buy from the touts who hang round the main stations; you'll pay well over the odds, quite often for a used ticket. Be sure to keep your ticket until the end of the journey; you'll be fined on the spot if you can't produce one. Only the *RER* has a choice of first- or second-class, although class distinctions are only in force 9am to 5pm.

If you are staying more than a day or two, it is more economical to have a **Carte Orange**, with a weekly coupon (*coupon hebdomadaire* or *coupon jaune*; get zones 1 and 2 to cover the city and close suburbs). It costs 59F, is valid for an unlimited number of journeys from Monday morning to Sunday evening, and is on sale at all métro stations and *tabacs* (you need a passport

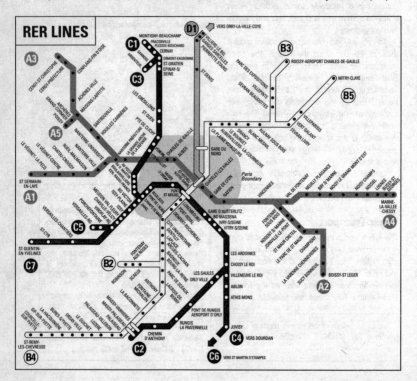

Touring Paris by Public Transport

The overground métro line on the southern route between Charles-de-Gaulle-Étoile and Nation (*ligne* 6) gives you views of the Eiffel Tower, the Île des Cygnes, the Invalides, the new National Library and the Finance Ministry. The northern route (*ligne* 2) is also above ground.

For La Voie Triomphale, take a trip on bus #73 between Grande Arche and the Musée d'Orsay. Bus #24 between Porte de Bercy and Gare St-Lazare follows the left bank of the Seine. Bus #20 from Gare de Lyon follows the Grands Boulevards and does a loop through the 1er and 2e *arrondissements*. Many more bus jouneys – outside rush hours – are worthwhile trips in themselves.

photo – 20F from the machines in the main stations). There is also a monthly coupon (*mensuel*) for 208F, and a cheaper *carte hebdomadaire*, which allows only two journeys a day for a week (40F).

Other possibilities are the 3- and 5-day visitors' coupons (**Paris Visites**) at 90F and 145F for Paris and close suburbs, or 200F and 275F to include the airports, Versailles and Disneyland Paris. The main advantage of these is that, unlike the *coupon hebdomadaire* whose validity runs unalterably from Monday to Sunday, they can begin on any day. They also allow you discounts on Paris boat trips, the Grande Arche, Parc Astérix, Musée Grevin, the top of Tour Montparnasse and the Cité des Sciences et de l'Industrie of between 20 and 35 percent.

All these tickets entitle you to unlimited travel on bus and métro. On the métro you put the coupon through the turnstile slot, but make sure to return it to its plastic folder; it is reusable throughout the period of its validity. On a bus you show the whole *carte* to the driver as you board – don't put it into the punching machine.

If it's late at night or you feel like treating yourself, don't hesitate to use the **taxis**. Their charges are very reasonable. To avoid being ripped off, check that the meter shows the appropriate fare rate. Even before you get into the taxi you can check by seeing which of the three small indicator lights on its roof is switched on. A (passenger side) indicates the daytime rate for Paris and the *boulevard périphérique*; B is the rate for Paris at night, on Sunday and on public holidays, and for the suburbs during the day; C

(driver's side) is the night rate for the suburbs. **Tipping** is not mandatory, but fifteen percent will be expected. Finding a taxi rank is usually better than trying to hail one down in the street. The large white light means the taxi is free; the orange light below means it's engaged. Average journeys within the city cost 35–60F. Taxi ranks will show phone numbers to call for that *arrondissement*.

Driving

Travelling around by **car**, in the daytime at least, is hardly worth it because of the difficulty of finding parking space, although the *Service de Stationnement de la Ville de Paris* (☎43.46.98.30; Mon–Fri 9am–noon & 1.30–5pm) will provide information about car parks and prices. Whatever you do, don't park in a bus lane or the *Axe Rouge* express routes (marked with a red square). Should you be **towed away** – and it's extremely expensive – you'll find your car in the pound belonging to that particular *arrondissement*. You'll have to phone the local town hall (*mairie*) to get the address.

In the event of a **breakdown** you can call *SOS Dépannage*, 28bis rue Pascal, 5e (☎47.07.99.99); *Aleveque Daniel*, 116 rue de la Convention, 15e (☎48.28.12.00); or *Aligre Dépannage*, 92 bd de Charonne, 20e (☎49.78.87.50), for round-the-clock assistance. Alternatively, ask the police.

For **car rental**, in addition to the big international companies like *Avis*, 5 rue Bixio, 7e (☎46.09.92.12); *Budget*, 4 av Franklin-D-Roosevelt, 8e (☎46.86.65.65); *Europcar*, 145 av Malakoff, 16e (☎30.43.82.82); *Hertz* (☎47.88.51.51); and *InterRent*, 87 rue la Boétie, 8e (☎40.74.00.07); some good local firms are: *Acar*, 77 rue Lagny, 20e; ☎43.79.54.54 (Mº Porte-de-Vincennes; Mon–Sat 8am–12.30pm & 2–7pm); also at 99 bd A-Blanqui, 13e (☎45.8.28.38), and 85 rue de la Chapelle, 18e (☎42.09.42.06); *Dergi et Cie*, 60 bd St-Marcel, 5e; ☎45.87.27.04 (Mº Gobelins; Mon–Sat 8am–7pm); *Locabest*, 9 rue Abel, 12e; ☎43.46.05.05 (Mº Gare-de-Lyon; Mon–Sat 7.30am–7pm); and *Rent a Car*, 79 rue de Bercy, 12e; ☎45.45.15.15 (Mº Bercy; Mon–Sat 8.30am–7pm).

Remember that you have to be eighteen years of age to drive in France, regardless of whether you hold a licence.

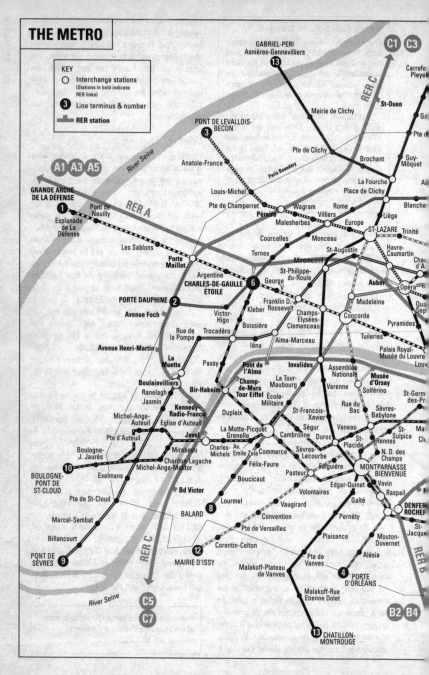

THE METRO

KEY
○ Interchange stations
(Stations in bold indicate RER links)
3 Line terminus & number
▨ RER station

A1 A3 A5

C1 C3

GABRIEL-PERI
Asnières-Gennevilliers
13

Mairie de Clichy

Carrefo
Pleye

St-Ouen

Ga

Pte de Clichy

Brochant

Guy-
Môquet

RER C

River Seine

PONT DE LEVALLOIS-
BECON
3

Anatole-France

Paris Boundary

La Fourche
Place de Clichy

Al

GRANDE ARCHE
DE LA DÉFENSE
1

Louis-Michel

Pte de Champerret

Wagram

Rome

Blanche

Pont de
Neuilly

RER A

Péreire

Villiers

Liège

ST-LAZARE

Trinité

Pte Dauphine

Esplanade
de La
Défense

Malesherbes

Europe

Les Sablons

Courcelles

Monceau

St-Augustin

Havre-
Caumartin

Chau
d'A

**Porte
Maillot**

Ternes

Miromesnil

Auber

Opéra

R

Argentine

**CHARLES-DE-GAULLE
ÉTOILE**

St-Philippe-
du-Roule

Madeleine

Qua
Sep

**PORTE DAUPHINE
2**

6

George
V

Franklin D.
Roosevelt

Champs-
Elysées-
Clemenceau

Concorde

Pyramides

Avenue Foch

Victor-
Hugo

Kleber

Boissière

Tuileries

Palais Royal-
Musée du Louvre

Rue de
la Pompe

Trocadéro

Iéna

Alma-Marceau

Louv

Avenue Henri-Martin

Passy

Pont de
l'Alma

Invalides

Assemblée
Nationale

**Musée
d'Orsay**

St-Germ
des-Pr

**La
Muette**

**Champ-
de-Mars
Tour Eiffel**

La Tour-
Maubourg

Varenne

Solférino

Boulainvilliers

Bir-Hakeim

École-
Militaire

Rue du
Bac

Sèvres-
Babylone

Ranelagh

Dupleix

St-Francois-
Xavier

Vaneau

St-
Sulpice

Ma
Cli

Jasmin

**Kennedy-
Radio-France**

La Motte-Picquet
Grenelle

Ségur

Duroc

St-
Placide

St-
Rennes

Michel-Ange-
Auteuil

Eglise d'Auteuil

Cambronne

Sèvres-
Lecourbe

N. D. des
Champs

Pte d'Auteuil

Javel

Charles-
Michels

Av.
Emile Zola

Commerce

Falguière

**MONTPARNASSE
BIENVENUE**

Boulogne-
J. Jaurès

Mirabeau

Félix-Faure

Pasteur

Edgar-Quinet

Vavin

10

Exelmans

Chardon-Lagache

Boucicaut

Volontaires

Gaîté

Raspail

BOULOGNE-
PONT DE
ST-CLOUD

Michel-Ange-Molitor

Bd Victor

8

Lourmel

Vaugirard

Pernéty

**DENFER
ROCHE**

Pte de St-Cloud

Convention

Plaisance

St-
Jacque

Marcel-Sembat

BALARD

Pte de Versailles

Mouton-
Duvernet

Billancourt

RER C

12

Corentin-Celton

Pte de
Vanves

Alésia

RER B

PONT DE
SÈVRES
9

MAIRIE D'ISSY

Malakoff-Plateau
de Vanves

4

**PORTE
D'ORLÉANS**

B2 B4

River Seine

C5

C7

Malakoff-Rue
Etienne Dolet

13 CHATILLON-
MONTROUGE

30

THE BASICS

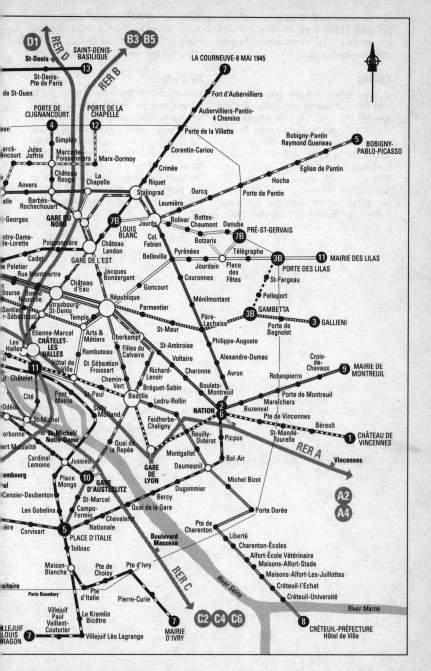

If you would like to fix things up in advance, in London, *Holiday Autos*, 25 Saville Row W1X 1AA (☎071 491 1111) have some of the most competitive rates going.

Cycling

If you are reckless enough to want to **cycle** and don't have your own machine, you can hire from *Paris-Vélo*, 2 rue du Fer-à-Moulin, 5e; ☎43.37.59.22 (Mº Censier-Daubenton; Mon–Sat 10am–7pm; closed public holidays); *Cycles Laurent*, 99 bd Voltaire, 11e (Mº République/ Oberkampf; Mon–Sat 10am–12.30pm & 2–7pm); *Paris By Cycle*, 9 rue de la Jonquière, 17e; ☎42.63.36.63 (Mº Porte de Clichy), and 78 rue de l'Ouest, 14e; ☎40.47.08.04 (Mº Gaîté/ Pernety); or, *Mountain Bike Trip*, place Étienne-

Pernet, 15e; ☎48.42.57.87 (Mº Félix-Faure). A deposit of around 2000F is usually required. Rental rates are around 100F for a day, 150F for 24hrs, 500F for a week.

By Boat

There remains one final mode of transport – by *Batobus* along the Seine. At the moment there are only five stops, though more are planned, and the service operates from April to September. The stops are: port de la Bourdonnais (Eiffel Tower), port de Solférino (Musée d'Orsay), quai Malaquais (Musée du Louvre), quai de Montebello (Notre-Dame) and quai de l'Hôtel de Ville. Boats run every 36 minutes from 10am to 7pm: total journey time is 21 minutes; tickets 15F a stop.

Information and Maps

In Paris, the **main tourist office** is at 127 avenue des Champs-Elysées, 8ᵉ; ☎ 49.52.53.54; fax 49.52.53.00 (Mᵒ Charles-de-Gaulle–Étoile; daily 9am–8pm all year round, except Dec 25, Jan 1 and May 1), where the efficient but overworked staff will answer questions from the predictable to the bizarre. There are **branch offices** at the main train stations: Austerlitz (Mon–Sat 8am–3pm), Est (May–Oct Mon–Sat 8am–9pm, otherwise Mon–Sat 8am–8pm), Lyon (May–Oct Mon–Sat 8am–9pm, otherwise Mon–Sat 8am–8pm), Nord (May–Oct Mon–Sat 8am–9pm & Sun 1–8pm, otherwise Mon–Sat 8am–8pm); and at the Eiffel Tower (daily May–Sept 11am–6pm).

For recorded **tourist information in English**, phone ☎ 47.20.88.89. Alternative sources of information are the **Hôtel de Ville information office** at 29 rue du Rivoli, 4ᵉ; ☎ 42.76.43.43 (Mᵒ Hôtel-de-Ville; Mon–Sat 9am–6pm) and electronic billboards in the streets.

For the clearest picture of the layout of the city the best **map** you can get is Michelin no. 10, the 1:10,000 Plan de Paris. More convenient is the pocket-sized Falkplan, which folds out only as you need it, or, if you're staying any length of time, one of the various A–Z street plans, which have a street index, bus route diagrams, useful

The French Government Tourist Office gives away large quantities of maps and glossy brochures for every region of France, including lists of hotels and campsites. For Paris, these include some useful fold-out leaflets detailing sights to see, markets, shops, museums, ideas for excursions, useful phone numbers and opening hours, as well as maps and more esoteric information like lists of Paris gardens and squares.

Paris Addresses and the Demise of the *Concierge*

The number after Paris addresses – 3ᵉ, 11ᵉ, etc – indicates the postal district or *arrondissement*. There are twenty of them altogether. The first, which is written 1ᵉʳ, is centred on the Louvre, with the rest unfurling outwards in a clockwise spiral – see map on p.58. They are an important aid to locating places, and their boundaries are clearly marked on all maps.

The vast majority of Parisians live in flats in apartment buildings, most of which date from the nineteenth century or earlier. They tend to be purpose-built, rather than the conversions typical of London terrace houses. Until very recently they were invariably guarded by a *concierge*, often, but not always, a woman who lived with her family – if she had one – in dark, pokey rooms beside the main entrance.

Paris *concierges* were a veritable institution. Besides being responsible for looking after the common areas, they took in the mail, relayed messages, ran errands, and, above all, kept a very beady eye on all comings and goings within the building and the adjacent streets. They ran an effective, if unofficial, neighbourhood watch, and a lightning-fast bush telegraph. They had a reputation for being ferocious, disapproving nosy-parkers. If not always loved individually, they were loved as an institution.

Sadly, they are now an endangered species, partly because stingy landlords won't pay their meagre salaries and partly because there is a general trend towards the dehumanization and depersonalization of life, in Paris as elsewhere.

Instead, most Parisian street doors are protected by *digicode* panels. If you don't know the code, you can't get in. So, when invited to someone's home, you have to remember to ask for the code.

addresses, and show car parks and one-way streets – all a great deal more useful than the tourist office free hand-outs. The information desk at Roissy airport, however, do provide a useful, free map.

Some of the A–Zs, like the *Cartes Taride*, include the nearer suburban areas. For a picture of the countryside around Paris – if you plan any of the excursions outlined in Chapter 20 – Michelin no. 196, Environs de Paris, is best.

French Government Tourist Offices

Australia
BNP Building 12th floor
12 Castlereagh St
Sydney NSW 2000 ☎612/231 5244

Canada
1981 av McGill College, Suite 490
Montréal, QUE H3A 2W9
☎514/288 4264, fax 514/845 4868

30 St Patrick St, Suite 700
Toronto ONT M5T 3A3
☎416/593 6427, fax 416/979 7587

Denmark
NY Ostergade 3.3
DK–1101 Copenhagen ☎33/11 49 12

Ireland
35 Lower Abbey St
Dublin 1 ☎1/703 4046, fax 01/874 7324

Netherlands
Prinsengr. 670
1017 KX Amsterdam
☎020/627 33 18, fax 020/620 33 39

Norway
Storgaten 10A
0155 Oslo 1 ☎22/42 33 87, fax 22/42 33 87

Sweden
Norrmalmstorg 1 Av
S11146 Stockholm ☎08/679 79 75

UK
178 Piccadilly
London W1V 0AL ☎0171/491 7622*

USA
610 Fifth Ave, Suite 222
New York, NY 10020-2452 ☎212/757 1125

645 North Michigan Ave
Chicago, ILL 60611-2836 ☎312/337 6301

9454 Wilshire Blvd
Beverly Hills, CA 90212-2967 ☎213/271 7838

Cedar Maple Plaza
2305 Cedar Springs Blvd
Dallas, TX 75201
☎214/720 4010, fax 214/720 0250

*In Britain, the FGTO has an information service, EuropAssistance, on a premium rate (Mon–Fri 9am–10pm, Sat 9am–5pm; 49p peak rate, 39p cheap rate). This is much easier to get through on; brochures will be sent without postage charge, and specific queries are quickly referred to the relevant organization.

Map outlets

UK

London: *National Map Centre*, 22–24 Caxton St, SW1 (☎0171/222 4945); *Stanfords*, 12–14 Long Acre, WC2 (☎0171/836 1321); *The Travellers Bookshop*, 25 Cecil Court, WC2 (☎0171/836 9132).

Edinburgh: *Thomas Nelson and Sons Ltd*, 51 York Place, EH1 3JD (☎0131/557 3011).

Glasgow: *John Smith and Sons*, 57–61 St Vincent St (☎0141/221 7472).

Maps by **mail or phone order** are available from *Stanfords* (☎0171/836 1321).

North America

Chicago: *Rand McNally*, 444 N Michigan Ave, IL 60611 (☎312/321-1751).

Montréal: *Ulysses Travel Bookshop*, 4176 St-Denis (☎514/289-0993).

New York: *British Travel Bookshop*, 551 5th Ave, NY 10176 (☎1-800/448-3039 or 212/490-6688); *The Complete Traveler Bookstore*, 199 Madison Ave, NY 10016 (☎212/685-9007); *Rand McNally*, 150 East 52nd St, NY 10022 (☎212/758-7488); *Traveler's Bookstore*, 22 West 52nd St, NY 10019 (☎212/664-0995).

San Francisco: *The Complete Traveler Bookstore*, 3207 Fillmore St, CA 92123 (☎415/923-1511); *Rand McNally*, 595 Market St, CA 94105 (☎415/777-3131).

Santa Barbara: *Map Link, Inc*, 25 East Mason St, CA 93101 (☎805/965-4402);

Seattle: *Elliot Bay Book Company*, 101 South Main St, WA 98104 (☎206/624-6600).

Toronto: *Open Air Books and Maps*, 25 Toronto St, M5R 2C1 (☎416/363-0719).

Vancouver: *World Wide Books and Maps*, 1247 Granville St (☎604/687-3320).

Washington DC: *Rand McNally*, 1201 Connecticut Ave NW, 20036 (☎202/223-6751).

Note: *Rand McNally* now has 24 stores across the US; call ☎1-800/333-0136 (ext 2111) for the address of your nearest store, or for **direct mail** maps.

Australia and New Zealand

Adelaide: *The Map Shop*, 16a Peel St, SA 5000 (☎08/231 2033).

Brisbane: *Hema*, 239 George St, QLD 4000 (☎07/221 4330).

Melbourne: *Bowyangs*, 372 Little Bourke St, VIC 3000 (☎03/670 4383).

Sydney: *Travel Bookshop*, 20 Bridge St, NSW 2000 (☎02/241 3554).

Perth: *Perth Map Centre*, 891 Hay St, WA 6000 (☎09/322 5733).

Costs, Money and Banks

Because of the relatively low cost of accommodation and eating out, at least by capital city standards, Paris is not an outrageously expensive place to visit. If you are one of two people sharing a hotel room, you can manage a reasonably comfortable existence, including restaurant, museum and café stops, on 500–600F per person per day (around £60–70/ $90–110). At the bottom line, by watching the pennies, staying at a hostel (115F for bed and breakfast) and being strong-willed about cups of coffee and culture, you could survive on as little as 250F (around £30/$45) a day, including a cheap restaurant meal – less if you limit eating to street snacks or market food.

For two or more people hotel **accommodation** can be almost as cheap as the hostels, though a sensible average estimate for a double room would be around 350F. As for food, you can spend as much or as little as you like. There are large numbers of reasonable, if not very exciting, **restaurants** with three- or four-course menus for between 75F and 150F. **Picnic fare**, obviously, is much less costly, especially when you buy in the markets and cheap supermarket chains. More sophisticated meals – takeaway salads and ready-to-(re)heat dishes – can be put together for reasonable prices if you shop at *charcuteries* (delis) and the equivalent counters of many supermarkets.

Transport within the city is inexpensive. The **Carte Orange**, for example, with a 59F weekly ticket (see p.28 for more details) gives you a week's unlimited travel on buses and métro.

Museums and monuments have become a lot more expensive in recent years and are likely to prove one of the biggest invisible wallet-eroders. Although **reduced admission** for young people to museums is a function of age – under 26 – not student status, it is worth carrying the *ISIC* (International Student Identity Card), if you are entitled to it, simply because of its universal acceptability as a proof of identity, which is not the case with a British *NUS* card. For reductions as someone over 60 years old you will need to carry your passport around with you. If you are going to do a lot of museum duty, it is worth considering buying a museum card (details on p.265).

Most importantly, budget-watchers need to be wary of nightlife and café-lounging; drinks in flash pubs and bars can quickly become a major expense.

Money

Travellers' cheques are one of the safest ways of carrying your money. Worldwide, they're available from almost any major bank (whether you have an account there or not), usually for a service charge of one percent on the amount purchased. Some banks take 1.25 or even 1.5 percent, and your own bank may offer cheques free of charge provided you meet certain conditions. Ask first, as you can easily make significant savings. *Thomas Cook, Visa* and *American Express* are the most widely recognized brands.

Europeans can also obtain *Eurocheques*, backed up with a card, which can be used for paying shop and restaurant bills in the same way as an ordinary cheque at home. With a PIN number, you can also use them in money machines which show the same symbol as on your card. Obtaining **French franc travellers' cheques** can be worthwhile: they can often be used as cash, and you should get the face value of the cheques when you change them, so commission is only paid on purchase. Banks being banks, however, this is not always the case.

Credit charge cards are widely accepted; just watch for the window stickers. *Visa/Barclaycard –*

known as the *Carte Bleue* in France – is almost universally recognized; *Access, Mastercard* – sometimes called *Eurocard* – and *American Express* rank considerably lower. *Switch* and *Delta* cards can be used in some money machines and all credit cards are gradually being linked up, so check with your bank or building society before you go. All money machines give you the choice of instructions in French or English. Also worth considering are post office **International Giro Cheques**, which work in a similar way to ordinary bank cheques, except that you can cash them through post offices, which are more common and have longer opening hours than banks.

Post offices will also cash *Eurocheques* (made out in francs) and US dollar travellers' cheques. You can also get cash over the counter with a *Visa* card.

Standard **banking hours** are 9am to 4.30pm; closed Saturday, Sunday, and public holidays. There are money-exchange bureaux open every day at Roissy and Orly airports (6.30am–11.30pm); at the train stations: Austerlitz (7am–9pm), Est (6.30am–10pm), Lyon (6.30am–11pm), Nord (6.30am–11pm), St-Lazare (8am–8pm); and in **Paris** at: 2 rue de l'Amiral-Coligny, 1er (M$^\circ$ Louvre-Rivoli; 11am–7pm); 2 rue de Marengo, 1er (M$^\circ$ Louvre-Rivoli; 11am–7pm), 151 rue St-Honoré, 1er (M$^\circ$ Palais-Royale; 11am–7pm); 2 place Vendôme, 1er (M$^\circ$ Opéra/Tuileries; 11am–7pm); and 2 place St-Michel, 5e (M$^\circ$ St-Michel; 11am–9pm). Banks will have a notice on the door if they do currency exchange. There are also automatic exchange machines at the airports and train stations, outside many money exchange bureaux and at the *Crédit du Nord*, 24 bd Sébastopol, 1er (M$^\circ$ Les Halles), and *CCF*, 115 av des Champs-Élysée, 8e (M$^\circ$ Georges V). Both these banks and *BNP*, 2 pl de l'Opéra, 2e (M$^\circ$ Opéra) will change all currencies and travellers' cheques. The automatic machines accept £10 and £20 notes as well as dollars and other European currency notes, but offer a very poor rate of exchange.

Rates of exchange and commission vary from bank to bank; the usual procedure is a one to two percent commission on travellers' cheques and a flat rate charge on cash. Be wary of banks claiming to charge no commission at all; often they are merely adjusting the exchange rate to their own advantage. On the whole, it is better to use banks than exchange bureaux.

In spite of the **money-exchange counters** and machines at train stations and airports, it is still a sensible precaution to buy some French francs before leaving home. The franc, abbreviated as F or sometimes FF, is divided into 100 centimes and comes in notes of 500F, 200F, 100F, 50F and 20F, and coins of 20F, 10F, 5F, 2F or 1F, and 50, 20 and 10 centimes.

Communications – Post, Phones and Media

Post

The French term for the post office is *la Poste* or *les PTT*; alternatively, *un bureau de poste* for a post office. The **main Paris post office** is at 52 rue du Louvre, 1er (Mº Étienne Marcel) and is the best place to have your mail sent, unless you have a particular branch office in mind. It's open 24 hours for *poste restante* and telephones. Letters should be addressed (preferably with the surname underlined and in capitals and initials, rather than forenames in full) to Poste Restante, 52 rue du Louvre, 75001 Paris.

To **collect your mail**, you need a passport or other convincing ID, and there'll be a small charge. You should ask for all your names to be checked, as filing systems are not brilliant.

Other post offices are open 8am–7pm, Monday to Friday, and 9am–noon on Saturday. For sending letters, remember that you can buy **stamps** (*timbres*) with less queuing from *tabacs*.

Parisian addresses

When writing to Parisian addresses, make up the postcode by adding the *arrondissement* number to the generic 750: so the 14e becomes 75014, Paris.

Telephones

You can make **international phone calls** from any box (*cabine*) and can receive calls wherever there's a blue logo of a ringing bell. A 50 unit (40F) and 120 unit (96F) **phone card** (called a *télécarte*) is fairly essential, since coin boxes are being phased out. Phone cards are available from *tabacs* and newsagents as well as post offices.

The **English-speaking operator** is available on ☎19.00.44 for the UK, and ☎19.00.11 for the US. Otherwise, to make an **international call**, put the money or card in first, dial ☎19, and wait for a tone; then dial the country code, followed by subscriber's number minus its initial 0. To call **from Paris to anywhere else in France**, dial ☎16, followed by all eight digits of the number (which includes the former area code – displayed in every *cabine*). To call **to a Paris number from anywhere else in France**, start by dialling ☎16-1.

To save fiddling around with coins or phone cards, post offices often have **metered booths** from which you can make calls connected by a clerk; you pay afterwards. To make a reverse-charge call, dial ☎19, wait for the tone, then dial 33 and the country code to speak to the bilingual operator. For directory enquiries, dial ☎12 for numbers within France; for international numbers, dial ☎19.33.12, followed by the relevant country code.

Peak rates are 73 centimes for six minute local calls, 2.19F a minute for places within 100km, and apply Mon–Fri 8am–12.30pm and 1.30–6pm & Sat 8am–12.30pm. Between Mon–Sat 12.30–1.30pm and Mon–Fri 6–9.30pm rates are thirty percent less. Between Mon–Sat 6–8am, Mon–Fri 9.30–10.30pm and Sun 6am–10.30pm rates are fifty percent less. Cheapest rates (65 percent less) are daily 10.30pm–6am.

To call TO Paris from the UK, the US, or virtually anywhere else in the world, dial ☎010 331 followed by the eight-digit number.

Faxes (télécopiés) can be sent but not received from main post offices.

Minitel

Every Paris phone subscriber has a minitel, an on-line computer allowing access through the phone lines to all kinds of directories, databases, chat lines etc. You will also find them in post offices, and looking up addresses and phone numbers is free (dial 11 and press *Connexion Fin*). Most organizations, from sports federations to government institutions to gay groups, have a code consisting of numbers and letters to call up information, leave messages, make reservations etc. You dial the number on the phone, wait for a fax-type tone, then type the letters on the keyboard, and finally, press Connexion Fin (the same key ends the connection). If you're at all computer literate and can understand basic keybord terms in French (*retour* – return, *envoi* – enter, etc) you shouldn't find them hard to use, and some friendly soul in the post office will probably help if you get stuck. Be warned that most services cost more than phone rates.

Newspapers and Periodicals

British newspapers, the *European*, and the *International Herald Tribune* are pretty widely on sale. The monthly Paris *Free Voice* produced by the American Church at 65 quai d'Orsay, 7ᵉ, has good listings, ads for flats, courses etc, and interesting articles on current events. It's available from the church and from English-language bookshops.

The **listings magazines** *Pariscope* and *L'Official des Spectacles* come out on Wednesdays, cost next to nothing, and are indispensable for knowing what's on. *Pariscope* in particular has a huge and comprehensive section on films.

Of the **French daily papers**, *Le Monde* is the most intellectual; it is widely respected, but is somewhat austere, making no concessions to such frivolities as pictures. *Libération* is moderately left-wing, independent, and more colloquial, with good, if choosy, coverage, while rigorous left-wing criticism of the French government comes from *L'Humanité*, the Communist Party paper. The other nationals, and the local paper

Le Quotidien de Paris, are all firmly right wing in their politics. Sporadic satirical publications appear from *Jalons*, a group inspired by the old Situationists, who organize such things as street demonstrations against the winter cold.

Weeklies of the *Newsweek/Time* model include the wide-ranging and socialist-inclined *Le Nouvel Observateur* and its right-wing counterpoint *L'Express*. *Globe* is a more exciting and less pompous weekly. The best investigative journalism is in the weekly satirical paper *Le Canard Enchainé*. *Charlie Hebdo* is a sort of *Private Eye* or *Spy Magazine* equivalent. **Monthlies** include *L'Autre Journal*, which covers culture as well as news, *Actuel*, which is good for current events. *Le Monde* publishes a beautifully designed monthly *Le Monde des Débats* – good, serious stuff – and there are, of course, all the French versions of *Vogue, Elle, Marie-Claire*, as well as *Paris-Match* for gossip about stars and the royal families.

"Moral" **censorship** of the press is rare. On the newsstands you'll find pornography of every shade, as well as covers featuring drugs, sex, blasphemy and bizarre forms of grossness alongside knitting patterns and DIY. You'll also find French **comics** – *bandes dessinées* – which often indulge these interests and are wonderful.

TV and Radio

French TV broadcasts six channels, three of them public, along with a good many more cable and satellite channels (see Chapter 19), which include the BBC World Service with *News, Newsnight, Eastenders* and other favourite programmes. If you've got a **radio**, you can tune into English-language news on the BBC World Service on 648khz or between 6.195 and 12.095MHz shortwave at intervals throughout the day and night. BBC Radio 4 from 5am to 11.45pm GMT and the World Service from 11.45pm to 5am GMT on 198KHz long wave, is usually quite clear, while the Voice of America transmits on 90.5, 98.8 and 102.4FM. Radio Classique (FM 101.1) is a classical music station with a minimum of chat and no commercials. For news in French, there's the state-run France Inter (FM 87.8), Europe 1 (FM 104.7) or round-the-clock news on France Infos (FM 105.5).

Business Hours and Public Holidays

Most shops, businesses, information services, museums and banks in Paris stay open all day. The exceptions are the smaller shops and enterprises. Basic hours of business are from 8 or 9am to 6.30 or 7.30pm. Sunday and Monday are standard closing days, though you can always find *boulangeries* and food shops which stay open – on Sunday normally until noon. The standard banking hours are 9am–4.30pm, closed Saturday and Sunday; for more details, see p.265.

Museums open between 9 and 10am and close between 5 and 6pm. Summer times may differ from winter times; if they do, both are indicated in the listings. Summer hours usually extend from mid-May or early June to mid-September, but sometimes they apply only during July and August, occasionally even from Palm Sunday to All Saints' Day. Don't be caught out by **closing days** – usually Tuesday or Monday, sometimes both. **Admission charges** can be a bit off-putting, though you can get reductions if you're under 26 or over 60 in some museums. **Churches** and **cathedrals** are almost always open all day, with charges only for the crypt, treasuries or cloister, and little fuss is made about how you're dressed.

One other factor can disrupt your plans. There are thirteen **national holidays** (*jours fériés*), when most shops and businesses, though not museums or restaurants, are closed. They are:

January 1

Good Friday (Alsace only)

Easter Sunday

Easter Monday

Ascension Day (forty days after Easter)

Whitsun (seventh Sunday after Easter, plus the Monday)

May 1

May 8 (VE Day)

July 14 (Bastille Day)

August 15 (Assumption of the Virgin Mary)

November 1 (All Saints' Day)

November 11 (1918 Armistice Day)

Christmas Day

Festivals and Events

With all that's going on in Paris, festivals – in the traditional "popular" sense – are no big deal. But there is an impressive array of arts events and, not to be missed for the politically interested, an inspired internationalist jamboree at the *Fête de l'Humanité*.

Popular Festivals and Fêtes

February – *Foire à la Feraille de Paris*. Antiques and bric-à-brac fair in the 12ᵉ (Parc Floral de Paris and the Bois de Vincennes).

Week before Lent – *Mardi Gras*. The *Mardi Gras* are enthusiastically celebrated in the south of France but go almost unnoticed in Paris. A few kids take the opportunity to cover unwary passers-by with flour.

End March, beginning April – *Festival International: Films des Femmes*. At Créteil; information from Maison des Arts, place Salvador-Allende, 9400 Créteil (☎49.80.18.88). This festival is just under twenty years old and gets better every year; tickets are cheap and you can vote for the awards.

April – *Foire du Trône*. A funfair located in the 12ᵉ, Pelouse de Reuilly and Bois de Vincennes.

May – *Marathon International de Paris*. Departs from Place de la Concorde, arrives at the Hippodrome de Vincennes 42km later.

Last week of May and first week of June – *Roland Garros tennis tournament*.

June – *Course des Garçons de Café*. Waiters' race in the streets of Paris with laden trays of alcohol. Departs from and arrives at the Hôtel de Ville, 1ᵉʳ.

June 21 (Summer Solstice) – *Fête de la Musique de Paris*. Midsummer's day usually sees parades, including the Gay Pride march, street theatre and amusements, and live bands throughout the city.

June – *Paris Villages*. Local festivities including regional folk dancing in various Paris neighbourhoods.

July – *Festival de Jazz*. International stars scattered around a variety of Paris venues.

End July – *Arrivée du Tour de France Cyclistes*. The Tour de France cyclists cross the finishing line, in the avenue des Champs-Élysées.

July 14 – *Bastille Day*. The 1789 surrender of the Bastille is celebrated in official pomp with parades of tanks down the Champs-Élysées, firework displays and concerts. At night there is dancing in the streets around place de la Bastille to good French bands.

July 15–Aug 15 – *Paris Quartier d'Été*. Music, cinema and theatre events around the city.

September – *Fête de l'Humanité*. (Admission 40F for three days; Mᵒ La Courneuve, then bus #177 or special shuttle from *RER*). Sponsored by the French Communist Party, this annual event just north of Paris at La Courneuve attracts people in their tens of thousands and of every political persuasion. Food and drink (all very cheap), and music and crafts from every corner of the globe, are the predominant features, rather than political platforms. Each French regional CP has a vast restaurant tent with regional specialities, French and foreign bands play on an open-air stage, and the event ends on Sunday night with an impressive firework display.

Autumn: Sept–Dec – *Festival d'Art Sacré*. Concerts and recitals of church music, much of it in Paris churches.

Autumn: end Sept to end Dec – *Festival d'Automne*. Theatre and music, including lots of eastern European companies, as well as American and Japanese; multilingual productions. Lots of avant-garde and multimedia stuff, most of it pretty exciting.

October – *Festival de Jazz de Paris*. Usually in the second half of the month and usually a feast of French and international music.

October – *Fêtes des Vendanges*. A grape harvest in the Montmartre vineyard, at the corner of rue des Saules and rue Saint-Vincent during the first weekend of the month.

October – *Foire Internationale d'Art Contemporain (FIAC)*. International contemporary art show.

October – *Prix de l'Arc de Triomphe*. Horse racing with high stakes.

November – *Mois de la Photo*. Photographic exhibitions are held in museums throughout the city.

November – *Salon d'Automne*. Art exhibition of new talent at the Grand Palais, avenue Winston-Churchill.

November – *Prix International de Danse*. Prestigious dancing title.

Feminist Contacts and Information

French culture remains stuck with myths about femininity that disable women to a far greater extent than in Britain, Holland or the USA, and although Parisian lesbians have a strong network, havens for non-lesbian feminists are few – the *Maison des Femmes*, the Marguerite Durand library and the *hammams* are about it.

Maison des Femmes

8 Cité Prost, off rue Chanzy, 11ᵉ; ☎43.48.24.91 (Mᵒ Faidherbe-Chaligny). Mon 6–8pm, Wed 3–8pm, Fri 6–8pm; Fri café 8pm–midnight.

A women's meeting place run by *Paris Féministe* they produce a fortnightly bulletin and also organize a wide range of events and actions, as well as being home to lesbian, anti-racist and North African women's groups; rape crisis and battered women's organizations also meet at the Maison.

This is by far the best place to come if you want to make contact with the movement. Don't be put off by the back-alley entrance, and though English speakers can't be guaranteed, you can count on a friendly reception. There's a cafeteria run by *MIEL – Hydromel –* operating for drinks and dinner most Friday evenings, occasional open days with exhibitions and concerts or discos, workshops and self-defence classes, discussions and film shows.

Centre Audio-Visuel Simone de Beauvoir

5 passage Pivert, 11ᵉ; ☎43.57.80.69 (Mᵒ Goncourt). Mon–Fri 10am–5pm.

An archive of audiovisual works by or about women, financed by de Beauvoir in her lifetime and maintained by her bequest. There are regular screenings (which you'll find listed in *Lesbia* magazine – see overleaf). Payment of a small fee allows you individual access to this comprehensive and compelling collection.

ARCL (Archives, Recherches et Cultures Lesbiennes)

Post box (BP) 362, 75526, Paris Cedex 11; answerphone ☎48.05.25.89. Fri 6–8pm – hours may change.

See under Gay and Lesbian Paris, p.46.

Bibliothèque Marguerite Durand

3rd floor, 79 rue Nationale, 13ᵉ (Mᵒ Tolbiac). Tues–Sat 2–6pm.

The first official feminist library in France, this carries the widest selection of contemporary and old periodicals, news clippings files, photographs, posters and etchings, documentation on current organizations, as well as books on every aspect of women's lives, past and present. It's a very pleasant place to sit and read, and admission is free; in order to consult publications you need to fill out a form and produce identification – the staff are very helpful.

Elletel

36-15-ELLETEL on the minitel (see p.39).

Information on women's groups, listings, message box (called *AGORA*), and information from the *Centre National d'Information sur le Droit des Femmes et des Familles*.

Feminism in France

During the Socialist government's first term in the early 1980s, Yvette Roudy's new Women's Ministry spent five years getting long-overdue equal pay and opportunity measures through parliament. Some funding was given to women's groups but the main emphasis was on legislation, including the provision of socialized health coverage for abortion. A law against degrading, discriminatory or violence-inciting images of women in the media was, however, thrown out by the National Assembly.

Meanwhile, the *MLF* (*Mouvement de Libération des Femmes – Women's Liberation Movement*) had been declared by the media to be dead and buried. There were no more Women's Day marches, no major demonstrations, no direct action. Feminist bookshops and cafés started closing, publications reached their last issue, and polls showed that young women leaving school were only interested in men and babies. As the Socialist policies ran out of steam, cuts in public spending and traditional ideas about the male breadwinner sent more and more women back to their homes and hungry husbands.

Under Chirac and the Gaullists, the *Ministère des Droits des Femmes* (Ministry of Women's Rights) was renamed as the *Ministère des Droits de l'Homme* (Ministry of the Rights of Man). The full title of the ministry included "the feminine condition" and "the family" but the irony of the implacably male gender bias of the French language went generally unremarked. The first woman prime minister, Edith Cresson (1991–92), had a disastrous time in office, but was rarely attacked on grounds of gender. Feminist *députés* in parliament did all they could to keep women's issues prominent but with no support from their colleagues, and little from the movement outside.

Feminist intellectuals – always the most prominent section of the French women's movement – have continued their *seminaires*, erudite publications and university feminist studies courses, while at the other end of the scale, women's refuges and rape crisis centres are still maintained, with some funding from the ministry. The *MLF* is occasionally seen on the streets, but disorganized and in much diminished numbers.

More recently a key mobilizing issue has again been abortion, with French women fearing the influence of the powerful US anti-abortion lobby on European public opinion. When a French company applied for a licence for the abortion pill RU486, the French *SPUC* initially forced them to withdraw it, with threats of violence, even death, to its employees. The male Minister for Health, however, declared RU486 to be "the moral property of women" and it has since been used by tens of thousands of women for terminations that are far safer and simpler than those by surgical methods. How much the minister was influenced by the needs of the French pharmaceutical industry rather than the needs of women is a matter for interpretation, but it was a significant victory nevertheless.

Feminists continue to be active in unions and political parties; male bastions in the arts and media have been under attack; in business and local government leading roles have been taken by a few women. But a combination of the expectations of the myth of feminism plus Catholicism mitigates against ideological equality at a very fundamental level: a woman president is still unthinkable, and Britain's Margaret Thatcher was always explained away by French feminists as a proto-male.

Publications and Media

There is no national feminist magazine or paper in France; instead nearly every group produces its own paper or review. Some are stapled, photocopied hand-outs issued at random intervals; others are regular, well-printed serials, with many of them linked to particular political parties.

- **Paris Féministe** (see *Maison des Femmes*, above) is a bimonthly carrying detailed listings for events and groups in Paris.
- **Suites des Cris** is a literary and artistic lesbian revue, available from *ARCL* (see p.46).
- **Marie Pas Claire** is produced by a group of young feminists.

- **Lesbia**, a monthly lesbian magazine, is the best general magazine for all feminists (see p.47).
- **Paris Plurielle** is a women's radio programme on 106.3MHz each Tuesday 7–8.30pm.

Emergencies

The **rape crisis number** is *SOS Viol* ☎05.05.95.95. It's staffed by members of the *Collectif Féministe Contre le Viol*, 4 Square St-Irénée, 11ᵉ; ☎45.82.73.00 (Mº St-Ambroise; Mon–Fri 10am–6pm). There are also the **battered women refuges**: *Centre Flora Tristan* (☎47.36.96.48) and *Halte Aide aux Femmes Battues* (☎43.48.20.40) – addresses available from the *Maison des Femmes* or the *mairies* (town halls) of each *arrondissement*. English-speakers are rare, so this may not be of much help, but if things do get bad you will at least get sympathy and an all-women environment, whereas going to the police may well be a further trauma.

SOS Help is a general **English-language helpline** and can provide information about English-speaking doctors, lawyers, etc.

Other Addresses

Feminist, lesbian or sympathetic commercial enterprises are listed in the relevant chapters of this book: these include bookshops in *Shops and Markets* (Chapter 17); cafés in *Eating and Drinking* (Chapter 13); clubs in *Music and Nightlife* (Chapter 18); *hammams* in *Daytime Amusements and Sports* (Chapter 15).

Organizations for both lesbian groups are given under Gay and Lesbian Paris, overleaf.

Gay and Lesbian Paris

Paris is one of Europe's major centres for gay men. New bars, clubs, restaurants, saunas and shops open all the time, and in the central street of the Marais, rue Ste-Croix-de-la-Bretonnerie, every other address is gay. Lesbians have much less choice here commercially, but there are networks of feminist groups and specific publications that cater for the well-organized lesbian community. The high spots of the calendar are the annual Gay Pride parade and festival and the Bastille Day Ball. Gay Pride is normally held on the Saturday closest to the summer solstice. It starts from the Bastille, and is a major carnival for both lesbians and gays. The Bastille Day Ball (July 13 10pm–dawn) is a wild open-air dance on the quai de la Tournelle, 5e (Mº Pont Marie), and is free for all to join in.

For a long time the emphasis of the gay community in Paris tended towards providing the requisites for a hedonistic lifestyle, rather than any very significant political campaigning. With the legal age of consent set at 15, and discrimination and harassment non-routine, protest was not a high priority.

Matters have changed, here as elsewhere, since the advent of AIDS (*SIDA* in French). The resulting homophobia, though not as extreme as in Britain or middle America, has nevertheless increased the suffering in the group statistically most at risk. The Pasteur Institute in Paris is at the forefront of research into the virus, though its gay patients have complained of being treated like cattle. A group of gay doctors and the association AIDES (*Association pour l'Entraide et l'Information SIDA*), however, have consistently provided sympathetic counselling and treatment, and the gay press has done a great deal to disseminate the facts about AIDS and to provide hope and encouragement. Lesbian organizations fight alongside gays on the general issue of anti-homosexuality while campaigning separately on the far more numerous and varied repressions to which women are subject.

In general, the French consider sexuality to be a private matter. Whether, for example, the former minister of culture, Jack Lang, is gay or not

is of no interest to commentators. On the whole, gays tend to be discreet outside specific gay venues, parades and the prime gay area between the Hôtel-de-Ville, the Bastille and Arts et Métiers. Gay-bashing is very uncommon.

Contacts and Information

Gay, lesbian or sympathetic commercial enterprises are listed in the relevant chapters of this book: bookshops in *Shops and Markets* (Chapter 17); bars in *Eating and Drinking* (Chapter 13); clubs in *Music and Nightlife* (Chapter 18). In addition, Paris has a huge number of gay organizations. Here we've listed the most prominent: for a fuller list, consult *Gai Pied's Guide Gai* (see opposite).

ARCL (Archives, Recherches et Cultures Lesbiennes), Post box (BP) 362, 75526, Paris Cedex 11; answerphone ☎48.05.25.89. Fri 6–8pm – hours may change. *ARCL* publish a yearly directory of lesbian and feminist addresses in France (available at the *Bibliothèque Marguerite Durand*) and a fairly regular bulletin. They also organize frequent meetings.

David & Jonathan, 92bis rue Picpus, 12e; ☎43.42.09.49 (Mº Michel-Bizot). 24hr answerphone for gay Christians.

GAGE, c/o *Les Mots à la Bouche* – see below (☎48.03.20.12). Gay students' group, meeting every Wednesday at the *Duplex* bar, 25 rue Michel-le-Comte, 3e (Mº Rambuteau; 8pm–midnight).

Gay Pride, see opposite under *Maison des Homosexualités*. Brings together all the organizations and media for the Gay Pride festival.

GPL (Gais pour les Libertés), ☎42.02.03.03. Left-wing campaigning group.

Maison des Femmes, 8 Cité Prost, off rue Chanzy, 11e; ☎43.48.24.91 (Mº Faidherbe-Chaligny). Mon 6–8pm, Wed 3–8pm, Fri 6–8pm; Fri café 8pm–midnight. Run by *Paris Féministe* (see p.44), this is the home of the *Groupe des Lesbiennes Féministes* and the *Mouvement d'Information et d'Expression des Lesbiennes*. A cafeteria operates on Friday nights, and there are occasional events organized.

Maison des Homosexualités, Staircase A, 3rd floor, 25 rue Michel-le-Comte, 3e; ☎ 42.77.72.77 (M° Rambuteau; Mon–Fri 5–9pm, Sat 2–6pm). Information and the umbrella address for several gay organizations, including *MAG*, which is an organization for 16–25-year olds and *Lesbiennes Internationales*.

Minitel .3615 GPS is the minitel number to dial for information on groups, contacts, messages etc. The service was set up by *Gai Pied* (see below). There are also any number of chat lines.

Media

Exit. Gay newspaper with useful addresses.

Fréquence Gaie, 98.2 FM. 24hr gay and lesbian radio station with music, news, chats, information on groups and events, etc.

Gageure. Small monthly mag for gay students, produced and distributed by *GAGE* (see opposite).

Gai Pied publishes the annual *Guide Gai*, which is the most comprehensive gay guide to France,

carrying a good selection of lesbian and gay addresses, with an English section.

Illico. A monthly with lonely hearts and Minitel numbers.

Lesbia. The most widely available lesbian publication, available from most newsagents. Each monthly issue features a wide range of articles, listings, reviews, lonely hearts and contacts.

Les Mots à la Bouche, 6 rue Ste-Croix-de-la-Bretonnerie, 4e (M° Hôtel-de-Ville). The main gay and lesbian bookshop with exhibition space and meeting rooms.

Rebel. Weekly culture and news.

SOS

Association des Médecins Gais (Association of gay doctors), 45 rue Sedaine, 11e; ☎ 48.05.81.71 (M° Bréguet-Sabin; Sat 2–4pm, Wed 6–8pm).

SOS Écoute Gaie, ☎ 48.06.19.11. Helpline run by *Associations des Médecins Gais*.

AIDS and safer sex

If Paris is the city of sex and romance, make sure it's safer by using condoms (*les préservatifs* or *capotes*), as Paris has the highest number of people suffering from AIDS of any city in Europe, and studies show that there are now almost equal numbers of heterosexual and homosexual people who are HIV positive. Among heterosexuals (excluding drug users), the number of women who are HIV positive overtook men in 1992.

The American Church offers an excellent **free counselling and support** service for people with

AIDS or who are HIV positive, a service called *FAACTS* (Free Anglo-American Counselling Treatment Support). Mon–Thurs 3–7pm; ☎ 47.05.07.99.

Free HIV tests, with counselling in French, are available in many hospitals and clinics, including the *Centre Médico-Social*, 3 rue Ridder, 14e; ☎ 45.43.83.78 (M° Plaisance); and at 218 rue Belleville, 20e; ☎ 47.97.40.49; and *SIDA Info Service (SIS)*; ☎ 05.36.66.36, a free 24hr nationwide telephone hotline.

Sexual and Racial Harassment

Women are almost bound to experience sexual harassment in Paris, where many men make a habit of looking you up and down and, more often than not, passing comment. Generally it is no worse than in Britain or North America, but problems arise in judging men without the familiar linguistic and cultural clues. If your French isn't good enough, how do you tell if a man is gabbling at you because you left your purse behind in a shop, or is inciting you to swear at him in English and be cuffed round the head for the insult? The answer is that you can't, but there are some pointers.

A "*Bonjour*" or "*Bonsoir*" on the street is almost always a pick-up line: if you return the greeting, you've left yourself open to a persistent monologue and a difficult brush-off job. On the other hand, it's not unusual to be offered a drink in a bar if you're on your own and not to be pestered afterwards, even if you accept. This is rarer in Paris than elsewhere in the country, but don't assume that any overture by a Frenchman is a come-on.

Late-night métros are nowhere near as unnerving as they are in London or New York, simply because the passenger numbers are significantly greater, and thanks to the fact that the French seem to be more inclined to intervene if nasty scenes do develop; groping and pushing up against you, however, are all too common on public transport.

Racism

France has its fair share of racist attitudes and behaviour. If you are Arab or look as if you might be, your chances of avoiding unpleasantness are very low. Hotels claim to be booked up, police demand your papers, and abuse from ordinary people is horribly frequent. In addition, being black, of whatever ethnic origin, can make entering the country difficult. Changes in passport regulations have put an end to outright refusal to let some British holidaymakers in, but customs and immigration officers can still be obstructive and malicious. In North African dominated areas of Paris such as the Goutte d'Or, identity checks by the police are common and not pleasant.

The main antiracist organization is *SOS Racisme*, 14 Cité Griset, 11e; ☎48.06.40.00 (Mᵒ Menilmontant), which organizes a rally and concert in Paris every June. Though it doesn't represent the majority of immigrants and their descendants in France (for rioting kids in the Paris suburbs, it's an irrelevant middle-class outfit), *SOS Racisme* has done a great deal over the last few years to raise consciousness amongst young white French people. See Contexts, p.403, for more details.

Trouble and the Police

Petty theft is pretty bad in the crowded hangouts of the capital, as in most major cities. Take normal precautions: keep your wallet in a front pocket or your handbag under your elbow, and if you have a car, don't leave anything of value in sight to entice the lightfingered.

If you should get attacked, hand over the money and dial the cancellation numbers for your travellers' cheques and credit cards:

American Express cards	☏ 47.77.72.00
American Express travellers' cheques	☏ 05.90.86.00
Visa	☏ 47.62.75.00
Eurocard	☏ 47.62.75.00
Barclaycard	☏ 47.62.75.00
Diners' Club	☏ 47.62.75.00
24hr UK number	☏ 0252/513500

Drivers face greater problems, most notoriously break-ins. Vehicles are rarely stolen, but tape-decks and luggage left in cars make tempting targets and foreign number plates and rented cars are easy to spot. Good insurance is the only answer, but even so, try not to leave any valuables in plain sight. If you have an accident while driving, officially you have to fill in and sign a *constat à l'aimable* (jointly agreed statement); car insurers are supposed to give you this with the policy, though in practice few seem to have heard of it.

For **non-criminal driving offences** such as speeding, the police can impose an on-the-spot fine. Should you be arrested on any charge, you have the right to contact your consulate (see box overleaf). Although the police here are not always as co-operative as they might be, it is their duty to assist you – likewise in the case of losing your passport or all your money. In the event of theft, you should report your loss promptly to the police at the *commissariat* of the *arrondissement* in which the theft took place and complete what is called a *constat de vol.* This is essential if you intend to make an insurance claim.

People caught smuggling or possessing drugs, even a few grammes of marijuana, are liable to find themselves in jail, and consulates will not be sympathetic. This is not to say that hard-drug consumption isn't a visible activity: there are scores of kids dealing in *poudre* (heroin) in Paris, and the authorities are unable to do much about it.

The Police

French police (in popular argot, *les flics*) are barely polite at the best of times, and can be extremely unpleasant if you get on the wrong side of them. In Paris, the city police force has an ugly history of cock-ups, including sporadic shootings of innocent people and brutality against "suspects" – often just ordinary teenagers and black people – whom they are prone to pull off the streets for identity checks. You can in fact be stopped at any time and asked to produce ID. If that does happen to you, it's highly inadvisable to be difficult or facetious.

The **two main types of police** – the *Police Nationale* and the *Gendarmerie Nationale* – are for all practical purposes indistinguishable. The *CRS* (Compagnies Républicaines de Sécurité), on the other hand, are an entirely different proposition. They are a mobile force of paramilitary heavies, used to guard sensitive embassies, "control" demonstrations, and generally intimidate the populace on those occasions when the public authorities judge that it is stepping out of line. They have earned themselves a reputation for extreme brutality over the years, particularly at those moments when the tensions inherent in the long civil war of French politics have reached boiling point – for instance, during the October 1961 demonstration against the proposed curfew for all North Africans living in Paris, when some 200 people were killed, and during the street battles and strikes of May 1968.

Foreign Consulates in Paris

Australia
4 rue Jean-Rey, 15^e
(M^o Bir-Hakeim) ☎ 49.59.33.00

Canada
35 av Montaigne, 8^e
(M^o Franklin-D-Roosevelt) ☎ 44.43.29.86

Denmark
77 av Marceau, 16^e
(M^o Étoile) ☎ 44.31.21.21

Ireland
12 av Foch, 16^e
(M^o Étoile) ☎ 45.00.22.16

Netherlands
7–9 rue Eblé, 7^e
(M^o St-François-Xavier) ☎ 43.06.61.88

New Zealand
7ter rue Léonardo-de-Vincei, 16^e
(M^o Victor-Hugo) ☎ 45.00.24.11

Norway
28 rue Bayard, 8^e
(M^o Franklin-D-Roosevelt) ☎ 47.23.72.78

Sweden
17 rue Barbet-de-Jouy, 7^e
(M^o Varenne) ☎ 44.18.88.00

UK
9 av Hoche, 8^e
(M^o Courcelles) ☎ 42.66.38.1/fax 40.76.02.87

US
2 rue St-Florentin, 1er
(M^o Concorde) ☎ 42.96.12.012

Work and Study

Specialists aside, most Britons and North Americans who manage to work and live in Paris do so on luck, brazenness and willingness to live in pretty grotty conditions. An exhausting combination of bar and club work, freelance translating, data processing, typing, busking, providing novel services like home-delivery fish'n'chips, teaching English or computer programming, dancing or modelling are some of the ways people get by. Great if you're into self-promotion and living hand-to-mouth, but if you're not, it might be wise to think twice.

France has a **minimum wage** (the *SMIC*, which is currently around 35F an hour. Employers, however, are likely to pay lower wages to temporary foreign workers who don't have easy legal resources. By law, however, all EU nationals are entitled to exactly the same pay, conditions and trade union rights as French nationals. It's also worth noting that if you're a full-time non-EU student in France (see overleaf), you can get a non-EU **work permit** for the following summer just so long as your visa is still valid.

Finding a job in a **French language school** is best done in advance. In Britain, jobs are often advertised in the *Guardian*'s "*Educational Extra*" and in the *Times Educational Supplement*. Late summer is usually the best time. You don't need fluent French to get a post, but a TEFL (Teaching English as a Foreign Language) qualification will

almost certainly be required. If you apply in advance, most schools will fix up the necessary papers for you. EU nationals don't need a work permit, but getting a *carte de séjour* and social security can still be tricky should employers refuse to help. It's quite feasible to find a teaching job once you're already in France, but you may have to accept semi-official status and no job security. For the addresses of schools, look under *Écoles de Langues* in the *Professions* directory of the local phone book. Offering private lessons (via university notice boards or classified ads), you'll have lots of competition, and it's hard to reach the people who can afford it, but it's always worth a try.

For **temporary work**, there's no substitute for checking the papers, pounding the streets and keeping an eye on the notice boards at the British (St George's English Church, 7 rue Vacquerie, 16ᵉ) and American (65 quai d'Orsay, 7ᵉ) churches. You could try the notice boards located in the offices of *CIDJ* at 102 quai Branly, 15ᵉ (Mᵒ Bir-Hakeim) and *CROUS*, 39 av Georges Bernanos, 5ᵉ (Mᵒ Port-Royal), both youth information agencies which advertise a number of temporary jobs for foreigners. The British Council Library at 9–11 rue de Constantine, 7ᵉ (☎ 45.55.95.95) has a similar notice board, and you may also pick up information here by word of mouth. Other good sources include the *Offres d'Emploi* in *Le Monde*, *Le Figaro* and the *International Herald Tribune*, as well as the notice board at the bookshop *Shakespeare & Co* (see p.306) where you can advertise for ten days for 10F.

Some people have found jobs selling magazines on the street and leafleting just by asking people already doing it for the agency address. The American/Irish/British bars and restaurants sometimes have vacancies. You'll need to speak French, look smart and be prepared to work very long hours. Obviously, the better your French, the better your chances are of finding work.

Although **working as an au pair** is easily set up through any number of agencies (lists are available from the closest French embassy or consulate and there are lots of ads in *The Lady* in the UK), this sort of work can be total misery if you end up with an unpleasant employer, with conditions, pay, and treatment the next worst thing to slavery. If you're determined to try – and it can be a very good way of learning the language – it's better to apply once in France, where you can at least meet the family first and check things out.

Claiming Benefit in Paris

Any British or EU citizen who has been signing on for **unemployment benefit** for a minimum period of four weeks at home, and intends to continue doing so in Paris, needs a letter of introduction from their own Social Security office, plus an E303 certificate of authorization (be sure to give them plenty of warning to prepare this). You must register within seven days with the *Agence Nationale pour l'Emploi (ANPE)*, whose offices are listed under *Administration du Travail et de l'Emploi* in the Yellow Pages or *ANPE* in the White Pages.

It's possible to claim benefit for up to three months while you look for work, but it can often take that amount of time for the paperwork to be processed. Information about social security is available on freephone ☎05.34.25.70 or from *Les Reseignements sur la Sécurité Sociale*, 69bis rue de Dunkerque, 9ᵉ (☎42.80.63.67).

Pensioners can arrange for their **pensions** to be paid in France, but not, unfortunately to receive French state pensions.

Studying

It's relatively easy to be a student in Paris. Foreigners pay no more than French nationals (around 1300F a year) to enrol in a course, but there's the cost of supporting yourself. Your *carte de séjour* and – for EU nationals – social security will be assured, and you'll be eligible for subsidized accommodation, meals, and all the student reductions. Few people want to do undergraduate degrees abroad, but for higher degrees or other diplomas, the range of options is enormous. Strict entry requirements, including an exam in French, apply only for undergraduate degrees.

Generally, French universities are much less formal than British ones and many people perfect their fluency in the language while studying. For full details and prospectuses, go to the Cultural Service of any French embassy or consulate (see p.18 for the addresses).

The embassies and consulates can also give details of language courses, at the Sorbonne, Alliance Française etc, which are often combined with lectures on French "civilization" and usually very costly. You'll find ads for lesser language courses at the notice boards detailed above.

Directory

AIRLINES *Air France*, 119 av des Champs-Élysées, 8ᵉ (reservations ☎45.35.61.61; arrivals information ☎43.20.13.55; departures information ☎43.20.14.55); *Air Inter*, 49 av des Champs-Elysées, 8ᵉ (☎45.46.90.00); *British Airways*, 12 rue Castiglione, 1ᵉʳ (☎47.78.14.14).

ALARM ☎3688 for a morning call.

BBC WORLD SERVICE 463m MW or on frequencies between 21m and 31m short wave at intervals throughout the day and night. Also on television via satellite. For more details, see p.39.

BIKE RENTAL see details on p.32.

CONTRACEPTIVES Condoms (*préservatifs* or *capotes*) have always been available at pharmacies, though contraception was only legalized in 1967. You can also get spermicidal cream and jelly (*dose contraceptive*), plus suppositories (*ovules, suppositoires*), and (with a prescription) the pill (*la pillule*), a diaphragm or IUD (*le sterilet*).

CUSTOMS With the Single European Market you can bring in and take out most things as long as you have paid tax on them in an EU country, and they are for personal consumption. Customs may be suspicious if they think you are going to resell goods (or break the chassis of your car). Limits still apply to drink and tobacco bought in duty free shops: 200 cigarettes, 250g tobacco or 50 cigars; 1 litre spirits or 2 litres fortified wine, or 2 litres sparkling wine and 2 litres table wine; 60ml perfume and 250ml toilet water.

ELECTRICITY 220V out of double, round-pin wall sockets. Electricity and gGas are supplied by *EDF–GDF* (*Electricité de France* ☎47.54.20.20; *Gaz de France*; ☎40.42.22.22; Mon–Fri 8.30am–4pm), who should be contacted concerning bills, gas problems or blackouts in an apartment building. For problems in individual flats, contact one of the emergency repair numbers listed in the *Pages Jaunes* (Yellow Pages).

EMERGENCY REPAIRS General agencies dealing with gas, electricity, plumbing, car repairs etc are listed under *SOS, Allo* or *Assistance – Dépannage* in the *Pages Jaunes* (Yellow Pages).

KIDS/BABIES Visiting Paris with children poses few travel problems. They're allowed in all bars and restaurants, most of whom will cook simpler food if you ask. Hotels charge by the room – there's a small supplement for an additional bed or cot. You'll have no difficulty finding disposable nappies, baby foods and milk powders. The *SNCF* charges half-fare on trains and buses for kids aged 4–12, nothing for under-4s. See Chapter 16 for full listings of activities.

LEFT LUGGAGE There are lockers at all train stations and consigne for bigger items or longer periods.

LEGAL ADVICE *SOS Avocats* (Mon–Fri 7–11.30pm; ☎43.29.33.00), free legal advice over the phone.

LOST BAGGAGE Airports: Orly (☎46.75.40.38); Roissy-Charles de Gaulle (☎48.62.12.12).

LOST PROPERTY *Bureau des Objets Trouvés*, 36 rue des Morillons, 15ᵉ; ☎45.31.14.80 (Mᵒ Convention). Mon, Wed & Fri 8.30am–5pm, Tues & Thurs 8.30am–8pm).

PETROL Some 24-hour filling stations are: *Esso*, 338 rue St-Honoré, 1ᵉʳ; *Antar*, 36 rue des Fossés-St-Bernard, 5ᵉ; *Esso*, 18 av des Champs-Élysées, 8ᵉ; *Shell*, 1 bd de la Chapelle, 10ᵉ; *Mobil*, 55 quai de la Rapée, 12ᵉ; *Mobil*, 47 bd de Vaugirard, 15ᵉ.

TALKING CLOCK ☎36.99.

TELEGRAMS by phone. Internal – ☎36.55; external – ☎05.33.44.41 (all languages).

TIME France is one hour ahead of Greenwich Mean Time throughout the year, except for a short period around the end of March and in September when the French change between summer and winter time, when it's the same as GMT. The dates of the time changes are announced in the media – watch out if you have planes or trains to catch around those periods.

TOILETS are usually to be found downstairs in bars, along with the phone, but they're often hole-in-the-ground squats and paper is rare.

TRAFFIC/ROAD CONDITIONS For Paris traffic jams listen to 90.4 FM (FIP) on the radio; for the *boulevard périphérique*, ring ☎42.76.52.52; for the Île de France, ring ☎48.99.33.33.

WEATHER For the Paris region: ☎36.65.00.00; rest of France: ☎36.69.01.01; international: ☎45.55.95.02.

The City

The Layout of the City

G eography, history and function have combined to give Paris a remarkably coherent and intelligible structure. The city lies in a basin surrounded by hills. It is very nearly circular, confined within the *boulevard périphérique*, which follows the line of the most recent, nineteenth-century fortifications. Through its middle, the **River Seine** flows east to west in a satisfying arc. At the hub of the circle, in the middle of the river, lies the kernel from which all the rest grew: the **Île de la Cité** (covered in Chapter 2). The city's oldest religious and secular institutions – the cathedral and the royal palace – stand right beside the river, which was itself both the city's *raison d'être* and its lifeline.

The royal palace of the **Louvre** lies on the north or **Right Bank** (*rive droite*) of the Seine, as the river flows. To the northwest runs the longest and grandest vista of the city – **La Voie Triomphale** (Chapter 3) – used by kings, emperors and presidents for the expression of royal and state power. It comprises the Tuileries gardens, the Champs-Élysées, the Arc de Triomphe, and La Grande Arche de la Défense, among other gestures of self-aggrandizement. To the north and east of that, clamped in an arc around the river, you'll find the commercial and financial quarters necessary to the everyday life of the state (covered in Chapter 4): the Stock Exchange, the Bank of France, the fashion and leather trades, jewellers, remnants of the medieval guilds, and what remains of the fruit, veg and meat market, the equivalent of London's Covent Garden, that was based in **Les Halles**. Just to the east of it, the **Marais** (Chapter 5) became the first really prestigious address for leading courtiers and businessmen; with the **Bastille**, it is now one of the liveliest areas of the city.

The south bank of the river, on the other hand, the so-called **Left Bank** (*rive gauche*; Chapter 6), developed quite differently. It owes its existence to the cathedral school of Notre-Dame, which spilled over from the Île de la Cité onto the south bank, and became the university of the Sorbonne, attracting scholars and students from all over the medieval world. Ever since then, it has been the

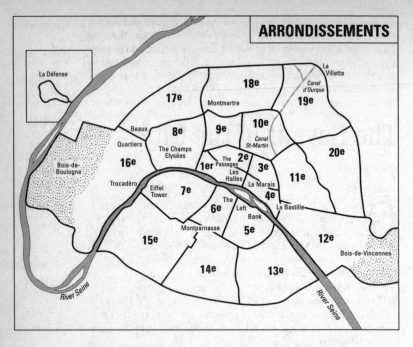

traditional domain of the intelligentsia, of academics, writers, artists, the cinema and the liberal professions.

The arrangement of the twenty *arrondissements* provides a pretty accurate guide to the structure and historical development of the city. Centred on the Louvre, they spiral outwards in a clockwise direction. The inner hub of the city comprises *arrondissements* 1er to 6^{e}, and it is here that most of the major sights and museums are to be found. The outer or higher-number *arrondissements* were mostly incorporated into the city in the nineteenth century. Those to the east accommodated mainly the poor and the working class, while the western ones held the aristocracy and the new rich. Most of them were outlying villages that were gradually swamped as industrialization and colonization brought growing wealth and labour-hunger to the city. Some, such as **Belleville**, **Montmartre** and **Passy**, have succeeded in retaining something of their separate village identity.

These historical divisions according to function and population substantially retain their validity to this day. The Right Bank still connotes business and commerce, the Left Bank arts and letters; west means bourgeois and smart, east means working class, immigrant and scruffy. In recent years, however, such neat arrangements have been increasingly disturbed as rising property values drive out the poor and open their traditional *quartiers* to gentrification.

One thing with which Paris is not particularly well endowed is **parks**. The largest, the **Bois de Boulogne** and the **Bois de Vincennes**, at the western and eastern limits of the city, do possess the odd small pockets of interest, but are largely anonymous sprawls. More enjoyable recreational spaces in Paris are the small squares and *places*, the *quais* along the banks of the Seine, and the bits of unexpected greenery encountered as you wander the streets. For a real break from the bustle of the city, it is best to try an out-of-town excursion, to the *château* of Vaux-le-Vicomte, for example, or the forest of Fontainebleau (see Chapter 20).

Orientation

Paris is strictly confined within the 78-square-kilometre limits of its *boulevard périphérique*; at its widest point it is only about 12km across, which, at a brisk pace, is not much more than two hours' walk. This marvellous compactness means that there is very little dross and tedium, and no lifeless and interminable residential areas. On the contrary, any walk across the city is very much action packed. You move in a trice from villagey Montmartre to the sleaze of Barbès, from the high-powered elegance of the Faubourg-St-Honoré to the frenetic and downmarket commercialism of Les Halles. You exchange vast subterranean shopping and entertainment complexes for chaotic and colourful *quartiers*, where West African textiles and teapots from the Maghreb are piled high behind narrow counters; you leave the maelstrom of the Right Bank expressway to find yourself alone by the brown waters of the Seine.

If you don't feel like walking, nothing could be easier than the excellent **public transport** system, detailed on p.27. Above ground, **buses** crisscross the city, each bus and each stop carrying a clear map of the route. Below ground the city is criss-crossed with **métro** lines (see map on pp.30–31), as well as the extra-quick *RER* trains (map on p.28). Stops are very frequent, so you are seldom more than a few minutes' walk away from the nearest station. The same tickets are valid on both métro and *RER*, and the cost of travel within the city and closest suburbs is flat-rate.

Chapter 2

Île de la Cité

T he Île de la Cité is where Paris began. The earliest settlements were sited here, as was the small Gallic town of Lutetia, overrun by Julius Caesar's troops in 52 BC. A natural defensive site commanding a major east–west river trade route, it

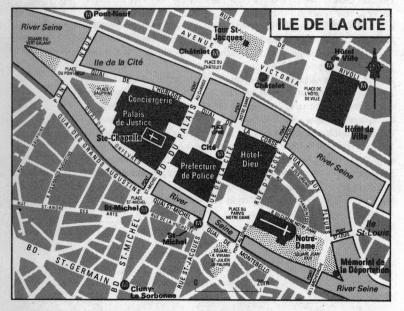

Île de la Cité: Listings

Restaurants
Au Rendez-vous des Camionneurs, 72 quai des Orfèvres, 1er.
Mº St-Michel.

Cafés and Bars
Taverne Henri IV, 13 place du Pont-Neuf, 1er.
Mº Pont-Neuf.

These establishments are reviewed in Chapter 13, Eating and Drinking, *on p.233.*

was an obvious candidate for a bright future. The Romans garrisoned it and laid out one of their standard military town plans, overlapping onto the Left Bank. While it never achieved any great political importance, they endowed it with an administrative centre which became the palace of the Merovingian kings in 508 AD, then of the counts of Paris, who in 987 became kings of France. So from the very beginning the Île has been close to the administrative heart of France.

Today the lure of the island lies in its tail-end – the **square du Vert-Galant, the quais, place Dauphine** and the **cathedral of Notre-Dame** itself. Haussmann demolished the central section in the nineteenth century, displacing some 25,000 people and virtually breaking the island's back by constructing four vast edifices in bland Baronial-Bureaucratick, which were largely given over to housing the law. He also perpetrated the litter-blown space in front of the cathedral, though that at least has the virtue of allowing a full-frontal view.

Pont-Neuf and the quais

If you arrive on the island by the **Pont-Neuf**, which despite its name is the city's oldest bridge (and the first to be constructed without the traditional medieval complement of houses on it), you'll see a statue of **Henri IV**, the king who commissioned it in 1607. It was during his reign that the first attempts were made to coordinate town planning in Paris.

Behind his statue, a flight of steps goes down to the **quais** and the **square du Vert-Galant**, a small tree-lined green enclosed within the triangular stern of the island. The name *Vert-Galant*, meaning a "green" or "lusty" gentleman, is supposed to celebrate Henri IV's success with women. The prime spot to occupy is the extreme point beneath a weeping willow – haunt of lovers, sparrows and sunbathers. On the north quay is the dock for the tourist river boats, *Bateaux-Vedettes du Pont-Neuf*.

Details of the Seine river boats are given on p.286.

Henri IV

Henri IV was, first of all, King of Navarre in the Pyrenees, a bastion of Protestantism. On becoming King of France in 1589, he was obliged to convert to Catholicism out of deference to the sensibilities of the majority of his new subjects. "Paris is worth a Mass", he is reputed to have said, somewhat cynically.

Henri's great aim was to reconstruct and reconcile France, and it was he who guaranteed the civil rights of the Protestants in 1598. When they were abrogated 100 years later by Louis XIV under the pressure of the Counter-Reformation, the Protestants scattered across the globe, from London's Spitalfields to the New World. As many of them were highly skilled craftsmen, their departure was a blow to the economy – as was the death and exile of so many Communards two hundred years later, who in their turn were also largely the working-class élite.

Sainte-Chapelle and the Conciergerie

On the other side of the bridge, across the street from the king, seventeenth-century houses flank the entrance to the sanded, chestnut-shaded place **Dauphine**, one of the city's most secluded and exclusive squares, where Simone Signoret lived until her death in 1985. The far end of the square is blocked by the dull mass of the **Palais de Justice**, which swallowed up the palace that was home to the French kings until Étienne Marcel's bloody revolt in 1358 frightened them off to the greater security of the Louvre. In earlier times it had been the Roman governors' residence, too.

The only part of the older complex that remains in its entirety is Louis IX's **Sainte-Chapelle** (daily April–Sept 9.30am–6.30pm; Oct–March 10am–5pm; 26F/17F/7F, combined ticket with Conciergerie 40F/30F/12F, closed bank holidays; M° Cité), built to house a collection of holy relics he had bought at extortionate rates from the bankrupt empire of Byzantium. It stands in a courtyard to the left of the main entrance (bd du Palais), looking somewhat squeezed by the proximity of the nineteenth-century law courts – which, incidentally, anyone is free to sit in on. Though much restored, the chapel remains one of the finest achievements of French Gothic (consecrated in 1248). Very tall in relation to its length, it looks like a cathedral choir lopped off and transformed into an independent building. Its most radical feature is its fragility: the reduction of structural masonry to a minimum to make way for a huge expanse of stunning **stained glass**. The impression inside is of being enclosed within the wings of myriad butterflies – the predominant colours are blue and red, and, in the later rose window, grass-green and blue.

It pays to get to the Sainte-Chapelle as early as possible. It attracts hordes of tourists, as does the **Conciergerie** (April–Sept 9.30am–6pm; Oct–March 10am–4.30pm; 26F/17F/7F, combined ticket with Sainte-Chapelle 40F/30F/12F, closed bank holidays), Paris's oldest prison, where Marie-Antoinette and, in their turn, the leading figures of the Revolution were incarcerated before execution. The chief interest of the Conciergerie is the enormous late Gothic **Salle des Gens d'Arme**, canteen and recreation room of the royal household staff. You miss little if you don't see Marie-Antoinette's cell and various other macabre mementoes of the guillotine's victims.

The original of Les Très Riches Heures is in the Musée Condé outside Paris – *see p.362.*

For the loveliest view of what the whole ensemble once looked like, you need to get hold of the postcard of the June illustration from the fifteenth-century Book of Hours known as *Les Très Riches Heures du Duc de Berry*, the most mouthwatering of all medieval illuminated manuscripts. It shows the palace with towers and chimneys and trellised rose garden and the Sainte-Chapelle touching the sky in the right-hand corner. The Seine laps the curtain wall where now the quai des Orfèvres ("goldsmiths") runs. In the foreground pollarded willows line the Left Bank, while barefoot peasant girls rake hay in stooks and their menfolk scythe light green swathes up the rue Dauphine. No sign of the square du Vert-Galant: it was just a swampy islet then, not to be joined to the rest of the Cité for another hundred years and more.

Place Lépine and Pont d'Arcole

If you keep along the north side of the island from the Conciergerie you come to place Lépine, named for the police boss who gave Paris' coppers their white truncheons and whistles. There is an exuberant **flower market** here six days a week, with **birds and pets** – cruelly caged – on Sunday.

Next bridge but one is the **Pont d'Arcole**, named for a young revolutionary killed in an attack on the Hôtel de Ville in the 1830 rising (see p.392), and beyond that the only bit of the Cité that survived Haussmann's attentions. In the streets hereabouts once flourished the cathedral school of Notre-Dame, forerunner of the Sorbonne.

Around the year 1200, one of the teachers was **Peter Abélard**, of Héloïse fame. A philosophical whizzkid and cocker of snooks at the establishment intellectuals of his time, he was very popular with his students and not at all with the authorities, who thought they caught a distinct whiff of heresy. Forced to leave the cathedral school, he set up shop on the Left Bank with his disciples and, in effect, founded the university of Paris. His love life was less success-ful, though much better known. While living near the rue Chanoinesse, behind the cathedral, he fell violently in love with his landlord's niece, Héloïse, and she with him. She had a baby, uncle had him castrated, and the story ended in convents, lifelong separa-tion and lengthy correspondence.

Abélard and Héloïse are buried in the Père-Lachaise cemetery – see p.180.

Notre-Dame

The **Cathédrale de Notre-Dame** itself (daily 9am–7pm, closed Sat 12.30–2pm; M° St-Michel) is so much photographed that seeing it even for the first time the edge of your response is somewhat dulled by familiarity. Yet it is truly impressive, that great H-shaped west front, with its strong vertical divisions counterbalanced by the hori-zontal emphasis of gallery and frieze, all centred by the rose window. It demands to be seen as a whole, though that can scarcely have been possible when the medieval houses clustered close about it. It is a solid, no-nonsense design, confessing its Romanesque ancestry. For the more fantastical kind of Gothic, look rather at the

Notre-Dame

north transept façade with its crocketed gables and huge fretted window-space.

Notre-Dame was begun in 1160 under the auspices of Bishop de Sully and completed around 1245. In the nineteenth century, Viollet-le-Duc carried out extensive renovation work, including remaking most of the statuary – the entire frieze of Old Testament kings, for instance – and adding the steeple and baleful-looking gargoyles, which you can see close-up if you brave the ascent of the **towers** (daily 10am–6pm; Oct–March closes 5pm; 31F/17F/6F, or 45F combined admission with *crypte archéologique* – see below). Ravaged by weather and pollution, the façade's beauty may still be partially masked by scaffolding put up for further restoration work.

The original statues are in the Musée National du Moyen-Age on p.273.

Inside, the immediately striking feature, if you can ignore the noise and movement, is the dramatic contrast between the darkness of the nave and the light falling on the first great clustered pillars of the choir, emphasizing the special nature of the sanctuary. It is the end walls of the transepts that admit all this light, nearly two-thirds glass, including two magnificent **rose windows** coloured in imperial purple. These, the vaulting, the soaring shafts reaching to the springs of the vaults, are all definite Gothic elements, yet, inside as out, there remains a strong sense of Romanesque in the stout round pillars of the nave and the general sense of four-squareness. Free guided tours lasting 1–1hr 30min take place in French every weekday at noon and Saturday at 2pm, and in English on Wednesday at noon. There are free organ concerts every Sunday at 5 or 5.30pm; four masses on Sunday morning and one at 6.30pm. The **trésor** (daily 9.30am–6pm; 15F/10F) is not really worth the entry fee.

Before you leave, walk round to the public garden at the east end for a view of the **flying buttresses** supporting the choir, and then along the riverside under the south transept, where you can sit in springtime with the cherry blossom drifting down. And say a prayer of gratitude that the city authorities had the sense to throw out President "Paris-must-adapt-itself-to-the-automobile" Pompidou's scheme for extending the quayside expressway along here.

Out in front of the cathedral, in the square separating it from Haussmann's police HQ, is what appears to be and smells like the entrance to an underground toilet. It is, in fact, a very well-displayed and interesting museum, the **crypte archéologique** (April–Sept 10am–5.30pm; Oct–March 10am–4.30pm; 26F/17F/6F, or 40F combined admission with tower), in which are revealed the remains of the church which predated the cathedral, as well as streets and houses of the Cité dating as far back as the Roman era.

Kilomètre zéro and Le Mémorial de la Déportation

On the pavement by the west door of Notre-Dame cathedral is a spot known as **kilomètre zéro**, from which all main road distances in France are calculated. For the Île de la Cité is the symbolic heart of the country, or at least of the France that in the school books fights wars, undergoes revolutions and launches space rockets.

It's fitting that the island should also be the symbolic tomb of the 200,000 French men and women who died in the Nazi concentration camps during World War II – Resistance fighters, Jews, forced labourers. Their moving memorial, **Le Mémorial de la Déportation**, is a kind of bunker-crypt, barely visible above ground, at the extreme eastern tip of the island. Stairs scarcely shoulder-wide descend into a space like a prison yard. A single aperture overlooks the brown waters of the Seine, barred by a grill whose spiky ends evoke the torments of the torture chamber. Above, nothing is visible but the sky and, dead centre, the spire of Notre-Dame. Inside, the sides of the tunnel-like crypt are studded with thousands of points of light representing the dead. Floor and ceiling are black and it ends in a black raw hole, with a single naked bulb hanging in the middle. Either side are empty barred cells. "They went to the other ends of the Earth and they have not returned. 200,000 French men and women swallowed up, exterminated, in the mists and darkness of the Nazi camps." Above the exit are the words "Forgive. Do not forget . . .".

La Voie Triomphale

La Voie Triomphale, or Triumphal Way, stretches in a dead straight line from the site of the original fortress in the Louvre, incorporating along the way some of the city's most famous landmarks – the Arc de Triomphe, the Champs-Élysées, place de la Concorde, the Tuileries and the Louvre pyramid. Its monumental constructions have been erected over the centuries by kings and emperors, presidents and corporations, to propagate French power and prestige.

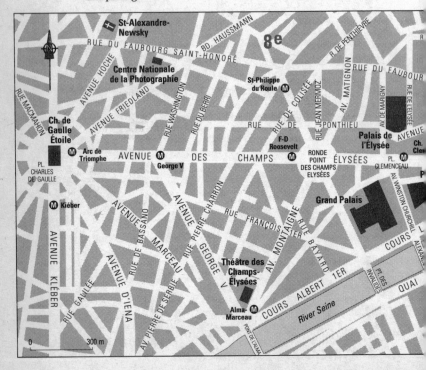

The tradition of self-aggrandizement dies hard, and has been given contemporary expression by an enormous, marble-clad cubic arch amid the skyscrapers at La Défense, a full nine kilometres out (see p.198), and the glass pyramid entrance in the central courtyard of the much-expanded Louvre. This latter project involved moving the Ministry of Finance out of the Louvre into vast new offices in the 12e *arrondissement*, digging up and rebuilding the foundations of the original medieval Louvre fortress and creating a new subterranean complex. Further works are underway on the Tuileries gardens, and the Champs-Élysées has been given more trees and wider pavements.

The Arc de Triomphe and the Champs-Élysées

The best view of this grandiose and simple geometry of kings to capital is from the top of the **Arc de Triomphe**, Napoléon's homage both to the armies of France and to himself (daily 10am–5pm; 31F, 20F for under-24s, 7F for under-7s; access from stairs on north corner of av des Champs-Élysées; Mº Charles-de-Gaulle–Étoile). The

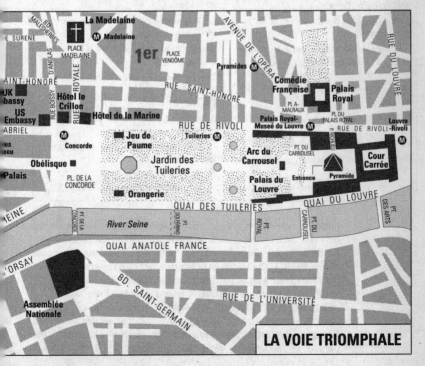

LA VOIE TRIOMPHALE

La Voie Triomphale: Listings

Restaurants

Aux Amis du Beaujolais, 28 rue d'Artois, 8e.
Mº George-V/St-Philippe-du-Roule.

L'Auvergnat 1900, 11 rue Jean-Mermoz, 8e.
Mº Franklin-Roosevelt/St-Philippe-du-Roule.

City Rock Café, 13 rue de Berri, 8e.
Mº George-V.

Le Dauphin, 167 rue St-Honoré, 1er.
Mº Palais-Royal–Musée-du-Louvre.

Dragons Élysées, 11 rue de Berri, 8e.
Mº George-V.

L'Élysées Bar Restaurant, 134 rue Faubourg St-Honoré, 8e.
Mº St-Philippe-du-Roule.

La Fermette Marbeuf 1900, 5 rue Marbeuf, 8e.
Mº Franklin-Roosevelt.

Foujita, 41 rue St-Roch, 1er.
Mº Pyramides/Tuileries.

Fouquet's, 99 av des Champs-Élysées, 8e.
Mº George-V.

Le Jardin du Royal Monceau, Hôtel Royal Monceau, 35 av Hoche, 8e.
Mº Charles-de-Gaulle/Étoile.

Prince de Galles, 33 av George V, 8e.
Mº George-V.

Le Relais du Sud-Ouest, 154 rue St-Honoré, 1er.
Mº Palais-Royal/Musée-du-Louvre.

Yvan, 1bis rue J-Mermoz, 8e.
Mº Franklin-Roosevelt.

Cafés and Bars

Angélina, 226 rue de Rivoli, 1er.
Mº Tuileries.

Ma Bourgogne, 133 bd Haussmann, 8e.
Mº Miromesnil.

La Boutique à Sandwiches, 12 rue du Colisée, 8e.
Mº St-Philippe-du-Roule.

Café de la Comédie, 153 rue Rivoli, 1er.
Mº Palais-Royal–Musée-du-Louvre.

Drugstore Élysées, 133 av des Champs-Élysées, 8e.
Mº Étoile.

Drugstore Matignon, 1 av Matignon, 8e.
Mº Franklin-Roosevelt.

E. Fahy Patissier, 165 rue du Faubourg-St-Honoré, 8e.
Mº St-Philippe-du-Roule/George V.

Fauchon, 24 place de la Madeleine, 8e.
Mº Madeleine.

Le Griffonier, 6 rue des Saussaires, 8e.
Mº Champs-Élysées.

Osaka, 163 rue St-Honoré, 1er.
Mº Palais-Royal.

Café de Poumone, allée Central, Jardin des Tuileries, 1er.
Mº Tuileries.

Restorama, Le Carrousel du Louvre, 1er.
Mº Louvre.

Virgin Megastore Café, 52 av des Champs-Élysées, 8e.
Mº Franklin-Roosevelt.

These establishments are reviewed in Chapter 13, Eating and Drinking, beginning on p.233.

emperor and his two royal successors spent ten million francs between them on this edifice, which victorious foreign armies would later use to humiliate the French. After the Prussians' triumphal march in 1871, the Parisians lit bonfires beneath the arch and down the Champs-Élysées to purify the stain of German boots.

From 1941 to 1944 Hitler's troops paraded daily around the swastika-decked monument – de Gaulle's arrival at the scene, come Liberation, was probably less effective than the earlier ashes and flames. In 1989 the French humiliated themselves with their grand parade of nations to mark the bicentennial of the French

Revolution. The symbol chosen for France was the locomotive which features in Émile Zola's novel, *La Bête Humaine*, about a railway worker who murders his wife.

Assuming there are no bizarre theatricals or armies in sight (on Bastille Day, the president proceeds down the Champs-Élysées accompanied by tanks, guns and flags), your attention is most likely to be caught not by the view, but by the mesmerizing traffic movements directly below you around **place de l'Étoile** – the world's first organized roundabout.

Of the twelve fat avenues making up the star (*étoile*) of the Place de l'Étoile, much the busiest is the avenue des Champs-Élysées, which disgorges and gobbles a phenomenal number of vehicles.

The glamour of the Champs-Élysées, particularly its upper end, may not be quite what it was, dominated as it is by airline offices, car showrooms, and bright, light shopping arcades. But there's still the *Lido* cabaret, *Fouquet's* high-class bar and restaurant, and plenty of cinemas and outrageously priced cafés to bring the punters in. At Christmas this is where the fairy lights go, and on December 31 everyone happily jams in, in their cars, to hoot in the New Year.

The new landscaping project has removed the avenue's side lanes where cars used to prowl in search of parking spaces, and now pedestrians have an equal share of the avenue's width, with shade from more trees. According to the municipality, cultural centres, hotels, and other "activities that participate in the tradition and prestige" of the Champs-Élysées would be encouraged to return, but a new Disney shop and more fast-food outlets are all that have appeared. At the Renault showrooms, by the way, is a display of cars, bikes and vans from the earliest days (free).

The stretch between the Rond-Point roundabout – whose Lalique glass fountains disappeared during the German occupation – and Concorde is bordered by chestnut trees and municipal flower beds, pleasant enough to stroll among, but not sufficiently dense to muffle the discomfiting squeal of accelerating tyres. The two massive buildings rising above the greenery to the south are the **Grand and Petit Palais**, with their overloaded Neoclassical exteriors, rail station roofs and exuberant flying statuary. They house a number of museums (see Chapter 14), and the Grand Palais is the address for major cultural exhibitions, curtailed at the moment due to major restoration works.

On the north side, combat police guard the high walls round the presidential **Élysée palace** and the line of ministries and embassies ending with the US in prime position on the corner of place de la Concorde. On Thursdays and at weekends you can see a stranger manifestation of the self-images of states in the **postage stamp market** at the corner of avenues Gabriel and Marigny.

Place de la Concorde, place Madeleine and the Tuileries

The Champs-Élysées' graceful gradients, like a landing flightpath, finish up eastwards at **place de la Concorde**, where more crazed traffic makes crossing over to the middle a death-defying task.

As it happens, some 1300 people did die here between 1793 and 1795, beneath the Revolutionary guillotine: Louis XVI, Marie-Antoinette, Danton and Robespierre among them. The centrepiece of the *place*, chosen like its name to make no comment on these events, is an obelisk from the temple of Luxor, offered as a favour-currying gesture by the viceroy of Egypt in 1829. It serves merely to pivot more geometry: the alignment of the French parliament, the Assemblée Nationale, on the far side of the Seine, with the church of the Madeleine at the end of rue Royale to the north. The Neoclassical *Hôtel Crillon* – ultimate luxury address for visitors to Paris – and its twin, the Ministry of the Navy, flank the entrance to rue Royale, which, needless to say, meets the Voie Triomphale at a precise right angle.

The **church of the Madeleine** is an obese Napoleonic structure on the classical temple model, ordered by the emperor as yet another monument to the glory of his army. It serves for *haut monde* weddings and for the perspective across place de la Concorde. There's a **flower market** every day except Monday along the east side of the church and a luxurious **Art Nouveau loo** by the métro at the junction of place and bd de la Madeleine. But the greatest appeal of place de la Madeleine is for rich gourmets and window-gazers. In the northeast corner are two blocks of the best food display in Paris – at *Fauchon's* – and, down the west side, you'll find the smaller *Hédiard's*, as well as caviar, truffle and spirit specialists.

Extensive listings of Parisian food shops can be found on p.312.

The symmetry of the Voie Triomphale continues into the formal layout of the **Tuileries** gardens, disrupted only by the bodies lounging on the grass, kids chasing their boats round the ponds, and gays cruising on the terrace overlooking the river. The two buildings flanking the garden at the Concorde end are the **Orangerie**, by the river, and the **Jeu de Paume** by rue du Rivoli. Long home to the state's Impressionist collection, the Jeu de Paume is now a modern art gallery. Workers doing the refit claimed to have found an eighteenth-century tennis ball in the rafters – a wild shot from the building's earliest days as a royal tennis court. The Orangerie houses a collection of Impressionists, including several Monet *Waterlilies*. It is going to be extended and will once again have an *orangerie* with orange and lemon trees as it did in the eighteenth and nineteenth centuries.

Full accounts of the artwork in the Orangerie and the Jeu de Paume are included in the Museums chapter on p.274.

The gardens themselves are not greatly exciting, with forlorn-looking trees, lichen-covered statues and too many expanses of

Place de la
Concorde,
place
Madeleine
and the
Tuileries

The Tuileries Gardens

The first garden to take the place of the medieval warren of tilemakers (*tuileries* in French) was Catherine de Médicis'. She had formal vegetable gardens, a labyrinth and a chequerboard of flowerbeds laid out in the 1570s, to be admired by the guests at her sumptuous parties. A hundred years later, Le Nôtre created the schema that exists to this day, of a central axis, round and octagonal pools and the *terrasses*. The sculptures from Versailles and Marly appeared here under Louis XV, and in the eighteenth century, the Tuileries were where flash Parisians came to preen and to party. In 1783 a hot air balloon was launched from the gardens – the height and breadth of the overgrown trees no doubt adding a certain *frisson* to the event. The first serious replanting was carried out after the Revolution – a 200-year-old plane tree with a three-metre circumference survives near the octagonal pool. In the nineteenth century, rare species were added to the garden, by now dominated by chestnut trees.

Dryness, disease and parasites, vandalism, lack of care and pollution have taken their toll on the trees of the Tuileries. A long and laborious project is now underway, with the aim of having three thousand healthy trees (of which five hundred will be newly planted) by the year 2000.

gravel, but major works are afoot, involving much tree surgery and replanting (see above). Many of the statues will be recast – and more added. There will be a certain amount of relandscaping, some harking back to Catherine de Médicis' garden, some adding new perspectives to the pyramid. The new Tuileries should be in shape by 1996. The temporary Passarelle Solférino, replacing the old Pont Solférino crossing the Seine from the Tuileries, was pulled down in 1993 for safety reasons, and a new beautiful footbridge should be in place by the end of 1996.

The Louvre

The *Grand Louvre* project was conceived by Mitterrand when he became president in 1981. He was following in the footsteps of François I, Catherine de Médicis, Louis XIV, Napoléon, and all the other kings, queens and emperors who have added to and altered Philippe-Auguste's original fortress, built to defend the city in 1200.

Twice in its history the Louvre has nearly been razed to the ground. Bernini, hired by Louis XIV's minister, Colbert, to redesign the palace, wanted to start from scratch, but lost the commission. In the mid-eighteenth century, with the court firmly established at Versailles, the Louvre had been taken over by artists and squatters, with a hundred different families living round the Cour Carrée. Louis XV's immediate response to such *lèse-majesté* was an urge to destroy the building, but he was dissuaded by his officials, thereby allowing it to become the scene of his son's humiliation at the hands of the revolutionaries in 1790.

The world-famous collections of the Louvre are covered in our Museums chapter on p.265.

The Louvre

Every alteration and addition up to 1988 created a surprisingly homogeneous building. It is not a very pretty one – though the Cour Carrée with its Renaissance grace and Three Musketeers associations is gasp-worthy – but with a grandeur, symmetry and Frenchness entirely suitable to this most historic of Parisian edifices.

Then came the **Pyramid**, bang in the centre of the palace in the Cour Napoléon, an extraordinary leap of daring and imagination. Chinese-born architect Ieoh Ming Pei's creation has no connection with its surroundings, except as a symbol of symmetry. And it is a lovely thing, a huge glass pyramid surrounded by a pool and fountains and three smaller pyramids. The view you get as you come out of the Cour Carrée through the Pavillon de l'Horloge is stunning, and at night, illuminated, the Pyramid is pure magic. In years to come it could even rival the Eiffel Tower, a hundred years its senior, as the symbol of the city. It has to be said, though, that the distorted view through the glass of the Pavillon de l'Horloge and the two Napoléon III wings is rather unpleasant. The poor pinkish-gold Arc du Carrousel, between the Louvre and the Tuileries, is now forlornly upstaged.

The next stage of the *Grand Louvre* project was the **Richelieu wing** on the north side, former home of the Finance Ministry. Its two courtyards have been glassed over and are visible from windows in the Passage Richelieu linking place du Palais-Royale and the Cour Napoléon. You get a better view of the famous Horses of Marly and Puget's monumental figures from this public passage than you do from within the museum itself. The Grand Projet is far from finished. All the façades of the palace are being cleaned, the lead replaced on the roofs, the statues restored... works will continue until 1997, if not beyond.

The other major development is underground – a vast space stretching from the Hall Napoléon, the main entrance to the museum, beneath the Pyramid to beyond the Arc du Carrousel. Known as the "Espaces Carrousel du Louvre", its central crossroads, place de la Pyramide Inversée, is fed with daylight through an inverted pyramid, a smaller model of the Pyramid.

From the Hall Napoléon, shops, restaurants, exhibition spaces – and bits of the old fortress's outer defences – make up the cold, classy and commercial "Carrousel du Louvre" gallery. Beyond are several auditoriums and conference halls, car and bus parking areas and new premises for the Louvre's research department, unique in the world for having its own particle accelerator to examine sub-atomic bits of works of art and archeological finds.

Before this subterranean complex was dug out, archeologists discovered Stone Age tools, remnants of an Iron Age farm growing lentils, peas, fruit and cereals, a house dating from 300 BC, a four-teenth-century manor house complete with wall-paintings and garden, and Catherine de Médicis' unfinished Tuileries Palace.

There will be direct access to the "Espace Carrousel du Louvre" from the métro and from place du Carrousel. The virtue of the new parking spaces will be to clear rue du Rivoli and place du Palais-Royale of the lines of coaches disgorging their passengers into the Louvre.

The Palais Royal

On the north side of the place du Palais-Royale, the **Palais Royal**, originally Richelieu's residence, houses various government and constitutional bodies and the **Comédie Française**, where the classics of French theatre are performed.

The palace gardens to the north were once the gastronomic, gambling and amusement hot spot of Paris. There was even a *café mécanique* where you sat at a table and sent your order down one of its legs, and were served via the other. The prohibition on public gambling in 1838 put an end to the fun, but the flats above the empty cafés remained desirable lodgings for the likes of Cocteau and Colette.

Folly has returned to the *palais* itself, however, in the form of black and white pillars in different sizes standing above flowing water in the main courtyard. The artist responsible, Daniel Buren, was commissioned in 1982 by Jack Lang, the socialist Minister of Culture. His Chirac-ian successor's decision to let the work go ahead caused paroxysms amongst self-styled guardians of the city's heritage and set an interesting precedent. After a legal wrangle, the court ruled that artists had the right to complete their creations.

Kids use the monochrome Brighton Rock look-a-likes as an adventure playground, the best game being to fish out the coins that people throw into the water with magnets on strings. Grown-ups perch on the pillars eating their lunch-time sandwiches or reading the paper. Though Buren's work has had many detractors, it has turned what used to be a car park into a popular pedestrian space.

When place du Palais-Royale is pedestrianized, under the auspices of I.M. Pei, you will be able to walk unhindered across the breadth of the 1er *arrondissement* from rue des Petits Champs to the Louvre, and then across the Passarelle Solférino to the Musée d'Orsay on the Left Bank.

Chapter 4

Right Bank Commerce, the Passages and Les Halles

I n the narrow streets of the 1er and 2e *arrondissements*, between the Louvre and the **Grands Boulevards**, the grandiose financial, cultural and political state institutions are surrounded by well-established commerce – the rag trade, newspapers, sex and well-heeled shopping. The most appealing features here are the nineteenth-century **passages**, shopping arcades long predating the concept of pedestrian precincts, with glass roofs, tiled floors and unobtrusive entrances. In contrast, the major **department stores** are next to the river and up in the 9e *arrondissement*, just north of the gaudy original **opera house**. For the seriously rich, however, the western end of the 1er and the streets to either side of the Champs-Élysées parade the wares of every top couturier, jeweller, art dealer and furnisher.

This is the area of Paris that has changed least in the last few decades: a mix of the monumental – the **Bourse**, **Banque de France**, **Bibliothèque Nationale** and **Opéra** – the traditional Grands Boulevards with their banks, brasseries and entertainment houses, and the intimacy of the Passages. It is both very chic and seedy. The great exception is **Les Halles**, once the food market of Paris, which no former trader would recognize. Of all the changes to the city in the last 25 years, the transformation of Les Halles is the least inspired, though it does provide some much-needed greenery and attracts the crowds.

The Grands Boulevards and the Opéra

The **Grands Boulevards** run from the Madeleine to République, then down to the Bastille. The western section, from the Madeleine to Porte St-Denis, follows the rampart built by Louis XIII. When its defensive purpose became redundant with the offensive foreign policy of Louis XIV, the walls were pulled down and the ditches filled in, leaving a wide promenade, which was given the name "*boulevard*" from the military term for the level part of a rampart. In the mid-eighteenth century, the boulevard became a fashionable place to be seen on horseback or in one's carriage, and gradually a fashionable place to have one's residence. The eastern section was far more entertaining, with street theatre, mime, juggling, puppets, waxworks and cafés of ill repute. It was known as the boulevard du Crime, and inevitably targeted by Haussmann, whose huge new crossroads – place de l'Opéra as well as place de la République – changed the physiognomy of the thoroughfare.

In the nineteenth century, the café clientele of the **boulevard des Italiens** set the trends for all of Paris, in manners, dress and what one could gossip about in public. The Grands Boulevards were cobbled; the first horse-drawn omnibus rattled from the Madeleine to the Bastille. From the bourgeois intellectuals in the west to the artisan fun-lovers to the east, this thoroughfare had the city's pulse. Even forty years ago, a visitor to Paris would have gone for a stroll along the Grands Boulevards to see "*Paris vivant*" as a matter of course. And today, for all the desperate traffic pollution and Burgerlands and grills, there are still theatres and cinemas (including the *Max Linder* and *Rex* – an extraordinary building inside and out, see p.336), the waxworks, and numerous brasseries and cafés, which, though not the chicest, most innovative or most amusing, still belong to the tradition of the Grands Boulevards, immortalized in the film *Les Enfants du Paradis*.

It was at 14 **bd des Capucines** that Paris first put on a movie, or animated photography, as the Lumière brothers' invention was called. An earlier artistic revolution took place at no. 35, where the first **Impressionist exhibition** was shown in Nadar's studio to an outraged art world. As one critic said of Monet's *Impression: Soleil Levant*, "it was worse than anyone had hitherto dared to paint". That was in 1874, only a year before the most preposterous building in the city was finally completed – the **Opéra de Paris**. Its architect, Charles Garnier, looks suitably foolish in a golden statue on the rue Auber side of his edifice, that so perfectly suited the by-then defunct court of Napoléon III. Excessively ornate and covering three acres in extent, it provided ample space for aristocratic preening, ceremonial pomp and the social intercourse of opera-goers, for whom the performance itself was a very secondary matter. The av de l'Opéra was built at the same time as its namesake – and left deliberately bereft of trees, which might mask the vista of the Opéra.

These days, with the Bastille opera open, the *Opéra Garnier* – as this is now called – is used almost exclusively for ballet. Rudolf Nureyev was director of the Paris Ballet here from 1983 to 1989, and the Opéra presented his last production, *La Bayadère* with the

Right Bank Commerce and the Passages: Listings

Restaurants

Chartier, 7 rue du Faubourg-Montmartre, 9e.
M° Montmartre.

Country Life, 6 rue Daunou, 2e.
M° Opéra.

Dilan, 13 rue Mandar, 2e.
M° Les Halles/Sentier.

Drouant, 18 rue Gaillon, 2e.
M° Opéra.

Drouot, 103 rue de Richelieu, 2e.
M° Richelieu-Drouot.

Le Grand Colbert, passage Colbert, rue Vivienne, 2e.
M° Bourse.

Le Grand Véfour, 17 rue de Beaujolais, 1er.
M° Pyramides.

L'Incroyable, 26 rue de Richelieu, 1er.
M° Palais-Royal.

Au Petit Riche, 25 rue Le Peletier, 9e.
M° Richelieu-Drouot.

Restaurant Végétarien Lacour, 3 rue Villedo, 1er.
M° Pyramides.

Le Vaudeville, 29 rue Vivienne, 2e.
M° Bourse.

Cafés and Bars

L'Arbre à Cannelle, 57 passage des Panoramas, 2e.
M° Rue-Montmartre.

Baalbeck, 16 rue de Mazagran, 10e.
M° Bonne-Nouvelle.

Le Bar de l'Entracte, corner of rue Montpensier and rue Beaujolais, 1er.
M° Palais-Royal–Musée-du-Louvre.

Aux Bons Crus, 7 rue des Petits-Champs, 1er.
M° Palais-Royal.

Cave Drouot, 8 rue Drouot, 9e.
M° Richelieu-Drouot.

La Champmeslé, 4 rue Chabanais, 2e.
M° Pyramides.

Du Croissant, corner of rue du Croissant and rue Montmartre, 2e.
M° Montmartre.

Flo, 7 cours des Petites-Écuries, 10e.
M° Château-d'Eau.

Le Grand Café Capucines, 4 bd des Capucines, 9e.
M° Opéra.

Kitty O'Shea's, 10 rue des Capucines, 2e.
M° Opéra.

Lina's Sandwiches, 50 rue Étienne-Marcel, 2e (M° Étienne-Marcel); 8 rue Marbeuf, 8e (M° Alma-Marceau).

La Micro-Brasserie, 106 rue de Richelieu, 2e.
M° Richelieu-Drouot.

La Muscade, Galerie de Montpensier, 1er.
M° Palais-Royale–Musée du Louvre.

Le Rubis, 10 rue du Marché-St-Honoré, 1er.
M° Pyramides.

Tigh Johnny, 55 rue Montmartre, 2e.
M° Sentier.

Village Gourmand, 16 rue des Petits-Champs, 2e.
M° Pyramides.

These establishments are reviewed in Chapter 13, Eating and Drinking, beginning on p.235.

Kirov, a few months before his death. At his funeral, in January 1993, the steps of the opera house were strewn with white flowers as his coffin was carried up to the foyer, and the orchestra played his favourite piece by Bach. This was Nureyev's home, the first place where he danced in the West, and the place where he took refuge after defecting from the Soviet Union in 1961. He is buried in the Russian Orthodox cemetery outside Paris in St-Geneviève-du-Bois.

By day you can visit the **interior** (daily 10am–5pm; 30F/18F), including the auditorium – as long as there are no rehearsals (best chance between 1 and 2pm) – whose ceiling is the work of Chagall. The classic horror movie, *The Phantom of the Opéra*, was set, though never filmed, here; a real underground stream lends credence to the tale.

To the north of the Opéra, on the barren bd du Haussmann, are two of the city's department stores, **Magasins du Printemps** and **Galeries Lafayette** (with the Paris branch of *Marks and Spencers* opposite). Though they still possess their proud, *fin-de-siècle* glass domes, much of the beauty of their interiors has been hacked away.

Boulevard des Italiens, running south of boulevard Haussmann from the Opéra to Richelieu-Drouot, has a fine selection of banking buildings. The *Crédit Lyonnais* (which broke records in 1994 for losing money) has its head branch at no. 19, with a huge gold clock surrounded by gigantic women in flowing disarray. The *Banque Nationale Populaire* has preserved the golden balconies and hunting friezes of the 1840s restaurant, the *Maison Dorée* at no. 20, next door to its sleek 1930s main building at no. 16.

The Passages

For decades the **passages** were left to crumble and decay. It was only very recently that the charms of being outside but inside, of walking on beautiful floors in a watery light, secluded from the mayhem of the city's streets, were rediscovered. Many, though by no means all, have now been rendered chic and immaculate – as they originally were – with mega-premiums on their leases. Their entrances, however, remain easy to miss, and you can surprise yourself by quite where you emerge at the other end. Many are closed at night and on Sundays.

The most homogeneous and aristocratic of the passages, with painted ceilings and panelled shopfronts divided by black marble columns, is **Galerie Véro-Dodat** (between rue Croix-des-Petits-Champs and rue Jean-Jacques Rousseau), named after the two pork butchers who set it up in 1824. It is still a little dilapidated with peeling paint on many of the shop fronts, and the recession has seen some of the old businesses close down. But at no. 26, Monsieur Capia still keeps a collection of antique dolls in a shop piled high with miscellaneous curios.

The **Banque de France** lies a short way northeast of Galerie Véro-Dodat. Rather than negotiating its massive bulk to reach the passages further north, it's more pleasant to walk through the gardens of the Palais Royal (see p.73). Rue Montpensier, running alongside the gardens to the west, is connected to rue Richelieu by several tiny passages, of which Hulot brings you out at the statue of Molière on the junction of rues Richelieu and Molière. A certain charm also lurks about rue de Beaujolais, bordering the northern end of the gardens, with its corner café looking on the Théâtre du Palais-Royal, the glimpses into *Le Grand Véfour* restaurant, and more short arcades leading up to rue des Petits-Champs.

On the other side of rue des Petits-Champs, just to the left as you come from rue de Beaujolais, is the forbidding wall of the **Bibliothèque Nationale**, the French equivalent of the British Museum library, soon to have an additional home in the 13e (see p.146). Temporary exhibitions here provide access to the more beautiful parts of the building, and you can also pay to see a display of coins and ancient treasures (Mon–Sat 1–5pm; 20F/12F). There's no restriction on entering the library, though without academic credentials you can't get your mits on any medieval manuscripts, sixteenth-century newspapers, Gutenberg bibles or Proust's private papers.

The library owns **Galerie Colbert**, one of two very upmarket passages linking rue Vivienne with rue des Petits-Champs. Gorgeously lit by bunches of bulbous lamps, Galerie Colbert shelters a collection of the library's sound recordings and theatrical publications, along with an expensive 1830s-style brasserie, *Le Grand Colbert*, where senior librarians and rich academics take their lunch breaks. The flamboyant décor of Grecian and marine motifs in the larger **Galerie Vivienne** entices you to buy Jean-Paul Gaultier or Yuki Torri gear, or to browse in the antiquarian bookshop, *Albert Petit Siroux*, that dates back to the passage's earliest days.

Three blocks west of the Bibliothèque Nationale is a totally different style of passage. The **passage Choiseul**, between rue des Petits-Champs and rue St-Augustin (and connected to rue Ste-Anne by passage Ste-Anne), is like a regular high street, with take-away food, cheap clothes shops, stationers, bars, and nothing as sleek as a *salon de thé* along its whole, considerable, length.

For a combination of chic and workaday you need to explore the **passage des Panoramas**, the grid of arcades north of the Bibliothèque Nationale, beyond rue St-Marc. The Panoramas are still in need of a little repair and there are no fancy mosaics for your feet. An old brasserie with carved wood panelling has been restored, and new restaurants are moving in, but there are still bric-à-brac shops, stamp dealers, an upper-crust printshop with its original 1867 fittings, and *Le Relax* bar where locals with their dogs sit at orange formica tables.

In **passage Jouffroy** across bd Montmartre, a M. Segas sells walking canes and theatrical antiques opposite a shop displaying every conceivable fitting and furnishing for a doll's house. Near the romantic *Hotel Chopin*, Paul Vulin spreads his second-hand books along the passageway. Crossing rue de la Grange-Batelière, you enter **passage Verdeau**, where a few of the old comic and camera dealers still trade alongside smart new art galleries and the *Pop Gril* snackbar, whose ceiling is studded with an ancient collection of wood and iron tools.

The tiny **passage des Princes** at the top of rue Richelieu has been stripped and awaits regentrification. Its erstwhile neighbour, the passage de l'Opéra, described in surreal detail by Louis Aragon in *Paris Peasant*, was eaten up by the completion of Haussmann's boulevards – a project that demolished scores of old passages.

While in this area, you could also take a look at what's up for auction at the Paris equivalent of *Christie's* and *Sotheby's*, the **Hôtel Drouot** (9 rue Drouot; M° Le Pelletier/Richelieu-Drouot). Details of the auctions are announced in listings magazines such as *Pariscope*, under the heading *Ventes aux Enchères*, and in the press. To spare any fear of unintended hand movements landing you in the bankruptcy courts, you can wander round looking at the goods before the action starts: 11am–6pm on the eve of the sale, 11am–noon on the day itself.

Returning to the 2e *arrondissement*, close to métro Étienne-Marcel, the three-storey **Grand-Cerf** between rue St-Denis and rue Dessoubs is stylistically the best of all the passages. Its wrought-iron work, glass roof and plain wood shop fronts have all been cleaned, and potted shrubs placed along its length. The only problem is the lack of tenants – just one *salon de thé, Thé S.F.*, hopefully awaits future clients.

As you exit from the passage du Grand-Cerf at rue Dessoubs you're faced with a mural entitled *La Ville Imaginaire*, inspired by Robert Mallet-Stevens. Fortunately this urban vision is not what is intended for this Montorgueil-St-Denis *quartier*, which is being pedestrianized. Already some streets have been recobbled, bollarded and fitted out with new rubbish bins, street signs and so forth. Finally, it seems, the wheel has turned full circle. The sense that inspired nineteenth-century planners to give pedestrians protection from mud and horse-drawn vehicles in the passages now gives protection on the streets from far more dangerous traffic.

Mallet-Stevens, a Cubist architect and contemporary of Le Corbusier, designed the entire rue Mallet-Stevens; see p.194.

Clothes, sex and stocks and shares

Mass-produced clothing is the business of **place du Caire**, the centre of the rag-trade district. The frenetic trading and deliveries of cloth, the food market on **rue des Petits-Carreaux**, and the general to-ing and fro-ing make a lively change from the office-bound quarters further west. Beneath an extraordinary pseudo-Egyptian façade of grotesque Pharaonic heads (a celebration of Napoléon's conquest of Egypt), an archway opens onto a series of arcades, the **passage du Caire**. These, contrary to any visible evidence, are the oldest of all the passages and entirely monopolized by wholesale clothes shops.

The garment business gets progressively more upmarket westwards from the trade area. The upper end of **rue Étienne-Marcel**, and Louis XlV's **place des Victoires**, adjoined to the north by the appealingly asymmetrical **place des Petits-Pères**, are the centre for new-name designer clothes, displayed to deter all those without the necessary funds. The boutiques on **rue St-Honoré** and its Faubourg extension have the established names, paralleled across the Champs-Élysées by those on **rue François-1er**, where Dior has at least four blocks on the corner with av Montaigne. *Pierre Marly*, optician's at 380 rue St-Honoré, and *Di Mauro*, bespoke shoemakers, 14 Faubourg St-Honoré, both have small museums dedicated to their crafts (see p.280 and p.279). The **place Vendôme**, with Napoléon high on a column clad with recycled Austro-Russian cannons, caters for the same pocketbook. Here you have all the fashionable accessories for *haute couture* – jewellery, perfumes, the original *Ritz*, a Rothschilds office and the Law and Order ministry.

After clothes, bodies are the most evident commodity on sale in the 1er and 2e *arrondissements*. However, **rue St-Denis**, which used to be the red light district of Paris, has been cleaned up. It is now a pedestrianized area, so kerb crawling has come to an end, and cafés like the new English *Frog and Rosbif* are replacing the old porn outlets. The prostitutes are still there for the moment – and the opiate-glazed eyes of so many of the women indicate the doubly vicious bind they're trapped in. But the 2e *arrondissement mairie* hopes they'll move further north, allowing rue St-Denis to become as upmarket as Les Halles. Around rue Ste-Anne, business is strictly gay, transvestite and under-age, and reaching the age of 13 or 14 invariably means redundancy. Such are the libertarian delights of Paris streetlife.

In the centre of the 2e stands the **Bourse** – the scene for dealing in stocks and shares, dollars and gold. The classical order of the façade utterly belies the scene within, which resembles nothing so much as an unruly boys' public school, with creaking floors, tottering pigeonholes and people scuttling about with bits of paper. You can enter the gallery above the dealing floor (Mon–Fri guided tours

---

Notable buildings in the 1er, 2e and 8e arrondissements

• **124 rue Réamur**, 2e, just east of rue Montmartre. M° Sentier.
Almost entirely metal with Art Nouveau curves, these industrial premises were probably the first to make a feature of its structure by revealing its riveted steel girders on the façade. Attributed to Georges Chedane, 1905.
• **Théâtre des Champs-Élysées**, 15 av Montaigne, 8e. M° Alma-Marceau.
Gold and gleaming white marble plus sculptures by Bourdelle cover this concrete creation of Auguste Perret and Henry van de Velde from 1913.
• **Mural, corner of rue Penthièvre and av Delcassé**, 8e. M° St-Philippe-du-Roule/Miromesnil.
If you look north down av Matignon from rue du Faubourg St-Honoré, you'll see a nineteenth-century apartment block painted by J.C. Decaux above two large clocks and rolling billboards.
• **Place du Marché St-Honoré**, 1er. M° Pyramides.
The horrible car park has been knocked down to be replaced by a glass hall of shops and offices designed by Ricardo Bofill. Should be finished by 1996.

at 1.30, 2, 2.30 and 3pm; 10F entry, ID needed), but you won't see the real financial sharks, who go elsewhere for their deals.

The status of the City of London is the French no. 2 grudge after the dominance of the English language, but short of changing the world's time zones, the Bourse de Paris will never rival Tokyo, New York or London. The antennae-topped building of the French news agency, AFP, overshadowing the Bourse from the south, gives a far more convincing impression of efficiency and alertness.

Les Halles

In 1969 the main **Les Halles market** was moved out to the suburbs after more than eight hundred years in the heart of the city. There was widespread opposition to the destruction of Victor Baltard's nineteenth-century pavilions, and considerable disquiet at what renovation of the area would mean. The authorities' excuse was the *RER* and métro interchange they had to have below. Digging began in 1971 and the hole was only finally filled at the end of the 1980s. Hardly any trace remains of the working-class quarter, with its night bars and bistros to serve the market traders. Rents now rival the 16e, and the all-night places serve and profit from salaried and speed-popping types. Les Halles is constantly promoted as the in-spot of Paris, where the cool and famous congregate. In fact, anyone with any sense and money hangs out in the traditional bour-geois *quartiers* to the west.

From Châtelet-Les Halles *RER*, you surface only after ascending from levels -4 to 0 of the **Forum des Halles** centre, which stretches underground from the Bourse du Commerce rotunda to rue Pierre-Lescot. The overground section comprises aquarium-like arcades of shops, enclosed by glass buttocks, with white steel creases sliding down to an imprisoned patio. To cover up for all this commerce, poetry, arts and crafts pavilions top two sides in a simple construc-tion – save for the mirrors – that just manages to be out of sync with the curves and hollows below.

The gardens have begun to outgrow their protective wire cages and the green space is providing a welcome respite. On the north side in front of St-Eustache, a giant head and hand still suggest the dislocation of this place. Beneath the garden, amidst the uninspiring shops, there's scope for such serious and appealing diversions as journeying through a simulated underwater world, swimming, watching games of billiards, discovering Paris through videos, and wandering through a tropical garden. Touch-screen computers, with French and English "menus", are on hand to guide you round.

Further details of the subterranean delights of the Forum can be found in Chapter 15.

After a spate of multi-levels, air-conditioning and artificial light, however, it's a relief to enter the high Gothic and Renaissance space of St-Eustache. A woman "preached" the abolition of marriage from the pulpit during the Commune, and the more recent history of the

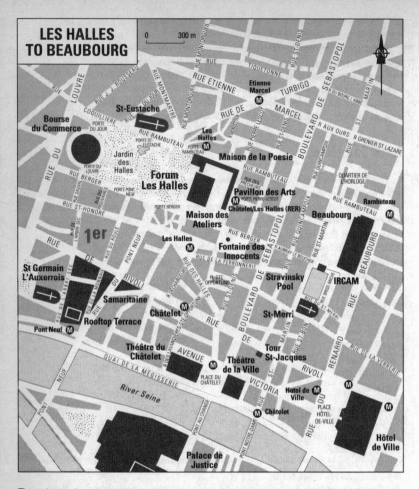

LES HALLES TO BEAUBOURG

0   300 m

RUE MONTORGUEIL

RUE TIQUETONNE

RUE ETIENNE MARCEL

Etienne Marcel Ⓜ

TURBIGO

BOULEVARD DE SEBASTOPOL

R DU BOURG L'ABBÉ

MARTIN

RUE J.J. ROUSSEAU

LOUVRE

RUE

COQUILLIÈRE

St-Eustache

RUE DU JOUR MONTMARTRE

RUE DE

MARCEL

RUE PIERRE LESCOT

RUE ST-DENIS

R GRENIER ST LAZARE

R AUX OURS

RUE QUINCAMPOIX

Bourse du Commerce

PORTE DU JOUR

RUE RAMBUTEAU

PORTE ST EUSTACHE

Les Halles

RUE ST-DENIS

Jardin des Halles

PORTE DU LOUVRE

RUE BERGER

PORTE ST RAMBUTEAU Ⓜ

Maison de la Poesie

QUARTIER DE L'HORLOGE

RUE DU

Forum Les Halles

RUE RAMBUTEAU

RUE DES PRÊCHEURS

RUE RAMBUTEAU

Rambuteau Ⓜ

PORTE PONT NEUF

Pavillon des Arts

PORTE PIERRE LESCOT

Beaubourg Ⓜ

RUE ST-HONORÉ

PORTE BERGER

Maison des Ateliers

Châtelet/Les Halles (RER)

Beaubourg

BEAUBOURG

1er

RUE DE L'ARBRE SEC

RUE DE L'ABOULE

PONT NEUF

Les Halles Ⓜ

RUE BERGER

BOULEVARD DE SEBASTOPOL

RUE ST-MARTIN

RUE

Fontaine des Innocents

R AUBRY LE BOUCHER

St Germain L'Auxerrois

RUE DE RIVOLI

RUE DE LA FERRONNERIE

Stravinsky Pool

IRCAM

RUE ST-MERRI

Samaritaine

RUE MONNAIE

RUE DES HALLES

PISTE OPPORTUNE

BOULEVARD DE SEBASTOPOL

St-Merri

RUE ST-MARTIN

RENARD

Châtelet

RUE DE RIVOLI

RUE ST-BON

Rooftop Terrace

Pont Neuf Ⓜ

Théâtre du Châtelet

AVENUE

Tour St-Jacques

RUE DE LA VERRERIE

PONT NEUF

QUAI DE LA MÉGISSERIE

Théâtre de la Ville

PLACE DU CHÂTELET

VICTORIA

RIVOLI

RUE ST-MARTIN

Hôtel de Ville Ⓜ

Ⓜ

River Seine

PONT AU CHANGE

Châtelet Ⓜ

PLACE HÔTEL-DE-VILLE

RUE DU

Hôtel de Ville

PONT NOTRE-DAME

Palace de Justice

The restaurants of Les Halles are keyed on the map on p.238.

area is depicted in a naive fresco in the chapelle St-Joseph, entitled *Le départ des fruits et légumes du coeur de Paris, le 28 février 1969.*

As an alternative to steel and glass troglodytism, you could join the throng around the **Fontaine des Innocents** and watch and listen to water cascading down its perfect Renaissance proportions (skate-boarders and boom-boxes permitting). Clowns imitating your move-ments for the amusement of everyone else are a regular hazard – or a delight, when you're not the victim.

There are always hundreds of people around the Forum, filling in time, hustling, or just loafing about. Pickpocketing and sexual harassment are pretty routine; the law plus canine arm are often in

evidence and at night it can be quite tense. The supposedly trendy
streets on the eastern side have plenty of cafés for breaks from the
shoving crowds. The area southwards to **place du Châtelet** teems
with jazz bars, nightclubs and restaurants, and is far more crowded
at 2am than 2pm.

*Music listings
for the area
around place
du Châtelet can
be found in
Chapter 18.*

North and south of Les Halles

Old food businesses survive to the north of Les Halles, along **rues
Montmartre, Montorgueil** and **Turbigo**. Strictly not for vegetarians, the shops and stalls feature wild boar, deer and feathered
friends, alongside *pâté de foie gras* and caviar. Professional chefs'
equipment is for sale as well (see p.314).

Les Halles

Once you retreat back towards the Louvre, streets like **de l'Arbre-Sec**, **Sauval** and **du Roule** revive the gentler attractions of pavement window-shopping while, on the riverfront, the three blocks of the **Samaritaine department store** (Mon, Thurs & Sat 9.30am–7pm; Tues & Fri 9.30am–8.30pm; Wed 9.30am–10.30pm) recall the days when art, not marketing psychology, determined the decoration of a store. It was built in 1903 in pure Art Nouveau style. The gold, green, and glass exteriors, and, inside, the brightly painted wrought-iron staircases and balconies against huge backdrops of ceramic floral patterns, have all been recently restored. Best of all is the view from the roof (take the lift to floor nine in Magasin 2 and then walk up two flights) – the most central high location in the city.

Chapter 5

Beaubourg, the Marais, Île St-Louis and the Bastille

T he **Centre Beaubourg** or Pompidou Centre, a few blocks away from Les Halles across boulevard Sébastopol, was a radical architectural breakthrough for its period – the 1970s – and an enduring, popular focus for the city. The **quartier du Beaubourg** is full of art galleries and cafés and is as lively as Les Halles by day and night. To the south, by the river, are the theatres of Châtelet and the town hall of Paris.

The **Marais**, to the east, and the **Île St-Louis** are the loveliest areas of central Paris. Their aristocratic mansions, the medieval lanes and Jewish quarter, and the plethora of small, appealing restaurants, shops and cafés have no major thoroughfares to disturb them.

The **Bastille** used to belong in spirit and in style to the working-class districts of eastern Paris. Since the building of the new opera house, it has become as fashionable a *quartier* as the Marais and very much one of Paris' central hot spots.

Beaubourg

For years after the 1977 opening of the **Centre Beaubourg** – the **Georges Pompidou national art and culture centre** – it was notorious as Paris' most outrageous building. The novel conception of architects Renzo Piano and Richard Rogers was to put all the infrastructure on the outside, leaving the maximum space for the interior. Painted in bright colours and with no monumental entrance – just a large, sloping piazza for buskers, magicians, clowns and anyone else to use as their stage – it was designed, in Richard Rogers' words, as "horizontal streets in the air". Talking about the building in 1994, Rogers said, "It's actually a reflection of 1968. I wouldn't have said this in 1971 when we did it, but looking back, I realize how much a reflection it was of my belief in being able to create a people's place. Our report presented it as 'a place for all

The interior spaces may be changed as the building undergoes extensive restoration work.

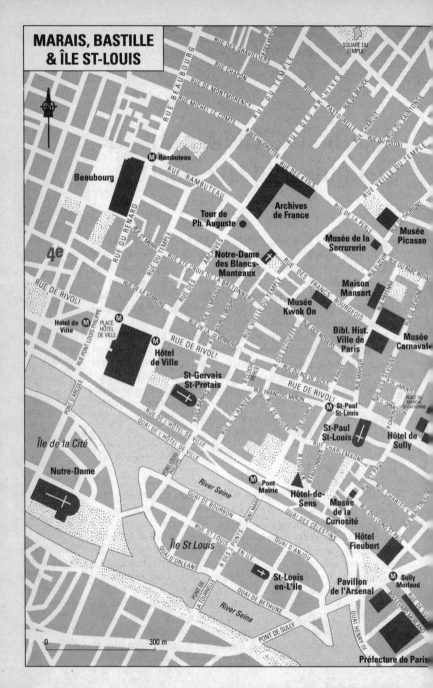

MARAIS, BASTILLE & ÎLE ST-LOUIS

RUE DES GRAVILLIERS
SQUARE DU TEMPLE
RUE CHAPON
RUE BEAUBOURG
RUE DE MONTMORENCY
RUE MICHEL LE COMTE
RUE DES ARCHIVES
RUE DE BEAUCE
RUE VERBOIS
RUE PASTOURELLE
RUE DU TEMPLE
RUE DE BRETAGNE
RUE CHARLOT
RUE DU POITOU
RUE DES MALCOURSES
RUE DU SANTONGE

Ⓜ Rambuteau
Beaubourg
RUE RAMBUTEAU
RUE DES 4 FILS
RUE VIELLE DU TEMPLE
RUE DE LA PERLE
RUE DE THORIGNY

Tour de Ph. Auguste ●
Archives de France
Musée de la Serrurerie
Musée Picasso

RUE DU RENARD
RUE ST-MERRI
RUE DU TEMPLE
HUE STE-CROIX DE LA BRETONNERIE
RUE DES ARCHIVES
4e
RUE DE RIVOLI
RUE DE LA VERRERIE
RUE DE LA VERRERIE

Notre-Dame des Blancs-Manteaux †
RUE DES FRANCS BOURGEOIS
Musée Kwok On
RUE VIELLE DU TEMPLE
Maison Mansart
RUE PAYENNE
RUE DE SEVIGNE
RUE DU PARC ROYAL
RUE ELZEVIR

Bibl. Hist. Ville de Paris
Musée Carnaval

Hôtel de Ville Ⓜ
PLACE HÔTEL DE VILLE
Ⓜ
RUE PONT LOUIS PHILIPPE
Hôtel de Ville
RUE DE RIVOLI
RUE DES ROSIERS
RUE DE SEVIGNE
RUE DE JARENTE

St-Gervais St-Protais †
RUE DE LA VERRERIE
RUE CLOCHE PERCE
RUE DU ROI DE SICILE
R. PAVEE
RUE MAHLER
PLACE DU MARCHE STE-CATHERINE
R. DE JARENTE
R. CARON

RUE DE RIVOLI
RUE FRANÇOIS MIRON
R. DU BOURG TIBOURG
RUE DES BARRES
RUE G. MASNIER
RUE DE FOURCY
R. CLOCHE PERCE
R. DE L'ORME ROSSON
Ⓜ **St-Paul St-Louis**

PONT D'ARCOLE
QUAI DE L'HÔTEL DE VILLE
Île de la Cité
Notre-Dame †
RUE FIGUIER
RUE CHARLEMAGNE
St-Paul St-Louis †
Hôtel de Sully
RUE ST-PAUL
RUE CHARLES V
RUE BEAUTREILLIS

PONT LOUIS PHILIPPE
PONT MARIE
Ⓜ **Pont Marie**
Hôtel-de-Sens
Musée de la Curiosité
RUE DES LIONS ST-PAUL
River Seine
QUAI DE BOURBON
QUAI DES CELESTINS
QUAI D'ANJOU

RUE ST-LOUIS EN L'ILE
Île St Louis
RUE DES 2 PONTS
QUAI D'ORLEANS
Hôtel Fieubert

PONT DE LA TOURNELLE
† **St-Louis en-L'Île**
QUAI DE BETHUNE
River Seine
Pavillon de l'Arsenal
Ⓜ **Sully Morland**
BOULEVARD MORLAND
RUE DE SULLY

0 ——— 300 m
QUAI HENRY IV
PONT DE SULLY
Préfecture de Paris

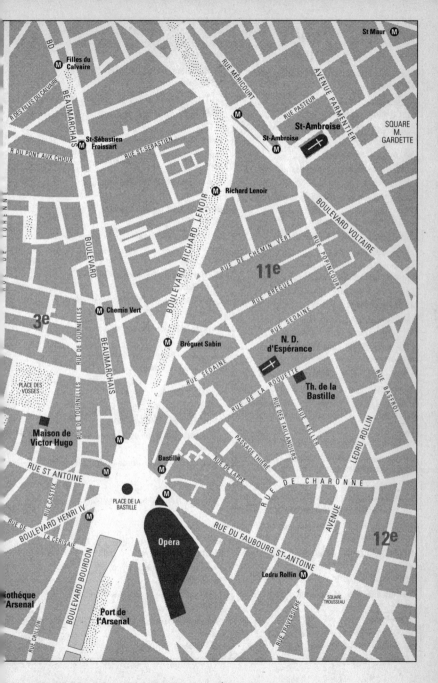

The Marais, Bastille and Île St-Louis: Listings

Restaurants

L'Abreuvoir, 68 rue de la Roquette, 11ᵉ.
Mᵒ Voltaire/Bastille.

L'Ambroisie, 9 pl Vosges, 4ᵉ.
Mᵒ Chemin-Vert/St-Paul.

Aquarius 1, 54 rue Ste-Croix-de-la-Bretonnerie, 4ᵉ.
Mᵒ St-Paul/Rambuteau.

Auberge de Jarente, 7 rue Jarente, 4ᵉ.
Mᵒ St-Paul.

Blue Elephant, 43–45 rue de la Roquette, 11ᵉ.
Mᵒ Bastille/Richard-Lenoir.

Bofinger, 3–7 rue de la Bastille, 3ᵉ.
Mᵒ Bastille.

La Canaille, 4 rue Crillon, 4ᵉ.
Mᵒ Sully-Morland/Bastille.

Chez Caroll Sinclair, 36 bd Henri-IV, 4ᵉ.
Mᵒ Sully Morland.

Le Castafiore, 51 rue St-Louis-en-l'Île, 4ᵉ.
Mᵒ Pont-Marie.

L'Enoteca, 25 rue Charles-V, 4ᵉ.
Mᵒ St-Paul.

L'Excuse, 14 rue Charles-V, 4ᵉ.
Mᵒ St-Paul.

Fleur de Lotus, 2 rue du Roi-de-Sicile, 4ᵉ.
Mᵒ St-Paul.

Goldenberg's, 7 rue des Rosiers, 4ᵉ.
Mᵒ St-Paul.

Le Gourmet de l'Île, 42 rue St-Louis-en-l'Île, 4ᵉ.
Mᵒ Pont-Marie.

Le Marais-Cage, 8 rue de Beauce, 3ᵉ.
Mᵒ Arts-et-Métiers/Filles-du-Calvaire.

Chez Nénesse, 17 rue Saintonge, 3ᵉ.
Mᵒ Arts-et-Métiers.

Nini Peau d'Chien, 24 rue des Taillandiers, 11ᵉ.
Mᵒ Bastille.

Le Palais de Fès, 41 rue du Roi-de-Sicile, 4ᵉ.
Mᵒ St-Paul.

Piccolo Teatro, 6 rue des Écouffes, 4ᵉ.
Mᵒ St-Paul.

Pitchi-Poï, 7 rue Caron, place du Marché-Ste-Catherine, 4ᵉ.
Mᵒ St-Paul.

Le Ravaillac, 10 rue du Roi-de-Sicile, 4ᵉ.
Mᵒ St-Paul.

La Truffe, 31 rue Vieille-du-Temple, 4ᵉ.
Mᵒ St-Paul.

Cafés and Bars

Bar Central, 33 rue Vieille-du-Temple, 4ᵉ.
Mᵒ St-Paul.

Bar de Jarente, 5 rue de Jarente, 4ᵉ.
Mᵒ St-Paul.

Berthillon, 31 rue St-Louis-en-l'Île, 4ᵉ.
Mᵒ Pont-Marie.

Le Bouchon du Marais, 15 rue François-Miron, 4ᵉ.
Mᵒ St-Paul.

Ma Bourgogne, 19 place des Vosges, 3ᵉ.
Mᵒ St-Paul.

Café de l'Industrie, 16 rue St-Sabin, 11ᵉ.
Mᵒ Bastille.

Café de la Plage, 59 rue de Charonne, 11ᵉ.
Mᵒ Bastille.

La Cane de Jouy, 8 rue de Jouy, 4ᵉ.
Mᵒ St-Paul/Pont-Marie.

Le Coude Fou, 12 rue du Bourg-Tibourg, 4ᵉ.
Mᵒ Hôtel-de-Ville.

Dame Tartine, 2 rue Brise-Miche, 4ᵉ.
Mᵒ Rambuteau/Hôtel-de-Ville.

L'Ébouillanté, 6 rue des Barres, 4ᵉ.
Mᵒ Hôtel-de-Ville.

Les Enfants Gatés, 43 rue des Francs-Bourgeois, 4ᵉ.
Mᵒ St-Paul.

Épices et Délices, 53 rue Vieille-du-Temple, 4ᵉ.
Mᵒ St-Paul.

La Fontaine, 1 rue de Charonne, 11ᵉ.
Mᵒ Bastille.

Fouquet's, 130 rue de Lyon, 12ᵉ.
Mᵒ Bastille.

Les Fous de l'Île, 33 rue des Deux-Ponts, 4ᵉ.
Mᵒ Pont-Marie.

Hollywood Canteen, 20 rue de la Roquette, 11ᵉ.
Mᵒ Bastille.

Iguana, 15 rue de la Roquette (corner rue Daval), 11ᵉ. Mᵒ Bastille.	**Sacha Finkelsztajn and Florence Finkelsztajn**, 27 rue des Rosiers, 4ᵉ. Both Mᵒ St-Paul.
L'Oiseau Bariolé, 16 rue Ste-Croix-de-la-Bretonnerie, 4ᵉ. Mᵒ Hôtel-de-Ville.	**Le St-Régis**, 92 rue St-Louis-en-l'Île, 4ᵉ. Mᵒ Pont-Marie.
Pause Café, 41 rue de Charonne, 11ᵉ. Mᵒ Ledru-Rollin.	**La Tartine**, 24 rue de Rivoli, 4ᵉ. Mᵒ St-Paul.
La Perla, 26 rue François-Miron, 4ᵉ. Mᵒ St-Paul.	**Le Taxi Jaune**, 13 rue Chapon, 3ᵉ. Mᵒ Arts-et-Métiers.
Au Petit Fer à Cheval, 30 rue Vieille-du-Temple, 4ᵉ. Mᵒ St-Paul.	**Le Temps des Cerises**, 31 rue de la Cerisaie, 4ᵉ. Mᵒ Bastille.
Le Pick-Clops, 16 rue Vieille-du-Temple, 4ᵉ. Mᵒ Hôtel-de-Ville.	**Le Trumilou**, 84 quai Hôtel-de-Ville, 4ᵉ. Mᵒ Pont-Marie.
La Pirada, 7 rue de Lappe, 11ᵉ. Mᵒ Bastille.	**Le Volcan de Sicile**, 62 rue du Roi-de-Sicile, 4ᵉ. Mᵒ Hôtel-de-Ville.
Le Quetzal, 10 rue de la Verrerie, 4ᵉ. Mᵒ St-Paul.	**Yahalom**, 22–24 rue des Rosiers, 4ᵉ. Mᵒ St-Paul.
Le Rouge Gorge, 8 rue St-Paul, 4ᵉ. Mᵒ St-Paul.	**Le Zinc**, 4 rue Caron, 4ᵉ. Mᵒ St-Paul.

These establishments are reviewed in Chapter 13, Eating and Drinking, *beginning on p.239.*

peoples, all creeds, all colours; a place for old and young'. We searched out things that were not specifically in the brief, areas for old people to be warm and read the newspaper and so on. We designed so that activities could overlap. We thought breadth of choice was very much part of a people's institution." Designed for 6000 visitors a day, it has had more like 25,000 – proof of its outstanding success as an enduringly popular building. But the overload of visitors and corrosion in the exterior steel has taken its toll. Discussions are going on as to how best to carry out renovation work – but nothing is to begin before 1997.

Inside the Centre

The centre is open, free (with admission charges for the exhibitions and art museum), every weekday except Tuesday from noon to 10pm, and at weekends from 10am to 10pm.

For details of Beaubourg's museum, cinema and activities for kids, see pp. 272, 337 & 300.

On the ground floor, the postcard selection and art bookshop betters anything on the streets outside, and there are usually some scattered artworks that you don't have to pay to see. Books, tapes, videos and international newspapers can be consulted for free at the **Bibliothèque Publique d'Information (BPI)** on the second floor. There are four more libraries: literature at ground level and on the second floor; plastic arts on the fourth floor; and documentation on the current main exhibition on the fifth.

The **escalator** is usually one long queue, but you should ride up this glass intestine at least once. As the circles of spectators on the plaza recede, a horizontal skyline appears: the Sacré-Coeur, St-Eustache, the Eiffel Tower, Notre-Dame, the Panthéon, the Tour St-Jacques with its solitary gargoyle, and La Défense menacing in the distance. From the platform at the top you can look down on the château-style chimneys of the Hôtel de Ville, with their flowerpot offspring sprouting all over the lower rooftops.

Back on the ground, the **visual entertainments** around Beaubourg don't appeal to every taste. There's the clanking gold *Défenseur du Temps* clock in the Quartier de l'Horloge; a *trompe-l'œil*, as you look along rue Aubry-le-Boucher from Beaubourg; a nine-digit timepiece counting down by milliseconds to the year 2000 on the south face of the centre; and colourful sculptures and fountains by Tinguely and Nicky de St-Phalle in the pool in front of **Église St-Merri**. This waterwork pays homage to Stravinsky and shows scant respect for passers-by; it is the ceiling for IRCAM, the centre for contemporary music. A new, overground extension to IRCAM has appeared, squeezed beside the old public baths on rue St-Merri. It's a Renzo Piano creation with a façade of stark terracotta marked like graph paper.

The activites of Pierre Boulez's IRCAM are described on p.332.

Quartier Beaubourg and the Hôtel de Ville

Where the *quartier* Beaubourg excels is in its choice of small **commercial art galleries**, in which you can browse to your heart's content for free. **Rue Quincampoix** is particularly full of promise, with photographic greats at *Zabriskie* (no. 37); multimedia installations at *Alain Oudin* (no. 47); the *Support-Surface* French movement of the Seventies at *Jean Fournier* (no. 44); and international stars at *Crousel-Robelin-Bama* (no. 40). Numbers 23 and 25 rue du Renard – respectively *Galerie Beaubourg*, for important contemporary works, and *Galerie Néotu*, for avant-garde furniture design – are both well worth a look. Just over rue Renard to the east, on rue St-Merri, is the *Galarie Maeght*, run by the Maeght Foundation in St-Paul-de-Vence. It sells works by Miró, Picasso, Giacometti and the like.

Rue Renard runs down to **place de l'Hôtel de Ville**, where the oppressively gleaming and gargantuan mansion is the seat of the city's local government. An illustrated history of the edifice, always a prime target in riots and revolutions, is displayed along the platform of the Châtelet métro on the Neuilly-Vincennes line.

The opponents to the establishments of kings and emperors created their alternative municipal governments at this building in 1789, 1848 and 1870. The poet Lamartine proclaimed the Second Republic here in 1848, and Gambetta the third in 1870. But with the defeat of the Commune in 1871, the conservatives, back in control, concluded that the Parisian municipal authority had to go, if order, property, morality and the suppression of the working class were to be maintained. For the next hundred years, Paris was ruled directly by the national government.

The next head of an independent municipality after the leaders of the Commune was **Jacques Chirac**, who became mayor in 1977. Although he hardly poses the same threat to the establishment, he has nonetheless been a constant source of irritation to President Mitterrand, and has run Paris as his own fiefdom with scant regard for other councillors. He even retained the mayorship while he was prime minister – a power base unequalled in French politics.

But whatever the political stakes, whatever the personal motives, Paris all too obviously enjoys dynamic local government: a shaming and glaring contrast to the shabby disenfranchisement of London.

The Marais

The **Marais** today comprises most of the 3^e and 4^e *arrondisse-ments*. But until the thirteenth century, when the Knights Templar set up house in its northern section, now known as the Quartier du Temple, and began to drain the land, it was uninhabitable riverside swamp – *marais* is the French for "swamp". It did not acquire the grand and aristocratic character that is now its hallmark until around 1600, when it became the object of royal patronage, especially after the construction of the place des Vosges – or place Royale, as it then was – by Henri IV in 1605.

Its apogee was relatively short-lived, however, for the aristocracy began to move away after the king removed his court to Versailles in the latter part of the seventeenth century, leaving their mansions to the trading classes, who were in turn displaced at the Revolution. Thereafter, the masses moved in. The mansions were transformed into multi-occupied slum tenements. Their fabric decayed and the streets degenerated into unserviced squalor – and stayed that way until the 1960s.

Since then, however, gentrification has proceeded apace, and the quarter is now a sought after enclave for media, arty and gay Parisians. Nonetheless, having largely escaped the depredations of modern development as well as the heavy-handed attentions of Baron Haussmann, the Marais remains one of the most seductive districts of Paris – old, secluded, as unthreatening by night as it is by day, and with as many alluring shops, bars and places to eat as you could wish for. The renovated mansions, their grandeur concealed by the narrow streets, have become museums, libraries, offices, and chic flats, flanked by shops selling designer clothes, house and garden accoutrements, works of art and one-off trinkets.

Through the middle, dividing it in two, runs the interminable **rue de Rivoli** and its continuation to Bastille, rue St-Antoine. South of this line is the Quartier St-Paul-St-Gervais, the riverside, the Arsenal, and the Île St-Louis. To the north, more homogeneous as well as more fun to walk around, are most of the shops and museums, **place des Vosges**, the **Jewish quarter** and the **Quartier du Temple**. The thing to do is to turn down every street. There is colour and detail everywhere: magnificent *portes cochères* (huge double carriage gates) with elaborate handles and knockers, stone and iron bollards to protect pedestrians from ruthless carriage drivers, cobbled courtyards, elegant iron railings and gates, sculpted house fronts, Chinese sweatshops, chichi boutiques, ethnic grocers – a wealth of interest.

The Marais hôtels and place des Vosges

The main lateral street of the northern part of the Marais, which also forms the boundary between the 3ᵉ and 4ᵉ *arrondissements*, is the **rue des Francs-Bourgeois**. Jack Kerouac translated it as "the street of the outspoken middle classes", which may be a fair description of the contemporary residents, but is inaccurate as a translation, for the

---

Place des Vosges

Royal patronage goes back to the days when a royal palace, the *Hôtel des Tournelles*, stood on the north side of what is now the place des Vosges. It remained in use until 1559. It was also the residence of the Duke of Bedford when he governed northern France in the name of England in the 1420s.

In 1559, **Henri II**, whose queen was Catherine de Médicis, concluded the treaty of Cateau-Cambrésis, and thereby ended his wars with the Holy Roman Empire. To cement the treaty he married his son to the Duke of Savoy and his daughter to Philip II of Spain. The double **wedding celebrations** took place near the place des Vosges. The finale was a **jousting tournament**, in which the king took part. He won two bouts, wearing the colours of his mistress, Diane de Poitiers, who watched, seated beside his wife. He then challenged the Duke of Montgomery, captain of his guards, who accidentally struck him in the eye, and he died after ten days of agony.

Montgomery fled to England, returned after some years to take part in the Wars of Religion on the Protestant side, was captured and, in violation of the terms of his surrender, was put to death by Catherine de Médicis. She also had the *Hôtel des Tournelles* demolished, and the space thus vacated became a huge **horse market**, trading between one and two thousand horses every Saturday. So it remained until Henri IV decided on the construction of his *place Royale*.

Since then its **name has changed many times**, reflecting the fluctuating fortunes of different political tendencies. It stayed place Royale until 1792, when it became, first, Fédérés, then Indivisibilité, then Vosges in 1800 (see opposite). It was changed back to Royale with the Restoration of the monarchy in 1814, to Vosges in 1831, Royale again through the Second Empire up to the Third Republic in 1870, then back to republican Vosges, which it has remained.

---

name means "people exempt from tax" and refers to the penurious inmates of a medieval almshouse that once stood on the site of no. 34.

At its western end, the street begins with the eighteenth-century magnificence of the **Palais Soubise**, which houses the *Archives de France*. Opposite, at the back of a driveway for the *Crédit Municipal* bank, you can see a pepperpot tower which was part of the city walls built by King Philippe-Auguste early in the thirteenth century to link up with his new fortress, the Louvre. Further along, past several more imposing façades and the peculiarly public *lycée* classrooms at no. 28, you can enter the courtyard of the **Hôtel d'Albret** (no. 29bis). This eighteenth-century mansion is home to the cultural department of the mayor of Paris. Tellingly, the dignified façade is blocked by a revolting sculptural column, a 1989 Bicentennial work by Bernard Pagès, resembling thorns and red and blue sticky tape.

The next landmarks on the street, at the junction with rue Payenne and rue Pavée, are two of the Marais' grandest *hôtels*, the sixteenth-century **Carnavalet** and **Lamoignon**, housing, respectively, the Musée Carnavalet and the Bibliothèque Historique de la Ville de Paris. Next to the Lamoignon, on rue Pavée – so called because it was among the first Paris streets to be paved, in 1450 – was the site of the **La Force prison**, where many of the Revolution's victims were incarcerated, including the Princesse de Lamballe, Marie-Antoinette's friend, who was lynched along with many others in the massacres of September 1792. Her head was presented on a stake to her friend.

Details of the Musée Carnavalet are given on p.281.

Voltaire's widowed niece, with whom he carried on a secret and passionate affair – "I kiss your cute little arse," he wrote to her, "and all the rest of you" – also lived in this street.

On the other side of rue des Francs-Bourgeois, rue Payenne leads up to the lovely gardens and houses of **rue du Parc-Royal** and on to **rue Thorigny**. Here, the magnificent classical façade of the seventeenth-century **Hôtel Salé**, built for a rich salt-tax collector, conceals the **Musée Picasso**.

The Musée Picasso is described on p.275.

Finally, across the traffic thoroughfare of the rue de Turenne, you reach the **place des Vosges**, a masterpiece of aristocratic elegance and the first example of planned development in the history of Paris. It is a vast square of symmetrical brick and stone mansions built over arcades. Undertaken in 1605 at the inspiration of **Henri IV**, it was inaugurated in 1612 for the wedding of Louis XIII and Anne of Austria. It is Louis' statue – or, rather, a replica of it – which stands hidden by chestnut trees in the middle of the grass and gravel gardens. Its original name was place Royale (see opposite); it was changed to Vosges in 1800 in honour of the *département*, which was the first to pay its share of the expenses of the Revolutionary wars.

Through all the vicissitudes of history, the *place* has never lost its cachet as a smart address. Among the many celebrities who made their homes here was **Victor Hugo**; his house, at no. 6, where he wrote much of *Les Misérables*, is now a museum. Today, more

The maison de Victor-Hugo is described on p.283.

than ever, expensive high heels tap through the arcades pausing at art, antique and fashion shops, while toddlers, octogenarians, schoolchildren, and workers on their lunch breaks sit or play in the garden, the only green space of any size in the locality.

From the southwest corner of the *place*, a door leads through to the formal château garden, orangerie, and exquisite Renaissance façade of the **Hôtel de Sully**. You can visit the temporary exhibitions mounted by the *Caisse Nationale des Monuments Historiques et des Sites* here or just pass through, nodding at the sphinxes on the stairs, to rue St-Antoine.

A short distance back to the west along rue St-Antoine, almost opposite the sixteenth-century **church of St-Paul**, which was inaugurated by Cardinal Richelieu, is another square. A complete contrast to the imposing formality of the place des Vosges, the tiny **place du Marché-Ste-Catherine** is a perfect example of that other great French architectural talent: an unerring eye for the intimate, the small-scale, the apparently accidental, and the irresistibly charming.

The Jewish quarter: rue des Rosiers

As the tide of chichification seeps remorselessly northwards up the Marais – at the time of writing the advance guard of galleries and design offices is washing around rues du Poitou and Pastorelle – the only remaining islet of genuine local, community life is in the city's main Jewish quarter, still centred around **rue des Rosiers**, just as it was in the twelfth century. Although the *hammam* has now succumbed to trendy clothes shops, and many of the little grocers, bakers, bookshops, and cafés are under pressure (for a long time local flats were kept empty, not for property speculation but to try to stem the middle-class invasion), the smells and sounds and the people on the streets are still largely Jewish. There is a distinctly Mediterranean flavour to the *quartier*, testimony to the influence of the **North African Sephardim**, who, since the end of the Second World War, have sought refuge here from the uncertainties of life in the French ex-colonies, replenishing the numbers of the ashkenazim, who, refugees already from the pogroms of eastern Europe, had been rounded up by the Nazis and the French police and transported back east to concentration camps.

If you sense a certain suspicion of outsiders in the area, it is because of the resurgence of French **anti-semitism** in recent years, and the still fresh memory of the bomb attacks, notably on synagogues and on *Goldenberg's* deli/restaurant in 1982. People died in these assaults, and *Front National* spray cans still periodically eject their obscenities on the walls and shop fronts.

Don't leave the area without wandering the surrounding streets: rue du Roi-de-Sicile, the minute **place Bourg-Tibourg** off rue du Rivoli, rue des Écouffes, rue Vieille-du-Temple, and rue Ste-Croix-de-la-Bretonnerie.

The Quartier du Temple

Ethnic, local, old-fashioned, working-class . . . By some peculiar and ironical shift in popular perceptions the values of these terms have been turned on their heads. Now they are accolades of approval instead of terms of disavowal and dismissal. The city streets they apply to cease to be mean and destitute, no-go areas for the self-respecting middle class. Their "discoverers" wax lyrical and nostalgic about the little workshops and the ordinary cafés and the "realness" of the people.

The **northern part of the Marais** is such a place. As you get beyond rue des Coutures-St-Gervais and rue du Perche, with its enticing congregation of brasseries, the aristocratic stone façades of the southern part give way to the humbler, though no less attractive, stucco and paint and thick-slatted shutters of seventeenth- and eighteenth-century streets bearing the names of the provinces of old rural France: **Beauce, Perche, Saintonge, Picardie**. Ordinary cafés and shops occupy the ground floors, while rag-trade workshops operate in the interior of the cobbled courtyards – for this is the centre of the wholesale clothes business.

Robespierre lived in the **rue de Saintonge**, at no. 64, demolished in 1834. In adjacent **rue Charlot**, at no. 6, you can watch an expert wind-instrument maker and repairer at work on his precious charges. Opposite, in the dead-end **ruelle de Sourdis**, one section of street has remained unchanged since its construction in 1626.

The Knights Templar

The military order of the Knights Templar was established in Jerusalem at the time of the Crusades to protect pilgrims to the Holy Land. Its members quickly became exceedingly rich and overweeningly powerful, with some nine thousand *commanderies* spread across Europe. They acquired land in the *marais* in Paris around 1140, and began to build. After the loss of Palestine in 1291, this fortress property, which covered the area now bounded by rues du Temple, Bretagne, Picardie and Béranger and constituted a separate town without the city walls, became their international headquarters, as the seat of their Grand Master.

They came to a sticky end, however, early in the fourteenth century, when King Philippe le Bel, alarmed at their power and in alliance with Pope Clement V, had them tried for sacrilege, blasphemy and sodomy. Fifty-four of them were burnt, including, in 1314, the Grand Master himself, in the presence of the king. And the order was abolished.

The Temple buildings continued to exist until the Revolution, with about four thousand inhabitants: a mixed population, consisting of artisans not subject to the the city's trade regulations, debtors seeking freedom from prosecution, and some rich residents of private *hôtels*. Louis XVI and the royal family were imprisoned in the keep in 1792 (see box overleaf). It was finally demolished in 1808 by Napoléon, determined to eradicate any possible focus for royalist nostalgia.

The Temple and Louis XVI

Louis XVI, Marie-Antoinette, their two children, and immediate family were imprisoned in the keep of the Knights Templar's ancient fortress in August 1792 by the Revolutionary government. By the end of 1794, when all the adults had been executed, the two children, a teenage girl and the nine- or ten-year-old dauphin – now, in the eyes of royalists, Louis XVII – remained there alone, in the charge of a family called Simon. Louis XVII was literally walled up, with no communication with other human beings, not even his sister, who was living on the floor above. He died in 1795, a half-crazed imbecile, and was buried in a public grave.

That, at least, is what appeared to be his fate. A number of clues, however, point to hocus-pocus. The doctor who certified the child's death kept a lock of his hair, but it was later found not to correspond with the colour of the young Louis XVII's hair, as remembered by his sister. Madame Simon confessed on her death-bed that she had substituted another child for Louis XVII. And a sympathetic sexton admitted that he had exhumed the body of this imbecile child and reburied it in the cloister of the Église Sainte-Marguerite in the Faubourg St-Antoine (see p.183), but when this body was dug up it was found to be that of an eighteen-year-old.

So what really happened? A plausible theory is that the real Louis XVII died early in 1794. But since Robespierre needed the heir to the throne as a hostage to menace internal and foreign royalist enemies with, he had Louis disposed of in secret and substituted the idiot.

Taking advantage of this atmosphere of uncertainty, 43 different people subsequently claimed to be Louis XVII.

Further along, on the corner of **rue du Perche**, a little classical façade on a leafy courtyard hides the Armenian church of Sainte-Croix, testimony to the many Armenians who sought refuge here from the Turkish pogroms of World War I. Further still, on the left and almost to the busy rue de Bretagne, is the easily missed entrance to the **Marché des Enfants-Rouges**, one of the smallest and least-known markets in Paris. On the far side you come out via tiny rue des Oiseaux into rue de Beauce, at the north end of which is the **Carreau du Temple**.

Nothing remains of the Knights Templar's installations beyond the name of **Temple**, although some of the fortifications survived until the Revolution, notably the keep. Now the only direct heirs of the old traditions are the markets and workshops; for the Temple was always a tax-free zone for non-guild craftsmen and a prosecution-free zone for debtors. The **Carreau** itself, which is a fine *halles*-like structure, shelters a daily clothes market with a heavy preponderance of leather gear. **Rue de la Corderie**, a pretty little street on the north side, opening into an otherworldly *place*, has a couple of pleasant cafés under the trees.

These streets have a genteel and somewhat provincial air about them. A block to the east it is a different story. **Rue du Temple**, itself lined with many beautiful houses dating back to the seven-

teenth century (no. 41, for instance, the *Hôtel Aigle d'Or*, is the
last surviving coaching inn of the period), is the dividing line, full
of fascinating little businesses trading in fashion accessories:
chains, buckles, bangles and beads – everything you can think of.
The streets to the east of it are narrow, dark, and riddled with
passages, the houses half-timbered and bulging with age. No. 3 **rue
Volta** is thought to be the oldest house in Paris, built around 1300.
Practically every house is a Chinese wholesale business, many of
them trading leather – and, on the face of it at least, not very
friendly. This was Paris' original **Chinatown**, fed by thousands of
immigrant workers brought in to fill the factories while French men
were being sent off to die in the trenches of the First World War. In
1865, at **44 rue des Gravilliers**, a tanner, an engraver, and a
bronze-worker opened the Paris office of the First International, set
up by Karl Marx in London in the previous year; the office was on
the ground floor in the courtyard.

South: the Quartier St-Paul-St-Gervais and the Pavillon de l'Arsenal

In the southern section of the Marais, **below rue de Rivoli/St-
Antoine**, the crooked steps and lanterns of rue Cloche-Perce, the
tottering timbered houses of **rue François-Miron**, the medieval
Acceuil des Jeunes en France buildings behind the church of St-
Gervais-St-Protais, and the smell of flowers and incense on **rue des
Barres**, all provide the opportunity to indulge in Paris picturesque.
The late Gothic **St-Gervais-St-Protais**, disappointingly battered and
severe from the outside, is more interesting inside, with some lovely
stained glass and an eighteenth-century organ. Between rues Fourcy
and François-Miron, the *Hôtel Hénault de Cantoube*, with its two-
storey *crypte*, is being turned into a European house of
photography.

Shift eastwards to the next tangle of streets and you'll find
modern, chi chi flats in the "**Village St-Paul**", with clusters of expensive antique shops in the courtyards off **rue St-Paul**. This part of the
Marais suffered a postwar hatchet job, and, although seventeenth-
and eighteenth-century magnificence is still in evidence, it lacks the
architectural cohesion of the Marais to the north. The fifteenth-
century **Hôtel de Sens** on the rue de Figuier (now a public library)
looks bizarre in its isolation.

*St Paul's new
museum of
magic is
detailed on
p.279.*

On rue du Petit-Musc there is an entertaining combination of
Thirties' modernism and nineteenth-century exuberance in the
Hôtel Fieubert (now a school). Diagonally opposite, at 21 bd
Morland, the **Pavillon de l'Arsenal** is an excellent addition to the
city's art of self-promotion, signalled by a sculpture of Rimbaud,
with his feet in front of his head, entitled *The man with his soles
in front*. The aim of the Pavillon (Tues–Sat 10.30am–6.30pm, Sun
11am–7pm; free) is to present **the city's current architectural**

**The Quartier
du Temple**

projects to the public and show how past and present developments have evolved as part and parcel of Parisian history. To this end they have a permanent exhibition of photographs, plans and models, including a model of the whole city with a spotlight to highlight a touch-screen choice of 30,000 images. The temporary exhibitions are equally impressive, and the best thing about the whole display is to see schools, industrial units and hospitals treated with the same respect as La Villette and La Grande Arche.

The **southeast corner of the 4ᵉ *arrondissement***, jutting out into the Seine, has its own distinct character. It's been taken up since the last century by the Célestins barracks and previously by the Arsenal, which used to overlook a third island in the Seine. Boulevard Morland was built in 1843, covering over the arm of the river which formed the Île de Louviers. The mad poet Gérard de Nerval escaped here as a boy and lived for days in a log cabin he made with wood scavenged from the island's timberyards. In the 1830s his more extrovert contemporaries – Victor Hugo, Liszt, Delacroix, Alexandre Dumas and co. – were using the library of the former residence of Louis XIV's artillery chief as a meeting place. While the literati discussed turning art to a revolutionary form, the locals were on the streets giving the authorities reason to build more barracks.

The Île St-Louis

Unlike its larger neighbour, the Île de la Cité (see p.60), the **Île St-Louis** has no monuments or museums, just high houses on single-lane streets, a school, a church, and assorted restaurants and cafés. A decade or so later than the Île de Louviers (see above), this island too was a Bohemian hang-out. The Hashashins club met every month at the **Hôtel Lauzun** at 17 quai d'Anjou, and Baudelaire lived for a while in the attic, which it was said he had decorated with stuffed snakes and crocodiles. Nowadays you only get to have your home on the island if you're the Aga Khan, the Pretender to the French throne, or an ex grand duke of Russia.

The Île St-Louis is chiefly memorable for most visitors for possessing the best sorbets in the world, chez *M. Berthillon*. Nothing can rival the taste of iced passion or kiwi fruit, guava, melon or whichever flavour – a sensation compared with which tasting ripe, fresh-picked fruit is but a shadow.

If you're looking for absolute seclusion, head for the **southern quais**, tightly clutching a triple-sorbet cornet as you descend the various steps, or climb over the low gate on the right of the garden across bd Henri-IV, to reach the best sunbathing spot in Paris. And even when Berthillon and his six concessionaries are closed, the island and its *quais* have their own very distinct charm.

The Bastille

The column surmounted by the "Spirit of Liberty" on **place de la Bastille** was erected to commemorate not the surrender of **the prison** with its last seven occupants in 1789, but the July Revolution of 1830, which replaced the autocratic Charles X with the "Citizen King" Louis-Philippe (see p.392). When he in turn fled in the more significant 1848 revolution, his throne was burnt beside the column and a new inscription added. Four months after the birth of the Second Republic in that year, the workers took to the streets. All of eastern Paris was barricaded, with the fiercest fighting on rue du Faubourg-St-Antoine. The rebellion was quelled with the usual massacres and deportation of survivors, but it is still the less contentious 1789 Bastille Day that France celebrates. Political protestors have always, however, used place de la Bastille as a rallying point, and still do.

The only visible remains of the Bastille prison were transported to square Henri-Galli at the end of bd Henri-IV.

The Bicentennial of the 1789 Revolution in 1989 was marked by the inauguration of a new opera house on place de la Bastille, the **Opéra-Bastille**. Mitterrand's pet project was the subject of the most virulent sequence of rows and resignations of any of the *grands projets*, and the finished building is proving inordinately expensive to run. Almost filling the entire block between rues de Lyon, Charenton and Moreau, it has shifted the focus of place de la Bastille. The column is no longer pivotal; in fact, it's easy to miss it altogether when dazzled by the night-time glare of lights emanating from the Opéra. One critic has described it as a "hippopotamus in a bathtub", and you can see his point. The architect, Carlos Off, was concerned that his design should not bring an overbearing monumentalism to place de la Bastille. The different depths and layers of the semicircular façade give a certain sense of the building stepping back, but self-effacing it is not. Time, use and familiarity have more or less reconciled it to its surroundings, and people happily sit on its steps, wander into its shops and libraries and camp out all night for the free performance on the fourteenth of July. When a giant condom was pulled over the Column of Liberty for AIDS awareness, old traditions and contemporary styles were truly wedded.

The opera's construction destroyed no small amount of low-rent housing, and the **quartier de la Bastille** is now trendier than Les Halles. But as with most speculative developments, the pace of change is uneven: old tool shops and ironmongers still survive alongside cocktail haunts and sushi bars; laundries and cobblers flank electronic notebooks outlets. You'll find art galleries clustered around rues Keller, Taillandiers and the adjoining stretch of rue de Charonne, and, on rue de Lappe, one survivor of that very Parisian tradition: the *bals musettes*, or dance halls of 1930s "*gai Paris*", frequented between the wars by Piaf, Jean Gabin and Rita Hayworth. It is the most famous, *Balajo*, founded by one Jo de

For a congenial snack next door to the market, try the down-to-earth wine bar Le Baron Rouge; see p.262.

The Bastille France, who introduced glitter and spectacle into what were then seedy gangster dives, and brought Parisians from the other side of the city to savour the rue de Lappe lowlife.

The rue de Lappe can still be as dodgy a place to be at night as it was in prewar days. The bouncers at clubs like the *Chapelle des Lombards*, and at *Balajo* itself, the heavy drug scene and the uneasy mix of local residents have taken the soul away from a street that ten years ago deserved the special affection that Parisians of all sorts gave it.

For moving beyond the Bastille further into the 11^e and 12^e *arrondissements*, see Chapter 10.

Chapter 6

The Left Bank

The term **Left Bank** (*rive gauche*) connotes Bohemian, dissident, intellectual – the radical student type, whether eighteen years of age or eighty. As a topographical term it refers particularly to their traditional haunts, the warren of medieval lanes round the **boulevards St-Michel** and **St-Germain**, known as the **Quartier Latin** because that was the language of the university sited there right up until 1789. In modern times its reputation for turbulence and innovation has been renewed by the activities of painters and writers like Picasso, Apollinaire, Breton, Henry Miller, Anaïs Nin and Hemingway after World War I; Camus, Sartre, Juliette Greco and the Existentialists after World War II; and the political turmoil of 1968, which escalated from student demonstrations and barricades to factory occupations, massive strikes and the near-overthrow of de Gaulle's presidency. This is not to say that the whole of Paris south of the Seine is the exclusive territory of revolutionaries and avant-gardists. It does, however, have a different and distinctive feel and appearance, noticeable as soon as you cross the river. And it's here, still, that the city's mythmakers principally gather: the writers, painters, philosophers, politicians, journalists, designers – the people who tell Paris what it is.

Quartier Latin

The pivotal point of the **Quartier Latin** is **place St-Michel**, where the tree-lined boulevard St-Michel begins. It has long lost its radical penniless chic, preferring harder commercial values. The cafés and shops are jammed with people, mainly young and in summer largely foreign. All the world's bobby-soxers unload here. The fountain in the *place* is a favourite meeting, not to say pick-up, spot. **Rue de la Huchette** – the Mecca of beats and bums in the post-World War II years, with its theatre still showing Ionesco's *Cantatrice Chauve* nearly forty years on – is given over to Greek restaurants of indifferent quality and inflated price, as is the adjoining rue Xavier-Privas,

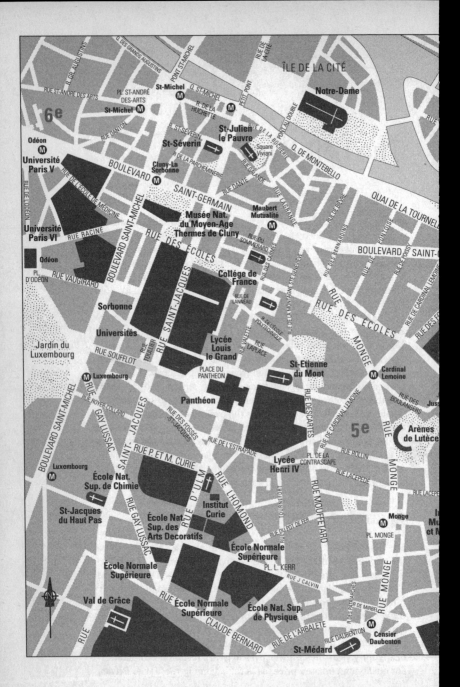

QUARTIER LATIN

Quartier Latin: Listings

Restaurants

Aleka, 187 rue St-Jacques, 5ᵉ.
RER Luxembourg.

Auberge des Deux Signes, 46 rue Galande, 5ᵉ.
Mᵒ St-Michel.

Bistro de la Sorbonne, 4 rue Toullier, 5ᵉ.
Mᵒ Luxembourg.

Brasserie Balzar, 49 rue des Écoles, 5ᵉ.
Mᵒ Maubert-Mutualité.

Le Grenier de Notre-Dame, 18 rue de la Bûcherie, 5ᵉ.
Mᵒ Maubert-Mutualité.

Inagiku, 14 rue Pontoise, 5ᵉ.
Mᵒ Maubert-Mutualité.

Chez Léna et Mimile, 32 rue Tournefort, 5ᵉ.
Mᵒ Consier-Daubenton.

Le Liban à la Mouff, 3 rue de l'Estrapade 5ᵉ.
Mᵒ Monge.

Perraudin, 157 rue St-Jacque, 5ᵉ
RER Luxembourg.
Mᵒ Jussieu.

Le Petit Prince, 12 rue Lanneau, 5ᵉ.
Mᵒ Maubert-Mutualité.

Restaurant A, 5 rue de Poissy, 5ᵉ.
Mᵒ Cardinal-Lemoine.

Le Refuge du Passé, 32 rue du Ter-á-Moulin, 5ᵉ.
Mᵒ Gobelins.

Student restaurants 8bis rue Cuvier, 5ᵉ (Mᵒ Jussieu); 31 rue Geoffroy-St-Hilaire, 5ᵉ (Mᵒ Censier-Daubenton); and 10 rue Jean-Calvin, 5ᵉ (Mᵒ Censier-Daubenton).

Tashi Delek, 4 rue des Fossés-St-Jacques, 5ᵉ.
Mᵒ Luxembourg.

Cafés and Bars

29 rue Linné (no name), 5ᵉ.
Mᵒ Jussieu.

Le Bâteau Ivre, 40 rue Descartes, 5ᵉ.
Mᵒ Cardinal-Lemoine.

Café des Arts, corner of place Contrescarpe and rue Lacépède, 5ᵉ.
Mᵒ Monge.

"Cafés and Bars" for the Quartier Latin are continued over the page.

*These establishments are reviewed in Chapter 13,
Eating and Drinking, beginning on p.243.*

Quartier Latin: Listings (continued)

Café de la Mosquée, 39 rue Geoffroy-St-Hilaire, 5e.
M^o Monge.

Café Notre-Dame, corner of quai St-Michel and rue St-Jacques, 5e.
M^o St-Michel.

Connolly's Corner, on the corner of rues Patriarches and Mirbel, 5e.
M^o Monge/Censier-Daubenton.

Le Crocodile, 6 rue Royer-Collard, 5e.
M^o Luxembourg.

La Fontaines, 9 rue Soufflot, 5e.
M^o Luxembourg.

La Fourmi Ailée, 8 rue du Fouarre, 5e.
M^o Maubert-Mutualité.

La Gueuze, 19 rue Soufflot, 5e.
M^o Luxembourg.

Le Piano Vache, 8 rue Laplace, 5e.
M^o Cardinal-Lemoine.

Les Pipos, 50 rue de la Montagne-Ste-Geneviève, 5e.
M^o Maubert-Mutualité/Cardinal-Lemoine.

Polly Magoo, 11 rue St-Jacques, 5e.
M^o St-Michel/Maubert-Mutualité.

Le Verre à Pied, 118bis rue Mouffetard, 5e.
M^o Censier-Daubenton.

Le Violon Dingue, 46 rue de la Montagne-Ste-Geneviève, 5e.
M^o Maubert-Mutalité.

Quartier Latin restaurant listings are given on p.243.

with the odd *couscous* joint thrown in. Connecting it to the riverside is the city's narrowest street, the **Chat-qui-Pêche**, alarmingly evocative of what Paris at its medieval worst must have looked like.

Rue St-Jacques and medieval churches

Things improve as you move away from the boulevard. At the end of rue de la Huchette, **rue St-Jacques** is aligned on the main street of Roman Paris. It gets its name from the medieval pilgrimage to the shrine of St-Jacques (St James) at Santiago de Compostela in northern Spain. This bit of hill was the first taste of the road for the millions who set out from the church of St-Jacques (only the tower remains) just across the river.

A short distance to the right, the mainly fifteenth-century **church of St-Séverin** (Mon–Thurs 11am–7.30pm, Fri & Sat 9am–10.30pm, Sun 9am–8pm) is one of the city's most elegant. Built in the Flamboyant Gothic style, it contains some splendidly virtuoso chiselwork in the pillars of the choir, as well as stained glass by the modern French painter Jean Bazaine.

Rue de la Parcheminerie to the north is where medieval scribes and parchment sellers used to congregate, hence its name. It's worth cricking your neck to look at the decorations on the façades, including that of no. 29 where the Canadian *Abbey Bookshop* continues the bookish tradition. Back towards the river, **square Viviani** with its welcome patch of grass and trees provides the most flattering of all views of Notre-Dame. The ancient listing tree propped on a concrete pillar by the church wall is reputed to be Paris' oldest, brought over from Guyana in 1680. The church itself, mutilated and disfigured, is **St-Julien-le-Pauvre**. The same age as Notre-Dame, it used to be the venue for university assemblies until some rumbustious students tore it apart in the 1500s. It's a quiet and intimate place, ideal for a moment's soulful reflection. For the last hundred years it has belonged to a Greek Catholic sect, whence the unexpected iconostasis screening the sanctuary. The hefty slabs of stone by the well at the entrance are all that remains of the Roman thoroughfare now overlain by rue St-Jacques.

The river bank and Institut du Monde Arabe

Round to the left on rue de la Bûcherie, the English bookshop **Shakespeare and Co.** is haunted by the shades of James Joyce and other great expatriate literati, though only by proxy, as Sylvia Beach, publisher of Joyce's *Ulysses*, had her original shop on rue de l'Odéon.

More books, postcards, prints, sheet music, records and assorted goods are on sale from the **bouquinistes**, who display their wares in green padlocked boxes hooked onto the parapet of the **riverside quais** – which, in spite of their romantic reputation, are not much fun to walk hereabouts, because of the traffic. Continuing upstream as far as the tip of the Île St-Louis, you come to the **Pont de Sully** with a dramatic view of the apse and steeple of Notre-Dame and the beginning of a riverside garden dotted with pieces of modern sculpture, known as the **Musée de Sculpture en Plein Air**.

At the end of the Pont de Sully, in the angle between quai St-Bernard and rue des Fossés-St-Bernard, shaming the hideous factory of the university Paris-VI next door, is the **Institut du Monde Arabe**, designed principally by Jean Nouvel. Its elegant glass and aluminium mass is cleft in two, with the riverfront half bowed and tapering to a knife-like prow, while the broad southern façade, comprising thousands of tiny light-sensitive shutters which open and close according to the brightness of the day, mimics with hi-tech ingenuity the *moucharabiyah* – the traditional Arab lattice-work balcony.

The institute is open daily except Monday, from 10am to 6pm. It houses a museum of Islamic art and artefacts, space for temporary exhibitions, a library, research, debate and publishing facilities, and an audio-visual centre. This last, the *Espace Image et Son* (Tues–Sun 1–6pm), is located in the basement and stores thousands of slides, photographs, films and recordings which you can access yourself. Film previews are shown, and in the *Salle d'Actualités* you can watch current news broadcasts from around the Arab world. When you need a rest, take the fastest lifts in Paris up to the ninth floor for expensive Lebanese eats or just a mint tea, with a brilliant view over the Seine that stretches from la Grande Arche to Buttes-Chaumont.

The museum of the Institut du Monde Arabe is described on p.276.

Place Maubert and the Sorbonne

Walking back along bd St-Germain towards bd St-Michel, past rue de Pontoise with its Art Deco swimming pool and primary school, you come to **place Maubert** (good market Tues, Thurs and Sat morning) at the foot of the **Montagne Ste-Geneviève**, the hill on which the Panthéon stands and the best strolling area this side of bd St-Michel. The best way in is either from the *place* or from the crossroads of boulevards St-Michel and St-Germain, where the walls of the third-century **Roman baths** are visible in the garden of the **Hôtel de Cluny**. A sixteenth-century mansion resembling an Oxford or Cambridge college, the *hôtel* was built by the abbots of the powerful Cluny monastery as their Paris pied-à-terre. It now houses a very beautiful museum of medieval art. There is no charge for entry to the quiet shady courtyard.

*The Musée
Nationale du
Moyen-Age is
described on
p.273.*

The grim-looking buildings on the other side of rue des Écoles are the **Sorbonne**, **Collège de France** – where Foucault, the specialist in sex and madness, taught – and **Lycée Louis-le-Grand**, which numbers Molière, Robespierre, Pompidou and Victor Hugo among its graduates and Sartre among its teachers. All these institutions are major constituents of the brilliant and mandarin world of French intellectual activity. You can put your nose in the Sorbonne courtyard without anyone objecting. The **Richelieu chapel**, dominating the uphill end and containing the tomb of the great cardinal, was the first Roman-influenced building in seventeenth-century Paris and set the trend for subsequent developments. Nearby, the traffic-free **place de la Sorbonne**, with its lime trees, cafés and student habitués, is a lovely place to sit.

The Panthéon and St-Étienne-du-Mont

Further up the hill, the broad rue Soufflot provides an appropriately grand perspective on the domed and porticoed **Panthéon**, Louis XV's thank-you to Sainte Geneviève, patron saint of Paris, for curing him of illness. Imposing enough at a distance, it is cold and uninteresting close to – not a friendly detail for the eye to rest on. The Revolution transformed it into a mausoleum for the great. It is deadly inside (April–Sept 10am–5.45pm; Oct–March 10am–noon & 2–4.45pm; closed Tues & public hols; 26F/17F), but there are, however, several cafés to warm the heart's cockles down towards the Luxembourg gardens, including the beer specialist, *La Gueuze*.

More interesting than the Panthéon is the mainly sixteenth-century church of **St-Étienne-du-Mont** on the corner of rue Clovis, with a façade combining Gothic, Renaissance and Baroque elements. The interior, if not exactly beautiful, is highly unexpected. The space is divided into three aisles by free-standing pillars connected by a narrow catwalk, and flooded with light by an exceptionally tall clerestory. Again, unusually – for they mainly fell victim to the destructive anti-clericalism of the Revolution – the church still possesses its rood screen, a broad low arch supporting a gallery reached by twining spiral stairs. There is some good seventeenth-century glass in the cloister. Further down rue Clovis, a huge piece of Philippe Auguste's **twelfth-century city walls** emerges from among the houses.

South of place du Panthéon, between rue Gay-Lussac and rue Lhomond, are more academic institutions: the École Normale Supérieure, a *grand école* that trains teachers and theorists and bred structuralism in the 1970s; the Curie and oceanographic institutes; and the *grands écoles* for chemistry, physics and decorative arts. Entry to the *grands écoles* is by exam following two years of preparation after the equivalent of A levels or a high school diploma, the *baccalauréat*. Started by Napoléon to provide professionally trained engineers and technicians, they are the most élitist aspect of French education. Graduates are treated with cringing respect and can expect to land highly paid jobs right away.

There is not much point in going further south on rue St-Jacques. The area is dull and lifeless once you are over the Gay-Lussac intersection, though Baroque enthusiasts might like to take a look at the seventeenth-century church of **Val-de-Grâce**, with its pedimented front and ornate cupola copied from St Peter's in Rome, while round the corner on bd de Port-Royal is another big **market** and several brasseries.

East of the Panthéon

More enticing wandering is to be had in the villagey streets east of the Panthéon. **Rue de la Montagne-Ste-Geneviève** climbs up from place Maubert across rue des Écoles to the gates of what used to be the **École Polytechnique**, the grandest of the *grands écoles* (see above) for entry to the top echelons of state power. The school has decamped to the suburbs, leaving its buildings to become the Ministry of Research and Technology– a trip down memory lane for many of its staff, no doubt. There's a sunny little café outside the gate and several restaurants in rue de l'École-Polytechnique facing the new ministry.

From here, **rue Descartes** runs into the tiny and once-attractive place de la Contrescarpe. An erstwhile arty hang-out, where Hemingway wrote – in the café *La Chope* – and Georges Brassens sang, it is now a bit of a dossers' rendezvous currently being re-landscaped. Just to the east on rue Lacépède is a municipal crèche, built in 1985, which has a lovely curved frontage inspired by the shape of a pregnant woman's belly.

The medieval **rue Mouffetard** begins here, a cobbled lane winding downhill to the church of **St-Médard**, once a country parish beside the now-covered River Bièvre. On the façade of no. 12 is a curious painted glass sign from the Golliwog era, depicting a Negro in striped trousers waiting on his mistress, with the unconvincing legend, "*Au Nègre Joyeux*". At no. 64, a shoe shop run by Georges the Armenian sells genuine Basque espadrilles and the last of the French wooden clogs or *sabots*. But most of the upper half of the street is given over to eating places, mainly Greek and little better than those of rue de la Huchette. Like any place devoted to the entertainment of tourists, it is rather soulless. The bottom half, however, with its sumptuous fruit and veg stalls, still maintains an authentic neighbourhood air. At the bottom, no. 130 has an extraordinary façade like a tapestry of a forest scene. On place des Patriarches, one block east, an old market hall has been replaced by a beautiful 1980s construction, containing low-cost flats and a gym, harking back to the old market while being unashamedly modern.

The Paris mosque and Jardin des Plantes

A little further east, across rue Monge, are some of the city's most agreeable surprises. Down rue Daubenton, past a delightful Arab shop selling sweets, spices and gaudy tea-glasses, you come to the crenellated walls of the **Paris mosque**, overtopped by greenery and a great square minaret. You can walk in the sunken garden and patios with their polychrome tiles and carved ceilings (9am–noon & 2–6pm; closed Fri & Muslim hols), but not the prayer room. There is a tearoom and restaurant, open to all, a *hammam*, and a shop selling clothes, bird cages and hubble-bubbles.

Opposite the mosque on rue Geoffroy-St-Hilaire, the hideous building belonging to the **Muséum National de l'Histoire Naturelle** (see p.284) was supposed to have been demolished to make way for a parvis leading up to the new *Galerie d'Évolution*, housed in a vast glass-domed metal-framed building contemporary with the Eiffel Tower. Its time will no doubt come, but for the moment you'll have to admire the new gallery from within the Jardin des Plantes.

You can enter the **Jardin des Plantes** (summer 7.30am–7.45pm; winter 8am–dusk; free) from the corner of rue Geoffroy St-Hilaire and rue Buffon, alongside the museum shop of wonderful books and postcards. The other entrances are further north on the corner with rue Cuvier, the main entrance on rue Cuvier itself or from quai St Bernard. On offer in the gardens are a small, cramped **zoo** (Mon–Sat summer daily 9am–6pm; winter 9am–5pm, Sun 9am–6.30pm all year; 25F/13F), botanical gardens, hothouses and museums of paleontology and mineralogy and evolution. Improvements are underway – particularly with regard to the overgrown mazes and trees that block the view across the river from the pergola – and it's a pretty enough space of greenery to while away the middle of a day. By the rue Cuvier entrance stands a fine Cedar of Lebanon planted in 1734, raised from seed sent over from Oxford Botanical Gardens, and a slice of an American sequoia more than 2000 years old with the birth of Christ and other historical events its life has encompassed marked on its rings. In the nearby physics labs Henri Becquerel discovered radioactivity in 1896, and two years later the Curies discovered radium – unwitting ancestors of the *force de frappe* (the French nuclear deterrent). Pierre Curie, incidentally, ended his days under the wheels of a brewer's dray on rue Dauphine.

A short distance away, with an entrance in rue de Navarre, rue des Arènes and another through a passage on rue Monge, is Paris' other Roman remain, the **Arènes de Lutèce**, an unexpected and peaceful backwater hidden from the street. It is a partly restored amphitheatre, with a *boules* pitch in the centre, benches, gardens and a kids' playground behind.

St-Germain

The northern half of the 6e *arrondissement*, asymmetrically centred on **place St-Germain-des-Prés**, is the most physically attractive, lively and stimulating square kilometre in the entire city. It's got the money, elegance and sophistication, but with it, also, an easy-going tolerance and simplicity that comes from a long association with the mould-breakers and trend-setters in the arts, philosophy, politics and the sciences. The aspiring and expiring are equally at home.

Across Pont des Arts

The most dramatic approach to St-Germain is to cross the river from the Louvre by the **Pont des Arts**, taking in the classic upstream view of the Île de la Cité, with barges moored at the quai de Conti, and the Tour St-Jacques and Hôtel de Ville breaking the skyline of the Right Bank.

The dome and pediment at the end of the bridge belong to the **Institut de France**, seat of the Académie Française, an august body of writers and scholars whose mission is to safeguard the purity of the French language. Recent creations include the excellent word *baladeur* for "Walkman", but rearguard actions against Anglo-Saxon terms in the sciences, information technology and management have been hopelessly ineffective.

This is the grandiose bit of the Left Bank riverfront. To the left is the **Hôtel des Monnaies**, redesigned as the Mint in the late eighteenth century. To the right is the **Beaux-Arts**, the school of Fine Art, whose students throng the *quais* on sunny days, sketch pads on knee.

The riverside

The riverside part of the quarter is cut lengthways by **rue St-André-des-Arts** and **rue Jacob**. It is full of bookshops, commercial art galleries, antique shops, cafés and restaurants. Poke your nose into courtyards and side streets. The houses are four to six storeys high, seventeenth- and eighteenth-century, some noble, some stiff, some bulging and skew, all painted in infinite gradations of grey, pearl and off-white. Broadly speaking, the further west the posher.

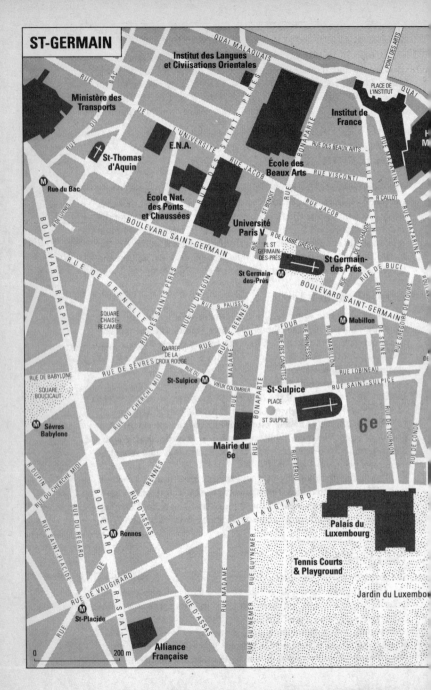

ST-GERMAIN

QUAI MALAQUAIS

Institut des Langues
et Civiisations Orientales

PONT DES ARTS

PLACE DE
L'INSTITUT

QUAI

Ministère des
Transports

RUE DU BAC

DE

RUE DES SAINTS PÈRES

RUE DE L'UNIVERSITÉ

Institut de
France

RUE BONAPARTE

St-Thomas
d'Aquin

E.N.A.

RUE JACOB

École des
Beaux Arts

RUE DES BEAUX ARTS

RUE VISCONTI

RUE MAZARINE

M Rue du Bac

RUE DES SAINTS PÈRES

RUE DE SEINE

R CALLOT

École Nat.
des Ponts
et Chaussées

RUE DU BAC

ST BENOIT

RUE JACOB

RUE DE L'ÉCHAUDE

Université
Paris V

R DE L'ABBÉ GRÉGOIRE

St Germain-
des Prés

RUE DE BUCI

BOULEVARD SAINT-GERMAIN

PL ST
GERMAIN-
DES-PRÉS

St Germain-
des-Prés M

RUE DE GRENELLE

BOULEVARD RASPAIL

RUE DE SÈVRES

RUE DES SAINTS PÈRES

RUE DU DRAGON

RUE B PALISSY

DU FOUR

BOULEVARD SAINT-GERMAIN

RUE GRÉGOIRE DE TOURS

M Mabillon

SQUARE
CHAISE-
RECAMIER

RUE DE RENNES

RUE DES CANETTES

RUE PRINCESSE

RUE MABILLON

RUE DE SEINE

CARREF
DE LA
CROIX ROUGE

RUE

RUE MADAME

RUE DU

RUE LOBINEAU

RUE DE BABYLONE

RUE DE SÈVRES

RUE DU CHERCHE MIDI

VIEUX COLOMBIER

RUE SAINT-SULPICE

SQUARE
BOUCICAUT

St-Sulpice M

RUE BONAPARTE

St-Sulpice

PLACE
ST SULPICE

RUE DE TOURNON

M Sèvres
Babylone

RUE FÉROU

6e

R DUPIN

Mairie du
6e

RUE

RUE DU CHERCHE MIDI

RUE DE RÉGARD

BOULEVARD

RENNES

RUE D'ASSAS

RUE MADAME

RUE GUYNEMER

RUE VAUGIRARD

Palais du
Luxembourg

M Rennes

RUE SAINT-PLACIDE

RUE DU REGARD

DE

RASPAIL

Tennis Courts
& Playground

RUE MADAME

Jardin du Luxembo

RUE DE VAUGIRARD

RUE D'ASSAS

RUE GUYNEMER

M St-Placide

0   200 m

Alliance
Française

St-Germain: Listings

Restaurants

Aux Charpentiers, 10 rue Mabillon, 6e.
Mº Mabillon.

Drugstore Saint-Germain, 149 bd St-Germain, 6e.
Mº St Germain-des-Prés.

Jacques Cagna, 14 rue des Grands-Augustins, 6e.
Mº Odéon/St-Michel.

Lipp, 151 bd St-Germain, 6e.
Mº St-Germain-des-Prés.

La Maison de la Lozère, 4 rue Hautefeuille, 6e.
Mº St-Michel.

La Maroussia, 9 rue de l'Éperon, 6e.
Mº Odéon.

Le Muniche, 22 rue Guillaume-Apollinaire, 6e.
Mº St-Germain-des-Prés.

Orestias, 4 rue Grégoire-de-Tours, 6e.
Mº Odéon.

Le Petit Mabillon, 6 rue Mabillon, 6e.
Mº Mabillon.

Le Petit Saint-Benoît, 4 rue Saint-Benoît, 6e.
Mº St-Germain-des-Prés.

Le Petit Vatel, 5 rue Lobineau, 6e. Mº Mabillon.

Le Petit Zinc, 11 rue Saint-Benoît, 6e.
Mº St-Germain-des-Prés.

Polidor, 41 rue Monsieur-le-Prince, 6e.
Mº Odéon.

Le Procope, 13 rue de l'Ancienne-Comédie, 6e.
Mº Odéon.

Restaurant des Arts, 73 rue de Seine, 6e.
Mº St-Germain-des-Prés.

Restaurant des Beaux-Arts, 11 rue Bonaparte, 6e.
Mº St-Germain-des-Prés.

Le Rôtisserie d'en Face, 2 rue Christine, 6e, Mº Odéon/St-Michel.

Student restaurants 55 rue Mazet, 6e (Mº Odéon); 92 rue d'Assas, 6e (Mº Port-Royal/Notre-Dame-des-Champs).

Village Bulgare, 8 rue de Nevers, 6e.
Mº Odéon/Pont-Neuf.

"Cafés and Bars" for St-Germain are listed over the page.

These establishments are reviewed in Chapter 13,
Eating and Drinking, *beginning on p.246.*

Historical associations are legion. Picasso painted *Guernica* in rue des Grands-Augustins. Molière started his career in rue Mazarine. Robespierre *et al.* split ideological hairs at the *Café Procope* in rue de l'Ancienne-Comédie. In rue Visconti Racine died, Delacroix painted and Balzac's printing business went bust. In parallel rue des Beaux-Arts, Oscar Wilde died, Corot and Ampère, father of amps, lived, and crazy poet Gérard de Nerval walked a lobster on a lead.

If you're looking for lunch, **place and rue St-André-des-Arts** offer a tempting concentration of places, from Tunisian sandwich joints to seafood extravagance, and a brilliant **food market** in rue Buci up towards bd St-Germain. Before you get to Buci, there's a little passage on the left, **Cour du Commerce**, between a *crêperie* and *Le Mazet* café. Marat had his printing press in the passage, while Dr Guillotin perfected his machine by lopping off sheep's heads in a loft next door. Since *Le Procope* was done up for the Bicentennial, with portraits of Voltaire and Robespierre on its back façade, a revolutionary theme has enveloped the passage. A couple of smaller courtyards open off it, revealing a stretch of Philippe Auguste's wall.

The Musée Delacroix is described on p.278.

An alternative corner for midday food or quiet is around rue de l'Abbaye and rue du Furstemberg, with a tiny square where **Delacroix's old studio** overlooking a secret garden has been converted into a museum (at no. 6).

This is also the beginning of some very **upmarket shopping territory**, in rue Jacob, rue de Seine and rue Bonaparte in particular. On the wall of no. 56 rue Jacob a plaque commemorates the signature of the Treaty of Independence between Britain and the US on September 23, 1783, by Benjamin Franklin, David Hartley and others. There are also cheap eating places at this end of the street, serving the university medical school by the intersection with rue des Saints-Pères.

The restaurants of St-Germain are keyed to a map on p.247.

Place St-Germain-des-Prés

Place St-Germain-des-Prés, the hub of the *quartier*, is only a stone's throw away, with the *Deux Magots* café on the corner and *Flore* just down the street. Both are renowned for the number of philosophico-politico-poetico-literary backsides that have shined their seats, like the snootier *Brasserie Lipp* across the boulevard, longtime haunt of the more successful practitioners of these trades, admission to whose hallowed portals has become somewhat easier since the decease of the crotchety old proprietor. All these establishments are extremely crowded in summer, expensive and far from peaceful. A place on the *terrasse* in summer will inevitably involve you in the attentions of buskers and street performers.

The tower opposite the *Deux Magots* belongs to the **church of St-Germain**, all that remains of an enormous Benedictine monastery. There has been a church on the site since the sixth century. The interior is best, its pure Romanesque lines still clear under the deforming paint of nineteenth-century frescoes. In the corner of the churchyard by the rue Bonaparte, a little Picasso head of a woman is dedicated to the memory of the poet Apollinaire.

St-Sulpice to the Odéon

South of bd St-Germain the streets round St-Sulpice are calm and classy. **Rue Mabillon** is pretty, with a row of old houses set back below the level of the modern street. There are two or three restaurants, including the old-fashioned *Aux Charpentiers*, decorated with models of rafters and roof-trees; it is the property of the Guild of Carpenters. On the left are the **halles St-Germain**, now incorporating a swimming pool, gym, auditorium and new commercial complex, on the site of a fifteenth-century market. Passing rue Lobineau you could be tempted by the delicious *pâtisserie* at no. 2. Rue St-Sulpice, where a shop called *L'Estrella* at no. 34 specializes in teas, coffees and jams, leads through to the front of the enormous **church of St-Sulpice**, with the popular *Café de la Mairie* on the sunny north side of the square.

The church, erected either side of 1700, is austerely classical, with a Doric colonnade surmounted by an Ionic, and Corinthian pilasters in the towers, only one of which is finished, where kestrels come to make their nests. The interior (there are some Delacroix frescoes in the first chapel on the right) is not to all tastes. But softened by the chestnut trees and fountain of the square, the ensemble is peaceful and harmonious. To the south, rue Férou, where a gentleman called Pottier composed the revolutionary anthem, the *Internationale*, in 1776, connects with **rue de Vaugirard**, Paris' longest street, and the **Luxembourg gardens** (see below).

The main attraction of **place St-Sulpice** is **Yves Saint Laurent Rive Gauche**, the most elegant fashion boutique on the Left Bank. That's on the corner of the ancient **rue des Canettes**. Further along the same side of the *place* there's Saint Laurent for men, and then it's Consume, Consume all the way, with your triple-gilt uranium-plated credit card, down rues Bonaparte, Madame, de Sèvres, de Grenelle, du Four, des Saints-Pères. . . . Hard to believe now, but smack in the middle of all this, at the carrefour de la Croix Rouge, there was a major barricade in 1871, fiercely defended by Eugène Varlin, one of the Commune's leading lights, later betrayed by a priest, half-beaten to death and shot by government troops on Montmartre hill.

For more on the Commune, see pp. 154 & 393.

These days you're more likely to be suffering from till-shock than shell-shock. You may feel safer in rue Princesse at the small, friendly and well-stocked American bookshop, *The Village Voice*, where you can browse through the latest literature and journals.

The least posh bit of the *quartier* is the eastern edge, where the university is firmly implanted, along bd St-Michel, with attendant scientific and medical bookshops, skeletons and instruments of torture, as well as a couple of weird and wonderful shops in rue Racine. But there is really no escape from elegance round here, as you'll see in rue Tournon and rue de l'Odéon, which leads to the Doric portico of the **Théâtre de l'Odéon** and back to the Luxembourg gardens by the rue de Médicis.

The Luxembourg palace and gardens

It was Marie de Médicis, Henri IV's widow, who had the **Jardin** and **Palais du Luxembourg** built to remind her of the Palazzo Pitti and Giardino di Boboli of her native Florence. The palace forms yet another of those familiar Parisian backdrops that no one pays much attention to, though there would be outrage if they were to disappear, not least from the members of the French senate who have their seat here. Opposite the gates, scarcely noticeable on the end wall of the colonnade of no. 36 rue de Vaugirard, is a metre rule, set up during the Revolution to guide the people in the introduction of the new metric system.

The gardens are the chief lung and recreation ground of the Left Bank, with tennis courts, pony rides, children's playground, *boules* pitch, yachts to rent on the pond and, in the wilder southeast corner, a miniature orchard of elaborately espaliered pear trees. With its strollers and mooners and garish *parterres* it has a distinctly

Mediterranean air on summer days, when the most contested spot is the shady Fontaine de Médicis in the northeast corner.

In the last week of September an "Expo-Automne" takes place in the Orangerie (entrance from 19 rue de Vaugirard, opposite rue Férou) where fruits, including the Luxembourg's own wonderful pears, and floral decorations are sold.

Chapter 7

Trocadéro, Eiffel Tower and Les Invalides

As you stand on the terrace of the **Palais de Chaillot** (place du Trocadéro) and look across the river to the **Tour Eiffel** and **École Militaire**, or let your gaze run from the ornate 1900 Pont Alexandre III along the grassy Esplanade to the **Hôtel des Invalides**, the vistas are absolutely splendid. But once you have said to yourself, "How magnificent!", that's it, more or less. This is town planning on the despotic scale, an assertion of power that takes no account of the small-scale interests and details of everyday lives.

The **7ᵉ** *arrondissement*, to which the Left Bank sections of these nineteenth- and twentieth-century urban landscapings belong, has the greatest concentration of ministries, embassies and official residences in Paris. The **Assemblée Nationale** is here, in the Palais Bourbon facing place de la Concorde across the river, and the entrance to the city's **sewers**. But there are corners of more amenable life – in **rue Babylone**, and in the streets between the Invalides and the Champs de Mars. There is also the best-used decommissioned railway station, the **Musée d'Orsay**, on the river bank towards St-Germain.

Of all the mega-monuments of this area, the best is, undoubtedly, the **Eiffel Tower**. No matter how many pictures, photos and models you have seen of it, or how many glimpses of it from other parts of the city, it is, when you get up close, an amazing structure.

The Palais de Chaillot

The **Palais de Chaillot** was built in 1937 like a latterday Pharaoh's mausoleum, on a site that has been a ruler's favourite since Catherine de Médicis constructed one of her playpens there in the early sixteenth century. Today's monster is home to several interesting museums (see pp.278, 281 & 282) and the *Théâtre National Populaire* company, founded by Jean Vilar. The enormous theatre, where diverse but usually radical productions are staged, lies under the *terrasse*. This is where to plant yourself, hassled by souvenir vendors, for the view across to the Eiffel Tower and École Militaire.

The **Palais de Tokyo**, contemporary with Chaillot and no less hideous, is a short way east on the Right Bank and houses rather better museums. From here you can reach the Eiffel Tower via the Passerelle Debilly footbridge and quai Branly.

The Palais de Chaillot

The museums of the Palais de Tokyo are reviewed on p. 273.

The Eiffel Tower

When completed in 1889, the **Tour Eiffel** was the tallest building in the world at 300m. Its 7000 tons of steel, in terms of pressure, sit as lightly on the ground as a child in a chair. Reactions to it were violent:

> *(We) protest with all our force, with all our indignation, in the name of unappreciated French taste, in the name of menaced French art and history, against the erection, in the very heart of our capital, of the useless and monstrous Eiffel Tower. . . . Is Paris going to be associated with the grotesque, mercantile imaginings of a constructor of machines?*

Eiffel himself thought it was beautiful. "The first principle of architectural aesthetics", he said, "prescribes that the basic lines of a structure must correspond precisely to its specified use. . . . To a certain extent the tower was formed by the wind itself." Needless to say, it stole the show at the 1889 Exposition, for which it had been constructed.

In 1986 the external night-time floodlighting was replaced by a system of illumination from within the tower's superstructure, so that it now looks at its magical best after dark, as light and fanciful as a filigree minaret. Going to the top by lift (9.30am–11pm) costs 53F (20F and 36F respectively for the first two levels) – so that it is only really worth the expense on an absolutely clear day. If you take the stairs (access to levels 1 and 2 only) the cost is 12F. The only reductions are for children under 12. Tickets give free entry to the audio-visual show about the tower on the first level.

Around the École Militaire

Stretching back from the legs of the tower, the long rectangular gardens of the **Champs de Mars** lead to the eighteenth-century buildings of the **École Militaire**, now the Staff College, originally founded in 1751 by Louis XV for the training of aristocratic army officers. No prizes for guessing who the most famous graduate was. A less illustrious but better loved French soldier has his name remembered in a

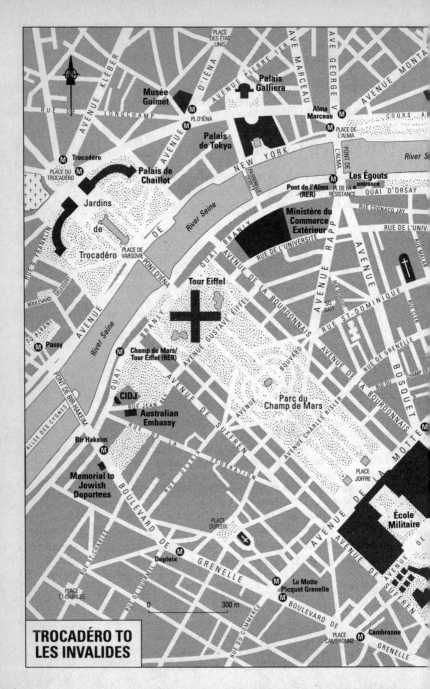

**TROCADÉRO TO
LES INVALIDES**

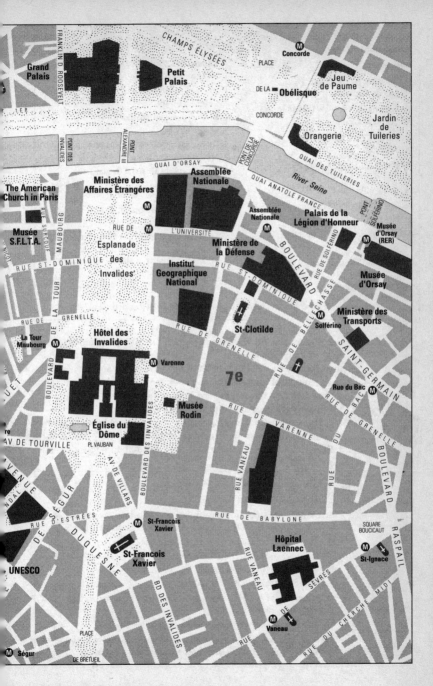

neighbouring street and square: Cambronne. He commanded the last surviving unit of Napoléon's Imperial Guard at Waterloo. Called on to surrender by the English, although surrounded and reduced to a bare handful of men, he shouted back into the darkness one word: *Merde* – Shit! – the commonest French swear word, known euphemistically ever since as *le mot de Cambronne*.

The surrounding *quartier* may be expensive and sought after as an address, but it remains uninteresting to look at – just like the UNESCO building at the back of the École Militaire. Controversial

Notable buildings in the 7e arrondissement

• **29 av Rapp.** *RER* Pont de l'Alma.

A really over-the-top Art Nouveau number with bulls' heads, turbaned women and revolting colour changes. Designed by Lavirotte, 1901.

• **Square Rapp**, off av Rapp. *RER* Pont de l'Alma.

A bizarre ensemble: more Lavirotte at no. 43, a trellis *trompe l'œil* and the Société Théosphique de France.

• **12 rue Sédillot.** *RER* Pont de l'Alma.

Art Nouveau and Art Deco elements in superb dormers and wrought iron grills and balconies.

• **Conservatoire de Musique**, 7 rue Jean-Nicot. M° Invalides.

Christian Portzamparc playing with a half-peeled tube of a tower and a window to its right that has some unspecific musical association.

at the time of its construction in 1958, it looks somewhat pedestrian, and badly weathered, today. It can be visited; some of the internal spaces are interesting and there are a number of art works, both inside and in the garden, the most noticeable being an enormous mobile by Alexander Calder. The most attractive feature is a quiet Japanese garden, to which you can repair on a summer's day to read a paper bought from the well-stocked kiosk in the foyer.

Most unexpected, therefore, in this rather austere *quartier*, to discover the wedge of **early nineteenth-century streets** between av Bosquet and the Invalides. Chief among them is the market street, **rue Cler**, with its cross streets, rue de Grenelle and rue St-Dominique, full of classy little shops, including a couple of *boulangeries* with their original painted glass panels.

Down on the quai: the American Church and the Sewers

Out on the river bank at quai d'Orsay, the **American church**, together with the American College in nearby av Bosquet (no. 31), is a nodal point in the well-organized life of the large American community. The notice board is plastered with job offers and demands. The people are friendly and helpful in all kinds of ways.

The other quayside attraction is the sewers, *les égouts* (entrance 50m east of the Pont de l'Alma and Quai d'Orsay junction; Sat–Wed 11am–5/6pm, last ticket an hour before closing, 24F/18F). Your nose will tell you all you need to know, if not the cadaverous pallor of the superannuated sewermen who wait on you. The guidebooks always bill this as an outing for kids; I doubt it. The visit consists of an unilluminating film, a small museum and a very brief look at some tunnels with a lot of smelly water swirling about. Cloacal appetites will get much more satisfaction from **Victor Hugo's description** in *Les Misérables*: twenty pages on the value of human excrement as manure (25 million francs' worth down the plughole in the 1860s), and the history, ancient and modern, including the sewage flood of 1802 and the first perilous survey of the system in 1805 and what it found – a piece of Marat's winding sheet and the skeleton of an orang-utan, among other things.

The film show is a laugh for its evasive gentility. It opens with misty sunrises, portraits of monarchs, and a breathless voice saying, "Paris, do you remember when you were little?" before relating how three million *baguettes*, 1000 tons of fruit, 100 tons of fish and so on make their daily progress through the guts of the city and end up here. As for the museum, serious students of urban planning could find some interesting items, if they were only allowed the time to look. In fact, I'd say, stay in the museum and skip the tour. Among other things there is an appropriate memorial to Louis Napoléon: an inscription beginning, "In the reign of His Majesty Napoléon III, Emperor of the French, the sewer of the rue de Rivoli . . .".

Les Invalides

The **Esplanade des Invalides**, striking due south from **Pont Alexandre III**, is a more attractive and uncluttered vista than Chaillot-École Militaire. The wide façade of the **Hôtel des Invalides**, topped by its distinctive dome, resplendent with new gilding to celebrate the bicentenary of the Revolution, fills the whole of the further end of the Esplanade. It was built as a home for invalided soldiers on the orders of Louis XIV. Under the dome are two churches, one for the soldiers, the other intended as a mausoleum for the king but now containing the mortal remains of Napoléon. The Hôtel (*son et lumière* in English, April–Sept) houses the vast **Musée de l'Armée**.

The Musée de l'Armée is described on p.280.

Both churches are cold and dreary inside. The **Église du Dôme**, in particular, is a supreme example of architectural pomposity. Corinthian columns and pilasters abound. The dome – pleasing enough from outside – is covered with paintings and flanked by four round chapels displaying the tombs of various luminaries. Napoléon himself lies in a hole in the floor in a cold smooth sarcophagus of red porphyry, enclosed within a gallery decorated with friezes of execrable taste and grovelling piety, captioned with quotations of awesome conceit from the great man: "Co-operate with the plans I have laid for the welfare of peoples"; "By its simplicity my code of law has done more good in France than all the laws which have preceded me"; "Wherever the shadow of my rule has fallen, it has left lasting traces of its value."

East towards St-Germain

The Musée Rodin is fully described on p.276.

Immediately east of the Invalides is the **Musée Rodin**, on the corner of rue de Varenne, housed in a beautiful eighteenth-century mansion which the sculptor leased from the state in return for the gift of all his work at his death. The garden, planted with sculptures, is quite as pretty as the house, with a pond and flowering shrubs and a superb view of the Invalides dome rising above the trees. The rest of the street, and the parallel rue de Grenelle, is full of aristocratic mansions, including the **Hôtel Matignon**, the prime minister's residence. At the further end, rue du Bac leads into rue de Sèvres, cutting across **rue de Babylone**, another of the *quartier*'s livelier streets, which begins at Sèvres-Babylone with the city's oldest department store, *Au Bon Marché*, renowned for its food halls, and ends with the crazy, rich man's folly, *La Pagode*, the city's most exotic cinema (see p.337) and one of its pleasantest *salons de thé*.

Newspapers reporting on French foreign policy use "the quai d'Orsay" to refer to the Ministère des Affaires Étrangères, which sits between the Esplanade des Invalides and the Palais Bourbon, home of the **Assemblée Nationale**. Napoléon, never a great one for democracy, had the riverfront façade of the Palais Bourbon done to match the pseudo-Greek of the Madeleine. The result is an entrance that suggests very little illumination within.

The same could perhaps be said of the **Musée d'Orsay**, a few blocks eastward on the riverfront, with its façade of bourgeois stone disguising the huge vault of steel and glass. Once inside, however, illumination is all-pervasive – from the vault and from the greatest collection of Impressionist paintings. The building was inaugurated as a railway station in time for the 1900 World Fair and continued to serve the stations of southwest France until 1939. The theatre troupe *Reynaud-Barrault*, in their squatting phase, staged several productions here. Orson Welles used it as the setting for his film of Kafka's *Trial*, with gigantically high narrow corridors filled with terrifying filing cabinets. De Gaulle used it to announce his coup d'état of May 19, 1958 – his messianic return to power to save the *patrie* from disintegration over the Algerian liberation war.

Notwithstanding this illustrious history, it was only saved from a hotel developer's bulldozer by the colossal wave of public indignation and remorse at the destruction of Les Halles. In the late 1980s the Italian architect Gae Aulenti was given the job of designing the new museum.

You'll find a full account of the Musée d'Orsay on p.270.

Chapter 8

Montparnasse and the south *arrondissements*

Montparnasse serves to divide the lands of the well-heeled opinion-formers and power-brokers of St-Germain and the 7e from the amorphous populations of the three southern *arrondissements*. Overscale developments from the 1950s to the present day have scarred some parts of this southern side of the city, but new spaces have also opened up and some of the contemporary smaller scale developments are delightful. There are pockets of Paris that have been allowed to evolve in a happily patchy way – **Pernety** and **Plaisance** in the 14e, the **rue du Commerce** in the 15e, and the **Butte aux Cailles** *quartier* in the 13e. These are genuinely pleasant places to explore, and well off the beaten tourist tracks.

Montparnasse

The **boulevard du Montparnasse** is firmly Left Bank with its celebrated **literary cafés**, as is **Montparnasse cemetery**, which scores high on famous figures, artistic and otherwise. The av de l'Observatoire firmly links the **Paris Observatory** with the northern side of bd du Montparnasse. The area round the station, dominated by the gigantic **Tour Montparnasse**, is a mix of worker's barracks and old-fashioned streets with theatres, markets and Antoine Bourdelle's atelier, now a museum.

Around the station

Montparnasse was once the great arrival and departure point for boat travellers across the Atlantic, impoverished emigrants as well as passengers on luxury cruises, and for Bretons seeking work in the capital. On place Bienvenue in front of the modern station you can still find Breton bands busking. But as a dramatic introduction or farewell to the capital, the scene is hardly auspicious. Despite a new fishbowl glass frontage with blue and grey bits of steel curving about, the station fails to impose, mainly because its prospect of the city is blocked by the colossal **Tour Montparnasse**. This has become one of the city's principal landmarks – at its best at night when the red staple-shaped corner lights give it a certain elegance. At 200 metres it held the record as Europe's tallest office building until it was overtaken by London Dockland's Canary Wharf. You can take a tour for less than it costs to go to the top of the Eiffel Tower (summer 9.30am–11pm; winter 10am–10pm; 40F/32F/24F, entrance on the north side), or you could spend the same amount on a drink in the 56th-storey bar – the lift ride is free – where you get a tremendous view westward over the city, especially at sunset.

In front of the tower, on **place du 18-juin-1940**, is an enormous, largely subterranean shopping complex, which holds a *Galeries Lafayette*, *C & A*, boutiques galore, snack bars, a sports centre and what-have-you – very convenient, if you like shopping underground.

On the front of the complex a plaque records the fact that this was the spot where General Leclerc of the Free French forces received the surrender of von Choltitz, the German general commanding Paris, on August 25, 1944. Under orders from Hitler to destroy the city before abandoning it, von Choltitz luckily decided to disobey. And the name of the *place* is also significant in French wartime history. It commemorates the date, June 18, 1940, when de Gaulle broadcast from London, calling on the people of France to continue the struggle in spite of the armistice signed with the Germans by Marshal Pétain.

Restaurants fill the final northern section of av du Maine after it surfaces from beneath place Bienvenue. On one of its side streets, rue Antoine-Bourdelle, a garden of sculptures invites you into the **Bourdelle museum**, recently given a major extension by Christian de Portzamparc. At the end of the street and to the right on rue Falguière are the stunning new offices of *Le Monde* newspaper. The building veers up and away from the line of the street in the smoothest of curves like the hull of a fantasy spaceship.

To the east of the station, the market on bd Edgar-Quinet provides down-to-earth clientele for cafés in the surrounding streets, in marked contrast to renowned establishments a stone's throw away on bd du Montparnasse. **Rue de la Gaité**, where Trotsky lived, is a slice of turn-of-the-century theatreland, with the newly restored *Théâtre Montparnasse* facing the *Théâtre Gaité-Montparnasse* and a fair share of porn outlets. At no. 17, *La Comedia Italienne* has cupids and *comedia della arte* characters on its violent pink exterior. The *Rive Gauche* at no. 8 has an equally spectacular frontage, and there's a mural illustrating the street as you look south from bd Edgar-Quinet.

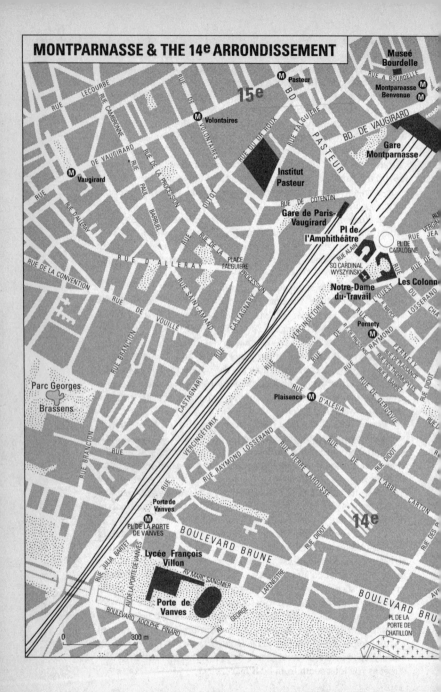

MONTPARNASSE & THE 14e ARRONDISSEMENT

Museé
Bourdelle

RUE A BOURDELLE

Montparnasse
Benvenue

RUE LECOURBE

15e

Pasteur

BD. DE VAUGIRARD

RUE CAMBRONNE

Volontaires

RUE DE VAUGIRARD

RUE DE VOLONTAIRES

RUE DU DR ROUX

RUE FALGUIÈRE

PASTEUR

Gare
Montparnasse

Vaugirard

RUE DE LA PROCESSION

RUE PAUL

RUE DUTOT

Institut
Pasteur

RUE DE COTENTIN

RUE D'ALÉSIA

RUE DE LA CONVENTION

RUE D'ALLERAY

RUE BARRAULT

PLACE
FALGUIÈRE

RUE SAINT-AMAND

RUE DE LA PROCESSION

Gare de Paris-
Vaugirard

Pl de
l'Amphithéâtre

PL DE
CATALOGNE

RUE ALAIN

SQ CARDINAL
WYSZYNSKI

Les Colonn

Notre-Dame
du-Travail

RUE DE VOUILLÉ

RUE DE

RUE CASTAGNARY

VERCINGÉTORIX

Pernety

RUE RAYMOND

PERNETY

RUE DIDOT

Parc Georges
Brassens

RUE BRANCION

RUE

CASTAGNARY

VERCINGÉTORIX

Plaisance

RUE D'ALÉSIA

RUE

RUE DE GERGOVIE

RUE PIERRE LAROUSSE

RUE DE

RUE DIDOT

L'ABBÉ
CARTON

RUE BRANCION

RUE

RUE

RUE RAYMOND LOSSERAND

14e

Porte de
Vanves

PL DE LA PORTE
DE VANVES

BOULEVARD BRUNE

RUE DIDOT

Lycée François
Villon

AV MARC SANGNIER

BOULEVARD BRU

RUE JULIA BARTET

AV DE LA PORTE DE VANVES

Porte de
Vanves

AV GEORGE

LAFENESTRE

PL DE LA
PORTE DE
CHATILLON

BOULEVARD ADOLPHE PINARD

0   300 m

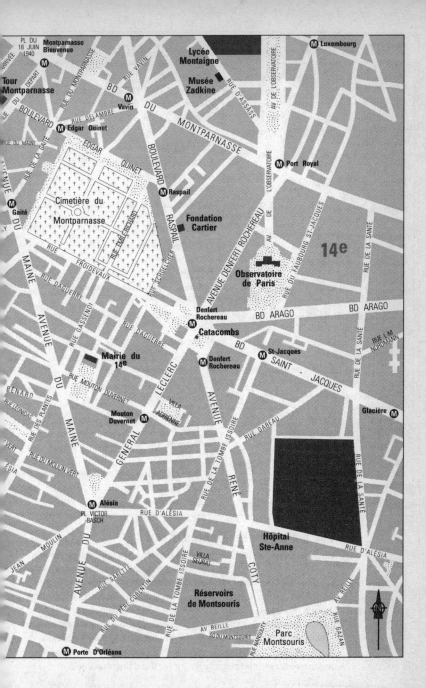

Montparnasse: Listings

Restaurants

Al Hana, 102 rue de l'Ouest, 14e.
Mo Pernety.

Aquarius 2, 40 rue Gergovie, 14e.
Mo Pernety.

Aux Artistes, 63 rue Falguière, 15e.
Mo Pasteur.

Le Berbère, 50 rue de Gergovie, 14e.
Mo Pernety.

Bergamote, 1 rue Niepce, 14e.
Mo Pernety.

Le Biniou, 3 av du Général-Leclerc, 14e.
Mo Denfert-Rochereau.

La Bûcherie, 138 bd du Montparnasse, 14e.
Mo Vavin/Port-Royal.

Chez Maria, 16 rue du Maine, 14e.
Mo Montparnasse.

La Coupole, 102 bd du Montparnasse, 14e.
Mo Vavin.

N'Zadette M'Foua, 152 rue du Château, 14e.
Mo Pernety.

L'Ostréade, 11 bd Vaugirard, 15e.
Mo Montparnasse.

Pavillon Montsouris, 20 rue Gazan, 14e.
RER Cité-Universitaire.

Phineas, 99 rue de l'Ouest, 14e.
Mo Pernety.

Au Rendez-vous des Camioneurs, 34 rue
des Plantes, 14e.
Mo Alésia.

La Route du Château, 123 rue du Château,
14e.
Mo Pernety.

Student restaurant at 13/17 rue Dareau.
Mo St-Jacques.

L'Univers, 73 rue d'Alésia (corner rue
Marguerin), 14e.
Mo Alésia.

Cafés and Bars

Au Chien Qui Fume, 19 bd du
Montparnasse, 14e.
Mo Duroc/Falguière.

Ciel de Paris, Tour Montparnasse, 33 av du
Maine, 15e.
Mo Montparnasse.

La Closerie des Lilas, 171 bd du
Montparnasse, 6e.
Mo Port-Royal.

Le Dôme, 108 bd du Montparnasse, 6e.
Mo Vavin.

L'Entrepot, 7–9 rue Francis-de-Pressensé,
14e.
Mo Pernety.

Mustangs, 84 bd du Montparnasse, 14e.
Mo Montparnasse-Bienvenue.

Le Rallye, 6 rue Daguerre, 14e.
Mo Denfert-Rochereau.

Le Rosebud, 11bis rue Delambre, 14e.
Mo Vavin.

Le Rotonde, 105 bd du Montparnasse, 6e.
Mo Vavin.

Le Select, 99 bd du Montparnasse, 6e.
Mo Vavin.

These establishments are reviewed in Chapter 13, Eating and Drinking, beginning on p.250.

The boulevard du Montparnasse

Most of the life of the Montparnasse *quartier* is concentrated around
place du 18-juin-1940, and along the immediate eastern stretch of the
boulevard. Like other Left Bank *quartiers*, Montparnasse still trades
on its association with the wild characters of the interwar artistic and
literary boom. Many were habitués of the cafés *Select*, *Coupole*,
Dôme, *Rotonde* and *Closerie des Lilas*, all still going strong on the
boulevard along with six multi-screen cinemas and several more in
the neighbouring streets. It stays up late and the pavements always
require concentrated negotiation, never mind the road itself.

> **Notable buildings around bd Montparnasse and the
> Montparnasse cemetery**
>
> • **26 rue Varin**, 6ᵉ. Mᵒ Vavin.
> A block of flats in white and blue tiles, with terraced balconies filled with
> exuberant gardens in the air. Built by Henri Sauvage in 1912.
> • **Rue Schœlcher and rue Froidevaux**. Mᵒ Raspail/Denfert-Rochereau.
> An excellent selection of nineteenth- and twentieth-century styles, of
> particular note being 5, 5bis and 11 rue Schœlcher, 11 and 23 rue
> Froidevaux, this last a 1930s block of artists' studios, with huge windows
> for northern light and fabulous ceramic mosaics.
> • **266 bd Raspail**, 14ᵉ. Mᵒ Raspail/Denfert-Rochereau.
> An interior design school with a marked Beaubourg influence: external
> stairs and blue pipe columns in front, plus the 1990s delight of glass and
> metal shuttering.
> • **259 bd Raspail**, 14ᵉ. Mᵒ Raspail/Denfert-Rochereau.
> The Cartier Foundation, designed by Jean Nouvel in 1994, with a predom-
> inance of glass. Trees grow between the glass building and a glass wall
> along the line of the street, attached by metal tubes. Next to it is a garden
> belonging to a Maison des Retraits, a haven of quiet between its old and
> new buildings.
> • **31 rue Campagne-Première**, 14ᵉ. Mᵒ Raspail.
> A myriad of earthernware tiles cover the concrete structure of these desir-
> able 1912 *appartements* with huge windows.

The animated part of the boulevard ends at **boulevard Raspail**,
where Rodin's *Balzac* broods over the traffic, though literary curiosity might take you down as far as the **Closerie des Lilas**, on the
corner of the tree-lined avenue connecting the Observatory and
Luxembourg gardens in a classic grand Parisian vista. Hemingway
used to come here to write, and Marshal Ney, one of Napoléon's
most glamorous generals, was killed by a royalist firing squad on
the pavement outside in 1815. He's still there, waving his sword,
idealized in stone. Hard by, dwarfed by apartment buildings at
100bis rue d'Assas, is the house and garden of the Russian sculptor
Ossip Zadkine, now a museum of his work and one of the most
delightful oases in the city.

*The Musée
Zadkine is
detailed on
p.279.*

Montparnasse cemetery and the catacombs

Just off to the southern side of bd Edgar-Quinet is the main entrance
to the **Montparnasse cemetery** (Mon–Fri 8am–6pm, Sat 8.30am–
6pm, Sun 9am–6pm), a gloomy city of the dead, with ranks of miniature temples, dreary and bizarre, and plenty of illustrious names for
spotters. To the right of the entrance, by the wall, is the unembel-
lished grave of Jean-Paul Sartre, who for the last few decades of his
life lived just a few yards away on bd Raspail.

Down av de l'Ouest, which follows the western wall of the cemetery, you'll find the tombs of Baudelaire (who has a more impressive
cenotaph by rue Émile-Richard on av Transversale), the painter

Soutine, Dadaist Tristan Tzara, sculptor Zadkine, and the fascist Pierre Laval, a member of Pétain's government who, after the war, was executed for treason, while in the throes of death from suicide. As an antidote, you can pay homage to Proudhon, the anarchist who coined the phrase "property is theft!", in Division 1 by the Carrefour du Rond-Point.

In the southwest corner of the cemetery is an old windmill, one of the seventeenth-century taverns frequented by the carousing, versifying students who gave the Montparnasse district its name of Parnassus.

Across rue Émile-Richard, in the eastern section of the cemetery, lie the mathematician Poincaré, car-maker André Citroën, Guy de Maupassant, César Frank, and the celebrated victim of turn-of-the-century French anti-semitism, Captain Dreyfus. Right in the northern corner is a tomb with a sculpture by Brancusi, *Le Baiser*, which makes a far sadder statement than the dramatic passionate scenes of grief adorning so many of the graves here. And, for the bizarre, by the wall along bd Raspail you can see the inventor of a safe gas lamp, Charles Pigeon, reading a book by the light of his lamp in bed with his sleeping wife.

If you are determined to spend your time among the dear departed, you can also get down into **the catacombs** (Tues–Fri 2–6pm, Sat & Sun 9–11am & 2–4pm; 27F/15F) in nearby **place Denfert-Rochereau**, formerly *place d'Enfer* – Hell Square. (The entrance is on the east side of the approach to av Général-Leclerc; don't go down in fancy new shoes – it's wet and gungy underfoot.) These are abandoned quarries stacked with millions of bones cleared from the old charnel houses in 1785, claustrophobic in the extreme, and cold to boot. Some years ago a slew of punks and art students developed a macabre taste for this as the ultimate party location, but the overseeing authorities, alas, soon put paid to that plan.

Discount clothes shops are reviewed on p.309.

Having surfaced, you will find yourself on rue Rémy-Dumoncel. From here you can stroll back over av du Général-Leclerc to the quiet little streets of clothes and crafts shops and cheap flats bordered by the cemetery and av du Maine (with a food market on rue Daguerre as well).

Or you can follow rue de la Tombe-Issoire to the **Observatoire de Paris**, where there's a garden open on summer afternoons (April–Aug 1–7pm; Sept to mid-Oct 1–4pm) in which to sit and admire the dome. From the 1660s, when the observatory was constructed, to 1884, all French maps had the zero meridian running through the middle of this building. After that date, they reluctantly agreed that 0° longitude should pass through a village in Normandy that happens to be due south of Greenwich. Visiting the Observatoire is a complicated procedure and all you'll see are old maps and instruments.

Commerce and convention: the 15e

Between the Montparnasse train tracks and the river lies the largest, most populated and characterless *arrondissement*, the 15e. It was in **rue du Commerce** that George Orwell worked as a dishwasher in a White Russian restaurant in the late Twenties, described in his *Down and Out in Paris and London*. Though there are still run-down and poor areas, an ever-widening stretch back from the river-front is plush high-rise with underground parking, serviced lifts and electronic security. A new park has appeared on the old Citroën works down in the southwest corner, while over towards the rail lines the **Parc Georges Brassens** is now well established on the former abattoir site.

The riverbank section

The western edge of the 15e *arrondissement* fronts the Seine from the Eiffel Tower to beyond Pont du Garigliano. It would be almost totally unrecognizable to anyone returning from a thirty-year absence.

Just off Pont de Bir-Hakeim at the beginning of bd de Grenelle, in a rather undignified enclosure sandwiched by high-rise buildings, a plaque commemorates the notorious **rafle du Vel d'Hiv**: the Nazi and French-aided round-up of 13,152 Parisian Jews in July 1942. Nine thousand of them, including four thousand children, were interned here at the now vanished cycle track for a week before being carted off to Auschwitz. Thirty adults were the only survivors.

Restaurants in the 15e are detailed on p.253.

The quaysides are pretty inaccessible, but out in midstream a narrow island, the **Allée des Cygnes,** joins the Pont de Grenelle and the double-decker road and rail bridge, Pont de Bir-Hakeim. It's a strange place to walk – it was one of Samuel Beckett's favourites – with just birds and trees and a scaled-down version of the **Statue of Liberty** at the downstream end. This was one of the four prelimi-nary models constructed between 1874 and 1884 by sculptor Auguste Bartholdi, with the help of Gustave Eiffel, before the finished article (originally intended for Alexandria in Egypt) was presented to New York. Contemporary photos show the final version, assembled in Bartholdi's rue de Chazelles workshop, towering over the houses of the 17e like a bizarre female King Kong.

The river bank down to Pont Mirabeau is marred by a sort of mini-Défense development of half-cocked futuristic towers with pretentious galactic names like Castor and Pollux, Vega and Orion, rising out of a litter-blown pedestrian platform some ten metres above street level.

Three major streets fan into the *arrondissement* from Rond-Point du Pont Mirabeau. Between rue Émile-Zola, demarcation line for the expensive tower block sector, and the long rue de la Convention lie the buildings of the **Imprimerie Nationale** – the

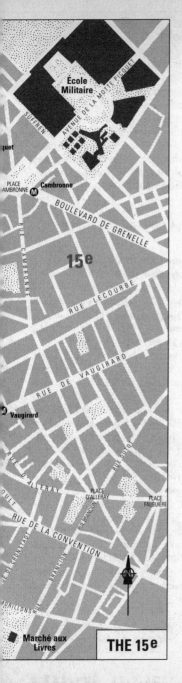

THE 15e

The 15e: Listings

Restaurants

Au Bélier d'Argent, 46 rue de Cronstadt, 15e.
Mº Porte-de-Vanves/Convention.

Le Clos Morillons, 50 rue Morillons, 15e.
Mº Porte-de-Vanves.

Le Commerce, 51 rue du Commerce, 15e.
Mº Émile-Zola.

Le Roi du Couscous, 48 rue de la Croix-Nivert, 15e.
Mº Cambronne.

Sampieru Corsu, 12 rue de l'Amiral-Roussin, 15e.
Mº Cambronne.

Student restaurant at 156 rue Vaugirard, 15e.
Mº Pasteur.

Cafés and Bars

JeThéMe, 4 rue d'Alleray, 15e.
Mº Vaugirard.

*These establishments are reviewed in Chapter 13,
Eating and Drinking, beginning on p.250.*

national printworks. Their shop (Mon–Fri 9am–6pm) on rue Paul
Hervieu displays some of their publications – beautifully bound art
books, musical scores, the *Rights of Man* on vellum and the current
general code on taxes. Two blocks east, on rue St-Charles is a
pocket of street life – rare for this side of the 15ᵉ – with small food
shops, including a branch of the upmarket *Hédiard* and an excellent *boulangerie* on the corner with rue Javel.

Whereas the yuppie apartment blocks end at Rond-Point du
Pont-Mirabeau, yuppie offices begin, notably the gleaming white,
smooth hulk of the TV company *Canal +*. At this point, the quayside road diverts underground – to the fury of Parisian cyclists who
now have to make a two kilometre detour. The reason for it was the
creation of the new Parc André-Citroën on the site of the old car
factory.

The Parc André-Citroën and Citroën-Cévennes quartier

The best thing about the **Parc André-Citroën** are the hothouses –
big glass boxes with mimosa, fish-tailed palms and other nice-
smelling shrubbery. The worst thing about it is that there's more
concrete here than greenery, including the absurdist extravagance
of an arch over the *RER* lines by the river, which is not a bridge,
just a decorative device. You will eventually be able to cross under
the lines and look at a "fragment du jardin" in the river itself.

The layout of the park is extremely formal, with split levels,
terraces, monumental plant holders, small enclosures and a series of
rather unsuccessful gardens dedicated to different colours – in
April, the red garden is full of white apple and pear blossom; the
only flower in the blue garden is the violent pink tulip, and the black
garden is full of green helibore. Near the entrance closest to Pont
Mirabeau, you can at least walk on the grass on plastic matting, and
on a cloud-scudding day, the top of the mirrored office block to the
south merges into the sky. The oddest thing is that no-one in Paris
seems to know about this park, and it's virtually empty.

Across rue Balard is the totally new *quartier du Citroën-
Cévennes*, with pedestrian streets, sports centres and youth clubs,
and the **Bibliothèque St-Charles**, a children's library on rue de la
Montagne d'Aulas. You can imagine Gutenburg – remembered in a
neighbouring street name – wearing a hat shaped like this peculiar
black building with slanting metallic bands. Built in 1990 and
designed by Franck Hammoutene, it has windows on only one side
and inside around a circular courtyard in which a cherry tree struggles up towards the light.

In the middle of the new developments is a slice of traditional
Paris – the **Grenelle cemetery**. In France, however influential and
with however many politicians in their pockets, developers cannot
touch a burial ground.

From the École Militaire to Parc Georges Brassens

If you start walking, say, in **avenue de la Motte-Picquet** by the École Militaire, you'll get the full flavour of the *quartier du Commerce*. That's the staid end, with brasseries full of officers from the École and the rather dreary **Village Suisse**, with 150 expensive antique shops (open Thurs–Mon) – all Louis Quinze and Second Empire. The nature of the *quartier* changes at **boulevard de Grenelle**, where the métro runs on iron piers above the street. Seedy hotels rent rooms by the month and the corner cafés offer cheap *plats du jour*. **Rue du Commerce** begins here, a lively, old-fashioned high street – once you're past the *Burger King* and *Uniprix* – full of small shops and peeling, shuttered houses. Scale and architecture give it a sunny, friendly atmosphere. The best-known cheap eating establishment is *Le Commerce* at no. 51, and there are other restaurants and interesting shops in the streets around.

Towards the end of the street, just past a fading Belle Époque butchers on the west side, is **place du Commerce**, with its trees and a bandstand in the middle, a model of old-fashioned petty-bourgeois respectability. Cafés and *pâtisseries* proliferate as rue du Commerce ends at place Étienne-Pernet, where cottagey houses still exist on the west side of the *place*. If you follow rue des Entrepreneurs east, past a beautiful apartment building at no. 109, you come to the surprisingly generous green space of **square Lambert**, with fountains and lawns overlooked by the prison-like premises of a *lycée* (top-stream secondary school).

If you carry on south, rue de la Croix-Nivert brings you to the **Porte de Versailles** where, at an informer's signal, government troops first entered the city in their final assault on the Commune on May 21, 1871. Today it is the site of several large **exhibition halls** where the *foires* are held – Agricultural Show, Ideal Home Exhibition and the like. Behind it, a few minutes' walk away past the headquarters of the French air force, is *Aquaboulevard*, the city's largest **leisure centre**, where the principal attraction is an artificial tropical lagoon complete with beaches and exotic plants and giant helter-skelter-type water chutes (see p.290).

More traditional relaxation – and for free – is on hand at **parc Georges Brassens**. The old Vaugirard abattoir was transformed into this park in the 1980s and it's a delight, especially for children. Two bronze bulls flank the main entrance on rue des Morillons. A pond surrounds the old abattoir clock tower. There is a garden of scented herbs and shrubs, designed principally for the blind (best in late spring), puppets and rocks and merry-go-rounds for the kids, a mountain stream with pine and birch trees, beehives, and a tiny terraced vineyard facing the sun behind the towering flats. The corrugated pyramid with a helter-skelter-like spiral is a new theatre, the *Silvia-Montfort*.

Book-lovers should take a look in the sheds of the old horse market between the park and rue Briançon where, every Saturday and Sunday morning, dozens of **book dealers** set out their genuinely interesting stock. The success of the park has rubbed off on **rue des Morillons** and **rue Briançon**. New restaurants and tea rooms have opened and old cafés have livened up.

On the east side of the park, in passage Dantzig off rue Dantzig, in a secluded garden, stands an unusual polygonal building known as **La Rûche**, the Beehive. It was designed by Eiffel as the wine pavilion for the 1900 trade fair and transported here from its original site in the Champs de Mars. It has been used ever since as artists' studios, rented by some of the biggest names in twentieth-century art, starting with Chagall, Modigliani and Léger.

If you're heading towards Montparnasse from here, take bus #89 rather than slogging it on foot. Close to place d'Alleray at 75–83 rue Alleray, an extraordinary church is being built – the first new church in Paris since the 1960s. If it sticks to the architectural models, the **Église de l'Arche d'Alliance** will be a cube on columns alongside a needle-thin tower, all encaged in a fretwork screen of stainless steel.

*For details of
the Pasteur
Museum, see
p.284.*

Further north, between rue du Docteur Roux and rue Falguière, is the **Pasteur Institute**, renowned for its founder, who more or less invented modern biology, and for its research into AIDS.

The 14e below Montparnasse

The 14e is one of the best of the outer *arrondissements*. While the area beside the train tracks immediately south of Gare Montparnasse has dramatically changed, old-fashioned networks of streets still exist in the **Pernety** and **Plaisance** *quartiers*, and between avs Réné-Coty and Général-Leclerc. In the early years of the century, so many outlawed Russian revolutionaries lived in the 14e that the Tsarist police ran a special Paris section to keep tabs on them. The 14e was also a favourite address for artists who could live in seclusion in the many *villas* (mews) built in the 1920s and 1930s.

Down in the southeast corner there's plenty of green space, in the **Parc Montsouris** and in the **Cité Universitaire**, home to more revolutionaries in their student days.

Pernety, Plaisance and down to the perimeter

Between avenue du Maine and the train tracks, the old working-class districts of **Plaisance** and **Pernety** have had whole swathes ravaged by redevelopment and the first arty-alternative phase of gentrification. While the latter does at least have the virtue of preserving the physical, if not the social, texture of the area, redevelopment has already completely transformed the western edge of the *quartier*. Had it not been for the efforts of the local campaign

The 14e below Montparnasse: Listings

Restaurants

Al Hana, 102 rue de l'Ouest, 14e.
Mº Pernety.

Aquarius 2, 40 rue Gergovie, 14e.
Mº Pernety.

Bergamote, 1 rue Niepce, 14e.
Mº Pernety.

Le Berbère, 50 rue de Gergovie, 14e.
Mº Pernety.

Le Biniou, 3 av du Général-Leclerc, 14e.
Mº Denfert-Rochereau.

N' Zadette M'Foua, 152 rue du Château, 14e.
Mº Pernety.

Pavillon Montsouris, 20 rue Gazan, 14e.
RER Cité-Universitaire.

Phineas, 99 rue de l'Ouest, 14e.
Mº Pernety.

Au Rendez-vous des Camioneurs, 34 rue des Plantes, 14e.
Mº Alésia.

La Route du Château, 123 rue du Château, 14e.
Mº Pernety.

Student restaurants at 13/17 rue Dareau (Mº St-Jacques); in the Cité Universitaire (*RER* Cité Universitaire).

L'Univers, 73 rue d'Alésia, 14e.
Mº Alésia.

Cafés and Bars

L'Entrepôt, 7–9 rue Francis-de-Pressensé, 14e.
Mº Pernety.

Le Rallye, 6 rue Daguerre, 14e.
Mº Denfert-Rochereau.

These establishments are reviewed in Chapter 13, Eating and Drinking, beginning on p.254.

group "Vivre dans le 14e", there would have been a motorway flanked by tower blocks all the way down to the *boulevard périphérique* from Montparnasse station.

Place de Catalogne, round the intersection of rue de Vercingétorix and rue du Château, is the hub of the newest and most upmarket transformation – a futuristic complex by the Catalan architect Ricardo Bofill. Local protest played its part in getting something more spectacular than plain grim blocks and towers, and Bofill's work certainly draws the attention better than the supremely gross new office blocks that bridge the train lines just north of place de Catalogne.

Water slides across an enormous tilted disc of cobbles in the centre of the *place* to form a fountain. Unfortunately, however, the attractiveness of the effect is marred by the traffic which hurtles around it, overlooked by Bofill's Neoclassical façades complete with metopes, triglyphs and pediments.

To the south, a great square arch leads through into a circular, lawn-filled courtyard bounded by glass walls punctuated by a colonnade of four-sided reflective glass columns with stone capitals, opening on the further side onto a vista of high-rise flats flanked by two massive Doric columns supporting nothing but sky – the whole know as **Les Colonnes**.

To the east, an amphitheatre (one of Bofill's favourite forms) towers over the church of Notre-Dame du Travail and a children's playground in square du Cardinal Wyszynski. From here and on down to past rue d'Alésia humans, rather than the imaginary giants Bofill builds for, are given precedence, with an open space alongside the tracks for playing *boules* or idling on benches. The interior of **Notre-Dame du Travail** testifies to the working-class congregation for which it was built in the 1890s. Combined with Art Nouveau elements are symbols of proletarian occupations and artisans' trades.

If you want to catch the flavour of what all the *quartier* used to be like, wander up **rue Raymond-Losserand** and **rue Didot** and look into the cross-streets, where offbeat shops, restaurants and clubs have proliferated alongside artisans' workshops and neighbourhood cafés. In the garden on the corner of rue Raymond-Losserand and rue d'Alésia is a Chagallesque mural of horses, doves, elephants and hunters, and further down rue Raymond-Losserand, at no. 168, the superbly proud and ugly building of the ancient Plaisance electricity substation. Plaisance still has its villagey mews like impasse Floriment, where Georges Brassens lived for many years. This is off **rue d'Alésia**, in the middle of the stretch between Plaisance métro and rue Didot, which plays host to a **food market** every Thursday and Sunday. Further east along rue d'Alésia, and particularly around place Victor-Basch, you'll find numerous good-value **clothes shops**, including many that sell discounted couturier numbers.

The area south of rue d'Alésia has less of a cosy Paris feel, but at the weekend it's worth heading down past the workers' flats on bd Brune for one of the city's best **junk markets**, spread along the pavements of av Marc-Sangnier and av Georges-Lafenestre and starting at daybreak (see p.317). The western end of the market peters out at place de la Porte de Vanves, where the city fortifications used to run until the 1920s when, despite talk of a green belt, most of the space gained by their demolition was given over to speculative building.

South from Denfert-Rochereau

From Denfert-Rochereau to Parc Montsouris, most of the space is taken up by *RER* lines, reservoirs and **Ste-Anne's psychiatric hospital**, where the great political philosopher Louis Althusser was incarcerated after murdering his wife. His autobiography, written in Ste-Anne's but published posthumously in 1992 because as a patient he had no right to publish, suggests that he would have preferred to have been tried and sent to prison. The plea of madness was, under French law, not a mitigating circumstance, but a denial altogether that a crime had taken place. His wife and victim, Hélène, had supported him through fits of severe mental illness for over thirty years. Some say she had had enough and threatened to leave him. A very sad and horrible story that was mercilessly exploited by the right-wing French press.

At the junction of rue d'Alésia and av Réné-Coty steep steps lead up into rue des Artistes and one of the most isolated spots in the city. At the end of the street, brambles grow over the fencing round the Montsouris reservoir. Dali, Lurgat, Miller, Durrell and other artists found homes here, in the cobbled *cul-de-sac* of **Villa Seurat**, off rue de la Tombe-Issoire. Lenin and his wife, Krupskaya, lived across the street at 4 rue Marie-Rose.

South of the reservoir are more secluded cobbled streets and mews. The square du Montsouris leads off av Reille, close by one of Corbusier's earliest Parisian commissions at no. 53, a studio for his painter friend Ozenfant, who styled the Hispano-Suiza cars of the 1920s. The roof has been altered, but not the Corbusier trademark of horizontal slices of windows. All manner of styles – even mock Norman farmhouse – can be spied along the verdant and secretive square du Montsouris, whose other entrance is on rue Nansouty. There are more *villas* off this street; Georges Braque lived at no. 6 in the one named after him.

Parc Montsouris was a favourite walking place of Lenin's, and no doubt of all the local artists, too. Its peculiarities include a meteorological office, a marker of the old meridian near bd Jourdan, and by the southwest entrance a kiosk run by the French Astronomy Association. Alas, the most surprising structure, a beautiful reproduction of the Bardo palace in Tunis, built for the 1867 *Exposition Universelle*, burnt down to the ground in half an hour just after restoration work had finished in the early 1990s. But it is still a good place to stroll, with its unlikely contours, winding paths and the cascade above the lake. Even the *RER* tracks cutting right through it fail to dent its charm – though park police, whistling at you for being on the grass, might.

On the other side of bd Jourdan, several thousand students from over one hundred different countries live in the curious array of buildings of the **Cité Universitaire**. The central Maison Internationale resembles the Marlinspike of Tintin books. The others reflect in their mixture of styles the diversity of the nations and peoples willing to subsidize foreign study. Armenia, Cuba, Indo-China and Monaco are neighbours at the western end; Japan, Brazil, Italy, India and Morocco gather together at the other; Cambodia is guarded by startling stone creatures next to the *boulevard périphérique*; Switzerland (designed by Le Corbusier during his stilts phase) and the US are the most popular for their relatively luxurious rooms; and the Collège Franco-Britannique is a red-brick monster.

The atmosphere is still very far from internationalist, but there are films, shows and other events (check the notice boards in the Maison Internationale) and you can eat cheaply in the cafeterias, if you have a student card.

The 13e

The tight-knit community on and around **rue Nationale** between bd Vincent-Auriol and the inner ring road never had much to hope for in the postwar days. But they made do with their crowded, rat-ridden, ramshackle slums, not just through lack of choice, but because life at least could be lived on the street – in the shops, the cafés (of which there were 48 on rue Nationale alone), and with the neighbours, who all shared the same conditions. Paris was another place, rarely ventured to. But, come the 1950s and 1960s, the city planners, here as elsewhere, came up with their sense-defying solution to the housing problem. Each tower-block flat is hygienic, secure and costly to run, the next-door neighbour is a stranger, and only a couple of cafés remain on rue Nationale. The architectural gloom of the southeastern half of the *arrondissement* is only alleviated by the gourmandize of the **Chinese quarter**, the admirable **Dunois jazz venue** (see p.329) and one or two clever new buildings.

West of avs d'Italie and des Gobelins – site of the famous tapestry works – there remains the almost untouched *quartier* of the **Butte-aux-Cailles** and little streets and cul-de-sacs of prewar houses and studios.

The eastern edge of the 13e along the riverfront is in the throes of mammoth development, involving the Bibliothèque de France, the Gare d'Austerlitz and everything in between. It is to be known as the "Seine Rive Gauche".

The 13e: Listings

Restaurants

Bol en Bois, 35 rue Pascal, 13e.
Mº Gobelins.

Chez Gladines, 30 rue des Cinq-Diamants, 13e.
Mº Corvisart.

Chez Grand-mère, 92 rue Broca, 13e.
Mº Gobelins.

Entoto, 143–145 rue Léon-Maurice-Nordmann, 13e.
Mº Glacière.

Hawaï, 87 av d'Ivry, 13e.
Mº Tolbiac.

Le Languedoc, 64 bd Port-Royal, 5e.
Mº Gobelins.

Lao-Thai, 128 rue de Tolbiac, 13e.
Mº Tolbiac.

Phuong Hoang, Terrasse des Olympiades, 52 rue du Javelot, 13e.
Mº Tolbiac.

Student restaurant, Cité Universitaire.
RER Cité Universitaire.

Le Temps des Cerises, 18–20 rue de la Butte-aux-Cailles, 13e.
Mº Place-d'Italie/Corvisart.

Thuy Huong and **Tricotin**, Kiosque de Choisy, 15 av de Choisy, 13e.
Mº Porte-de-Choisy.

Cafés and Bars

La Folie en Tête, 33 rue de la Butte-aux-Cailles, 13e.
Mº Place-d'Italie/Corvisart.

Le Merle Moqueur, 11 rue de la Butte-aux-Cailles, 13e.
Mº Place-d'Italie/Corvisart.

These establishments are reviewed in Chapter 13, Eating and Drinking, *beginning on p.254.*

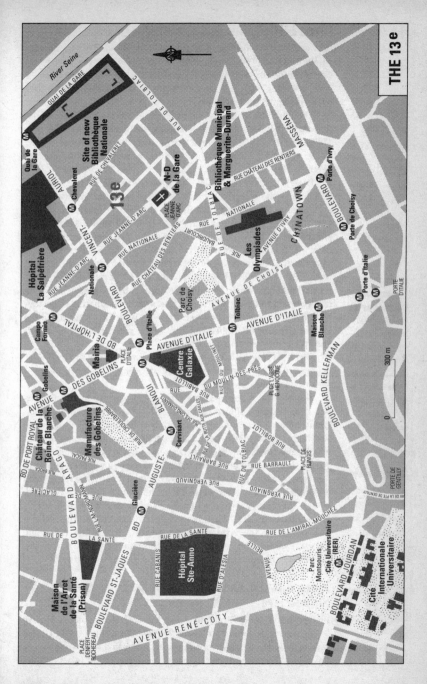

River Seine

QUAI DE LA GARE

RUE DE TOLBIAC

Quai de
la Gare

Ⓜ Chevaleret

RUE DE CHEVALERET

Site of new
Bibliothèque
Nationale

13e

✝ N-D
de la Gare

PLACE
JEANNE-D'ARC

Hôpital
La Salpêtrière

RUE JEANNE-D'ARC

RUE JEANNE-D'ARC

RUE NATIONALE

RUE CHÂTEAU DES RENTIERS

Bibliothèque Municipal
& Marguerite-Durand

RUE CHÂTEAU DES RENTIERS

MASSÉNA

Ⓜ Porte d'Ivry

RUE DE TOLBIAC

RUE NATIONALE

RUE BAUDRICOURT

AVENUE D'IVRY

CHINATOWN

Ⓜ Nationale

BOULEVARD VINCENT-

Les
Olympiades

Ⓜ Porte de Choisy

Ⓜ Porte d'Italie

Parc de
Choisy

AVENUE DE CHOISY

Ⓜ Tolbiac

AVENUE D'ITALIE

Maison
Blanche

Ⓜ Porte d'Italie

PORTE
D'ITALIE

Campo
Formio

BD DE L'HÔPITAL

AVENUE D'ITALIE

RUE DU MOULIN-DES-PRÉS

AVENUE D'ITALIE

Ⓜ Place d'Italie

PLACE
D'ITALIE

Mairie

Centre
Galaxie

BOULEVARD KELLERMAN

Ⓜ Gobelins

DES GOBELINS

RUE BOBILLOT

RUE BABILLOT

P. DE L'ABBÉ
G. HÉNOCQUE

Château de la
Reine Blanche

AVENUE DES GOBELINS

Manufacture
des Gobelins

RUE DE BOUSSINGAULT

BLANQUI

Ⓜ Corvisart

RUE DE LA BUTTE AUX CAILLES

RUE BOBILLOT

AV DE LA PTE DE GENTILLY

BD DE PORT ROYAL

BOULEVARD ARAGO

RUE BROCA

RUE DE LA

GLACIÈRE

AUGUSTE-

RUE VERGNIAUD

RUE DE TOLBIAC

RUE BARRAULT

PLACE
DE RUNGIS

PORTE DE
GENTILLY

RUE PASCAL

RUE DE BOULEVARD

RUE VANDRÉZANNE

RUE VERGNIAUD

RUE BARRAULT

Ⓜ Glacière

BD

RUE DE LA SANTÉ

RUE DE L'AMIRAL-MOUCHEZ

RÉILLE

Maison
de l'Arret
de la Santé
(Prison)

RUE DE
LA SANTÉ

RUE CABANIS

Hôpital
Ste-Anne

RUE DE

AVENUE

Parc
Montsouris.

Cité Universitaire
(RER)

BOULEVARD JOURDAN

Cité
Internationale
Universitaire.

PLACE
DENFERT-
ROCHEREAU

BOULEVARD ST-JACQUES

BOULEVARD ST-JAQUES

RUE D'ALESIA

AVENUE RENÉ-COTY

0   300 m

Butte-aux-Cailles and the old quartiers

Between rue de Tolbiac and the stretch of bd Auguste-Blanqui where the food market is held, from place d'Italie to beyond Corvisart métro, there's a hill – the *butte* – on which the quails – *cailles* – must once have perched, nested or been hunted, to give the street and *quartier* its name.

Though there's highrise along rue Bobillot, the top floors of the five-storey houses on **rue de la Buttes-aux-Cailles**, typical of pre-1960s Paris, have views north across the city to the Sacré Coeur. Rents are not cheap, and it's far from being a working-class neighbourhood.

Recently, lamp posts have been added to rue de la Butte-aux-Cailles and the street recobbled, a suspicious sign that the many long-term residents may come under pressure to move on. It still has, however, book, bric-à-brac, wine and food shops, a *boulangerie* and newsagents, and one of the green Art Nouveau municipal drinking fountains, donated to the city by Sir Richard Wallace. There's a community action centre, a co-operative jazz bar and restaurant (*La Folie en Tête* at no. 33 and *Le Temps des Cerise* at no. 18) and nine other bars and restaurants besides, most of which stay open till the early hours. And that's without counting the establishments on the streets between rue de la Butte-aux-Cailles and the market street of bd August-Blanqui, which you can reach by a path and steps from rue des Cinq-Diamants.

South of rue Tolbiac, small houses with fancy brickwork or decorative timbers have remained intact: aroune Temps al between rues Boussingault and Brillat-Savarin.

North of bd Auguste-Blanqui, rue Léon-Maurice-Nordmann has two semi-private cobbled alleyways off it, the **Cité Verte** in which Henry Moore once had a studio, and the **Cité des Vignes**, opposite. The high wall along rue de la Santé encloses a remand prison, from which a spectacular helicopter escape was made in 1986.

To the east, just behind the Gobelins (see below), is an exquisite fairytale octagonal tower and gateway hemmed in by workshops and lock-ups. It is all that remains of the **Château de la Reine Blanche**, where, it is said, the young Charles VI of France went mad after a riotous party in 1393 when he was nearly burnt alive. The château was rebuilt in the sixteenth century, from which the remaining structures date. You can take a look through a gateway on rue des Gobelins or through the courtyard at 4 rue Gustave-Geffroy.

Le Temps de Cerise was a famous song of the late 1870s, popular for referring to the heady days of the recently defeated Commune, at a time when it was not possible to talk openly.

Place d'Italie, the Gobelins workshops and La Salpêtrière

Place d'Italie, the central junction of the 13e, has the ornate *Mairie* of the *arrondissement* to its north side, and a huge white edifice with a tangled coloured wire appendage housing a new cinema to the south. It's one of those Parisian roundabouts that takes half-an-hour to cross on foot. In the 1848 revolution it was barricaded and the scene of one short-lived victory of the Left. A government general and his officers were allowed through the barricade, only to be surrounded and dragged off to the police station, where the commander was persuaded to write an order of retreat and a letter promising three million francs for the poor of Paris. Needless to say, neither was honoured and the reprisals were heavy. Many of those involved in the uprising were tanners, laundry-workers or dye-makers, with their workplace the banks of the Bièvre River. This was covered over in 1910 (creating rues Berbier-du-Mets and Croulebarbe) as a health hazard, the main source of pollution being the dyes from the **Gobelins tapestry workshops** at 42 av des Gobelins, in operation here for some four hundred years. Tapestries are still being made by the same methods on cartoons by contemporary painters – a painfully slow process that you can watch (guided visits Tues, Wed & Thurs 2 & 2.45pm; 26F/17F; Mº Gobelins).

Between bd St-Marcel and bd Vincent-Auriol, the buildings are ornate and bourgeois, dominated by the immense **Hôpital de la Salpêtrière**, built under Louis XIV to dispose of the dispossessed. It later became a psychiatric hospital, fulfilling the same function. Jean Charcot, who believed that susceptibility to hypnosis proved hysteria, staged his theatrical demonstrations here, with Freud one of his greatly interested witnesses. If you ask very nicely in the Bibliothèque Charcot (block 6, red route), the librarian may show you a book of photographs of the desperate female victims of these experiments.

For a more positive statement on women, take a look at the building at 5 rue Jules-Breton, which declares in large letters on its façade, "In humanity, woman has the same duties as man. She must have the same rights in the family and in society."

Tolbiac and Chinatown

The area between rue de Tolbiac, av de Choisy and bd Masséna is the colourful **Chinatown of Paris**, with no concessions to organic matter, unless it's to be unceremoniously ingested. From rue Tolbiac, just east of rue Baudricourt, some steps lead up to a concrete platform, known as *Les Olympiades*, where the tower blocks hide a clutch brilliant Asiatic restaurants and sundry arcades with Chinese high-street businesses – travel agents, video libraries, hairdressers and bowling alleys – where no transactions seem to be carried out in French. Exiting onto av d'Ivry, you'll find the **Tang-Frères supermarket** and a larger **covered market**, where birds circle above the mind- and stomach-boggling goodies. Chinese, Laotian, Cambodian, Thai and Vietnamese shops and restaurants fill both av d'Ivry and av de Choisy all the way down to the city limits, many of them in shopping mazes on the ground floors of tower blocks.

The restaurants of Chinatown are detailed on p.252.

In case you should think this is all too materialistic, head into the underground service road, rue du Disque, just by the escalators up to the *Olympiades* at 66 av d'Ivry. Red and gold lanterns announce the entrance to a Buddhist temple. Community activities go on there as well as worship, and no-one will mind you going in.

Back on rue de Tolbiac on the corner with rue Nationale, there's a wonderful municipal library in a steel-frame curved building with a giant, framed, semitransparent photograph on the rue Nationale side. It houses the **Bibliothèque Marguerite Durand**, the first official feminist library in France (see p.43), and has newspapers and a video auditorium.

If you prefer to relax outside, the square de Choisy, on the north side of rue de Tolbiac, has outdoor ping-pong tables with concrete nets, archery targets, and birds and trees. There are more good modern buildings near here: Christian de Portzamparc's public housing estate on rue des Hautes-Formes, and, at 106 rue du Château-des-Rentiers, a ten-storey block of public flats whose façade on rue Jean-Colly has a map of the *quartier* in coloured tiles and pipes to show the métro lines.

There's little point in heading further east (unless you're a serious Le Corbusier fan – his Salvation Army building, blackened by traffic pollution, is at the end of rue Cantagrel at no. 12). However, in a few years, rue de Tolbiac will reach the Seine, not through trainlines and marshalling yards, crumbling warehouses and sinister empty spaces, but alongside what might be one of the loveliest new monuments of Paris.

"Seine Rive Gauche"

The new **Bibliothèque Nationale de France** has four glass L-shaped towers, 100m high, at each corner of an open space the size of sixteen football pitches, around a sunken garden. The architect is a young Frenchman, Dominique Perrault, who was virtually unknown prior to winning the competition.

In 1991 the bd Vincent-Auriol end of the site was squatted by African families evicted from their homes north of the river. Their tent city inspired great public sympathy and concern for the plight of the homeless in the city. It was used as a political football between Chirac and Mitterrand and the protesters were eventually moved off by heavy-handed police action. There have been protests that of the housing to be built alongside the library, only a third will be municipally owned. "Irregularities" in the awarding of contracts have led to prosecutions and the transparent towers have had shutters added after senior figures in the librarian and academic worlds accused the design of being entirely unsuited to the storing of books and papers.

But despite all these problems, the building works should be finished in March 1995 and the most advanced library in the world will open to everyone – not just card-carrying academics – in

November 1996. If you want to discover more about it, you can look at photos, architectural models and a video in the *Acceuil Cité Chantier* on the site (access from 139 quai de la Gare; Mº quai de la Gare; Mon–Thurs 10am–5pm, Fri–Sun 10am–6pm; free).

Whether the recession will allow the rest of the **Seine Rive Gauche** to be completed is another matter. There's all the fancy housing around the library, a whole new sector from bd Vincent-Auriol to the glass hall of Austerlitz Station (for when the *TGV* lines are completed between 2000 and 2005) and a new bridge across the Seine.

The competition entries from world-famous architects for the Austerlitz development and models of the different housing blocks are displayed in the **Tipi** (Tues–Sun 2–7pm; free), a conical tent on the south side of bd Vincent-Auriol close by quai de la Gare métro station. There are also plans and drawings from the past when this area was just the plain of Ivry with farms and windmills. They were a bit crazy then too – a floating footbridge of pagodas was proposed for where the new Pont Charles-de-Gaulle is planned.

Chapter 9

Montmartre and Northern Paris

Montmartre lies in the middle of the largely petit bourgeois and working-class 18^e *arrondissement*, respectable round the slopes of the hill or *Butte Montmartre*, distinctly less so around **Pigalle** on the northern edge of the 9^e *arrondissement* and towards the **Gare du Nord** and **Gare de l'Est** into the 10^e *arrondissement*, where the colourful bazaar-like shops and depressing slums of the **Goutte d'Or** crowd along the train tracks. On its northern edge, across the so-called "plain of Montmartre", lies the extensive **St-Ouen flea market**. To the west, between av de Clichy and the St-Lazare train lines, is the little-explored Batignolles *quartier*.

Montmartre

At 130m, the **Butte Montmartre** is the highest point in Paris. All the various theories as to the origin of its name have a Roman connection. It could be a corruption of *Mons Martyrum*, the Martyrs' hill – the martyrs being Saint Denis and his companions. On the other hand, it might have been named *Mons Mercurii*, in honour of a Roman shrine to Mercury, or possibly *Mons Martis*, after a shrine to Mars.

In spite of being one of the city's chief tourist attractions, it manages to retain the quiet, almost secretive, air of its rural origins. Only incorporated into the city in the mid-nineteenth century, it received its first major influx of population from the poor displaced by Haussmann's rebuilding programme. Its **heyday** was from the last years of the century to World War I, when its rustic charms and low rents attracted crowds of artists. Although that traditional population of workers and artists has largely been supplanted by a more chic and prosperous class of Bohemian, the *quartier*'s physical appearance has changed little, thanks largely to the warren of **plas-**

ter-of-Paris quarries that perforate its bowels and render the ground too unstable for new building.

The **most popular access** route is via the rue de Steinkerque and the steps below the Sacré-Cœur (the funicular railway from place Suzanne-Valadon is covered by the *Carte Orange*). But for a quieter approach you can go up via place des Abbesses or rue Lepic, and still have the streets to yourself.

Place des Abbesses to the Butte

Place des Abbesses is postcard-pretty, with one of the few complete surviving **Guimard Art Nouveau métro entrances** (transferred from the Hôtel de Ville): the glass porch as well as the railings and the slightly obscene orange-tongued lanterns. The bizarre-looking **church of St-Jean-l'Évangéliste** on the downhill side of the *place* had the distinction of being the first concrete church in France (1904), its internal structure remarkably pleasing in spite of the questionable taste of the decoration.

East from the *place*, at the Chapelle des Auxiliatrices in rue Yvonne-Le-Tac, Ignatius Loyola founded the **Jesuit** movement in 1534. It is also supposed to be the place where **Saint Denis**, the first Bishop of Paris, had his head chopped off by the Romans around 250 AD. He is said to have carried it until he dropped, on the site of the cathedral of St-Denis, in what is now a traditionally Communist suburb north of the city. Just beyond the end of the street, in the beautiful little **place Dullin**, the *Théâtre de l'Atelier* is still going strong after nearly two centuries.

To continue from place des Abbesses to the top of the Butte, there is a choice of two quiet and attractive routes. You can either climb up **rue de la Vieuville** and the stairs in rue Drevet to the minuscule **place du Calvaire**, which has a lovely view back over the city, or go up **rue Tholozé**, then right below the **Moulin de la Galette** – the last survivor of Montmartre's forty-odd windmills, immortalized by Renoir – into rue des Norvins.

Artistic associations abound hereabouts. Zola, Berlioz, Turgenev, Seurat, Degas and Van Gogh lived in the area. Picasso, Braque and Juan Gris invented Cubism in an old piano factory in place Émile-Goudeau, known as the **Bateau-Lavoir**, still serving as artists' studios, though the original building burnt down some years ago. It was here that Picasso painted *Les Demoiselles d'Avignon*. And Toulouse-Lautrec's inspiration, the **Moulin Rouge**, survives also, albeit a mere shadow of its former self, on the corner of bd de Clichy and place Blanche.

Rue Lepic begins here, its winding contours recalling the lane that once served the plaster quarry wagons. A busy market occupies the lower part of the street, but once above rue des Abbesses it reverts to a mixture of tranquil and furtive elegance. Round the corner above rue Tourlaque a flight of steps and a muddy path

The Salvador Dali museum is opened at 11 rue Poulbot, adjacent to place du Calvaire; see p.278.

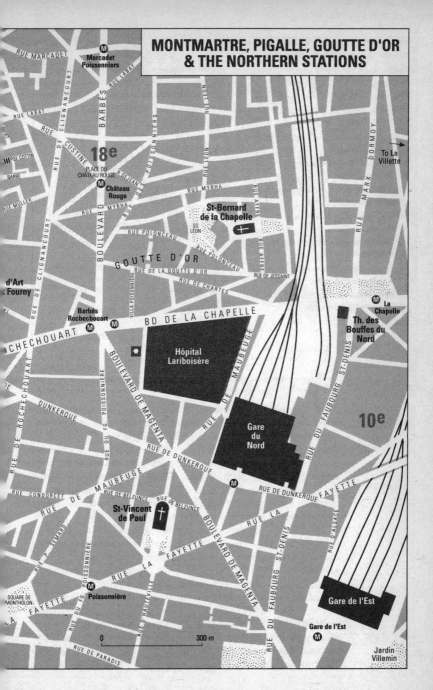

Montmartre, Pigalle, Goutte d'Or and the northern stations: Listings

Restaurants

L'Assiette, 78 rue Labat, 18ᵉ.
Mº Château-Rouge.

Baalbeck, 16 rue de Mazagran, 10ᵉ.
Mº Bonne-Nouelle.

Flo, 7 cours des Petites-Écuries, 10ᵉ.
Mº Château d'Eau.

L'Indiscreto, 10 rue Lambert, 18ᵉ.
Mº Château-Rouge.

Chez Ginette, 101 rue Caulaincourt, 18ᵉ.
Mº Lamarck-Caulaincourt.

Au Grain de Folie, 24 rue La Vieuville, 18ᵉ.
Mº Abbesses.

L'Homme Tranquille, 81 rue des Martyrs, 18ᵉ.
Mº Abbesses.

Julien, 16 rue du Faubourg St-Denis, 10ᵉ.
Mº Strasbourg–St-Denis.

Le Maquis, 69 rue Caulaincourt, 18ᵉ.
Mº Lamarck-Caulaincourt.

À Napoli, 4 rue Dancourt, 18ᵉ.
Mº Anvers/Abbesses.

À la Pomponnette, 42 rue Lepic, 18ᵉ.
Mº Blanche.

Quasne Shineen, 14 rue du Faubourg St-Denis, 10ᵉ.
Mº Strasbourg–St-Denis.

Terminus Nord, 23 rue de Dunkerque, 10ᵉ.
Mº Gare-du-Nord.

Cafés and Bars

Le Dépanneur, 27 rue Fontaine, 9ᵉ.
Mº Pigalle.

Aux Deux-Théâtres, 18 rue Blanche, 9ᵉ.
Mº Blanche.

Aux Négociants, 27 rue Lambert (corner rue Custine), 18ᵉ.
Mº Château-Rouge.

La Petite Charlotte, 24 rue des Abbesses, 18ᵉ.
Mº Abbesses.

Le Pigalle, place Pigalle, 18ᵉ.
Mº Pigalle.

Le Refuge, corner rue Lamarck & rue de la Fontaine-du-But, 18ᵉ.
Mº Lamarck-Caulaincourt.

These establishments are reviewed in Chapter 13, Eating and Drinking, *beginning on p.255.*

sneak between gardens to **av Junot**, where the still delectable actress, Anouk Aimée, has her home. To the left is the secluded and exclusive cul-de-sac **Villa Léandre**. To the right, the Cubist house of Dadaist poet Tristan Tzara stands on the corner of another exclusive enclave of houses and gardens, the **Hameau des Artistes**, while higher up the street, with the best view of the Moulin de la Galette, the **square Suzanne-Buisson** provides a gentle haven for young and old alike, with a sunken *boules* pitch overlooked by a statue of Saint Denis clutching his head to his breast.

Further on, **rue des Saules** tips steeply down the north side of the Butte past the terraces of tiny **Montmartre vineyard**, harvesting about 1500kg of grapes at the beginning of October, which, in turn, makes about 1500 bottles of wine. To the right **rue Cortot** cuts through to the water tower, whose distinctive form, together with that of the Sacré-Cœur, is one of the landmarks of the city's skyline.

At 12 rue Cortot, a pretty old house with a grassy courtyard and magnificent view from the back over the vineyard and the northern reaches of the city, was occupied at different times by Renoir, Dufy, Suzanne Valadon and her mad son, Utrillo. It is now the **Musée de Montmartre** (Tues–Sun 11am–6pm; 25F/15F), whose disappointing exhibits (nearly all the works by major artists are reproductions) attempt to recreate the atmosphere of Montmartre's pioneering heyday. It does, however, have interesting temporary exhibitions.

Next to the vineyard on **rue St-Vincent** is a patch of totally over-grown ground, which looks like a vacant lot awaiting the builders. It is, in fact, the **garden of the museum**, officially left wild since 1985, to allow a space for the natural development of Paris' native flora and fauna (April–Oct Mon 4–6pm, except during school and public hols, and Sat 2–6pm; free; further information from Paris Espace Nature, ☎43.28.47.63). Berlioz lived just beyond it with his English wife, in the corner house on the steps of rue du Mont-Cenis, whence there is a magnificent view northwards along the canyon of the steps, as well as back up towards place du Calvaire. The steps are perfect sepia-romantic Montmartre: a double handrail runs down the centre, with the lampposts between. The streets below are among the quietest and least touristy in Montmartre.

Place du Tertre to Sacré-Cœur

The heart of Montmartre, the **place du Tertre**, photogenic but totally bogus, is jammed with tourists, overpriced restaurants and "artists" doing quick portraits while you wait. Its trees, until recently under threat of destruction for safety reasons by overzealous offi-cialdom, have been saved by the well-orchestrated protests of its influential residents.

Between place du Tertre and the Sacré-Cœur, the **church of St-Pierre** – the oldest in Paris, along with St-Germain-des-Prés – is all that remains of a Benedictine convent which occupied the Butte Montmartre from the twelfth century on. Though much altered, it still retains its Romanesque and early Gothic feel. In it are four ancient columns, two by the door and two in the choir, leftovers from the Roman shrine that stood on the hill. It also still has its cemetery, which dates from Merovingian times.

As for its neighbour, the **Sacré-Cœur**, graceless and vulgar pastiche though it is, its white pimply domes are an essential part of the Paris skyline. Construction was started in the 1870s on the initiative of the Catholic Church to atone for the "crimes" of the Commune. The thwarted opposition, which included Clemenceau, eventually got its revenge by naming the space at the foot of the monumental staircase **square Willette**, after the local artist who turned out on inauguration day to shout, "Long live the devil!".

The best thing about the Sacré-Cœur is the **view from the top** (summer 9am–7pm; winter closes 6pm). It costs 15F, is almost as high as the Eiffel Tower, and you can see the layout of the whole city, how it lies in a wide, flat basin ringed by low hills, with the high-rise blocks in the southeastern corner, on the heights of Belleville, La Défense in the west, and the tall flat faces of the subur-ban workers' barracks like slabs of tombstone in the hazy beyond.

To the south and east of the Sacré-Cœur, the slopes of the Butte drop much more steeply down towards bd Barbès and the Goutte d'Or (see below). Directly below are the gardens of square Willette, milling with tourists. If you want to avoid the crowds, there's the stepped rue Utrillo and rue Paul Albert, which joins rue Ronsard along the edge of the gardens. The circular **Halles St-Pierre** on rue Ronsard (Tues–Sat 10am–10pm, Sun & Mon 10am–6pm; museums 22F/16F each or 35F/ 28F for both) hosts changing exhibitions in a *musée en herbe* for children and in the **Musée d'Art Naïf Max Fourny**, with works from all over the world. There's also an auditorium with film, theatre, music and dance, a bookshop and a cheap cafeteria with the day's

---

The Paris Commune

On March 18, 1871, in the **place du Tertre**, Montmartre's most illustrious mayor and future prime minister of France, **Georges Clemenceau**, flapped about trying to prevent the bloodshed that gave birth to the Paris Commune and the ensuing civil war with the national government.

On that day, Adolphe Thiers' government dispatched a body of troops under General Lecomte to take possession of 170 guns, which had been assembled at Montmartre by the National Guard in order to prevent them falling into German hands. Although the troops seized the guns easily in the dark before dawn, they had forgotten to bring any horses to tow them away. That gave Louise Michel, the great woman revolutionary, time to raise the alarm.

A large and angry crowd gathered, fearing another restoration of empire or monarchy such as had happened after the 1848 revolution. They persuaded the troops to take no action and arrested General Lecomte, along with another general, Clément Thomas, who was in bad odour with the people because of his part in the brutal repression of the 1848 republican uprising.

The two generals were shot and mutilated in the garden of **no. 36 rue du Chevalier-de-la-Barre** behind the Sacré-Cœur. By the following morning, the government had decamped in fear to Versailles, leaving the Hôtel de Ville and the whole of the city in the hands of the National Guard, who then proclaimed the Commune.

Divided among themselves and isolated from the rest of France, the *Communards* only finally succumbed to government assault after a week's bloody street-fighting between May 21 and 28. No one knows how many of them died; certainly no fewer than 20,000, with another 10,000 executed or deported. By way of government revenge, Eugène Varlin, one of the founder members of the First International and a leading light in the Commune, was shot on the self-same spot where the two generals had been killed just a few weeks before.

It was a working-class revolt, as the particulars of those involved clearly demonstrate, but it hardly had time to be as socialist as subsequent mythologizing would have it. The terrible cost of repression had long-term effects on the French working-class movement, both in terms of numbers lost and psychologically. For, after it, not to be revolutionary could only appear a betrayal of the dead.

For more details of the German siege of Paris and on the Commune, see p.393.

papers to read. It's a great place, totally ignored by the tourists being disgorged from their coaches only yards away.

Outside, in **rue Ronsard**, masked by overhanging greenery, are the now-sealed entrances to the quarries where plaster of Paris was extracted, and which were used as shelters and refuges by the revolutionaries of 1848.

The Montmartre cemetery

West of the Butte, near the beginning of rue Caulaincourt in place Clichy, lies the **Montmartre cemetery** (Mon–Fri 8am–5.30pm, Sat 8am–8.30pm, Sun 8am–9pm). Tucked down below street level in the hollow of an old quarry, it is a tangle of trees and funerary pomposity, more intimate and less melancholy than Père-Lachaise or Montparnasse.

The illustrious dead include Zola, Stendhal, Berlioz, Degas, Feydeau, Offenbach, Dalida and François Truffaut. There is also a large Jewish section by the east wall. The entrance is on av Rachel under rue Caulaincourt, next to an antique cast-iron poor-box – *Tronc pour les Pauvres*.

Next to the cemetery, with its entrance on rue Carpeaux, the **Hôpital Bretonneau** – a curious assembly of brick and iron-frame pavilions condemned to demolition due to subsidence – has been given a temporary reprieve by being loaned to an organization called *Usines Ephémères*, whose *raison d'être* is to recuperate old buildings for use as studios and performance spaces by young artists and musicians, both French and foreign. Its original lease has been extended, so there will continue to be free shows and exhibitions.

The cemeteries of Père-Lachaise and Montparnasse are detailed on pp.180 and 131.

Batignolles and the eastern 17e

East of Montmartre cemetery, in a district bounded by the St-Lazare train lines, marshalling yards, and av de Clichy, is the "village" of Batignolles. Its heart is rue des Batignolles and it is sufficiently conscious of its uniqueness to have formed an association for the preservation of its *caractère villageois*. The poet Verlaine was brought up here, and Stéphane Mallarmé lived on bd des Batignolles. At the northern end of the street, the attractive semicircular **place Félix-Lobligeois** frames the colonnaded church of **Ste-Marie-des-Batignolles**, its entrance modelled on the Madeleine; behind the church the tired and trampled greenery of **square Batignolles** stretches back to the big rail marshalling yards. On the corner of the *place*, the modern *L'Endroit* bar attracts the bourgeois kids of the neighbourhood until 2am.

From rue des Batignolles, rue Legendre and rue des Dames lead southeast across the train lines to **rue de Lévis** and one of the city's

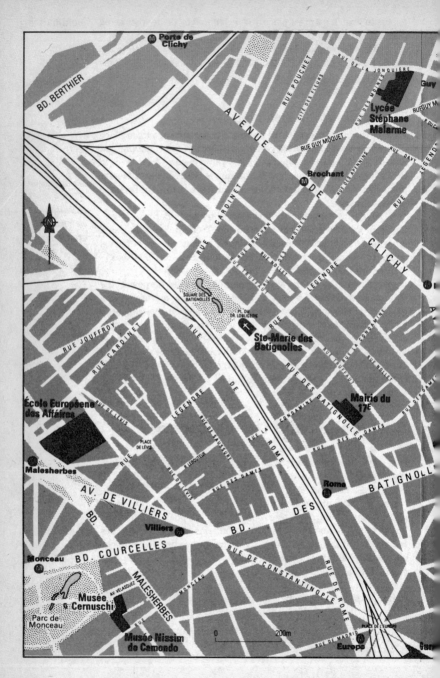

BATIGNOLLES

most flamboyant and appetizing food and clothes markets, held every day except Monday.

To the northeast, the long **rue des Moines** leads towards Guy-Môquet, with a covered market on the corner of rue Lemercier. This is the working-class Paris of the movies: all small, animated, friendly shops, four- to five-storey houses in shades of peeling grey, and brown-stained bars, where men drink standing at the "zinc".

Across avenue de Clichy, round **rue de La Jonquière**, the quiet streets are redolent of petit bourgeois North African respectability, interspersed with decidedly upper-crust enclaves. The latter are typified by the film-set perfection of the **Cité des Fleurs**, a residential lane of magnificent private houses and gardens that would not look out of place in London's Chelsea.

From Guy-Môquet, it's a short walk to rue Lamarck, which will take you up to Montmartre, or back along avenue de St-Ouen to rue du Capitaine-Madon, leading through to the wall of the Montmartre cemetery. In the heart of this cobbled alley, with washing strung at the windows, the ancient *Hôtel Beau-Lieu* still survives. Ramshackle and peeling, on a tiny courtyard full of plants, it epitomizes the kind-hearted, instinctively arty, sepia Paris that every romantic visitor secretly cherishes. Most of the guests have been there years.

The Batignolles and dog cemeteries

Right at the frontier of the 17ᵉ and Clichy, under the *périphérique*, lies the little-visited **Cimetière des Batignolles**, with the graves of André Breton, Verlaine and Blaise Cendrars (Mᵒ Porte-de-Clichy).

A great deal curiouser, and more lugubrious, is the **dog cemetery** on the banks of the Seine at Asnières (the first "s" is not pronounced). It is accessible on the same métro line, about fifteen minutes' walk from Mᵒ Mairie-de-Clichy along boulevard Jaurès, then left at the far end of Pont de Clichy.

Privately owned, the **Cimetière des Chiens** (mid-March to mid-Oct 10am–noon & 3–7pm; mid-Oct to mid-March 10am–noon & 2–5pm; closed Tues & hols) occupies a tree-shaded ridgelet that was once an island in the river. It is full of tiny graves decked with plastic flowers. Most of them, going back to 1900, belong to dogs and cats, many with epigraphs of the kind: "To Fifi, the only consolation of my wretched existence". There is a surprising preponderance of Anglo-Saxon names – *Boy*, *Pussy*, *Dick*, *Jack*: a tribute perhaps to the peculiarly English sentimentality about animals. Among the more exotic cadavers are a Muscovite bear, a wolf, a lioness, the 1920 Grand National winner, and the French *Rintintin*, vintage 1933.

The flea market of St-Ouen

In spite of the "St-Ouen" in its name, it is actually the **Porte de Clignancourt** – the old gateway to the Channel – which gives access

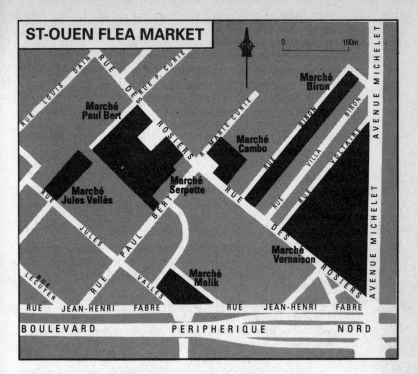

ST-OUEN FLEA MARKET

Marché Biron

Marché Paul Bert

Marché Cambo

Marché Jules Vallès

Marché Serpette

Marché Vernaison

Marché Malik

RUE LOUIS DAIN

RUE DES

RUE P. CURIE

RUE MARIE CURIE

RUE BIRON

VILLA

VOLTAIRE

AVENUE MICHELET

AVENUE MICHELET

RUE

RUE DES

RUE ROSIERS

RUE JULES

RUE PAUL BERT

VALLES

RUE LECUYER

RUE JEAN-HENRI FABRE

RUE JEAN-HENRI FABRE

BOULEVARD PERIPHERIQUE NORD

0 100m

to the market of St-Ouen, and not the Porte de St-Ouen itself. The market is located on the northern edge of the 18ᵉ *arrondissement*, now hard up against the *boulevard périphérique*.

Officially open from 7.30am to 7pm – unofficially, from 5am – the **puces de St-Ouen** claims to be the largest flea market in the world, the name "flea" deriving from the state of the second-hand mattresses, clothes and other junk sold here when the market first operated in the free-fire zone outside the city walls.

Nowadays, however, it is predominantly a proper – and very expensive – antiques market, selling mainly furniture but also such trendy "junk" as old café counters, telephones, traffic lights, posters, juke boxes and petrol pumps, with what is left of the rag-and-bone element confined to the further reaches of **rue Fabre and rue Lécuyer**.

First impressions as you arrive from the métro are that there is nothing for sale but jeans and leather jackets. There are, however, seven official markets within the complex: Marché **Biron**, selling serious and expensive antique furniture; Marché **Cambo**, next to Biron, also with expensive furniture; Marché **Vernaison** – the oldest – which has the most diverse collection of old and new furniture and knick-knacks; Marché **Paul-Bert**, offering modern furniture, china etc; Marché **Malik**, with mostly clothes, some high-class couturier stuff, and a lot of uninteresting new items; Marché **Serpette**, specializing in 1900–30; and Marché **Jules-Vallès**, which is the cheapest, most junk-like and most likely to throw up an unexpected treasure.

It can be fun to wander around, but it's foolish to expect any bargains. In some ways the streets of St-Ouen beyond the market are just as interesting for the glimpse they give of a tempo of living long vanished from the city itself. Should hunger overtake you, there is a touristy *restaurant-buvette* in the centre of Marché Vernaison, *Chez Louisette*, where the great gypsy jazz guitarist, Django Reinhardt, sometimes played. But for more dependable, as well as cheaper, eating, it's best to go to one of the brasseries on av Michelet just outside the market, or back on bd Ornano.

Pigalle

From place Clichy in the west to Barbès-Rochechouart in the east, the hill of Montmartre is underlined by the sleazy **boulevards of Clichy and Rochechouart**, the centre of the roadway often occupied by bumper-car pistes and other funfair sideshows. **At the Barbès end**, where the métro clatters by on iron trestles, the crowds teem round the *Tati* department stores, the cheapest in the city, while the pavements are thick with Arab and African street vendors offering watches, trinkets and textiles. The best place to watch is from the stairs to the Barbès métro.

At the **place Clichy** end, tour buses from all over Europe feed their contents into massive hotels. In the middle, between **place Blanche** and **place Pigalle**, sex shows, sex shops, and prostitutes, both male and female, keep alive the tawdry, tarnished image of the Naughty Nineties. You won't find the golden-hearted whores and Bohemian artists of popular tradition, but, as with any red-light district, the tourists have to be shown it, or so their tour guides think.

It is an area in which respectability and sleaze rub very close shoulders. On **place Pigalle** itself, huge anatomical blow-ups (unveiled only after dark in deference to the residents' sensibilities) assail the senses on the very corner of one of the city's most elegant private *villas*, **avenue Frochot**. In the adjacent streets – **rues Douai, Victor-Massé, Houdon** – specialist music shops (this is *the* area for instruments and sound systems) and grey house façades are interspersed with tiny ill-lit bars where "hostesses" lurk in compli-cated tackle, ready to snatch at passing prey.

South of Pigalle

The rest of the 9ᵉ *arrondissement*, which stretches south of Pigalle, is rather dull, with the exception of some blocks of streets round **place St-Georges**, where Thiers, president of the Third Republic, lived in a house which is now a library (rebuilt after being burned by the Commune). In the centre of the *place* stands a statue of the nineteenth-century cartoonist Gavarni, who made a speciality of lampooning the mistresses that were *de rigueur* for bourgeois males of the time. This was the mistresses' *quartier* – they were known as *lorettes* after the nearby church of Notre-Dame-de-Lorette.

Place Toudouze, rue Clauzel, rue Milton and **rue Rodier** are also worth a look, and **rue St-Lazare**, between the St-Lazare station and the hideous church of Ste-Trinité, is a welcome swathe of activity amid the residential calm. Close by is the bizarre and little-visited museum dedicated to the works of the Symbolist painter **Gustave Moreau** (see p.279), opposite rue de la Tour-des-Dames, where two or three gracious mansions and gardens recall the days when this was the very edge of the city.

Cabarets and sex: around Pigalle

For many foreigners, Paris is still synonymous with a use of the stage perpetuated by those mythical names the *Moulin Rouge*, *Folies Bergères* and *Lido*. These **cabarets**, which flash their presence from the Champs-Élysées to bd Montmartre, predate the film industry, though it appears as if the glittering Hollywood musicals of the 1930s are their inspiration rather than their offspring. They define an area of pornography that would have trouble titillating a prudish Anglo-Saxon, and, though the audience is mainly male, the whole event is to live sex shows what glossy fashion reviews are to "girlie" mags. Apart from seeing a lot of bare breasts, your average coached-in tourist may well feel he has not got what he paid (rather excessively) for. All the more easy prey for the pimps of Pigalle.

The *Lido*, for example, takes breaks from multicoloured plumage and illuminated distant flesh to bring on a conjuror to play tricks with the clothes and possessions of the audience. Then back come the computer-choreographed "Bluebell Girls", in a technical tour-de-force of light show, music and a moving stage transporting the thighs and breasts to more faraway exotica – the sea, a volcano, ice or Pacific island. The scale is far too spectacular to be a dirty macs' night out.

The *Moulin Rouge* is of the same ilk with its "Doriss Girls", and still trades on its Toulouse-Lautrec painted fame as the place for "the most celebrated can-can in the world". The oldest cabaret, the *Folies Bergères*, closed down in 1992, but reopened in 1993 with a new pastiche show starring a drag artist as the lead chorus "girl".

At the *Crazy Horse* the theatrical experience convinces the audience that they are watching art and the prettiest girls in Paris. In the ranks of defences for using images of female bits to promote, sell, lure and exploit, Frenchmen are particular in putting "art and beauty" in the front line. In upholding the body suspended and pouting, weak and whimpering, usually nude and always immaculate, they claim to protect the femininity, beauty and desirability of the Frenchwoman as she would wish it herself.

Moving from the glamour cabarets to the **"Life Sex"** and **"Ultra-hard Life Sex"** venues (never "Live Sex" for some reason) is to leave the world of elegant gloss and exportable Frenchness for a world of sealed-cover porn that knows no cultural borders.

The Goutte d'Or and the northern stations

Continuing east from Pigalle, bd Rochechouart becomes bd de la Chapelle, along the north side of which, between **bd Barbès** and the **Gare du Nord** railway lines, stretches the poetically named, crumbling and squalid quarter of the **Goutte d'Or**. The name – the *Drop of Gold* – derives from the vineyard that occupied this site in medieval times. Since World War I, however, when large numbers of North Africans were first imported to replenish the ranks of Frenchmen dying in the trenches, it has gradually become an immigrant ghetto.

In the late 1950s and early 1960s, during the Algerian war, few middle- class Parisians would have dreamt of entering the *quartier*, not just for its reputation for score-settling, prostitution and drugs, but because of the clandestine activity of the Algerian National Liberation Front (FLN). In fact, the new residents of the *quartier* had far better reason to fear the respectable "law-abiding" French.

Many of the buildings remain in a lamentable state of decay. While artists, writers and others have moved in, attracted by the only affordable property left in the city, a major programme of pulling down, rebuilding and cleaning up is underway. As the physical backdrop changes, so inevitably does the character of the *quartier*. Much of **rue de la Goutte d'Or** itself is new, including a lovely nursery school on the corner with rue Islettes. For the moment, however, rue de la Goutte-d'Or and its tributary lanes – especially to the north: rue Myrha, rue Léon, the Marché Dejean, rue Polonceau (with its basement mosque at no. 55), and the cobbled alley and gardens of **Villa Poissonnière** – remain distinctly North African and poor.

Washing hangs from every balcony and tiny shops sell snazzy cloth and jewellery as well as traditional *djellabas*. The windows of the *pâtissiers* are stacked with trays of equally brightly coloured cakes and pastries. Sheep's heads grin from the slabs of the halal butchers. The grocers shovel their wares from barrels and sacks,

---

The 1961 massacre

On October 17, 1961, the FLN organized a peaceful demonstration in Paris against the curfew imposed on all Arab French two weeks before. The métro Bonne-Nouvelle was one of the gathering points for the march, and it was here that a thousand unarmed women, men and children were tear-gassed, fired upon and clubbed to the ground by the police. In Neuilly, where Algerians from the suburbs had gathered, the police fired into the crowd with sub-machine guns for 45 minutes; bodies were thrown into the Seine, and sixty arrested protestors were murdered in the police headquarters on Île de la Cité. No police were ever prosecuted in this most appalling event in Paris' postwar history. There was almost complete media silence and details only became public in the 1980s, despite hundreds of eyewitnesses.

---

and the plangent sounds of Arab music echo evocatively from the record shops. In the playground of square Léon, there's authorized graffiti tagging and three brilliant murals. It's a funny place to sit, as the play areas are cordoned off with high mauve painted grills. The cafés and bars of the Goutte d'Or tend to be too small and intimate to appeal to outsiders, but you'd certainly be able to find a good mint tea.

The stations and faubourgs

On the **south side of bd de la Chapelle** lie the big northern stations, the **Gare du Nord** (serving the Channel ports and places north) and **Gare de l'Est** (serving northeastern and eastern France and eastern Europe), with the major traffic thoroughfares, bd de Magenta and bd de Strasbourg, both bustling, noisy, and not in themselves of much interest.

To the right of the Gare d'Est as you face the station, a high wall encloses the gardens of **square Villemin**, which once belonged to the Couvent des Récollets – the near wreck of building along rue du Faubourg St-Martin. The same campaign groups that saved the gardens for public use (entrance on rue des Récollets), including a 200-day occupation to stop the bulldozers, are now focusing on the convent. Various projects are in the air and local people fear the building will deteriorate beyond the point of repair. However, given their success with the gardens, they may well win this one too.

On a little street off rue du Faubourg St-Martin further down is one of the three remaining makers of brass musical instruments in France. Antoine Courtois moved to 8 rue de Nancy in 1856 – the same business had made the cavalry trumpets for Napoléon's army.

The liveliest part of the quarter is the **rue du Faubourg-St-Denis**, full, especially towards the lower end, of *charcuteries*, butchers, greengrocers and foreign delicatessens, as well as a number of restaurants, including the *Brasserie Julien* and *Brasserie Flo*, the latter in an old-world stableyard, the cour des Petites-Écuries. Spanning the end of the street is the **Porte St-Denis**, a triumphal arch built in 1672 on the Roman model to celebrate the victories of Louis XIV. Feeling secure behind Vauban's extensive frontier fortifications, Louis demolished Charles V's city walls and created a swathe of leafy promenades, where the Grands Boulevards now run. In place of the city gates he planned a series of triumphal arches, of which this and the neighbouring **Porte St-Martin**, at the end of rue du Faubourg-St-Martin, were the first.

The Brasserie Julien *and the* Brasserie Flo *are reviewd on p.257.*

The whole area between the two *faubourgs* through to the provincial **rue du Faubourg-Poissonnière** is honeycombed with passages and courtyards. China and glass enthusiasts should take a walk along **rue de Paradis**, whose shops specialize in such wares, with the *Baccarat* firm's **Musée du Cristal** at no. 30 (see p.279), tucked away behind the classical façade of Louis XV's *cristallerie*.

Close by at no. 18, the magnificent mosaic and tiled façade of
Monsieur Boulanger's Choisy-le-Roi tileworks shop is now the
entrance to an art gallery, *Le Monde d'Art* (Tues–Sat 1–7.30pm,
Mon 2–7pm). You can go inside and admire more exuberant ceramics featuring peacock tails and flamingoes on the stairs and floors.

Across bd Bonne-Nouvelle are the *passages* of place du Caine
and rue St-Denis leading down to Les Halles (see Chapter 4).

Chapter 10

Eastern Paris

P aris east of the Canal St-Martin has always been a working class area, from the establishment of the Faubourg St-Antoine as the workshop of the city in the fifteenth century, to the colonization of the old villages of Belleville, Ménilmontant, and Charonne by the French rural poor in the mid-nineteenth century. These were the populations that supplied the manpower for the great rebellions of the last century: the insurrections of 1830, 1832, 1848, and 1851, and the short-lived **Commune** of 1871, which divided the city in two, with the centre and west battling to preserve the status quo against the oppressed and radical east. Even in the 1789 Revolution, when Belleville, Ménilmontant and Charonne were still just villages, the most progressive demands came from the artisans of the Faubourg-St-Antoine.

Until quite recently, in the demonology of bourgeois Parisians, there was nothing more to be feared than the *"descente de Belleville"*: the descent from the heights of Belleville of the revolutionary mob, with imagined knives clenched between their teeth. It was in order to contain this threat that so much of the Canal St-Martin, a natural line of defence, was covered over by **Baron Haussmann** in 1860.

Today, precious little stands in remembrance of these events. The *Mur des Fédérés* in Père-Lachaise cemetery records the death of 147 *Communards*; the Bastille column and its inscription commemorate 1830 and 1848; a few streets bear the names of the people's leaders. But nothing you now see in the 11e, for instance, suggests its history as the most fought-over *arrondissement* in the city.

Indeed, the physical backdrop itself is also slowly disappearing. Narrow streets and artisans' houses still survive in **Belleville**, **Ménilmontant**, and off the **Canal St-Martin**, but many of the crumbling, dank, damp and insanitary houses have now been demolished. Earlier rebuilding produced shelving-unit apartment blocks, but in recent years the new constructions have shown far more imagination and sensitivity.

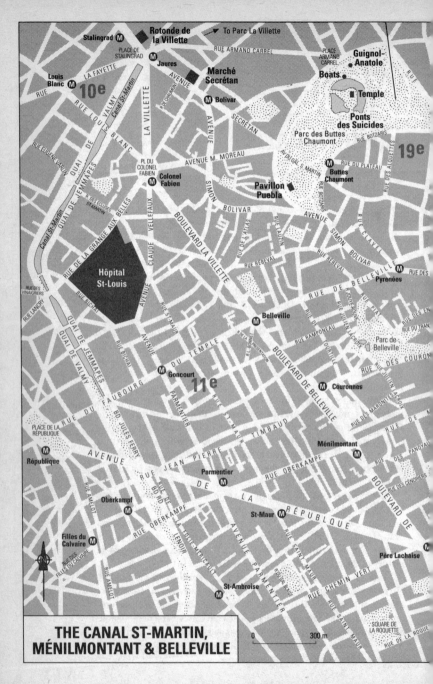

THE CANAL ST-MARTIN,
MÉNILMONTANT & BELLEVILLE

Canal St-Martin, Belleville and Ménilmontant: Listings

Restaurants

Anjou-Normandie, 13 rue de la Folie-Méricault, 11e.
Mº St-Ambroise.

Astier, 44 rue Jean-Pierre Timbaud, 11e.
Mº Parmentier.

Chez Jean, 38 rue Boyer (near corner with rue de Ménilmontant), 20e.
Mº Gambetta/Ménilmontant.

Chez Justine, 96 rue Oberkampf, 11e.
Mº St-Maur/Ménilmontant.

À la Courtille, 1 rue des Envierges, 20e.
Mº Pyrénées.

Égée, 19 rue de Ménilmontant, 20e.
Mº Ménilmontant.

L'Europe Centrale, 6 rue de la Présentation (corner Louis-Bonnet), 11e.
Mº Belleville.

La Fontaine aux Roses, 27 av Gambetta, 20e.
Mº Père-Lachaise.

Au Gigot Fin, 56 rue de Lancry (close to the canal), 10e.

Louis Valy, 49 rue Orfila, 20e.
Mº Gambetta/Pelleport.

L'Occitanie, 96 rue Oberkampf, 11e.
Mº St-Maur/Ménilmontant.

Le Pacifique, 35 rue de Belleville, 20e.
Mº Belleville.

Au Pavillon Puebla, Parc des Buttes-Chaumont, 19e.
Mº Buttes-Chaumont.

Pho-Dong-Huong, 14 rue Louis-Bonnet, 11e.
Mº Belleville.

Le Polonia, 3 rue Chaumont, 19e.
Mº Jaurès.

Le Président, 19 rue Louis-Bonnet, 11e.
Mº Belleville.

Aux Rendez-Vous des Amis, 10 av Père-Lachaise, 20e.
Mº Gambetta.

"Cafés and Bars" for Canal St-Martin, Belleville and Ménilmontant are listed over the page.

These establishments are reviewed in Chapter 13,
Eating and Drinking, *beginning on p.257.*

Restaurant de Bourgogne, 26 rue des
Vinaigriers, 10ᵉ.
Mᵒ Jacques-Bonsergent.

Le Royal Belleville, 19 rue Louis-Bonnet,
11ᵉ.
Mᵒ Belleville.

Aux Tables de la Fontaine, 33 rue Jean-
Pierre-Timbaud, 11ᵉ.
Mᵒ Parmentier.

Taï Yen, 5 rue de Belleville, 20ᵉ.
Mᵒ Belleville.

Taverna Restaurant, 50 rue Piat, 20ᵉ.
Mᵒ Pyrénées.

Au Trou Normand, 9 rue Jean-Pierre
Timbaud, 11ᵉ.
Mᵒ Filles-du-Calvaire/Oberkampf/
République.

Au Val de Loire, 149 rue Amelot, 11ᵉ.
Mᵒ République.

Cafés and Bars

Le Baratin, 3 rue Jouye-Rouve, 20ᵉ.
Mᵒ Pyrénées.

Cithea, 114 rue Oberkampf, 11ᵉ.
Mᵒ Ménilmontant.

Le Clown Bar, 114 rue Amelot, 11ᵉ.
Mᵒ Filles-du-Calvaire.

La Divette de Valmy, 71 quai de Valmy,
10ᵉ.
Mᵒ Jacques-Bonsergent.

Les Envierges, 11 rue des Envierges, 20ᵉ.
Mᵒ Pyrénées.

L'Opus, 167 quai de Valmy, 10ᵉ.
Mᵒ Château-Landon.

La Patache, 60 rue de Lancry, 10ᵉ.
Mᵒ Jacques-Bonsergent.

Le Vieux Belleville, 12 rue des Envierges,
20ᵉ.
Mᵒ Pyrénées.

Though some of the new is public housing, redevelopments
have inevitably shifted old populations out and encouraged new arty
and media intelligentsia in. The old character of these most Parisian
areas of the city is gradually being effaced. It doesn't happen overnight, however, and they continue to provide some of the most
fascinating urban landscapes in the city. **Belleville** remains the most
extraordinary mix of races and cultures. **Rue du Faubourg-St-
Antoine** is still full of cabinet-makers and joiners.

Only La Villette up in the city's northeast corner in the 19ᵉ and
Bercy along the Seine in the 12ᵉ have been totally transformed.

Place de la République and the Canal St-Martin

Abutting three *arrondissements* – the 3ᵉ, 10ᵉ and the 11ᵉ – the
grimly barren **place de la République** is one of the largest roundabouts in Paris. It was designed as a pivotal point in Haussmann's
counter-insurgency road scheme. An army barracks dominated the
north side, and still does. From it seven major streets radiate, cutting
through the then-inflammable neighbourhoods of working-class
Paris to make this the most blatant example of Napoléon III's political town planning. In order to build it, Haussmann destroyed a
number of popular theatres, including the *Funambules* of *Les
Enfants du Paradis* fame, and Daguerre's unique diorama.

The motivation for covering over the Canal St-Martin from Bastille to rue du Faubourg-du-Temple with the bd Richard-Lenoir was similar. Completed in 1825, the canal was built as a short-cut for the river traffic to lop off the great western loop of the Seine around Paris. Spanned by six swing-bridges, which could easily be jammed open, it formed a splendid natural defence for the rebellious quarters of eastern Paris in times of trouble.

The streets to either side of bd Richard-Lenoir have a fine selection of eating places and make for pleasant wandering. Some possibilities to incorporate into a walk are the iced cake looks of the **Cirque d'Hiver** (the circus) just by Filles du Calvaire métro; a multilayered mural of literature on rue Nicolas-Appert (east of the boulevard between M° Richard-Lenoir and M° Bréguet-Sabins); or the gilt and mirrored *boulangerie* selling Viennese, French and English bread on the corner of rues Chemin-Vert and Popincourt (M° St-Ambroise).

Canal St-Martin

The **southern stretch** of the revealed canal is the most attractive. Plane trees line the cobbled *quais*, and elegant high-arched footbridges punctuate the spaces between the locks, where you can still watch the occasional barge slowly rising or sinking to the next level. The canalside houses are solid bourgeois-looking residences of the mid-nineteenth century. Although small back-street workshops and businesses still exist, gentrification and modernization are well advanced. The idea of canal frontage has clearly put a light in the developers' eyes, although you can at least be thankful it has not been turned into the motorway envisaged by President Pompidou.

Ancient corners do continue to exist. Down the steps to **rue des Vinaigriers**, the shoemakers' union has its headquarters, *Fédération Nationale des Artisans de la Chaussure*, behind a Second Empire shop front, with fluted wooden pilasters crowned with capitals of grapes and a gilded Bacchus. Across the street, the

---

The Montfaucon gallows

Long ago, rue de la Grange-aux-Belles was a dusty track leading uphill, past fields, on the way to Germany. Where no. 53 now stands, a path led to the top of a small hillock. Here, in 1325, on the king's orders, an enormous gallows was built, consisting of a plinth 6m high, on which stood sixteen stone pillars 10m high. These were joined by chains, and from the chains malefactors were hanged in clusters. They were left there until they disintegrated, by way of an example, and they stank so badly that when the wind blew from the northeast, they infected the nostrils of the far-off city.

This practice continued until the seventeenth century. Bones and other remains from the pit into which they were thrown were found during the building of a garage in 1954.

surely geriatric *Cercle National des Garibaldiens* still has a meeting place, and at no. 35 *Poursin* has been making brass buckles since 1830.

On the other side of the canal, in the rustic-sounding **rue de la Grange-aux-Belles**, the *Le Pont-Tournant* (the Swing-Bridge) café name evokes the canal's more vigorous youth. Traditionally, the bargees came from the north, whence the name of the **Hôtel du Nord** at 102 quai de Jemappes, made famous by Marcel Carné's film starring Arletty and Jean Gabin. For a long time there was talk of transforming it into a movie museum, but now, with its façade restored, it has been incorporated into a block of modern apartments.

Local residents are very active in defence of their neighbourhood – the **square Villemin** gardens abutting the canal just above rue des Récollets (see p.163) being one successful instance. The magazine *La Gazette du Canal*, on sale locally, publicizes local campaigns and gives good addresses of cafés, restaurants and events in the area.

Just behind the square is one of the finest and least visited buildings in Paris, the early seventeenth-century **Hôpital St-Louis**, built in the same style as the **place des Vosges** (see p.94). Although it still functions as a hospital, you can walk through into its quiet central courtyard to admire the elegant brick and stone façades and steep-pitched roofs.

At the back of the hospital, on rue Juliette-Dodu, an unprepossessing building houses one of the key centres in world research into human genetics. The **Centre des Études du Polymorphism Humain** was financed by the art business of its founder's wife and studies DNA from 40 families – French, Venezuelan, Amish and Mormon.

Place de Stalingrad and Bassin de la Villette

Along the northern section of the canal to La Villette, both banks have now been thoroughly sanitized. The one major improvement has been the restoration of the **place de Stalingrad**, which has been sanded and grassed.

The stone work of the **Rotonde de la Villette** here – which was one of the toll houses designed by the architect, Ledoux, as part of Louis XVI's scheme to tax all goods entering the city – has been recently scrubbed clean. Then, every road out of the city had a customs post or *barrière* linked by a 6-metre high wall, known as *Le Mur des Fermiers-Généraux* – a major irritant in the run-up to the 1789 Revolution. It is a clean-cut, Roman-inspired building with a Doric portico and pediments surmounted by a rotunda.

One of the side effects of the general clean-up has been to enhance the elegant aerial stretch of métro, supported on Neoclassical iron and stone pillars, which backs the toll house. Looking back from further up the Bassin de la Villette, it provides a focus for an impressive new monumental vista.

> **Place du Colonel-Fabien**
>
> Colonel Fabien, who gave his name to the *place* where the French
> Communist Party has its HQ, was the *nom de guerre* of Pierre Georges.
> He committed the first official act of Communist armed resistance against
> the Nazis on August 21, 1941, by shooting a German sailor on the plat-
> form of the Barbès-Rochechouart métro station. This was in reprisal for
> the execution of Samuel Tyszelmann, a Jewish Polish Resistance worker
> who had carried out the first recorded act of sabotage by stealing some
> dynamite a few days previously.

Recobbled, and with its dockside buildings converted into
offices for **canal boat trips** (see p.287), the Bassin has lost all
vestiges of its former status as France's premier port. The old port-
side restaurant *Au Rendez-vous de la Marine* is still going,
however, and on Sundays and holidays people stroll along by the
quais, play *boules*, fish or canoe and row in the dock. At rue de
Crimée, a **hydraulic bridge** (1885) marks the end of the dock and
the beginning of the **Canal de l'Ourcq**. To the east, the burrowing
slums of the rue de Flandres are coming down, and it's all a bit of a
wasteland from here up to the junction of canals, where a rearing
megachain hotel, as ugly as they come, faces the architectural
cacophony across the water of Paris' most extravagant high-tech
park, the Parc de la Villette.

La Villette

All the meat for Paris used to come from **La Villette**. Slaughtering
and butchering, and industries for the abattoirs' and meat markets'
by-products, provided plenty of jobs for the dense population of the
area. After work, people would amuse themselves by betting on
cockfights, skating or swimming, and eating in the area's numerous
restaurants famed for their fresh meat.

New refrigeration techniques making a centralized meat industry redundant emerged just as vast sums of money had been spent
modernizing La Villette in the 1960s. A new abattoir of gigantic
proportions was almost complete. The only solution was to switch
course completely and go on pouring billions into La Villette, to
create a music, art and science complex that would stun the world
with Parisian brilliance. President Giscard d'Estaing started the
project, and Mitterrand's successor will probably preside over whatever the finishing touches end up being.

When the **Parc de la Villette** first opened in 1985, it was
extraordinary and brilliant. The abandoned abattoir had become
the **Cité des Sciences et de l'Industrie**. In front of it balanced the
Géode, a bubble of reflecting steel dropped from an intergalactic
game of *boules* into this strange wilderness in which the only other
new building was the inflatable **Zénith** rock music stadium sited by
a sculpted, bright-red aeroplane descending on a concrete column.

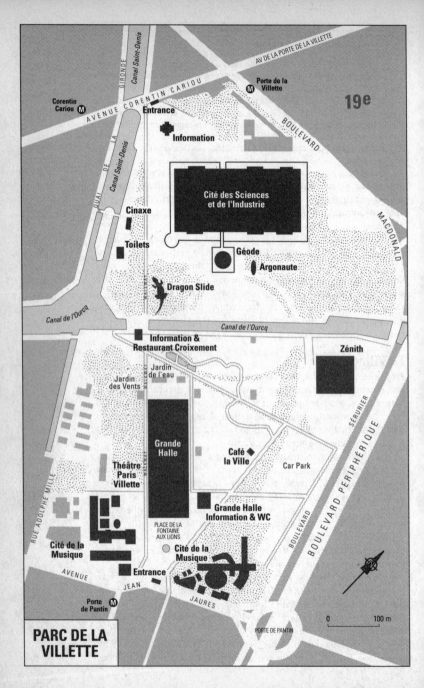

PARC DE LA
VILLETTE

> **Parc de la Villette: Listings**
>
> Cafés and Bars
>
> Café de la Ville, Parc de la Villette, between the Grande Salle and the Zenith, 19ᵉ. Mᵒ Porte-de-Pantin/Corentin-Cariou.
>
> *This establishment is reviewed in Chapter 13,* Eating and Drinking, *beginning on p.258.*

To the south was one of the nineteenth-century iron-framed market halls, the **Grand Salle** (to be used for art festivals and trade and fashion shows), flanked at its southern end by two smaller contemporaries, the Pavillon Janvier and the Théâtre Paris Villette. Finally there was a dragon slide, assembled out of recycled cable drums and pipes. The idea that all this would soon be surrounded by enormous gardens was too good to be true.

The theatre is now hidden behind the **Cité de la Musique**, designed by the ever-prevalent Christian de Portzamparc, and spread across two blocks on av Jean-Jaurès. The one to the right (as you look from the avenue), scheduled to open very shortly, will have the main concert hall, the Musée de la Musique, and commercial outlets for everything to do with music-making. Its separate buildings form a satisfying cake-slice wedge pointing down to the Porte de Pantin entrance of the park.

The **Conservatoire National Supérieur de Musique** (the national music academy), on the left, intentionally bears no relation or symmetry to its twin. It combines waves and funnels, irregular polygons and nonparallel lines, gangways, greenhouses and aggressively slit windows. Mr Portzamparc is proud of the confusion of its corridors and passageways: "You search, you discover", he says – and presumably you miss your lesson. The curving roof, he says, is like a Gregorian chant. What is impressive, when you think about it, is that contemporary engineering and technology can keep such buildings standing up.

A 900-metre walkway shelter runs in a straight line from the side of the Conservatoire, past the Grande Salle, through the complicated metal bridge over the canal de l'Ourcq, past the dragon slide, now messed up with steel tube supports, and on between the Cité des Sciences and the Cinaxe simulation cinema, all the way to the av Corenlin-Cariou entrance.

On the **south side of the canal**, bizarrely landscaped gardens feature giant bits of a bicycle as if half buried in the ground. Thirty bright red cubic follies by Bernard Tschumi – the man mainly responsible for the park's design – punctuate the park (providing space for cafés, crèches, expos, first aid and information centres).

One of the oddest things about this enormous park is that it feels so cramped. The various thematic gardens are all small; the tree-lined paths don't go very far. There is not much greenery here at all.

A play area just east of the Grande Salle for little kiddies, Le Jardin des Vents, could have been three times the size and it would still be full.

Bernard Tschumi's concept of a futuristic park expressly dispensed with the eighteenth- and nineteenth-century idea of relaxation, and was to be for "activity". What, in fact, is going on here (and in the Cité de la Musique) is a landscaping and architectural expression of deconstructivism. This, more or less, is the idea that the only way to approach artistic creation is to back off from the old-fashioned idea of unity, meaning and purpose, to "deconstruct" the work into its disparate elements, thereby opening up all possible interpretations.

So – as one "activity" – you could walk around speculating on different meanings: is this the collapse of the environment?; the death of the collective?; the displacement of the individual and the end of revolution?; the overcrowding of the globe? Alternatively, you can just keep walking around feeling more and more exhausted and confused.

Full details of the science museum, Géode, Cinaxe, Argonaute submarine and Zénith are on p.271 and p.301.

Cité des Sciences et de l'Industrie

In contrast, the Cité des Sciences is a classically modern rectangular box – the form of the concrete hulk of the abandoned abattoir that provides its structure. Equally Modernist are the giant walls of glass hanging beneath a dark blue lattice of steel. White walkways accelerate out of the building towards the Géode across a moat level with the underground floors. It would be fortress-like were it not for its transparency and the fact that its vast volume – nearly four times the size of Beaubourg – is sunk into a pit. But it would still be too cold,

---

Notable buildings in the 19e *arrondissement*

The area around Parc de la Villette has had more development than any other area of the city, almost all of it on a large scale. A few highlights are:
• **Agence pour la Propriété** (City Cleaning Department), 17 rue Raymond-Radiguet. M° Crimée.
Renzo Piano, 1988. A long glass façade decorated with curved metal grids reveals the activities within.
• **Métropole 19**, 138–140 rue d'Aubervilliers. M° Crimée.
Jodry and Viguier, 1988. An industrial building housing small eco-friendly businesses; again lots of glass and galvanized steel with rounded towers for the lifts. The best view is through the service road.
• **145 rue de l'Ourcq**. M° Crimée/Coventin-Cariou.
Maison-Haute and Levy, 1980. A warehouse converted into flats with a beautiful shared space of plant-filled balconies and walkways. You may have to ring to get in.
• **School**, corner of rues Cambrai and de l'Ourcq. M° Crimée.
Mitrofanoff, 1986. An opening in the gleaming white façade reveals a multi-coloured mosaiced column in a typical 1980s interior-exterior formation.

complicated and threatening in its dimensions to approach were it not for the reflecting Géode drawing you towards it.

Access to La Villette

The Parc de la Villette is accessible from Mᵒ Porte-de-la-Villette on av Corentin-Cariou to the north, from the canal de l'Ourcq's quai de la Marine to the west (see p.171) or from Mᵒ Porte-de-Pantin on av Jean-Jaurès to the south. There are information centres by the northern entrance and by the canal bridge.

Belleville, Ménilmontant and Charonne

The old villages of **Belleville**, **Ménilmontant**, and **Charonne**, only incorporated into the city in 1860, are strung out along the western slopes of a ridge that rises steadily from the Seine at Bercy to an altitude of 128m near Belleville's Place des Fêtes, the highest point in Paris after Montmartre. The quickest and easiest way to see them is to take a trip on the **#26 bus** from the Gare du Nord, getting on and off at strategic points all along the **avenue de Simon-Bolivar and rue des Pyrénées**, which between them run the whole length of the ridge to Porte de Vincennes.

At the northern end of the Belleville heights, a shortish walk from La Villette, is the **parc des Buttes-Chaumont** (Mᵒ Buttes-Chaumont/ Botzaris; bus #26, stop Botzaris/Buttes-Chaumont). It was constructed under the guidance of Haussmann in the 1860s to camouflage what until then had been a desolate warren of disused quarries, rubbish dumps and miserable shacks. The sculpted, beak-shaped park stays open all night and, equally rarely for Paris, you're not cautioned off the grass.

At its centre, a huge rock upholds a delicate Corinthian temple. You can cross the lake that surrounds it, via a suspension bridge, or take the shorter *Pont des Suicides*. This, according to Louis Aragon, the literary grand old man of the French Communist Party,

> . . . *before metal grills were erected along its sides, claimed victims even from passers-by who had had no intention whatsoever of killing themselves but were suddenly tempted by the abyss . . . . And just see how docile people turn out to be: no one any longer jumps off this easily negotiable parapet.*
>
> Le Paysan de Paris

Perhaps the attraction for suicides and roving Commie writers is the unlikeliness of this park, with its views of the Sacré-Cœur and beyond, its grotto of stalactites, and the fences of concrete moulded

Claude Chappe and the rue du Télégraphe

The **rue du Télégraphe** is named in memory of Claude Chappe's invention of the optical telegraph. Chappe first tested his device here in September 1792, in a corner of the Belleville cemetery. When word of his activities got out, he was nearly lynched by a mob that assumed he was trying to signal to the king, who was at that time imprisoned in the Temple (see p.98). Eventually two lines were set up, from Belleville to Strasbourg and the east, and from Montmartre to Lille and the north. By 1840 it was possible to send a message to Calais in three minutes, via 27 relays, and to Strasbourg in seven minutes, using 46 relays.

to imitate wood – for that matter, its very existence, in this corner of a city so badly deprived of green space. There are enticements, too, for kids and other lovers of life (see p.298).

Belleville

East of the parc des Buttes-Chaumont between rue de Crimée and place Rhin et Danube, dozens of cobbled and gardened *villas* lead off from rue Miguel Hidalgo, rue du Général Brunet, rue de la Liberté, rue de l'Égalité and rue de Mouzaïa. It is so light and airy here, you wonder why places like Arteuil and Passy should ever have seemed so much more desirable. Heading south, the first main street you meet is the **rue de Belleville**. Close to its highest point is the **place des Fêtes**, still with a market, though no longer festive. Once the village green, it is now totally unrecognizable under concrete tower blocks and shopping parades, a terrible monument to the unimaginative redevelopment of the 1960s and 1970s. But things improve as you descend the steepening gradient towards rue des Pyrénées. Round the church of St-Jean de Belleville, among the *boulangeries* and *charcuteries*, you could be in the busy main street of any French provincial town.

Below rue des Pyrénées, bits of old Belleville remain – very, very dilapidated – alongside the new. On the wall of no. 72 a plaque

La descente de la Courtille

The name "*Courtille*" comes from *courti*, a Picard dialect word for "garden". The heights of Belleville were known as *La Haute Courtille* in the nineteenth century, while the lower part around rue du Faubourg-du-Temple and rue de la Fontaine-au-Roi was *La Basse Courtille*. Both were full of boozers and dance halls, where people flocked from the city on high days and holidays.

The wildest revels of the year took place on the night of Mardi Gras, when thousands of masked people turned out to celebrate the end of the *carnaval*. Next morning – Ash Wednesday – they descended in drunken procession from Belleville to the city, in up to a thousand horsedrawn vehicles: *la descente de la Courtille*.

commemorates the birth of the legendary *chanteuse*, Édith Piaf, although she was in fact found abandoned as a baby here on the steps.

A little lower, the cobbled **rue Piat** climbs past the beautiful wrought-iron gate of the jungly **Villa Otoz** to the newly created **Parc de Belleville**. From the terrace at the junction with rue des Envierges there is a fantastic view across the city, especially at sunset. At your feet the small park descends in a series of terraces and waterfalls, a total success compared with the nondescript development of a decade ago. Inevitably it has brought the establishment of one or two rather posh eating/drinking places in its wake.

Continuing straight ahead, a path crosses the top of the park past a minuscule vineyard and turns into steps that drop down to **rue des Couronnes**. Some of the adjacent streets are worth a wander for a feel of the changing times: rue de la Mare, rue des Envierges, rue des Cascades, with two or three beautiful old houses in overgrown gardens, alongside new housing that follows the height and curves of the streets and newly reopened passages between them.

Between the bottom of the park and bd de Belleville the squalid, rotting housing, combined with a teeming street life, has been almost erased but not completely. The local organization for the defence of Belleville fought hard for restoration rather than demolition and for preserving the little cafés, restos and shops that gave the *quartier* its animation. Rue Ramponeau has an historic record of resistance: at the junction with rue de Tourtille the very last barricade of the Commune was defended singlehandedly for fifteen minutes by the last fighting *Communard*, before he melted away – to write a book about it all.

The restaurants of Belleville are detailed on p.259.

It is also in these streets and on the boulevard that the strong ethnic diversity of Belleville becomes apparent. Rue Ramponeau, for example, is still full of – though for how long it's hard to say – kosher shops, belonging to Sephardic Jews from Tunisia. Around the rue du Faubourg-du-Temple/bd de Belleville crossroads there are dozens of Chinese restaurants, with a scattering of restaurants owned by east Europeans (descendants of refugees from nineteenth-century pogroms in Russia and Poland, and the twentieth-century atrocities of the Nazis), Turks and Greeks. On the boulevard, especially during the Tuesday and Friday morning market, you see women from Mali, Gambia, and Zaire, often wearing their local dress, and men in burnouses, who look as if they still had the arid ridges of the High Atlas in their mind's eye. And all this diversity is reflected in the produce on sale.

The boulevard is now lined with dramatic new architecture employing jutting triangles, curves and the occasional reference to the roof lines of nineteenth-century Parisian blocks. But the old hangs in there too. At no. 63, *Le Berry* – with a leaping zebra above its name – has been, since 1961, the only venue for films and shows in the area, and a place where little-known musicians and theatre

**Belleville,
Ménilmontant
and
Charonne**

The bygone eastern villages

Before redevelopment, the human scale of the houses, the cobbled lanes, the individual gardens, the numerous stairways, and local shops and cafés perfectly integrated with the housing, combined with the superb hillside location, gave the area a unique charm – quite the equal of Montmartre – and without the touristy commercialism.

For a picture of what it was like, there is no more evocative record than the atmospheric photographs of Willy Ronis, if you can lay hands on a copy. But there is still on-the-ground evidence, in addition to the little cul-de-sacs of terraced houses and gardens north of rue des Pyrénées. There are alleys so narrow that nothing but the knife-grinder's tricycle could fit down them, like **passage de la Duée**, 17 rue de la Duée, and detached little houses, like 97 rue Villiers d'Adam. You can also see the less romantic side of life in the grim neo-Gothic fortress housing estates of 140 rue de Ménilmontant, built in 1925 for the influx of rural populations after World War I, and the 1913 Villa Stendhal, off rue Stendhal. Right over to the east, near the Porte Bagnolet, however, workers in 1908 were provided with housing almost unmatched in the city. From place Octave-Chanute, wide stone steps, bordered by lanterns, lead up to a miraculous little sequence of streets of terraced houses and gardens, some with Art Nouveau glass porches, fancy brickwork and the shade of lilac and cherry trees.

companies could perform in public. Local musicians are trying to fend off the actions of the building's owner, who has been using strongarm tactics, including ransacking the projection room, in order to clear the building for development.

The combination of old and new continues in Basse Belleville in the large triangle of streets below bd de Belleville, bounded by rue du Faubourg-du-Temple (the most lively) and avenue de la République. Zany high-tech metal and glass at 117 rue Faubourg-du-Temple co-exists with small unchanged business premises in the Cour des Bretons. Goods still cost around half the price that they do in shops in the centre of the city, despite a number of increasingly fashionable restaurants. Here there is still a good mix of French and immigrant, workshop, residence and commerce. And the houses are built on the traditional pattern, with passages and courtyards burrowing within courtyards.

Ménilmontant

Like Belleville, the *quartier* of Ménilmontant aligns itself along one long, straight, steep street, the rue de Ménilmontant. It has always been less dilapidated than Belleville. Though it has its black spots, it is somehow more respectable.

For half its length the **rue de Ménilmontant** is a busy, multi-racial shopping street, full of traditional, small shops and snack bars, the continuation of the equally busy rue Oberkampf. The upper reaches, above rue Sorbier, are quieter. There, as you look back, you find yourself dead in line with the rooftop of the Centre Beaubourg, a measure of how high you are above the rest of the city.

Like Belleville, the area closest to bd Belleville has been almost completely demolished and rebuilt – on a small scale around courtyards with open spaces for kids to play. Centred around rue des Amandiers, it's all a bit squeaky clean and unweathered as yet, and the café count has dropped to near zero. **Rue Eliza-Berry** turns into steps alongside the extraordinary *France Telecom* building, topped with great bunches of masts and facing a lovely small park on rue Sorbier.

If you cross the park, take a right, then a left into rue Boyer, you'll find the splendid mosaiced and sculpted constructivist façade of **La Bellevilloise** at no. 25, built for the *PCF* in 1925 to celebrate fifty years of work and science. Saved from demolition by a preservation order, it is now home to a theatre school.

A short way before it, a delightful lane of village houses and gardens, **rue Laurence-Savart**, climbs up to rue du Retrait and rue des Pyrénées opposite the poetically named alley of sighs, the passage des Soupirs.

There is more melancholy poetry near the northeast corner of the Père-Lachaise cemetery, where the last crumbling houses of the **rue des Partants** (the street of the departers) offer the most poignantly evocative streetscape in the *quartier*. But only the **street names** echo the long-vanished orchards and rustic pursuits of the villagers: *Amandiers* (almond trees), *Pruniers* (plum trees), *Mûriers* (mulberry trees), *Pressoir* (wine press).

Rue des Pyrénées, the main cross-route through the *quartier*, is itself redolent of the provinces, getting busier as it approaches place Gambetta. The post office at no. 248 has a big ceramic wallpiece by the sculptor Zadkine. Close by place Gambetta, on rue Malte, is the big glass frontage of the **Théâtre National de la Colline**, built in 1987 to replace the dingy old cinema that used to house the theatre. You can snack in its cafeteria and pick up the beautifully produced and illustrated brochures on current productions.

Charonne

If you like unexpected and unvisited corners of cities, take a walk from the avenue du Père-Lachaise entrance to the cemetery along rue des Rondeaux, the street that follows the cemetery wall with a very desirable residence for exhibitionists at no. 26.

Cross rue des Pyrénées by the bridge in rue Renouvier, turn right on rue Stendhal (Villa Stendhal is opposite – see box opposite), past the underground reservoir that serves as a gigantic header tank for the stop-cocks that wash the city's gutters, and go down the steps at the end to rue de Bagnolet. Alternatively, take rue Lisfranc off rue

For more on the catacombs and underground Paris, see p.132.

**Belleville,
Ménilmontant
and
Charonne**

Stendhal and left on rue Prairies then left again on rue de Baguolet. It's a longer way round, but **rue des Prairies** has excellent examples of sensitive and imaginative infill. The new buildings have a pleasing variety of designs and colours, with bright tiling and ochre shades of cladding.

In place St-Blaise is the perfect little church of **St-Germain-de-Charonne**. It has changed little since it served a village, and its Romanesque belfry not at all, since the thirteenth century. Unique among Paris churches, with the exception of St-Pierre in Montmartre, it has its own graveyard, in which several hundred murdered *Communards* were buried after being accidentally disinterred during the construction of a reservoir in 1897. Otherwise, charnel houses were the norm, with the bones emptied into the catacombs as more space was required. It was not until the nineteenth century that public cemeteries appeared on the scene, the most famous being **Père-Lachaise** (see below).

Opposite the church, the old cobbled village high street, **rue St-Blaise**, is one of the prettiest in Paris, or was until it was prettified further, its face-lift eradicating the charm it once had. Beyond place des Grès, the argument for infill, for preserving and creating the new, is clear. Everything has been rebuilt; it is hard and harsh and the few cafés are full of young men aggressively jolting at arcade games.

Rue de Vitruve, however, which crosses rue St-Blaise at place Grès, has a great new swimming pool and the Artignan youth hostel to the north, and to the south, at no. 39, a school, built in 1982. Designed by Jacques Bardet, the school's rectangular mass is broken up by open air segments, enclosed only by the structural steel lattice of the building over which plants are supposed to spread – though there's very little sign of them yet. But the best thing is hidden round the corner, visible as you approach from rue des Pyrénées. It's a huge sculptured **salamander** and its footprints mounted on the windowless side of a building on rue R.A. Marquet. Engraved above the street sign, it says: "A legend is told that a salamander, after passing by the square where it would have left a long trail, set off towards rue R.A. Marquet and stopped to rest on a corner of rue Vitruve."

Père-Lachaise cemetery

The cimetière Père-Lachaise (daily 7.30am–6pm; M° Gambetta/ Père-Lachaise/Alexandre-Dumas) is like a miniature city devastated by a neutron bomb: a great number of dead, empty houses and temples of every size and style, and exhausted survivors, some congregating aimlessly, some searching persistently for their favourite famous dead in an arrangement of numbered divisions that is neither entirely haphazard nor strictly systematic.

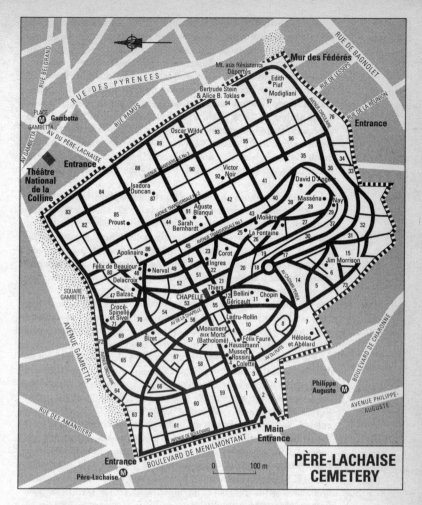

PÈRE-LACHAISE CEMETERY

Rue de Bagnolet

Mur des Fédérés

ML aux Résistants
Déportés

Edith
Piaf

Gertrude Stein
& Alice B. Toklas
94

Modigliani
97

Rue des Pyrénées

Rue de Lesseps

Rue de la Réunion

Rue Belgrand

Rue Ramus

76

Entrance

PLACE
GAMBETTA

Gambetta

GAMBETTA

Oscar Wilde

93

89

96

AV DU PÈRE-LACHAISE

35

34

AV GAMBETTA

Entrance

88

Victor
Noir

Avenue Transversale No 3

90

92

95

36

33

Théâtre
National
de la
Colline

84

Isadora
Duncan
87

41

David D'Angers

28

Masséna

Nay

83

85

Auguste
Blanqui
91

42

40

39

29

Avenue Transversale No 2

43

Molière

27

37

32

82

Proust

44

Sarah
Bernhardt

Avenue Transversale No 1

25

La Fontaine
26

30

31

Apolinaire

86

45

23

Corot

19

17

15

Félix de Beaujour

50

Ingres
22

20

18

Jim Morrison

SQUARE
GAMBETTA

Nerval

49

51

21

6

Delacroix

48

52

Thiers

14

73

47 Balzac

CHAPELLE

53

55

12 Bellini

Géricault

Chopin

5

Crocé-
Spinelle
et Sivel
71

70

54

AV DE LA CHAPELLE

56

Ledru-Rollin
10

7

Avenue Gambetta

69

Bizet

68

Monument
aux Morts
(Bataholomé)

57

8

Héloïse
et Abélard

Félix Faure

Haussmann
Musset

65

67

58

Rossini
Colette

AV DU PUITS

66

59

Philippe
Auguste

64

60

Avenue Philippe-
Auguste

Rue des Amandiers

63

62

61

Main
Entrance

Avenue de Boulevard

Entrance

Boulevard de Ménilmontant

0   100 m

Père-Lachaise

Boulevard de Charonne

AV CASIMIR PÉRIER

Avenue Circulaire

Père-Lachaise cemetery was opened in 1804, after an urgent
stop had been put on further burials in the then overflowing city
cemeteries and churchyards. It was an incredibly successful piece of
land speculation. Nicolas Frochot, the urban planner who bought
the land, persuaded the civil authorities to have **Molière**, **La
Fontaine**, **Abélard** and **Héloïse** reburied in his new cemetery. To be
interred in Père-Lachaise quickly became the ultimate status symbol
for the rich and successful. Ironically Frochot, even sold a plot to
the original owner for considerably more money than the price he
had paid for the entire site. Even today, the rates are still extremely
high.

Some of the most celebrated dead have unremarkable tombs while those whose fame died with them or who were nonentities to start with have the most expressive monuments. Swarms flock to ex-Doors lead singer **Jim Morrison's tomb** in Division 6, where a motley assembly of devotees roll spliffs against a backdrop of Doors' lyrics and declarations of love and drug consumption, graffitied in every western language on every stone in sight. *Femme fatale* **Colette's** tomb, close to the main entrance in division 4, is very plain though always covered in flowers. The same is true for the divine **Sarah Bernhardt's** (division 44) and the great *chanteuse* **Edith Piaf's** (division 97). **Marcel Proust** lies in his family's conventional tomb (division 85), which honours the medical fame of his father.

In contrast, one **Jean Pezon**, a lion tamer, is shown riding his pet lion, which ate him (division 86). In division 92, nineteenth-century journalist **Victor Noir** – shot for daring to criticize a relative of Napoléon III – lies flat on his back, fully clothed, his top hat fallen by his feet. His prostrate figure has been a magnet not for anti-censorship campaigners, but for infertile women rubbing themselves against him as a sexual charm. Close by, a forgotten and unlamented French diplomat must turn in his grave with envy – he provided himself with an enormous tapering phallus, admirably higher than the trees around it in division 48. In division 71 two men lie together hand in hand – not a gay couple (as far as anyone knows); but a pair of balloonists who went so high they died from lack of oxygen.

Other bed scenes include **Félix Faure** (division 4), French president, who died in the arms of his mistress in the Elysée palace in 1899. Draped in a French flag like a sheet, his head is raised and his hand seems to be groping the flag pole as if it might be his lover. **Gericault** reclines on cushions of stone (division 12), paint palette in hand, his neck and bony face taut with concentration. Close by is the relaxed figure of **Jean Carriès**, a model maker, in felt hat and overalls, holding one of his figures in the palm of his hand. For a more fearsome view of death there's the tomb of a French judge, **Raphaël Roger**, in division 94, where a figure cowled from head to foot stands sentinel beneath a pointed arch. Or the poet in division 6 bursting out of his granite block.

Painter **Corot** (division 24) and novelist **Balzac** (division 48) both have superb busts, Balzac looking particularly satisfied with his life. **Chopin** (division 11) has a willowy muse weeping for his loss. The most impressive of the individual tombs is **Oscar Wilde's**, for which Jacob Epstein sculpted a strange Pharaonic winged messenger. The inscription is a grim verse from *The Ballad of Reading Gaol.*

Approaching Oscar Wilde's grave from the centre of the cemetery, you pass the tomb of **Auguste Blanqui** (division 91), after whom so many French streets are named. Described by Karl Marx as the nineteenth century's greatest revolutionary, he served his time in jail – 33 years in all – for his political activities that spanned the 1830 Revolution to the Paris Commune.

Below Blanqui's and Wilde's graves – along with Victor Noir, Edith Piaf and Raphaël Roger – you'll find in division 96 the grave of **Modigliani** and his lover **Jeanne Herbuterne**, who killed herself in crazed grief a few days after he died in agony from meningitis. **Laura Marx**, Karl's daughter, and her husband **Paul Lafargue**, who committed suicide together in 1911, lie in this southeast corner of the cemetery too (division 76).

But it is the monuments to the collective, violent deaths that have the power to change a sunny outing to Père-Lachaise into a much more sombre experience. In division 97, you'll find the memorials to **those who died in the Nazi concentration camps**, to executed **Resistance fighters** and to those who were never accounted for in the genocide of the last world war. The sculptures are relentless in their images of inhumanity, of people forced to collaborate in their own degradation and death.

Finally, there is the **Mur des Fedérés** (division 76), the wall where the last troops of the Paris Commune were lined up and shot in the final days of the battle. The man who ordered their execution, **Adolphe Thiers**, lies in the centre of the cemetery in division 55.

Defeat is everywhere: the oppressed and their oppressors are interred with the same ritual, in the same illustrious spot; the relative riches and fame as unequal among the tombs of the dead as they are in the lives of the living.

A good map of the cemetery is available for 10F in the newsagent and flower shop on av Père-Lachaise and at outlets near the main entrance on bd de Ménilmontant. You'll find that the rue de la Réunion and around place Gambetta are the best places to seek out sustenance.

Down to the Faubourg St-Antoine

Heading back to Bastille from Père-Lachaise, **rue de la Roquette and rue de Charonne** are the principal thoroughfares. There's nothing particularly special about the numerous passages and ragged streets that lead off into the lower 11ᵉ *arrondissement*, except that they are utterly Parisian, with the odd detail of a building, the obscurity of a shop's speciality, the display of vegetables in a simple greengrocer's, the sunlight on a café table, or the graffiti on a Second Empire street fountain to charm an aimless wanderer. And the occasional reminder of the sheer political toughness of French working-class tradition, as in the plaque on some flats in rue de la Folie-Regnault commemorating the first FTP (Francs-Tireurs Partisans) Resistance group, which used to meet here until it was betrayed and its members executed in 1941. Square de la Roquette was the site of an old prison, where 4000 members of the

BASTILLE TO NATION

Cimetière du
Père-Lachaise

RUE DE BAGNOLET

Alexandre
Dumas Ⓜ

CHARONNE

20e

ORE DUMAS

BOULEVARD

AV PHILIPPE-AUGUSTE

Avron Ⓜ

RUE DE MONTREUIL

DE CHARONNE

PLACE DE

Triomphe de
la République

AV DU TRÔNE

Nation Ⓜ LA NATION

COURS DE
VINCENNES

BD DE PICPUS

AVENUE DE BEL AIR

AVENUE DE ST-MANDE

0   300 m

Félix Eboué

**To the Faubourg St-Antoine and the north-
ern 12e arrondissement: Listings**

Restaurants

Les Amognes, 243 rue du Faubourg-St-Antoine,
11e.
Mo Faidherbe-Chaligny.

Chardenoux, 1 rue Jules-Vallès, 11e.
Mo Charonne.

Les Cinq Points Cardinaux, 14 rue Jean-Macé,
11e.
Mo Faidherbe-Chaligny/Charonne.

Les Demoiselles de Charonne, 4 rue Léon-Frot,
11e.
Mo Charonne.

L'Ébauchoir, 43-45 rue de Cîteaux, 12e.
Mo Faidherbe-Chaligny.

Au Limonaire, 88 rue de Charenton, 12e.
Mo Ledru-Rollin, Gare-de-Lyon.

La Mansouria, 11 rue Faidherbe, 11e.
Mo Faidherbe-Chaligny.

Palais de la Femme, 94 rue de Charonne, 11e.
Mo Charonne/Faidherbe-Chaligny.

Le Train Bleu, 1st floor, Gare de Lyon, 20 bd
Diderot, 12e.
Mo Gare-de-Lyon.

Cafés and Bars

Le Baron Rouge, 1 rue Théophile-Roussel, 12e.
Mo Ledru-Rollin.

Jacques-Mélac, 42 rue Léon-Frot, 11e.
Mo Charonne.

Le Penty Bar, corner of pl d'Aligre and rue
Emilio-Castellar, 12e.

*These establishments are reviewed in Chapter 13,
Eating and Drinking, beginning on p.260.*

Resistance were imprisoned in 1944. The low, foreboding gateway on rue de la Roquette has been preserved in their memory.

South of rue de Charonne, between rue St-Bernard and impasse Charrière, stands the rustic-looking **church of Ste-Marguerite**, with a garden beside it dedicated to the memory of Raoul Nordling, the Swedish consul who persuaded the retreating Germans not to blow up Paris in 1944.

The church itself (Mon–Sat 8am–noon & 3–7.30pm, Sun 8.30am–noon & 5–7.30pm) was built in 1624 to accommodate the growing population of the *faubourg*, which was about 40,000 in 1710 and 100,000 in 1900. The sculptures on the transept pediments were made by its first full-blown parish priest. Inside it is wide-bodied, low, and quiet, with a very local and un-urban feel, as if it were still out in the fields. The stained-glass windows record a very local history: the visit of Pope Pius VII in 1802, in Paris for Napoléon's coronation; the miraculous cure of a Madame Delafosse in the rue de Charonne on May 31, 1725; the fatal wounding of Monseigneur Affre, the archbishop of Paris, in the course of a street battle in the *faubourg* on June 25, 1848; the murder of sixteen Carmelite nuns at the Barrière du Trône in 1794 (presumably, more revolutionary anti-clericalism); the *quartier*'s dead in World War I.

In the now disued cemetery of Ste-Marguerite, the story goes – though no one has been able to prove it – lies the body of Louis XVII, the ten-year-old heir of the guillotined Louis XVI, who died in the Temple prison (see box on p.98). The cemetery also received the dead from the Bastille prison.

From square R-Nordling, rue de la Forge Royale – with the *Casbah* nightclub magnificently decorated in North African style at no. 18 – takes you down to rue du Faubourg St-Antoine. Or you can continue down rue de Charonne past an excellent mural entitled "Kubisme" at no. 50, and hit the stretch of Faubourg St-Antoine that has a series of courtyards, mews and alleyways, providing quiet havens for the Bastille traffic. No. 54, for example, has ivy and roses curtaining three shops, window boxes on every storey, and lemon trees in tubs tilted on the cobbles.

After Louis XI licensed the establishment of craftsmen in the fifteenth century, the *faubourg* became the principal working-class *quartier* of Paris, cradle of revolutions and mother of street-fighters. From its beginnings the principal trade associated with it has been **furniture-making**, and this was where the classic styles of French furniture – Louis Quatorze, Louis Quinze, Second Empire – were developed. The maze of interconnecting yards and passages are still full of the workshops of the related trades: marquetry, stainers, polishers, inlayers etc, many of which are still producing those styles.

To the east, rue du Faubourg-St-Antoine ends at place de la Nation, along with bd Voltaire that cuts diagonally right across the 11e *arrondissement* and the continuation of bd de Ménilmontant.

The *place* is adorned with the Triumph of the Republic bronze, and, at the start of the Cours de Vincennes, the bizarre ensemble of two medieval monarchs, looking very small and sheepish in pens on the top of two high columns. During the Revolution, when the old name of place du Trône become place du Trône-Renversé (the overturned throne), more people were guillotined here than on the more notorious execution site of place de la Concorde.

The 12ᵉ arrondissement

South of the Ledru-Rollin métro station on rue du Faubourg-St-Antoine, a small tangle of streets survives between the Bastille Opera, place d'Aligre and the major building works around the **Gare du Lyon**. On rue Traversière, at no 55, the *Librairie Ekmecic* is dedicated to the former Yugoslavia, and further north along the street is a Yugoslav deli. The *boulangerie* on the corner of rues Charenton and Emilio-Castelar has beautiful painted glass panels – and good bread. **Place d'Aligre**, centre of opposition to the demolition of the Opera House, has a raucous daily market (except Monday) with food in and around the covered *halles* and secondhand clothes and junk, as well as cheap and friendly cafés, on the *place*.

To the south, along av Daumesnil, the main artery of the 12ᵉ, runs the old railway viaduct. The brickwork has now been scrubbed clean and new antique shops are appearing under the arches. Plans for a pedestrian promenade and bicycle track along the top may still materialize. Opposite one of the new shops, at 64 av Daumesnil, you'll find a superb Lebanese *pâtisserie*, *Arnaout*, selling Turkish delight and other sweet mouthfuls in small quantities. Further down, amidst the new apartment blocks of passage Gatbois, is a particularly good mural depicting the movement of a little girl dancing.

A short way south of av Daumesnil is the gorgeous nineteenth-century extravaganza of the Gare du Lyon, hemmed in on its southern flank by building works for an interchange on the new Météor underground line, and by the office blocks of quai de la Rapée. This stretch of the river has long been a business quarter, but in the last ten years or so the whole quayside right out to the *périphérique* has gradually been subjected to more and more major developments.

Just downstream of the Pont de Bercy is the **Ministère des Finances**, built in 1988 after the treasury staff had finally agreed to move out of the *Richelieu* wing of the Louvre. It stretches like a giant loading bridge from above the river (where higher bureaucrats and ministers arrive by boat) to rue de Bercy, a distance of some 400 metres. Kafka would have loved it, and contemporary Czechs would probably imagine the hand of Stalin on it. The best view of the monster is from the Charles-de-Gaulle–Nation métro line as it crosses the Pont de Bercy.

From the métro – which also gives good views of the new National Library on the opposite bank – you can see, on the east side of bd de Bercy, the **Palais Omnisports de Bercy**. Built in 1983, its concrete bunker frame, clad with sloping lawns, covers a vast arena used for sporting and cultural events. Beyond it used to be the old Bercy warehouses, where for centuries the capital's wine supplies were unloaded from river barges. This is now being turned into a huge park, with neat little flower beds around the few old buildings that have been preserved. In the course of demolition and excavation, archeologists unearthed the remains of Neolithic dugout boats, dwellings and other bits and pieces dating back to around 4000 BC, adding an extra dimension to the city's history.

New buildings surround the park, from the ugly megahotels rearing up beside the Palais Omnisports to the line of steel and reflecting glass offices at the eastern end. On the north side, on rue Jean-Paul Belmondo, is the new **American Centre** (decamped from bd Raspail), designed by one of America's most fashionable architects, Frank O. Gehry. Constructed from zinc, glass and limestone, it resembles a falling pack of cards – according to Gehry, the inspiration was Matisse's collages done "with a simple pair of scissors". The centre has a cinema, theatre, exhibition and lecture spaces, and twenty-odd flats for visiting American artists.

All this new grand-scale development of Bercy is to match the emerging "Seine Rive Gauche" (see Chapter 8) on the opposite bank. In the minds of the planners the whole of eastern Paris is to become the new ultramodern, high-tech zone of the city, between the two "poles" of La Villette and the "Seine Rive Gauche". For the moment, however, Bercy is cut off from the rest of the 12e *arrondissement* by the rail tracks of the Gare du Lyon and the Gare de Paris-Bercy (the motorail station). You can walk under the lines along bd de Bercy or rue Proudhon but it's not much fun. The only bus is the #62 from Pont de Tolbiac and place Lachambeaudie to place Félix-Eboué, and all the new building works may disrupt its route.

North of the tracks, on the eastern intersection of av Daunesnil and rue de Charenton, stands the ebullient *mairie* of the 12e, with a particularly splendid rear side on rue Bignon. A short way down rue Charenton, at no. 119–120, a block built in 1911 has sculpted figures of a tired miner, sailor, industrial worker and farm labourer holding up the heavy weight of the window bays.

The traditional work in this area used to be at the freight station of Reuilly to the north of the *mairie*. This has now become the **Jardin de Reuilly**, a large circle of grass that you can walk, sleep or play on, with water gardens and a kids' playground, and statues baring their rears to av Daumensnil. There's a sundial with the hours marked on the ground (and, in typical French fashion, details of the calculation methods, the movements of the earth, the history of sundials and so on engraved on it), and a lovely wooden footbridge that crosses over the park to the new pedestrian allée

Vivaldi. This is not a very exciting street architecturally – and the old Gare du Reuilly looks miserably anachronistic at the far end – but it's a gentle way of reaching the Daumesnil métro stop by the smug lions of place Félix-Eboué.

The 12ᵉ arrondissement

Just beyond the *place*, continuing down av Daumesnil, an extremely narrow brickwork façade, topped by the tallest bell tower in Paris, conceals the vast cupola – filling the whole block behind the street – of the **Église du Saint-Esprit**. It was built in 1931 in memory of the colonial missionaries. The Roman Catholic Church was worried by the possible reaction of the anticlerical, communist sympathies of the local residents, hence the disguise of its enormous dimensions. Between rues Tournéux and Fecamp, one block down from the church, one of the city's grim 1920s housing estates has been cleaned up and restored.

Another peculiar church, St-Éloi, built in 1968, lies north of the Jardin de Reuilly on pl M. de Fontenay, off rue de Reuilly (M° Montgallet). Its ground plan is a right-angle triangle with the altar positioned at one of the nonright-angled corners, and it feels like an industrial building. Both outside and inside are clad with lacquered aluminium leaves, in honour of Saint Éloi, patron saint of jewellers and iron workers who lived in this area in the seventh century.

The bizarre collection of the Musée des Arts Africains et Océaniens are detailed on p.275.

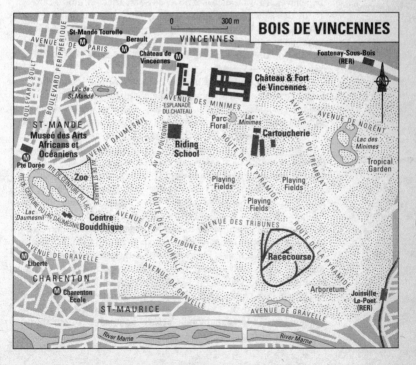

The 12ᵉ arrondissement

Close by the church, on the other side of rue de Reuilly, is one of the most perfect mews in Paris, the **impasse Mousset**. Roses, clematis, wisteria and honeysuckle wind across telegraph lines and up the whitewashed walls of tiny houses. A rusted hotel sign advertising wines and liqueurs as well as beds still hangs from one of the houses. You can hear children playing in hidden gardens; there are no designer offices here, just homes, the odd artist's studio and a small, still busy, printworks.

Vincennes

To reach the **Bois de Vincennes** which belongs to the 12ᵉ, you can take bus #86 from rue du Faubourg St-Antoine, or more directly bus #46 which runs along rue de Reuilly and the last stretch of av Daumesnil. On the other side of Porte Dorée, bus #46 passes the **Musée des Arts Africains et Océaniens,** with its 1930s colonial façade of jungles, hard-working natives and the place names of the French Empire representing the "overseas contribution to the capital". The bus next stops at the **Parc Zoologique** (summer 9am–6pm, winter 9am–5.30pm; 35F/20F), which was one of the first zoos to replace cages with trenches and give the animals room to exercise themselves. The entrance is at 53 av de St-Maurice (Mᵒ Porte-Dorée).

In summer, the Parc Floral hosts any number of fun things to do for kids; see p.297.

In the **Bois de Vincennes** itself, you can spend an afternoon **boating** on Lac Daumesnil (just by the zoo), or rent a bike from the same place and take some stale *baguette* to the ducks on Lac des Minimes on the other side of the wood (also reached by bus #112 from Château-de-Vincennes métro).

The fenced enclave on the southern side of Lac Daumesnil is a **Buddhist centre** with a Tibetan temple, Vietnamese chapel and international pagoda, and all occasionally visitable (information on ☎40.04.98.06). As far as real woods go, the *bois* opens out and flowers once you're east of av de St-Maurice, but the area is so overrun with roads that countryside sensations don't stand much chance. *Boules* competitions are popular, however – there's usually a collection of devotees between route de la Tourelle and av du Polygone.

To the north, near the château, the **Parc Floral** (Mon–Fri & Sun 9.30am–6.30pm, Sat in summer 9.30am–10pm, in winter 9.30am–6.30pm; 10F entrance; bus #112 from Mᵒ Château-de-Vincennes) testifies to the strict French art in landscape gardening. But the flowers are very pleasant, with lily ponds and a Four Season Garden for all-year displays. There are also plenty of kids' activities (see Chapter 16). Although this is itself a wood, tree lovers are encouraged to visit the arboretum (Mon, Wed & Fri 1–4.30pm; route de la Pyramide: *RER* Joinville-le-Pont), where eighty different species of greenery are tended.

To the east of the Parc Floral is the **Cartoucherie de Vincennes**, an old ammunitions factory, now home to four theatre companies including the radical *Théâtre du Soleil* (see p.340).

On the northern edge of the *bois*, the **Château de Vincennes**, royal medieval residence, then state prison, porcelain factory, weapons dump and military training school, is still undergoing restoration work started by Napoléon III. A real behemoth of a building, it's unlikely to be beautified by the removal of the nineteenth-century gun positions or any amount of stone-scrubbing.

Chapter 11

Western Paris

T he **Beaux Quartiers** of western Paris are essentially the 16ᵉ and 17ᵉ *arrondissements*. The 16ᵉ is aristocratic and rich; the 17ᵉ, or at least the southern part of it, bourgeois and rich, embodying the staid, cautious values of the nineteenth-century manufacturing and trading classes. The northern half of the 16ᵉ, towards place Victor-Hugo and place de l'Étoile, is leafy and distinctly metropolitan in feel. The southern part, round the old villages of **Auteuil** and **Passy**, has an almost provincial air, and is full of pleasant surprises for the walker. One good peg on which to hang a walk is a visit to the **Musée Marmottan** in avenue Raphaël, with its marvellous collection of late Monets. There are also several interesting pieces of turn-of-the-century and early **twentieth-century architecture** scattered through the district, especially by Hector Guimard (designer of the swirly green Art Nouveau métro stations) and by Le Corbusier and Mallet-Stevens, architects of the first "Cubist" buildings.

Auteuil

The ideal place to start an architectural exploration of the Beaux Quartiers is the **Église d'Auteuil** métro station. Around this area are several of Hector Guimard's **Art Nouveau** buildings: at 34 rue Boileau, 8 av de la Villa-de-la-Réunion, 41 rue Lagache-Chardon, 142 av de Versailles, and 39 bd Exelmans.

The house at 34 rue Boileau was one of Guimard's first commissions in 1891. A high fence, creepers and a huge satellite dish obscure much of the view, but you can see some of the decorative tile work under the eaves and around the doors and windows. Close by, at no. 40, the Algerian embassy with Islamic motifs stands at the corner of the leafy *villa* called the Hameau Boileau. Further down on this fascinating street, just before you reach bd Exelmans, is a bizarre but successful combination of 1970s Western architecture with traditional Vietnamese elements of a pagoda roof and earthen-

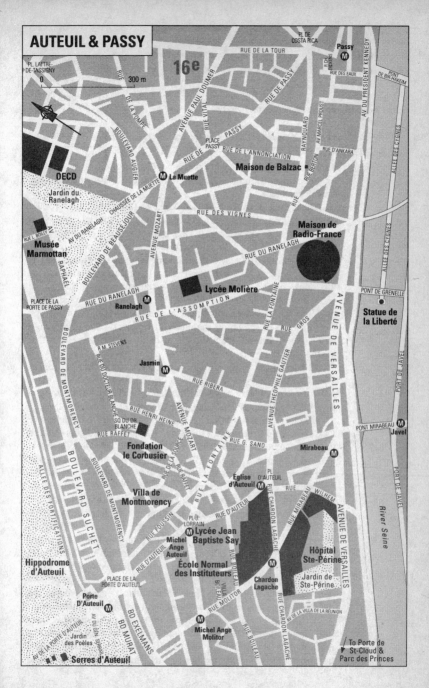

AUTEUIL & PASSY

PL. LATTRE-
DE-TASSIGNY

0   300 m

16e

PL. DE
COSTA RICA

RUE DE LA TOUR

Passy Ⓜ

DECD

Jardin du
Ranelagh

La Muette Ⓜ

PLACE
PASSY

RUE DE PASSY

RUE DE L'ANNONCIATION

Maison de Balzac

Musée
Marmottan

RUE DES VIGNES

Maison de
Radio-France

Lycée Molière

RUE DU RANELAGH

RUE DU RANELAGH

Ranelagh Ⓜ

PLACE DE LA
PORTE DE PASSY

RUE DE L'ASSOMPTION

R.M. STEVENS

Statue de
la Liberté

PONT DE GRENELLE

Jasmin Ⓜ

RUE RIBERA

RUE HENRI HEINE

SQ DU DR
BLANCHE

RUE RAFFET

RUE G. SAND

Fondation
le Corbusier

PONT MIRABEAU   Ⓜ Javel

Mirabeau Ⓜ

Villa de
Montmorency

Église
d'Auteuil Ⓜ

PL
D'AUTEUIL

Hippodrome
d'Auteuil

PL DU
LORRAIN

Lycée Jean
Baptiste Say

Michel
Ange
Auteuil Ⓜ

École Normal
des Instituteurs

Hôpital
Ste-Périne

Jardin de
Ste-Périne

Chardon
Lagache

PLACE DE LA
PORTE D'AUTEUIL

Porte
D'Auteuil Ⓜ

Jardin
des Poêles

Michel Ange Ⓜ
Molitor

To Porte de
St-Cloud &
Parc des Princes

Serres d'Auteuil

ware tiles at no. 62. If you continue along rue Boileau beyond bd Exelmans, you'll find a series of charming *villas* backing onto the Auteuil cemetery.

The Guimard block at 142 av Versailles (1905) has the typically bulging, heaving effect of Art Nouveau buildings, which at worst can make you feel almost seasick. It's just by the Exelmans crossroads (on bus #72's route) and a short way from Villa de la Réunion. If you're heading back up to Église d'Auteuil from here you can cut across the surprisingly large **Jardin de Ste-Périne**, once the rural residence of the monks of Ste Geneviève's abbey, established here in 1109. The entrances are opposite 135 av Versailles and alongside the hospital on rue Mirabeau, just north of the rue Chardon-Lagache junction.

For more of the life of the *quartier*, follow the old village high street, **rue d'Auteuil**, from the métro exit to **place Lorrain**, which hosts a Saturday market.

In rue Poussin, just off the *place*, carriage gates open on to **Villa Montmorency**, a typical 16ᵉ *villa*, in the sense of a sort of private village of leafy lanes and English-style gardens. Gide and the Goncourt brothers of Prix fame lived in this one.

Behind it, in a cul-de-sac on the right of rue du Dr-Blanche, are **Le Corbusier's first private houses** (1923), the Villa Jeanneret and the Villa La Roche, now the *Fondation Le Corbusier* (Mon–Fri 10am–12.30pm & 1.30–6pm, Fri closes 5pm; closed Aug). They are built in strictly Cubist style, very plain, with windows in bands. The only extravagance is the raising of one wing of the Villa La Roche on piers and its curved frontage. It looks commonplace enough now, but what a contrast to anything that had gone before. Further along rue du Dr-Blanche, the tiny rue Mallet-Stevens was built entirely by Robert Mallet-Stevens (see p.81), also in Cubist style. No. 12, where Mallet-Stevens had his offices, has been altered, along with other houses in the street, but you can still see the architectural intention – familiar enough today – of sculpting the entire street space as a unity. To continue on to the **Musée Marmottan**, a subway under the disused *Petite Ceinture* rail line brings you out by avenue Raphael.

Returning to place Lorraine, **rue de la Fontaine**, running from the *place* to the *Radio-France* building, has Guimard buildings at nos. 14, 17, 19, 21 and 60. No. 14 is the most famous: the "Castel Béranger" (1898) with exuberant Art Nouveau decoration and shapes in the bay windows, the roofline and the chimney. No. 60 is worth a look too, and at no. 65, there's a huge block of artists' studios by Henri Sauvage (1926) with a fascinating colour scheme, influenced by Cubism.

Poets, greenhouses and the Albert Kahn garden

East of Porte d'Auteuil are two gardens: the **Jardin des Poètes** (M° Porte d'Auteuil, sortie bd Murat, entrance on av du Général Sarrail; 9am–6pm; free) and the **Jardin des Serres d'Auteuil** (main entrance at 3 av de la Porte d'Auteuil; daily 10am–5/6pm; 3F or you can enter from the Jardin des Poètes). You can't escape the traffic noise completely, but the Jardin des Poètes is extremely tranquil. Famous French poets are remembered by a verse (mostly of a pastoral nature) engraved on small stones surrounded by little flower beds. A statue of Victor Hugo by Rodin, almost obscured by a laurel bush, stands in the middle of this very informal garden. Approaching the Auteuil garden and its greenhouses (*serres*) from the Jardin des Poètes, you pass the delightful potting sheds with rickety wooden blinds that every Parisian park has hidden somewhere. Then you're into a formal garden, beautifully laid out around the big old-fashioned metal frame greenhouses. There may be a special exhibition on – azaleas in April, for example – in which case there'll be an extra entrance fee for the greenhouses. Check first in *Pariscope*.

Directly beyond the Jardin des Serres d'Auteuil is the Stade Roland Garros, venue for the French tennis championships. To the south is the main football and rugby stadium, the Parc des Princes.

The **Jardin Albert Kahn** (Tues–Sun 11am–6/7pm; winter closed; 20F/12F; ☎46.04.52.80) is in the neighbouring suburb of Boulogne-Billancourt at 14 rue du Port (M° Pont St-Cloud–Boulogne). You enter the gardens through a small museum (same hours as gardens) dedicated to temporary exhibitions of *"Les Archives de la Planète"* – photographs and films collected by the banker and philanthropist Albert Kahn between 1909 and 1931 to record human activities and ways of life that he knew would soon disappear for ever. His aim in the garden was to combine English, French, Japanese and other styles to demonstrate the possibility of a harmonious, peaceful world. It is an enchanting place, with rhododendrons and camelias under blue cedars, a rose garden and an espaliered orchard, a forest of Moroccan pines and streams with Japanese bridges beside pagoda tea houses, Buddhas and pyramids of pebbles. A palm hot house has been turned into a very chic *salon de thé*, serving such delights as pear liqueur and *marrons glacés* sorbet. Beside the exit on rue des Abondances there's a *boulangerie* that does good sandwiches for half the price of the garden's *salon de thé*.

Passy

Passy too offers scope for a good meandering walk, from place du Trocadéro (cemetery enthusiasts can take a look at the **Cimetière de Passy**, which holds the graves of Manet and Berthe Morisot) to Balzac's house, and up rue de Passy to the Marmottan museum.

If you start in **rue Franklin**, take a left after place de Costa-Rica and go down the steps into square Alboni, a patch of garden enclosed by tall apartment buildings as solid as banks. Here the métro line emerges from what used to be a vine-covered hillside beneath your feet at the Passy stop – more like a country station – before rumbling out across the river by the Pont de Bir-Hakeim.

Below the station, in **rue des Eaux**, Parisians used to come to take the Passy waters, and today the street is enclosed by a canyon of monied apartments, which dwarf the eighteenth-century houses of **square Charles-Dickens**. In one of them, burrowing back into the cellars of a vanished monastery, the **Musée du Vin** puts on a disappointing display of viticultural odds and bobs (*dégustation*, if you need it). Its vaults connect with the ancient quarry tunnels – not visitable – from which the stone for Notre-Dame was hewn.

If you continue along the foot of the Passy hill, on av Marcel-Proust, you arrive in the cobbled **rue d'Ankara** at the gates of an eighteenth-century château half-hidden by greenery and screened by a high wall. It's a brave punter who will march resolutely up to the gate and peer in with the confident air of the connoisseur. And you'd better make it convincing, for all the time your nose is pressed between the bars, at least four armed guards are watching the small of your back intently, fingers on the trigger. This is the Turkish embassy, and there's not even a parked car to obstruct the field of fire. It was once a clinic where the pioneering Dr Blanche tried to treat the mad Maupassant and Gérard de Nerval, among others; before that it was the home of Marie-Antoinette's friend, the Princesse de Lamballe.

From the gates, **rue Berton**, a cobbled path with its gas lights still in place, follows round the ivy-covered garden wall. By an old green-shuttered house, a boundary stone bears the date 1731. Apart from the embassy security, there is nothing to give away that it is not still 1731 in this tiny backwater. The house was **Balzac's** (Tues–Sun 10am–noon & 2.30–5.40pm; free Sun) in the 1840s, and contains memorabilia and a library. The entrance is from rue Raynouard, down a flight of steps into a dank garden overshadowed at one end by a singularly unattractive block of flats built, and lived in, by the architect Auguste Perret, father of French concrete.

There's more about the Maison de Balzac on p.282.

Across the street, even here, in the heart of Passy, **rue de l'Annonciation**, where once you could have had your Bechstein repaired or your furniture lacquered, is being violated by the developers. At the further end, at **place de Passy**, you join the old high street, **rue de Passy**, which leads past a parade of eye-catching boutiques to **métro La Muette**, from where Chaussée de la Muette leads into the Ranelagh gardens (with a rather engaging sculpture of La Fontaine with the eagle and fox) and the Musée Marmottan.

Bois de Boulogne

The **Bois de Boulogne**, running all down the west side of the 16e, is supposedly modelled on London's Hyde Park, in a very French interpretation. It offers all sorts of facilities: the **Jardin d'Acclimatation** with lots of attractions for kids; the excellent **Musée National des Arts et Traditions Populaires** (p.281); the **Parc de Bagatelle**, with beautiful displays of tulips, hyacinths and daffodils in early April, irises in May, waterlilies and roses at the end of June; a riding school; **bike rental** at the entrance to the Jardin d'Acclimatation; **boating** on the Lac Inférieur; **race courses** at Longchamp and Auteuil. The best, and wildest, part for walking is towards the southwest corner.

Activities for children in the Bois de Boulogne are covered on p.297.

When the Bois de Boulogne opened in the eighteenth century, it was popularly said that *"Les mariages du bois de Boulogne ne se font pas devant Monsieur le Curé"* – "Unions cemented in the Bois de Boulogne do not take place in the presence of a priest." Today's

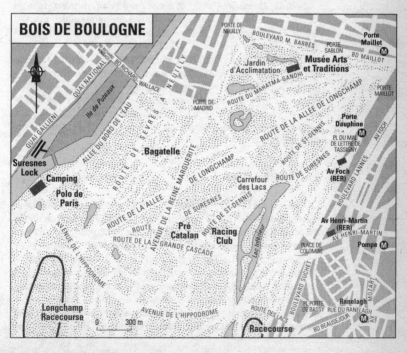

after-dark unions are no less disreputable, the speciality in particular of Brazilian transvestites – but don't be tempted to go in for any night-time sightseeing. This can be a very dangerous place.

Around the Étoile

Twelve avenues make up the star of the Étoile, or place Charles-de-Gaulle, with the Arc de Triomphe at its centre (see Chapter 3). The northern 16e and eastern 17e *arrondissements* through which the avenues fan are cold and soulless, and the huge apartments here are empty much of the time as their owners – royal, exiled royal, ex-royal or just extremely rich – move between their other residences dotted about the globe.

The best avenue to start wandering down – apart from the Champs-Élysées – is the northerly av Wagram. Devotees of Art Nouveau can stop in front of no. 34, Jules Lavirotte's design of 1904, to see if they can honestly persist in saying the style is beautiful. Less taxing aesthetic judgements are called for in front of the flower market and cafés of place des Ternes, the first big junction on av Wagram where rue du Faubourg St-Honoré begins. If you take this street and then the second left – you're in the 8e *arrondissement* now – you can admire the five gold onion domes of the Cathédrale Alexandre-Nevski at 6 rue Daru before turning right on rue de Courcelles, which brings you to the enormous gilded gates of the av Hoche entrance to **Parc Monceau**. The park has a roller-skating rink and kids' play facilities, but, basically, it's a formal garden with antique colonnades and artificial grots. Half the people who command the heights of the French economy spent their infancy there, promenaded in prams by proper nannies. In avenue Velasquez on the far side, the **Musée Cernuschi** houses a small collection of ancient Chinese art (see p.278) bequeathed to the state by the banker Cernuschi, who nearly lost his life for giving money to the Commune.

La Défense

La Grande Arche, six kilometres out from the Arc de Triomphe at the far end of the Voie Triomphale, has put **La Défense** high on the list of places to which visitors to Paris must pay homage. It is a beautiful and astounding structure, a 112m hollow cube, clad in white marble and angled a few degrees out from the Voie Triomphale. Suspended within the hollow, which could enclose Notre-Dame with ease, are the open lift shafts and a "cloud" panoply. Unlike other new Parisian monuments, La Grande Arche is a pure and graceful example of design wedded to innovative engineering, putting it on a par with the Eiffel Tower. Its Danish architect, Johan Otto von

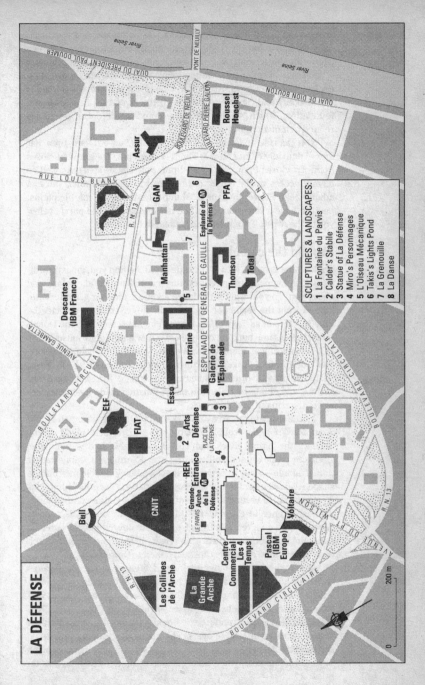

LA DÉFENSE

SCULPTURES & LANDSCAPES:

1 La Fontaine du Parvis
2 Calder's Stabile
3 Statue of La Défense
4 Miro's Personnages
5 L'Oiseau Mécanique
6 Takis's Lights Pond
7 La Grenouille
8 La Danse

River Seine

QUAI DU PRÉSIDENT PAUL DOUMER

PONT DE NEUILLY

River Seine

QUAI DE DION BOUTON

Roussel
Hoechst

Assur

BOULEVARD DE NEUILLY

BOULEVARD PIERRE GALON

RUE LOUIS BLANC

R. N. 13

GAN

6

PFA

R. N. 13

Manhattan

7

Esplanade de
la Défense

Descartes
(IBM France)

Thomson

Total

AVENUE GAMBETTA

ESPLANADE DU GÉNÉRAL DE GAULLE

Lorraine

5

Esso

Galerie de
l'Esplanade

1

3

BOULEVARD CIRCULAIRE

ELF

FIAT

Arts
Défense

2

PLACE DE
LA DÉFENSE

4

RER
Entrance

Grande
Arche
de la
Défense

LE PARVIS

CNIT

Bull

Voltaire

AVENUE DU PT. WILSON

R. N. 13

Les Collines
de l'Arche

La
Grande
Arche

Centre
Commercial
Les 4
Temps

Pascal
(IBM
Europe)

BOULEVARD CIRCULAIRE

R. N. 13

0   200 m

LA DÉFENSE

Spreckelsen, died before the building was completed – it was originally intended for the 1989 Bicentennial, but squabbles between Chirac and Mitterrand over its use delayed the project. It now houses a government ministry, international businesses, an information centre on the European Union, "*Sources d'Europe*" (Mon–Fri 10am–6pm) and, in the roof section, the *Arche de la Fraternité* foundation, which stages exhibitions and conferences on issues related to human rights.

You can ride up to the roof for 35F/25F (Sun–Fri 9am–6pm, Sat 9am–7pm; July & Aug Mon & Thurs closes 7pm, Tues & Wed closes 5pm, Fri closes 9pm, Sat 10am–9pm, Sun 10am–7pm). As well as having access to the *Arche de la Fraternité* exhibitions, you can admire Jean-Pierre Raynaud's "Map of the Heavens" marble patios, and, on a clear day, scan from the marble path on the parvis below you to the Arc de Triomphe, and beyond to the Louvre.

Around the complex

Details of shows at the Dôme-Imax are on p.337.

Back on the ground, with La Grande Arche behind you, an extraordinary monument to twentieth-century capitalism stands before and above you. To your right is the latest addition: another galactic *boule* lobbed from the realms of higher technology, come to displace La Villette's *Géode* as the world's largest cinema screen. It's the Dôme-Imax, in the same building complex as a new automobile museum.

In front of you, along the axis of the Voie Triomphale, an assortment of towers – token apartment blocks, offices of ELF, Esso, IBM, banks, and other businesses – compete for size, dazzle of surface and ability to make you dizzy. Finance made flesh, they are worth the trip out in themselves.

Mercifully, too, **bizarre artworks** lighten the nightmarish mood. **Joan Miró**'s giant wobbly creatures bemoan their misfit status beneath the biting edges and curveless heights of the buildings. Opposite is **Alexander Calder**'s red iron offering – a stabile rather than a mobile – while in between the two, a black marble metronome shape releases a goal-less line across the parvis. **Torricini**'s huge fat frog screams to escape to a nice quiet pond. A statue commemorating the **defence of Paris** in 1870 (for which the district is named) perches on a concrete plinth in front of a coloured plastic waterfall and fountain pool, while, nearer the river, disembodied people clutch each other round endlessly repeated concrete flowerbeds.

Inside the public buildings, **Art Défense**, alongside Agam's waterworks, displays models and photographs of the artworks, with a map to locate them and a guide for 15F (daily 10am–7pm), as well as temporary exhibitions (daily except Tues noon–7pm). The **CNIT building**, next to La Grande Arche, looks a bit like a covered stadium with businesses instead of seats. The pitch, all gleaming granite, is softened by slender bamboo trees; all the serious activity takes place beyond the far goal, where every major computer company has an office. There's also a *FNAC*, and overpriced cafés and brasseries. Less damaging to the pocket, if unhealthy for the soul, is the **Quatre-Temps** commercial centre, the biggest of its ilk in Europe, across the parvis, opposite. To minimize the encounter, enter from the left-hand doors, and you'll find crêperies, pizzerias and cafés without having to leave ground level.

New skyscrapers are still being built, but the glut of unrented office space, along with recession-led fears of new investment, have begun to bite. Plans for a *"tour sans fin"* – a tower without end – by Jean Nouvel, which would have a needle point disappearing into the clouds, have had to be put on hold until at least 1996.

Access to La Défense

Grande Arche de la Défense lies on *RER* line A and is the terminus of the no. 1 métro line. One stop before is the Esplanade de la Défense. Both are within zone 2.

Île de la Jatte and Île de Chatou

Below La Défense, the **Île de la Jatte** floats in the Seine just off rich and leafy Neuilly, an ideal venue for a romantic riverside walk. From the Pont de Levallois, near the métro, a flight of steps descends to the tip of the island. Formerly an industrial site, it is now part public garden (Mon–Fri 8.30am–6pm, Sat & Sun 10am–8pm), and part stylish new housing development. What remains of the island's erstwhile rustic character is to be found along the tree-lined boulevard de Levallois, where a line of Heath-Robinson houses and workshops quietly moulders away. On the right, a former *manège* has become the smart *Café de la Jatte*, while beside the bridge the pricey *Guinguette de Neuilly* restaurant still flourishes.

A long narrow island in a loop of the Seine further downstream, the **Île de Chatou** was once a rustic spot where Parisians came on the newly opened rail line to row, dine and flirt at the riverside *guinguettes* (eating and dancing establishments). The one *guinguette* to survive, just below the Pont de Chatou road bridge, is the **Maison Fournaise**. This was a favourite haunt of Renoir, Monet, Manet, Van Gogh, Seurat, Sisley, Courbet . . . half of them were in love with the proprietor's daughter, Alphonsine. One of Renoir's best-known canvases, *Le Déjeuner des Canotiers*, shows his friends lunching on the balcony. Vlaminck and his fellow-Fauves, Derain and Matisse, were also *habitués*.

It was from the Île de Chatou that Vlaminck set off for the 1905 Salon des Indépendants with the truckload of paintings that caused the critics to coin the term Fauvism.

Derelict for many years, the *Maison Fournaise* has recently reopened, restored and refurbished, as a very agreeable **restaurant** (see p.263). The outbuildings have been renovated too and house a small museum of memorabilia from this artistic past (Wed–Sun 11am–5pm; permanent exhibition 15F, temporary exhibition 25F). It's a great site, with a huge plane tree shading the river bank and a view of the barges racing downstream on the current.

Gustave Flourens

One of the boldest and most colourful of the Commune's commanders met his death on the Île de Chatou – **Gustave Flourens**, commander of the Red Belleville battalions. Although far from being a proletarian himself – he was of upper-class stock – he was a flamboyant champion of freedom, who had already taken part in Crete's attempts to throw off the Turkish yoke in the 1860s – thus his preferred uniform and arm, a Grecian kilt and *yataghan*. Impatient with the inertia of his colleagues, he led an attack on the government forces at Versailles. He continued, when others fell back. Surrounded and outnumbered, he was captured and had his head split in twain.

The downstream end of the island is now a park, tapering away into a tree-lined tail hardly wider than the path. The upstream end is spooky in the extreme. A track, black with oil and ooze and littered with assorted junk, bumps along past yellowed grass and bald poplar trees to a group of ruined houses stacked with beat-up cars.

Beyond the rail bridge, a louche-looking chalet, guarded by Alsatians, stands beside the track. A concrete block saying "No Entry" in home-made lettering bars the way. There are rumours that the house contains paintings, maybe frescoes, by important artists.

If you're bold enough to pass the Alsatians, there's a view from the head of the island of the old market gardens on the right bank and the decaying industrial landscape of Nanterre on the left.

Access to the island is from the **Rueil-Malmaison RER** stop. Take the Sortie av Albert 1, go left out of the station and right along the dual carriageway on to the bridge (10min walk). Bizarrely, there's a twice-yearly ham and antiques fair on the island, which could be fun to check out (March and September).

Paris: Listings

Accommodation

The hotels and hostels of Paris are often heavily booked, so it's wise to reserve a place well ahead of time, if you can. If not, there are two agencies to turn to for help: the tourist board's *Bureaux d'Accueil*, and the youth-oriented *Accueil des Jeunes en France (AJF)*. The former charges a small commission (from 20F for a hotel; 8F for a hostel); its function is to bale you out of last-minute difficulty rather than find the most economical deal. The *AJF* guarantees to find you a room – in a hostel (around 110F B&B) if you arrive early enough, or in a hotel (240F upwards). You pay for the accommodation, plus a 10F fee, and you receive vouchers to take to the establishment.

The best area for budget priced hotels is the 11^e. There are bargains in the 17e as well, but they are a lot further from the centre, where cheapies fill up quickly and need reserving well in advance. Not all hotels accept credit cards – you may have to send an international money order with your reservation.

Bureaux d'Accueil

Office du Tourisme, 127 av des Champs-Élysées, 8e; ☎47.23.61.72 (M^o Charles-de-Gaulle-Étoile). 9am–8pm throughout the year, except Dec 25, Jan 1 and May 1.

Gare d'Austerlitz, bd de l'Hôpital, 13e; ☎45.84.91.70. Mon–Sat 8am–3pm.

Gare de l'Est, bd de Strasbourg, 10e; ☎46.07.17.73. Summer Mon–Sat 8am–9pm; off season Mon–Sat 8am–8pm.

Gare de Lyon, 20 bd Diderot, 12e; ☎43.43.33.24. Summer Mon–Sat 8am–9pm; off season Mon–Sat 8am–8pm.

Gare du Nord, 18 rue de Dunkerque, 10^e; ☎45.26.94.82. Summer Mon–Sat 8am–9pm; off season Mon–Sat 8am–8pm.

Gare Montparnasse, pl R-Dautry, 15^e; ☎43.22.19.19. Summer Mon–Sat 8am–9pm; off season Mon–Sat 8am–9pm.

Tour Eiffel, Champ de Mars, 7^e; ☎45.51.22.15 (*RER* Champs-de-Mars-Tour Eiffel). May–Sept 11am–6pm.

24-hour information in English: ☎49.52.53.56.

Accueil des Jeunes en France

Gare du Nord, Nouvelle gare banlieue; ☎42.85.86.19. June–Sept 7.30am–9pm.

Each year, the Paris hoteliers' organization publishes a list of the most heavily booked periods for accommodation, which is available from *FGTO* offices (see p.34). The list is based on the dates of the *salons* or trade fairs; September and October are invariably the worst months, otherwise dates vary slightly from year to year. It is worth checking them out when planning a trip.

Accommodation

Beaubourg, 119 rue St-Martin, opposite Centre Beaubourg, 4e; ☎42.77.87.80 (Mº Châtelet-Les Halles). All year Mon–Sat 9.30am–5.30/6pm. This office can also be used as a forwarding address for mail.

Quartier Latin, 139 bd St-Michel, 5e; ☎43.54.95.86 (Mº Port-Royal). March–Oct Tues–Sat 10am–6pm.

If you're seriously interested in **a long stay on a low budget,** then it would be worth checking out the various basic and star-less hotels you'll see as you go about the streets, especially in less central districts. Many only let rooms by the month, often catering for immigrant workers, at very low prices.

Hotels

If you value your independence and have your own preferred choice of location, there's obviously more scope in booking a hotel yourself than in using the official reservation services.

There are a great many in all price categories and Paris scores heavily, especially in relation to London, in the still considerable, if dwindling, number of small **family-run hotels with budget priced rooms.**

The hotels listed in this section have been arranged by *arrondissement*, and divided into the following **seven price categories:**

① up to 160F
② 160–220F
③ 220–300F
④ 300–400F
⑤ 400–500F
⑥ 500–650F
⑦ over 650F

The prices given are for the cheapest double rooms normally available in high season. Most hotels have different kinds of rooms at differing prices; where the range in any one establishment is particularly large, we have used more than one symbol; eg ②–⑤.

Most of the hotels in the cheapest category are perfectly adequate. That means the sheets are clean, you can wash decently and there isn't a brothel on the floor below. There won't be much luxury, however. Price seems to be chiefly a function of location, the relative newness of the paintwork, the glitziness of the reception area, and the presence or absence of a lift. Most small Paris hotels are in converted old buildings, so the stairs are often dark and the rooms

cramped, with a view onto an internal courtyard, and the decor hardly spanking new.

We've assumed that most visitors come to Paris to see the city and will treat their hotel simply as a convenient and inexpensive place to spend a few of the night hours. Where we think conditions are at the limit of what most people will accept, we say **"basic".**

All hotel room prices have to be displayed somewhere prominent, in the entrance or by the reception desk usually. **Certain standard terms recur.** *Eau courante (EC)* means a room with washbasin only, *cabinet de toilette (CT)* means basin and bidet. In both cases there will be communal toilets on the landing and probably a shower as well. *Douche/WC* and *Bain/WC* mean that you have a shower or bath as well as toilet in the room. A room with a *grand lit* (double bed) is invariably cheaper than one with *deux lits* (two separate beds).

Breakfast (*petit déjeuner* or *PD*) is sometimes included (*compris*) in the room price and is sometimes extra (*en sus*) – the amount varies between about 25F and 45F per person. It isn't supposed to be obligatory, though some hotels may make a sour face when you decline to give it. Always make it clear whether you want breakfast or not when you take the room. It's usually a fairly indifferent continental breakfast, and you'll get a fresher, cheaper one at the local café.

A new municipal tax is now payable from 1F to 5F a night.

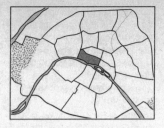

1er

Hôtel Vauvilliers, 6 rue Vauvilliers, 1er; ☎42.36.89.08 (Mº Châtelet/Les Halles/Louvre).

Need to book well in advance for this well-established cheapie. ①–②.

Hôtel St-Honoré, 85 rue St-Honoré, 1er; ☎42.36.20.38, fax 42.21.44.08 (Mº Châtelet-les-Halles/Louvre).
Conveniently close to the heart of things but being done up, so prices may rise. ③–④.

Hôtel Henri IV, 25 place Dauphine, 1er; ☎43.54.44.53 (Mº Pont-Neuf/Cité).
An ancient and well-known cheapie in the beautiful place Dauphine at the sharp end of the Île de la Cité. Nothing more luxurious than *cabinet de toilette* and now somewhat run down. Essential to book. ②.

Hôtel de Lille, 8 rue du Pélican, 1er; ☎42.33.33.42 (Mº Louvre/Les Halles/Palais-Royal).
Very small and a bargain for the area. ②–③.

Hôtel Lion d'Or, 5 rue de la Sourdière, 1er; ☎42.60.79.04, fax 42.60.09.14 (Mº Tuileries).
Spartan, but clean, friendly and very central. ③–④.

Hôtel de la Vallée, 84 rue St-Denis, 1er; ☎42.36.46.99 (Mº Étienne-Marcel/Châtelet).
Great location, absolutely smack in the middle of Les Halles. Perfectly adequate rooms. ③.

Hôtel Montpensier, 12 rue de Richelieu, 1er; ☎42.96.28.50, fax 42.86.02.70 (Mº Palais-Royal).
Characterless but convenient. ③–④.

Hôtel Flor Rivoli, 13 rue des Deux Boules, 1er; ☎42.33.49.60, fax 40.41.05.43 (Mº Châtelet).
Tucked away behind the rue de Rivoli, just by the métro entrance. ④.

Hôtel Washington Opéra, 50 rue de Richelieu, 1er; ☎42.96.68.06 (Mº Palais-Royal).
Pleasant and comfortable. ④–⑤.

Agora, 7 rue Cossonerie, 1er; ☎42.33.46.02, fax 42.33.80.99 (Mº Les Halles/Châtelet).
Charmming, peaceful hotel. ⑤–⑦.

Ducs d'Anjou, 1 rue Ste-Opportune, 1er; ☎42.36.92.24, fax 42.36.16.63 (Mº Châtelet).
A carefully renovated old building overlooking the endlessly crowded place Ste-Opportune in the middle of Les Halles nightlife district. ⑥.

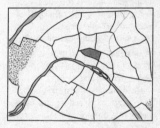

2e

Hôtel de France, 11 rue Marie-Stuart, 2e; ☎42.36.35.33 (Mº Châtelet-Les Halles/Sentier).
Don't be put off by exterior. Bargain prices, perfectly clean, and a great location. ②.

Hôtel Tiquetonne, 6 rue Tiquetonne, 2e; ☎42.36.94.58 (Mº Étienne-Marcel).
Bargain prices – 160–220F – but situated in a somewhat sleazy location: close to the red-light bit of rue St-Denis. ②–③.

Les Noailles, 9 rue Michodière, 2e; ☎47.42.92.90, fax 49.24.92.71 (Mº Opéra/4 Septembre).
Contemporary styling with traditional pleasures of garden and *terrasse*. ⑥–⑦.

Accommodation

The price categories used in this chapter are as follows:

① up to 160a

② 160–220F

③ 220–300F

④ 300–400F

⑤ 400–500F

⑥ 500–600F

.⑦ over 600F

For a fuller explanation, see opposite.

Accommodation

3e

Hôtel du Marais, 16 rue de Beauce, 3e;
☎ 42.72.30.26 (M° Arts-et-Métiers/Filles-du-Calvaire).
The genuine article: a prewar Paris chea-pie, untouched, with brown spiral stairs, iron handrail, tiled floors and Turkish loos. Primitive, certainly, but clean, with very nice *patron*, who runs a similarly old-fashioned bar downstairs. Quiet medieval street. ①.

Grand Hôtel des Arts et Métiers, 4 rue Borda, 3e; ☎ 48.87.73.89, fax 48.87.66.58 (M° Arts-et-Métiers).
Pleasant, well located and cheap. ②.

Hôtel Picard, 26 rue de Picardie, 3e; ☎ 48.87.53.82, fax 48.87.02.56 (M° Arts-et-Métiers/Filles-du-Calvaire).
Clean, comfortable and a great location. Run by a charming and very accommo-dating Pole, overlooking the Carreau du Temple. ③.

Hôtel de Saintonge le Marais, 16 rue de Saintonge, 3e; ☎ 42.77.91.13, fax 48.87.76.41 (M° Filles-du-Calvaire).
On the edge of the Marais, near the Picasso Museum. A soothing stay. ⑤–⑥.

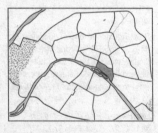

4e

Hôtel Moderne, 3 rue Caron, 4e; ☎ 48.87.97.05 (M° St-Paul/Bastille).

Much better than the first impression of the staircase would suggest, and the price is amazing for this area. ①.

Grand Hôtel du Loiret, 8 rue des Mauvais-Garçons, 4e; ☎ 48.87.77.00 (M° Hôtel-de-Ville).
Simple, but offering very good value for the price. ②.

Le Palais de Fes, 41 rue du Roi-de-Sicile, 4e; ☎ 42.72.03.68 (M° St-Paul/Hôtel-de-Ville).
Very cheap for the area: rather basic, with restaurant downstairs. ③.

Castex Hôtel, 5 rue Castex, 4e; ☎ 42.72.31.52 (M° Bastille/Sully-Morland).
Renovated building in a quiet street on the edge of the Marais. ④.

Grand Hôtel Jeanne d'Arc, 3 rue de Jarente, 4e; ☎ 48.87.62.11, fax 48.87.37.31 (M° St-Paul).
Clean, quiet and attractive. Necessary to reserve. ④.

Hôtel Sévigné, 2 rue Mahler, 4e; ☎ 42.72.76.17 (M° St-Paul).
Very comfortable and agreeable hotel, much frequented by foreigners and consequently overbooked. ④.

L'Hôtel du Septième Art, 20 rue St-Paul, 4e; ☎ 42.77.04.03, fax 42.77.69.10 (M° St-Paul/Pont-Marie).
Decorated with posters and photos from old movies. Pleasant and comfortable. The stairs and bathrooms live up to the black-and-white-movie style. Every room equipped with a safe. ⑤.

Hôtel Central Marais, 33 rue Vieille du Temple, 4e; ☎ 48.87.56.08, fax 42.77.06.27 (M° Hôtel-de-Ville).
The only gay hotel in Paris. Women welcome. ⑤.

Hôtel des Célestins, 1 rue Charles-V, 4e; ☎ 48.87.87.04 (M° Sully-Morland).
A very comfortable sleep in a restored seventeenth-century mansion. ⑥.

Grand Hôtel Mahler, 5 rue Mahler, 4e; ☎ 42.72.60.92, fax 42.72.25.37 (M° St-Paul).
Right in the heart of the Marais; recently renovated seventeenth-century vaulted wine cellar to breakfast in. ⑦.

Hôtel de Lutèce, 65 rue St-Louis-en-l'Île, 4e; ☎43.26.23.52, fax 43.29.60.25 (Mº Pont-Marie).
Small but exquisite rooms on the most desirable island in France. ⑦.

5e

Hôtel du Commerce, 14 rue de la Montagne-Ste-Geneviève, 5e; ☎43.54.89.69, fax 43.54.89.69 (Mº Maubert-Mutualité).
Renowned if somewhat gloomy cheapie. Nothing over 140F, in spite of the location in the heart of the Latin Quarter. Run by a charming old lady. Communal washing and toilets. No reservations, lots of competition. Turn up early in the morning. ①.

Hôtel des Alliés, 20 rue Berthollet, 5e; ☎43.31.47.52, fax 45.35.13.92 (Mº Censier-Daubenton).
Simple and clean, and bargain prices. ②.

Hôtel des Carmes, 5 rue des Carmes, 5e; ☎43.29.78.40, fax 43.29.57.17 (Mº Maubert-Mutualité).
A well-established, good-value tourist hotel. ③.

Hôtel le Central, 6 rue Descartes, 5e; ☎46.33.57.93 (Mº Maubert-Mutualité/Cardinal-Lemoine).
Clean and decent accommodation in a typically Parisian old house on top of the Montagne Ste-Geneviève, overlooking the gates of the former École Polytechnique. One of a dying breed. ③.

Hôtel Marignan, 13 rue du Sommerard, 5e; ☎43.54.63.81 (Mº Maubert-Mutualité).
One of the best bargains in town. Totally sympathetic to the needs of rucksack-toting foreigners, especially from Australia and NZ. Free laundry and ironing facilities,

plus a room to eat your own food in − plates provided. Even the maid speaks English. No reservations − turn up early. Rooms for two, three and four people. A three will take you close to 350F. ③.

Hôtel Esmeralda, 4 rue St-Julien-le-Pauvre, 5e; ☎43.54.19.20, fax 40.51.00.68 (Mº St-Michel/Maubert-Mutualité).
A discreet and ancient house on square Viviani with a superb view of Notre-Dame. Most rooms are 350−500F, though there are several much cheaper ones. ②−⑤.

Hôtel St-Jacques, 35 rue des Écoles, 5e; ☎43.26.82.53, fax 43.25.65.50 (Mº Maubert-Mutualité/Odéon).
Reasonable anchorage in the heart of the district. ②−④.

Royal Cardinal Hôtel, 1 rue des Écoles, 5e; ☎43.26.83.64, fax 44.07.22.32 (Mº Jussieu/Cardinal-Lemoine).
A comfortable and unexciting two-star, used to foreigners. ④.

Hôtel Gay-Lussac, 29 rue Gay-Lussac, 5e; ☎43.54.23.96 (Mº Luxembourg).
Still excellent value for the area. Need to book at least a week in advance. ④.

Grand-Hôtel St-Michel, 19 rue Cujas, 5e; ☎46.33.33.02 (Mº Odéon/Cluny).
Comfortable hotel, in a great location between the Panthéon and the Luxembourg gardens. ④−⑤.

Grand Hôtel Oriental, 2 rue d'Arras, 5e; ☎43.54.38.12., fax 40.51.86.78 (Mº Jussieu/Cardinal-Lemoine/Maubert-Mutualité).
Recently refurbished like so many of the old cheapies, but still quite a bargain for this locality − and nice people, too. ④.

Hôtel des Grandes Écoles, 75 rue du Cardinal-Lemoine, 5e; ☎43.26.79.23 (Mº Cardinal-Lemoine).
Refurbished, and comfortable, in a great location with a most attractive garden. ⑤.

Hôtel Mont-Blanc, 28 rue de la Huchette, 5e; ☎43.54.22.29, fax 46.34.14.56 (Mº St-Michel).
Another face-lift and higher prices, but a great if noisy location, a stone's throw from Notre-Dame. ⑤.

Accommodation

The price categories used in this chapter are as follows:
① up to 160F
② 160−220F
③ 220−300F
④ 300−400F
⑤ 400−500F
⑥ 500−600F
⑦ over 600F
For a fuller explanation, see p.208.

Accommodation

Hôtel de la Sorbonne, 6 rue Victor-Cousin, 5e; ☎ 43.54.58.08, fax 40.51.05.18 (Mᵒ Luxembourg).
An attractive old building, quiet, comfortable and close to the Luxembourg gardens. ⑤.

Le Jardin des Plantes, 5 rue Linné, 5e; ☎ 47.07.06.20, fax 47.07.62.74 (Mᵒ Jussieu).
Small, friendly hotel with a rooftop terrace for breakfasting. ⑤–⑦.

Hôtel des 3 Collèges, 16 rue Cujas, 5e; ☎ 43.54.67.30, fax 46.34.02.99 (Mᵒ Luxembourg).
Light and airy. ⑤–⑥.

Agora St-Germain, 42 rue des Bernardins, 5e; ☎ 46.34.13.00, fax 46.34.75.05 (Mᵒ Maubert-Mutualité).
Very pleasant and comfortable. ⑦.

6e

Hôtel de Nesle, 7 rue de Nesle, 6e; ☎ 43.54.62.41 (Mᵒ St-Michel).
Hippy haven. No reservations – arrive before 10am. ②–③.

Le Petit Trianon, 2 rue de l'Ancienne-Comédie, 6e; ☎ 43.54.94.64 (Mᵒ Odéon).
Adequate accommodation, right in the heart of things. ③–④.

Hôtel St-Michel, 17 rue Gît-le-Coeur, 6e; ☎ 43.26.98.70 (Mᵒ St-Michel).
Simple, but perfectly adequate. Great location in a very attractive old street close to the river. ③–④.

Hôtel St-Placide, 6 rue St-Placide, 6e; ☎ 45.48.80.08, fax 45.44.70.32 (Mᵒ Rennes/St-Placide).
Clean and adequate accommodation, right between Montparnasse and St-Germain. ④.

Hôtel du Dragon, 36 rue du Dragon, 6e; ☎ 45.48.51.05 (Mᵒ St-Germain-des-Prés/Sèvres-Babylone).
Great location and nice people. ③–④.

Hôtel Michelet Odéon, 6 place de l'Odéon, 6e; ☎ 46.34.27.80, fax 46.34.55.35 (Mᵒ Odéon/Luxembourg).
Another fantastic location. ⑤.

Welcome Hotel, 66 rue Seine, 6e; ☎ 46.34.24.80, fax 40.46.81.59 (Mᵒ Odéon).
Simple and quiet. ⑤.

Hôtel Récamier, 3bis place St-Sulpice, 6e; ☎ 43.26.04.89 (Mᵒ St-Sulpice/St-Germain).
Comfortable, and superbly sited. ⑥.

Hôtel des Marronniers, 21 rue Jacob, 6e; ☎ 43.25.30.60, fax 40.46 83.56 (Mᵒ St-Germain-des-Prés).
This three-star costs more than our usual prices, but it is a delightful place with a dining room overlooking a secret garden. Good for a special occasion. ⑥–⑦.

Hôtel de l'Odéon, 13 rue St-Sulpice, 6e; ☎ 43.25.70.11, fax 43.29.97.34 (Mᵒ St-Sulpice).
Old-fashioned luxury. ⑦.

Hôtel de l'Angleterre, 44 rue Jacob, 6e; ☎ 42.60.34.72, fax 42.60.16.93 (Mᵒ St-Germain-des-Prés).
Classy and elegant, this was once the British Embassy. Later Hemingway lived in room 14. ⑦.

7e

Grand Hôtel Lévèque, 29 rue Cler, 7e; ☎ 47.05.49.15, fax 45.50.49.36 (Mᵒ École-Militaire/Latour-Maubourg).
Clean and decent; nice people, who speak some English. Good location smack in the middle of the rue Cler market. Book one month ahead. ②–③.

Splendid Hôtel, 29 av de Tourville, 7e; ☎ 45.51.24.77, fax 44.18.94.60 (Mº École-Militaire).
A little noisy, but a great area with views, from the top floor, of the Eiffel Tower and Invalides. Some singles much cheaper than the standard 670F upwards. ③–⑦.

Hôtel du Palais Bourbon, 49 rue de Bourgogne, 7e; ☎ 45.51.63.32, fax 45.55.20.21 (Mº Varenne).
A handsome old building in a sunny street by the Musée Rodin. Rooms are spacious and light. ③–④.

Hôtel Solferino, 91 rue de Lille, 7e; ☎ 47.05.85.54, fax 45.55.51.16 (Mº Bac).
Attractive place, featuring an old-fashioned cage-lift. ③–⑥.

Hôtel du Centre, 24bis rue Cler, 7e; ☎ 47.05.52.53, fax 40.62.95.66 (Mº École-Militaire).
An old-fashioned, no-frills establishment in a posh and attractive neighbourhood. Need to reserve two weeks in advance. ④.

Hôtel du Champs-de-Mars, 7 rue du Champs-de-Mars, 7e; ☎ 45.51.52.30 (Mº École-Militaire).
Good comfortable accommodation in a quiet street off av Bosquet. Closed second week in August. ④–⑤.

Hôtel Malar, 29 rue Malar, 7e; ☎ 45.51.38.46, fax 45.51.38.46 (Mº Latour-Maubourg/Invalides).
Small, with slightly pokey rooms, but in a very attractive street close to the river. Prices include breakfast for two. ④.

Royal Phare Hôtel, 40 av de la Motte-Picquet, 7e; ☎ 47.05.57.30, fax 45.51.64.41 (Mº École-Militaire).
A bit impersonal, but very convenient and has some good views. Also, close to rue Cler and its sumptuous market. ④.

Le Pavillon, 54 rue St-Dominique, 7e; ☎ 45.51.42.87, fax 45.51.32.79 (Mº Invalides/Latour-Maubourg).
A tiny former convent set back from the tempting shops of the rue St-Dominique in a leafy courtyard. A lovely setting, but the rooms are a little pokey for the price: 420F. ⑤–⑥.

Hôtel de la Tulipe, 33 rue Malar, 7e; ☎ 45.51.67.21, fax 47.53.96.37 (Mº Latour-Maubourg).
Patio for summer breakfast and drinks. Beamy and cottagey. But as with all hotels in this area you are paying for the location rather than great luxury. ⑤.

Hôtel de Beaune, 29 rue de Beaune, 7e; ☎ 42.61.24.89, fax 49.27.02.12 (Mº Bac).
A very pretty, ideally located hotel. ⑥.

Hôtel Bersoly's St-Germain, 28 rue de Lille, 7e; ☎ 42.60.73.79, fax 49.27.05.55 (Mº Bac).
Small but exquisite rooms each named after an artist. Impeccable service. ⑦.

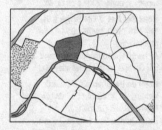

8e

Hôtel d'Artois, 94 rue la Boétie, 8e; ☎ 43.59.84.12 (Mº St-Philippe-du-Roule).
One of the cheapest in this smartest part of town. ③–⑤.

Hôtel de la Paix, 22 rue Roquépine, 8e; ☎ 42.65.14.36 (Mº St-Augustine).
A bit gloomy, but in a very Parisian fashion. ④.

Hôtel d'Albion, 15 rue Penthièvre, 8e; ☎ 42.65.84.15, fax 49.24.03.47 (Mº Miromesnil/Champs-Élysées).
Uninspired decor but a beautiful little garden. ④–⑤.

Hôtel de Penthièvre, 21 rue Penthièvre, 8e; ☎ 43.59.87.63, fax 45.62.00.76 (Mº Miromesnil/Champs-Élysées).
Good value for the location; pleasant management and beautiful Siamese cat always stalking the foyer. ④–⑤.

Hôtel de L'Élysée, 12 rue des Saussaies, 8e; ☎ 42.65.29.25, fax 42.65.64.28 (Mº St-Philippe-du-Roule).
Chandeliers and four-posters – classic luxury. ⑦.

Accommodation

The price categories used in this chapter are as follows:

① *up to 160F*
② *160–220F*
③ *220–300F*
④ *300–400F*
⑤ *400–500F*
⑥ *500–600F*
⑦ *over 600F*
For a fuller explanation, see p.208.

Accommodation

9e

Hôtel des Trois Poussins, 15 rue Clauzel, 9e; ☎ 48.74.38.20 (Mº St-Georges).
At the foot of Montmartre is this reliable cheapie. You can book rooms for the month at under 200F a night. ③.

Hôtel des Arts, 7 Cité Bergère, 9e; ☎ 42.46.73.30, fax 48.00.94.42 (Mº Montmartre).
A charming and friendly hotel and one of the cheaper in this quiet alley. ④.

Hôtel de Beauharnais, 51 rue de la Victoire, 9e; ☎ 48.74.71.13 (Mº Le Peletier/Havre-Caumartin).
Louis Quinze, First Empire . . . every room decorated in a different period style. ④.

Hôtel des Croisés, 63 rue St-Lazare, 9e; ☎ 48.74.78.24, fax 49.95.04.43 (Mº Trinité).
Low on mod cons but great on style: a hotch-potch of different periods. ④.

Hôtel Imperial, 45 rue de la Victoire, 9e; ☎ 48.74.10.47 (Mº Le Peletier/Chaussée d'Antin).
Young, efficient manager speaking excellent English. Fairly nondescript rooms but acceptable. ④.

Hôtel St-Louis, 8 rue Boisson, 9e; ☎ 42.49.18.85 (Mº Goncourt).
Very pleasant. modern building. ④.

Mondial Hôtel, 21 rue Notre-Dame-de-Lorette, 9e; ☎ 48.78.60.47 (Mº St-Georges).
Acceptable, if uninspired, and by the lovely pl St-Georges. Rooms for four under 500F. ④.

Parrotel Paris-Montholon, 11bis rue Pierre-Sémard, 9e; ☎ 48.78.28.94, fax 42.80.11.15 (Mº Poissonnière).

Reasonable value for money, though the rooms are a little small and dark. ④–⑤.

Hôtel St-Louis, 8 rue Boisson St-Louis, 9e; ☎ 42.49.18.85 (Mº Goncourt).
Modern building, very pleasant. ④.

Hôtel Chopin, 46 passage Jouffroy, 9e; ☎ 47.70.58.10., fax 42.47.00.70 (Mº Montmartre).
Entrance on bd Montmartre, near the rue du Faubourg-Montmartre. A splendid period building in the old *passage*. ⑤.

Hôtel du Léman, 20 rue Trévise, 9e; ☎ 42.46.50.66, fax 48.24.27.59 (Mº Montmartre).
Tiny rooms but a delightful address. ⑤–⑦.

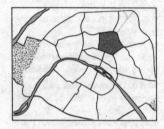

10e

Hôtel Savoy, 9 rue Jarry, 10e; ☎ 47.70.03.72 (Mº Gare-de-l'Est, Château-d'Eau).
Pokey and basic but still very cheap. ①.

Hôtel du Jura, 6 rue de Jarry, 10e; ☎ 47.70.06.66 (Mº Gare-de-l'Est, Château-d'Eau).
Primitive, but friendly and decent. ①–②.

Hôtel Jarry, 4 rue Jarry, 10e; ☎ 47.70.70.38 (Mº Gare-de-l'Est, Château-d'Eau).
First impression is gloomy, but the rooms are okay. ②–③.

Sibour Hôtel, 4 rue Sibour, 10e; ☎ 46.07.20.74, fax 46.07.37.17 (Mº Gare-de-l'Est).
Good value, if characterless. ②–③.

Adix Hôtel, 30 rue Lucien-Sampaix, 10e; ☎ 42.08.19.74, fax 42.08.27.28 (Mº Bonsergent).

In a pleasant street close to the St-Martin canal. Reasonable value for money, including three-person rooms at 515F. ④–⑤.

Belta Hôtel Résidence, 46 rue Lucien-Sampaix, 10ᵉ; ☎46.07.23.87, fax 42.09.87.27 (Mº Gare-de-l'Est).
Good location on the St-Martin canal bank. Totally renovated in bland airport style, but is still comfortable. ⑤–⑥.

Hôtel St-Laurent, 5 rue St-Laurent, 10ᵉ; ☎42.09.83.50, fax 42.09.83.50 (Mº Gare-de-l'Est).
A comfortable base close to the stations, with some fine views of the city from the top floor. ⑥.

11ᵉ

Hôtel de l'Europe, 10 rue Louis-Bonnet, 11ᵉ; ☎43.57.17.49 (Mº Belleville).
A very basic flop. ①.

Mary's Hotel, 15 rue de Malte, 11ᵉ; ☎47.00.81.70, fax 47.00.58.06 (Mº République).
Dull, but clean and cheap. ②–③.

Hôtel des Arts, 2 rue Godefroy-Cavaignac, 11ᵉ; ☎43.79.72.57 (Mº Voltaire).
Not much charm, but hospitable and acceptable at the price. ②–④.

Hôtel de la Nouvelle France, 31 rue Keller, 11ᵉ; ☎47.00.40.74 (Mº Bréguet-Sabin).
An old-fashioned and basic hotel. ②.

Hôtel de Vienne, 43 rue de Malte, 11ᵉ; ☎48.05.44.42 (Mº République/Oberkampf).
Very pleasant and good-value cheapie, and nice people. ②.

Cosmo's Hotel, 35 rue Jean-Pierre Timbaud, 11ᵉ; ☎43.57.25.88 (Mº Parmentier).

Clean and decent, and with good restaurants nearby. ②–③.

Grand Hôtel Amelot, 54 rue Amelot, 11ᵉ; ☎48.06.15.19 (Mº St-Sébastien-Froissart).
Reasonable rooms, and a good location near the Bastille. ③.

Hôtel de Nevers, 53 rue de Malte, 11ᵉ; ☎47.00.56.18 (Mº République/Oberkampf).
Clean and decent accommodation run by very sympathetic proprietor. Excellent breakfasts. ③–④.

Hôtel Parmentier, 91 rue Oberkampf, 11ᵉ; ☎43.57.02.09 (Mº Parmentier).
Clean and friendly. Better to get a room on the courtyard if you can; the street side is a little noisy. ③.

Plessis-Hôtel, 25 rue du Grand-Prieuré, 11ᵉ; ☎47.00.13.38 (Mº République/Oberkampf).
A friendly, good-value hotel. ③.

Garden Hôtel, 1 rue du Général-Blaise, 11ᵉ; ☎47.00.57.93 (Mº St-Ambroise).
Comfortable but a little overpriced at 300F, even if it is located on the pleasant Square Parmentier. ④–⑤.

Hôtel du Nord et de l'Est, 49 rue de Malte, 11ᵉ; ☎47.00.71.70, fax 43.57.51.16 (Mº République/Oberkampf).
Ordinary, decent accommodation. ④.

Hôtel St-Martin, 12 rue Léon-Frot, 11ᵉ; ☎43.71.09.14 (Mº Boulets-Montreuil).
Boring neighbourhood, but a nice hotel – friendly with all the mod cons. ④.

Pax Hotel, 12 rue de Charonne, 11ᵉ; ☎47.00.40.98 (Mº Ledru-Rollin/Bastille).
A reasonable establishment if you want to be in the centre of the Bastille's night-life. ③–④.

Hôtel Beaumarchais, 3 rue Oberkampf, 11ᵉ; ☎43.38.16.16, fax 43.38.32.86 (Mº Filles du Calvaire/Oberkampf).
All rooms with bathrooms and a complimentary copy of *Libération* newspaper every day. Pleasant. ④.

Méridional, 36 bd Richard-Lenoir, 11ᵉ; ☎48.05.75.00, fax 43.57.42.85 (Mº Bréguet-Sabin).
Attractive with light rooms and a garden. ⑥–⑦.

Accommodation

The price categories used in this chapter are as follows:
① up to 160F
② 160–220F
③ 220–300F
④ 300–400F
⑤ 400–500F
⑥ 500–600F
⑦ over 600F
For a fuller explanation, see p.208.

Accommodation

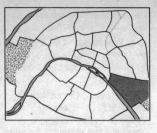

12ᵉ

Paris Hôtel, 93 rue de Charenton, 12ᵉ; ☎46.28.13.63 (Mº Ledru-Rollin/Gare de Lyon).
Basic. ①.

Grand Hôtel Doré, 201 av Daumesnil 12ᵉ; ☎43.43.66.89, fax 43.43.65.20 (Mº Daumesnil).
Not very central but smart for the price. ④.

Hôtel des Pyrénées, 204 rue du Faubourg-St-Antoine, 12ᵉ; ☎43.72. 07.46, fax 43.72.98.45 (Mº Faidherbe-Chaligny).
Comfortable and quiet behind its posh reception area. ④.

Hôtel du Midi, 31 rue Traversière, 12ᵉ; ☎43.07.88.68 (Mº Ledru-Rollin).
Close to the Gare du Lyon and very nice. ③–④.

Hôtel Saphir, 35 rue de Citeaux, 12ᵉ; ☎43.07.77.28, fax 43.46.67.45 (Mº Faidherbe-Chaligny).
On a quiet street of the Faubourg St-Antoine. No special charms but comfortable. ⑤.

13ᵉ

Arian Hôtel, 102 av de Choisy, 13ᵉ; ☎45.70.76.00 (Mº Tolbiac).
Boring but cheap. ②.

Hôtel de la Place des Alpes, 2 place des Alpes, 13ᵉ; ☎45.35.14.14 (Mº Place-d'Italie).
Agreeable enough for the price. ③.

Hôtel des Arts, 8 rue Coypel, 13ᵉ; ☎47.07.76.32, fax 43.31.18.09 (Mº Place d'Italie).
Very decent, modest but modern hotel. ③.

Hôtel Verlaine, 51 rue Bobillot, 13ᵉ; ☎45.89.56.14 (Mº Place-d'Italie).
Comfortable and clean. ③–④.

Résidence Les Gobelins, 9 rue des Gobelins, 13ᵉ; ☎47.07.26.90, fax 43.31.44.05 (Mº Les Gobelins).
Delightful establishment, but well known so needs booking well in advance. ⑤.

14ᵉ

Ouest Hotel, 27 rue de Gergovie, 14ᵉ; ☎45.42.64.99, fax 45.42.46.65 (Mº Pernety).
Basic. ②.

Savoy Hôtel, 16 rue Fermat, 14ᵉ; ☎43.22.60.63 (Mº Denfert-Rochereau/Gaîté).
Closes 1am. Basic. ②.

Hôtel de la Loire, 39bis rue du Moulin-Vert, 14ᵉ; ☎45.40.66.88, fax 45.40.89.07 (Mº Alésia/Plaisance).
Decent cheapie on a very quiet street, with a little garden for breakfast. ③.

Hôtel Le Royal, 49 rue Raymond-Losserand, 14ᵉ; ☎43.22.14.04 (Mº Pernety/Gaîté).
Reasonable bargain in the middle of the old 14ᵉ. ③.

Virginia Hotel, 66 rue du Père Corentin, 14ᵉ; ☎45.40.70.90, fax 45.40.95.21 (Mº Pte d'Orléans).
Quiet part of town some way from the centre but very good value. ③–④.

Hôtel du Parc, 6 rue Jolivet, 14e;
☎ 43.20.95.54, fax 42.79.82.62 (Mº
Montparnasse/Edgar-Quinet).
On a pleasant quiet square behind
Montparnasse, but no longer the knock-
down bargain it used to be. ④–⑤.

Alésia-Montparnasse, 84 rue Raymond-
Losserand, 14e; ☎ 45.42.16.03, fax
45.42.11.60 (Mº Pernety/Gaîté).
Comfortable, well-placed hotel. ⑥.

15e

Mondial Hôtel, 136 bd de Grenelle, 15e;
☎ 45.79.73.57, fax 45.79.58.65 (Mº La
Motte-Picquet).
Friendly and decent, with large rooms
and good views in spite of a rather grim
appearance. Right under the raised métro.
Prices include breakfast. ③.

Pratic Hôtel, 20 rue de l'Ingénieur-Keller,
15e; ☎ 45.77.70.58, fax 40.59.43.75 (Mº
Charles-Michels).
Very nice: clean and friendly. Still some
rooms under 220F. Close to the Eiffel
Tower. ③.

Tourisme Hôtel, 66 av de la Motte-
Picquet, 15e; ☎ 47.34.28.01, fax
47.83.66.54 (Mº La Motte-Picquet).
The building itself is an unprepossessing
barrack-like structure on the corner of bd
de Grenelle, but once you're inside the
rooms are fine. ④.

Hôtel Ini, 159 bd Lefebvre, 15e;
☎ 48.28.18.35, fax 48.28.11.21 (Mº Porte-
de-Vanves).
Comfortable rooms – attractively situated on
a pleasant tree-lined exterior boulevard. ④.

Hôtel King, 1 rue de Chambéry, 15e;
☎ 45.33.99.06, fax 42.50.02.34 (Mº Porte-
de-Vanves/Convention).

Quiet and decent hotel, located
conveniently close to the Parc Georges-
Brassens. ⑤.

Hôtel Fondary, 30 rue Fondary, 15e;
☎ 45.75.14.75, fax 45.75.84.42 (Mº
Émile-Zola).
Quiet and agreeable location. Doubles
around 400F. ⑤.

Hôtel Wallace, 89 rue Fondary, 15e;
☎ 45.78.83.30, fax 40.58.19.43 (Mº
Émile-Zola).
Unpretentious and charming place with a
pretty garden in the courtyard. ⑥.

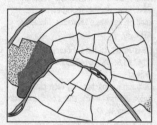

16e

Hameau de Passy, 48 rue Passy, 16e;
☎ 42.88.47.55, fax 42.30.83.72 (Mº
Muette).
Tucked away in a mews – utterly
peaceful and with faultless service.
⑥–⑦.

Hôtel Pergolèse, 3 rue Pergolèse, 16e;
☎ 40.67.96.77, fax 45.00.42.60 (Mº
Argentine).
Modern and very stylish design in a classic *Beaux Quartiers* building. ⑦.

17e

Hôtel Gauthey, 5 rue Gauthey, 17e;
☎ 46.27.15.48 (Mº Brochant).
Basic but clean. ①.

Accommodation

*The price
categories used
in this chapter
are as follows:*

① *up to 160F*

② *160–220F*

③ *220–300F*

④ *300–400F*

⑤ *400–500F*

⑥ *500–600F*

⑦ *over 600F*
*For a fuller
explanation,
see p.208.*

Accommodation

Studios–Hôtel des Batignolles, 36 rue des Batignolles, 17e; ☎42.94.27.66 (Mº Rome/Place Clichy).
A pretty grotty hotel, but it's redeeming feature is that it's very cheap. ①.

Hôtel Avenir-Jonquière, 23 rue de la Jonquière, 17e; ☎46.27.83.41 (Mº Guy-Môquet).
Clean, friendly establishment. offering bargain accommodation. ②.

Hôtel des Batignolles, 26–28 rue des Batignolles, 17e; ☎43.87.70.40 (Mº Rome/Place-Clichy).
A quiet and very reasonable establishment in a neighbourhood that prides itself on its village character. Triples for 370F. ④.

Lévis-Hôtel, 16 rue Lebouteux, 17e; ☎47.63.86.38, fax 40.53.00.92 (Mº Villiers).
Only ten rooms, but very nice, clean and quiet, in a small side street off the rue de Lévis market. ④.

Hôtel du Roi René, 72 place Félix-Lobligeois, 17e; ☎42.26.72.73, fax 42.63.74.99 (Mº Rome/Villiers).
A mid-priced hotel in a very nice location by a mini-Greek temple and public garden. ⑤.

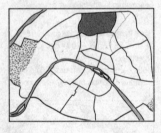

18e

Idéal Hôtel, 3 rue des Trois-Frères, 18e; ☎46.06.63.63 (Mº Abbesses).
Marvellous location on the slopes of Montmartre. Cheap and clean. A real bargain. ①–③.

Hôtel New Montmartre, 7 rue Paul Albert, 18e; ☎46.06.03.03, fax 46.06.73.28 (Mº Anvers/Château Rouge).
Just east of the Sacré-Cœur; light and roomy. ②.

Style Hôtel, 8 rue Ganneron, 18e; ☎45.22.37.59 (Mº Place de Clichy).
Wooden floors, marble fireplaces, a secluded internal courtyard, nice people – great value. ②–③.

Hôtel André Gill, 4 rue André-Gill, 18e; ☎42.62.48.48, fax 42.62.77.92 (Mº Pigalle/Abbesses).
Low prices for very adequate rooms in a great location on the slopes of Montmartre. It's very quiet too, in a dead-end alley off rue des Martyrs. ③.

Hôtel Tholozé, 24 rue Tholozé, 18e; ☎46.06.74.83 (Mº Blanche/Abbesses).
A genuine bargain – clean, friendly and quiet, in a steep, quiet street below the Moulin de la Galette. ③.

La Résidence Montmartre, 10 rue Burcq, 18e; ☎46.06.51.91, fax 42.52.82.59 (Mº Abbesses).
A smart and comfortable hotel. ⑥.

19e

Hôtel Le Richemont, 22 rue de Joinville, 19e; ☎44.89.21.00 (Mº Crimé).
A most unlikely place, but a real bargain in a brand new modern block close to the Canal St-Martin and La Villette. ②.

Bolivar, 5 av Simon-Bolivar, 19e; ☎42.08.16.87, fax 42.45.37.17 (Mº Bolivar).
Close to the Parc des Buttes-Chaumont. Fairly basic. ②–③.

Hôtel Rhin et Danube, 3 pl Rhin-et-Danube, 19e; ☎42.45.10.13, fax 42.06.88.82 (Mº Danube).
Way out of the centre but on the airy heights of Belleville and geared to self-catering. The only disadvantage is the building works on the square which should be finished by mid-1995. ④.

20e

Hôtel Fleury, 28 rue Villiers de-l'Isle-Adam, 20e; ☎43.61.51.70 (Mº Gambetta). Unmodernized but cheap. The manager is a bit deaf. ②.

Hôtel Tamaris, 14 rue des Maraîchers, 20e; ☎43.72.85.48 (Mº Porte de Vincennes). Simple, clean, and attractive, and run by nice people. Extremely good value at 135–258F. Close to métro and terminus of 26 bus route from Gare du Nord. Closed mid-July to mid-August. ②–③.

Ermitage Hôtel, 42bis rue de l'Ermitage, 20e; ☎46.36.23.44 (Mº Jourdain). A clean and decent cheap hotel, close to the leafy, provincial rue des Pyrénées. ③.

Mary's, 118 rue Orfila, 20e; ☎43.61.51.68 (Mº Pelleport). Simple, clean and friendly; but good value. A little far out, at the rue Pelleport end of rue Orfila. ②.

Hôtel Nadaud, 8 rue de la Bidassoa, 20e; ☎46.36.87.79 (Mº Gambetta). Very good value, close to the Père-Lachaise cemetery. Closed Aug. ③.

Hôtel Pyrénées-Gambetta, 12 rue Père-Lachaise, 20e; ☎47.97.76.57, fax 47.97.17.61 (Mº Gambetta). Perfect for anyone passionate about the Père-Lachaise cemetery. Very pleasant. ④.

Hostels, Foyers and Campsites

Youth Hostels

The cheapest youth accommodation is to be found in the hostels run by the **French** Youth Hostel Association, for which you need International YHA membership (no age limit), and those connected with the **MIJE** (Maison Internationale de la Jeunesse et des Étudiants) and **UCRIF** (Union des Centres de Rencontres Internationaux de France). Current costs for bed and breakfast are: youth hostels 106–126F, MIJE hostels 115F and UCRIF between 100F and 200F. The determining factor is whether you have an individual or shared room. There is no effective age limit at either.

There are only two **youth hostels** in Paris proper and it's advisable to book ahead in summer (send a cheque or postal order to cover the cost of the first night):

Jules Ferry, 8 bd Jules-Ferry, 11e; ☎43.57.55.60, fax 40.21.79.92 (Mº République).

In the lively and colourful area at the foot of the Belleville hill. When full, they will help you find a bed elsewhere for the same price.

D'Artagnan, 80 rue Vitruve, 20e; ☎43.61.08.75, fax 43.61.09.12 (Mº Porte-de-Bagnolet).

A pleasant modern building on the edge of the city in Charonne.

The **Cité des Sciences**, just out of the city to the northeast, is the closest suburban hostel: 24 rue des Sept-Arpents 93310, Le Pré-St-Gervais; ☎48.43.26.82 (Mº Hoche). Other suburban hostels are less conveniently located. They include:

3 rue Marcel-Duhamel, Arpajon; ☎64.90.28.85. RER ligne C4 to Arpajon.

125 av Villeneuve-Saint-Georges, Choisy-le-Roi; ☎48.90.92.30 (RER ligne C from St-Michel to Choisy-le-Roi, and bus #182 direction Villeneuve-Triage, station "Auberge de Jeunesse").

Points d'Accueil Jeunesse, allée des Matelots, route de St-Cyr, 7800 Versailles ☎30.21.84.85 (RER ligne C to Versailles-Chantiers, then bus P).

Open mid-June to mid-Sept. 16–26-year-olds only.

Accommodation

The price categories used in this chapter are as follows:
① up to 160F
② 160–220F
③ 220–300F
④ 300–400F
⑤ 400–500F
⑥ 500–600F
⑦ over 600F
For a fuller explanation, see p.208.

Accommodation

Foyers

The MIJE's *foyers*, which cannot be booked in advance and where the maximum length of stay is seven days, are:

Résidence Bastille, 151 av Ledru-Rollin, 11e; ☎ 43.79.53.86 (Mº Ledru-Rollin/Bastille/Voltaire).

Le Fourcy, 6 rue de Fourcy, 4e; ☎ 42.74.23.45 (Mº St-Paul).

Le Fauconnier, 11 rue du Fauconnier, 4e; ☎ 42.74.23.45 (Mº St-Paul/Pont-Marie).

Maubuisson, 12 rue des Barres, 4e; ☎ 42.72.23.45 (Mº Pont-Marie/Hôtel-de-Ville).

François Miron, 6 rue François-Miron, 4e (Mº Hôtel-de-Ville). Annexe of above.

The latter four are superbly and very centrally situated, occupying historic buildings in the Marais.

Other *foyers* include:

Résidence Coubertin, 53 rue Lhomond, 5e; ☎ 43.36.18.12 (Mº Censier-Daubenton). July & Aug only.

Résidence Luxembourg, 270 rue St-Jacques, 5e; ☎ 43.25.06.20 (Mº Luxembourg/Port-Royal). July–Sept only.

Cité Universitaire, bd Jourdan, 14e; ☎ 45.89.68.52 (*RER* Cité Universitaire). Mon–Fri 9am–5pm.
The student campus can provide a list of the different *maisons* or *fondations* that let out rooms during the summer holidays. These include the *Maison des États-Unis* (☎ 45.89.35.79) and the *Collège Franco-Britannique* (☎ 44.16.24.00). Costs vary from around 120F to 140F a night.

UCRIF has at its disposal **eleven hostels** in or close to Paris, for which there is no advance booking. *UCRIF* advises you either to phone direct to the hostels on arrival in Paris or go to their main office at 4 rue Jean-Jacques-Rousseau, 1er; ☎ 42.60.42.40. Mon–Fri 10am–6pm.

BVJ (Bureau de Voyages de la Jeunesse) Centre International de Paris/Louvre, 20 rue Jean-Jacques-Rousseau, 1er; ☎ 42.36.88.18, fax 42.33.40.53 (Mº Louvre/Châtelet-Les Halles).

BVJ Centre International de Paris/Opéra, 11 rue Thérèse, 1er; ☎ 42.60.77.23, fax 42.33.40.53 (Mº Pyramides/Palais-Royal).

BVJ Centre International de Paris/Les Halles, 5 rue du Pélican, 1er; ☎ 40.26.92.45, fax 42.33.40.53 (Mº Louvre/Châtelet-Les Halles/Palais-Royal).

BVJ Centre International de Paris/Quartier Latin, 44 rue des Bernardins, 5e; ☎ 43.29.34.80, fax 42.33.40.53 (Mº Maubert-Mutualité).

Maison des Clubs UNESCO de Paris, 43 rue de la Glacière, 13e; ☎ 43.36.00.63, fax 45.35.05.96 (Mº Glacière).

Centre d'Accueil et d'Animation Paris 20e, 46 rue Louis-Lumière, 20e; ☎ 43.61.24.51 (Mº Porte-de-Bagnolet/Porte-de-Montreuil).

Centre International de Séjour de Paris (CISP) Kellermann, 17 bd Kellermann, 13e; ☎ 45.80.70.76 (Mº Porte-d'Italie).

Centre International de Séjour de Paris (CISP) Maurice Ravel, 6 av Maurice-Ravel, 12e; ☎ 43.43.19.01, fax 43.44.45.30 (Mº Porte-de-Vincennes).

Foyer International d'Accueil de Paris Jean Monnet, 30 rue Cabanis, 14e; ☎ 45.89.89.15, fax 45.81.63.91 (Mº Glacière).

Centre International de Séjour Léo Lagrange, 107 rue Martre, Clichy; ☎ 42.70.03.22 (Mº Mairie-de-Clichy).

All the above provide canteen meals for around 50F.

Further possibilities include more hostel-type accommodation, notably:

Auberge Ste-Marguerite, 10 rue Trousseau, 11e; ☎ 47.00.62.00, fax 47.00.33.16 (Mº Bastille/Ledru-Rollin). No card necessary. 90F B&B.

Aloha Hostel, 1 rue Borromé, 15e; ☎ 42.73.03.03 (Mº Volontaires). Same management as *Three Ducks* opposite. 85F. Arrive by 9am to book.

Association des Étudiants Protestants de Paris (Protestant Student Association),

46 rue de Vaugirard, 6e; ☎43.33.23.30 (M° Luxembourg).
Open to people aged 18–25 of all nationalities and creeds. No advance booking; turn up or phone on the day – early. Maximum stay five weeks. Current cost is 10F membership (valid for subsequent visits) and 65F for bed and breakfast, plus 150F deposit. Friendly, but pretty basic.

CROUS, Académie de Paris, 39 av Georges-Bernanos, 5e; ☎40.51.36.00 (M° Port-Royal).
This is the organization which controls student accommodation in Paris and lets free space during university vacations.

Maison Internationale des Jeunes, 4 rue Titon, 11e; ☎43.71.99.21, fax 43.71.78.58 (M° Faidherbe-Chaligny).
For 18–30-year-olds. Operates like a youth hostel, but does not require YHA membership. 110F B&B.

Three Ducks Hostel, 6 pl Étienne-Pernet, 15e; ☎48.42.04.05 (M° Emile-Zola).
A private youth hostel, with no age limit – though as the warden says himself, it's mainly young and noisy. Lock-out 11am–5pm, curfew at 1am. 85F – some rooms for couples. Kitchen facilities. It's necessary to book between May and Oct: send the price of the first night.

Young and Happy Hostel, 80 rue Mouffetard, 5e; ☎45.35.09.53, fax 47.07.22.24 (M° Monge/Censier-Daubenton).
Turn up between 8pm and 10pm to book. Noisy, basic and studenty. 95F B&B.

For Women Only

Palais de la Femme, 94 rue de Charonne, 11e; ☎43.71.11.27, fax 43.71.15.55 (M° Charonne/Faidherbe-Chaligny).
Salvation Army hostel, where there is usually room, especially in summer, in the absence of regular residents, but you need to book in advance, preferably in writing. Current cost 85F for a bed; self-service meal about 30F.

Résidence Orfila, 65 rue Orfila, 20e; ☎46.36.82.80 (M° Gambetta/Pelleport).
Up to age 24 except in July and August when there are no restrictions. May to Sept-ember are the best months for vacancies. Current cost is around 90F for B&B. There are cooking facilities and the possibility of an evening meal. Nice "villagey" location not far from Père-Lachaise cemetery.

Foyer des Jeunes Filles, 234 rue Tolbiac, 13e; ☎45.89.06.42, fax 43.71.78.58 (M° Glacière).
18–25-year-olds only. Excellent facilities. 100F.

For sundry other addresses try the **CIDJ** office's information files at 101 quai Branly, 15e (M° Bir-Hakeim).

Camping

With the exception of the one in the Bois de Boulogne, most of Paris' **campsites** are some way out of the city.

Camping du Bois de Boulogne, Allée du Bord-de-l'Eau, 16e (M° Porte-Maillot and bus #244 to Route des Moulins). April–Oct; camping shuttle bus 10F; ☎45.24.30.00.
Much the most central campsite, next to the River Seine in the Bois de Boulogne, and usually booked out in summer. 60–80F for a tent. The ground is pebbly, but the site is well equipped and has a useful information office.

Camping du Parc de la Colline (March 15–Oct 15; slightly further east than the above), Route de Lagny, 77200 Torcy; ☎60.05.42.32 (*RER ligne A4* to Torcy, then bus #421 to stop Le Clos).

Camping du Parc-Étang (April to end Sept; southwest of Paris), Base de Loisirs, 78180 Montigny-le-Bretonneux; ☎30.58.56.20 (*RER ligne C* St-Quentin-en-Yvelines. Métro connections for *RER ligne C* at Invalides, St-Michel, Gare d'Austerlitz).

The tourist office can provide details of other campsites.

Bed and Breakfast

Finally, there remains the possibility of Bed and Breakfast in people's houses.

Accommodation

Accommodation

Two organizations to contact are: **France Lodge**, 5 rue du Faubourg Montmartre, 9e; ☎ 42.46.68.19. From 85F plus 85F annual membership.

Bed and breakfast, 7 rue Campagne-Première, 14e; ☎ 43.35.11.26. 2 days' minimum stay: 130–350F plus 50F annual membership.

Chapter 15

Eating and Drinking

As in the rest of France, Parisian cooking has art status, the top chefs are stars, and dining out is a national pastime, whether it's at the bistro on the corner or at a famed house of *haute cuisine*. In recent years, prices at the top end of the market have come down – with some superb-value midday menus on offer – while the quality at the bottom end, particularly in the tourist hotspots, has sunk. Our advice to gourmets is to snack it out for a few days, then go for a blow-out (but don't forget that wine with a 220F menu can easily send the bill to 400F).

Paris is also renowned for its foreign cuisine. There are numerous excellent Thai, Chinese and Vietnamese establishments and you will find restaurants of Caribbean, Middle Eastern, Central African and western and eastern European origin, along with Kurdish, Afghan, Japanese and even Tibetan.

Like other Latin Europeans, the French seldom separate the major pleasures of eating and drinking. Drinking is never an end in itself, as it so often is for Anglo-Saxons, and drink other than wine is referred to as 'apéritifs' and 'digestifs'. There are in consequence thousands of establishments in Paris where you can both eat and drink. In order to simplify matters, we have divided them into two broad categories: **Restaurants** and **Cafés and Bars**. The former is fairly unambiguous. "Cafés and Bars", on the other hand, includes places which offer anything from a sandwich to a full-blown meal, or no food at all.

You will find the listings which follow arranged in alphabetical order under the same geographical headings as are used in Chapters 2 to 11. By way of an introduction, we have included a description of the kinds of food and drink you might expect to find in the various kinds of establishment, as well as some indication of the conventions which surround eating and drinking in France.

You will find boxes following that list vegetarian (p.233), ethnic (p.252), and late-night (p.261) restaurants in Paris.

Cafés and Bars

In our "Cafés and Bars" category in the listings which follow, we've included cafés, café-bars, café-brasseries, *salons de thé*, *bistrots à vin*, cocktail-type bars, and beer cellars/pubs. Of these, the last two are the only ones where you may not find anything to eat.

Some brasseries are more restaurant than café (see p.226), but otherwise they have little to distinguish them from cafés and café-bars. The principal difference is that anything with "brasserie" in the title is going to serve proper meals in addition to the usual range of sandwiches, snacks, alcoholic and non-alcoholic drinks. *Salons de thé* and *bistrots à vin*, on the other hand, do have a distinctive identity, and it is not adequately conveyed by the standard English translations, tearoom and wine bar; for details, see over the page.

Eating and Drinking

There's really no difference between a café and a bar. Although the number of them in Paris is said to be decreasing rapidly, you still see them everywhere: big ones, small ones, scruffy ones, stylish ones, snobby ones, arty ones. They line the streets and cluster thickly around crossroads and squares.

Many **bars and cafés** advertise *les snacks* or *un casse-croûte* (a bite) with pictures of omelettes, fried eggs, hot dogs or various sandwiches displayed on the pavement outside. But, even when they don't, they will usually make you a half or a third of a *baguette* (French bread stick), buttered or filled with cheese or meat (*une tartine/au beurre/au jambon* etc). This, or a croissant, with hot chocolate or coffee, is generally the best way to eat **breakfast** – and cheaper than the rate charged by most hotels. (Brasseries also are possibilities for cups of coffee, eggs, snacks and other breakfast- or brunch-type food.)

If you **stand at the counter**, which is always cheaper than sitting down, you may see a **basket of croissants** or some hard-boiled eggs (they're usually gone by 9.30 or 10am). The drill is to help yourself – the waiter will keep an eye on how many you've eaten and bill you accordingly.

Coffee is invariably espresso and very strong. *Un café* or *un express* is black; *un crème* is with milk; *un grand café* or *un grand crème* is a large cup. In the morning you could also ask for *un café au lait* – espresso in a large cup or bowl filled up with hot milk. *Un déca*, decaffeinated coffee, is very widely available. Drinkers of **tea** (*thé*), nine times out of ten, have to settle for *Lipton's* tea-bags. To have milk with it, ask for *un peu de lait frais* (some fresh milk). **Hot chocolate** (*chocolat chaud*) is a better bet and can be had in any café.

Many cafés, you will find, also offer reasonably priced **lunches**. These usually consist of salads, the more substantial kind of snack such as *croque-monsieur* or *croque-madames* (both of which are variations on the grilled-cheese sandwich), a **plat du jour** (chef's daily special), or a **formule**, which is a limited or no-choice set menu.

Full price lists have to be displayed in every bar or café by law, usually without the fifteen percent service charge added, but detailing separately the prices for consuming at the bar (*au comptoir*), sitting down (*la salle*), or on the terrace (*la terrasse*) – all progressively more expensive. You pay when you leave, unless your waiter is just going off shift, and you can sit for hours over just one cup of coffee.

Liquor, soft and hard

All cafés and bars serve a full range of alcoholic and non-alcoholic drinks throughout the day. Although on the whole there is much less drunkenness than in Britain, it is still common to see people starting their day with a beer, cognac or *coup de rouge* (glass of red wine). A *café cogna'* is the popular combination of a cup of espresso and a glass of cognac.

On the soft drink front, bottled fruit juices and the universal standard canned lemonades, Cokes (*Coca*) and clones are available. You can also get freshly squeezed orange and lemon juice (*orange/citron pressé*). Particularly French are the various **sirops**, diluted with water to make cool eye-catching drinks with traffic-light colours, such as *menthe* (peppermint) and *grenadine* (pomegranate). Bottles of **spring water** (*eau minérale*; *pétillante* for sparkling, *plate* for still) are widely drunk, from the best-selling Perrier to the most obscure spa product.

Characteristically French **apéritifs** are the aniseed drinks – *pastis*, in French – *Pernod* and *Ricard*. Like Greek *ouzo*, they turn cloudy when diluted with water and ice cubes (*glaçons*) – very refreshing and not expensive. Two other drinks designed to stimulate the appetite are *Pineau* (cognac and grape juice) and *Kir* (white wine with a dash of blackcurrant syrup – or champagne for a *Kir Royal*).

Beers are the familiar Belgian and German brands, plus home-grown ones from Alsace. Draught (*à la pression*, usually *Kronenbourg*) is the cheapest drink you can have next to coffee and wine. Ask for *un demi* (one third of a litre). For a wider choice of draughts and bottles you need to go to the special beer-drinking establishments, or English/Irish-style pubs found in abundance in Paris. A light summertime option is shandy (*une panachée*).

As for the harder stuff, there are dozens of **eaux de vie** (brandies distilled from fruit) and **liqueurs**, in addition to the classic cognacs or Armagnac. Among less familiar names, try *Poire William* (pear brandy), *Marc* (a spirit distilled from grape pulp), the *grappa*-like Basque *Izarra*, or just point to the bottle with the most attractive colour. Measures are generous, but they don't come cheap: the same applies for imported spirits like whisky, always called *scotch*.

Eating and Drinking

Wine

Wine – *vin* – is drunk at just about every meal or social occasion. Red is *rouge*, white *blanc*, or there's *rosé*. *Vin de table* or *vin ordinaire* – table wine – is always cheap and generally drinkable.

AC (Appellation d'Origine Contrôlée) wines are another matter. They can be excellent value at the lower end of the price scale, where favourable French taxes keep prices down to 15–25F a bottle, but move much above it and you're soon paying serious prices for serious bottles.

Restaurant mark-ups of *AC* wines can be outrageous. Popular *AC* wines found on most restaurant lists include Côtes du Rhône (from the Rhône valley), St-Émilion and Médoc (from Bordeaux), Beaujolais and very upmarket Burgundy.

The **basic wine terms** are *brut*, very dry; *sec*, dry; *demi-sec*, sweet; *doux*, very sweet; *mousseux*, sparkling; *méthode champenoise*, mature and sparkling. There are grape varieties as well, but the complexities of the subject take up volumes.

A glass of wine at a bar is simply *un verre de rouge* or *un verre de blanc*. If it is an *AC* wine you may have the choice of *un ballon* (a large round glass).

Eating and Drinking

Tisanes

Tisanes or *infusions* are the generic terms for **herb teas**. Every café serves them. They are particularly soothing after overeating or overdrinking, as well as for stomach upsets. The more common ones are *verveine* (verbena), *tilleul* (lime blossom), *menthe* (mint) and *camomile*.

Salons de thé

Salons de thé are a relatively new-fangled invention. They are chicer and more refined than anything suggested by "tearoom". They crop up characteristically in both established upper-class haunts and wherever a new part of town has been gentrified. They serve everything from light midday meals, brunches, salads, and quiches to rich confections of cake and ice cream. The oldest is *Angélina's*, with its marble cake-frosting exterior. More exotic and relaxed are *La Pagode* and *La Mosquée*, in the two least Parisian of the city's buildings.

Bistrots à vins

Bistrots à vins, unlike *salons de thé*, are an ancient institution, traditionally working-class sawdust-on-the-floor drinking haunts.

Some genuine *bistrots* still exist, such as *La Tartine*, *Le Rubis* and *Le Baron Rouge*, unpretentious and catering for everyone. The newer generation, however, who ironically owe their existence in large part to the English influence, have a distinctly yuppified flavour, and are far from cheap. Most serve at least a limited range of dishes or *plats*, often deriving from a particular regional *cuisine*, and specialize in the less usual and less commercial wines, again often from a particular region. Some, like *Le Baron Rouge*, sell good, inexpensive wine from the barrel, if you bring your own containers. The basic idea is to enable you to try wines by the glass.

Restaurants

In terms of quality and price, there's nothing to choose between restaurants (or *auberges* or *relais*, as they sometimes call themselves) and brasseries. The distinction is that brasseries, which often resemble cafés, serve quicker meals and at most hours of the day, while restaurants tend to stick to the **traditional meal times** of noon until 2pm, and 7pm until 9.30 or 10.30pm.

The latest time at which you can walk into a restaurant and order is usually about 9.30 or 10pm, although once ensconced you can often remain well into the night. (Hours – last orders – are stated in the listings below, and unusually or specifically **late-night places** are included in the box on p.261.) After 9pm or so, some restaurants serve only à

Snacks and picnics

For those occasions when you don't want – or can't face – a full meal, Paris offers numerous **street stalls and stand-up sandwich bars**. In addition to the indigenous *frites* (French fries), *crêpes*, *galettes* (wholewheat pancakes), *gauffres* (waffles), and fresh sandwiches, there are Tunisian snacks like *brik à l'oeuf* (a fried pastry with an egg inside), *merguez* (spicy North African sausage), Greek *souvlaki* (kebabs), Middle Eastern *falafel* (deep-fried chickpea balls with salad), Japanese titbits, and all manner of good things from the eastern European delicatessens.

For **picnics and takeaway food**, head for either a **charcuterie** proper, or the delicatessen counter in a good supermarket. Although, strictly, specializing in pork-based preparations like salami and ham, most *charcuteries* stock a wide range of cold cuts, *pâtés*, *terrines*, ready-made salads, and fully prepared main courses. These are not exclusively meaty, either: artichokes *à la grecque*, stuffed tomatoes and *paellas* are common. You buy by weight, by the slice (*tranche*) or by the carton (*barquette*).

---

la carte meals, which invariably work out more expensive than eating the set menu. For the more upmarket places, it's wise to make **reservations** – easily done on the same day. When hunting, avoid places that are half-empty at peak time, and treat the business of sizing up different menus as an enjoyable appetizer in itself.

Prices

You should find a display of prices and what you get for them posted outside every restaurant. Normally, there is a choice between one or more *menus fixes*, where the number of courses for the stated price is fixed and the choice accordingly limited. Currently there are numerous **fixed-price menus under 80F**, particularly at lunchtime, providing staple dishes of varying quality.

At that price, menus will be three courses with a choice of four to six entrées, three main courses, and three or four desserts. They will be fairly standard dishes, such as steak and chips (*steak frites*), chicken and chips (*poulet frites*), or various preparations of offal. Look for the *plat du jour*, which may be a regional dish and more appealing. You will also find *formules*, usually choices of a main dish plus starter or dessert.

Service compris or *s.c.* means the **service charge** is included. *Service non compris, s.n.c.,* or *service en sus* means it isn't, and you need to calculate an additional fifteen percent. **Wine** (*vin*) or a drink (*boisson*) may be included, though it is unlikely on menus under 100F. When ordering **house wine** (*vin ordinaire*), ask for *un pichet* (a small jug); they come in quarter- (*un quart*) or half-litres (*un demi*). **A bottle of wine** can easily add 80F to the bill.

The more you pay, the greater the choice. **Menus between 150F and 200F** offer a significantly more interesting range of dishes, including, probably, some regional and other specialities, and once **over 200F** you should get some serious gourmet satisfaction. **Eating *à la carte***, of course, gives you access to everything that is on offer, plus complete freedom to construct your meal as you choose. But it will cost a great deal more. One simple and perfectly legitimate ploy is to have just one course instead of the expected three or more. There is no minimum charge.

Student restaurants

Anyone holding an **International Student Card** or *Carte Jeune* (for which you have to be under 26) is eligible to apply for tickets for the **university restaurants** under the direction of *CROUS de Paris*. A list of addresses, which includes numerous cafeterias and brasseries, is obtainable from their offices at 39 av Georges-Bernanos, 5e (Mº Port-Royal). The meal tickets, however, come in units of ten and are only obtainable from and valid for each particular restaurant – worthwhile, if you are not bothered by the restrictions, for you can get a square meal for 12.30F.

Eating and Drinking

Chain restaurants

There are a number of French restaurant chains with addresses all over the city. Service is usually quick and there's no need to book.

The best is **L'Amanguier**, open daily till midnight with a wide-choice 110F menu and an 88F *formule*. At 20 bd Montmartre, 9e; 46 bd Montparnasse, 15e; 51 rue du Théâtre, 15e; and 43 av des Ternes, 17e.

La Criée specializes in seafood and fish and is also dependable; menus at 119F with wine and 79F without, and addresses throughout the centre. Open till 1am.

Batifol, with 15 establishments throughout Paris, is fine but not very exciting, and **Hippopotamus** (13 addresses) though a lot cheaper, is not particularly good. **Le Bistro Romain** has gone downhill and is desperately trying to wean back its old clientele with cheaper menus.

Eating and Drinking

A List of Foods and Dishes

Basics

Pain	Bread	*Vinaigre*	Vinegar
Beurre	Butter	*Bouteille*	Bottle
Oeufs	Eggs	*Verre*	Glass
Lait	Milk	*Fourchette*	Fork
Huile	Oil	*Couteau*	Knife
Poivre	Pepper	*Cuillère*	Spoon
Sel	Salt	*Table*	Table
Sucre	Sugar	*L'Addition*	The bill

Snacks

Crêpe	Pancake (sweet)	*Omelette . . .*	Omelette . . .
au sucre	with sugar	*nature*	plain
au citron	with lemon	*aux fines herbes*	with herbs
au miel	with honey	*au fromage*	with cheese
à la confiture	with jam	*Salade de . . .*	Salad of . . .
aux oeufs	with eggs	*tomates*	tomatoes
à la crème	with chestnut	*betteraves*	beetroot
de marrons	purée	*concombres*	cucumber
Galette	Buckwheat (savoury) pancake	*carottes rapées*	grated carrots

Other fillings/salads:

Un sandwich/ une baguette . . .	A sandwich . . .

Anchois	Anchovy
Andouillette	Tripe sausage
Boudin	Black pudding
Coeurs de palmiers	Palm hearts
Fonds d'artichauts	Artichoke hearts
Hareng	Herring
Langue	Tongue
Poulet	Chicken
Thon	Tuna fish

jambon	with ham
fromage	with cheese
saucisson	with sausage
à l'ail	with garlic
au poivre	with pepper
pâté	with pâté
(de campagne)	(country-style)
croque-monsieur	Grilled cheese and ham sandwich
croque-madame	Grilled cheese and bacon, sausage, chicken or an egg

And some terms:

Chauffé	Heated
Cuit	Cooked
Cru	Raw
Emballé	Wrapped
À emporter	Takeaway
Fumé	Smoked
Salé	Salted/spicy
Sucré	Sweet

Oeufs	Eggs
au plat	Fried eggs
à la coque	Boiled eggs
durs	Hard-boiled eggs
brouillés	Scrambled eggs

Soups (*soupes*) and starters (*hors d'oeuvres*)

Bisque	Shellfish soup	*Velouté*	Thick soup, usually made with fish or poultry
Bouillabaisse	Marseillais fish soup		
Bouillon	Broth or stock		
Bourride	Thick fish soup		
Consommé	Clear soup		
Pistou	Parmesan, basil and garlic paste added to soup	**Starters**	
		Assiette anglaise	Plate of cold meats
		Crudités	Raw vegetables with dressings
Potage	Thick vegetable soup		
Rouille	Red pepper, garlic and saffron mayonnaise with fish soup	*Hors d'oeuvres variés*	Combination of the above, plus smoked or marinated fish

Fish (*poisson*), seafood (*fruits de mer*) and shellfish (*crustaces* or *coquillages*)

Eating and Drinking

Anchois	Anchovies	*Moules (marinière)*	Mussels (with shallots in white wine sauce)
Anguilles	Eels		
Barbue	Brill		
Bigourneau	Periwinkle	*Oursin*	Sea urchin
Brème	Bream	*Palourdes*	Clams
Cabillaud	Cod	*Praires*	Small clams
Calmar	Squid	*Raie*	Skate
Carrelet	Plaice	*Rouget*	Red mullet
Claire	Type of oyster	*Saumon*	Salmon
Colin	Hake	*Sole*	Sole
Congre	Conger eel	*Thon*	Tuna
Coques	Cockles	*Truite*	Trout
Coquilles St-Jacques	Scallops	*Turbot*	Turbot
Crabe	Crab	**Terms: (Fish)**	
Crevettes grises	Shrimps	*Aïoli*	Garlic mayonnaise served with salt cod and other fish
Crevettes roses	Prawns		
Daurade	Sea bream		
Eperlan	Smelt or whitebait	*Béarnaise*	Sauce made with egg yolks, white wine, shallots and vinegar
Escargots	Snails		
Flétan	Halibut		
Friture	Assorted fried fish	*Beignets*	Fritters
Gambas	King prawns	*Darne*	Fillet or steak
Hareng	Herring	*La douzaine*	A dozen
Homard	Lobster	*Frit*	Fried
Huîtres	Oysters	*Friture*	Deep fried small fish
Langouste	Spiny lobster	*Fumé*	Smoked
Langoustines	Saltwater crayfish (scampi)	*Fumet*	Fish stock
		Gigot de Mer	Large fish baked whole
Limande	Lemon sole	*Grillé*	Grilled
Lotte	Burbot	*Hollandaise*	Butter and vinegar sauce
Lotte de mer	Monkfish		
Loup de mer	Sea bass	*À la meunière*	In a butter, lemon and parsley sauce
Louvine, loubine	Similar to sea bass		
Maquereau	Mackerel	*Mousse/ mousseline*	Mousse
Merlan	Whiting	*Quenelles*	Light dumplings

Meat (*viande*) and poultry (*volaille*)

Agneau (de pré-salé)	Lamb (grazed on salt marshes)	*Contrefilet*	Sirloin roast
		Coquelet	Cockerel
Andouille, andouillette	Tripe sausage	*Dinde, dindon*	Turkey
		Entrecôte	Ribsteak
Boeuf	Beef	*Faux filet*	Sirloin steak
Bifteck	Steak	*Foie*	Liver
Boudin blanc	Sausage of white meats	*Foie gras*	Fattened (duck/ goose) liver
Boudin noir	Black pudding	*Gigot (d'agneau)*	Leg (of lamb)
Caille	Quail	*Grillade*	Grilled meat
Canard	Duck	*Hâchis*	Chopped meat or mince hamburger
Caneton	Duckling		

Eating and Drinking

Meat and poultry (continued)

Langue	Tongue	*Poussin*	Baby chicken
Lapin, lapereau	Rabbit, young rabbit	*Ris*	Sweetbreads
Lard, lardons	Bacon, diced bacon	*Rognons*	Kidneys
Lièvre	Hare	*Rognons blancs*	Testicles
Merguez	Spicy, red sausage	*Sanglier*	Wild boar
Mouton	Mutton	*Tête de veau*	Calf's head (in jelly)
Museau de veau	Calf's muzzle	*Tournedos*	Thick slices of fillet
Oie	Goose	*Tripes*	Tripe
Os	Bone	*Veau*	Veal
Porc	Pork	*Venaison*	Venison
Poulet	Chicken		

Meat and poultry – dishes and terms

Boeuf bourguignon	Beef stew with burgundy, onions and mushrooms	*Farci*	Stuffed
		Au feu de bois	Cooked over wood fire
Canard à l'orange	Roast duck with an orange-and-wine sauce	*Au four*	Baked
		Garni	With vegetables
		Gésier	Gizzard
Cassoulet	A casserole of beans and meat	*Grillé*	Grilled
		Magret de canard	Duck breast
Coq au vin	Chicken cooked until it falls off the bone with wine, onions and mushrooms	*Marmite*	Casserole
		Mijoté	Stewed
		Museau	Muzzle
		Rôti	Roast
		Sauté	Lightly cooked in butter
Steak au poivre (vert/rouge)	Steak in a black (green/red) peppercorn sauce		
		For steaks:	
		Bleu	Almost raw
Steak tartare	Raw chopped beef, topped with a raw egg yolk	*Saignant*	Rare
		À point	Medium
		Bien cuit	Well done
Terms:		*Très bien cuit*	Very well cooked
Blanquette, daube, estouffade, hochepôt, navarin and *ragoût*	All are types of stew	*Brochette*	Kebab
		Garnishes and sauces:	
		Beurre blanc	Sauce of white wine and shallots, with butter
Aile	Wing		
Carré	Best end of neck, chop or cutlet	*Chasseur*	White wine, mushrooms and shallots
Civit	Game stew	*Diable*	Strong mustard seasoning
Confit	Meat preserve		
Côte	Chop, cutlet or rib	*Forestière*	With bacon and mushroom
Cou	Neck		
Cuisse	Thigh or leg	*Fricassée*	Rich, creamy sauce
Epaule	Shoulder	*Mornay*	Cheese sauce
Médaillon	Round piece	*Pays d'Auge*	Cream and cider
Pavé	Thick slice	*Piquante*	Gherkins or capers, vinegar and shallots
En croûte	In pastry		
		Provençale	Tomatoes, garlic, olive oil and herbs

Vegetables (*légumes*), herbs (*herbes*) and spices (*épices*), etc.

Eating and Drinking

Ail	Garlic	*Rouges*	Kidney
Algue	Seaweed	*Beurres*	Butter
Anis	Aniseed	*Laurier*	Bay leaf
Artichaut	Artichoke	*Lentilles*	Lentils
Asperges	Asparagus	*Maïs*	Corn
Avocat	Avocado	*Menthe*	Mint
Basilic	Basil	*Moutarde*	Mustard
Betterave	Beetroot	*Oignon*	Onion
Carotte	Carrot	*Pâte*	Pasta or pastry
Céleri	Celery	*Persil*	Parsley
Champignons,	Mushrooms of	*Petits pois*	Peas
cèpes,	various kinds	*Piment*	Pimento
chanterelles		*Pois chiche*	Chickpeas
Chou (rouge)	(Red) cabbage	*Pois mange-tout*	Snow peas
Choufleur	Cauliflower	*Pignons*	Pine nuts
Ciboulettes	Chives	*Poireau*	Leek
Concombre	Cucumber	*Poivron*	Sweet pepper
Cornichon	Gherkin	*(vert, rouge)*	(green, red)
Échalotes	Shallots	*Pommes (de terre)*	Potatoes
Endive	Chicory	*Primeurs*	Spring vegetables
Épinards	Spinach	*Radis*	Radishes
Estragon	Tarragon	*Riz*	Rice
Fenouil	Fennel	*Safran*	Saffron
Flageolet	White beans	*Salade verte*	Green salad
Gingembre	Ginger	*Sarrasin*	Buckwheat
Haricots	Beans	*Tomate*	Tomato
Verts	String (French)	*Truffes*	Truffles

Vegetables – dishes and terms

Beignet	Fritter	*Jardinière*	With mixed diced
Farci	Stuffed		vegetables
Gratiné	Browned with cheese or	*Sauté*	Lightly fried in butter
	butter	*À la vapeur*	Steamed
À la	Sautéed in butter	*Je suis*	I'm a vegetarian.
parisienne	(potatoes); with white	*végétarien(ne).*	
	wine sauce and shallots	*Il y a quelques*	Are there any
Parmentier	With potatoes	*plats sans viande?*	non-meat dishes?

Fruits (*fruits*) and nuts (*noix*)

Abricot	Apricot	*Fraises (de bois)*	Strawberries (wild)
Amandes	Almonds	*Framboises*	Raspberries
Ananas	Pineapple	*Fruit de la passion*	Passion fruit
Banane	Banana	*Groseilles*	Redcurrants and
Brugnon, nectarine	Nectarine		gooseberries
Cacahouète	Peanut	*Mangue*	Mango
Cassis	Blackcurrants	*Marrons*	Chestnuts
Cérises	Cherries	*Melon*	Melon
Citron	Lemon	*Myrtilles*	Bilberries
Citron vert	Lime	*Noisette*	Hazelnut
Figues	Figs	*Noix*	Nuts

Eating and Drinking

Fruits and nuts (continued)

Orange	Orange	*Raisins*	Grapes
Pamplemousse	Grapefruit	**Terms:**	
Pêche (blanche)	(White) peach	*Beignets*	Fritters
Pistache	Pistachio	*Compôte de . . .*	Stewed . . .
Poire	Pear	*Coulis*	Sauce
Pomme	Apple	*Flambé*	Set aflame in
Prune	Plum		alcohol
Pruneau	Prune	*Frappé*	Iced

Desserts (*desserts* or *entremets*) and pastries (*pâtisserie*)

Bombe	A moulded ice-cream dessert	*Parfait*	Frozen mousse, sometimes ice cream
Brioche	Sweet, high yeast breakfast roll	*Petit Suisse*	A smooth mixture of cream and curds
Charlotte	Custard and fruit in lining of almond fingers	*Petits fours*	Bite-sized cakes/pastries
Crème Chantilly	Vanilla-flavoured and sweetened whipped cream	*Poires Belle Hélène*	Pears and ice cream in chocolate sauce
		Yaourt, yogourt	Yoghurt
Crème fraîche	Sour cream	**Terms:**	
Crème pâtissière	Thick eggy pastry-filling	*Barquette*	Small boat-shaped flan
Crêpe suzette	Thin pancake with orange juice and liqueur	*Bavarois*	Refers to the mould, could be a mousse or custard
Fromage blanc	Cream cheese		
Glace	Ice cream	*Coupe*	A serving of ice cream
Île flottante/ oeufs à la neige	Soft meringues floating on custard	*Crêpe*	Pancake
		Galette	Buckwheat pancake
Macarons	Macaroons	*Gênoise*	Rich sponge cake
Madeleine	Small sponge cake	*Sablé*	Shortbread biscuit
Marrons Mont Blanc	Chestnut purée and cream on a rum-soaked sponge cake	*Savarin*	A filled, ring-shaped cake
		Tarte	Tart
		Tartelette	Small tart
Mousse au chocolat	Chocolate mousse	*Truffes*	Truffles, the chocolate or liqueur variety
Palmiers	Caramelized puff pastries		

Cheese (*fromage*)

There are over 400 types of French cheese, most of them named after their place of origin. *Chèvre* is goat's cheese. *Le plateau de fromages* is the cheeseboard, and bread – but not butter – is served with it.

And one final note: always call the waiter or waitress *Monsieur* or *Madame* (*Mademoiselle* if a young woman), never *garçon*, no matter what you've been taught in school.

Paris for Vegetarians

Vegetarians will find that French chefs have not yet caught on to the idea that tasty and nutritious meals do not need to be based on meat or fish. Consequently, the chances of finding vegetarian main dishes on the menus of regular restaurants are not good. However, even if you don't eat fish, it is possible to have a vegetarian meal at even the most meat-oriented brasserie by choosing dishes from among the starters (*crudités*, for example, are nearly always available) and soups, or by asking for an omelette.

As far as specifically **vegetarian restaurants** are concerned, the list is brief. All the establishments listed below are reviewed in the pages which follow.

Aquarius 1, 54 rue Ste-Croix-de-la-Bretonnerie, 4ᵉ. p.241.

Aquarius 2, 40 rue Gergovie, 14ᵉ. p.254.

Bol en Bois, 35 rue Pascal, 13ᵉ. p.255.

Country Life, 6 rue Daunou, 2ᵉ. p.236.

Les Fines Herbes, 38 rue Nollet, 17ᵉ. p.257.

Au Grain de Folie, 24 rue de La Vieuville, 18ᵉ. p.256.

Le Grenier de Notre-Dame, 18 rue de la Bûcherie, 5ᵉ. p.245.

Joy in Food, 2 rue Truffaut, 17ᵉ. p.257.

Le Petit Légume, 36 rue Boulangers, 5ᵉ. p.246.

Piccolo Teatro, 6 rue des Écouffes, 4ᵉ. p.241.

La Truffe, 31 rue Vieille-du-Temple, 4ᵉ. p.241.

Restaurant Végétarien Lacour, 3 rue Villedo, 1ᵉʳ. p.237.

Chapter 2: Île de la Cité

CAFÉS AND BARS

Taverne Henri IV, 13 place du Pont-Neuf, 1ᵉʳ (Mº Pont-Neuf). Mon–Fri noon–9.30pm, Sat noon–4.30pm; closed Aug. One of the good older wine bars, opposite Henri IV's statue. Yves Montand used to come here when Simone Signoret lived in the adjacent place Dauphine. Full of lawyers from the Palais de Justice. The food is good but a bit pricy if you have a full meal. Plates of meats and cheeses around 70F, sandwiches 25F, wine 25–50F a glass.

RESTAURANTS

Au Rendez-vous des Camionneurs, 72 quai des Orfèvres, 1ᵉʳ; ☎43.54.88.74 (Mº St-Michel). Daily noon–2pm, 7–11.30pm. Crowded, traditional establishment serving snails, steaks and scallops. 130–180F.

Chapter 3: La Voie Triomphale

CAFÉS AND BARS

Angélina, 226 rue de Rivoli, 1ᵉʳ (Mº Tuileries). Daily l0am–7pm; closed Aug. A long-established gilded cage, where the well-coiffed sip the best hot chocolate in town. *Pâtisseries* and other desserts of the same high quality. Not cheap.

Ma Bourgogne, 133 bd Haussmann, 8ᵉ (Mº Miromesnil). Mon–Fri 7am–10pm; closed July. A place for pre-siesta glasses of Burgundy; *plats du jour* as well, and meals at 150–200F.

La Boutique à Sandwiches, 12 rue du Colisée, 8ᵉ (Mº St-Philippe-du-Roule). Mon–Sat 11.45am–11.30pm; closed Aug. Not the best sandwiches in the world, but certainly cheap for this part of town, plus *raclette* and *steak frites* for under 80F at the counter.

Café de la Comédie, 153 rue Rivoli, 1ᵉʳ (Mº Palais-Royal–Musée-du-Louvre). Tues–Sun 10am–midnight. Small café opposite the Comédie Française, complete with a mirror painted with theatrical scenes at the back.

Drugstore Élysées, 133 av des Champs-Élysées, 8ᵉ (Mº Étoile). Daily 9am–2am. All day salads, sandwiches, *plats du jour*, full-blown meals and huge, delicious desserts are available from the three drugstores (see p.248), along with books,

Eating and Drinking

Some of Paris' top gourmet restaurants are listed on p.263.

See p.261 for a list of cafés and restaurants which stay open late.

Eating and Drinking

Some of Paris' top gourmet restaurants are listed on p.263.

newspapers, tobacco, and a multitude of fripperies. Prices are very reasonable and the food much better than the décor would suggest.

Drugstore Matignon, 1 av Matignon, 8ᵉ (Mº Franklin-Roosevelt). Daily 10am–midnight; closed mid-Aug.

E. Fahy Patissier, 165 rue du Faubourg-St-Honoré, 8ᵉ (Mº St-Philippe-du-Roule/George V). Open weekdays at midday. A boulangerie selling sandwiches, tarts, quiches, ready-made salads to take away or eat in a corner at the back.

Fauchon, 24 place de la Madeleine, 8ᵉ (Mº Madeleine). Mon–Sat 9.45am–6.30pm. Narrow and uncomfortable counters at which to gobble wonderful *pâtisseries, plats du jour* and sandwiches – at a price.

Le Griffonier, 6 rue des Saussaires, 8ᵉ (Mº Champs-Élysées). Mon–Fri 10am–8pm. Well-paid office types in this small wine bar with a good selection of Loire wines at 18–20F a glass.

Osaka, 163 rue St-Honoré, 1ᵉʳ (Mº Palais-Royal). Daily 11.30am–8.15pm. Japanese snack bar with meals for 60F. More expensive sushi, sushimi and tempura bar on the left.

Café de Poumone, allée Central, Jardin des Tuileries, 1ᵉʳ (Mº Tuileries). Temporary café installed for the duration of the replanting.

Restorama, Le Carrousel du Louvre, 1ᵉʳ (Mº Louvre). Daily 9am–9pm. One vast underground fast food eating hall served by over a dozen different outlets: rotisseries, hamburgers, pizzas, Tex-Mex, Chinese, Lebanese, Japanese, crêperies, salad bars ... easy to eat for under 40F. Access from pl du Carrousel or the Louvre pyramid.

Rose Thé, 91 rue St-Honoré, 1ᵉʳ (Mº Louvre-Rivoli). Mon–Fri noon–7pm. Calm and tranquil *salon de thé* in a courtyard of antique shops and faded bric-à-brac. Teas, milkshakes, *tartes aux fruits*, salads, etc. A *cocktail tonique* of fresh fruit juice is 32F.

Virgin Megastore Café, 52 av des Champs-Élysées, 8ᵉ (Mº Franklin-Roosevelt). Daily 10am–11.30pm. As

popular as the store; coffee and snacks – *tapas* around 35F, sandwiches for 28F – or meals for around 150F.

RESTAURANTS

Aux Amis du Beaujolais, 28 rue d'Artois, 8ᵉ; ☎45.63.92.21 (Mº George-V/St-Philippe-du-Roule). Mon–Sat till 9pm; closed middle two weeks of July. If you can fathom the hand-written menu, you'll find good traditional French dishes of stews and sautéed steaks, and Beaujolais. Around 150F.

L'Auvergnat 1900, 11 rue Jean-Mermoz, 8ᵉ; ☎43.59.21.47 (Mº Franklin-Roosevelt/St-Philippe-du-Roule). Mon–Fri noon–2.30pm & 7–10.20pm. The decor, like the food, is solid and substantial. *Cassoulets, confits de canard, patés*, wild mushrooms and other Auvergnat goodies. 115F menu, *carte* 240F.

City Rock Café, 13 rue de Berri, 8ᵉ; ☎47.23.07.72 (Mº George-V). Daily noon–2am. As over the top as its Dragon neighbour, this American restaurant is dedicated to rock. Gold guitar motifs on the steps and doors, plus a wax Monroe in the window, make it hard to miss. Genuine articles belonging to the greats – cars, clothes, guitars – are on show; standard American fare – hamburgers, chile con carne, mega-salads – are on the menu. 65F menu at midday, *carte* 160F. Downstairs is a club (see *Nightlife*).

Le Dauphin, 167 rue St-Honoré, 1ᵉʳ; ☎42.60.40.11 (Mº Palais-Royal–Musée-du-Louvre). Daily noon–2.30pm & 7–11.30pm (June–Oct until 12.30am). A genuine bistro with menus under 100F. Seafood platter for 167F. Excellent *lapereau* (young rabbit) *à la grand-mère* and *magnet de canard*.

Dragons Élysées, 11 rue de Berri, 8ᵉ; ☎42.89.85.10 (Mº George-V). Daily till 11.30pm. The Chinese-Thai cuisine encompasses dim-sum, curried seafood and baked mussels, but the overriding attraction is the extraordinary décor. Beneath a floor of glass tiles water runs from pool to pool inhabited by exotic fish. Water even pours down part of one wall, and on the ceiling pinpoints of light imitate stars. And all this amid the usual chinoiserie of red lanterns and black furniture. 75F menu, 200F Thai seafood menu, *carte* 250F.

L'Élysées Bar Restaurant, 134 rue Faubourg St-Honoré, 8e (Mº St-Philippe-du-Roule). Tues–Sat noon–2.30pm & 7–9.30pm. Tables outside for *gigot d'agneau* (72F) and *steak tartare frites* (73F). If you don't fancy it, there's the *Lord Sandwich* bar next door.

La Fermette Marbeuf 1900, 5 rue Marbeuf, 8e; ☎47.23.31.31 (Mº Franklin-Roosevelt). Daily until 11.30pm. Try to eat in the tiled and domed inner room, where the original Art Nouveau décor has been restored. A rather well-heeled clientele, foreign as well as French, but not stuffy. A good inclusive menu for 160F; *carte* up to 350F.

Foujita, 41 rue St-Roch, 1er; ☎42.61.42.93 (Mº Tuileries/Pyramides). Mon–Sat noon–2.15pm & 7.30–10pm. Closed mid-Aug. One of the cheaper but best Japanese restaurants, as evidenced by the numbers of Japanese eating here. Quick and crowded; soup, sushis, rice and tea for 85F at lunchtime; plate of sushis or sushamis for under 100F.

Fouquet's, 99 av des Champs-Élysées, 8e; ☎47.23.70.60 (Mº George-V). Daily until midnight. A long-established and expensive watering-hole for ageing stars, politicians, newspaper editors, and advertising barons. The restaurant upstairs (which is closed weekends and mid-July to Aug) is more expensive than the terrace "grill," but both are outrageous. At around 350F you're paying for the past and present clientele, the prime site on the Champs-Élysées, and the snobbishness of the whole affair.

Le Jardin du Royal Monceau, Hôtel Royal Monceau, 35 av Hoche, 8e (Mº Charles-de-Gaulle/Étoile). Daily noon–2.30pm & 7–11pm. Seriously good food in a luxury hotel. *A la carte* would set you back 500F or more but there's a midday menu for 280F.

Prince de Galles, 33 av George V, 8e; ☎47.23.55.11 (Mº George-V). Daily noon–2.30pm & 7–10.30pm. A choice of three

entrées, three main courses and three puds in very classy surroundings for under 200F – so long as you only drink water.

Le Relais du Sud-Ouest, 154 rue St-Honoré, 1er; ☎42.60.62.01 (Mº Palais-Royal/Musée-du-Louvre). Mon–Sat till 10.30pm. An ancient map of the southwest of France hangs on the wall; there's an old kitchen range, and traditional southwest specialities are served at candlelit tables. Good value on the 80F menu.

Yvan, 1bis rue J-Mermoz, 8e; ☎43.59.18.40 (Mº Franklin-Roosevelt). Mon–Sat noon–2.30pm & 7pm–midnight, closed Sat lunchtime. Fish specialities and pigeon with polenta attract a stylish clientele. Extremely good food and menus at 168F, 188F and 238F.

Eating and Drinking

See p.233 for a list of vegetarian restaurants in Paris.

Chapter 4: Right Bank Commerce, the Passages and Les Halles

Right Bank Commerce and the Passages

CAFÉS AND BARS

L'Arbre à Cannelle, 57 passage des Panoramas, 2e (Mº Rue-Montmartre). Mon–Sat till 6pm. Exquisite wooden panelling, frescoes and painted ceilings; puddings, flans and *assiettes gourmandes* for 54–70F.

Le Bar de l'Entracte, on the corner of rue Montpensier and rue Beaujolais, 1er (Mº Palais-Royal–Musée-du-Louvre). Tues–Sat 10am–2am. Theatre people, bankers and journalists come for quick snacks of *gratin de pomme de terre* and Auvergnat ham, in this almost traffic-free spot. Fills up to bursting during the intervals at the Palais-Royal theatre just down the road.

Aux Bons Crus, 7 rue des Petits-Champs, 1er (Mº Palais-Royal). Mon–Fri 8am–10pm, Sat 8.30am–6pm. A relaxed workaday place which has been serving good wines and cheese, sausage and ham for over eighty years. Wine from 10F a glass; plate of cold meats from 30F.

Cave Drouot, 8 rue Drouot, 9e (Mº Richelieu-Drouot). Mon–Fri 8am–10pm;

Our glossary of French food and dishes begins on p.228.

Eating and Drinking

*Some of Paris'
top gourmet
restaurants are
listed on p.263.*

closed July 14–Sept 1. By the Druoot auction rooms. Excellent wines and a reasonably priced restaurant with *plats du jour* and *charcuterie*.

La Champmeslé, 4 rue Chabanais, 2e (Mº Pyramides). Mon–Sat 11am–2am, Sun 5pm–2am. Lesbian bar with two rooms reserved for women, and one room for mixed company. Cocktails (from 45F), picture/photo exhibitions, and Thurs night cabaret.

Du Croissant, corner of rue du Croissant and rue Montmartre, 2e (Mº Montmartre). On July 31, 1914, the Socialist and pacifist leader Jean Jaurès was assassinated in this café for his anti war activities. The table he was sitting at still remains.

Le Grand Café Capucines, 4 bd des Capucines, 9e (Mº Opéra). A favourite all-nighter with over-the-top Belle Époque décor and excellent seafood. Boulevard prices mean 20F for an espresso.

Kitty O'Shea's, 10 rue des Capucines, 2e (Mº Opéra). Noon–1.30am. An Irish pub with excellent Guinness and Smithwicks. A favourite haunt of the Irish expats. The *John Jameson* restaurant upstairs serves high-quality Gaelic food, including seafood flown in from Galway, at a price.

Lina's Sandwiches, 50 rue Étienne-Marcel, 2e (Mº Étienne-Marcel), and 8 rue Marbeuf, 8e (Mº Alma-Marceau). Mon–Sat 9.30am–5pm. A spacious, stylish place for your designer shopping break. Sandwiches from 18 to 40F.

La Micro-Brasserie, 106 rue de Richelieu, 2e (Mº Richelieu-Drouot). Mon–Sat 8am–2am. A beer cellar that brews its own beer on the spot and offers *moules* and *frites* for 40F.

La Muscade, Galerie de Montpensier, 1er (Mº Palais-Royale–Musée du Louvre). Smart café in the Palais Royale gardens. Ace chocolate macaroons as well as meals.

Le Rubis, 10 rue du Marché-St-Honoré, 1er (Mº Pyramides). Mon–Fri 7am–10pm, Sat 8am–4pm. Closed mid-Aug. One of the oldest wine bars, it enjoys a reputation for having among the best wines, plus excellent snacks and *plats du jour*.

Very small and very crowded. Glasses of wine from 10F.

Tigh Johnny, 55 rue Montmartre, 2e (Mº Sentier). Daily 4pm–1.30am, last orders 12.30am. A mostly Irish clientele at this bar that serves a reasonably priced Guinness and sometimes has impromptu Celtic bands.

Village Gourmand, 16 rue des Petits-Champs, 2e (Mº Pyramides). *Foie gras* or goose *rillettes* on fancy bread to take away. From 22F.

RESTAURANTS

Chartier, 7 rue du Faubourg-Montmartre, 9e; ☎47.70.86.29 (Mº Montmartre). Until 9.30pm. Brown linoleum floor, dark-stained woodwork, brass hat-racks, clusters of white globes suspended from the high ceiling, mirrors, waiters in long aprons – the original décor of a turn-of-the-century soup kitchen. Worth seeing and, though crowded and rushed, the food is not bad at all. Under 100F.

Country Life, 6 rue Daunou, 2e; ☎42.97.48.51 (Mº Opéra). Mon–Sat 11.30am–2.30pm only. Vegetarian soup, *hors d'oeuvres*, lasagne and salad for under 60F. Menu details gluten and soya contents. No alcohol, no smoking.

Dilan, 13 rue Mandar, 2e; ☎42.21.46.38 (Mº Les Halles/Sentier). Daily noon–2pm & 7.30–11pm. Closed Sun midday. An excellent-value Kurdish restaurant. Beautiful starters, stuffed aubergines (*babaqunuc*), fish with yoghurt and courgettes (*kanarya*). Midday menu 60F.

Drouant, 18 rue Gaillon, 2e; ☎47 65.15.16 (Mº Opéra). Till 12.30am. A top-notch restaurant with a variety of dining places, including the 'café' which offers a 230F menu until 12.30am at the weekend.

Drouot, 103 rue de Richelieu, 2e; ☎42.96.68.23 (Mº Richelieu-Drouot). Daily noon–3pm & 6.30–10pm. Admirably cheap and good food, served at a frantic pace, in an Art Deco décor. Menu around 80F.

Le Grand Colbert, passage Colbert, rue Vivienne, 2e; ☎42.86.87.88 (Mº Bourse).

Daily noon–2pm & 7.30pm–1am. Closed mid-July to mid-Aug. In the same high style as the *passage* in which it's situated. Solid French cooking – *canard confit* and *andouillette* – and a 155F menu including the wine.

Le Grand Véfour, 17 rue de Beaujolais, 1er; ☎42.96.56.27 (M⁰ Pyramides). Mon–Fri 12.30–2pm & 7.30–10pm, Sat 7.30–10pm. The carved wooden ceilings, frescoes, velvet hangings and late eighteenth-century chairs haven't changed since Napoléon brought Josephine here. Considering the luxuriance of the *cuisine*, the lunchtime menu for 305F is a cinch. Go *à la carte* and the bill could top 800F.

L'Incroyable, 26 rue de Richelieu, 1er; ☎42.96.24.64 (M⁰ Palais-Royal). Tues–Thurs lunchtime & 6.30–9pm, Sat & Mon lunch only; closed Sun & two weeks at Christmas. Hidden in a tiny passage, a very pleasant restaurant serving decent meals for 60F at midday and 70F in the evening.

Au Petit Riche, 25 rue Le Peletier, 9e; ☎47.70.68.68 (M⁰ Richelieu-Drouot). Mon–Sat until 12.15am, closed second half of Aug. A long-established restaurant with a mirrored 1900s interior. Prompt and attentive service, good food. Very much a business hangout. Menu at 180F.

Restaurant Végétarien Lacour, 3 rue Villedo, 1er; ☎42.96.08.33 (M⁰ Pyramides). Mon–Sat noon–2pm. Vegetarian lunches for under 50F.

Le Vaudeville, 29 rue Vivienne, 2e; ☎40.20.04.62 (M⁰ Bourse). Until 2am. A lively late-night brasserie, where it's often necessary to queue. Good food, attractive marble-and-mosaic interior. *Carte* from 150F. 119F and 159F menus midday, evening 189F.

Les Halles

CAFÉS AND BARS

Asia Express, corner of rues Étienne-Marcel and St-Denis (M⁰ Etienne-Marcel). Chinese and Vietnamese stand-up self-service amidst the St-Denis sex shops. Dishes 28–32F. Beware the *Phō* soup special, festooned with floating testicles.

Café Costes, 4 rue Berger, 1er (M⁰ Châtelet-Les Halles). Tedious, overpriced, shallow and ugly. The design of the loos is original, but has failed to take account of the effect water smears have on glass.

À la Cloche des Halles, 28 rue Coquillière, 1er (M⁰ Châtelet-Les Halles/Louvre). Open till 8.30pm. Closed Sat evening and Sun. The bell hanging over this little wine bar is the one that used to mark the end of trading in the market halls. Though today's noise is from traffic on this busy corner, you are assured of some very fine wines.

Le Cochon à l'Oreille, 15 rue Montmartre, 1er (M⁰ Châtelet-Les Halles/Étienne-Marcel). Mon–Sat 7am–5pm. This classic little café, with raffeta chairs outside and scenes of the old market in ceramic tiles inside, opens early for the local fishmongers and meat traders.

L'Eustache, 37 rue Berger, Ier (M⁰ Les Halles). Daily till 2am. In marked contrast to the trendy *Le Comptoir* next door, a traditional brasserie. *Plats du jours* 60–80F.

The James Joyce, 5 rue du Jour, 1er (M⁰ Châtelet-Les Halles). Noon–3.30pm & 7pm–1am. Authentic Irish paraphernalia – *Freeman's Journal* and pics of Dublin on the wall, and on the quieter edge of Les Halles. Jazz some weekend evenings.

Chez Jo-Jo et Michele, 79 rue St-Honoré, 1er (M⁰ Louvre-Rivoli). Mon–Sat noon–2pm. A left-over from the market days where local butchers eat. Excellent meat. 69F menu.

Au Père Tranquille, on the corner of rues Pierre-Lescot and des Pécheurs, 1er (M⁰ Châtelet-Les Halles). Open till 2am. One of the big Les Halles cafés, overlooking the favoured stage where clowns make fools of passers-by against the backdrop of the horrid mirror structures. Expensive.

Au Pomelle, 19 rue du Roule, 1er (M⁰ Louvre-Rivoli). Tiny old-fashioned bar with a low zinc counter and newspapers on wooden batons.

Self-Service de la Samaritaine, Magasin 2, rue de la Monnaie, 1er (M⁰ Pont-Neuf). Open summer only, Mon–Sat 11.30am–3pm. In the number two *magasin*. The view over the Seine is probably more of

Eating and Drinking

See p.252 for a list of the various ethnic restaurants in Paris.

Eating and Drinking

an attraction than the food, though that isn't bad for the price (around 70F menu).

Le Sous-Bock, 49 rue St-Honoré, 1er (M° Châtelet-Les Halles). 11am–5am. Hundreds of bottled beers (around 33F a pint) and whiskies to sample with simple, inexpensive food. Mussels a speciality (40–50F). Frequented by night owls.

Au Trappiste, 4 rue St-Denis, 1er (M° Châtelet). Daily 11am–2am. Numerous draught beers include *Jenlain*, France's best-known *bière de garde*, Belgian *Blanche Riva* and *Kriek* from the *Mort Subite*

(Sudden Death) brewery – plus mussels and *frites* for 45F and various *tartines*.

RESTAURANTS

Aux Deux Saules, 91 rue St-Denis, 1er; ☎ 42.36.46.57 (M° Châtelet-Les Halles). Daily until 1am. Cheap if unexciting dishes. A leftover from the days of the market. The tile work representing same is the best feature. 69F menu.

L'Escargot Montorgueil, 38 rue Montorgueil, 1er; ☎ 42.36.83.51 (M° Étienne-Marcel/Les Halles). Daily till 11pm.

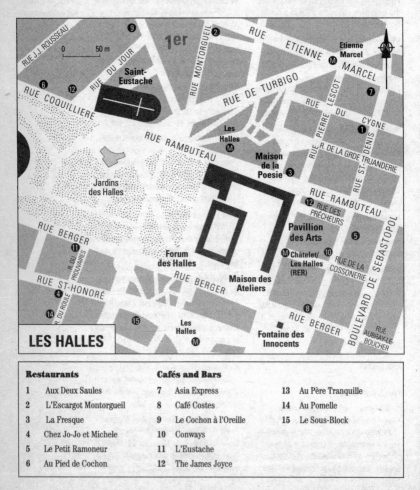

LES HALLES

Restaurants		Cafés and Bars			
1	Aux Deux Saules	7	Asia Express	13	Au Père Tranquille
2	L'Escargot Montorgueil	8	Café Costes	14	Au Pomelle
3	La Fresque	9	Le Cochon à l'Oreille	15	Le Sous-Block
4	Chez Jo-Jo et Michele	10	Conways		
5	Le Petit Ramoneur	11	L'Eustache		
6	Au Pied de Cochon	12	The James Joyce		

Closed mid-Aug. Sumptuous decor and snails the speciality. 180F midday menu, otherwise hugely expensive.

La Fresque, 100 rue Rambuteau, 1er; ☎42.33.17.56 (Mº Etienne-Marcel/Les Halles). Daily till midnight. Closed Sun midday. Nicely dingy with the old decor of a snail merchant's hall appearing through the gloom. 65F midday menu with wine. *Carte* 120F.

Le Petit Ramoneur, 74 rue St-Denis, 1er; ☎42.36.39.24 (Mº Châtelet-Les Halles). Mon–Fri until 9.30pm. Closed end Aug. Elbow-rubbing cheapie in good bistro tradition, with cheap wine that's better than table wine. Crowded, but a welcome and genuine relief in Les Halles. 63F menu.

Au Pied de Cochon, 6 rue Coquillière, 1er; ☎42.36.11.75 (Mº Châtelet-Les Halles). Open 24 hours. For extravagant middle-of-the-night pork chops and oysters. Seafood platter 192F. *Carte* up to 300F.

Le Terminus du Châtelet, 5 rue des Lavandières-St-Opportune, 1er; ☎45.08.50.44 (Mº Châtelet). Mon–Sat noon–2pm & 7–10.30pm. Closed Sat evening. Tucked away south of the rue de Rivoli, a tiny charming bistro. Lovely cheese and nut salads and dry sausage at lunchtime. Around 150F for full meal.

Chapter 5: Beaubourg, the Mairas, Île St-Louis and the Bastille

Beaubourg and Hôtel de Ville

CAFÉS AND BARS

Café Beaubourg, 43 rue St-Merri, 4e (Mº Rambuteau). Until 2am. Post-modernist clone of the earlier Philippe Starck *Café Costes*. It's expensive and the service is sour. It shares its rival's loo fetish; they are better here.

Dame Tartine, 2 rue Brise-Miche, 4e (Mº Rambuteau/Hôtel-de-Ville). Daily noon–11.30pm. Overlooking the Stravinsky pool, serving particularly delicious open toasted sandwiches (27–30F). Inside, decorated with kids' pictures.

Le Petit Marcel, 63 rue Rambuteau, 3e (Mº Rambuteau). Mon–Sat, until 2am. Speckled tabletops, mirrors and Art Nouveau tiles, cracked and faded ceiling and about eight square metres of drinking space. Friendly barman and "local" atmosphere.

Self-Service Beaubourg, 5th floor, Centre Pompidou, 4e (Mº Rambuteau). Wed–Sun noon–9.30pm. Cheap beer, coffee and snacks; no extra for sitting down on the *terrasse* with superb views.

RESTAURANTS

Le Farafina, 12 rue Quincampoix, 4e; ☎48.04.50.52 (Mº Châtelet/Hôtel-de-Ville). Tues–Sun 8pm–dawn. *Maffé* (Senegalese meat or fish stew) and *yassa* (chicken and lime) but the main attraction is live African music. Not for the retiring. Around 200F.

The Marais

CAFÉS AND BARS

Bar Central, 33 rue Vieille-du-Temple (corner rue Ste-Croix-de-la-Bretonnerie), 4e (Mº St-Paul). Noon–2am. One of the most popular gay bars in the Marais.

Bar de Jarente, 5 rue de Jarente, 4e (Mº St-Paul). A lovely old-fashioned café-bar remaining nonchalantly indifferent to the shifting trends that surround it.

Le Bouchon du Marais, 15 rue François-Miron, 4e; ☎48.87.44.13 (Mº St-Paul). 10am–3pm & 7.30pm–2am; closed Sun. A small relaxed wine *bistrot*, serving the patron's own wines from Touraine. Sandwiches as well as meals. 70F–180F.

Ma Bourgogne, 19 place des Vosges, 3e (Mº St-Paul). Open daily until 12.30am or 1am in summertime. A quiet and agreeable arty cafe with tables under the arcades on the northwest corner of the square. Best in the morning when the sun hits this side of the square. Serves somewhat pricy meals too.

La Cane de Jouy, 8 rue de Jouy, 4e; ☎42.78.38.86 (Mº St-Paul/Pont-Marie). Daily until 10.30pm; mornings only on

Eating and Drinking

See p.233 for a list of vegetarian restaurants in Paris.

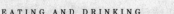

Eating and Drinking

See p.261 for a list of cafés and restaurants which stay open late.

Our glossary of French food and dishes begins on p.228.

Mondays. A very pretty shop selling *pâtés* and other special goodies from southwest France, as well as serving food. 43F midday menu, evening meal 180–200F.

Le Coude Fou, 12 rue du Bourg-Tibourg, 4e (Mº Hôtel-de-Ville). Noon–4pm & 6pm–midnight; Happy Hour 5–7pm weekdays; closed Sun lunchtime. A popular and rather pricey wine bar, which serves some good and unusual wines, along with *charcuterie* and cheese to match.

L'Ébouillanté, 6 rue des Barres, 4e (Mº Hôtel-de-Ville). Tues–Sun noon–9pm. Tiny *salon de thé* in picturesque street behind the church of St-Gervais, with reasonable prices and simple fare – chocolate cakes and *pâtisseries* as well as savoury dishes. *Plats du jour* for 60F.

Les Enfants Gatés, 43 rue des Francs-Bourgeois, 4e (Mº St-Paul). Deep armchairs, painting exhibitions and snacks like goat's cheese and tarragon tart (40F).

Épices et Délices, 53 rue Vieille-du-Temple, 4e (Mº St-Paul). Daily to midnight. Restaurant and *salon de thé* with very pleasant service and food. Aubergine *gratin* 60F.

L'Oiseau Bariolé, 16 rue Ste-Croix-de-la-Bretonnerie, 4e (Mº Hôtel-de-Ville). Open until 2am. Small, friendly café-bar, full of Americans. Serves *plats du jour*, salads, Breton cider, omelettes.

La Perla, 26 rue François-Miron (corner rue du Pont-Louis-Philippe), 4e (Mº St-Paul). Noon–2am. A spacious trendy corner café specializing in things Mexican. The tequila cocktails are specially good (average price 48F). Snacks from around 40F, and meals too, though these are best avoided.

Au Petit Fer à Cheval, 30 rue Vieille-du-Temple, 4e (Mº St-Paul). Mon–Fri 9am–2am, Sat–Sun 11am–2am; food noon–midnight. Very attractive small *bistrot*/bar with trad décor. Good wine, excellent *gigot d'agneau à romarin* for 58F and other good-value *plats*.

Le Pick-Clops, 16 rue Vieille-du-Temple, 4e (Mº Hôtel-de-Ville). Daily until 2am. An attractive easy-going bar on the corner of

rue du Roi-de-Sicile, popular with the youngish and hippish.

Le Quetzal, 10 rue de la Verrerie (corner rue Moussy), 4e (Mº St-Paul). Daily until 3am. A fashionable and stylish gay bar, with space for dancing.

Le Rouge Gorge, 8 rue St-Paul, 4e (Mº St-Paul). Mon–Sat noon–2pm. The young and enthusiastic clientele sip familiar wines and snack on *chèvre chaud* and smoked salmon salad, or tuck into more substantial fare (*plats du jour* around 60F), while listening to jazz or classical music.

Sacha Finkelsztajn and Florence Finkelsztajn, 27 rue des Rosiers, 4e (Wed–Sun 9.30am–1.30pm & 3–7.30pm) and 24 rue des Écouffes, 4e (Mon & Thurs–Sun 9.30am–1.30pm & 3–7.30pm). Both Mº St-Paul. Marvellous for takeaway snacks and goodies: gorgeous east European breads, cakes, *gefilte* fish, aubergine purée, tarama, *blinis* and *borscht*.

La Tartine, 24 rue de Rivoli, 4e (Mº St-Paul). Wed–Mon until 10pm. Closed Aug. The genuine 1900s article, which still cuts across class boundaries in its clientele. A good selection of affordable wines, plus excellent cheese and *saucisson* with *pain de campagne*.

Le Temps des Cerises, 31 rue de la Cerisaie, 4e (Mº Bastille). Mon–Fri until 8pm; food at midday only. Closed Aug. It is hard to say what is so appealing about this café, with its dirty yellow décor, old posters and prints of *vieux Paris*, save that the *patronne* knows most of the clientele, who are young, relaxed and not the dreaded *branchés*. There's a cheap *menu fixe*. See p.144 for a note on the origin of the name.

Le Trumilou, 84 quai Hôtel-de-Ville 4e; ☎42.77.63.98 (Mº Pont-Marie). Daily to 11pm. The Parisian equivalent of a diner. Pigs trotters, Lyonnais sausage and wonderful sweet chestnut charlotte, all served with wit and panache. 65F and 80F menus. *À la carte* close to 200F.

Le Volcan de Sicile, 62 rue du Roi-de-Sicile, 4e (Mº Hôtel-de-Ville). Flooded with sunshine at midday, this is *the* café to sit and sip on the corner of the exquisite and minuscule place Tibourg.

Yahalom, 22–24 rue des Rosiers, 4e (Mº St-Paul). Kosher *falafel* 25F; *plats du jour* 45F.

Le Zinc, 4 rue Caron, 4e (Mº St-Paul). 11am–2am, Sun 8.30am–6pm. A small intimate modern bar – with food costing 60–80F – close to the lovely place du Marché-Ste-Catherine.

RESTAURANTS

L'Ambroisie, 9 pl Vosges, 4e; ☎42.78.51.45 (Mº Chemin-Vert/St-Paul). Daily till 10.30pm. Closed first 3 weeks in August and Sun & Mon during school holidays. Scoring 19 out of 20 in the gourmet's bible *Gault et Millau*, this is exquisite food in an exquisite location, and costs 700F upwards. Booking imperative.

Aquarius 1, 54 rue Ste-Croix-de-la-Bretonnerie, 4e; ☎48.87.48.71 (Mº St-Paul/Rambuteau). Mon–Sat noon–9.45pm. Austere and penitential vegetarian restaurant: no alcohol, no smoking, and a leavening of Rosicrucianism. Menu at 51F.

Auberge de Jarente, 7 rue Jarente, 4e; ☎42.77.49.35 (Mº St-Paul). Tues–Sat noon–2.30pm & 6.30–10.30pm. Closed Aug. A hospitable and friendly Basque restaurant, serving first-class food: *cassoulet*, hare stew, king prawns in whisky, *magret de canard*, and *piperade* – the Basque omelette. Menues at 130F and 170F.

Chez Caroll Sinclair, 36 bd Henri-IV, 4e; ☎42.72.17.09 (Mº Sully Morland). Open until 11.30pm. Closed Sat midday and Sun evening. Beautiful fish dishes including seafood soup and excellent desserts. Over 200F *à la carte* but 150F midday weekday menu with wine and 177F evening menu.

L'Enoteca, 25 rue Charles-V, 4e; ☎42.78.91.44 (Mº St-Paul). Open noon–2am. A very pleasant and fashionable Italian *bistrot à vins*. Plats between 60F and 70F.

L'Excuse, 14 rue Charles-V, 4e; ☎42.77.98.97 (Mº St-Paul). Noon–2pm & 7.30–11pm; closed Sun. The cuisine is *nouvelle*-ish, as refined and elegant as the very pretty décor. One menu at 145F, otherwise a good deal more. A good place for a quiet but stylish date.

Fleur de Lotus, 2 rue du Roi-de-Sicile, 4e; ☎42.78.74.90 (Mº St-Paul). 11am–3pm & 5.30–10.30pm. Closed Sun & the last fortnight in Aug. A tiny and attractive Vietnamese where you eat excellent food for under 120F.

Goldenberg's, 7 rue des Rosiers, 4e; ☎48.87.20.16 (Mº St-Paul). Daily until 11pm. The best-known Jewish restaurant in the capital; its *borscht*, *blinis*, potato strudels, *zakouski*, and other central European dishes are a treat. Around 200F.

Le Palais de Fès, 41 rue du Roi-de-Sicile, 4e; ☎42.72.03.68 (Mº St-Paul). Daily until 10.30pm. Delicious lamb *tagines* with plums and almonds for 80F, stewed quail and menu at 65F.

Piccolo Teatro, 6 rue des Écouffes, 4e; ☎42.72.17.79 (Mº St-Paul). Wed–Sun noon–3pm & 7–11pm. Closed Aug. A vegetarian restaurant with *assiette végétarienne* at 58F; lunch menus at 54F and 74F, evening at 85F and 110F.

Pitchi-Poï, 7 rue Caron (in the corner of place du Marché-Ste-Catherine), 4e; ☎42.77.46.15 (Mº St-Paul). Noon–3pm & 7.30–11pm. Polish/Jewish *cuisine*: excellent food and sympathetic ambience – lovely location. Around 160F; menu at 140F and an *assiette végétarienne* for 81F.

Le Ravaillac, 10 rue du Roi-de-Sicile, 4e; ☎42.72.885.85 (Mº St-Paul). Noon–3pm & 7–10.30pm; closed Sun, Mon lunchtime & Aug. Long-established Polish restaurant. Specialities include meat *perushkis*, beef Stroganoff, and *choucroute*. Excellent quality for the price – around 100F.

La Truffe, 31 rue Vieille-du-Temple, 4e; ☎42.71.08.39 (Mº St-Paul). Daily noon–4pm & 7.30–11pm. A vegetarian specializing in mushrooms as well as lentil and cheese dishes and delicious fruit tarts.

Eating and Drinking

See p.252 for a list of the various ethnic restaurants in Paris.

Eating and Drinking

See p.233 for a list of vegetarian restaurants in Paris.

Quartier du Temple

CAFÉS AND BARS

Le Taxi Jaune, 13 rue Chapon, 3e (Mº Arts-et-Métiers). Mon–Sat until 11pm. An ordinary café, made special by the odd poster, good taped rock and new wave music. Interesting food, until 11.30pm; lunchtime menu at 68F with wine, evening menu 89F, cocktails 35F. Offers the occasional concert.

RESTAURANTS

Le Marais-Cage, 8 rue de Beauce, 3e; ☎48.87.31.20 (Mº Arts-et-Métiers/Filles-du-Calvaire). Noon–2.15pm & 7–10.30pm; closed Sat noon, Sun and Aug. Friendly and popular West Indian restaurant; good food, with prices a little on the high side – 150–200F.

Chez Nénesse, 17 rue Saintonge, 3e; ☎42.78.46.49 (Mº Arts-et-Métiers). Mon–Fri noon–3pm & 7.30–10.15pm. Closed Aug. Doe steak in bilberry sauce and figs stuffed with cream of almonds are two of the unique delights of this restaurant, along with home-made chips on Thursday lunchtimes. Under 100F midday, over 200F for dinner.

Île St-Louis

CAFÉS AND BARS

Berthillon, 31 rue St-Louis-en-l'Île, 4e (Mº Pont-Marie). Wed–Sun 10am–8pm. Long queues for these very best of ice creams and sorbets (18F a triple), which are made and sold here on the Île St-Louis. Also available at *Lady Jane* and *Le Flore-en-l'Île*, both on quai d'Orléans, as well as at four other island sites listed on the door.

Les Fous de l'Île, 33 rue des Deux-Ponts, 4e (Mº Pont-Marie). Light lunches in bookish surroundings for around 50–60F, tea and cakes till 7pm and dinner until 11pm. Closed Mon.

Le St-Régis, 92 rue St-Louis-en-l'Île, 4e (Mº Pont-Marie). An unpretentious brasserie opposite the Pont St-Louis with view of Notre-Dame. *Plats du jour* around 75F.

RESTAURANTS

Le Castafiore, 51 rue St-Louis-en-l'Île, 4e; ☎43.54.78.62 (Mº Pont-Marie). Daily till 10.30pm. Italian specialities. Very pleasant *patron*. 98F menu before 8.30pm, 158F after.

Le Gourmet de l'Île, 42 rue St-Louis-en-l'Île, 4e; ☎43.26.79.27 (Mº Pont-Marie). Wed–Sun noon–2pm & 7–10pm. A bargain four-course menu for 125F, including wonderful stuffed mussels.

Bastille

CAFÉS AND BARS

Café de l'Industrie, 16 rue St-Sabin, 11e (Mº Bastille). 9am–2am; closed Sun. Rugs on the floor around solid old wooden tables, miscellaneous objects on the walls, and a young, unpretentious crowd enjoying the lack of chrome, minimalism or Philippe Starck. One of the best Bastille addresses. *Plats du jour* from 38F.

Café de la Plage, 59 rue de Charonne, 11e (Mº Bastille). Tues–Sun until 2am. A multiracial clientele and as many women as men in this low-ceilinged, friendly, youthful and often very crowded Irish-run bar. Jazz club downstairs.

La Fontaine, 1 rue de Charonne, 11e (Mº Bastille). Gentrified, as are all the cafés hereabouts, but not too self-conscious or expensive. On the corner of rue du Faubourg-St-Antoine by the fountain.

Fouquet's, 130 rue de Lyon, 12e (Mº Bastille). Till midnight. Closed Sat & Sun midday. A smart and expensive café-restaurant underneath the new Opéra, sister establishment to the Champs-Elysées *Fouquet's*. But with perfect French courtesy they will leave you undisturbed for hours with a 15F coffee. Menu, including wine, at 165F.

Hollywood Canteen, 20 rue de la Roquette, 11e (Mº Bastille). Flossed-up Fifties style American bar: milk shakes, ham-burgers (19–35F), cocktails, brownies etc.

Iguana, 15 rue de la Roquette (corner rue Daval), 11e (Mº Bastille). Mon–Sat 10am–4am. A place to be seen in. Décor of trellises, colonial fans, and brushed bronze bar. The clientele studies récherché art reviews.

Pause Café, 41 rue de Charonne (corner rue Keller), 11e (Mº Ledru-Rollin). Tues–Sat 8am–2am, Sun till 9pm. A new and fashionable Bastille café, down among the galleries.

La Pirada, 7 rue de Lappe, 11e; ☎47.00.73.61 (Mº Bastille). Till 2am, Sun till 5pm. Designer *tapas* bar for the designer people of the new Bastille; live music. 60–120F. 68F menu at midday.

RESTAURANTS

L'Abreuvoir, 68 rue de la Roquette (corner rue des Taillandiers), 11e; ☎43.57.71.74 (Mº Voltaire/Bastille). Lunchtime, & evenings until 1am; closed Sun midday. Traditional cooking. Local restaurant from pre-trendy days. Midday menu at 59F, otherwise around 120F.

Blue Elephant, 43–45 rue de la Roquette, 11e; ☎47.00.42.00 (Mº Bastille/Richard-Lenoir). Daily to midnight. Closed Sun evening. Superb Thai restaurant in tropical forest décor. Worth every centime. 150F midday menu, otherwise over 250F.

Bofinger, 3–7 rue de la Bastille, 3e; ☎42.72.87.82 (Mº Bastille). Daily until 1am. A well-established and popular turn-of-the-century brasserie, with original décor, serving the archetypal fare of sauerkraut and seafood. Menu at 149F, otherwise over 200F.

La Canaille, 4 rue Crillon, 4e; ☎42.78.09.71 (Mº Sully-Morland/Bastille). Mon–Sat lunchtime & 7.30pm–midnight. Bar in front, restaurant behind, decorated with revolutionary posters invoking rather more durable old-fashioned values than the usual contemporary fast-buck stuff. The food is simple, traditional and well cooked. Delightful, friendly atmosphere. There are 85F and 125F evening menus, and *à la carte* at 140F.

Nini Peau d'Chien, 24 rue des Taillandiers, 11e; ☎47.00.45.35 (Mº Bastille). 11.30am–2.30pm & 8-11pm; closed Sun & Mon. The charm of the two proprietors makes up for the scatty service and very mediocre main courses

at this boisterous and well-heeled gay and lesbian restaurant. Good starters include a very light and tasty *terrine craillée de St-Jacques* and *amourettes* (spinal marrow). Lunchtime menu at 59F, evening menu 119F.

Chapter 6: The Left Bank

Quartier Latin

CAFÉS AND BARS

29 rue Linné (no name), 5e (Mº Jussieu). Very cheap sandwiches and a 30F midday menu of Asian food.

Le Bâteau Ivre, 40 rue Descartes, 5e (Mº Cardinal-Lemoine). Closed Mon. Happy hour is 4–8pm at this small bar just clear of the Mouffetard tourist hot spot.

Café des Arts, corner of place Contrescarpe and rue Lacépède, 5e (Mº Monge). Prettier cups and cheaper coffee than its touristy neighbour *La Chope*.

Café de la Mosquée, 39 rue Geoffroy-St-Hilaire, 5e (Mº Monge). Mon–Thurs, Sat & Sun 10am–9.30pm. Closed Aug. In fine weather you can drink mint tea and eat sweet cakes beside a fountain and assorted fig trees in the courtyard of this Paris mosque – a delightful haven of calm. The interior of the salon is beautifully Arabic with cats curled up on the seats. You can have meals in the adjoining restaurant.

Café Notre-Dame, corner of quai St-Michel and rue St-Jacques, 5e (Mº St-Michel). With a view right across to the cathedral. Lenin used to drink here.

Connolly's Corner, on the corner of rues Patriarches and Mirbel, 5e (Mº Monge/Censier-Daubenton). Noon–1am, Sat noon–4am. An Irish bar with darts, *Smithwicks*, and not a lot of space, but plenty of atmosphere. Very smoky.

Le Crocodile, 6 rue Royer-Collard, 5e (Mº Luxembourg). Mon–Sat 10.30pm–2am; closed Aug. Small, rather tattered old-fashioned bar. Not at all salubrious despite the 45F and upwards cocktails, but good fun.

La Fontaines, 9 rue Soufflot, 5e (Mº Luxembourg). Mon–Sat until 10.30pm.

Eating and Drinking

The cafés and restaurants of the Quartier Latin are keyed on our special map over the page.

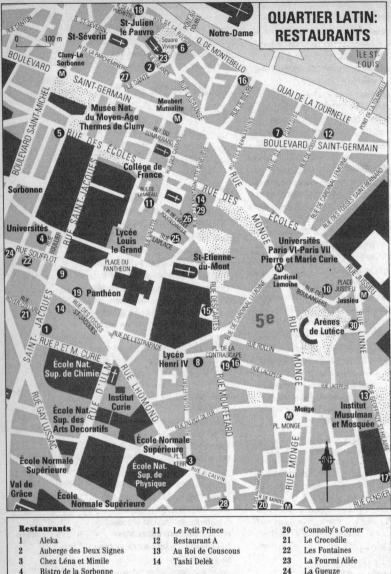

QUARTIER LATIN: RESTAURANTS

Restaurants	
1	Aleka
2	Auberge des Deux Signes
3	Chez Léna et Mimile
4	Bistro de la Sorbonne
5	Brasserie Balzar
6	Le Grenier de Notre-Dame
7	Inagiku
8	Le Liban à la Mouff
9	Perraudin
10	Le Petit Légume

11	Le Petit Prince
12	Restaurant A
13	Au Roi de Couscous
14	Tashi Delek
Cafés and Bars	
15	Le Bâteau Ivre
16	Café des Arts
17	Café de la Mosquée
18	Café Notre-Dame
19	La Chope

20	Connolly's Corner
21	Le Crocodile
22	Les Fontaines
23	La Fourmi Ailée
24	La Gueuze
25	Le Piano Vache
26	Les Pipos
27	Polly Magoo
28	La Verre à Pied
29	Le Violon Dingue
30	29 Rue Linné

Serving huge seafood salads, roast rabbit in mustard sauce and chicken fricassé with morilles mushrooms. Up to 200F for a full meal.

La Fourmi Ailée, 8 rue du Fouarre, 5e (Mº Maubert-Mutualité). Noon–7pm. Closed Tues. Simple, light fare – including brunch on Saturday and Sunday – in this feminist bookshop-cum-*salon-de-thé*. Around 60F for tea and a cake.

La Gueuze, 19 rue Soufflot, 5e (Mº Luxembourg). Mon–Sat noon–2am. Comfy surroundings – lots of wood and stained glass. Kitchen specials are *pierrades*: dishes cooked on hot stones. Numerous bottles and several draughts, including cherry beer. Close to the university with lots of student habitués.

Le Piano Vache, 8 rue Laplace, 5e (Mº Cardinal-Lemoine). 9am–1.30am, Sat & Sun evenings only. Venerable student bar with canned music and relaxed atmosphere.

Les Pipos, 50 rue de la Montagne-Ste-Geneviève, 5e (Mº Maubert-Mutualité/Cardinal-Lemoine). Old carved wooden bar and sculpted chimney piece, its own wines, and a long-established position opposite the gates of the former *grand école*.

Polly Magoo, 11 rue St-Jacques, 5e (Mº St-Michel/Maubert-Mutualité). A scruffy all-nighter frequented by chess addicts.

Le Verre à Pied, 118bis rue Mouffetard, 5e (Mº Monge). Closed Sun afternoon, Mon & mid-July to Aug. An unchanged, old-fashioned café-bar with cheap drinks.

Le Violon Dingue, 46 rue de la Montagne-Ste-Geneviève, 5e (Mº Maubert-Mutualité). Mon & Wed–Sun 6pm–1am. Happy hour 6–9pm. A long dark student pub, noisy and friendly.

RESTAURANTS

Aleka, 187 rue St-Jacques, 5e; ☎44.07.02.75 (*RER* Luxembourg). 10am–midnight. Fresh and simple combinations – *brochettes*, rice, salads, followed by *crêpes* – sometimes served by the champion roller-skating sons of the proprietors. *Plats* under 80F. Greek wines and ouzo.

Auberge des Deux Signes, 46 rue Galande, 5e; ☎43.25.00.46 (Mº St-Michel). Closed Sat midday, Sun & Aug. A medieval setting and for once, an interesting choice on the *menus fixes* at 140F and 230F.

Bistro de la Sorbonne, 4 rue Toullier, 5e; ☎43.54.41.49 (Mº Luxembourg). Mon–Sat until 11pm. Help-yourself starters and salads, good ices and *crêpes flambées*. Copious portions. Crowded and attractive student ambience. 70F menu at lunchtime, including wine and service; 95F in the evening.

Brasserie Balzar, 49 rue des Écoles, 5e; ☎43.54.13.67 (Mº Maubert-Mutualité). Daily until 12.30am; closed Aug. A traditional literary-bourgeois brasserie, frequented by the intelligentsia of the Latin Quarter. About 170F.

Le Grenier de Notre-Dame, 18 rue de la Bûcherie, 5e (Mº Maubert-Mutalité). Daily noon–11.30pm. Some veggies love this place, others hate it. Substantial fare including couscous, fried tofu, cauliflower cheese. Menus at 75F, 105F and 140F.

Inagiku, 14 rue Pontoise, 5e; ☎43.54.70.07 (Mº Maubert-Mutualité). Mon–Sat till 11pm. Authentic Japanese: 4 pieces sushi 65F, 108F midday menu.

Chez Léna et Mimile, 32 rue Tournefort, 5e; ☎47.07.72.47 (Mº Consier-Daubenton). Until 11pm. Closed Sat & Sun midday. The south-facing high *terrasse* is the main attraction, and the 185F menu with wine and coffee included is excellent. Also 98F menu.

Le Liban à la Mouff, 3 rue de l'Estrapade 5e; ☎47.07.29.99 (Mº Monge). Closed Tues & Wed midday. A pleasant and unusually cheap Lebanese restaurant. *Kafta* 60F, wonderful milk pudding *mouhallabiah* 28F, large *mezze* for four 440F.

Perraudin, 157 rue St-Jacques, 5e; ☎46.33.15.75. (*RER* Luxembourg). Mon & Sat 7.00–10.30pm, Tues–Fri noon–2pm & 7.30–10.15pm. A well-known traditional *bistrot* with a midday menu at 60F; *carte* around 150F.

Eating and Drinking

See p.261 for a list of cafés and restaurants which stay open late.

See p.252 for a list of the various ethnic restaurants in Paris.

Eating and Drinking

See p.261 for a list of cafés and restaurants which stay open late.

Le Petit Légume, 36 rue Boulangers, 5e (Mº Jussieu). Mon–Fri 9.30am–10pm. Vegetarian restaurant; perhaps not one of the greatest veggie addresses, but useful if you're stuck. *Plats* around 48F.

Le Petit Prince, 12 rue Lanneau, 5e; ☎43.54.77.26 (Mº Maubert-Mutualité). Evenings only, until 12.30am. Good food in a restaurant full of Latin Quarter charm in one of the *quartier's* oldest lanes. Menus at 82F and 148F.

Le Refuge du Passé, 32 rue du Fer-à-Moulin, 5e; ☎47.07.29.91 (Mº Les Gobelins). Till midnight. Closed Sun & Mon midday. Stuffed full of bric-à-brac and musical instruments, this is a rare home for French *chansons*. Decent food from southwest France – 115F midday menu with wine, 150F evening menu.

Restaurant A, 5 rue de Poissy, 5e; ☎46.33.85.54 (Mº Cardinal-Lemoine). Tues–Sun until 11pm. Good and unusual Chinese dishes with vegetables sculpted into flowers and animals. Menu at 108F; *carte* 200F plus.

Student restaurants The "Resto-U's" for which those with student cards can buy tickets (books of ten/12.30F a meal) are at: 8bis rue Cuvier, 5e (Mº Jussieu); 39 av G-Bernanos, 5e (Mº Port-Royal); 31 rue Geoffroy-St-Hilaire, 5e (Mº Censier-Daubenton); and 10 rue Jean-Calvin, 5e (Mº Censier-Daubenton). Not all serve both midday and evening meals, and times change with each term. Full details can be had from the student organization, *CROUS* (☎40.51.36.00). Though the food is not wonderful, it is certainly filling, and you can't complain for the price. Tickets are available in the entrances to the restaurants, and some are less fussy than others about student credentials, and will sell tickets to anyone for 24.60F (in *carnets* of ten).

Tashi Delek, 4 rue des Fossés-St-Jacques, 5e; ☎43.26.55.55 (Mº Luxembourg). Lunchtime and evenings until 10.30pm. An enjoyable Tibetan restaurant – run by refugees – where you can eat for as little as 50F, without wine. On the 125F menu you can try the wonderful *beignets* of chicken with ginger sauce.

St-Germain

CAFÉS AND BARS

Le 10, 10 rue de l'Odéon, 6e (Mº Odéon). Daily 5.30pm–2am. The beer here is very cheap, which is why it attracts youth, particularly foreigners. Old posters, a juke box, and a lot of chatting-up.

L'Alsace à Paris, 9 place St-André-des-Arts, 6e; ☎43.26.21.48 (Mº St-Michel). A very busy and well-worn brasserie, with menus at 110F, 130F and 180F – but also delicious and cheap *tartes flambées* like thin pizzas that you can also take away.

L'Assignat, 7 rue Guénégaud, 6e (Mº Pont-Neuf). Mon–Sat 7.30am–8.30pm, closed July. Zinc counter, bar stools, bar football and young regulars in an untouristy café close to quai des Augustins. 25F for a sandwich and a glass of wine.

Le Bonaparte, corner rue Bonaparte and place St-Germain (Mº St-Germain-des-Prés). Meeting place for the quartier's intellectuals, quieter and less touristy than *Deux Magots* or *Flore*.

Café de la Mairie, place St-Sulpice, 6e (Mº St-Sulpice). A peaceful, pleasant, youthful café on the sunny north side of the square.

À la Cour de Rohan, Cour du Commerce, off rues St-André-des-Arts & Ancienne-Comédie, 6e (Mº Odéon). Tues–Fri noon–7pm, Sat & Sun 3–7pm; closed Aug. A genteel, chintzy drawing-room atmosphere in a picturesque eighteenth-century alley close to bd St-Germain. Cakes, *tartes*, poached eggs, etc. No smoking. 95F menu.

Les Deux Magots, 170 bd St-Germain, 6e (Mº St-Germain-des-Prés). Open until 2am; closed Aug. Right on the corner of place St-Germain-des-Prés, it too owes its reputation to the intellos of the Left Bank, past and present. In summertime it picks up a lot of foreigners seeking the exact location of the spirit of French culture, and buskers galore play to the packed terrace.

L'Écluse, 15 quai des Grands-Augustins, 6e (Mº St-Michel). Noon–2am. Forerunner of the new generation of wine bars, with décor and atmosphere in authentic traditional style – just lacking the workmen to spit on the floor. Small and intimate: a very agreeable place to sit and sip. It has spawned several offspring, none of which is as pleasant.

Le Flore, 172 bd St-Germain, 6e (Mº St-Germain-des-Prés). Open until 2am; closed July. The great rival and immediate neighbour of *Deux Magots*, with a very similar clientele.

Chez Georges, 11 rue des Canettes, 6e (Mº Mabillon). Tues–Sat noon–2am; closed July 14–Aug 15. An attractive wine-bar in the spit-on-the-floor mode, with its old shop front still intact in a narrow leading street off place St-Sulpice.

Lina's Sandwiches, 27 rue St-Sulpice, 6e (Mº Odéon). Same outfit as at 50 rue Étienne-Marcel, 2e. See above under "Right Bank Commerce and Passages".

Eating and Drinking

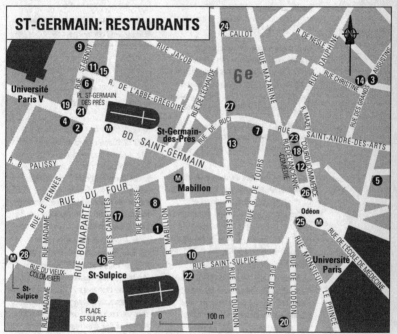

Restaurants

1	Aux Charpentiers	11	Le Petit Zinc	19	Les Deux Magots
2	Drugstore St-Germain	12	Le Procope	20	Le 10
3	Jacques Cagna	13	Restaurant des Arts	21	Le Flore
4	Lipp	14	La Rôtisserie d'en Face	22	Lina's Sandwiches
5	La Maroussia			23	Le Mazet
6	Le Muniche	**Cafés and Bars**		24	La Palette
7	Orestias	15	Le Bonaparte	25	La Pinte
8	Le Petit Mabillon	16	Café de la Mairie	26	Pub St-Germain
9	Le Petit St-Benoît	17	Chez Georges	27	La Table d'Italie
10	Le Petit Vatel	18	À la Cour de Rohan	28	Au Vieux Colombier

Eating and Drinking

See p.261 for a list of cafés and restaurants which stay open late.

Le Mazet, 60 rue St-André-des-Arts, 6ᵉ (Mᵒ Odéon). Mon–Thurs 10am–2am; Fri and Sat until 3.30am; closed Sun. A well-known hang-out for buskers (with a lock-up for their instruments) and heavy drinkers. What about a *bière brûlée* for an evil concoction – it's flambéed with gin.

La Paillote, 45 rue Monsieur-le-Prince, 6ᵉ (*RER* Luxembourg/Mᵒ Odéon). Mon–Sat 9pm till dawn. Closed Aug. *The* late-night bar for jazz fans, with one of the best collections of recorded jazz in the city. Drinks around 38F.

La Palette, 43 rue de Seine, 6ᵉ (Mᵒ Odéon). Mon–Sat 8am–2am. Once-famous Beaux Arts student hang-out, now more for art dealers and their customers. The service can be uncivil, but the murals and every detail of the décor are superb.

La Pinte, 13 carrefour de l'Odéon, 6ᵉ (Mᵒ Odéon). 6.30pm–2am; closed Aug. Boozy and crowded beer cellar, with piano and jazz.

Pub Saint-Germain, 17 rue de l'Ancienne-Comédie, 6ᵉ (Mᵒ Odéon). Open 24 hours. 21 draught beers and hundreds of bottles. Huge, crowded, and expensive. Hot food at mealtimes, otherwise cold snacks. For a taste of "real" French beer try *ch'ti* (patois for northerner), a *bière de garde* from the Pas-de-Calais.

La Table d'Italie, 69 rue de Seine, 6ᵉ (Mᵒ Mabillon/St-Germain-des-Prés). Italian pasta, snacks, etc at the counter, plus a grocery selling pasta and other Italian delicatessen products. 98F menu.

La Taverne de Nesle, 32 rue Dauphine, 6ᵉ (Mᵒ Odéon). 7am–5am. Vast selection of beers. Full of local night birds. Cocktails from 40F.

Au Vieux Colombier, 65 rue des Rennes, 6ᵉ (Mᵒ St-Sulpice). An Art Deco café on the corner of rue du Vieux-Colombier, with enamelled dove medallions, ice-cream cone lights and stained green wooden frames for the windows.

RESTAURANTS

Aux Charpentiers, 10 rue Mabillon, 6ᵉ; ☎43.26.30.05 (Mᵒ Mabillon). Mon–Sat until 11pm; closed hols. A friendly, old-fashioned place belonging to the *Compagnons des Charpentiers* (Carpenters' Guild), with appropriate décor of roof-trees and tie beams. Traditional *plats du jour* are their forte. Around 220F.

Drugstore Saint-Germain, 149 bd St-Germain, 6ᵉ Mᵒ St-Germain-des-Prés. Until 2am. The best of the drugstores for food. Basics include steak tartare, and *langoustines* done to a T.

Jacques Cagna, 14 rue des Grands-Augustins, 6ᵉ; ☎43.54.54.48 (Mᵒ Odéon/St-Michel). Closed Sun, Mon midday and 3 weeks in Aug. Till 10.30pm. Classy surroundings for very classy food – Scottish beef with Périgord truffles and the like for 700F upwards *à la carte*. But a midday menu for 260F.

Lipp, 151 bd St-Germain, 6ᵉ; ☎45.48.53.91 (Mᵒ St-Germain-des-Prés). Until 12.30am; closed mid-July to mid-Aug. A 1900s brasserie, one of the best-known establishments on the Left Bank, haunt of the successful and famous. Rather more welcoming now that its sour old owner has died and been replaced by a niece. 200–250F. No reservations; be prepared to wait.

La Maison de la Lozère, 4 rue Hautefeuille, 6ᵉ; ☎43.54.26.64 (Mᵒ St-Michel). Tues–Sat until 10.30pm, Sun lunchtime only; closed mid-July to mid-Aug & the last week in Dec. A scrubbed-wood restaurant serving up the cuisine, cheeses etc of the Lozère *département*. Menus at 86F (lunchtime only during the week, wine included), 115F and 141F. Excellent omelettes for under 50F.

La Maroussia, 9 rue de l'Éperon, 6ᵉ; ☎43.54.47.02 (Mᵒ Odéon). Tues–Fri lunchtime & 7.30–11pm, Sat & Mon evenings only; closed three weeks in Aug. Polish and Ukrainian dishes – *bigos* (sausage and cabbage stew), *shashlik* (kebabs), salmon *kulibiak* (soup) and *zakouskis* (cold hors d'oeuvres). 150F menu; 230F *carte*. Music Sat and Wed evening.

Le Muniche, 22 rue Guillaume-Apollinaire, 6ᵉ; ☎46.33.62.09 (Mᵒ St-Germain-des-Prés). Noon–2am. A crowded old-style brasserie with an oyster bar, mirrors and theatre posters on the walls and good old French offal concoctions on the menu. 140F menu.

Orestias, 4 rue Grégoire-de-Tours, 6e; ☎43.54.62.01 (Mº Odéon). Mon–Sat lunchtime & evening until 11pm. A mixture of Greek and French cuisine. Good helpings and very cheap – with a menu at 44F (weekdays only).

Le Petit Mabillon, 6 rue Mabillon, 6e; ☎43.54.08.41 (Mº Mabillon). Mon evening until 11.30pm, Tues–Sat lunchtime & evening until 11.30pm; closed mid-Dec to mid-Jan. Decent and straightforward Italian menu for 75F.

Le Petit Saint-Benoît, 4 rue Saint-Benoît, 6e; ☎42.60.27.92 (Mº St-Germain-des-Prés). Mon–Fri lunchtime & 7–l0pm. A simple, genuine and very appealing local for the neighbourhood's chattering classes. Serves solid traditional fare in a brown-stained, aproned atmosphere – for about 120F.

Le Petit Vatel, 5 rue Lobineau, 6e; ☎43.54.28.49 (Mº Mabillon). Mon–Sat lunchtime & 7pm–midnight, Sun evenings only. A tiny, matey place with good plain home-cooking, including a vegetarian *plat* – for around 60F.

Le Petit Zinc, 11 rue Saint-Benoît, 6e; ☎46.33.51.66 (Mº St-Germain-des-Prés). Noon–2am. Excellent traditional dishes, especially seafood, in stunning new Art Nouveau premises, complete with white fringed parasols over the pavement tables. Not cheap – midday menu 158F, seafood platter 440F for two.

Polidor, 41 rue Monsieur-le-Prince, 6e; ☎43.26.95.34 (Mº Odéon). Mon–Sat until 1am, Sun until 11pm. A traditional *bistrot*, whose visitors' book, they say, boasts more of history's big names than all the glittering palaces put together. Not as cheap as it was in James Joyce's day but good food and great atmosphere. Lunches at 55F during the week and an excellent l00F evening menu.

Le Procope, 13 rue de l'Ancienne-Comédie, 6e; ☎43.26.99.20 (Mº Odéon). Daily noon–1am. This was the first establishment to serve coffee in Paris. Over 300 years it has retained its reputation as the place for powerful intellectuals. Its present décor dates from the Bicentennial of the Revolution, and citizens are still offered 69F and 98F menus – before 7pm. After that it's 289F until 11pm when a 119F menu is on offer.

Restaurant des Arts, 73 rue de Seine, 6e. (Mº St-Germain-des-Prés). Mon–Thurs till 9pm, Fri lunchtime only; closed Aug. Menu at 78F. A small, crowded, friendly place with simple, homely meals. Young and old, well-heeled, and not at all.

Restaurant des Beaux-Arts, 11 rue Bonaparte, 6e; ☎43.26.92.64 (Mº St-Germain-des-Prés). Daily lunchtime & evening until 10.45pm. The traditional hang-out of the art students from the Beaux-Arts across the way. Menu at 69F including wine. The choice is wide, the portions generous, and the queues long in high season; the atmosphere is generally good, though the waitresses can get pretty tetchy.

Le Rôtisserie d'en Face, 2 rue Christine, 6e; ☎43.26.40.98 (Mº Odéon/St-Michel). An annexe to *Jacques Cagna* (see p.248). Excellent grilled meats. 220F menu for two, midday menu 145F in a rather too business-like atmosphere.

Student restaurants at 55 rue Mazet, 6e (Mº Odéon) and 92 rue d'Assas, 6e (Mº Port-Royal/Notre-Dame-des-Champs). See under Quartier Latin, p.246, for details.

Village Bulgare, 8 rue de Nevers, 6 e; ☎43.25.08.75 (Mº Odéon/Pont-Neuf). Noon–2pm & 7.30–10pm; closed Sun evening & Mon midday. The only Bulgarian restaurant in France. Specialities include *kebabtcheta* (veal and lamb stew), *cirène au four* (baked sheep's milk cheese with vegetables), yoghurt and Gamza wine. 80F menu, *à la carte* 150F.

Chapter 7: Trocadéro, Eiffel Tower and Les Invalides

CAFÉS AND BARS

Kléber, place du Trocadéro, 16e (Mº Trocadéro). Open until dawn. Good for

Eating and Drinking

Some of Paris' top gourmet restaurants are listed on p.263.

See p.252 for a list of the various ethnic restaurants in Paris.

Eating and Drinking

Some of Paris'
top gourmet
restaurants are
listed on p.263.

cinematic views of the Eiffel Tower catching the first light or morning mist filling the valley of the Seine.

La Pagode, 57bis rue de Babylone, 7e (Mº François-Xavier/Sèvres-Babylone). 4–9.45pm, Sun 2–8pm. A real-life pagoda (see p.337) – one of the most beautiful buildings in Paris in which to have tea. Tables in the Chinese garden in summer.

Restaurant du Museé d'Orsay, 1 rue Bellechasse, 7e (RER Musée d'Orsay/Mº Solférino). Tues, Wed & Fri–Sat 11.30am–2.15pm, 4–5.30pm & 7–9.45pm; Thurs 11.30am–2.15pm & 7–9.45pm; Sun 11.30am–2.15pm & 4–5.30pm. Superb views over the Seine in the museum's rooftop restaurant. Hors d'oeuvres, dessert and wine for 72F. Quick and friendly service.

Sancerre, 22 av Rapp, 7e (Mº Alma-Marceau). Wine shop and bar serving glasses of Sancerre from 22F and sandwiches at 16–219F. Try the rosé (and other Loire wines).

Le Suffren, corner of avs Motte-Piquet and Suffren, 15e (Mº École-Militaire/La Motte-Piquet). Big café-brasserie distinguished by serving dark Swiss chocolate bar with its *café crème*, and being the only obvious place to sit down after walking the length of the École Militaire.

Veggie, 38 rue de Verneuil, 7e. Mon–Fri 10.30am–2.30pm & 4.30–7.30pm. Organic take-away from health food shop near the Musée d'Orsay.

RESTAURANTS

L'Ami Jean, 27 rue Malar, 7e; ☎47.05.86.89 (Mº Latour-Maubourg). Mon–Sat lunchtime & 7–10.30pm. Closed Aug. Pleasant ambience, if rather hurried, and good Basque food for around 130–150F.

Au Babylone, 13 rue de Babylone, 7e; ☎45.48.72.13 (Mº Sèvres-Babylone). Mon–Sat lunchtime only; closed Aug. Lots of old-fashioned charm and basics like *rôti de veau*, steak etc, plus wine on the 80F menu.

Le Basilic, 2 rue Casimir-Périer, 7e; ☎44.18.94.64 (Mº Solférino). Daily noon–2.30pm & 7.30–11.30pm. Very classy

with lots of polished brass and a terrace overlooking the apse of Ste-Clotilde. Specialities such as lamb from Sisteron in salt and basil will set you back 88F. Count on 200F for a full meal.

Le Bourdonnais, 113 av La Bourdonnais, 7e; ☎47.05.47.06 (Mº École-Militaire). Till 11pm. A gem of a restaurant and a high-class one at that. À la carte costs around 400F, but there's a superb midday menu including wine for 220F, evening menu 280F.

Le Las Cases, 27 rue Bellechasse, 7e (Mº Solferino). An ordinary brasserie with a good selection of dishes and a 52F lunchtime menu.

Escale de Saigon, 24 rue Bosquet, 7e; ☎45.51.60.14 (Mº École-Militaire). Mon–Sat noon–2.30pm & 7–10.30pm. A small and inexpensive local Vietnamese, with a 47F menu.

Au Pied de Fouet, 45 rue de Babylone, 7e; ☎47.05.12.27 (Mº St-François-Xavier/Sèvres-Babylone). Mon–Fri 12–2pm & 7–8.50pm, Sat 12–2pm; closed Aug. Good food and a great little place. Little is the operative word: there are just four tables and no reservations. Around 110F.

Thoumieux, 79 rue St-Dominique, 7e; ☎47.05.49.75 (Mº Latour-Maubourg). Lunchtime & 7–11.30pm. A large and popular establishment in this rather smart district, with traditional brasserie service. A menu at 57F, usually offal, otherwise you have to be careful to get away with less than 180F.

Chapter 8: Montparnasse and the Southern Arrondissements

Montparnasse

CAFÉS AND BARS

Au Chien Qui Fume, 19 bd du Montparnasse, 14e (Mº Duroc/Falguière). Named after a real dog, it's an old and ordinary café – a refuge from its tourist-haunted famous neighbours.

Ciel de Paris, Tour Montparnasse, 33 av du Maine, 15e (Mº Montparnasse). *Salon* de thé 4.30–6pm; piano bar 11pm–1.30am, Fri & Sat till 2am; restaurant till midnight. The bar has a tremendous view over the western part of the city and into the setting sun, but it's not cheap: 33F for an orange juice, cocktails 52–60F and menus from 195F.

La Closerie des Lilas, 171 bd du Montparnasse, 6e (Mº Port-Royal). 10am–1am. The smartest, artiest, classiest one of all, with excellent cocktails. No bum's paradise – it's pricy. The tables are name-plated after celebrated habitués (Verlaine, Mallarmé, Lenin, Modigliani, Léger, Strindberg), and there's a pianist in residence.

Le Dôme, 108 bd du Montparnasse, 6e (Mº Vavin). Tues–Sun until 1am. Next door to *La Coupole* and another of Sartre's haunts. Beautiful terrace which is where you have to be if you just want to drink.

Mustangs, 84 bd du Montparnasse, 14e (Mº Montparnasse-Bienvenue). Daily 9am–5am. Young crowd and happy atmosphere. A good place to finish up the evening after night-clubbing in St-Germain. Tex-Mex food, cocktails and beers.

Le Rosebud, 11 bis rue Delambre, 14e (Mº Vavin). Open till 3am. Cheaper cocktails than on the boulevard (around 45F) and the clientele usually make an amusing spectacle.

Le Rotonde, 105 bd du Montparnasse, 6e (Mº Vavin). Another of the grand old Montparnasse establishments, with the names of the departed famous on the menu: Lenin, Trotsky, etc.

Le Select, 99 bd du Montparnasse, 6e (Mº Vavin). Open until 3am. The least spoilt of the Montparnasse cafés and more of a traditional café than the rest.

Tea and Tattered Pages, 24, rue Mayet, 6e (Mº Duroc). Daily 11am–7pm. Rather a long way from anywhere, and looks as if it's a knitting shop from the outside. But inside you can have tea and cakes, speak English and browse through a very good selection of cheap second-hand English books.

RESTAURANTS

La Bûcherie, 138 bd du Montparnasse, 14e; ☎43.20.47.87 (Mº Vavin/Port-Royal). Butcher's shop décor (minus the carcasses), waiters in butchers' aprons, menus on leather . . . and ace steaks. Up to 150F.

La Coupole, 102 bd du Montparnasse, 14e; ☎43.20.14.20 (Mº Vavin). 7.30–10.30am for breakfast, then noon–2am. The largest and perhaps the most famous and enduring arty-chic Parisian hang-out for dining, dancing and debate. It has been lavishly renovated by the prince of Paris' turn-of-the-century brasseries, Jean-Paul Bucher of *Flo* and *Julien* fame . . . but it ain't the same, say the old habitués. Some complain that the lighting is now too bright, that the intimacy is gone and the food gone downhill. Others say the opposite. Either way its future is assured, even if it's for who has eaten there rather than who's to be seen tonight. One definite improvement is an after 11pm menu at 109F including wine. *Carte* 170–310F. Dancing 3–7pm weekends (Sat 60F, Sun 80F) and 9.30pm–4am Fri & Sat (90F).

Chez Maria, 16 rue du Maine, 14e; ☎43.20.84.61 (Mº Montparnasse). Evenings only, 8.30pm–1am. Zinc bar, candlelight, posters, paper tablecloths – an intimate gloom that appeals to arty theatre creatures after hours. Very pleasant. Around 170F.

L'Ostréade, 11 bd Vaugirard, 15e; ☎43.21.87.41 (Mº Montparnasse). Daily to 11pm. A newish seafood brasserie with *tapas* on a 75F formule and excellent oysters. Around 175F for a full whack.

The 15e

CAFÉS AND BARS

JeThéMe, 4 rue d'Alleray, 15e (Mº Vaugirard). Tues–Sat 10.30am–7pm; closed Aug. Despite the obnoxious name and the nostalgic décor (plagues of most Parisian *salons de thé*), the sweets, salads and snacks are good, and served at reasonable prices and with rare grace. Also sells coffee, tea and chocolate to take away.

Eating and Drinking

See p.233 for a list of vegetarian restaurants in Paris.

See p.261 for a list of cafés and restaurants which stay open late.

Eating and Drinking

See p.233 for a list of vegetarian restaurants in Paris.

Ethnic Restaurants In Paris

Our selection of the ethnic restaurants of Paris can only scratch the surface of what's available. **North African** places are widely distributed throughout the city; apart from rue Xavier-Privas in the Latin Quarter, where the trade is chiefly tourists, the heaviest concentration is the Little Maghreb district along boulevard de Belleville. **Indo-Chinese** restaurants are also widely scattered, with notable concentrations around av de la Porte-de-Choisy in the 13e and in the Belleville Chinatown. The **Greeks** are tightly corralled, in rue de la Huchette, rue Xavier-Privas and along rue Mouffetard, all in the 5e, and, frankly, a rip-off.

AFRICAN AND NORTH AFRICAN

Le Berbère, 50 rue de Gergovie, 14ᵉ. North African. p.254.

Entoto, 143–145 rue Léon-Maurice-Nordmann, 13ᵉ. Ethiopian. p.255.

Le Farafina, 12 rue Quincampoix, 4ᵉ Central African. 4ᵉ. p.339.

Fouta Toro, 3 rue du Nord, 18ᵉ. Senegalese. p.256.

La Mansouria, 11 rue Faidherbe-Chaligny, 11ᵉ. Moroccan. p.260.

N'Zadette M'Foua, 152 rue du Château, 14ᵉ. Congolese. p.254.

Au Port de Pidjiguiti, 28 rue Étex, 18ᵉ. Co-operative, run by a village in Guinea-Bissau. p.256.

Le Roi de Couscous, 48 rue de la Croix-Nivert, 15ᵉ. North African. p.253.

CARRIBEAN

Le Marais-Cage, 8 rue de Beauce, 3ᵉ. p.242.

EAST EUROPEAN

L'Europe Centrale, 6 rue de la Présentation (corner Louis-Bonnet), 11ᵉ. Jewish/East European. p.259.

La Maroussia, 9 rue de l'Éperon, 6ᵉ. Polish and Ukrainian. p.248.

Pitchi-Poï, 7 rue Caron, 4ᵉ. Polish/Jewish. p.241.

Le Polonia, 3 rue Chaumont, 19ᵉ. Polish. p.260.

Le Ravaillac, 10 rue du Roi-de-Sicile, 4ᵉ. Polish. p.241.

Village Bulgare, 8 rue de Nevers, 6ᵉ. Bulgarian. p.249.

GREEK

Égée, 19 rue de Ménilmontant, 20ᵉ. p.259.

Orestias, 4 rue Grégoire-de-Tours, 6ᵉ. p.249.

ITALIAN

La Castafiore, 51 rue St-Louis-en-L'Île, 4ᵉ. p.241.

L'Enoteca, 25 rue Charles-V, 4ᵉ. p.241.

L'Indiscreto, 10 rue Lambert, 18ᵉ. p.256.

Le Petit Mabillon, 6 rue Mabillon, 6ᵉ. p.249.

INDO-CHINESE

Asia Express, corner of rues Étienne-Marcel and St-Denis, 2ᵉ. Chinese and Vietnamese. p.237.

Blue Elephant, 43–45 rue de la Roquette, 11ᵉ. p.243.

Dragons Élysées, 11 rue de Berri, 8ᵉ. Chinese-Thai. p.234.

Escale de Saigon, 24 rue Bosquet, 7ᵉ. Vietnamese. p.250.

Fleur de Lotus, 2 rue du Roi-de-Sicile, 4ᵉ. Vietnamese. p.241.

Hawaï, 87 av d'Ivry, 13ᵉ. Vietnamese. p.255.

Lao-Thai, 128 rue de Tolbiac, 13ᵉ. Thai and Laotian. p.255.

Le Pacifique, 35 rue de Belleville, 20ᵉ. Chinese. p.259.

Pho-Dong-Huong, 14 rue Louis-Bonnet, 11ᵉ. Chinese. p.259.

Phuong Hoang, Terrasse des Olympiades, 52 rue du Javelot, 13ᵉ. Vietnamese, Thai and Singaporean. p.255.

Eating and Drinking

Ethnic Restaurants in Paris (continued)

Restaurant A, 5 rue de Poissy, 5e. Chinese. p.246.

Le Royal Belleville and **Le Président**, 19 rue Louis-Bonnet, 11e. Chinese. p.260.

Taï Yen, 5 rue de Belleville, 20e. Thai. p.260.

Thuy Huong, Kiosque de Choisy, 15 av de Choisy, 13e. Chinese and Cambodian. p.255.

JAPANESE

Foujita, 45 rue St-Roch, 1er. p.235.

Inagiku, 14 rue Pontoise, 5e. p.245.

Osaka, 163 rue St-Honoré, 1er. p.234.

JEWISH

Goldenberg's, 7 rue des Rosiers, 4e. p.241.

Pitchi-Poï, 7 rue Caron, 4e. p.241.

KURDISH

Dilan, 13 rue Mandar, 2e. p.236.

LEBANESE

Al Hana, 102 rue de l'Ouest, 14e. p.254.

Baalbeck, 16 rue Mazagran, l0e. p.257.

Le Liban à la Mouff, 3 rue de l'Estrapade, 5e. p.245.

TIBETAN

Tashi Delek, 4 rue des Fossés-St-Jacques, 5e. p.246.

TURKISH

Taverna Restaurant, 50 rue Piat, 20e. p.260.

RESTAURANTS

Aux Artistes, 63 rue Falguière, 15e; ☎43.22.05.39 (M° Pasteur). Mon–Fri lunchtime & 7.15pm–1am, Sat 7.15pm–1am only. An old-time cheapie that has seen many a poor artist in its day. Still crowded and popular, serving a menu at 75F.

Au Bélier d'Argent, 46 rue de Cronstadt, 15e; ☎48.28.17.57 (M° Porte-de-Vanves/Convention). Opposite the entrance to the Parc Georges-Brassens with specialities from the Landes region, including fondue of duck bits and pieces in béarnaise, green pepper, honey, bilberry and mustard sauces (150F). Otherwise 98.50F.

Le Clos Morillons, 50 rue Morillons, 15e; ☎48.28.04.37 (M° Porte-de-Vanves). Mon–Fri 12.15–2.15pm & 8–10.15pm; Sat 8–10.30pm. Rabbit stuffed with aubergines, veal in lemon and almond purée and some alluring fish dishes. Menus at 160F and 285F.

Le Commerce, 51 rue du Commerce, 15e; ☎45.75.03.27 (M° Émile-Zola). Daily noon–3pm & 6.30–midnight. A double-storey restaurant that has been catering for *le petit peuple* for over a hundred years.

Still varied, nourishing and cheap. Midday menu 100F; *plats du jour* 55–65F; 88F and 114F *formules*; *carte* around 145F.

Le Roi du Couscous, 48 rue de la Croix-Nivert, 15e; ☎47.83.93.67 (M° Cambronne). Particularly good semolina for the couscous and generous *tagines*. Reasonable prices.

Sampieru Corsu, 12 rue de l'Amiral-Roussin, 15e (M° Cambronne). Mon–Fri lunchtimes & 7–9.30pm. Decorated with the posters and passionate declarations of international socialism, this restaurant has as its purpose the provision of meals for the homeless, the unemployed, the low-paid. The principle is that you pay what you can and it is left to your conscience how you settle the bill. The minimum requested is 36F for a three-course meal with wine. However poor you might feel, as a tourist in Paris you should be able to pay more. The restaurant only survives on the generosity of its supporters, and it's a wonderful place.

Student restaurant at 156 rue Vaugirard, 15e (M° Pasteur). See p.246 and p.227, for details.

Eating and Drinking

See p.261 for a list of cafés and restaurants which stay open late.

The 14e

CAFÉS AND BARS

L'Entrepot, 7–9 rue Francis-de-Pressensé, 14e (M° Pernety). Mon–Sat 2–11.30pm. Cinema with a spacious café, 58F midday menu, 95F and 125F evening menus.

Le Rallye, 6 rue Daguerre, 14e (M° Denfert-Rochereau). Tues–Sat until 8pm; closed Aug. A good place to recover from the Catacombs or Montparnasse cemetery. The patron offers a bottle for tasting; gulping the lot would be considered bad form. Good cheese and *saucisson*.

RESTAURANTS

Al Hana, 102 rue de l'Ouest, 14e; ☎45.42.35.36 (M° Pernety). Excellent-value Lebanese food. *Mezzes* for two 150F, for four 350F.

Aquarius 2, 40 rue Gergovie, 14e; ☎45.41.36.88 (M° Pernety). Mon–Sat noon–3pm & 7–10.30pm. Imaginative vegetarian meals served with proper Parisian bustle. 60F menu.

Le Berbère, 50 rue de Gergovie, 14e; ☎45.42.10.29 (M° Pernety). Daily, lunchtime & evenings until 10pm. A very unprepossessing place décor-wise, but serves wholesome, unfussy and cheap North African food. Couscous from 60F.

Bergamote, 1 rue Niepce, 14e; ☎43.22.79.47 (M° Pernety). Tues–Sat lunchtime & evenings until 11pm; closed Aug. A small and sympathetic bistro, in a quiet, ungentrified street off rue de l'Ouest. Only about ten tables; you need to book weekends. There are 61F and 100F *formules* at lunchtime, 125F in the evening; *carte* around 160F.

Le Biniou, 3 av du Général-Leclerc, 14e; ☎43.27.20.40 (M° Denfert-Rochereau). Mon–Fri midday & 6.45–10pm. Lots of delicious *crêpes*, from 15F to 50F.

N'Zadette M'Foua, 152 rue du Château, 14e; ☎43.22.00.16 (M° Pernety). Mon–Sat evenings, until midnight. A small and tasty Congolese restaurant – *manioc*, *maboké*, etc. Reservations required weekends. Around 120F.

Pavillon Montsouris, 20 rue Gazan, 14e; ☎45.88.38.52 (*RER* Cité-Universitaire).

12.15–2.30pm & 7.45–10.30pm. A special treat for summer days, sitting on the terrace overlooking the park, choosing from a menu featuring truffles, *foie gras* and the divine *pêche blanche rôtie à la glace vanille*. Menus at 185F and 255F.

Phineas, 99 rue de l'Ouest, 14e; ☎45.41.33.50 (M° Pernety). Mon–Sat 9am–11pm; closed Mon midday. A gallery-restaurant specializing in plates of food arranged into funny faces. Several veggie dishes and a friendly atmosphere. A good one for kids and under 130F.

Au Rendez-vous des Camioneurs, 34 rue des Plantes, 14e; ☎45.40.43.36 (M° Alésia). Mon–Fri lunchtime & 6–9.30pm; closed Aug. No lorry drivers any more, but good food for under 100F; menu at 60F and a quarter of wine 5F. Wise to book.

La Route du Château, 123 rue du Château, 14e; ☎43.20.09.59 (M° Pernety). Mon lunchtimes only, Tues–Sat lunchtimes and evenings until 12.30am; closed Aug. Linen tablecloths, a rose on your table, an old-fashioned *bistrot* atmosphere. The food is good, beautifully prepared and cooked – try the thin slice of rumpsteak (well over 150F). Menu at 80F.

Student restaurants at 13/17 rue Dareau (M° St-Jacques) and in the Cité Universitaire (*RER* Cité Universitaire). See p.246 and p.227 for details.

L'Univers, 73 rue d'Alésia (corner rue Marguerin), 14e; ☎43.27.17.71 (M° Alési). Solid cooking; 71F for simple three-course menu, 98F for *formule*. Excellent-value Sancerre rosé at 126F.

The 13e

CAFÉS AND BARS

La Folie en Tête, 33 rue de la Butte-aux-Cailles, 13e (M° Place-d'Italie/Corvisart). Mon–Sat 10am–2am. Cheap beer, sandwiches and midday *plat du jour* from some of the people who used to run *Le Merle Mocqueur* and *Le Temps des Cerises*. Jazz Thursday nights; *chansons* Friday and Saturday. A very warm and laid-back address.

Le Merle Moqueur, 11 rue des Buttes-aux-Cailles, 13e (M° Place-d'Italie/

Corvisart). 9pm–1am. Still going strong and still popular, along with its neighbouring bar-restaurants, **Le Diapason** (no. 15), **Chez Michel** (no. 15), **Resto des Bons Amis** (no. 13) and **Le Palmier** (no. 13).

RESTAURANTS

Bol en Bois, 35 rue Pascal, 13e; ☎47.07.27.24 (Mº Gobelins). Mon–Sat noon–2.30pm & 7–10pm. Macrobiotic veg and fish restaurant in a street being taken over by veggie/Buddhist concerns. 95F menu, *carte* 110F. Generous portions.

Entoto, 143–145 rue Léon-Maurice-Nordmann, 13e; ☎45.87.08.51 (Mº Glacière). Tues–Sat 7.30–10pm. An Ethiopian restaurant where you can share plates, using *indjera* (bread) rather than knives and forks. Veggie and meat dishes, some of them spiced with very hot pepper called *mitmita*. Around 150F.

Chez Gladines, 30 rue des Cinq-Diamants, 13e; ☎45.83.53.34 (Mº Corvisart). Tues–Sun 7.30am–1.30am. This small corner *bistrot* is always welcoming. Excellent wines and dishes from the southwest. The mashed/fried potato is a must and goes best with *magret de canard* (58F). Around 100F for a full meal.

Chez Grand-mère, 92 rue Broca, 13e; ☎47.07.13.65 (Mº Gobelins). Closed Sun. Excellent *terrines* and stuffed trout. 70F midday menu, 115F evening menu.

Hawaï, 87 av d'Ivry, 13e; ☎45.86.91.90 (Mº Tolbiac). 11am–10pm; closed Thurs. Everyday Vietnamese food, well appreciated by the locals. Particularly good Tonkinese soups, *dim sum* and brochettes. Around 100F.

Le Languedoc, 64 bd Port-Royal, 5e; ☎47.07.24.47 (Mº Gobelins). Thurs–Mon till 10pm. Closed Aug. Just in the 5e, but closer to the Gobelins than the Latin Quarter. A traditional checked tablecloth bistro with an illegible menu on which you might decipher frogs legs, snails, *museau de boeuf* etc. Good value for a 105F menu including wine.

Lao-Thai, 128 rue de Tolbiac, 13e; ☎43.31.98.10 (Mº Tolbiac). Thurs–Tues 11.30–2.30 & 7–11pm. Big glass-fronted

resto on a busy interchange. Finely spiced Thai and Laotian food, with coconut, ginger and lemon grass flavours. Around 120F.

Phuong Hoang, Terrasse des Olympiades, 52 rue du Javelot, 13e; ☎45.84.75.07 (Mº Tolbiac: take the escalator up from rue Tolbiac). Mon–Fri noon–2.30pm & 7–11.30pm. Like most of its neighbours this is a family business and the quality varies depending on which uncle, nephew or niece is at the stove that day. Vietnamese, Thai and Singapore specialities on lunch menus at 50F and 68F; *carte* 100–150F. If it's full or doesn't take your fancy, try *Le Grand Mandarin* or *L'Oiseau de Paradis* nearby.

Student restaurant 105 bd de l'Hôpital, 13e (Mº St-Marcel). See under Latin Quarter for details.

Le Temps des Cerises, 18–20 rue de la Butte-aux-Cailles, 13e; ☎45.89.69.48 (Mº Place-d'Italie/Corvisart). Mon–Fri noon–2pm & 7–11pm, Sat 7–11pm. A well-established workers' co-op with elbow-to-elbow seating and a different daily choice of imaginative dishes. 58F and 112F menus.

Thuy Huong and **Tricotin**, Kiosque de Choisy, 15 av de Choisy, 13e; ☎45.86.87.07 and ☎45.84.74.44 (Mº Porte-de-Choisy). Noon–2.30pm & 7–10.30pm; closed Thurs. *Thuy Huong* is in the inner courtyard of this Chinese shopping centre and is more of a café. *Tricotin* has two restaurants, visible from the avenue, no. 1 specializing in Thai dishes, no. 2 in the other Asiatic cuisines. Not easy to work out what's on the menu (*méduse*, by the way, is jellyfish), but you can depend on the *dim sum*, the duck dishes and the Vietnamese rice pancakes. Around 120F, or 70F at *Thuy Huong*.

Chapter 9: Montmartre and Northern Paris

Montmartre

CAFÉS AND BARS

Aux Négociants, 27 rue Lambert (corner rue Custine), 18e; ☎46.06.15.11 (Mº Château-Rouge). Lunchtime and evenings

Eating and Drinking

Our glossary of French food and dishes begins on p.228.

Eating and Drinking

See p.261 for a list of cafés and restaurants which stay open late.

Tues, Thurs, Fri until 10pm; closed Sat, Sun, public holidays, and Aug. An intimate and friendly *bistrot à vins* with a selection of well-cooked *plats* and good wines: around 130F for a full meal. The clientele is vaguely arty-intellectual. Wise to book.

La Petite Charlotte, 24 rue des Abbesses, 18e (Mº Abbesses). Tues–Sun to 8pm. Crêpes, *pâtisseries* and 58F *formule* on sunny tables.

Le Refuge, corner of rue Lamarck and the steps of rue de la Fontaine-du-But, 18e (Mº Lamarck-Caulaincourt). A gentle café stop with a long view west down rue Lamarck to the country beyond.

RESTAURANTS

L'Assiette, 78 rue Labat, 18e; ☎42.59.06.63 (Mº Château-Rouge). Closed Wed and Sat midday. A bit out of the way but very friendly, with an 82F menu, delicious *champignons forestières*, chocolate charlotte and a beef stroganoff which might not be on the menu but the chef will cook especially for you if she has a spare filet.

Fouta Toro, 3 rue du Nord, 18e; ☎42.55.42.73 (Mº Marcadet-Poissonniers). 8pm–midnight; closed Tues. A tiny, crowded, welcoming Senegalese diner in a very scruffy run-down alley northeast of Montmartre. No more than 70F all in. Unless you come at the 8pm opening time, or after about 10.30pm, you'll almost certainly have to wait.

Chez Ginette, 101 rue Caulaincourt, 18e; ☎46.06.01.49 (Mº Lamarck-Caulaincourt). Lunchtime, and evenings until 11.30pm; closed Sun & Aug. Decent food in a traditional "Parisian" environment, with live piano and dancing. *Carte* around 150F; lunchtime menu at 75F. Wise to book.

Au Grain de Folie, 24 rue La Vieuville, 18e; ☎42.58.15.57 (Mº Abbesses). 12.30–2.30pm & 7–11.30pm. Tiny, simple and cheap, with just the sort of traditional atmosphere that you would hope for from Montmartre. Vegetarian. Soup and tart 60F, menu 100F.

L'Homme Tranquille, 81 rue des Martyrs, 18e; ☎42.54.56.28 (Mº Abbesses).

Evenings only, 7–11.30pm; closed Sun, Mon & Aug. Simple and pleasant *bistrot* ambience, with imaginative French dishes, including chicken in honey, coriander and lemon. Around 150F.

L'Indiscreto, 10 rue Lambert, 18e; ☎42.52.22.40 (Mº Château-Rouge). Lunchtime, & evenings until 10.30pm; closed Sun, Mon lunchtime. Really good Italian food and beautiful décor, with a menu at 125F.

Le Maquis, 69 rue Caulaincourt, 18e; ☎42.59.76.07 (Mº Lamarck-Caulaincourt). Lunchtime, and evenings until 10pm; closed Sun & Mon. Lunchtime menu at 63F; *carte* around 180F. A gently elegant and courteous place.

Marie-Louise, 52 rue Championnet, 18e; ☎46.06.86.55 (Mº Simplon). Lunchtime, and evenings until 9.30pm; closed Sun, Mon & Aug. A place with a well-deserved reputation. A bit of a trek north, but very much worth the journey for a special meal, for the traditional French cuisine is excellent. Menu at 120F, otherwise around 200F. The dish to try is *bœuf à la ficelle* (poached beef).

À Napoli, 4 rue Dancourt, 18e; ☎42.23.93.66 (Mº Anvers/Abbesses). Noon–2.30pm & 6–11pm. Clean and simple, with an Italian flavour, and very good-value food. Menu at 62F, otherwise around 100F.

À la Pomponnette, 42 rue Lepic, 18e; ☎46.06.08.36 (Mº Blanche). Lunchtime, and evenings until 9.30pm; closed Sun evening, Mon & Aug. A genuine old Montmartre *bistrot*, with posters, drawings, zinc-top bar, nicotine stains etc. The food is excellent, but will cost you going on 200F *à la carte*; good menu including wine at 150F.

Au Port de Pidjiguiti, 28 rue Étex, 18e; ☎42.26.71.77 (Mº Guy-Môquet). Lunchtime, and evenings until 11pm; closed Mon & Jan. Very pleasant atmosphere and excellent food for about 80F. It is run by a village in Guinea-Bissau, whose inhabitants take turns in staffing the restaurant; the proceeds go to the village. Good-value wine list.

Batignolles

CAFÉS AND BARS

Bar Belge, 75 av de St-Ouen, 17ᵉ (Mº Guy-Môquet). Tues–Sun 3.30pm–1am. Belgian beers and *moules frites* for 60F, *coq au vin* 70F and *poulet aux cèpes* 65F.

L'Endroit, 67 place Félix-Lobligeois, 17ᵉ; ☎42.29.50.00 (Mº Rome/La Fourche). Noon–2am; closed Sun. A smartish late-night bar serving the local youth. Drinks from about 50F.

RESTAURANTS

Les Fines Herbes, 38 rue Nollet, 17ᵉ; ☎43.87.05.41 (Mº Place-Clichy/La Fourche). Lunchtime only, 11.30am–3pm; closed Mon & Sun. A pleasant little veggie, with *plats* at 25–36F. No smoking.

Joy in Food, 2 rue Truffaut, 17ᵉ; ☎43.87.96.79 (Mº Place-Clichy). Mon–Sat lunchtime, also evenings Tues, Fri & Sat. Minuscule veggie, with its mind on higher things: open meditation sessions at 8pm Wed. Good food and inexpensive.

Pigalle

CAFÉS AND BARS

Le Dépanneur, 27 rue Fontaine, 9ᵉ; ☎40.16.40.20 (Mº Pigalle). A relaxed and fashionable all-night bar in black and chrome, just off place Pigalle.

Le Pigalle, place Pigalle, 18ᵉ (Mº Pigalle). 24-hr bar, brasserie and tabac. A classic, complete with 1950s décor. Prices go up after 10pm.

RESTAURANTS

Aux Deux-Théâtres, 18 rue Blanche, 9ᵉ; ☎45.26.41.43 (Mº Blanche). Daily till 12.30am. A place to lash out on champagne, oysters, lobster, gooey desserts affordably. Menu at 165F. Best to go early and book for later.

The Stations and Faubourgs

CAFÉS AND BARS

Quasre Shireen, 14 rue Faubourg-St-Denis, 10ᵉ (Mº Strasbourg-St-Denis). Fast-food Indian cheapie with rice and curry for 25F, samosas 5F.

RESTAURANTS

Baalbeck, 16 rue de Mazagran, 10ᵉ; ☎47.70.70.02 (Mº Bonne-Nouvelle). Lunchtime & 8pm–midnight. Much liked by the moneyed refugees, a Lebanese restaurant with dozens of appetizers. For 555F you can have a representative selection for four, with *arak* to drink. Sticky Levantine/Turkish cakes too. Very busy, so make a reservation or go early.

Flo, 7 cours des Petites-Écuries, 10ᵉ; ☎47.70.13.59 (Mº Château-d'Eau). Until 1.30am. Handsome old-time brasserie, all dark-stained wood, mirrors, and glass partitions, in attractive courtyard off rue du Faubourg-St-Denis. You eat elbow to elbow at long tables, served by waiters in ankle-length aprons. Excellent food and atmosphere. From around 200F; really good value menus at 110F and 159F midday, 185F evenings.

Julien, 16 rue du Faubourg St-Denis, 10ᵉ; ☎47.70.12.06 (Mº Strasbourg-St-Denis). Until 1.30am. Part of the same enterprise as *Flo*, with an even more splendid décor. Same good Alsatian – vaguely Germanic – cuisine; same prices and similarly crowded. From around 200F, with a 110F menu including wine after 11pm.

Terminus Nord, 23 rue de Dunkerque, 10ᵉ; ☎42.85.05.15 (Mº Gare-du-Nord). Daily until 12.30am. A magnificent 1920s brasserie where a full meal costs around 250F, but where you could easily satisfy your hunger with just a main course – an excellent steak, for example – and still enjoy the décor for considerably less money.

Chapter 10: Eastern Paris

République and the Canal St-Martin

CAFÉS AND BARS

Le Clown Bar, 114 rue Amelot, 11ᵉ (Mº Filles-du-Calvaire). Sun–Fri till 11.15pm. Where the circus professionals go.

La Divette de Valmy, 71 quai de Valmy, 10ᵉ (Mº Jacques-Bonsergent). An ordinary

Eating and Drinking

Some of Paris' top gourmet restaurants are listed on p.263.

Eating and Drinking

See p.233 for a list of vegetarian restaurants in Paris.

café-brasserie at the foot of one of the arching canal bridges. A lovely spot in the afternoon sun.

L'Opus, 167 quai de Valmy, 10e (Mo Château-Landon). 8pm–4am; closed Sun. A stylish modern-chintzy atmosphere in a barn-like space. Listen to live classical music (from 10pm) while you sip your cocktails – or dine, in the rather expensive restaurant. Drinks 65–80F average, plus 50F surcharge for the music.

La Patache, 60 rue de Lancry, 10e (Mo Jacques-Bonsergent). An atmospheric café-bar, survivor from the neighbourhood's pre-gentrification days.

RESTAURANTS

Anjou-Normandie, 13 rue de la Foli-Méricault, 11e; ☎47.00.30.59 (Mo St-Ambroise). Tues-Fri till 9pm. Pure ingredients and renowned for its patés and *andouillettes*. 140F and 150F menus. Best to book.

Astier, 44 rue Jean-Pierre Timbaud, 11e; ☎43.57.16.35 (Mo Parmentier). Mon–Fri until 10pm; closed Aug, two weeks in May and two weeks at Christmas. Very successful and very popular. Simple décor, unstuffy atmosphere, and the food renowned for its freshness and refinement. Essential to book. Menu at 130F.

Au Gigot Fin, 56 rue de Lancry (close to the canal), 10e; ☎42.08.38.81. Lunchtime, and evenings until 10pm; closed Sat lunchtime & Sun. Another very Parisian old-timer, like the *Bourgogne*, with solid country fare. Midday menu at 85F, evening menus at 110F and 175F, otherwise around 200F.

Au Rendez-Vous de la Marine, 114 quai de la Loire, 19e; ☎42.49.33.40 (Mo Jaurès). Lunchtime & evenings until 10pm; closed Sun, Mon & Aug. A busy successful old-time restaurant on the east bank of the Bassin de la Villette, renowned for its meat and desserts. A really good meal for around 150F. Need to book.

Restaurant de Bourgogne, 26 rue des Vinaigriers, 10e; ☎46.07.07.91 (Mo Jacques-Bonsergent). Lunchtime, and evenings until 10pm; closed Sat evening, Sun and Aug. Homely old-fashioned

restaurant with midday menu at 50F and evening menu at 60F. Still has a strong local character in spite of the changing nature of the area.

Aux Tables de la Fontaine, 33 rue Jean-Pierre-Timbaud 11e; ☎43.57.26.00 (Mo Parmentier). Mon–Fri lunchtimes and evenings, Sat evenings only; closed mid-Aug to mid-Sept. Excellent food, and good choice. Midday offer of kir, main dish and coffee for 60F, otherwise 135F. Nice location on the corner of a shady *place*, opposite *Astier's*.

Au Trou Normand, 9 rue Jean-Pierre Timbaud, 11e; ☎48.05.80.23 (Mo Filles-du-Calvaire/Oberkampf/République). Mon–Fri lunchtimes & evenings until 9.30pm, Sat evening only; closed Aug. A small, totally unpretentious and very attractive local *bistrot*, serving good traditional food at knock-down prices. Dinner around 70F.

Au Val de Loire, 149 rue Amelot, 11e; ☎47.00.34.11 (Mo République). Noon–2.30pm & 6.30–9.45pm; closed Sun & Aug. Simple and good food in pleasant surroundings. Menus at 56F and 110F.

La Villette

CAFÉS AND BARS

Café de la Ville, Parc de la Villette, between the Grande Salle and the Zenith, 19e (Mo Porte-de-Pantin/Corentin-Cariou). Open in summer only. In one of the Tschumi follies with an interior designed by Philippe Starck.

Belleville, Menilmontant, Charonne and Père Lachaise

CAFÉS AND BARS

Le Baratin, 3 rue Jouye-Rouve, 20e (Mo Pyrénées). Tues-Fri noon–midnight, Sat & Sun 5pm–midnight. *Bistrot à vins.* Friendly, unpretentious place with a good mix of people, locals and alternative types. Good selection of lesser known wines and whiskies. Midday menu 59F, *à la carte* 150F.

Cithea, 114 rue Oberkampf, 11e (Mo Ménilmontant). Daily 9pm–2am. Bar and venue next door for Afro funk, funk reggae, world beat, jazz fusion, etc. Cocktails 40F.

Les Envierges, 11 rue des Envierges, 20ᵉ (Mº Pyrénées). Wed–Fri noon–midnight, Sat & Sun noon–8pm. *Bistrot à vins*. Another purveyor of good-quality lesser known wines to connoisseurs. An attractive bar – though more a place to taste and buy wine than eat – in a great location above the Parc de Belleville.

Tabac-Charonne, 120 rue de Bagnolet., 20ᵉ (Mº Porte de Bagnolet). Beautiful old café in Charonne village, with fading painted panels.

Le Vieux Belleville, 12 rue des Envierges, 20ᵉ; ☎ 44.62.92.66 (Mº Pyrénées). 7am–11pm; closed Sun. An old-fashioned café, simple and attractive. A good alternative if the smarter and more fashionable *Courtille* opposite is full. Around 120F. *Plats du jours* 65F.

RESTAURANTS

À la Courtille, 1 rue des Envierges, 20ᵉ; ☎ 46.36.51.59 (Mº Pyrénées). Lunchtime, and evenings until 11.30pm. Slightly stark modern interior, but good traditional cuisine in an unbeatable situation overlooking the delightful new Parc de Belleville. Get a pavement table on a summer evening and you'll have the best restaurant view in Paris. Midday menus 70F and 100F, *à la carte* 200F.

Égée, 19 rue de Ménilmontant, 20ᵉ; ☎ 43.58.70.26 (Mº Ménilmontant). Noon–2.30pm & 7.30–11.30pm. Greek and Turkish specialities served with fresh home-made bread. Lunch menu at just 45F, eating *à la carte* is more like 120F.

L'Europe Centrale, 6 rue de la Présentation (corner Louis-Bonnet), 11ᵉ; ☎ 43.57.10.12 (Mº Belleville). Lunchtime & evenings; closed Wed & Aug. Jewish-east European cuisine – genuine, but not exactly cheap, at 120–150F. Specialist *pâtisserie* and take-away adjoining.

La Fontaine aux Roses, 27 av Gambetta, 20ᵉ; ☎ 46.36.74.75 (Mº Père-Lachaise). Till 10pm. Closed Mon, Sun midday & Aug. Small and beautiful restaurant with first-rate midday menu of 103F and

evening 156F, both including kir royale, wine and coffee.

Chez Jean, 38 rue Boyer (near corner with rue de Ménilmontant), 20ᵉ; ☎ 47.97.44.58 (Mº Gambetta/Ménilmontant). Mon–Fri lunchtime & evenings till 10pm. Closed Sat midday and first half of Aug. A charming, friendly, intimate place, with a small but carefully chosen menu. Fun. 54F midday menu, 120F *à la carte*.

Chez Justine, 96 rue Oberkampf, 11ᵉ; ☎ 43.57.44.03 (Mº St-Maur/Ménilmontant). Mon lunchtimes only, Tues–Sat lunchtimes and evenings until 10.30pm; closed Aug. Good, substantial traditional cooking, decent wines for around 100F a bottle and a homely cheerful atmosphere. Menus at 68F midday and 85F and 135F evenings.

Louis Valy, 49 rue Orfila, 20ᵉ; ☎ 46.36.73.60 (Gambetta/Pelleport). Lunchtime only, closed Sun & Aug. Good terrines, meat dishes and cheeses in generous helpings and a very convivial atmosphere. Menu at 140F.

L'Occitanie, 96 rue Oberkampf, 11ᵉ; ☎ 48.06.46.98 (Mº St-Maur/Ménilmontant). Mon–Fri lunchtimes and evenings to 10.30pm, Sat pm only; closed second half of July. Copious homely southwestern food, featuring duck in many guises in a simple, friendly atmosphere. Menus from 59F to 198F.

Le Pacifique, 35 rue de Belleville, 20ᵉ; ☎ 42.49.66.80 (Mº Belleville). 11am–1am. A huge Chinese eating house with variable culinary standards, but low prices. 120F *à la carte*.

Au Pavillon Puebla, Parc des Buttes-Chaumont, 19ᵉ; ☎ 42.08.92.62 (Mº Buttes-Chaumont). Tues–Sat noon–10pm. Luxury cuisine in an old hunting lodge. Poached lobster, stuffed baby squid, duck with *foie gras* and spicy oyster raviolis are some of the *à la carte* delights. Around 400F *à la carte*, midday menus at 180F, evening menus 230F.

Pho-Dong-Huong, 14 rue Louis-Bonnet, 11ᵉ; ☎ 43.57.42.81 (Mº Belleville). Noon–10.30pm; closed Tues. Spotlessly clean Vietnamese resto, where all dishes are under 50F and come with piles of fresh

Eating and Drinking

See p.261 for a list of cafés and restaurants which stay open late.

Eating and Drinking

Some of Paris' top gourmet restaurants are listed on p.263.

green leaves. Spicy soups, crispy pancakes, but slow service.

Le Polonia, 3 rue Chaumont, 19e; ☎42.40.38.97 (Mº Jaurès). Lunchtime & evenings until 10.30pm; closed Sun pm, Mon & Aug. Don't be put off by the grubby exterior – underneath hotel of the same name. Inside there's a jovial Polish welcome and good Polish dishes for as little as 50F, though 100–120F might be more realistic.

Aux Rendez-Vous des Amis, 10 av Père-Lachaise, 20e; ☎47.97.72.16 (Mº Gambetta). Lunchtime only, noon–2.30pm; closed Sun and mid-July to mid-Aug. Unprepossessing surroundings for very good, simple and satisfying family cooking – at around 80F, menu at 59F.

Le Royal Belleville, 19 rue Louis-Bonnet, 11e (☎43.38.22.72) and **Le Président** (☎47.00.17.18) the floor above – entrance on rue-du-Faubourg-du-Temple (Mº Belleville). 11am–2am. A dramatic blood-red double staircase leads up to *Le Président*, the more expensive of these two cavernous Chinese restaurants. You go for the atmosphere and décor rather than the food, though the spring rolls and rum banana fritters are acceptable. The Thai dishes at *Le Président* are not very special. Between 100F and 150F.

Taï Yen, 5 rue de Belleville, 20e; ☎42.41.44.16 (Mº Belleville). 11.30am–1am. You can admire the koi carps like embroidered satin cushions idling round their aquarium while you wait for the copious soups and steamed specialities. 60F menu, 100F *à la carte*.

Taverna Restaurant, 50 rue Piat, 20e; ☎40.33.07.20 (Mº Pyrénées). A homely and friendly local Turkish restaurant close to the Parc de Belleville. Around 90F including wine.

To the Faubourg St-Antoine

CAFÉS AND BARS

Jacques-Mélac, 42 rue Léon-Frot, 11e; ☎43.70.59.27 (Mº Charonne). 8.30am–8pm (10pm Tues and Thurs); closed Sat & Sun and mid-July to mid-Aug. Some way off the beaten track (between Père-

Lachaise and place Léon-Blum) but a highly reputed and very popular *bistrot à vins* whose patron even makes his own wine – the solitary vine winds round the front of the shop (harvest celebrations in the second half of Sept: said to be great fun). The food (*plats* around 38F), wines and atmosphere are great, but you can't book, so it pays to get there early.

RESTAURANTS

Les Amognes, 243 rue du Faubourg-St-Antoine, 11e; ☎43.72.73.05 (Mº Faidherbe-Chaligny). Tues–Sat noon–2.30pm & 7.30–11pm; closed 3 weeks in Aug. Excellent and interesting food in a very popular place. Need to book. A menu at 160F, otherwise well over 200F.

Chardenoux, 1 rue Jules-Vallès, 11e; ☎43.71.49.52 (Mº Charonne). Mon–Fri noon–2.30pm & 8–10.30pm; closed July. An authentic oldie, with engraved mirrors dating back to 1900, that still serves solid meaty fare like calf kidneys grilled in mustard. Around 200F.

Les Cinq Points Cardinaux, 14 rue Jean-Macé, 11e; ☎43.71.47.22 (Mº Faidherbe-Chaligny/Charonne). Noon–2pm & 7–10pm. An excellent, simple, old-time *bistrot*, still mainly frequented by locals and decorated with the old tools of their trades. Prices under 55F for lunch; menus 57F and 95F in the evening. The snails in basil and the profiteroles are worth trying.

Les Demoiselles de Charonne, 44 rue Léon-Frot, 11e; ☎40.09.03.93 (Mº Charonne). Lunchtime only; closed Sat and Sun. Delicious old-time home-cooking. Menu at 81F, plus cheaper *formules*.

La Mansouria, 11 rue Faidherbe-Chaligny, 11e; ☎43.71.00.16 (Mº Faidherbe-Chaligny). Lunchtimes, and evenings until 11.30pm; closed Sun, and Mon lunch-time, plus a fortnight in Aug. An excellent and elegant Moroccan restaurant, with the cheapest menu at 99F; otherwise around 170F. Excellent Moroccan crêpes and tagines.

Palais de la Femme, 94 rue de Charonne, 11e; ☎43.71.11.27 (Mº Charonne/Faidherbe-Chaligny). Daily 11.30am–2.30pm & 6.30–8pm. A good

Late-night Paris

For bars and brasseries in Paris to stay open after midnight is not unusual; the list below comprises cafés and bars open after 2am, and restaurants open beyond midnight.

Eating and Drinking

CAFÉS AND BARS

Connolly's Corner, corner of rues Patriarches and Mirbel, 5ᵉ. Until 4am. p.243.

Le Dépanneur, 27 rue Fontaine, 9ᵉ. All-nighter. p.257.

Drugstore Élysées, 133 av des Champs-Élysées, 8ᵉ (p.233); **Drugstore Matignon**, 1 av Matignon, 8ᵉ (p.234); and **Drugstore Saint-Germain**, 149 bd St-Germain, 6ᵉ (p.248). All until 2am.

Le Grand Café Capucines, 4 bd des Capucines, 9ᵉ. All-nighter. p.236.

Iguana, 15 rue de la Roquette, 11ᵉ. Till 4am. p.242.

Kléber, place du Trocadéro, 16ᵉ. Until dawn. p.249.

Le Mazet, 6 rue St-André-des-Arts, 6ᵉ. Until 2am; Fri & Sat until 3.30am. p.248.

Mustangs, 84 bd Montparnasse, 14ᵉ. Til 4am. p.251.

L'Opus, 167 quai de Valmy, 10ᵉ. Till 4am. p.258.

La Paillote, 45 Monsieur-Le-Prince, 6ᵉ. Til dawn. p.248.

Le Pigalle, place Pigalle, 18ᵉ. Till 5am. p.257.

Polly Magoo, 11 rue St-Jacques, 5ᵉ. All-nighter. p.245.

Pub Saint-Germain, 17 rue de l'Ancienne-Comédie, 6ᵉ. 24-hr. p.248.

Le Quetzal, 10 rue de la Verrerie, 4ᵉ. Till 3am. p.240.

Le Rosebud, 11bis rue Delambre, 14ᵉ. Until 3am. p.251.

Le Select, 99 bd du Montparnasse, 6ᵉ. Until 3am. p.251.

Le Sous-Bock, 49 rue St-Honoré, 1ᵉʳ. Until 5am. p.238.

La Taverne de Nesle, 32 rue Dauphine, 6ᵉ. Until 5am. p.248.

RESTAURANTS

Aux Deux Théâtres, 18 rue Blanche, 9ᵉ. Til 12.30 am. p.257.

L'Abreuvoir, 68 rue de la Roquette, 11ᵉ. Till 1am. p.243.

Aux Artistes, 63 rue Falguière, 15ᵉ. Until 12.30am. p.253.

Baalbeck, 16 rue Mazagran, 10ᵉ. Until 1am. p.257.

Bofinger, 3–7 rue de la Bastille, 3ᵉ. Until 1am. p.243.

City Rock Café, 13 rue de Berri, 8ᵉ. Until 2am. p.234.

La Coupole, 102 bd du Montparnasse, 14ᵉ. Until 2am. p.251.

Aux Deux Saules, 91 rue St-Denis, 1ᵉʳ. Until 1am. p.238.

Drouant – the "café" – 18 rue Gaillon, 2ᵉ. Just after midnight. p.236.

L'Enoteca, 25 rue Charles V, 4ᵉ. Till 2am. p.241.

Le Farafina, 12 rue Quincampoix, 4ᵉ. Till 4am or later. p.239.

Flo, 7 cours des Petites-Écuries, 10ᵉ. Until 1.30am. p.257.

Fouta Toro, 3 rue du Nord, 18ᵉ. Until 1am. p.256.

Chez Gladines, 30 rue des Cinq-Diamants, 13ᵉ. Until 2am. p.255.

Julien, 16 rue du Faubourg-St-Denis, 10ᵉ. Until 1.30am. p.257.

Lipp, 151 bd St-Germain, 6ᵉ. Until 12.30am. p.248.

Chez Maria, 16 rue du Maine, 14ᵉ. Until 1am. p.251.

Le Muniche, 22 rue Guillaume-Apollinaire, 6ᵉ. Until 3am. p.248.

Le Pacifique, 35 rue de Belleville, 20ᵉ. Until 1am. p.259.

Le Petit Prince, 12 rue Lanneau, 5ᵉ. Until 12.30am. p.246.

Le Petit Zinc, 11 rue Saint-Benoît, 6ᵉ. Until 3am. p.249.

Au Pied de Cochon, 6 rue Coquillière, 1ᵉʳ. 24-hr. p.239.

Eating and Drinking

See p.252 for a list of the various ethnic restaurants in Paris.

Late night Paris (continued)

Polidor, 41 rue Monsieur-le-Prince, 6e. Until 1am. p.249.

Le Procope 13 rue de l'Ancienne-Comédie, 6e. Until 1am. p.249.

La Route du Château, 123 rue du Château, 14e. Until 12.30am. p.254.

Le Royal Belleville/Le Président, 19 rue Louis-Bonnet, 11e. Until 2am. p.260.

Terminus Nord, 23 rue de Dunkerque, 10e. Until 12.30am. p.257.

Taï Yen, 5 rue de Belleville, 20e. Until 1am. p.260.

Le Vaudeville, 29 rue Vivienne, 2e. Until 2am. p.237.

---

self-service restaurant in the women's hostel, run separately and open to all. Good solid meals for less than 50F.

The 12e

CAFÉS AND BARS

Le Baron Rouge, 1 rue Théophile-Roussel (corner of place d'Aligre market), 12e (Mº Ledru-Rollin). 10am–2pm & 5–9.30pm; closed Sun evening and Mon. Another real popular and local bar, as close as you'll find to the spit-on-the-floor stereotype of the old movies. As well as the wines – you can fill your own containers from the barrel for around 16F per litre – it serves a few snacks of cheese, *foie gras*, and *charcuterie* to the shoppers and workers of the Aligre market.

Le Penty Bar, corner of pl d'Aligre and rue Emilio-Castellar, 12e. Small, old-fashioned café making no concessions to 1990s sanitation and still only 5F for a sit-down cup of coffee.

Un Temps pour Tout, 42 allée Vivaldi, 12e (Mº Daumesnil). Daily till 1am. Glasshouse café-resto near the new Reuilly gardens with crêpes, salads, ice creams, as well as full meals. Reasonable prices.

RESTAURANTS

L'Ébauchoir, 43-45 rue de Cîteaux, 12e; ☎43.42.49.31 (Mº Faidherbe-Chaligny). Mon–Sat until 10.30pm. Good *bistrot* fare in a sympathetic atmosphere; menu at 58F. Best to book for the evening.

Au Limonaire, 88 rue de Charenton, 12e; ☎43.43.49.14 (Mº Ledru-Rollin/Gare-de-

Lyon). Noon–2.30pm & 8–10pm; closed Aug. Interesting food and wine in a beautiful old-fashioned café, adorned with musical instruments (entertainment in second half of week after 10pm: traditional French singing, etc). Lunchtime *plats* for around 50F; dinner 90–150F.

Le Phonograph, corner rues Montgallet and Charenton, 12e (Mº Montgallet). Very tucked away in the shadow of new developments. Salmon and lentils, *magret de canard*, generous *chèvre chaud*. Nouvelle cuisine-ish and good. The piano and accordion are played some nights. Around 200F.

Le Train Bleu, 1st floor, Gare de Lyon, 20 bd Diderot, 12e; ☎43.43.09.06 (Mº Gare-de-Lyon). Daily until 10pm. You pay not for the food but the ludicrous *fin-de-siècle* stucco and murals of popular train destinations. Lunch menu at 195F, otherwise inflated *à la carte* prices.

Seine Rive-Gauche

CAFÉS AND BARS

Mimado, on the new Bibliothèque Nationale site, bd Vincent-Auriol, 13e (Mº Quai de la Gare). Omelettes and chips and sandwiches, 52F menu, in a portacabin near the "Tipi".

Chapter 11: Western Paris

Auteuil and Passy

CAFÉS AND BARS

Le Coquelin Aîné, 67 rue de Passy, 16e (Mº Muette). Tues–Sat 9am–6.30pm. An elegant café on place Passy, meeting place of gilded youth and age. Excellent salads, *tartes*, cakes, at a price – this is not for paupers. 110F menu from noon to 2.30pm.

RESTAURANTS

Les Chauffeurs, 8 chaussée de la Muette, 16e; ☎42.88.50.05 (Mº Muette). Daily noon–2.30pm & 7.30–10pm. You can't beat the 59F menu (not available Sun) for this part of the world.

Jean-Claude Ferrero, 38 rue Vital, 16e; ☎45.04.42.42. (Mº Passy). Closed first 2 weeks in May & last 3 weeks in Aug. A gourmet heaven run by the chef who introduced menus dedicated to mushrooms and truffles. Mushrooms in a delectable sauce are included on the 220F midday menu. *À la carte* 450F upwards.

The 17e

RESTAURANTS

Natacha, 35 rue Guersant, 17e; ☎45.74.23.86 (Mº Porte-Maillot). Lunchtime, and evenings until 10.30pm (11.30pm on Sat); closed Sun, Sat noon and Aug 10–20. A bit out of the way, beyond the place des Ternes, but a great bargain. For 75F at midday or 95F in the

evening, you can help yourself to hors d'oeuvres and wine, with three other very respectable courses to follow. Not surprisingly, it pulls in the crowds. Best to be early.

Sangria, 13bis rue Vernier, 17e; ☎45.74.78.74 (Mº Porte-de-Champerret). As at *Natacha*, for 75F at midday and 85F in the evening you can help yourself to starters and wine in addition to enjoying three other courses. Also very popular and crowded, and just has the edge over *Natacha*.

Île de Chatou

RESTAURANTS

Restaurant Fournaise, Île de Chatou. ☎30.71.41.91 (*RER ligne A2* to Rueil-Malmaison, then a 10-minute walk right along the dual carriageway to the bridge). Lunchtime, and evenings until 10pm; closed Sun evening in winter. There is a menu at 150F; the *carte* is more like 200–250F. The food is good, but it is above all the location you come for (see p.201). The restaurant, now beautifully restored, was a favourite haunt of the Impressionists and is the subject of Renoir's painting *Le Déjeuner des Canotiers*. The verandah, which features in the painting, is still there, shaded by a magnificent riverside plane tree. A real treat for a lunchtime in spring or dinner on a warm summer night.

Eating and Drinking

See p.261 for a list of cafés and restaurants which stay open late.

Over the Top . . . The Gourmet Restaurants of Paris

If you're feeling slightly crazed – or you happen on a winning lottery ticket – there are, of course, some really spectacular Parisian restaurants. For *nouvelle cuisine* at its very best *Robuchon* (32 rue de Longchamp, 16e), *Lucas Carton* (9 place de la Madeleine, 8e), and *Taillevent* (15 rue Lamenais, 8e) are said to be the pinnacles of gastronomic experience and not just for bills that can reach 10,000F for two. For pride of place if not so much for *plats* there's *Jules Vernes* on the second floor of the Eiffel Tower. Unfortunately, the moment's madness that might inspire you to eat in any of these restaurants would most likely come months too late for you to make reservations.

Chapter 14

Museums and Galleries

You may find there is sufficient visual stimulation to be gained from just wandering the streets of Paris, without feeling the need to explore the city's **galleries and museums**. It's certainly questionable whether the Louvre, for example, can compete in pleasure with the Marais, the *quais* or parts of the Latin Quarter. But if established art appeals to you at all, the Paris collections are not to be missed.

The most popular are the various **museums of modern art**: in the Beaubourg Pompidou Centre, Palais de Tokyo and Musée Picasso, and, for the brilliantly represented opening stages, in the **Musée d'Orsay, Orangerie** and **Marmottan**. Since Paris was the well-rocked cradle of Impressionism, Fauvism, Cubism, Surrealism and Symbolism, there's both justice and relevance in such a multitude of works being here. No less breathtaking, going back to earlier cultural roots, are some of the medieval works in the **Musée National du Moyen-Age** (the old *Musée Cluny*), including the glorious *La Dame à la Licorne* tapestry. **Contemporary art** has a new home in the remodelled galleries of the Jeu de Paume.

Among the city's extraordinary number of technical, historical, social and applied art museums, pride of place must go to the dazzling **Cité des Sciences**, radical in both concept and architecture – and fun. If any answer were needed to Euro Disney, this is it. Entertaining too, if more conventional, is the **Musée National des Arts et Traditions Populaires**, its equivalent for

the past. Some of the smaller ones are dedicated to a single person – Balzac, Hugo, Piaf – and others to very particular subjects – spectacles, counterfeits, tobacco. We've detailed all but a very few of the smallest and most highly specialized, such as the freemasonry and lawyers' museums, details can be obtained from the tourist office. A few others, like **Le Corbusier, Montmartre**, the **Pavillon de l'Arsenal**, the **Gobelins** and the **Bibliothèque Nationale** have been incorporated in the text in the relevant chapters. **Out-of-town museums** are detailed in Chapter 20, *Day Trips from Paris*.

The Big Four – **Louvre, d'Orsay, Cité des Sciences** and **Beaubourg** – are described first. The remainder of the city's museums follow under five headings: Art, Fashion and Fripperies, History, Performance Arts and Literature, and Science and Industry. The museums in the suburbs and beyond come at the end.

Admission prices vary, but all have gone up considerably in the last few years: the Cité des Sciences is the most expensive at 45F; the rest range from around 15F to 35F. Some museums offer student reductions for which the only acceptable ID is an ISIC international student card. This can still be refused, however, if you're obviously over 25, despite claims to the contrary. Other museums, such as the Louvre and d'Orsay, offer the *tarif reduit* to those aged between 18 and 25 and over 60, for which you'll need to show your passport, and free entry for the under-18s.

If you're going to visit a great many museums in a short time, it's worth buying the *Carte Musées et Monuments* pass (60F 1-day; 120F 3-day; 170F 5-day; available from *RER* stations and museums), which is valid for 65 museums and monuments in and around Paris, and allows you to bypass the ticket queues.

The Louvre and most other state-owned museums **close** on Tuesday and some have **half-price admission** on Sunday; the city-owned museums **close** on Monday and some have **free admission** on Sunday. Opening days and hours are all given below.

Lastly, keep an eye out for **temporary exhibitions**, some of which match any of Paris' regular collections. Beaubourg, the Grand Palais and the Grande Salle at La Villette have the major ones, well advertised by posters and detailed in *Pariscope* and the other listings magazines. Many of the museums and commercial galleries host themed exhibitions during the various arts festivals (see p.41–42). The **commercial galleries** (heavily concentrated in the Beaubourg and St-Germain

areas and detailed in Chapters 5 and 6) are always good for a look-in, which of course you can do without charge.

The Louvre

Pyramide, Cour Napoléon, Palais du Louvre, 1er (Mº Palais-Royal–Musée du Louvre/Louvre-Rivoli).

Thurs–Sun 9am–6pm, Wed 9am–10pm. Richelieu wing, Histoire du Louvre rooms, Medieval Louvre Wed till 10pm; temporary exhibitions 10am–10pm; bookshop, restaurant, cafés 9.30am–10pm. Everything closed Tues. Last tickets 45min before closing time; tickets valid all day, re-entry allowed. Admission 40F, after 3pm and all day Sun 20F; under-18s free.

"You walked for a quarter of a mile through works of fine art; the very floors echoed the sounds of immortality . . . It was the crowning and consecration of art . . . These works instead of being taken from their respective countries were given to the world and to the mind and heart of man from whence they sprung . . ."

William Hazlitt, writing of the Louvre in 1802, goes on, in equally florid style, to

Museums
and Galleries

If queues at the main pyramid entrance seem dauntingly long, check whether the alternative entrance at the western end of Denon is open.

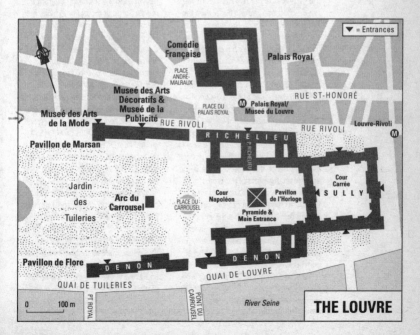

Museums and Galleries

There's more about the Palais du Louvre itself on p.71.

proclaim this museum as the beginning of a new age when artistic masterpieces would be the inheritance of all, no longer the preserve of kings and nobility. Novel the Louvre certainly was. The palace, hung with the private collections of monarchs and their ministers, was first opened to the public in 1793, during the Revolution. Within a decade Napoléon had made it the largest art collection on earth with takings from his empire.

However inspiring it might have been then, the Louvre has been a bit of a nightmare over the last few decades, requiring heroic willpower and stamina to find one work of art that you want to see among the 30,000. The new **"Grand Louvre"**, which was finally inaugurated by President Mitterrand in the autumn of 1988 and is now more or less complete, has failed to solve the problems.

The pyramid is now the main entrance, covering a subterranean but day-lit concourse – the **Hall Napoléon** – with lifts and escalators leading into the three wings of the building, each with four floors: the *entresol* (the level reached from the escalators in the Hall Napoléon), the *rez-de-chaussée* (ground floor), then the first and second floors. The three wings are *Sully* (around the Cour Carrée), *Denon* (the south wing) and *Richelieu* (the north wing). These are then divided into ten numbered areas, subdivided into numbered rooms and colour-coded for the main categories of the collection (see below). The trouble with the Louvre has always been horizontal not vertical orientation and distance, so the access up from the *Hall Napoléon* doesn't get you very far. The signing system, including the giant electronic billboards in the *Hall Napoléon*, and the arrangement of the works, remains as mysterious and frustrating as ever. Most works – but not all – are now in their definitive place, but the insurmountable problem is that the Louvre is just too big. When you need a break, you still have to get back down to the ticket concourse to find a cup of coffee.

One bonus from all the building works has been the opportunity to excavate the remains of the **medieval Louvre** –

Philippe Auguste's twelfth-century fortress and Charles V's fourteenth-century palace conversion – under the Cour Carrée. These are now on show along with a permanent exhibition on the history of the Louvre, from the Middle Ages up to the current transformations. The medieval Louvre is all on the *entresol, Sully,* and easy to find.

The **seven basic categories** of the museum's collections are: three lots of antiquities, sculpture, painting, applied and graphic arts. Each category spreads over more than one wing (except Egyptian Antiquities – all are in *Sully*) and several floors. The free handbook (in English) gives details. **Oriental Antiquities** – including the newly presented Islamic Art collection – covers the Sumerian, Babylonian, Assyrian and Phoenician civilizations, plus the art of ancient Persia. **Egyptian Antiquities** contains jewellery, domestic objects, sandals, sarcophagi and dozens of examples of the delicate naturalism of Egyptian decorative technique, such as the wall tiles depicting a piebald calf galloping through fields of papyrus and a duck taking off from a marsh. Some of the major exhibits are: the pink granite *Mastaba Sphinx*, the *Kneeling Scribe* statue (*Sully* ground floor 2 and 5), a wooden statue of *Chancellor Nakhti*, the *god Amon,* protector of Tutankhamun, a bust of *Amenophis IV*, *Sethi I* and the *goddess Hathor*.

The **Greek and Roman Antiquities** include the *Winged Victory of Samothrace* (*Denon* first floor, at the top of the great staircase) and the *Venus de Milo* (*Sully* ground floor 9), biggest crowd-pullers in the museum after the *Mona Lisa. Venus*, striking a classic model's pose, is one of the great sexpots of all time. She dates from the late second century BC. Her antecedents are all on display, too, from the delightful *Dame d'Auxerre* (seventh century BC) and the fifth-century BC bronze *Apollo of Piombino*, still looking straight ahead in the archaic manner, to the classical perfection of the *Athlete of Benevento* and the beautiful *Ephebe of Agde*. In the Roman section are some very attractive mosaics from Asia Minor and luminous frescoes from Pompeii and Herculaneum, which already seem to foreshadow the decorative lightness of touch of a Botticelli still 1000 years and more away.

The **Applied Arts** collection is heavily weighted on the side of vulgar imperial opulence. Beautifully crafted and extravagantly expensive pieces of furniture arouse no aesthetic response whatever, just an appalled calculation of the cost. The same has to be said of the renowned cabinet-maker Boulle's work (active round 1700), immediately recognizable by the heavy square shapes and lavish use of inlays in copper, bronze and pewter and such ecologically catastrophic exuberance as entire doors of tortoiseshell. There are also several acres of tapestry – all of the very first quality and workmanship, but a chore to look at. Relief has to be sought in the smaller, less public items: Marie-Antoinette's travelling case, for example, fitted up with the intricacy of a jigsaw to take an array of bottles, vials and other queenly necessaries. Or the carved Parisian ivories of the thirteenth century: angels with rouged cheeks, and the Virgin pulling a sharp little nipple from her dress to suckle the Babe. Or the Limoges enamels and even earlier Byzantine ivories.

The **Sculpture section** covers the entire development of the art in France from Romanesque to Rodin, all in the new *Richelieu* wing, and Italian and Northern European sculpture in *Denon*, including Michelangelo's *Slaves*, designed for the tomb of Pope Julius II (*Denon* ground floor 10). The huge glass-covered courtyards of the *Richelieu* wing – the Cour Marly with the Marly Horses that once graced place de la Concorde, and the Cour Puget with Puget's *Milon de Crotone* as the centrepiece – are very impressive. But it's a bit too grandiose and overwhelming – the view from the passage Richelieu (see Chapter 3) is better. Upstairs, on the second floor, Napoléon III's apartments of flock wallpaper, matching upholstery and vast chandeliers, are now open to view. You can see why the Finance Ministry was so reluctant to move out.

The largest and most indigestible section by far is the **paintings**: French from the year dot to mid-nineteenth century, with Italians, Dutch, Germans, Flemish and Spanish represented too. Among them are many paintings so familiar from reproduction in advertisements and on chocolate boxes that it is a surprise to see them on a wall in a frame. And unless you're an art historian, it is hard to make much sense of the parade of mythological scenes, classical ruins, piteous piety, acrobatic saints and sheer dry academicism. A portrait, a domestic scene, a still life, is a real relief. Walking by with eyes selectively shut is probably the best advice. At least the lighting is much improved, with all the paintings on the first and second floors, and the ceilings designed by a specialized CAD programme to maximize and unify the natural light.

The early Italians (*Denon* first floor 5 & 7) are the most interesting part of the collection, at least up to Leonardo and the sixteenth century. Giotto, Fra Angelico, Uccello's *Battle of San Romano*, Mantegna, Botticelli, Filippo Lippi, Raphael . . . all the big names are represented. It is partly their period, but there is still an innate classical restraint which is more appealing to modern taste than the exuberance and grandiloquence of the eighteenth and nineteenth centuries. If you want to get near the *Mona Lisa* (*Denon* first floor 5), go first or last thing in the day. No one, incidentally, pays the slightest bit of attention to the other Leonardos right alongside, including the *Virgin of the Rocks*.

Access to the *Hall Napoléon* and its shops, information services, audiovisual shows and so on, is free (so long as the Louvre queues do not preclude access to the pyramid). You can reach it through passage Richelieu from rue de Rivoli, from the underground car park, or through the Tuileries, taking the spiral staircase down from the base of the pyramid.

The Palais du Louvre houses three other museums – decorative arts, fashion and publicity – listed under "The Rest of the Art" and "Fashion and Fripperies" on p.276 and p.279.

Museums and Galleries

MUSEUMS

1 M. National des Arts et Traditions Populaires
2 Centre Nationale de la Photographie
3 M. Arménien et M. d'Ennery
4 M. des Contrefaçons
5 M. Marmottan
6 Atelier d'Henri Bouchard
7 Maison de Belzac
8 M. de Radio-France
9 Palais Chaillot (M.du Cinéma, M. des
   Monuments Français et M. de l'Homme)
10 M. Guimet
11 M. des Costumes
12 Palais de Tokyo (M. d'Art Moderne
   de la Ville de Paris)
13 M. Intercoiffure
14 M. Cernushi
15 M. du Bottier
16 M. de S.E.I.T.A
17 M. de l'Armée
18 M. d'Orsay
19 M. Rodin
20 M. Valentin-Haüy
21 M. Bourdelle
22 M. de la Poste
23 M. Musée Pasteur
24 M. Branly
25 M. Ernest-Hébert
26 M. Zadkine
27 M. Delacroix
28 M. National du Moyen Age
29 M. de la Préfecture de Police
30 Institut du Monde Arabe
31 M. Assistance Publique
32 Orangerie
33 Jeu de Paume
34 M. des Lunettes
35 M. Cognacq-Jay
36 M. de la Perfumerie
37 M. Gustave Moreau
38 M. Renan-Scheffer
39 M. Art juif
40 M. de Montmartre
41 M. d'Art Naïf Max Fourny
42 M. Grévin I
43 M. du Cristal
44 M. des Arts de la Mode (Louvre)
45 M. des Arts Décoratifs (Louvre)
46 M. de la Publicité (Louvre)
47 Centre Culturel des Halles
   (M. Grévin II/M. Holographie)
48 M. National Techniques
49 Beaubourg
50 M. des Instruments de Musique Mécanique
51 M. de la Serrurerie
52 M. Kwok-On
53 M. Picasso
54 M. Carnavelet
55 M. de l'Histoire de France
56 Maison Victor Hugo
57 M. de la Curiosité
58 M. Adam Mickiewicz
59 Pavillon de l'Arsenal
60 M. Arts Africains et Océaniens
61 M. Edith Piaf
62 Cité de la Musique
63 Cité des Sciences
64 Centre International de l'Automobile

Museums and Galleries

Musée d'Orsay

1 rue de Bellechasse/quai Anatole-France (for major exhibitions), 7ᵉ (Mº Solférino/RER Musée d'Orsay). Tues, Wed, Fri & Sat 9/10am–6pm, Thurs 9/10am–9.45pm, Sun 9am–6pm; closed Mon. Admission 36F, 18–25s and over-60s 24F, under-18s free; Sun 20F (no reductions); free guided tours in English by staff lecturer 11am & 2pm.

The conversion of the disused train station, the Gare d'Orsay, into the Musée d'Orsay marked a major advance in the reorganization of the capital's art collections. It houses the painting and sculpture of the immediately pre-modern period, 1848–1914, bridging the gap between the Louvre and the Centre Beaubourg. Its focus is the cobweb-clearing, eye-cleansing collection of **Impressionists** rescued from the cramped corridors of the Jeu de Paume – though not, unavoidably, from the coach parties and gangs of brats. Scarcely less electrifying are the works of the **Post-Impressionists** brought in from the Palais de Tokyo.

The **general layout** is as follows. On the ground floor, the **mid-nineteenth-century sculptors**, including Barye, caster of super-naturalistic bronze animals, occupy the centre gallery. To their right, a few canvases by Ingres and Delacroix (the bulk of whose work is in the Louvre) serve to illustrate **the transition from the early nineteenth century**. Puvis de Chavannes, Gustave Moreau, the Symbolists and early Degas follow, while in the galleries to the left Daumier, Corot, Millet and the Realist school lead on to the **first Impressionist works**, including Manet's *Déjeuner sur l'Herbe*, which sent the critics into apoplexies of rage and disgust when it appeared in 1863. *Olympia* is here too, equally controversial at the time, for the colour contrasts and sensual surfaces, rather than the content, though the black cat was considered peculiar.

To get the chronological continuation you have to go straight up to the top level, where numerous landscapes and outdoor scenes by **Renoir, Sisley, Pissarro** and **Monet** owe much of their brilliance to the novel practice of setting up easels in the open to catch a momentary light. Monet's *Waterlilies* are here in abundance, too, along with five of his Rouen cathedral series, each painted in different light conditions.

Le Berceau (1872), by Morisot, the only woman in the early group of Impressionists, is one of the few to have a complex human emotion as its subject – perfectly synthesized within the classic techniques of the movement. A very different touch, all shimmering light and wide brush strokes, is to be seen in Renoir's depiction of a good time being had by all in *Le Moulin de la Galette* – a favourite Sunday afternoon out on the Butte Montmartre.

Cézanne, a step removed from the preoccupations of the mainstream Impressionists, is also wonderfully represented. One of the canvases most revealing of his art is *Still life with apples and oranges* (1895–1900), in which the background abandons perspective while the fruit has an extraordinary reality.

The rest of this level is given over to the various **offspring of Impressionism**. Among a number of pointilliste works by Seurat and others is Signac's horrible *Entrée du Port de Marseille*. There's Gauguin, post- and pre-Tahiti, as well as some very attractive derivatives like Georges Lacombe's carved wood panels; several superb Bonnards and Vuillards and lots of Toulouse-Lautrec at his caricaturial night-clubbing best – one large canvas including a rear view of Oscar Wilde at his grossest. Plus all the blinding colours and disturbing rhythms of the **Van Goghs**.

The middle level takes in Rodin and other **late nineteenth-century sculptors**, three rooms of superb **Art Nouveau** furniture and *objets*, and, lastly, some Matisses and Klimts to mark the **transition to the moderns** in the Beaubourg collection.

The design of the Musée d'Orsay is, without doubt, very clever, and the art works have been given the best lighting you could wish for. But many people find the space overdesigned, the sequences of galleries on the upper floors too intense, and the ground floor so marbled it feels like a tomb. It's certainly better than the Jeu de Paume, but the exuberance of the paintings, the desire that a glimpse of one can give you to skip across the room, cannot but be dampened by the seriousness of these surroundings.

Cité des Sciences et de l'Industrie

Parc de la Villette, 30 av Corentin-Cariou, 19e (Mº Porte de la Villette). Tues–Sun 10am–6pm; everything closed Mon. Cité pass giving access to Explora, planetarium, Cinéma Louis-Lumière, Salle Jean-Painlevé and mediathèque screens, aquarium and Argonaute: 45F, reduced tarif 35F, under-7s free; Géode Tues–Sun 10am–8pm: 50F/37F (some films are more), combined ticket with Cité 85F/72F (available from Géode only); Inventorium and Cité des Enfants (see p.301) 15F and 20F extra; Cinaxe 27F/22F.

This is the science museum to end all science museums, and worth visiting for the interior of the building alone: all glass and stainless steel, crows-nests and cantilevered platforms, bridges and suspended walkways, the different levels linked by lifts and escalators around a huge central space open to the full 40m height of the roof. It may be colossal, but you are more likely to lose yourself mentally rather than physically, and come out after several hours reeling with images and ideas, while possibly none the wiser about DNA, quasars, bacteria reproduction, curved space or rocket launching.

The **permanent exhibition**, called *Explora*, takes up the top two floors and is divided into thirty units (pick up a detailed plan from the *Accueil général Explora* on *niveau 1*). These cover different subjects such as sounds, robots, computer science, expression and behaviour, oceans, energy, light, the environment, mathematics, space, language etc. The emphasis, as the name suggests, is on exploring; the means used are interactive computers, multimedia displays, videos, holograms, animated models and games. Most of the explanations and instructions are in English as well as French; one exception, unfortunately, is the *Jeux de Lumière* –

"light games", a whole series of experiments to do with colour, optical illusions, refraction etc. But then you can treat working out what you're supposed to do as an experiment in itself.

A classic example of chaos theory introduces the maths section: a wheel of glasses rotating below a stream of water in which the switch between clockwise and anticlockwise motion is entirely unpredictable. An "inertial carousel"– a revolving drum (2–6pm only) provides a four-minute insight into the strange transformations of objects in motion. In *Expressions et comportements* you can intervene in stories acted out on videos, changing the behaviour of the characters to engineer a different outcome. Hydroponic plants grow for real in the *green bridge* across the central space. You can steer robots through mazes; make music by your own movements; try out a flight simulation; watch computer-guided puppet shows and holograms of different periods' visions of the universe; and stare at two slabs of wall parting company at the rate of two centimetres a year – enacting the gradual estrangement of Europe and America.

When all this interrogation and stimulation becomes too much, you can relax at the café within *Explora* (by the planetarium on *niveau 2*), where the cheapest sit-down cup of coffee in the city is served and even smoking is allowed. When you want your head to start reeling again, just join the queue for the **planetarium** (shows at 11am, 12 noon, 2pm, 3pm, 4pm and 5pm).

Back on the ground floor the **Cinéma Louis-Lumière** shows a short stereoscopic film at 11.30am, 2pm, 3.30 pm, 4pm and 4.30pm. There are more films downstairs (level S1) in the **Salle Jean-Painlevé** and **Salle Les Shadoks** (specially for kids), while you can call up your own choices at the individual consoles in the **Mediathèque**. For details of the **Cité des Enfants** and **Inventorium** (for which you have to be accompanied by a child), see p.301.

On the bottom floor of the building (S2) with access to the Géode, Argonaute,

**Museums
and Galleries**

Cinaxe and the rest of the park, there's a café-restaurant arranged around the rather small, by La Villette standards, **aquarium**.

On top of all this are the **temporary exhibitions**, in which a general subject is treated, historically and philosophically as well as scientifically, often using contemporary works of art as commentary, and allowing you hands-on experiments.

A Walkman guide in English is available at the counter in the main hall (around 15F), and includes details of the architecture, explanations for *Explora* and the soundtrack for the Planetarium shows.

The entire building is **accessible by wheelchair** (as is the park with escalators at the bridge across the canal); the *Médiathèque* has a **Braille** room; and there are **signers** (in FSL).

Outside, the **Argonaute** is a real 1957 French military submarine in which you can clamber about, discover masses of facts about underwater transportation, and view the park through the periscope. The **Géode** shows films shot on the 180° Omnimax system (see *Film, Theatre and Dance* chapter, p.337), while the **Cinaxe** combines 70mm film shot at 30 frames a second with seats that move, so that a bobsleigh ride down the Cresta Run, for example, not only looks unbelievably real, but feels it too.

Beaubourg: Musée National d'Art Moderne

Centre Beaubourg, rue St-Martin/rue du Renard, 4ᵉ (Mᵒ Rambuteau/Hôtel-de-Ville). Centre open Mon & Wed–Fri noon–10pm, Sat & Sun 10am–10pm; closed Tues. Free entry but there are admission charges for the permanent collections (except Sun 10am–2pm) and temporary exhibitions: Musée National d'Art Moderne Wed, Thurs, Mon noon–6pm; Fri noon–10pm, Sat & Sun 10am–6pm; 30F/20F; Galeries Contemporaines 20F; day pass for exhibitions and permanent collections 57F/40F.

The Musée National d'Art Moderne on the fourth floor of Beaubourg is second to none. The art is exclusively twentieth-century and constantly expanding. Contemporary movements and works dated the year before last find their place

here along with the late-Impressionists, Fauvists, Cubists, Figuratives, Abstractionists and the rest of this century's First World art trends. The lighting and spacing is superb, but only a fraction of the whole collection is hung at any one time.

One of the earliest paintings is Henri Rousseau's *La Charmeuse de Serpent* (1907), an extraordinary, idiosyncratic beginning. In a different world, Picasso's *Femme Assise* of 1909 brings in the reduced colours and double dimensions of Cubism, presented in its fuller development by Braque's *L'Homme à la Guitare* (1914) and, later, in Léger's solid balancing act, *Les Acrobates en Gris* (1942–44).

Among **Abstracts**, there's the sensuous rhythm of colour in Sonia Delauney's *Prismes Électriques* (1914) and a good number of Kandinskys at his most harmonious and playful. Dali disturbs, amuses or irritates with *Six apparitions de Lénine sur un piano* (1931), and there are more surrealist images from Magritte and de Chirico.

Moving to the **Expressionists**, one of the most compulsive pictures – of 1920s' female emancipation as viewed by a male contemporary – is the portrait of the journalist Sylvia von Harden by Otto Dix. The gender of the sleeping woman in *Le Rêve* by Matisse has no importance – it is the human body at its most relaxed that the artist has painted.

Jumping forward, to Francis Bacon, you find the tension and the torment of the human body and mind in the portraits, and – no matter that the figure is minute – in *Van Gogh in Landscape* (1957). Squashed-up cars, lines and squares, wrapped-up grand pianos and Warhol's *Electric chair* (1966) are there to be seen, while, for a reminder that contemporary art can still hold its roots, there's the classic subject of *Le Peintre et son modèle* by Balthus in 1980–81.

There are temporary exhibitions of photographs, drawings, collages and prints in the **Salle d'Art Graphique** and **Salon Photo**, part of the permanent collections of the museum. If your grasp of French is sufficient you can take advantage of the **audiovisual presentations** on the major artistic movements of this century, or the **films**, projected several times daily, on contemporary art, on current exhibitions or as experimental art in themselves.

On the mezzanine floor (down the stairs to the right of the plaza doors) are the **Galeries Contemporaines** where the overspill of the museum's contemporary collection gets rotated and young artists get a viewing. The **Grande Galerie** right at the top of the building is where the big-time exhibitions are held. They usually last several months, are extremely well publicized, and can, occasionally, be brilliant. Yet more temporary shows on equally diverse themes take place in the basement **Centre de Création Industrielle**.

Beaubourg also has an excellent cinema (see p.337), a reference library including foreign newspapers open to all, a record library where you can take a music break, a snack bar and restaurant (with seating on the roof), a bookshop, dance and theatre space, and kids' workshop (see p.300).

The Rest of the Art

Musée d'Art Moderne de la Ville de Paris

Palais de Tokyo east wing, 11 av du Président-Wilson, 16ᵉ (Mᵒ Iéna/Alma-Marceau). Tues–Fri 10am–5.30pm, Sat & Sun 10am–7pm, Wed till 8.30pm in summer; closed Mon & hols. 27F/14F, under-18s free.

The problem with reviewing Paris' own Musée d'Art Moderne is that it is difficult to predict which works will be on display and where, for this gallery suffers from seemingly chronic St Vitus' Dance. But you can rest assured that the museum's schools and trends of **twentieth-century art** will always be richly represented by artists such as Vlaminck, Zadkine, Picasso, Braque, Juan Gris, Valadon, Matisse, Dufy, Utrillo, both Delaunays, Chagall, Modigliani, Léger and many others, as well as by sculpture and painting by contemporary artists.

Among the most spectacular works on permanent show are Robert and Sonia Delaunay's huge whirling wheels and cogs of rainbow colour (which are now displayed in the ground floor corridor); the pale leaping figures of Matisse's *La Danse*; and Dufy's enormous mural, *La Fée Électricité* (done for the electricity board), illustrating the story of electricity from Aristotle to the then modern power station, in 250 lyrical, colourful panels filling three entire walls.

The upper floors of the gallery are reserved for all sorts of contemporary and experimental work, including music and photography.

On sale in the bookshop are a number of artists' designs, among them a set of Sonia Delaunay's playing cards, guaranteed to rejuvenate the most jaded card-sharp. Next to it is an excellent and reasonably priced snack bar.

Musée National du Moyen-Age

6 place Paul-Painlevé, off rue des Écoles, 5ᵉ (Mᵒ Cluny-La Sorbonne/St-Michel). Wed–Mon 9.15am–5.45pm; closed Tues. 27F/18F, under-18s free; half-price Sun.

If you have always found tapestries boring, this treasure house of medieval art may well provide the flash of enlightenment. The numerous beauties in the former Musée de Cluny include a marvellous depiction of the grape harvest; a Resurrection embroidered in gold and silver thread, with sleeping guards in medieval armour; and a whole room of sixteenth-century Dutch tapestries, full of flowers and birds, a woman spinning while a cat plays with the end of the thread, a lover making advances, and a pretty woman in her bath, overflowing into a duck pond.

But the greatest wonder of all is *La Dame à la Licorne* – The Lady with the Unicorn: six enigmatic scenes featuring a beautiful woman flanked by a lion and a unicorn. Dating from the late fifteenth century, and perhaps made in Brussels, it is quite simply the most stunning piece of art you are likely to see in many a long day. The ground of each panel is a delicate red worked with a thousand tiny flowers, birds and animals. In the centre, on a green island, equally flowery and

Museums and Galleries

**Museums
and Galleries**

framed by stylized trees, the young woman plays a portable organ, takes a sweet from a proffered box, makes a necklace of carnations, while a pet monkey, perched on the rim of a basket of flowers, holds one to his nose . . .

Unfortunately, the lighting and general atmosphere of this museum are a trifle gloomy, and it doesn't yet feature on the list for dramatic renovations, but nevertheless it's a treat (and generally uncrowded).

Jeu de Paume

Jardins des Tuileries, Place de la Concorde, 8e (Mº Place-de-la-Concorde). Tues noon–9.30pm, Wed–Fri noon–7pm, Sat & Sun 10am–7pm; closed Mon. 32F/25F (more for some exhibitions), under-13s free.

The transformation of the Jeu de Paume into an exhibition space for contemporary art has been so successful that it seems almost a shame not to put the Impressionists back. The height of the building has been emphasized in the design of the staircase and in the galleries, which have all been given plain white walls and parquet flooring.

The exhibitions policy is far from conservative: under the heading *Générique 1. Désordres*, one gallery was given over to Jana Sterbak's *Flesh Dress for an Albino Anorexic*, a dress made of pieces of sewn-together steak. The room was infused with a strong perfume of lilies, whose purpose only became apparent once you were close enough to realize that the material was not a rich, sculpted velvet. On the wall hung a big colour photograph of a model wearing the dress, fresh.

Don't be put off, however: truly shocking works of arts are few and far between, and the Jeu de Paume would think itself lucky to have such a coup again.

The Orangerie

Jardins des Tuileries, Place de la Concorde, 1er (Mº Concorde). Wed–Mon 9.45am–5.15pm; closed Tues. 33F/24F.

The Orangerie, on the south side of the Tuileries terrace overlooking place de la Concorde, is one of the museums people

tend to forget about, despite its two oval rooms arranged by **Monet** as panoramas for his largest waterlily paintings. In addition, there are works by no more than a dozen other **Impressionist** artists – Matisse, Cézanne, Utrillo, Modigliani, Renoir, Soutine and Sisley among them.

This is a private collection, inherited by the state with the stipulation that it should always stay together. Consequently none of the pictures were moved to the Musée d'Orsay, and the Orangerie remains one of the top treats of Paris art museums.

Cézanne's southern landscapes, the portraits by Van Dongen, Utrillo and Derain of Paul Guillaume and Jean Walter, whose taste this collection represents, the massive nudes of Picasso, Monet's *Argenteuil* and Sisley's *Le Chemin de Montbuisson*, are the cherries on the cake of this visual feast. What's more, you don't need marathon endurance to cover the lot and get back to your favourites for a second look.

Musée Marmottan

2 rue Louis-Boilly, off av Raphael, 16e (Mº Muette). Tues–Sun 10am–5.30pm; closed Mon. 35F/15F.

The Marmottan house itself is interesting, with some splendid pieces of First Empire pomposity: chairs with golden sphinxes for armrests, candelabra of complicated headdresses and twining serpents. There is a small and beautiful collection of thirteenth- to sixteenth-century manuscript illuminations, but the star of the show is the collection of **Monet paintings** bequeathed by the artist's son. Among them is the canvas entitled *Impression, Soleil Levant* (Impression, Sunrise), an 1872 rendering of a misty sunrise over Le Havre, whose title the critics usurped to give the Impressionist movement its name. There's a dazzling collection of canvases from Monet's last years at Giverny. They include several *Nymphéas* (Waterlilies), *Le Pont Japonais*, *L'Allée des Rosiers*, *La Saule Pleureur*, where rich colours are laid on in thick, excited whorls and lines. To all intents and purposes, these are abstractions – so much more "advanced" than the work of, say, Renoir, Monet's exact contemporary.

Impression, Soleil Levant was stolen from the gallery in October 1985, along with eight other paintings. After a police operation lasting five years and going as far afield as Japan, the paintings were discovered in a villa in southern Corsica, and are back on show – with greatly tightened security measures.

Musée des Arts Africains et Océaniens

293 av Daumesnil, 12e (Mº Porte-Dorée). Mon & Wed–Fri 10am–noon & 1.30–5.15pm, Sat & Sun 10–6pm; closed Tues. 27F/18F; Sun half-price.

This strange museum – one of the least crowded in the city – has an African gold brooch of curled-up sleeping crocodiles on one floor and, in the basement, five live crocodiles in a tiny pit surrounded by tanks of tropical fishes. Imperialism is much in evidence in a gathering of culture and creatures from the old French colonies: hardly any of the black African artefacts are dated, as the collection predates European acknowledgement of history on that continent, and the captions are a bit suspicious too. These masks and statues, furniture, adornments and tools should be exhibited with paintings by Expressionists, Cubists and Surrealists to see in which direction inspiration went. Picasso and friends certainly came here often. And though casual tourists might not respond with a bit of painting or sculpture, they should find a lot to enjoy.

Musée Picasso

Hôtel Salé, 5 rue de Thorigny, 3e (Mº St-Paul/ Chemin-Vert). Wed 9.15am–10pm, Mon & Thurs–Sun 9.15am–5.15pm; closed Tues. 26F/ 18–25s 17F, under-18s free, Sun 17F.

The French are justly proud of this 1980s art museum. The grandiloquent seventeenth-century mansion, the Hôtel Salé, was restored and restructured at a cost to the government of £3–4m. The spacious, undaunting interior is admirably suited to its contents: the largest collection of Picassos anywhere. A large proportion of the works were personally owned by Picasso at the time of his death, and the

state had first option on them in lieu of taxes owed. They include all the different media he used, the paintings he bought or was given by his contemporaries, his African masks and sculptures, photographs, letters and other personal memorabilia.

All of which said, it's a bit disappointing. These are not Picasso's most enjoyable works – the museums of the Côte d'Azur and the Picasso gallery in Barcelona are more exciting. But the collection does leave you with a definite sense of the man and his life in conjunction with his production. This is partly because these were the works he wanted to keep. The paintings of his wives, lovers and families are some of the gentlest and most endearing: the portraits of *Marie-Thérèse* and *Claude dessinant, Françoise et Paloma*, for example. Throughout the chronological sequence, the photographs are vital in showing this charismatic (and highly photogenic) man seen at work and at play by friends and family.

The portrait of *Dora Maar*, like that of *Marie-Thérèse*, was painted in 1937, during the Spanish Civil War when Picasso was going through his worst personal and political crises. This is the period when emotion and passion play hardest on his paintings and they are by far the best (though *Guernica* is in Madrid, not here). A decade later, Picasso was a member of the Communist Party – his cards are on show along with a drawing entitled *Staline à la Santé* (Here's to Stalin), and his delegate credentials for the 1948 World Congress of Peace. The *Massacre en Corée* (1951) demonstrates the lasting pacifist commitment in his work.

Temporary exhibitions will bring to the Hôtel Salé works from the periods least represented: the Pink Period, Cubism (despite some fine examples here, including a large collection of collages), the immediate postwar period and the 1950s and 1960s.

The modern museological accoutrements are all provided: audiovisuals and films in a special cinema, biographical and critical details displayed in each room and a library.

Museums and Galleries

Museums and Galleries

Musée Rodin

Hôtel Biron, 77 rue de Varenne, 7ᵉ (just to the east of the Invalides) (Mᵒ Varenne). Tues–Sun 10am–5/5.45pm; closed Mon. 27F/18F, garden only 5F.

This collection represents the whole of Rodin's work. Major projects like *Les Bourgeois de Calais, Le Penseur, Balzac, La Porte de l'Enfer, Ugolini et fils* are exhibited in the garden – the latter forming the centrepiece of the ornamental pond. Indoors (and very crowded) are works in marble like *Le Baiser, La Main de Dieu, La Cathédrale* – those two perfectly poised, almost sentient, hands. There is something particularly fascinating about those works, such as *Romeo and Juliet* and *La Centauresse*, which are only, as it were, half-created, not totally liberated from the raw block of stone.

There is a reasonably priced café in the garden.

Musée des Arts Décoratifs

Palais du Louvre, 107 rue de Rivoli, 1ᵉʳ (Mᵒ Palais-Royale–Musée du Louvre). Wed–Sat 12.30–6pm, Sun noon–6pm; closed Mon & Tues. 25F/16F; disabled access.

This is an enormous museum, except by the standards of the building housing it – the Louvre – of which it takes up the Tuileries end of the north wing. It is, however, being reorganized and alterations will be going on until 1997. The contents are the furnishings, fittings, and objects of French interiors: beds, blankets, cupboards, tools, stained glass and lampshades, in fact almost anything that illustrates the decorative skills from the Middle Ages to the 1990s.

The meagre contemporary section has been added to recently – principally works by French, Italian and Japanese designers, including, inevitably, Philippe Starck. The rest of the twentieth century (also on the first floor) is fascinating – a bedroom by Guimard, Jeanne Lanvin's Art Deco apartments, and a salon created by Georges Hoentschel for the 1900 *Expo Universelle*. You can work your way back through the nineteenth century's fascination with the foreign and love of vivid colouring (fourth floor), to the intricate

wood-carving of the eighteenth century (third floor), to seventeenth-century marquetry and Renaissance tapestries and ivories (second floor).

A section on the third floor is dedicated to toys throughout the ages, with changing exhibitions. The museum shop, with books, clothes, accessories, playing cards and other amusements, is good, though not cheap.

Institut du Monde Arabe

1 rue Fossés-St-Bernard, 5ᵉ (Mᵒ Jussieu/Cardinal Lemoine). Tues–Sun 10am–6pm; closed Mon. 25F/20F (30F for temporary exhibitions).

Spread over seven spacious floors, the museum of the Institut du Monde Arabe has something of the atmosphere of a mosque – a rarefied place where you can talk and walk or think and study, at ease in the gracefulness of the building. There is a great deal of information, in the form of interactive videos and sheets (in both French and English) which you can take with you, while the choice of exhibits is extremely select.

Weights and measures, celestial globes, astrolabes, compasses and sundials along with the grinding and mixing implements for medicines illustrate an early period of Arab scientific research between 750 and 1258 AD. There are coins from an even earlier era, and illuminated manuscripts with fairy-tale pictures. Among the half a dozen or so exquisite silk carpets, one, of sixteenth-century Persian origin, has arabesques of flowers and birds with a swirling movement far removed from the static geometries usually associated with oriental carpet design. Ceramics and the tools of calligraphy and cookery are also represented.

On the ground floor are **contemporary paintings and sculpture** from the Arab world. Many of these have an emotional charge lacking in most Western contemporary art. Perhaps it is the political context that makes, for example, the brilliant bands of colour denoting sea, sand and city in Saliba Douaihy's *Beirut-Mediterranean*, painted during the Civil War in Beirut, such a powerful statement. Sami Mohamed Al-Saleh's bronze sculpture *Sabra and Chatila* would represent profound agony in any context, but the reference is there. Not all the paintings, by any means, address political 'issues'. They represent a wonderful diversity of the main artistic movements currently being explored in the Arab world.

Musée-Fondation Dapper

50 av Victor-Hugo, 16ᵉ (Mᵉ Étoile). Daily 11am–7pm during exhibitions. 15F/7.50F, free Wed.

The art of precolonial Africa is presented in superb temporary exhibitions based around a region, a period or a particular aspect of culture. Check *Pariscope* etc, for details. The library is open to students and researchers.

Grand and Petit Palais

Av W-Churchill, 8ᵉ (Mᵉ Champs-Elysées-Clemenceau). Grand Palais Mon & Thurs–Sun 10am–8pm, Wed 10am–10pm; prices vary depending on the exhibition, reduced rate Mon; closed Tues; Petit Palais Tues–Sun 10am–5.40pm; closed Mon & hols. 26F/14F.

The **Grand Palais** holds major temporary art exhibitions, good ones being evident from the queues stretching down avenue Churchill. *Pariscope* and co. will have details, and you'll probably see plenty of posters around. Two years of work on the roof and nave is planned, so exhibitions may be limited.

In the **Petit Palais**, whose entrance hall is a brazenly extravagant painted dome, you'll find the Beaux Arts museum, which on first impressions seems to be a collection of leftovers, from every period from the Renaissance to the 1920s, after the other main galleries have taken their pick.

However, the Petit Palais does have some gems. Monet's *Coucher de Soleil à Lavacourt* and Boudin's *Coup de Vent au Havre* stand out against some rather boring Renoirs, Morisots, Cezannes and Manets. There's the ultimate seductive actress pose of *Sarah Bernhardt* painted by Georges Clairin, and you'll also find a sculpture of her many years later, downstairs between galleries *Zoubaloff* and *Dutuit*.

Ugly furniture and fantasy jewellery of the Art Nouveau period, effete eighteenth-century furniture, the plaster models

designed for the Madeleine church in the early nineteenth century, and vast canvases recording Paris street battles during the 1830 and 1848 revolutions, trumpeting the victory of the Tricolour, are other potential attractions of this collection.

Musée Nationale des Arts Asiatiques – Guimet

6 place d'Iéna, 16ᵉ (Mᵉ Iéna). Wed–Mon 9.45am–5.15pm; 27F/18F, Sun half-price; closed Tues & hols.

Little visited, this features a huge and beautifully displayed collection of Oriental art, from China, India, Japan, Tibet and southeast Asia. There is a particularly fine collection of Chinese porcelain on the top floor.

Centre National de la Photographie

Hôtel Salomon de Rothschild, 11 rue Berryer, 8ᵉ (Mᵉ George V). Daily except Tues noon–7pm. 30F/15F.

Temporary exhibitions in a superb classical mansion. Check *Pariscope* for details.

Individual artists and smaller museums

Musée d'Art Juif

42 rue des Saules, 18ᵉ (Mᵉ Lamarck-Caulaincourt). Sun–Thurs 3–6pm; closed Fri, Sat & Aug. 30F/20F.

Some contemporary art, models of the great synagogues, and numerous objects to do with worship, supplemented by temporary exhibitions.

Atelier d'Henri Bouchard

25 rue de l'Yvette, 16ᵉ (Mᵉ Jasmin). Wed & Sat only, 2–7pm. 25F/15F.

The preserved studio of a sculptor (1875–1960), exhibiting works in bronze, stone, wood and marble.

Musée Bourdelle

16 rue Antoine-Bourdelle, 15ᵉ (Mᵉ Montparnasse/Falguière). Tues–Sun 10am–5.45pm; closed Mon & hols. 27F/19F.

The work of the early twentieth-century sculptor, including casts, drawings and tools, in his studio-house, and a new

**Museums
and Galleries**

extension in which you can see studies for the great works such as the homage to Mickiewicz and *L'Épogée Polonaise*.

Musée Cernuschi

7 av Velasquez, 17ᵉ (by east gate of Parc Monceau); Mº Monceau/Villiers. Tues–Sun 10am–5.40pm; closed Mon & hols. 25F/18F.

A small collection of ancient Chinese art with some exquisite pieces, but of fairly specialized interest.

Musée Cognacq-Jay

Hôtel Donon, 8 rue Elzévir, 3ᵉ (Mº St-Paul/ Chemin-Vert/Rambuteau). Tues–Sun 10am– 5.40pm; closed Mon & hols. 17F/9F.

For lovers of European art of the eighteenth century – Canaletto, Fragonard, Tiepolo – and early Rembrandt. Also porcelain, furniture and aristocratic trinkets in a matching setting of wood-panelled rooms.

Musée Salvador Dali

9–11 rue Poulbot (place du Tertre), 18ᵉ (Mº Abbesses). Daily 10am–7pm. 35F/25F.

An underground museum, all in black with atmospheric sound effects, which shows less well-known, though still very familiar, Dali works: watercolour illustrations for books – *Alice in Wonderland*, Dante's *Inferno* – and small sculptures of soft watches, melting snails and other phantasms from the incomprehensible mind of the self-promoting master. A must for Dali lovers.

Musée Delacroix

6 rue Furstemburg, 6ᵉ (Mº St-Germain-des-Prés). Mon & Wed-Fri 9.45am–12.30pm & 2–5.15pm, Sat & Sun 9.45am–5.15pm; closed Tues. 19F/ 15F.

Delacroix lived and worked here from 1857 till his death in 1863. Some attractive watercolours, illustrations from Hamlet and a couple of versions of a lion hunt hang in the painter's old studio, but there's nothing much in the way of major work.

Musée Nissim de Camondo

63, rue Monceau, 8ᵉ (Mº Villiers/Monceau). Wed–Sun 10am–noon & 2–5pm; closed Mon & Tues. 20F/14F.

It's only worth forking out for the Musée Nissim de Camondo if you share Count Camondo's taste for eighteenth-century French aristocratic luxuries: tapestries, paintings, gilded furniture, and tableware of the porcelain and solid silver variety. The museum is named after the count's son, killed while flying missions for France in World War I.

Musée de l'Holographie

15 Grand-Balcon, niveau -1, Forum des Halles, 1ᵉʳ (Mº/RER Châtelet-Les Halles). Mon–Sat 10am–7pm, Sun & hols 1–7pm. 32F/26F/15F.

Like most holography museums to date, this one is less exciting than you expect, the fault lying primarily with the state of the art. But one or two of the holograms are more inspired than women winking as you pass, and there are also works where artists have combined holograms with painting. The most impressive technically are the reproductions of museum treasures; just like the originals, you can't touch them.

Musée Jacquemart-André

158 bd Haussmann, 8ᵉ (Mº Miromesnil/St-Philippe-du-Roule). Wed–Sun 1–6.30pm; closed Mon & Tues. 35F/25F.

The ceilings of the staircase and three of the rooms of this museum are decorated with Tiepolo frescoes. His French contemporaries of the eighteenth century hang in the ground-floor rooms as well as his fellow Venetian, Canaletto. The collection contains several Rembrandts and, best of all, fifteenth- and sixteenth-century Italian genius in the works of Botticelli, Donatello, Mantegna, Tintoretto, Titian and Uccello.

Musée des Monuments Français

Palais de Chaillot, place du Trocadéro, 16ᵉ (Mº Trocadéro). Wed–Mon 10am–5.30pm; temporary exhibitions 10.30am–7pm, Wed till 9pm; closed Tues & hols. 21F/14F.

In the east wing of the Palais de Chaillot, the Musée des Monuments Français comprises full-scale reproductions of the most important church sculpture from Romanesque to Renaissance. All the major sites are represented. This is an ideal place to familiarize yourself with the styles and periods of monumental sculpture in France. Also included are repros of the major frescoes.

Musée Gustave Moreau

14 rue de la Rochefoucauld, 9e (M° Trinité). Mon & Thurs–Sun 10am–12.45pm & 2–5.15pm, Wed 11am–5.15pm; closed Tues & hols. 17F/11F.

An out-of-the-way bizarre, overcrowded collection of cluttered, joyless paintings by the Symbolist Gustave Moreau. If you know you like him, go along. Otherwise, give it a miss.

Espace Photographique de Paris

4–8 Grande Galerie, niveau -1, Porte Pont-Neuf, Forum des Halles, 1er (M°/RER Châtelet-Les Halles). Tues–Fri 1–6pm, Sat & Sun 1–7pm. 16F/8F.

A space for photographic art with changing exhibitions of the greats – Cartier-Bresson, Brandt, Cameron etc – as well as the lesser known.

Musée Valentin-Haüy

5 rue Duroc, 7e (M° Duroc). Tues & Wed only 2.30–5pm; closed July & Aug. Free.

Not for the blind but about them – the aids devised over the years as well as art and objects made by blind people.

Musée Zadkine

100bis rue d'Assas, 6e (M° Vavin). Tues–Sun 10am–5.40pm; closed Mon & hols. 17F/9F.

In Zadkine's own house and garden – a secret, private garden hidden away among tall apartment blocks. His angular Cubist bronzes are sheltered by the trees or emerge from a clump of bamboos. The rustic cottage, like the garden, is full of his sculptures. A place you want to linger in.

Fashion and fripperies

Musée des Arts de la Mode et du Textile

Palais du Louvre, 109 rue de Rivoli, 1er (M° Palais-Royal). Wed–Sat 12.30–6pm, Sun noon–6pm; closed Mon & Tues. 30F/20F.

Like everything else in the Palais du Louvre, this fashion museum is being extended, and it should re-open at the end of 1995. Hours may change.

Musée de la Curiosité

11 rue St-Paul, 4e (M° St-Paul/Sully-Morland). Wed, Sat & Sun 2–7pm. 45F/30F.

A delightful new museum dealing with magic and illusion. A few tricks are explained – the museum does not want to encourage any occult or supernatural beliefs – but conjurers' professional secrets are protected, so don't expect to glean all the answers. Automatons, distorting mirrors and optical illusions, things that float on thin air, a box for sawing people in half – they're all on view with examples from the eighteenth and nineteenth centuries, as well as contemporary magicians' tools.

The best fun is a live demonstration of the art (every 30min from 2.30–6pm) by the highly skilled Monsieur Cadiarc, who speaks excellent English and whose sleight of hand is mesmerizing.

The museum shop sells books on conjuring and magic cards, wands, boxes, scarves etc. Groups of schoolchildren tend to visit on Wednesdays, so best to visit at weekends.

Musée du Cristal

30bis rue de Paradis, 10e (M° Gare de l'Est/Château-d'Eau). Mon–Fri 9am–5.30/6pm, Sat 10am–noon & 2–5pm; closed Sun & hols. Free.

The most intricate and beautiful examples of crystal glass from the manufacturers *Baccarat* in a modern building behind a seventeenth-century arcade.

Di Mauro Mini Musée du Bottier

14 rue du Faubourg St-Honoré (escalier B in the courtyard on the right), 8e (M° Madeleine). Mon–Sat 10am–6pm; free.

A collection of shoes and boots from the 1920s to the present day housed in a shop, though hardly an ordinary shop. Three generations of the Italian family Di Mauro have been making one-off handmade shoes for the rich and famous here since 1939, and current prices range from 5800F to 9000F. One of the earliest exhibits is a pair of man's crocodile shoes with

Museums and Galleries

Museums and Galleries

baby croc arms as ties (1928). There are 1930s ski boots, the court shoes made for the present owner's widowed aunt in 1940 with the Italian colours and a framed photograph of the uncle as a buckle, and 1944 court shoes with the flags of the Four Powers.

The collection is not just of historical interest: customers often see an old style they like and ask for a variant of it. Behind the mirrored door, three old craftsmen work away on a tiny bench surrounded by shelves of all the clientele's shoe lasts.

If there are customers to attend to, the owner will not be able to give a guided tour (French or Italian only), but as long as there is not a crowd, you are free to take a look.

Musée Pierre Marly des Lunettes et Lorgnettes de Jadis

380 rue St-Honoré, 1er (M⁰ Place de la Concorde/Madeleine). Tues–Sat 9am–1pm & 2–7pm; closed Sun, Mon & Aug. Free.

Don't look for a museum. This superb collection of focusing aids resides in an ordinary optician's shop, with nothing on the outside to advertise its existence. The exhibits span pretty much the whole history of the subject, from the first medieval corrective lenses to modern times, taking in binoculars, microscopes and telescopes on the way. Many items are miniature masterpieces: bejewelled, inlaid, enamelled and embroidered – an intricate art that readily accommodated itself to the gimmickry its rich patrons demanded. There are, for example, lenses set in the hinges of fans and the pommels of gentlemen's canes, and one lorgnette case pops open to reveal an eighteenth-century dame sitting on a swing about a waterfall. A special collection consists of pieces that have sat upon the bridges of the famous: Audrey Hepburn, the Dalai Lama, Sophia Loren and ex-President Giscard.

Musée de la Mode et du Costume

Palais Galliera, 10 av Pierre ler-de-Serbie, 16e (M⁰ léna/Alma-Marceau). Tues–Sun 10am–5.40pm; closed Mon. 30F.

Clothes and fashion accessories of the rich and powerful, from the eighteenth

century to present day, exhibited in temporary thematic exhibitions. They last about six months and during change-overs (usually in May and Nov) the museum is closed.

Musée de la Publicité

Palais du Louvre, 107 rue de Rivoli, 1er (M⁰ Palais-Royal–Musée du Louvre). Mon & Wed–Sat 12.30–6pm, Sun noon–6pm; closed Tues. 25F/16F.

Publicity posters, adverts and TV and radio commercials are presented in temporary exhibitions, concentrating either on the art, the product or the psychological techniques. This museum is being reorganized, so hours may change.

SEITA

12 rue Surcouf, 7e (M⁰ Invalides/Latour-Maubourg). Mon–Sat 11am–6pm; closed Sun & hols. Free.

The state tobacco company has this small and, unfortunately, delightful museum in its offices, presenting the pleasures of smoking and none of the harm, with pipes and pouches from every continent – early Gauloise packets, painted *tabac* signs and, best of all, a slide show of tobacco in painting from the seventeenth century to now.

History and social sciences

Musée de l'Armée

Hôtel des Invalides, 7e (M⁰ Invalides/Latour-Maubourg/École-Militaire). Daily 10am–5pm. 34F/24F; no hats to be worn.

France's national war museum is enormous. The largest part is devoted to the uniforms and weaponry of Napoléon's armies; Napoléon's personal items include his campaign tent and bed, and even his dog, stuffed. Later French wars are represented, too, through paintings, maps and engravings. Sections on the two world wars are good, with deportation and resistance covered as well as battles. Some of the oddest exhibits are Secret Service sabotage devices – for instance, a rat and a lump of coal stuffed with explosives.

Musée Arménien and Musée d'Ennery

59 av Foch, 16ᵉ (Mº Porte-Dauphine). Sun & Thurs 2–6pm; closed Aug. Free.

On the ground floor, artefacts, art and historical documents of the Armenian people from the Middle Ages to the genocide by the Turks at the start of this century. On the floors above, the personal acquisitions of a nineteenth-century popular novelist: Chinese and Japanese objects including thousands of painted and sculpted buttons.

Musée de l'Homme

Palais de Chaillot, place du Trocadéro, 16ᵉ (Mº Trocadéro). 9.45am–5.15pm; closed Tues & hols. 25F/15F.

In the last couple of years, culture minister Jack Lang has waved his multimillion-franc wand over this once dusty collection with its rank upon rank of scratched glass cases. After a renovation on the scale of the d'Orsay museum, the new Musée de l'Homme is very flash, full of high-tech facilities and still oblivious to the problem of its title excluding half the world.

It's a gigantic museum, as befits its subject. Anthropology, ethnology, paleontology, along with more recent studies in genetics and linguistics are dealt with (plus musical instruments with a concert programme), from the year dot and from Polynesia to the Arctic. You've got to be selective unless you want to camp overnight among the mummified Incas, Menton Man's skeleton, hosts of African masks or Descartes' skull.

Musée National des Arts et Traditions Populaires

6 av du Mahatma-Gandhi, Bois de Boulogne (beside main entrance to Jardin d'Acclimatation), 16ᵉ (Mº Les Sablons/Porte-Maillot). 9.45am–5.15pm; closed Tues. 20F/14F, Sun 14F (28F/19F with exhibition).

If you have any interest in the beautiful and highly specialized skills, techniques and artefacts developed in the long ages that preceded industrialization, standardization and mass-production, then you should find this museum fascinating.

Boat-building, shepherding, farming, weaving, blacksmithing, pottery, stone-cutting, games, clairvoyance . . . all beautifully illustrated and displayed. Downstairs, there is a study section with cases and cases of implements of different kinds, and cubicles where you can call up explanatory slide shows at the touch of a switch.

Musée de l'Assistance Publique

Hôtel de Miramion, 47 quai de la Tournelle, 5ᵉ (Mº Maubert). Tues–Sat 10am–5pm; closed Sun, Mon, hols & Aug. 20F/10F.

The history of Paris hospitals from the Middle Ages to the present with pictures, pharmaceutical containers, surgical instruments and decrees relating to public health.

Musée Carnavalet

23 rue de Sévigné, 3ᵉ (Mº St-Paul). Tues–Sun 10am–5.40pm, Thurs till 8.30pm; closed Mon & hols. 26F/14F (35F/25F with exhibitions), disabled access.

A Renaissance mansion in the Marais presents the history of Paris as viewed and lived by royalty, aristocrats and the bourgeoisie mainly from François I to 1900, but with a new section spanning Roman times to the Middle Ages. The rooms for 1789–95 are full of sacred mementos: models of the Bastille, original Declarations of the Rights of Man and the Citizen, Tricolours and liberty caps, sculpted allegories of Reason, crockery with revolutionary slogans, glorious models of the guillotine, and execution orders to make you shed a tear for the royalists as well.

In the rest of the gilded rooms, the display of paintings, maps and models of Paris is too exhaustive to give you an overall picture of the city changing. And unless you have the historical details to hand, it's hard to get intrigued by any one period. Some of the set pieces – the Belle Époque interiors of one of the cafés on the Grands Boulevards and Fouquet the jeweller's shop of the same date – are quite fun, but you can see similar in the real city. That is the problem with this museum – competing with its own subject.

Museums and Galleries

Museums and Galleries

Musée Grévin I

10 bd Montmartre, 9ᵉ (Mº Montmartre). Daily 1–7pm, during school hols 10am–6pm; no admissions after 6pm. 48F, under-14s 34F.

The main Paris waxworks are nothing like as extensive as London's, and only worth it if you are desperate to do something with the kids and can afford to throw money around. The ticket includes a ten-minute conjuring act.

Musée Grévin II

Grand Balcon, Forum des Halles, niveau 1, 1ᵉʳ (Mº/RER Châtelet-Les Halles). Mon–Sat 10.30am–6.45pm, Sun & hols 1–6.30pm. 42F, under-14s 32F.

One up on the wax statue parade of the parent museum, but typically didactic. It shows a series of wax-model scenes of French brilliance at the turn of the century, with automatically opening and closing doors around each montage to prevent you from skipping any part of the voice-over and animation.

Musée de l'Histoire de France

Archives Nationales, 60 rue des Francs-Bourgeois, 3ᵉ (Mº Rambuteau/St-Paul). Wed–Mon 1.45–5.45pm; closed Tues & hols. 15F/10F.

Some of the authentic bits of paper that fill the vaults of the Archives Nationales: wills, edicts, and papal bulls; a medieval English monarch's challenge to his French counterpart to stake his kingdom on a duel; Henry VIII's RSVP to the Field of the Cloth of Gold invite; fragile cross-Channel treaties; Joan of Arc's trial proceedings with a doodled impression of her in the margin; and recent legislation and constitutions. The Revolution section includes the book of samples from which Marie-Antoinette chose her dress each morning, and a Republican children's alphabet where J stands for Jean-Jacques Rousseau and L for labourer. It's scholarly stuff (and no English translations), but the early documents are very pretty, dangling seals and penned in delicate and illegible hands.

Musée de la Marine

Palais de Chaillot, place du Trocadéro, 16ᵉ (Mº Trocadéro). Wed–Sun 10am–6pm. Closed Mon & Tues 45F/25F.

Beautiful models of French ships, ancient and modern, warlike and commercial.

Musée de la Préfecture de Police

1bis rue des Carmes, 5ᵉ (Mº Maubert). Mon–Fri 9am–5pm, Sat 10am–5pm; closed Sun & hols. Free.

The history of the Paris police force, as presented in this collection of uniforms, arms and papers, stops at 1944 and is, as you might expect, all of the "legendary criminals" variety.

Performance arts, literature and sport

Maison de Balzac

47 rue Raynouard, 16ᵉ (Mº Passy/La Muette.) Tues–Sun 10am–5.40pm; closed Mon & hols. 17F/9F.

Contains several portraits and caricatures of the writer and a library of works by him, his contemporaries and his critics. Balzac lived here between 1840 and 1847, but literary grandees seem to share the common fate of not leaving ghosts.

Musée du Cinéma Henri Langlois

Palais de Chaillot (East Wing on river side, pending new palace arrangements), place du Trocadéro, 16ᵉ (Mº Trocadéro). Guided tours only Wed–Sun at 10am, 11am, 2pm, 3pm & 4pm; closed Mon, Tues & hols. 25F.

Plans are afoot for a completely new cinema museum further to stun the poor overwhelmed tourist in Paris. In the meantime, this tour of costumes, sets, cameras, projectors, etc, from magic lanterns to the latest Depardieu performance, ending with a showing of a rare movie from the archives, is a must for *cinéastes*.

Centre Culturel des Halles

Terrasse du Forum des Halles, 101 rue Rambuteau, 1ᵉʳ (Mº/RER Châtelet-Les Halles). Tues–Sun 11.30am–6.30pm; closed Mon & hols. Prices vary.

Temporary exhibitions, events and workshops of poetry, crafts and arts take cover beneath the queasy strictured structures above the Forum: in the **Maison de la Poésie**, **Pavillon des Arts** and **Maison des Ateliers**.

Musée Instrumental

See p.173 for details of opening.

Several thousand musical instruments, dating from the Renaissance onwards and owned by the Paris Conservatory, are waiting to move into the Cité de la Musique in the Parc de la Villette.

Instruments de Musique Mécanique

Impasse Berthaud, 3e (Mº Rambuteau). Sat, Sun & hols only, one-hour guided visits 2–7pm; 25F, under 12s 15F.

Barrel organs, gramophones and automata with demonstrations.

Musée Kwok-On

41 rue des Francs-Bourgeois, 4e (Mº St-Paul/ Rambuteau). Mon–Fri 10am–5.30pm; closed hols. 15F/10F.

Changing exhibitions feature the popular arts of southern Asia – the musical instruments, festival decorations, religious objects, and, most of all, the costumes, puppets, masks and stage models for theatre, in eleven different countries stretching from Japan to Turkey. The collection includes such things as figures for the Indonesian and Indian Theatres of Shadows, Peking Opera costumes and storytellers' scrolls from Bengal. The colour is overwhelming and the unfamiliarity shaming – much recommended.

Musée Adam Mickiewicz

6 quai d'Orléans, 4e (Mº Pont-Marie). Guided tours only Tues, Thurs & Fri at 2pm, 3pm, 4pm & 5pm; closed mid-July to mid-Sept. Free.

A tiny museum commemorating one of the greatest Polish poets, a Romantic and nationalist who came to France in 1832 unable to bear the partitioned non-existence of his homeland. On the first floor, a room is dedicated to another exile and friend of Mickiewicz, **Chopin**. It contains some of the composer's furniture, a few scores, a death mask, and the only surviving daguerreotype of Chopin as a young man.

Musée Édith Piaf

5 rue Créspin-du-Gast, 11e (Mº Ménilmontant/St-Maur). Admission by appointment only:

☎ 43.55.52.72. Mon–Thurs 1–6pm; closed July. Free.

Édith Piaf was not an acquisitive person. The few clothes, letters, toys, paintings and photographs that she left are almost all here, along with every one of the recordings, in a flat lived in by her devoted friend Bernard Marchois. It is he who will show you round and tell you stories about her.

Musée Renan-Scheffer/La Vie Romantique

16 rue Chaptal, 9e (Mº Pigalle/St-Georges). Tues–Sun 10am–5.45pm; closed Mon & hols. 35F/ 25F.

Changing exhibitions focus on the life of intellectuals and literati in the nineteenth century. The permanent collection looks at just one thinker, writer and activist of that century – **George Sand**. Her jewels and trinkets are on show, rather than her manuscripts, but there are some beautiful drawings, by Delacroix, Ingres and Sand herself.

Musée du Sport Français

Parc des Princes, 24 rue du Commandant-Guilbaud (Mº Porte-de-St-Cloud). Mon, Tues, Thurs, Fri & Sun 9.30am–12.30pm & 2–5pm; closed Wed, Sat & hols. 20F/10F.

Books, posters, paintings and sculptures to do with the history of French sport are exhibited here on a rotating basis, along with trophies and boots, caps, racquets and gloves worn by the famous, and the vanity case of the greatest French Wimbledon champion, Suzanne Lenglen.

Maison de Victor-Hugo

6 place des Vosges, 4e (Mº Bastille/Chemin-Vert). Tues–Sun 10am–5.45pm; closed Mon & hols. 17F.

This museum is saved by the fact that Hugo decorated and drew, as well as wrote. Many of his ink drawings are exhibited and there's an extraordinary Japanese dining room he put together for his lover's house. That apart, the usual portraits, manuscripts and memorabilia shed sparse light on the man and his work.

Museums and Galleries

Museums
and Galleries

Science and industry

La Colline de l'Automobile

1 place du Dôme, La Défense (Mº Grande Arche de la Défense). Daily noon–7pm. 36F/30F.

A car museum, with 100 models illuminating developments from the earliest times until the present day.

Palais de la Découverte

Grand Palais, av Franklin-D-Roosevelt, 8e (Mº Champs-Elysées-Clemenceau/Franklin-D-Roosevelt). Tues–Sat 9.30am–6pm, Sun & hols 10am–7pm; closed Mon. 22F/11F.

This, the old science museum, has brightened itself up considerably since the Cité des Sciences came on the scene. It can't really compete but it does have plenty of interactive exhibits, some very good temporary exhibitions, and an excellent planetarium (15F/10F supplement; check *Pariscope* and co. for times).

Musée Branly

21 rue d'Assas, 6e (Mº St-Placide). Mon–Fri 9am–noon & 2–5pm; closed July & Aug. By appointment only, ☎49.54.52.00. Free.

In the 1890s Marconi used Branly's invention of an electric wave detector – the first coherer – to set up the startling system of communication which didn't need wires. The coherer in question is exhibited along with other pieces from the physicist's experiments.

Musée de la Contrefaçon

16 rue de la Faisanderie, 16º (Mº Porte-Dauphine). Mon & Wed 2–4.30pm, Fri 9.30am–noon; closed Tues, Thurs & weekends. Free.

One of the odder ones – examples of imitation products, labels and brand marks trying to pass off as the "genuine article".

Muséum d'Histoire Naturelle

Jardin des Plantes, 57 rue Cuvier, 5e (Mº Austerlitz/Jussieu).

Entomologie *Mon & Wed–Fri 2–5pm, 12F/8F;* **Paléontologie** *Wed–Sun 10am–5pm, 25F/15F;* **Minérologie** *Wed–Sun 10am–5pm, 25F/15F;* **Paléobotanique** *Sat & Sun April–Sept 11am–6pm, 15F/10F;* **Evolution** *10am–6pm, Thurs till 10pm, 40F/30F; disabled access to most areas.*

The four musty old galleries have been upstaged by **La Galerie d'Évolution** in the old Galerie de Zoologie overlooking rue Geffroy-St-Hilaire. The first of its kind in the world, it reveals the diversity of species and their habitats, the history and science of evolution, and the relations between human beings and nature. And all that within a secular cathedral of glass and steel contemporary with the Eiffel Tower.

Musée Pasteur

Institute Pasteur, 25 rue du Docteur-Roux, 7e (Mº Volontaires/Pasteur); Mon–Fri 2–5.30pm; closed weekends & Aug. 11F/8F; pass needed to enter the building – available from the office opposite.

Guided tours (English version available) of the apartment, scientific souvenirs and Byzantine-style mausoleum of Dr Pasteur, the great nineteenth-century chemist-biologist who created the science of microbiology by discovering how fermentation worked (hence the term "pasteurization"). The main nonscientific interest in the museum is in seeing the sombre interior decoration (plus innovative plumbing) of the nineteenth-century Parisian middleclass.

Musée de la Poste

34 bd de Vaugirard, 15e (Mº Montparnasse). Mon–Sat 10am–6pm; closed Sun & hols. 25F/12.50F.

Not just stamps, though plenty of those. Also the history of sending messages, from the earliest times to the present.

Musée de Radio-France

116 av du Président-Kennedy, 16e (Mº Passy/Ranelagh/Mirabeau). Mon–Sat guided visits at 10.30am, 11.30am, 2.30pm, 3.30pm, 4.30pm; closed Sun & hols. 14F/7F.

A wide assortment of models, machines and documents, covering the history of broadcasting, and housed in the national TV and radio building.

Musée de la Serrure Bricard

Hôtel Libéral-Bruand, 1 rue de la Perle, 3e (Mº Chemin-Vert/Rambuteau). Mon–Fri 2–5pm; closed Sat, Sun & holidays. 15F.

This collection of elaborate and artistic locks throughout the ages includes the

Napoleonic fittings for his palace doors (the one for the Tuileries bashed in by revolutionaries), locks that trapped your hand or shot your head off if you tried a false key, and a seventeenth-century masterpiece made by a craftsman under lock and key for four years. The rest of the exhibits are pretty boring, though the setting in a Marais mansion is some compensation.

Musée National des Techniques

292 rue St-Martin, 3e (Mo Réaumur-Sébastopol/ Arts-et-Métiers). Tues–Sun 10am–5.30pm; closed Mon & hols. Free while renovation works are in progress.

Until 1996, only Lavoisier's laboratory and the astronomy and clock rooms are open while the huge early Gothic chapel is restored and all the other museum spaces revamped.

Museums
and Galleries

A Day-Tripper's Guide to Outlying Museums

Chapter 20, *Day Trips from Paris*, includes details of several more museums within a day's excursion from central Paris. Among the more interesting are:

Musée d'Art et d'Histoire at St-Denis. Local archeology and Commune documents; p.355.

Musée Condé and **Musée Vivant du Cheval** at Chantilly. Live horses and lots of paraphernalia, at the château which also contains the magnificent medieval *Très Riches Heures du Duc de Berry*; p.362.

Musée de l'Air et de l'Espace at Le Bourget. Planes and spacecraft from Lindbergh to Apollo 13 displayed in Paris' original airport; p.364.

Musée des Antiquités Nationales at St-Germain-en-Laye. Evocative archeological displays, from cave-dwellers onwards; p.365.

Musée de l'Île de France at Sceaux. Local history, from kings to artists; p.365.

Musée National de la Céramique at Sèvres. Ceramics from all over the world as well as the local stuff; p.366.

Chapter 15

Daytime Amusements and Sports

For details on the cinemas of Paris, see Chapter 19.

When it's cold and wet, and you've had enough of peering at museums, monuments and the dripping panes of shop fronts and café vistas, don't despair or retreat back to your hotel. There are saunas to soak in, roller- and ice-skating rinks to fall on, music halls inviting you to dance the tango, bowling alleys, billiards, swimming pools and gyms. You can take advantage of the Parisian love of high technology to call up a choice of music and videos on CD-Rom or examine, in old-fashioned style, obscure picture books in medieval libraries.

If you're feeling brave, you could also change your hairstyle, indulge in a total body tonic, take up yoga or take your first steps as a ballerina. You could even learn how to concoct sublime French dishes at a professional cookery school. And when the weather isn't so bad, you can go for a ride in a boat or perhaps even a helicopter if you've had a successful flutter on the horses in the Bois de Boulogne.

Paris' range of **sports**, both for spectators and participants, is also outlined below. For additional possibilities, check *L'Officiel des Spectacles* (the best of the listings magazines for sports facilities) or, to see which major sporting events may be taking place during your stay, *L'Équipe*, the daily sports newspaper. The highlight of the calendar is, of course, the triumphal arrival of cycling's Tour de France in July.

Boat trips, balloon and heli rides

Seeing Paris by boat is one of the city's most popular and durable tourist experiences – and a lot of fun, if the mood grabs you. Seeing it from the air is even better.

Bateaux-Mouches

From the *quais* or the bridges, after the night has fallen, the sudden appearance of a bulging *Bateau-Mouche*, blaring its multilingual commentaries and dazzling with its floodlights, can come as a nasty shock to anyone indulging in romantic contemplations. But one way of avoiding the ugly sight of these hulking hulls is to get on one yourself. You may not be able to escape the trite narration, but the evening rides certainly give a superb and very glamorous close-up view of the classic Seine-side buildings.

Bateaux-Mouches start from the *Embarcadère du Pont de l'Alma* on the right bank in the 8e, Mº Alma-Marceau (reservations ☎ 42.25.96.10, information ☎ 40.76.99.99). The rides, which usually last between an hour and an hour and a quarter, depart every half-hour from 10am until noon and from 2pm until 11pm; winter departures at 11am, 2.30, 4 and 9pm only (40F, under-16s 20F; after 8pm 50F/20F). Make sure you avoid the outrageously priced lunch and dinner trips, for which "correct" dress is mandatory. The main **competitors** to the *Bateaux-Mouches* are *Bateaux Parisiens*, *Bateaux-Vedettes de Paris* and *Bateaux-Vedettes du Pont Neuf*. They're all much of a muchness, and can be found detailed in *Pariscope* etc under *Promenades*.

One alternative way of riding on the Seine, which spares you the commentaries, is the *Batobus*, a river transport system operating from April to September between port de la Bourdonnais by the Eiffel Tower and quai de l'Hôtel-de-Ville, stopping at port de Solférino (by the Musée d'Orsay), quai Malaquais (by the Pont des Arts, the footbridge to the Louvre) and quai de Montebello (by Notre-Dame). The service runs from 10am until 7pm, about every three-quarters of an hour, and costs 12F per stop or 60F for a day pass.

Canal trips

Less overtly tourist fodder than the *bateaux-mouches* and their clones are the **canal boat trips**. *Canauxrama* (reservations ☎ 42.39.15.00) chugs up and down between the Port de l'Arsenal (opposite 50 bd de la Bastille, 12e; Mº Bastille) and the Bassin de la Villette (13bis quai de la Loire, 19e; Mº Jaurès) on the Canal St-Martin. Departs every day at 9.15am and 2.45pm from La Villette and at 9.45am and 2.30pm from the Bastille. At the Bastille end is a long tunnel from which you don't surface till the 10e *arrondissement*. The ride lasts three hours – not a bad bargain for 75F (students 60F, under 12s 45F, under 6s free; no reductions weekends or holiday afternoons). The company also runs day trips along the Canal de l'Ourcq, west as far as Meaux, with a coach back (for 200F).

A more stylish vessel for exploring the canal is the **catamaran** of *Paris-Canal*, with trips between the Musée d'Orsay (quai Anatole-France by the Pont Solférino, 7e; Mº Solférino) and the Parc de la Villette (Park Information Centre on the canal by the bridge between the Grande Salle and the Cité des Sciences, 19e; Mº Porte-de-Pantin), which also last three hours. The catamaran departs from the Musée d'Orsay at 9.30am daily, and

2.25pm Saturday and Sunday; Parc de la Villette departures are 2.30pm daily, and 10am Saturday and Sunday; 90F, 12–25-year-olds 70F (except Sunday and holiday afternoons), 6–12-year-olds 55F; reservations ☎ 42.40.96.97. One Saturday a month the company runs night-time cruises with a live New Orleans jazz band (250F per person, includes drinks).

Paris by helicopter or balloon

Having seen Paris from the water, the next step up is Paris from the air. A helicopter tour above all the city's sights is somewhat prohibitive, but if whirly-gig rides turn you on as much or more than a four-star meal or a stalls seat at the theatre, then a quick loop around La Défense is on. The two companies operating are *Héli-France* (Mon–Fri 8am–8pm, Sat & Sun 9am–6pm; ☎ 45.54.95.11) and *Hélicap* (Mon–Fri 9am–7pm; ☎ 45.57.75.51), both at the *Héliport de Paris*, 4 av de la Porte-de-Sèvres, 15e; Mº Balard. A twenty-minute trip will set you back about 550F per person.

For an even classier and far more extravagant overview, how about going up in a **balloon**? *Air Ballon Communication*, 12 rue Bonaparte, 6e (☎ 43.29.14.13), can oblige.

Afternoon tangos

One pastime to fill the afternoon hours that might not cross your mind is a *bal musette*. The dance halls where they take place were the between-the-wars solution in the down-and-out parts of *Gay Paree* to depression, dole and the demise of the Popular Front. They crossed social scales, too, with film stars and jaded aristocrats coming to indulge in a bit of rough. Three or four generations of owners later, only **Balajo** remains in the rue de Lappe, still attracting a partially working-class clientele, and running both afternoon and evening sessions. Turn up on a Monday afternoon and you'll find people dancing to abandon, cheek-to-cheek, couple squashed against couple. Their clothes aren't smart, their French isn't academy, men dance with women, and everyone drinks.

Daytime Amusements and Sports

Daytime Amusements and Sports

For details of evening activities at Balajo *and* Chez Gégène, *see p.325.*

Less conducive to participation, but potentially entertaining, are the **tea dances**, a much more genteel or camp experience than the *bals musettes*.

Balajo, 9 rue de Lappe, 11e (Mº Bastille). Open in the afternoon Mon, Fri & Sat 3–6.30pm, before reopening at 10pm for the evening session. The original venue. Music, all recorded, is a mixture of waltz, tango, java, disco and rock. Admission price is around 30F.

Chez Gégène, 162bis quai de Polangis, Joinville-Le-Pont; ☎48.83.29.43 (*RER* Joinville-Le-Pont). Just across the Marne from the Bois de Vincennes. Midday *bals musettes* at weekends from March to October, but ring first to check. High-class rétro dancing in a 1900-style *guinguette*.

La Coupole, 102 bd Montparnasse, 14e. ☎43.20.14.20 (Mº Vavin). Sat, Sun & holidays 3–7pm.

La Java, 105 rue du Faubourg-du-Temple, 10e (Mº Belleville). Sun 2–7pm (55F) for a tea dance in the oldest of the dance halls. *La Java* is being renovated; times and prices may change.

Le New-Look, 40 rue des Blancs-Manteaux, 4e. ☎42.71.03.29 (Mº Rambuteau). Sun 5–11pm (30F). Lesbian tea dance in one of the Marais' gay clubs.

Retro République, 23 rue du Faubourg du Temple, 10e (Mº République). Daily 2–6.30pm, weekday 30F including drink.

Le Rex Club, 5 bd Poissonnière, 2e. ☎42.36.10.96 (Mº Montmartre). Tues–Sat 2–7pm. Tangos etc for couples of all ages at one of the city's best-known rock venues.

Le Palace, 8 rue du Faubourg-Montmartre, 9e. ☎42.46.10.87 (Mº Rue Montmartre). Gay tea dance every Sunday afternoon, 5pm onwards; entry 40F before 6pm, 69F after; drinks from 50F.

Musical and visual discoveries

If you want, you can listen to CDs or watch videos all day in public places. If you're not feeling well and your hotel room has a video, you can call up *Reels on Wheels* for English videos plus Indian or Tex-Mex food (☎40.38.39.83 for north of the river; ☎45.67.64.99 for south). Libraries can offer unexpected delights, too, and you don't have to pay to browse through any of the municipal collections.

FNAC, 4 place de la Bastille, 11e (Mº Bastille). Mon-Sat 10am–8pm; Wed and Fri until 10pm. FNAC's newest music shop has touch-screen access to a limited but interesting selection of CDs. Once you've donned the headphones, touch the square on the screen reading "*Touchez l'écran*". If you then touch first "*Répérages FNAC*", then "*Variétés Françaises*", then "*Rock*", you'll end up with a list of recent French rock recordings which you can listen to, adjusting the volume or flicking forwards by touching arrows. "*Sommaire*" takes you back to the previous list. Of course you can choose medieval church music, jazz or Pierre Boulez instead – it's very simple and when the shop isn't crowded you can spend as long as you like for free.

Jean Paul Gaultier (Galerie Vivienne, 2e; Mº Bourse) and **Nina Ricci** (39 av Montaigne, 8e; Mº Alma-Marceau) both have catwalk videos, visible in the case of *JPG* from peepholes in the *passage* as well as in the shop.

Vidéothèque de Paris, 2 Grande Gallerie, Porte St-Eustache, Forum des Halles, 1er (*RER* Châtelet-Les Halles). (Information ☎44.76.63.44.) Tues–Sun 12.30–8.30pm. Even more sophisticated than FNAC. For 30F/25F you can watch any of the four videos or films screened each day, and, in the *Salle Pierre Emmanuel*, make your own selection from 4000 film clips, newsreel footage, commercials, documentaries, soaps etc from 1896 to the present day. All the material is connected to Paris in some way, and you can make your choice – on your individual screen and keyboard – via a Paris place-name, an actor, a director, a date and so on. Don't be put off by the laboratory atmosphere or by the idea that this can't be for just anyone to play with. It is, and there are instructions in English at the desk and a friendly "librarian" to help you out. Once you're in the complex you can go back and forth between the projection rooms, the *Salle Pierre Emmanuel* and a café, open 12.30–6pm.

Virgin Megastore, 52 av des Champs-Elysées, 8e (Mº George V). Mon–Thurs 10am–midnight, Fri & Sat 10am–1pm. No sophisticated computers here: you just grab the headphones of whichever one of the hundred hooked-up CDs takes your fancy, or the headphones for one of the feature film videos being screened, and pretend you're on a transatlantic flight.

Libraries

Bibliothèque André-Malraux, 78 bd Raspail, 6e (Mº Rennes). Books on the cinema.

Bibliothèque des Arts Graphiques, Mairie, 78 rue Bonaparte, 6e (Mº St-Sulpice). Specializes in the history of book design and production.

Bibliothèque Forney, Hôtel de Sens, 1 rue du Figuier, 4e (Mº Pont-Marie). Medieval building filled with volumes on fine and applied arts.

Bibliothèque Publique d'Information (BPI), 2nd floor, Centre Pompidou (Beaubourg), 4e (Mº Rambuteau). Everything, including foreign newspapers, and a free language learning lab if you feel like brushing up on your French, Mandarin or Euskara.

The Body Beautiful

Parisians are, predictably, keen on twisting, stretching and straining muscles, while competing in style rather than scores. Aerobics, dance workouts and anti-stress fitness programmes are big business, along with the other well-established trends of yoga, tai-chi and martial arts.

Fitness venues

Many fitness club activities are organized in courses or involve a minimum month's or year's subscription (the big gym chains like *Garden Gym* and *Gymnase Club* are financially prohibitive, and even the exceptions are costly enough to excuse you. But if your last meal has left you feeling you need it, here are some options.

Académie de Danse à Magenta, 62 bd Magenta, 10e (Mº Gare-de-l'Est). All types of dance and a free trial.

Centre de Danse du Marais, 41 rue du Temple, 4e. ☎42.77.58.19 (Mº Hôtel-de-Ville). 9am–9pm. You can try out rock 'n 'roll, folkloric dance classes from the East, tap-dancing, modern dance, physical expression or flamenco. Expect to pay around 70F per session.

Centre de Danse de Paris, Salle Pleyel, 252 rue du Faubourg-St-Honoré, 8e (Mº

Getting to grips with gastronomy

Most cookery courses in the capital are designed for aspiring pros, cost an arm and a leg, and last several weeks, if not months. But you can watch demonstrations at *Le Cordon Bleu* and, if it happens to be November or December, get some hands-on experience chez *Le Comptoir Corrézien*.

Le Cordon Bleu
8 rue Léon-Delhomme, 15e
Mº Vaugirard   ☎48.56.06.06
Mon–Fri 9am–7pm.

Full-time courses here cost around 30,000F a term, but for a mere 140F you can spend two and a half hours watching a *grand chef* do the business (English translations sometimes available). Demonstration programmes vary, so you need to check with the school and reserve a place.

Le Comptoir Corrézien
8 rue des Volontaires, 15e
Mº Volontaires   ☎47.83.52.97
Tues–Sat 9am–1.30pm & 3.30–8pm, Mon 3.30–8pm.

This is a shop selling regional duck, goose and wild mushroom concoctions, whose proprietor, Chantal Larnaudie, runs two-hour courses for 150F, Tuesdays, Thursdays and Fridays during November and December. Check with the shop for times, and to book.

Daytime Amusements and Sports

Étoile–Charles-de-Gaulle/Ternes). Mon–Sat 8.45am–8pm. Offers professional classes in contemporary dance and ballet, including some for beginners. Costs are around 70F per session.

Centre Inter Sivananda de Yoga Vedanta, 123 bd de Sebastopol, 2e.☎ 40.26.77.49 (Mº Strasbourg-St-Denis). 11am–9.30pm. First lesson is free.

Espace Vit'Halles, place Beaubourg, 48 rue Rambuteau, 3e. ☎ 42.77.21.71 (RER Châtelet-Les Halles). Mon–Fri 9am–10pm, Sat 11am–7pm, Sun 11am–3pm. Back across boulevard Sebastopol, Vit'Halles charges 150F, for which fanatics can spend a day doing every kind of tendon-shattering gyration. It's divided into four "work zones:" the parquet, gym floor, body-building room, and the multi-gym room. Détente – relaxation – is also provided for with a sauna, hammam, solarium and diet bar. For 80F you can have access to these and one floor session.

Swimming

For straightforward exercise, and for around 20F, you can go swimming in any of Paris' **municipal baths**, but check first in L'Officiel des Spectacles for opening times (under Activités Sportives) as varying hours are given over to schools and clubs. These are among the best:

Les Amiraux, 6 rue Hermann-Lachapelle, 18e (Mº Simplon). Municipal pool.

Armand-Massard, 66 bd Montparnasse, 15e (Mº Vavin). Municipal pool.

Bernard-Lafay, 79 rue de la Jonquière, 17e (Mº Guy-Moquet). Municipal pool.

Butte aux Cailles, 5 place Verlaine, 13e (Mº Place-d'Italie). Housed in a 1920s brick building with an Art Déco ceiling, recently spruced up. One of the pleasantest swims in the city.

Château-Landon, 31 rue du Château-Landon, 10e (Mº Château-Landon). Municipal pool.

Henry-de-Montherlant, 32 bd Lannes, 16e (Mº Porte-Dauphine). Two pools, a terrace for sunbathing, a solarium, and the Bois de Boulogne close by. Under 10F.

Jean Taris, 16 rue de Thouin, 5e (Mº Cardinal-Lemoine). An unchlorinated pool in the centre of the Latin Quarter and a student favourite.

Georges-Vallerey Tourelles, 148 av Gambetta, 20e (Mº St-Fargeau). Municipal pool.

Piscine Susanne Berlioux/Les Halles, 10 place de la Rotonde, niveau 3, Porte du Jour, Forum des Halles, 1er (RER Châtelet-Les Halles). A 50m pool with a vaulted concrete ceiling and a glass wall looking through to the tropical garden.

Privately run pools

Non-municipal pools are usually twice as expensive or more, but some have their attractions.

Aquaboulevard, 4 rue Louis-Armand, 15e. ☎ 40.60.10.00 (Mº Balard/RER Boulevard-Victor). Daily 8am–midnight. An American-style vast multisports complex. The pool has wave machines and water slides, and costs 68F weekdays and 75F weekends (49F/55F for children) for a four-hour session.

Deligny, 25 quai Anatole-France, 7e (Mº Chambre-des-Députés). The ultimate Parisian pool; crowded but an amusing, if expensive, spectacle of rich bodies sunning themselves on the vast deck above the Seine. 50F, students 45F.

Molitor, 2–8 av de la Porte-Molitor (Mº Porte-d'Auteuil). For outside bathing, try this 1930s pool on the edge of the Bois de Boulogne.

Pontoise, 19 rue de Pontoise, 5e (Mº Maubert-Mutualité). Features night sessions from 9pm until midnight Mon–Thurs, and sometimes nude swimming. Rates under 20F.

Roger-Le Gall, 34 bd Carnot, 12e (Mº Porte-de-Vincennes). Most of the extras are reserved for club members but anyone can swim in the pool (covered in winter and open in summer).

Hairdressing salons

The range is as wide – style-wise and price-wise – as you'd expect in this supremely fashion-conscious city.

Alexandre, for women at 3 av Matignon, 8ᵉ. ☎42.25.57.90 (Mᵒ Franklin-Roosevelt). Also for men at 29 rue Marbeuf, 8e. ☎42.25.29.41 (Mᵒ Alma-Marceau). The long-established haut-coiffeur of Paris could be an intimidating experience unless you're wearing Yves St-Laurent or Gaultier. Wash-cut-and-blow-dries for women are not that expensive considering the *clientèle* – around 450F – but the men's salon, with saunas, massage, manicure, pedicure, etc, would cost you your beautified arm and leg.

Desfossé, 19 av Matignon, 8ᵉ. ☎43.59.95.13 (Mᵒ St-Philippe-du-Roule). Men can spend three hours having their hair, hands, feet and skin attended to at this equally upmarket address – hair 230F, full works 375F.

Jacques Dessange, 37 av Franklin-Roosevelt, 8ᵉ. ☎43.59.31.31 (Mᵒ Franklin-Roosevelt). And at 13 other addresses. Less classic, but still very smart, this is Charlotte Rampling's favourite cutter; around 450F for wash, cut and blow-dry.

Jean-Marc Maniatis, 35 rue de Sèvres, 6ᵉ. ☎45.44.16.39 (Mᵒ Sèvres-Babylone). Younger and less established beauties come here for the renowned and meticulous cutting. You can have a free cut by a trainee – if they like the look of your hair. Pop in and find out.

Cheaper cuts – and schools

The more run-of-the-mill Paris hairdressers may be more appealing. Around Les Halles, the Bastille and St-Germain many salons go for maximum visibility, so you can watch what's being done and take your pick. It's always a gamble anyway, and it could be fun trying out your French in the intimate trivial chit-chat that all hairdressers insist on. Book a couple of days in advance.

Various salons or schools offer free wash-cut-and-blow-dries to those bold enough to act as guinea-pigs for new cuts or inexperienced trainees. These include the following:

Jean-Louis Déforges Académie, 71 bd Richard-Lenoir, 11ᵉ. ☎43.55.56.67 (Mᵒ Richard-Lenoir). Monsieur Déforges may be wandering around criticizing his train-

ees, in which case your cut will take much longer. Around 45F.

Jean-Louis David, 5 rue Cambon, 1ᵉʳ. ☎42.97.51.71 (Mᵒ Concorde). You need to go to the salon to make an appointment for a free cut by a trainee. There are other branches at 27 rue de la Ferronnerie, 1ᵉʳ; 160bis rue du Temple, 3ᵉ; 58 rue St-Antoine, 4ᵉ; 7 rue Monge, 5ᵉ; and 82 rue de Rennes, 6ᵉ, where you can go for a regular cut – no appointments, just turn up and wait. Prices around 135F for women and 75F for men. Open Tues–Sat 10am–7pm.

École Jacques Dessange, 24 rue St-Augustin, 2ᵉ. ☎47.42.24.73 (Mᵒ 4-Septembre). Mon–Wed, by appointment. 35F.

Jean-Marc Maniatis, 35 rue de Sèvres, 6ᵉ. ☎45.44.16.39 (Mᵒ Sèvres-Babylone). See above.

Hammams

A steam bath and a massage may be as necessary after a trip to the Louvre as after intentional physical exercise. The *hammams*, or Turkish baths, are one of the unexpected delights of Paris. Much more luxurious than the standard Swedish sauna, these are places to linger and chat.

Les Bains d'Odessa, 5 rue d'Odessa, 14ᵉ. ☎43.20.91.21 (Mᵒ Montparnasse). Women: Mon & Thurs–Sat 10.30am–9pm; men: Mon, Tues & Thurs–Sat 9.30am–9pm. 83F for steambath and sauna; jacuzzi 120F, massage 110F. The oldest *hammam* in the city, which you reach through a courtyard decorated with shells and cupids.

Cleopatra Club, 53 bd de Belleville, 11ᵉ. ☎43.57.34.32 (Mᵒ Belleville). Tues–Sun 10am–6pm. Women only. 70F for a sauna, 130F for massage. Very relaxed hammam with beautiful tiling and mint tea served.

Hammam de la Mosquée, 39 rue Geoffroy-St-Hilaire, 5ᵉ. ☎43.31.18.14 (Mᵒ Censier-Daubenton). Women: Mon & Wed 11am–8pm, Thurs 11am–9pm, Sat 10am–8pm; men: Fri 11am–8pm & Sun 10am–8pm; closed Aug. You can order

Daytime Amusements and Sports

mint tea and honey cakes after your baths, around a fountain in a marble and cedar-wood-covered courtyard. It's very good value for 65F (massage 50F extra) and a very unintimidating experience if you've never taken a public bath before.

Participatory sports

Ice- and roller-skating, skateboarding, jogging, bowling, billiards, *boules* – it's all here to be enjoyed.

Skating and skateboarding

If it's your ankles and shock absorbers you want to exercise, get on the ice at the city's only **ice rink**. The *Patinoire des Buttes-Chaumont* (30 rue Edouard-Pailleron, 19e; ☎42.08.72.20; Mº Bolivar) is open Mon, Tues, Thurs 3–9pm; Wed 10am–9pm; Fri 3pm–midnight; Sat 10am–midnight; Sun 10am–6pm. Admission is 25F, 20F for children, plus 16F for skate rental.

Roller-skating has a special disco rink at *La Main Jaune* (pl de la Porte-de-Champerret, 17e; Mº Champerret) Wed, Sat & Sun 2.30–7pm, 40F plus 15F skate rental. Fri & Sat disco sessions 10pm–dawn; 70F plus 15F skate rental.

The main official **outdoor roller-skating and skateboarding** arena is the concourse of the Palais de Chaillot (Mº Trocadéro), though Les Halles (around the Fontaine des Innocents) and the Beaubourg piazza are both equally popular.

Jogging – and the marathon

The **Paris Marathon** is held in May over a route from place de la Concorde to Vincennes. If you want to join in and need details and equipment, the best place for information is a shop owned by a dedicated marathon runner, *Marathon* (29 rue de Chazelles, 17e; ☎42.27.48.18; Mº Monceau). A shorter race, *Les 20km de Paris*, takes place mid-October and begins and ends at the Eiffel Tower.

If you feel compelled to **run or jog** by yourself, take great care with the traffic. The Jardin du Luxembourg, Tuileries and Champs de Mars, which are particularly popular with Parisian joggers, all provide decent, varied runs, and are more or less

flat. If you want to run hills, head for the Parc des Buttes-Chaumont in the 19e or Parc Montsouris in the 14e for plenty of suitably punishing gradients. If you have easy access to them, the Bois de Boulogne and the Bois de Vincennes are the largest open spaces, but very cut through with roads.

Cycling

Very few people cycle in Paris, with good reason, although in these days of traffic congestion their numbers are increasing. There are several outlets for renting bikes, as well as touring clubs which organize day outings. You can usually rent by the hour, the day, the weekend or for a week. Prices vary depending on the type of bike, but are usually around 25–30F per hour and up to 400F for the week. You will need a credit card or at least 2000F by way of a deposit.

Cycle rental

Bois de Boulogne near the Porte de Sablons entrance (Mº Les Sablons). For rides through the wood.

Cycles Laurent, 9 bd Voltaire, 11e (Mº République/Oberkampf). Mon–Sat 10am–7pm.

Mountain Bike Trip, 6 place Étienne-Pernet, 15e. ☎48.42.57.87 (Mº Félix-Faure). 90F a day.

Paris by Cycle, 78 rue de l'Ouest, 14e (Mº Gaîté/Pernety). Mon–Fri 8.30am–7.30pm.

Paris-Vélo, 2 rue du Fer-à-Moulin, 5e (Mº Gobelins). Mon–Sat 10am–12.30pm & 2–7pm.

Cycle trips

Paris by Cycle and *Mountain Bike Trip* (see above) both arrange outings. The latter run a daily discovering-Paris-by-bike tour in English, starting at 11am and returning around 5pm, with a lunch stop in the Quartier Latin. The cost, which includes bike rental, guide and insurance, is 118F. The following specialist companies are also worth contacting.

Bicy-Club, 8 place de la Porte-de-Champerret. ☎47.66.55.92 (Mº Porte-de-Champerret). Weekdays only. Arranges assorted expeditions into the outlying countryside.

Vélonature, 5 rue St-Victor, 5ᵉ. ☎ 40.46.87.65 (Mᵒ Cardinal Lemoine/Maubert-Mutualité). Very friendly team organizing cycling trips everywhere from the Himalayas to the Fôret de Fontainebleau. Sunday trips out to Versailles, Chantilly, Rambouillet, Fontainebleau etc cost between 150F and 210F, including lunch but not bike rental (120F extra).

Bowling alleys

There's nothing particularly Parisian about bowling alleys, but they exist and they're popular, should the urge to scuttle skittles take you. Prices vary between 16F and 20F a session, double where you have to rent shoes, and more at weekends.

Bowling de Montparnasse, 25 rue Commandant-Mouchotte, 14ᵉ. ☎ 43.21.61.32 (Mᵒ Montparnasse-Bienvenue). Daily 10am–2am. A complex with sixteen lanes. Entertainment is complete, with bar, brasserie, pool tables and video games.

Bowling-Académie de Billard, 66 av d'Ivry, 13ᵉ. ☎ 45.86.55.52 (Mᵒ Tolbiac). Daily 2pm–2am. Entrance by escalators to Olympiades. Attracts an active and young clientele to roll the balls in Chinatown. With bar billiards and pool alongside.

Bowling Mouffetard, Centre-Commercial Mouffetard-Monge, 73 rue Mouffetard, 5ᵉ. ☎ 43.31.09.35 (Mᵒ Monge). Daily 11am–2am. The cheapest in town, well favoured by students, with bar and billiards.

Bowling de Paris, Jardin d'Acclimatation, Bois de Boulogne. ☎ 40.67.94.00 (Mᵒ Sablons). Daily 11am–2am. Popular with the chic types west of town.

Billiards

Billiards, unlike bowling, is an original and ancient French game played with three balls and no pockets. Pool, or American billiards as the French call it, is also played. If you want to watch or try your hand (for around 50F per hour plus deposits of around 100F), head for one of the following:

Académie de Clichy-Montmartre, 84 rue de Clichy, 9ᵉ (Mᵒ Clichy). Daily 1.30–11.30pm. The chicest billiard hall in Europe, where the players look like they've stepped out of a 1940s movie (or a *Men in Vogue* ad) and the décor is all ancient gilded mirrors, high ceilings and panelled walls.

Académie de Paris, 47 av de Wagram, 17ᵉ (Mᵒ Ternes). Mon–Fri 12.30–11pm, Sat & Sun 2–11pm.

Blue-Billard, 111 rue St-Maur, 11ᵉ (Mᵒ Parmentier). Daily 5pm–2am. Cocktails, chess and backgammon as well as billiards, in arty-intellectual hang-out close to Belleville.

Bowling-Académie de Billard, 66 av d'Ivry, 13ᵉ (Mᵒ Tolbiac). Daily 2pm–2am. See above.

Bowling Mouffetard, 73 rue Mouffetard, 5ᵉ (Mᵒ Monge). See above.

Salle des Billards des Halles, niveau 2, Porte du Jour, Forum des Halles, 1ᵉʳ (*RER* Châtelet-Les Halles). Members only, but you can watch experts play; Mon–Fri noon–8pm, Sat noon–8pm, Sun 1–8pm.

Boules

The classic French game involving balls, *boules* or *pétanque*, is best performed (or watched) at the *Arènes de Lutèce* (see p.111) and the Bois de Vincennes. On balmy summer evenings you're likely to see it played in any of the city's parks and gardens.

Rock climbing

The best training wall in Paris is at the *Centre Sportif Poissonnier*, 2 rue Jean-Cocteau, 18ᵉ.(☎ 42.51.24.68 (Mᵒ Porte-de-Clignancourt). It's 23m high, with corridors and chimneys. There's another wall in *Aquaboulevard* (see below) and one for kids in the sports and camping shop, *Au Vieux Campeur*, in rue des Écoles (see Chapter 16).

Other sports

Tennis, squash, golf, skiing on artificial slopes, archery, canoeing, fishing, windsurfing, water-skiing and parachuting –

Daytime Amusements and Sports

Daytime Amusements and Sports

you name it, you can do it, in or around the city. Whether you'll want to spend the time and money on booking and renting equipment is another matter. If you're determined, you'll find some details in *L'Officiel des Spectacles* etc, or you can ring *Allo Sports* on ☎42.76.54.54 (Mon–Fri 10.30am–5pm) or pay a visit to the *Direction Jeunesse et Sports* (25 bd Bourdon, 4e; Mº Bastille; Mon–Fri 10am–5.30pm). These are both municipal outfits, so the places they have listed will all be subsidized and cheapish.

Of the private clubs and complexes, *Aquaboulevard*, 4 rue Louis-Armand, 15e (Mº Balard/RER Boulevard Victor) is the newest and biggest, with squash and tennis courts, a climbing wall, golf tees, aquatic diversions, *hammams*, dance floors, shops, restaurants and other money-extracting paraphernalia. Some sample prices are: tennis 150–200F per hour; squash 60F per half-hour.

> One sport that is not really worth trying in Paris is **horse-riding**. You need to have all the gear with you and a licence, the *Carte Nationale de Cavalier*, before you can mount.

Spectator sports

Paris' best football team, *Paris St-Germain*, are currently resurgent in the French league, and the capital retains a special status, too, in the rugby, cycling and tennis worlds. Horse racing is as serious a pursuit as in Britain or North America.

Cycling

The biggest event of the French sporting year is the grand finale of the *Tour de France*, which ends in a sweep along the Champs-Élysées in the third week of July. In theory the last day of the race is a competitive time-trial, but most years this amounts to a triumphal procession, the overall winner of the *Tour* having long since been determined. Only very rarely does Paris witness memorable scenes such as those of 1989, when American Greg Lemond snatched the coveted *mail-*

lot jaune (the winner's yellow jersey) on the final day.

Football and rugby

The *Parc des Princes* (24 rue du Commandant-Guilbaud, 16e; ☎40.71.91.91 or ☎48.74.84.75; Mº Porte-de-St-Cloud) is the capital's main stadium for both rugby union and football events, and home ground to the first-division Paris football team *Paris-SG (St-Germain)* and the rugby champions, *Le Racing*.

Tennis

The French equivalent of Britain's Wimbledon, *Roland-Garros*, lies between the Parc des Princes and the Bois de Boulogne, with the ace address of 2 av Gordon-Bennett, 16e (☎47.43.00.47; Mº Porte-d'Auteuil). The French Tennis Open, one of the four major events which together comprise the Grand Slam, takes place in the last week of May and first week of June, and tickets need to be reserved before February. A few are sold each day, but only for the unseeded matches. Unlike Wimbledon, you can't get near the main courts once inside the turnstiles.

Athletics and other sports

The *Palais des Omnisports Paris-Bercy (POPB)* at 8 bd Bercy, 12e (☎43.42.01.23) hosts all manner of sporting events, including athletics, cycling, handball, dressage and show-jumping, ice hockey, ballroom dancing, judo and motorcross. Keep an eye on the sports pages of the newspapers (except *Le Monde*, which has no sports coverage at all) and you might find something on that interests you. The complex holds 17,000 people, so you've a fair chance of getting a ticket at the door, championships excepted.

Horse racing

Being a spectator at a horse race could make a healthy change from looking at art treasures. If you want to fathom the **betting system**, any bar or café with the letters *PMU* will take your money on a three-horse bet, known as *le tiercé*. The

biggest races are the *Prix de la République* and the *Grand Prix de L'Arc de Triomphe* on the first and last Sundays in October at Auteuil and Longchamp. The week starting the last Sunday in June sees nine big events, at Auteuil, Longchamp, St-Cloud and Chantilly (see p.361). **Trotting races**, with the jockeys in chariots, run from August to September on the Route de la Ferme in the Bois de Vincennes.

St-Cloud Champ de Courses is in the Parc de St-Cloud off Allée de Chamillard. *Auteuil* is off the route d'Auteuil, and *Longchamp* off the route des Tribunes, both in the Bois de Boulogne. *L'Humanité* and *Paris-Turf* carry details, and admission charges are around 25F.

Daytime Amusements and Sports

Chapter 16

Kids' Stuff

For details on
Disneyland
Paris, see
p.371.

Paris is often considered a strictly adult city, with little to engage or entertain energetic kids. Keeping teenagers amused is certainly as hard in Paris as it is anywhere, but, for the younger ones, there is a lot on offer, in addition to Disneyland Paris (see Chapter 21).

You shouldn't underestimate the sheer attraction of Paris' vibrant sense of life, with its diversity of sights and sounds so far removed from typical British and American cities. But neither should you expect kids to be enthralled by "doing" the Louvre, Notre-Dame and the Invalides. There are museums and monuments to excite most children, as well as play-grounds, puppet shows, wonderful shops

and high-tech treats. The French are also extremely welcoming to children, so there's never a problem being in cafés, bars or restaurants.

If your offspring know that **Disneyland Paris** is just outside the city, you probably won't be able to do anything with them until they've been there. If you can keep its existence a secret, so much the better, but at least take them to the **Cité des Sciences** at La Villette as a contrast.

In this chapter we assess the principal outdoor spaces and indoor attractions Paris can offer your kids, as well as shops specializing in items for children and special events such as theatre perfor-mances and circuses.

Paris With Babies

You will have little problem in getting hold of essentials for babies. Familiar brands of baby food are available in the supermarkets, as well as disposable nappies (*couches à jeter*) etc. After hours, you can get most goods from late-night pharmacies (see p.21).

Getting around with a pushchair poses the same problems as in most big cities. The métro is particularly bad, with its constant flights of stairs (and few escalators), diffi-cult turnstiles and very stiff doors. One particular place to avoid is the Louvre: taking a buggy in there is like trying to pothole with a rucksack.

For emergency medical care, see under "Health and Insurance", p.21.

Baby-sitters

The most reliable baby-sitting agency is *Ababa*, 8 av du Maine, 15e; ☎45.49.46.46, which has English speakers and charges around 29F per hour plus agency fees of 59F and taxis home after the métro stops running. Other possibilities include *Kid Service* (☎42.96.04.12; 29F per hour plus 55F fees) or individual notices at the American Church, 65 quai d'Orsay, 6e (M° Invalides), the *Alliance Française*, 101 bd Raspail, 6e (M° St-Placide) or *CIDJ* (101 quai Branly, 15e; ☎44.49.12.00; M° Bir-Hakeim. If you know someone who has a phone, you could dial up Babysitting on "*Elletel*" via their minitel.

The most useful **sources of information**, for current shows, exhibitions and events, are the special sections in the listings magazines, "*Pour les jeunes*" in *Pariscope* and "*Jeunes*" in *L'Officiel des Spectacles*. The best place for **details of organized activities**, whether sports, courses or local youth clubs, is the *Centre d'Information et de Documentation de la Jeunesse (CIDJ)*, 101 quai Branly, 15ᵉ; ☎44.49.12.00 (Mº Bir-Hakeim; Mon–Sat 10am–6pm). The Mairie of Paris also provides information about sports and special events at the *Kiosque Paris-jeunes*, 25 bd Bourdon, 4ᵉ; ☎42.76.22.60 (Mon–Fri 10am–5.30pm).

Parks, gardens and zoos

The parks and gardens within the city cater well for younger kids, though some may find the activities too structured or even twee. One of the most standard forms of entertainment is puppet shows and *Guignol*, the French equivalent of Punch and Judy. Adventure playgrounds hardly exist, and there aren't, on the whole, any open spaces for spontaneous games of football, baseball or cricket. French sport tends to be thoroughly organized (see Chapter 15).

The real star attraction for young children has to be the **Jardin d'Acclimatation**, though you can also let your kids off the leash at the **Jardin des Plantes**, 57 rue Cuvier, 5ᵉ; ☎40.79.30.00 (Mº Jussieu/Monge; 7.30 or 8am until dusk) with a small zoo (9am–5/6pm), a playground, hothouses and plenty of greenery. The **Bois de Vincennes** has a better zoo, 53 av de St-Maurice, 12ᵉ; ☎43.43.84.95 (Mº Porte-Dorée; summer 9am–6pm, winter 9am–5.30pm; 30F/15F; free for children under 6; see p.190).

Jardin d'Acclimatation

In the Bois de Boulogne by Porte des Sablon; ☎40.67.90.82 (Mº Sablons/Porte-Maillot). 10F; under-16s 5F, under-3s free; rides from 4.50–7F. Daily 10am–6pm, with special attractions Wed, Sat and Sun and all week during school holidays, including a little train to take you there from Mº Porte-Maillot (behind the

L'Orée du Bois restaurant; every 10min, 1.30–6pm; 9F).

The garden is a cross between funfair, zoo and amusement park, with temptations ranging from bumper cars, go-karts, pony and camel rides, to sea lions, birds, bears and monkeys; a magical mini-canal ride (*la rivière enchantée*), distorting mirrors, scaled-down farm buildings, a puppet theatre and a superb collection of antique dolls at the **Grande Maison des Poupées**. Astérix and friends may be explaining life in their Gaulish village, or Babar the world of the elephants – created by archeologists in the **Musée en Herbe**. If not, there'll be some other kid-compelling exhibition with game sheets (also in English), workshops and demonstrations of traditional crafts. And if they just want to watch and listen, the **Théâtre du Jardin pour l'Enfance et la Jeunesse** puts on musicals and ballets.

Outside the *jardin*, in the **Bois de Boulogne**, older children can amuse themselves with mini-golf and bowling, or boating on the Lac Inférieur. By the entrance to the *jardin* there's **bike rental** for roaming the wood's cycle trails.

Parc Floral

In the Bois de Vincennes, on rte de la Pyramide. ☎43.43.92.95 (Mº Château-de-Vincennes, then bus #112). Daily 9.30am–10pm; Oct–Feb closes 6.30pm; admission 10F; 5F for 6–10-year-olds, plus supplements for some activities; free for under-6s and over 65s. A little train tours all the gardens (April–Oct Wed–Sun 10.30am–5pm; 5F).

There's always fun and games to be had at the Parc Floral, on the other side of the Bois de Vincennes to the zoo. The excellent playground has slides, swings, ping-pong and pedal carts; a few paying extras like mini-golf, an electric car circuit, and pony rides (April–Oct daily 2–6pm); and clowns, puppets and magicians on summer weekends. Most of the activities are free and in general you'll be far less out of pocket after an afternoon here than at the Jardin d'Acclimatation. Also in the park is a children's theatre, the

Kids' Stuff

Kids' Stuff

Théâtre Astral, which may have mime, clowns or other not-too-verbal shows.

Jardin des Halles

105 rue Rambuteau. ☎45.08.07.18 (M°/ RER Châtelet-Les Halles). 7–11-year-olds only; Tues–Sat 10am–6pm, Sun 1–6pm; closed Mon; winter closing 4pm; closed in bad weather; 2.50F per hour.

Right in the centre of town at Les Halles, and great if you want to lose your charges for the odd hour. A whole series of fantasy landscapes fill this small but cleverly designed space. On Wednesday animators organize adventure games; and at all times the children are super-vised by professional child-carers. You may have to reserve a place an hour or so in advance. On Saturday morning you can go in and play too.

Other parks, squares and public gardens

All of these assorted open spaces can offer play areas, puppets or, at the very least, a bit of room to run around in, and are open from 7.30 or 8am till dusk. **Guignol and puppet shows** take place on Wednesday and weekend afternoons (and more frequently in the summer holidays).

Buttes-Chaumont, 19e. ☎42.40.88.66 (M° Buttes-Chaumont/Botzaris). Donkey-drawn carts, puppets, grassy slopes to roll down (see p.175).

Champs-de-Mars, 7e. ☎48.56.01.44 (M° École-Militaire). Puppet shows.

Jardin du Luxembourg, 6e. ☎43.26.46.47 (M° St-Placide/Notre-Dame-des-Champs/ RER Luxembourg). A large playground, pony rides, toy boat rental, bicycle track, roller-skating rink, and puppets (see p.116).

Jardin du Ranelagh, av Ingres, 16e (M° Muette). Donkey-carts, *Guignol*, pony-rides, cycle track, roller-skating rink and playground.

Jardins du Trocadéro, place du Trocadéro, 16e (M° Trocadéro). Roller-skating, skateboarding and aquarium.

Parc Georges-Brassens, rue des Morillons, 15e (M° Convention/Porte-de-Vanves). Climbing rocks, puppets, pony rides, artificial river, playground and scented herb gardens (see p.137).

Parc Monceau, bd de Courcelles, 17e. ☎42.67.04.63 (M° Monceau). Roller-skating rink (see p.198).

Parc Montsouris, bd Jourdan, 14e (M° Glacière/RER Cité-Universitaire). Puppet shows by the lake (see p.141).

Parc de la Villette, 19e (M° Corentin-Cariou/Porte-de-la-Villette/Porte-de-Pantin). The Dragon slide is the best in Paris. There are also curious gardens and sculptures (see p.173), plus a real-life submarine and high-tech movies in the Géode and Cinaxe outside the Cité des Sciences (see p.301).

Food for Kids

Junk-food addicts no longer have any problems in Paris. *McDonald's*, *Quick Hamburger* and their clones are to be found all over the city. The French-style *"fast foude"* chain, *Hippopotamus*, is slightly healthier (at 1 bd des Capucines, 2e, and throughout the centre of the city; 54F *menu enfants*, daily 11.30am until after midnight). At *Chicago Meatpackers*, 8 rue Coquillière, 1er, ☎40.28.02.33 (daily 11.45am–1am; 50F children's menu) a dining room with giant electric trains is reserved for kids. They're given balloons and drawing equipment, and on Wednesday, Saturday and Sunday lunchtimes (every day during holidays) there are mime, music or magic shows.

Other restaurants are usually good at providing small portions or allowing children to share dishes. The drugstores (see Chapter 13) have special children's menus, and are good for ice creams, too. In fact, keeping away from ice creams rather than finding them is the main problem in Paris. One thing to remember with steaks, hamburgers etc is that the French serve them rare unless you ask for them *"bien cuit"*.

Funfairs

One last outdoor thrill – funfairs – are, alas, few and far between. There's usually a **merry-go-round** at the Forum des Halles and beneath Tour St-Jacques at Châtelet, with ones for smaller children on place de la République, at the Rond-Point des Champs-Elysées by avenue Matignon, and at place de la Nation. Very occasionally, rue de Rivoli around Mº St-Paul hosts a mini-fairground.

Fantasy worlds and theme parks

Disneyland Paris (see p.371) has now put all the other fantasy worlds and theme parks of Paris into the shade. And unfortunately it's the only one with direct transport links. But, if you're prepared to make the effort, **Parc Astérix** is better mind-fodder and cheaper than Disney.

If outer space is the kids' prime interest, then bear in mind the two **planetariums**, in the Palais de la Découverte (see p.284) and the Cité des Sciences (see p.271). The latter is the best adventure land of all for kids who enjoy working things out for themselves. If their minds are more tuned to basic matters, an excursion into the catacombs or even the sewers might be an idea.

Other possibilities could include the various river and canal trips detailed in Chapter 15.

The Catacombs and the Sewers

Horror fanatics and ghouls should get a really satisfying shudder from the **catacombs** at 1 place Denfert-Rochereau, 14e· ☎43.22.47.63 (*RER* Denfert-Rochereau; Tues–Fri 2–6pm, Sat & Sun 9–11am & 2–4pm; closed holidays and Mondays; 27F/ 15F), though perhaps you should read p.132 first.

The archetypal pre-teen fixation, on the other hand, might find fulfilment in the sewers – **les égouts**, at place de la Résistance, on the corner of quai d'Orsay and the Pont de l'Alma; ☎47.05.10.29. (Mº Alma-Marceau; guided tours Sat–Wed, 11am–5/6pm; 24F/19F) – see p.123.

Parc Astérix

In Plailly, 38km north of Paris off the A1 auto-route, most easily reached by half-hourly shuttle bus from RER Roissy-Charles-de-Gaulle (ligne B). April–June Mon–Fri 10am–6pm, weekends 10am–7pm; July and Aug daily 10am–7pm; Sept & Oct Wed and weekends only 10am–6pm. Phone to check. Closed mid-Oct to March. Admission is 150F, 3–12s 105F, under-3s free.

Kids' Stuff

A Via Antiqua shopping street, with buildings from every country in the Roman empire, leads to a Roman town where gladiators play comic battles and dodgem chariots line up for races. There's a legionaries' camp where incompetent soldiers attempt to keep watch, and a wave-manipulated lake which you cross on galleys and longships. In the Gaulish village, Getafix mixes his potions, Obelix slavers over boars, Astérix plots further sorties against the occupiers, and the dreadful bard is exiled up a tree. In another area, street scenes of Paris show the city changing from Roman Lutetia to the present-day capital. All sorts of rides are on offer (with long queues for the best ones); dolphins and sea lions perform tricks for the crowds; there are parades and jugglers; restaurants for every budget; and most of the actors speak English (even if they occasionally get confused with the variations on the names). Information about Parc Astérix in the UK is available on ☎01242/236 169.

Circus, film and theatre

Language being less of a barrier for smaller children, the younger your kids, the more likely they are to appreciate Paris' many special theatre shows and films. There's also mime and the circus, which need no translations.

Circus

Circuses, unlike funfairs, are taken seriously in France. They come under the heading of culture as performance art (and there are no qualms about performing animals).

Some circuses have permanent venues, of which the most beautiful in Paris is the nineteenth-century *Cirque*

Kids' Stuff

Details of the Dôme-Imax are given on p.337.

d'Hiver Bouglione (see below). You'll find details of the seasonal ones under "*Cirques*" in *Pariscope* etc, and there may well be visiting circuses from Warsaw or Moscow.

Cirque d'Hiver Bouglione, 110 rue Amelot, 11ᵉ. The strolling players and fairy lights beneath the dome welcome circus-goers from October to January (and TV and fashion shows the rest of the year).

Cirque National Alexis Gruss. Performs at various venues between October and mid-February.

Cirque Bormann Diana Moreno. ☎45.00.23.01. This touring circus crops up at several different locations during its two seasons: April–June & Sept–Dec. From 60F/50F.

Cirque de Paris, on the corner of av Hoche and av de la Commune-de-Paris, Nanterre; ☎47.24.11.70 (*RER* Nanterre-Ville). A dream day out; for 235F+ adults, 195F+ children, you can spend an entire day at the circus (Nov–June Wed, Sun & school holidays 10am–5pm). In the morning you are initiated into the arts of juggling, walking the tightrope, clowning and make-up. You have lunch in the ring with your artist tutors, then join the spectators for the show, after which, if you're lucky, the lion-tamer will take you round to meet his cats. You can, if you prefer, just attend the show at 3pm (70–155F/45–95F), but if so, you'd better not let the kids know what they have missed.

Theatre

Several **theatres**, apart from the ones in the *Parc Floral* and the *Jardin d'Acclimatation*, specialize in shows for children.

The *Blancs Manteaux* and *Point Virgule* in the Marais, *Au Bec Fin* in the 1ᵉʳ, *Le Dunois* in the 13ᵉ, and the *Bateau Théâtre* moored by the Passerelle des Arts, all have excellent reputations, but it's doubtful how much pleasure your children will get unless they're bilingual. Still, it's worth checking in the listings magazines for any magic, mime, dance or music shows.

You'll find full details of Paris theatres in Chapter 19.

Cinema

There are many cinemas showing cartoons and children's films, but if they're foreign they are inevitably dubbed into French. Listings of the main Parisian cinemas are given in Chapter 19. The pleasure of an Omnimax projection at La Géode in La Villette or Dôme-Imax at La Défense, however, is greatly enhanced by not understanding the commentary. The Cinaxe projection at La Villette simulates motion to accompany high-definition film (see p.338). Films at the Louis-Lumière cinema (also in the Cité des Sciences – see below) may be less accessible, but you can ask at the enquiry desk for advice.

Museums

The best treat for children of every age from three upwards is the **Cité des Sciences** in the Parc de la Villette. All the other museums, despite entertaining collections and special activities and workshops for children, pale into insignificance. So beware that, if you visit the Cité on your first day, your offspring may decide that's where they want to stay.

Given kids' particular and sometimes peculiar tastes, the choice of other museums and monuments is best left to them, though the **Musée des Enfants** itself, which boringly purveys sentimental images of childhood, is certainly one to avoid. On the other hand, don't forget the gargoyles of Notre-Dame, and the aquariums at the **Musée des Arts Africains et Océaniens** (see p.275) and beneath the **Palais de Chaillot** (place du Trocadéro, 16ᵉ; Mº Trocadéro; daily 10am–5.30pm).

Certain museums have **children's workshops**, giving you the freedom to enjoy the sort of things that bore most children to tears. When they've exhausted **Beaubourg's** free attractions – the performers on the plaza and the building in itself – you can deposit 6- to 14-year-olds in the *Atelier des Enfants* (Wed & Sat 2–3.30pm & 3.45–5pm; free for visitors to the art museum; some English-speaking animators) where they can create their own art and play games. The **Musée**

d'Art Moderne de la Ville de Paris has
special exhibitions and workshops in its
children's section (Wed, Sat & Sun;
entrance 14 av de New-York). The **Musée
d'Orsay** provides worksheets (English
promised) for 8- to 12-year-olds that
make them explore every aspect of the
building. Other municipal museums with
sessions for kids include the **Musée
Carnavalet, Musée de la Mode et du
Costume** and the **Petit Palais**; costs are
around 25F.

Full details of all the state museums'
activities for children, which are all
included in the admission charge, are
published in *Objectif Musée*, a booklet
available from the museums or from the
Direction des Musées de France (34 quai
du Louvre, 1er; closed Tues).

Cité des Sciences et de l'Industrie

*Parc de la Villette, 19e. ☎ 40.05.80.00 (Mº Porte-
de-la-Villette). Tues–Sun 10am–6pm; Cité pass
giving access to Explora, planetarium, Cinéma
Louis-Lumière, Salle Jean-Painlevé and mediathèque screens, aquarium and Argonaute: 45F,
reduced tarif 35F; Géode Tues–Sun 10am–8pm:
50F/37F (some films are more), combined ticket
with Cité 85F/72F (available from Géode only);
Cité des Enfants ground floor, limited numbers
for hour and a half sessions Mon–Fri 11.30am,
1.30pm & 3.30pm, weekends 10.30am,
12.30pm, 2.30pm & 4.30pm; 20F extra., no
charge for accompanying adult. Cinaxe 27F/22F;
everything closed on Monday.*

The **Cité des Enfants**, the Cité's special
section for children, divided between 3–6
and 5–12-year-olds, is totally engaging.
The kids can touch and smell and feel
inside things, play about with water,
construct buildings on a miniature
construction site complete with cranes,
hard hats and barrows, experiment with
sound and light, and carry out genetic
tests with computers. They can listen to
different languages by inserting telephones into the appropriate country on a
globe and put together their own television news. Everything, including the
butterfly park, is on an appropriate scale
and the whole area is beautifully organized and managed. If you haven't got a
child it's worth borrowing one to get in
here. While queuing you can translate the

United Nations' Rights of Children to your
charges.

The rest of the museum is also pretty
good for kids, and if you want to wander
round the park, or see an exhibition at the
Grande Salle without them, there are two
"follies" where they can be dumped. *La
Petite Folie*, across the canal from the Cité,
is a game-filled crèche for 2- to 5-year-
olds (Wed–Sun 1.30–7.30pm; 3hr maximum stay; bookings ☎ 42.40.15.10; 18F
per hour). The *Folie Arts Plastiques* near
the *Grande Salle* is a painting workshop
for 7- to 10-year-olds (Sat & Sun 2–
5.30pm; bookings ☎ 40.40.03.22; 50F).

Shops

If your offspring belong to the modern
breed of sophisticated consumers, then
keeping them away from shops will be
your biggest saving. This can be difficult
given the Parisian art of enticing window
displays, practised to the full on every
other street. Children with an eye for
clothes are certain to spy boots or gloves
or dresses without which life will not be
worth living. Huge cuddly animals, gleaming models, and the height of fashionable
sports equipment will beckon them from
every turn, not to mention ice creams,
waffles, chips and pancakes. The only
goodies you are safe from are high-tech
toys, of which France seems to offer a
particularly poor selection.

However, the brats may get the better
of you, or you may decide to treat them
anyway. So here's a small selection of
shops to seek out, be dragged into or to
avoid at all costs.

Books

Among shops stocking a good selection
of English books are the following, but be
warned: they're expensive.

Brentano's, 37 av de l'Opéra, 2e (Mº
Opéra). Mon–Sat 10am–7pm.

Chantelivre, 13 rue de Sèvres, 6e (Mº
Sèvres-Babylone). Mon 1–6.50pm, Tues–
Sat 10am–6.50pm; closed Mon in Aug. A
huge selection of everything to do with
and for children, including good picture
books for the younger ones, an English

Kids' Stuff

*The Cité des
Sciences et de
l'Industrie is
described in
full on p.271.*

Kids' Stuff

section, a play area and drawing and mime classes.

Galignani, 224 rue de Rivoli, 1er (M^o Tuileries). Mon–Sat 9.30am–7pm.

W H Smith, 248 rue de Rivoli, 1er (M^o Concorde). Mon–Sat 9.30am–7pm.

Tea and Tattered Pages, 24 rue Mayet, 6e (M^o Duvoc). Daily 11am–7pm. The English bookshop and *salon de thé* has a storyteller every Wed morning 11am–noon, suitable for 3–7-year-olds. ☎40.65.94.35 for more details.

Toys and games

As well as the wide assortment of shops listed below, which range from kites to masks and puppets to train sets, it's worth bearing in mind that if children have enjoyed a museum they'll probably want what's on offer in the museum shops. The boutiques at **Beaubourg** and the **Cité des Sciences** have wonderful books, models, games, scientific instruments and toys covering a wide price range.

Ali Baba, 29 av de Tourville, 7e (M^o Varenne/St-François-Xavier). Mon–Sat 10am–7pm. Traditional toy store covering three floors – for all ages.

Art et Joie, 74 rue de Maubeuge, 9e (M^o Poissonnière). Mon–Fri 9.30am–6.30pm, Sat 10am–12.30pm; closed Aug. Everything you need for painting, modelling, graphic design, pottery and every other art and craft.

Boutique D.A.C., 10 rue du Cardinal-Lemoine, 5e (M^o Cardinal-Lemoine). Tues–Sat 10am–7.30pm; closed Aug. Musical boxes, puppets, wooden dolls.

Le Ciel Est à Tout le Monde, 10 rue Gay-Lussac, 5e (M^o Luxembourg); 7 av Trudaine, 9e (M^o Anvers). Tues–Sat 10am–7pm; closed Mon. The best kite shop in Europe also sells frisbees, boomerangs etc, and, next door, books, slippers, mobiles and traditional wooden toys.

Au Cotillon Moderne, 13 bd Voltaire, 11e (M^o Oberkampf). Mon–Sat 10am–6.30pm; closed Aug. Celluloid and supple plastic masks of animals, characters from fiction, politicians etc, trinkets, festoons and other party paraphernalia.

Les Cousins d'Alice, 36 rue Daguerre, 14e (M^o Gaîté/Edgar-Quinet). Tues–Sat 10am–1pm & 3–7pm, Sun 11am–1pm; closed Aug. Alice in Wonderland decorations, toys, games, puzzles and mobiles, plus a general range of books and records.

Deyrolle, 46 rue du Bac, 7e (M^o Bac). Mon–Sat 9am–12.30pm & 2–6.30pm. The best-known taxidermist: insects, butterflies, stuffed animals – from the biggest to the smallest, plus rocks and fossils. Fun to look at.

Magie Moderne, 8 rue des Carmes, 5e (M^o Maubert-Mutualité). Tues–Sat 10am–8pm; Sun, Mon and hols 10am–7,30pm. A magician's paradise.

La Pelucherie, 84 av des Champs-Elysées, 8e (M^o George-V/Franklin-D-Roosevelt). Tues–Sat 10am–midnight, Mon 10am–7.30pm, Sun and hols 11.30am–7.30pm. The top cuddly toy consortium. Expensive but worth a look.

Au Nain Bleu, 406–410 rue St-Honoré, 8e (M^o Concorde). Mon–Sat 9.45am–6.30pm; closed Mon in Aug. The Paris equivalent of London's *Hamley's* – a large store completely devoted to toys of all kinds.

Puzzles d'Art, 116 rue du Château, 14e (M^o Pernéty). Mon–Fri 8.30am–8pm, Sat 11am–8pm. Exactly what the name says; with workshop on the premises.

Pains d'Épices, 29 passage Jouffroy, 9e (M^o Montmartre). Mon 2–7pm, Tues–Sat 10am–7pm. Fabulous dolls' house necessities from furniture to wine glasses, and puppets.

Renault - Salles des Expositions, 51–52 av des Champs-Elysées, 8e (M^o Franklin-D-Roosevelt). Mon–Sat 9.30am–6pm. The main Paris showrooms have a collection of Renault cars from prewar to recent Formula Ones, which you can look at without pretending you want to buy a new one.

Rigodon, 13 rue Racine, 6e (M^o Odéon). Tues–Sat 10.30am–7pm; Mon 2.30–7pm; closed Aug. A weird and wonderful wizard's cave filled to the brim with marionettes, puppets, horror masks and other spooks.

Si Tu Veux, 68 galerie Vivienne, 2ᵉ (Mᵒ Bourse). Mon–Sat 11am–7pm. Well-made traditional toys plus do-it-yourself and ready-made costumes.

Le Train Bleu, 55 rue St-Placide, 6ᵉ (Mᵒ St-Placide). Mon 2–7pm, Tues–Sat 10am–7pm. Also at Centre Beaugrenelle, 16 rue Linois, 15e (Mᵒ Charles-Michels; Tues–Sun 10am–7.30pm); and 2 & 6 av Mozart, 16e (Mᵒ Ranelagh; Mon 2–7pm, Tues–Sat 10am–7pm). A fairly expensive chain with the biggest array at St-Placide; good on electric trains, remote control vehicles and other things you don't want to carry home with you.

Virgin Megastore, 52 av des Champs-Elysées, 8ᵉ (Mᵒ George-V). Mon–Thurs 10am–midnight; Fri & Sat 10am–1am. As well as all the cassettes and CDs to listen to, there's a Nintendo Gameboy to play with, but the Sega Super Entertainment console is not in fact hooked up to a machine.

Clothes

Besides the specialist shops we list here, most of the big department stores and the discount stores have children's sections (see Chapter 17, *Shops and Markets*). Of the latter, *Tati* and *Monoprix* are the cheapest places to go for vital clothing purchases.

Agnès B, 2 rue du Jour, 1ᵉʳ (Mᵒ/*RER* Châtelet-Les Halles). Mon–Sat 10.30am–7pm. Very fashionable, desirable and unaffordable, with lovely animal rocking chairs for the kids to sit in and ponder over their image.

Baby Dior, 28 av Montaigne, 8ᵉ (Mᵒ Alma-Marceau/F-Roosevelt). Mon–Sat 10am–6.30pm. Even more unaffordable,

less desirable but entertaining – the prices, most of all.

Dipaki, 46 rue de l'Université, 7ᵉ (Mᵒ Bac). Mon–Sat 10am–6.45pm. Also at 23 other addresses. Dependable, hard-wearing and reasonably priced clothes for up to 14-year-olds.

Gullipy, 66 rue de Babylone, 7ᵉ (Mᵒ St-François-Xavier). Mon–Fri 9am–7pm, Sat 11am–1pm. Fun accessories for children, as well as clothes – satchels, bags, wallets etc.

Junior Gaultier, 7 rue du Jour, 1ᵉʳ (Mᵒ/*RER* Châtelet-Les Halles). Mon–Fri 10am–7pm, Sat 11am–7pm. Horror movie decor to bring the brats in. The clothes are cheaper than the adult range.

Nic et Pouf, 32 rue du Four, 6ᵉ (Mᵒ St-Germain-des-Près). Mon–Sat 10.15am–7pm; closed Mon in Aug. All the top-name designers for the kiddies of all the top names. Good stuff, though not cheap.

Pom d'Api, 13 rue du Jour, 1ᵉʳ (Mᵒ/*RER* Châtelet-Les Halles). Mon–Sat 10.30am–7pm. Also at 28 rue du Four, 6ᵉ (Mᵒ St-Germain-des-Près; Mon–Sat 10am–7pm) and 6 rue Guichard, 16ᵉ (Mᵒ La Muette; Mon–Fri 10am–1pm & 2–7.30pm, Sat 10am–7.30pm). The most colourful, imaginative and well-made shoes for kids in Paris (up to size 40/7, and from 250F) and exquisite chairs in the shapes of swans, dogs for the little ones to sit on while they try them on.

Au Vieux Campeur, 48 rue des Écoles, 5ᵉ, Mᵒ Cluny-La Sorbonne. Tues, Thurs, Fri 10.30am–7.30pm, Wed 10.30am–10pm, Sat 10am–7.30pm. The best camping and sporting equipment range in Paris, spread over several shops in the *quartier*. The special attraction for kids is a climbing wall.

Kids' Stuff

Chapter 17

Shops and Markets

Flair for style and design is as evident in the shops of Paris as it is in other aspects of the city's life. Parisians' fierce attachment to their small local traders, especially when it comes to food, has kept alive a wonderful variety, despite the pressures to concentrate consumption in gargantuan underground and multistorey complexes.

Even if you don't plan – or can't afford – to buy, Parisian shops are one of the chief delights of the city. Some of the most entertaining and tempting are those small cluttered affairs which reflect their owners' particular passions. You'll find traders in offbeat merchandise in every *quartier*.

Markets, too, are grand spectacle. Mouthwatering arrays of food from half the countries of the globe, intoxicating in their colour, shape and smell, assail the senses in even the drabbest parts of town. In Belleville and the Goutte d'Or North Africa predominates, Southeast Asia in the 13e *arrondissement*. Though the food is perhaps the best offering of the Paris markets, there are also street

Toyshops, and shops selling children's clothes and books are detailed in Chapter 16.

markets dedicated to secondhand goods (the *marchés aux puces*), clothes and textiles, flowers, birds, books and stamps.

Shops

The most distinctive and unusual shopping possibilities are in the nineteenth-century arcades of the *passages* in the 2e and 9e *arrondissements*, almost all now smartly renovated. On the streets proper, the square kilometre around place St-Germain-des-Prés is hard to beat, packed with books, antiques, gorgeous garments, artworks and playthings.

Les Halles is another well-shopped district, with its focus the submarine shopping complex of the Forum des Halles, good for everything from records through to designer clothes. The aristocratic **Marais** and the new trendies' *quartier* of the **Bastille** have filled up with dinky little boutiques, arty and specialist shops and galleries. For window-shopping the really moneyed Parisian *haute couture* – Hermès and the like – the two traditional areas are avenue Montaigne, rue François 1er and rue du Faubourg-St-Honoré in the 8e and avenue Victor-Hugo in the 16e. The fashionable newer designers, lead by the Japanese, are to be found around place des Victoires in the 1er and 2e.

For food and essentials, the cheapest supermarket chains are *Ed l'Épicier* and *Franprix*. Other last-minute or convenience shopping is probably best at *FNAC* shops (for books and records) and the big department stores (for everything else).

Opening hours

Shop opening hours are variable throughout the city, but most tend to stay open comparatively late – until 7 or 8pm as often as not – and to close for up to two hours at lunchtime, somewhere between noon and 3pm. Most are closed on Sunday, many on Monday as well.

Art and design

If you want to get an idea of what is going on in the world of contemporary art, you should take a look at the **commercial art galleries**. They are concentrated in four main areas: in the 8^e, especially in and around avenue Matignon; in the Marais; around the Bastille; and in Saint-Germain.

There are literally hundreds of galleries, and for an idea of who is being exhibited where, you'll need to consult the booklet *Rive Droite Rive Gauche*, available from the galleries themselves or from more upmarket hotels, or *Pariscope*, which carries details of major exhibitions under *Expositions* and *Galeries*. Entry to the commercial galleries is free to all.

Design

A small selection of places where contemporary and the best of twentieth-century design can be seen is listed below. Also worth checking out are the shops of the art and design museums, and the rue St-Paul with a particularly high concentration of shops specializing in particular periods.

VIA (Valorisation de l'Innovation dans l'Ameublement), cour du Commerce-St-André, 6e (M^o Odéon). Mon–Sat 10.30am–7pm. The *VIA*'s function is to promote and assist young designers with a variety of exhibitions.

Collectania, 2 place du Palais-Royal, 1er (M^o Palais-Royal–Musée-du-Louvre). In the middle of the Louvre des Antiquaires (see below): tableware and furniture by big European names.

En Attendant les Barbares, 50 rue Étienne-Marcel, 2e (M^o Châtelet-Les Halles). Tues–Fri 10.30am–7pm; Mon 10.30am–1pm, 2–7pm; Sat 11am–6.30pm. The style known as neo-Barbarian: Baroque gilding on bizarre experimental forms. Nothing you'd actually trust your weight to, but fun to look at.

Espace Loggia, 94 rue du Bac, 6e (M^o Rue-du-Bac). Tues–Sat 11am–7pm, Mon 2–7pm. Also at 21 av de Friedland, 8^e (M^o George-V). Closed two weeks in Aug.

Shops and Markets

Late-night Shopping

The three **Drugstores** (see p.233 and p.248 for addresses) are open for books, newspapers, tobacco and all kinds of gift gadgetry until 2am every night.

In addition, you could try:

Prisunic supermarket, 52 av des Champs-Élysée, 8e (M^o Franklin-D-Roosevelt). Open till midnight Tues–Sat.

Boulangerie de l'Ancienne-Comédie, 10 rue de l'Ancienne-Comédie, 6e (M^o Odéon). Mon–Sat open 24hrs.

Le Cochon Rose, 44 bd de Clichy, 17e (M^o Blanche/Pigalle). Grocers open 6pm–6am daily except Thursday.

Kiosque, place de l'Étoile, 8e (M^o Charles-de-Gaulle–Étoile). Newsagents open 24hrs daily.

Tabacs

Le Terminus, 10 rue St-Denis, 1e (M^o Châtelet/Les Halles). Daily to 2am.

La Favourite Bar-Tabac, 3 bd St-Michel, 5e (M^o St-Michel). *Tabac* open daily to 2am.

Old Navy, 150 bd St-Germain, 6e (M^o St-Germain-des-Prés). Open till 5am.

Le Pigalle, 22 bd de Clichy, 18e (M^o Blanche.) Open till 4.30am.

Shell Garage, 6 bd Raspail, 7e (M^o Rue-du-Bac). 24-hr food shop and garage.

Petrol stations open all night:

Elf, 42 rue Beaubourg, 3e.

Shell, 82 rue Réaumur, 2e; 1–5 bd de la Chapelle, 10e.

Total, 103 av des Champs-Élysées, 8e.

Shops and Markets

Our Books section on p.405 recommends dozens of excellent books about Paris.

Chairs, chairs, chairs . . . from Louis XIII to contemporary.

Eugénie Seigneur, 16 rue Charlot, 3e (Mº République). The place to take your print or original for a highly unique frame.

Galerie Documents, 53 rue de Seine, 6e (Mº Odéon). Tues–Sat 10.30am–12.30pm, 2.30–7pm. Best antique posters.

Louvre des Antiquaires, 2 place du Palais-Royal, 1er (Mº Palais-Royal-Musée-du-Louvre). Tues–Sun 11am–7pm; closed Sun in July and Aug. An enormous antiques and furniture hypermarket, where you can pick up anything from a Mycenean seal ring to an Art Nouveau vase – for a price.

Bookshops

Books are not cheap in France – foreign books least of all. But don't let that stop you browsing. The best areas are the Seine *quais* with their rows of stalls perched against the river parapet and the narrow streets of the Quartier Latin, but don't neglect the array of specialist shops listed below.

English-language books

Abbey Bookshop/La Librairie Canadienne, 29 rue de la Parcheminerie, 5e (Mº St-Michel). Mon–Thurs 11am–10pm, Fri & Sat 11am–midnight, Sun 3–8pm. A Canadian bookshop round the corner from *Shakespeare & Co.* with lots of secondhand British and North American fiction; good social and political science sections; knowledgeable and helpful staff . . . and free coffee.

Attica, 23 Jean-de-Beauvais, 5e (Mº Maubert-Mutualité). 10.30am–12.30pm, 1.30–7pm; closed Mon. Most reasonably priced English-language books in Paris – literature rather than best-sellers.

Brentano's, 37 av de l'Opéra, 2e (Mº Opéra). Mon–Sat 10am–7pm. English and American books. Good section for kids.

FNAC Librairie Internationale, 71 bd St-Germain, 6e (Mº Cluny/RER St-Michel). 10am–8pm; closed Sun. Literally hundreds of foreign newspapers and magazines and tens of thousands of foreign books.

Galignani, 224 rue de Rivoli, 1er (Mº Concorde.) Mon–Sat 9.30am–7pm. Good range, including children's books.

Shakespeare & Co., 37 rue de la Bûcherie, 5e (Mº Maubert-Mutualité). Noon–midnight every day. A cosy, friendly, famous literary haunt, with the biggest selection of secondhand English books in town. Also poetry readings and such.

W H Smith, 248 rue de Rivoli, 1er (Mº Concorde). Mon–Sat 9am–7pm. Wide range of books and newspapers.

Village Voice, 6 rue Princesse, 6e (Mº Mabillon). Tues–Sat 11am–8pm, Mon 2–8pm. Principally poetry and modern literature, both British and American.

Books in French

For general French titles, the biggest and most convenient shop has to be the *FNAC* in the Forum des Halles, though it's hardly the most congenial of places. If you fancy a prolonged session of browsing, the other general bookstores below are probably more suitable.

Le Divan, 39 rue Bonaparte, 6e (Mº St-Germain-des-Prés). Mon–Sat 10am–7.30pm.

FNAC, at the Forum des Halles, *niveau 2*, Porte Pierre-Lescot (Mº RER Châtelet-Les Halles). Also at 136 rue de Rennes, 6e (Mº Montparnasse); 26 av des Termes, 17e (Mº Termes); and *CNIT*, 2 place de la Défense (Mº La Défense). Mon–Sat 10am–7.30pm. Lots of *Bandes Dessinées*, guidebooks and maps among everything else.

Gallimard, 15 bd Raspail, 7e (Mº Sèvres-Babylone). Mon–Sat 10am–7pm. The shop of the great French publisher.

Gibert Jeune, 6 place St-Michel, 5e and 27 quai St-Michel, 5e (Mº St-Michel). Mon–Sat 9.30am–7.30pm. With lots of sales, some English books and secondhand, too. These are the number-one suppliers of school and university set books.

La Hune, 170 bd St-Germain, 6e (Mº St-Germain-des-Prés). Mon–Sat 10am–midnight. One of the biggest and best.

Secondhand and antiquarian

In addition to the *quais*, you might try:
Albert Petit Siroux, Galerie Vivienne, 2e

(Mº Bourse). New and secondhand books, including musty leather-bound volumes on Paris and France. Mon–Sat 11am–7pm.

Giraud-Badin, 22 rue Guynemer, 6ᵉ (Mº Notre-Dame-des-Champs). 9am–1pm, 2–6pm; closed Sun, Tues and August. These are books which belong in museum collections – with prices to match.

L'Introuvable, 25 rue Juliette-Dodu, 10ᵉ (Mº Colonel-Fabien). Tues–Sat 11am–1pm & 3–7pm. All sorts stocked, but particular specialization is detective, crime, spy and SF stories.

Gibert Jeune, see opposite.

African/Third World

L'Harmattan, 16 rue des Écoles, 5ᵉ (Mº Maubert-Mutualité). Mon–Sat 10am–12.30pm & 1.30–7pm. Excellent, very knowledgeable bookshop, especially good for Arab/North African literature (in French). Publisher, too.

Art and architecture

Artcurial, 9 av Matignon, 8e (Mº Franklin-D-Roosevelt). Mon–Sat 10.30am–7.15pm; closed two weeks in Aug. *The* art bookshop in Paris – French and foreign editions. There is also a gallery, which puts on interesting exhibitions.

Librairie du Musée des Arts Décoratifs, 107 rue de Rivoli, 1ᵉʳ (Mº Palais-Royal). Wed–Sun 12.30–6pm. Design, posters, architecture, graphics, etc.

Librairie du Musée d'Art Moderne de la Ville de Paris, Palais de Tokyo, 11 av du Président-Wilson, 16ᵉ (Mº Iéna). Tues–Sun 10am–5.30pm. Specialist publications on modern art, including foreign works.

Librairie de l'École des Beaux Arts, 13 quai Malaquais, 6ᵉ (Mº St-Germain-des-Prés). Mon–Fri 10am–6pm; closed Aug. The bookshop of the national Fine Art school: own publications, posters, reproductions, postcards, etc.

Autographs

Librairie de l'Abbaye, 27 rue Bonaparte, 6ᵉ (Mº St-Germain-des-Prés). Tues–Sat 10am–12.30pm & 2–7pm; closed Aug.

Signatures of the famous. Good for a browse.

Comics/*Bandes dessinées*

Album, 60 rue Monsieur-le-Prince, 6ᵉ (Mº Odéon). Also at 6–8 rue Dante, 5ᵉ (Mº Maubert-Mutualité). Tues–Sat 10am–8pm. Vast collection of French, US and oher comics, some of them the rarest editions with original artwork.

Bloody Mary, 212 rue St-Jacques, 5ᵉ (*RER* Luxembourg); 18 rue Linné, 5ᵉ (Mº Jussieu). 10.30am–7.30pm. Stacks of comics in both establishments.

Boulinier, 20 bd St-Michel, 6ᵉ (Mº St-Michel). Mon–Sat 10am–7.30pm. Renowned for its selection of new and secondhand comics, including many that are difficult to obtain. Good collection of secondhand CDs now as well.

La Terrasse de Gutenberg, 9 rue Emilio-Castelar, 12ᵉ (Mº Ledru-Rollin). Mon 2.30–8pm, Tues–Sun 10am–7.30pm. Excellent collection of fine and graphic art, including *bandes dessinées*, plus photographs, postcards and general books. Near the Bastille.

Cookery, Gardening, Crafts

Librairie Gourmande, 4 rue Dante, 6ᵉ (Mº Maubert-Mutualité). Mon–Sat 10am–7pm, Sun 2.30–7pm. The very last word in books about cooking.

La Maison Rustique, 26 rue Jacob, 6ᵉ (Mº St-Germain-des-Prés). Mon–Sat 10am–7pm. Books – many in English – on all kinds of country and outdoor interests, from gardening to pruning olive trees and identifying wild flowers and birds.

Feminist

La Brèche, 9 rue de Tunis, 11ᵉ (Mº Nation). Mon 2–8pm, Tues–Sat noon–8pm. Feminist books and journals. Run by the *Ligue Communiste Révolutionnaire*.

La Fourmi Ailée, 8 rue du Fouarre, 6ᵉ (Mº Maubert-Mutualité). Daily noon–7pm. Left-wing bookshop and *salon de thé*, stocking most feminist reviews.

Shops and Markets

Shops and Markets

Librairie Anima, 3 rue Ravignan, 18ᵉ (Mᵒ Abbesses).

Gay and lesbian

Les Mots à la Bouche, 6 rue Ste-Croix-de-la-Bretonnerie, 4ᵉ (Mᵒ St-Paul). Mon–Fri 11am–11pm, Sat 11am–midnight. Literature, psychology etc: books and magazines – some in English. Includes some lesbian literature. They speak English well.

Kiosque Forum, 10 rue Pierre-Lescot, 1ᵉʳ (Mᵒ Châtelet-Les Halles). Daily 8am–midnight. Newsagents carrying a wide range of gay and lesbian literature.

Leftist avant-garde

Actualités, 38 rue Dauphine, 6ᵉ (Mᵒ Odéon). Tues–Sat 11am–1pm & 2–7pm. Literature (foreign included), philosophy, *bandes dessinées* (especially US comic books), etc.

Parallèles, 47 rue St-Honoré, 1ᵉʳ (Mᵒ Châtelet-Les Halles). Mon–Sat 10am–7pm. The place to go for green, feminist, anti-racist, 57 brands of socialist publications. As well as most of the "underground" press, you can pick up info on current events, demos etc. Good too on music and comics.

Performing arts

Librairie Bonaparte, 31 rue Bonaparte, 6ᵉ (Mᵒ St-Germain-des-Prés). Mon–Sat 9am–7pm; closed Aug. Exhaustive stock of books on ballet, theatre, opera, puppets, music hall, *chansonniers* etc.

Clair Obscur, 161 rue St-Martin, 3ᵉ (Mᵒ Rambuteau). Mon–Sat 11am–8pm. Wonderful film fanatics' stuff: stacks of movie-star stills and posters. Books on cinema and theatre, plus masks and puppets.

Les Feux de la Rampe, 2 rue de Luynes, 7ᵉ (Mᵒ Bac). Tues–Sat 11am–1pm & 2.30–7pm; closed three weeks in July and Aug 15. Books, scripts, stills, etc.

Poetry

L'Arbre Voyageur, 55 rue Mouffetard, 5ᵉ (Mᵒ Monge). Mon 2.30–7.30pm, Tues–Thurs 11am–8pm, Fri & Sat 11am–midnight. Poetry from all over the world, plus readings, discussions and exhibitions.

L'Envers du Miroir, 19 rue de Seine, 6ᵉ (Mᵒ Mabillon). Tues–Sat 2–7pm; closed Aug. Some fine and rare editions of modern poetry, as well as periodicals.

Travel

L'Astrolabe, 46 rue de Provence, 9ᵉ (Mᵒ Le Peletier). Mon–Sat 9am–7pm. Every conceivable map, French and foreign; guidebooks; climbing and hiking guides; sailing, natural history etc.

Institut Géographique National (IGN), 107 rue La Boétie, 8ᵉ (Mᵒ Miromesnil). Mon–Fri 9.30am–7pm, Sat 10.30am–12.30pm & 2–5.30pm. The French Ordnance Survey: the best for maps of France and the entire world, plus guidebooks, *GR* route descriptions, satellite photos, day packs, map holders, etc.

Ulysse, 26 rue St-Louis-en-l'Île, 4ᵉ (Mᵒ Sully-Morland). Tues–Sat 2–8pm. Travel books, maps, guides.

Clothes

There may be no way you can get to see the *haute couture* shows (see the box opposite), but there's nothing to prevent you trying on fabulously expensive creations by famous couturiers in rue du Faubourg-St-Honoré, avenue François-1ᵉʳ and avenue Victor-Hugo – apart from the intimidating scorn of the assistants and the awesome chill of the marble portals. Likewise, you can treat the **younger designers** round place des Victoires and in the Marais and Saint-Germain area as sightseeing. The long-time darling of the glitterati is **Azzedine Alaïa**, for whom the likes of Christy Turlington model for free. He is to fashion what Jean Nouvel is to architecture and Philippe Starck to interior design – together they form the triumvirate of Paris style. **Jean-Paul Gaultier** remains as popular as ever for his anti-fashion fashion, famous model **Inès de la Fressange** produces her own lines and new foreign designers like **Jil Sander** from Germany are competing with the wares of Japanese stylists.

End-of-line and old stock of the couturiers are sold all year round in discount shops listed below. For clothes to buy without the fancy labels the best area is the 6e: round rue de Rennes, rue de Sèvres and, in particular, rue St-Placide and rue St-Dominique in the neighbouring 7e. The department stores *Galeries Lafayette* and *Au Printemps* have good selections of designer *prêt-à-porter*; **the Forum des Halles** is chock-a-block with clothes shops but at less competitive prices; and individual boutiques are taking over more and more of the **Marais** and the **Bastille** around rue de la Roquette.

The Les Halles end of rue de Rivoli has plenty of chain stores, including a *Monoprix* supermarket for essentials, or you can get even better bargains in the **rag-trade district** round place du Caire or place de la République, with a *Printemps* on the north side, *Tati* on the south, and the adjacent rues Meslay and Notre-Dame-de-Nazareth full of **shoe** and **clothes** shops respectively. For **jewellery** – gems and plastic – try rue du Temple and rue Montmorency.

The sales take place in January and July, with up to forty percent reductions on designer clothes. This still leaves prices running into hundreds of pounds, but if you want to blow out on something bizarre and beautiful these are the months to do it. The sales in the more run-of-the-mill shops don't offer significant reductions.

Discount

The highest concentration of shops selling end-of-line and last year's models at thirty- to fifty-percent reductions are in rue d'Alésia in the 14e and rue St-Placide in the 6e. Though before you get too excited, remember that twenty percent off £500 still leaves a hefty bill. Not that all items are as expensive as that. The best times of year to join the scrums are after the new collections have come out in January and October.

Cacharel Stock, 114 rue d'Alésia, 14e (Mº Alésia). Mon 2–7.30pm, Tues–Sat 10am–7.30pm. 30–40 percent off last season's stock. Men, women and kids.

La Clef des Marques, 99 rue St-Dominique, 7e (Mº Varenne). Mon noon–7pm, Tues–Fri 10am–noon, 3–7pm, Sat 10am–1pm, 2–7pm. Huge store with wide choice of clothes for men and women.

Dorothée Bis, 76 rue d'Alésia, 14e (Mº Alésia). Mon 2–7pm, Tues–Sat 10.15am–

Shops and Markets

The common signs you see in clothes stores, vente en gros *and* vente en détail *(or* vente aux particuliers*), mean wholesale and retail, respectively.*

The Haute Couture Shows

Invitations to the January and July *haute couture* shows go out exclusively to the elite of the world's fashion editors and to the 2000 or so clients for whom price tags between £10,000 and £100,000 for a dress represent a mere day or week or two's unearned income. *Hello*, *Ola* and the like have a field day as the top hotels, restaurants and palace venues disgorge famous bodies cloaked in famous names. Mrs Ex-Trump thrills the press by saying husbands come and go but couturiers are worth hanging on to, and every arbiter of taste and style maintains the myth that fashion is the height of human attainment.

The truth, of course, is that the catwalks and the clientele are there to promote more mass-consumed products, and the recession has taken its toll. 1991 was a near-disaster, with the "Gulf Princess" sector of the market keeping a low profile and the Americans too frightened of bombs on Concorde to attend. 1992 and 1993 brought far chiller winds, and the scene has hardly improved since: the hitherto minimum requirements for *haute couture* status, of employing 20 skilled workers and showing 75 garments a year, have been reduced by nearly half, and collections can now be shown on video instead of live. The sacrosanct dates of the spring and autumn shows are to be brought forward for the convenience of the big department store buyers. And, in high-handed fashion, the workers who are to lose their jobs have not so far been involved in the discussion.

Shops and Markets

The Big Names In Paris Fashion

Prices at Paris's big-name fashion emporia are well into the stratosphere. The addresses below are those of the main or most conveniently located shops.

Agnès B, 6 rue du Jour, 1er (Mo Châtelet/Les Halles).

Azzedine Alaïa, 7 rue de Moussy, 4e (Mo Hôtel-de-Ville).

Giorgio Armani, 6 & 25 place Vendôme, 1er (Mo Opéra).

Balenciaga, 10 av George-V, 8e (Mo Alma-Marceau).

Balmain, 44 rue François-1er, 8e (Mo George-V).

Cacharel, 5 place des Victoires, 1er (Mo Bourse).

Pierre Cardin, 59 rue du Faubourg-St-Honoré, 8e (Mo Madeleine).

Carven, 6 rond-point des Champs-Élysées, 8e (Mo Franklin-D-Roosevelt).

Castelbajac, 31 place du Marché-St-Honoré, 1er (Mo Pyramides).

Cerruti, 1 and 15 place de la Madeleine, 8e (Mo Madeleine).

Chanel, 31 rue Cambon, 1er (Mo Madeleine).

Chloé, 60 rue du Faubourg-St-Honoré, 8e (Mo Madeleine).

Comme des Garçons, 40–42 rue Étienne-Marcel, 2e (Mo Châtelet/Les Halles).

Courrèges, 40 rue François-1er, 8e (Mo George-V).

Dior, 32 av Montaigne, 8e (Mo Franklin-D-Roosevelt).

Dorothée Bis, 46 rue Étienne-Marcel, 1er (Mo Châtelet/Les Halles).

Louis Féraud, 88 rue du Faubourg-St-Honoré, 8e (Mo Madeleine).

Inès de la Fressange, 14 av Matignon, 8e (Mo Alma-Marceau).

J-P Gaultier, 6 rue Vivienne, 2e (Mo Bourse).

Givenchy, 8 av George-V, 8e (Mo Alma-Marceau).

Kenzo, 3 place des Victoires, 1er (Mo Bourse).

Emanuelle Khan, 2 rue de Tournon, 6e (Mo Odéon).

Christian Lacroix, 73 rue du Faubourg-St-Honoré, 8e (Mo Concorde).

Karl Lagerfeld, 19 rue du Faubourg-St-Honoré, 8e; 51 rue François-1er, 8e (Mo Concorde).

Lanvin, 2 rue du Faubourg-St-Honoré, 8e (Mo Concorde).

Ted Lapidus, 35 rue François-1er, 8e (Mo Franklin-D-Roosevelt).

Guy Laroche, 30 rue du Faubourg-St-Honoré, 8e (Mo Concorde).

Issey Miyake, 3 place des Vosges, 4e (Mo St-Paul).

Claude Montana, 3 rue des Petits-Champs, 1er (Mo Bourse/Pyramides).

Thierry Mugler, 10 place des Victoires, 2e (Mo Bourse).

Myrène de Prémonville, 38 rue de Bac, 7e (Mo Rue du Bac).

Paco Rabanne, 7 rue du Cherche-Midi, 6e (Mo Sèvres-Babylone).

Nina Ricci, 39 av Montaigne, 8e (Mo Alma-Marceau).

Sonia Rykiel, 175 bd St-Germain, 6e (Mo St-Germain-des-Prés).

Saint-Laurent, 38 rue du Faubourg-St-Honoré, 8e (Mo Concorde); 6 place St-Sulpice, 6e (Mo St-Sulpice/Mabillon).

Jil Sander, 52 av Montaigne, 8e (Mo Franklin-D-Roosevelt).

Jean-Louis Scherrer, 51 av Montaigne, 8e (Mo Franklin-D-Roosevelt).

Junko Shimada, 54 rue Étienne-Marcel, 1er (Mo Châtelet/Les Halles).

Ungaro, 2 av Montaigne, 8e (Mo Alma-Marceau).

Valentino, 17–19 av Montaigne, 8e (Mo Alma-Marceau).

Gianni Versace, 62 rue du Faubourg-St-Honoré, 8e (Mo Concorde).

7pm. 25-percent discounts. Women and kids.

Stock 2, 92 rue d'Alésia, 14e (M^o Alésia). Mon–Sat 10am–7pm. 30-percent reductions on Daniel Hechter's end-of-line items.

Le Mouton à Cinq Pattes, 8 & 18 rue St-Placide, 6e, and **L'Annexe** (for men) at no. 48 (M^o Sèvres-Babylone). Mon 2–7pm, Tues–Sat 10am–7pm. Popular discount store, with discounts on a wide range of big names.

Jean-Louis Scherrer Stock, 29 av Ledru-Rollin, 12e (M^o Gare-de-Lyon). Summer Sun–Fri 10am–7pm, winter Mon & Tues and Thurs–Sat 10am–7pm. 50–60 percent off last season's clothes and up to 80 percent off older ones.

Toutes Griffes Dehors, 76 rue St-Dominique, 7e (M^o Latour-Maubourg) and 84 rue de Sèvres, 6e (M^o Duroc). End-of-lines from *Guy Laroche* among others.

Secondhand and *rétro*

Rétro means period clothes, mostly unsold factory stock from the 1950s and 1960s, though some shops specialize in expensive high fashion articles from as far back as the 1920s. Plain secondhand stuff is referred to as *fripe* – not especially interesting compared with London and dominated by the US combat jacket style. The best place to look is probably the Porte de Montreuil flea market (see p.371).

L'Apache, 45 rue Vieille-du-Temple, 3e (M^o Hôtel-de-Ville). Mon 2–7pm, Tues–Sat 11am–7.30pm. A big selection of 1920–1950s popular fashions.

Derrière les Fagots, 8 rue des Abbesses, 18e (M^o Abbesses). Tues–Sat 11.30am–7.30pm. A gold mine of 1960s clothes and accessories in, on the whole, very good condition. Reasonable prices.

Halle aux Fringues Rétro, 16 rue de Montreuil, 11e (M^o Faidherbe-Chaligny). 10am–7pm; closed Sun & Mon am. Classy 1940s–1960s clothes; hats of all descriptions, and kimonos.

Rag Time, 23 rue du Roule, 1er (M^o Louvre). Mon–Sat 2.30–7.30pm. A veritable museum of superb dresses and high-

fashion articles from the Twenties to the Fifties. Some for hire. Expensive.

Réciproque, 89, 93, 95, 101 & 123 rue de la Pompe, 16e (M^o Pompe). Tues–Sat 10am–6.45pm. *Haute couture*: for women at no. 95; accessories and coats for men at no. 101; more accessories and coats for women at no. 123.

Rétro Activité, 38 rue du Vertbois, 3e (M^o Temple). Tues–Sat noon–7pm. Dresses from the 1930s to 1960s, and men's suits from the Fifties and Sixties – unbelievably cheap.

Tati

Tati is in a class by itself, the cheapest of cheap clothes stores and always thronged with people. Addresses are: 2–30 bd Rochechouart, 18e (M^o Barbès-Rochechouart); 140 rue de Rennes, 6e (M^o St-Placide); and 13 place de la République, 11e (M^o République).

Department stores and hypermarkets

Paris' two largest **department stores**, *Printemps* and *Galeries Lafayette*, are right next door to each other near the St-Lazare station, and between them there's not much they don't have. Less enticing for its wares, perhaps, but a visual knock-out, is the renovated *Samaritaine*. Best for food is *Au Bon Marché*.

In addition, Paris has its share of **hypermarkets** – giant shopping complexes – of which the *Forum des Halles* in the 1er, the *Centre Maine-Montparnasse* in the 14e and the *Quatre-Saisons* in La Défense are the biggest.

Bazar de l'Hôtel de Ville (BHV), 52–64 rue de Rivoli, 4e (M^o Hôtel-de-Ville). Daily 9.30am–7pm. Mon, Wed 9.30am–10pm. Only two years younger than the *Bon Marché* and noted in particular for its DIY department and cheap self-service restaurant overlooking the Seine. Less elegant in appearance than some of its rivals, perhaps, but the value for money is pretty good.

Au Bon Marché, 38 rue de Sèvres, 7e (M^o Sèvres-Babylone). Mon–Fri 9.30am–6.30pm, Sat 9.30am–7pm. Paris' oldest

Shops and Markets

For shops selling children's clothes, see Chapter 16.

Shops and Markets

department store, founded in 1852. The prices are lower on average than at the chicer *Galeries Lafayette* and *Printemps*, and the tone is more mass-market middle class. It has an excellent kids' department and a renowned food hall.

Galeries Lafayette, 40 bd Haussmann, 9ᵉ (Mº Havre-Caumartin). Mon–Sat 9.30am–6.45pm. The store's forte is high fashion. Two complete floors are given over to the latest creations by leading designers for men, women and children. Then there's household stuff, tableware, furniture, a host of big names in men's and women's accessories, a huge *parfumerie*, etc – all under a superb 1900 dome.

Au Printemps, 64 bd Haussmann, 9ᵉ (Mº Havre-Caumartin). Mon–Sat 9.30am–7pm. Books, records, a *parfumerie* even bigger than the rival *Galeries Lafayette*'s. Excellent fashion department for women – less so for men.

La Samaritaine, 75 rue de Rivoli, 1ᵉʳ (Mº Rivoli). 9.30am–7pm/Thurs 10pm. The biggest of the department stores, spread over three buildings, whose boast is to provide anything anyone could possibly want. It aims downmarket of the previous two. *Magasin 3* is wholly devoted to sport. You get a superb view of the Seine from the tenth-floor terrace, which is closed from October to March.

Food

The general standard of food shops throughout the capital is remarkably high, both in quality and presentation: a feast for the eyes quite as much as the palate. These listings are for **the specialist places**, many of which are veritable palaces of gluttony and very expensive. Markets are detailed in a separate section at the end of this chapter.

The equivalents of *Harrods*' food hall are to be found at **Fauchon's** on place de la Madeleine and the **Grande Épicerie** in the *Bon Marché* department store, each with exhibits to rival the best of the capital's museums. Then, there are one-product specialists whom gourmets will cross the city for: *Poilâne's* or *Ganachaud's* for bread, *Barthélémy* for

cheese, *La Maison de l'Escargot* for snails, *Émile's* for fish.

As for buying food with a view to economic eating, you will be best off shopping at the street markets or supermarkets – though save your bread-buying at least for the local *boulangerie* and let yourself be tempted once in a while by the apple *chaussons*, *pains aux raisins*, *pains au chocolat*, *tartes aux fraises* and countless other goodies. **Useful supermarkets** with branches throughout the city are *Félix Potin*, *Prisunic* and *Monoprix*. The cheapest supermarket chain is *Ed Discount*; choice, inevitably, is limited, but they do some things very well – jams, for instance.

Next door to the *Tang Frères* emporium in Chinatown (see below under "Markets") is the *Supermarché Paris Store*, 21 av d'Ivry, 13ᵉ (Mº Porte d'Italie), daily 9.30am–7pm, one of the best Chinese supermarkets selling everything from teacups to ampules of royal jelly and ginseng. Other branches at 12 bd de la Villette, 19ᵉ (Mº Belleville), and 8–10 rue de l'Evangile, 18ᵉ (Mº Marx-Dornoy).

Bread

La Flûte Gana, 226 rue des Pyrénées, 20ᵉ (Mº Gambetta). Mon–Sat 7.30am–1.30pm & 2.30–8pm. Run by the daughters of Ganachaud; the two shops are very close. Start the day with a *pain biologique* and you'll live a hundred years, guaranteed.

Ganachaud, 150–154 rue de Ménilmontant, 20ᵉ (Mº Pelleport). Tues 2.30–8pm, Wed–Sat 7.30am–8pm, Sun 7.30am–1.30pm; closed Mon & Aug. Although father Ganachaud has left the business, the new owners continue his recipes and the bread is still out of this world.

Poilâne, 8 rue du Cherche-Midi, 6ᵉ (Mº Sèvres-Babylone). Mon–Sat 7.15am–8.15pm. More marvellous bread, which is baked to ancient and secret family recipes. These are shared with brother Max, who has shops at 29 rue de l'Ouest, 14ᵉ (Mº Gaîté/Pernety; Mon–Sat 7.15am–8pm) and 87 rue Brancion, 15ᵉ (Mº Porte-de-Vanves; Mon–Sat 7.15am–8pm).

Poujauran, 20 rue Jean-Nicot, 7e (M⁰ Latour-Maubourg). Tues–Sat 8am–8.30pm; closed Aug. The shop itself is exquisite, with its original painted glass panels and tiles. The bread is excellent – there are several different kinds – and so too are the *pâtisseries*.

Charcuterie

Divay, 50 rue du Faubourg-St-Denis, 10e (M⁰ Château-d'Eau). Tues & Thurs–Sat 7.30am–1pm & 4–7.30pm, Wed & Sun 7.30am–1pm; closed Mon. *Foie gras, choucroute, saucisson* and such.

Aux Ducs de Gascogne, 4 rue du Marché-St-Honoré, 1er (M⁰ Pyramides). Mon–Sat 10am–7pm. Further branches at: 112 bd Haussmann, 8e (M⁰ St-Augustin; 10am–7pm; closed Sun and Mon am); 111 rue St-Antoine, 4e (M⁰ St-Paul; 9.30am–2pm & 3–8pm; closed Sun and Mon am); 21 rue de la Convention, 15e (M⁰ Boucicaut; 9.30am–1pm & 4–8pm; closed Sun and Mon am); 41 rue des Gatines, 20e (M⁰ Gambetta; 9am–12.45pm & 3–8pm; closed Sun and Mon am). An excellent chain with numerous southwestern products like preserved fruits in Armagnac, *foie gras*, conserves, hams and so forth.

Goldenberg's, 7 rue des Rosiers, 4e (M⁰ St-Paul). Daily 9am–2am, Sat 9am–2am. Superlative Jewish deli and restaurant.

Ets Bruneau, 6 rue Montmartre, 1er (M⁰ Châtelet-Les Halles). Tues–Sun 8am–6pm. Specialist in products from the Landes region, *pâtés* in particular: Bayonne hams, goose and duck pâtés, conserves, etc.

Maison de la Truffe, 19 place de la Madeleine, 8e (M⁰ Madeleine). Mon–Sat 9am–9pm. Truffles, of course, and more from the Dordogne and Landes.

Cheese

Barthélémy, 51 rue de Grenelle, 7e (M⁰ Bac). Tues–Fri 8.30am–1pm & 3.30–7.30pm, Sat 8.30am–1pm & 3.30–6.30pm; closed Aug. Purveyors of cheeses to the rich and powerful; orders can be faxed.

Carmès et Fils, 24 rue de Lévis, 17e (M⁰ Villiers). Tues–Sat 8.30am–1pm & 4–7.30pm, Sun 8.30am–1pm; closed Aug. In the rue de Lévis market. A family of experts, who bring on many of the cheeses in their own cellars and can advise you exactly which one is ripe for the picking. Said to be the only place in Paris where you can buy (whole) Cheddar cheeses.

Maison du Fromage, 62 rue de Sèvres, 6e (M⁰ Sèvres-Babylone). Mon–Fri 9am–1pm & 3–7.30pm, Sat 9am–7.45pm. Specializes in goat, sheep and mountain cheeses.

Chocolates and *pâtisseries*

Debauve et Gallais, 30 rue des Saints-Pères, 6e (M⁰ St-Germain-des-Prés). Mon–Sat 10am–7pm. A beautiful and ancient shop, specializing since time began in chocolate and elaborate sweets.

À la Mère de Famille, 35 rue du Faubourg-Montmartre, 9e (M⁰ Le Peletier). Tues–Sat 8.30am–1.30pm & 3–7pm. A nineteenth-century *confiserie* selling

Shops and Markets

Any list of the food shops of Paris has to have at its head the two **palaces**:

Fauchon, 26 place de la Madeleine, 8e (M⁰ Madeleine). Mon–Sat 9.40am–7pm/ summer 10pm. An amazing range of extravagantly beautiful groceries, fruit and veg, *charcuterie*, wines both French and foreign . . . almost anything you can think of. The quality is assured by blind testing which all suppliers have to submit to. Just the place for presents of tea, jam, truffles, chocolates, exotic vinegars, mustards and so forth. A self-service, too.

Hédiard, 21 place de la Madeleine, 8e (M⁰ Madeleine). Mon–Sat 9.30am–9pm/ Sat 10pm. Since 1854, the aristocrat's grocer, with sales staff as deferential as servants, as long as you don't try to reach down items for yourself. Superlative quality. Among the other branches are those at 126 rue du Bac, 7e; 106 bd de Courcelles, 17e; and Forum des Halles, level-1.

Shops and Markets

marrons glacés, prunes from Agen, dried fruit, sweets, chocolates and even some wines.

Ladurée, 16 rue Royale, 8e (Mº Madeleine). Mon–Sat 8.30am–7pm. Delectable and pricey *pâtisseries*.

Le Moule à Gâteaux – chain of good *pâtisseries*. Addresses include 111 rue Mouffetard, 5e (Mº Censier-Daubenton); 17 rue Daguerre, 14e (Mº Denfert-Rochereau); 25 rue de Lévis, 17e (Mº Villiers); 53 rue des Abbesses, 18e (Mº Abbesses). All are open Tues–Sat 8am–8pm, Sun 8am–2pm; closed Mon.

Pâtisserie Stohrer, 51 rue Montorgueil, 2er (Mº Sentier). Tues–Sat 8am–8pm. Bread, *pâtisseries*, chocolate and *charcuterie*. Discover what standard-fare *pain aux raisins* should really taste like.

Herbs, spices and dried foods

Aux Cinq Continents, 75 rue de la Roquette, 11e (Mº Bastille). Tues–Fri 9.30am–1.30pm & 3.30–10pm; Sun 9.30am–1.30pm, Mon 3.30–10pm. Boxes, trays, sacks of rice, pulses, herbs, spices, tarama, vine leaves, etc, from the world over, plus alcohol.

Izraël, 30 rue François-Miron, 4e (Mº St-Paul). Tues–Sat 9.30am–1pm & 2.30–7pm. Another cosmopolitan emporium of goodies from all round the globe.

Honey

Les Abeilles, 21 rue de la Butte-aux-Cailles, 13e (Mº Corvisart/Place d'Italie). Tues–Sat 11am–8pm. Honey from all over France and further afield, sold by an experieced bee keeper. Pots from 23F to 43F.

Kitchen equipment

Au Bain Marie, 10 rue Boissy-d'Anglas, 8e (Mº Concorde). Mon–Sat 10am–7pm. An Aladdin's cave of things for the kitchen: pots, pans, books, antiques, napkins.

E Dehillerin, 51 rue Jean-Jacques-Rousseau, 1er (Mº Châtelet-Les Halles). Mon–Sat 8am–6pm. Laid out like a traditional ironmonger's: no fancy displays, prices buried in catalogues, but good-quality stock at reasonable prices.

MORA, 13 rue Montmartre, 1er (Mº Châtelet-Les Halles). Mon–Fri 8.30am–5.45pm, Sat 8.30am–1pm. An exhaustive collection of tools of the trade for the top professionals.

Salmon, seafood and caviar

In addition to the establishments below, more caviar, along with truffles, *foie gras* etc, is to be found at the lower end of rue Montmartre by the Forum des Halles in the 1er.

Comptoir du Saumon, 60 rue François-Miron, 4e (Mº St-Paul). Mon–Sat 10am–10pm. Salmon especially, but eels and trout and all things fishy as well. Plus a very agreeable small restaurant in which to do some tasting.

Caviar Kaspia, 17 place de la Madeleine, 8e (Mº Madeleine). 9am–12.30am. Blinis, smoked salmon and Beluga caviar.

Petrossian, 18 bd de Latour-Maubourg, 7e (Mº Latour-Maubourg). 10am–7pm. More gilt-edge fish eggs, but other Russian and French delicacies too.

Snails

La Maison de l'Escargot, 79 rue Fondary, 15e (Mº Dupleix). Tues–Sat 8.30am–8pm, Sun 9am–1pm. The most delicious snails and stuffings in town. Here they sauce and re-shell them while you wait. There is a restaurant for *dégustation* opposite at no. 70 (55–65F, with a glass of wine).

Vegetarian

Diététique D J Fayer, 45 rue St-Paul, 4e (Mº St-Paul). Tues–Sat 9am–1.30pm, 2.45–8.45pm. One of the city's oldest specialists, selling dietary, macrobiotic, and vegetarian products.

Wine

Le Baron Rouge, 1 rue Théophile-Roussel, 12e (Mº Ledru-Rollin). Tues–Sat 10am–2pm & 5–9.30pm, Sun 10am–2pm. A good selection of dependable lower-range French wines. Very drinkable *Merlot* at 16F a litre, if you bring your own containers.

Les Caves St-Antoine, 95 rue St-Antoine, 4e (Mº St-Paul). Mon–Sat 9am–1pm, 3–

8pm; Sun 9am–1pm. Another small amicable outfit.

Aux Caves Royales, 137 bd de l'Hôpital, 13e (Mº Campo-Formio). 9.30am–1pm, 3.30–7.45pm; closed Sun pm & Mon in Aug. Another good selection of wines, from 17F a litre.

Maison de la Vigne et du Vin de France, 21 rue François 1er (Mº Franklin-D-Roosevelt). Mon–Fri 9.30am–12.30pm & 1.30–6.30pm. The headquarters of the French wine industry with information about all the wine regions, wine tasting and a shop. English spoken.

Michel Renaud, 12 place de la Nation, 12e (Mº Nation). 9am–1pm & 2–8.30pm; closed Sun pm and Mon. Superb value and a huge selection of French and Spanish wines (drinkable plonk for around £1 a bottle), champagnes and Armagnac.

Music

Records, cassettes and CDs are not particularly cheap in Paris, but you may come across selections that are novel enough to tempt you. Like the live music to be heard, Brazilian, Caribbean, Antillais, African and Arab albums that would be **specialist rarities** in London, as well as every kind of jazz, abound in Paris. Secondhand bargains can be scratchy treats – anything from the Red Army choir singing the *Marseillaise* to African drummers on skins made from spider ovaries. **The flea markets**, St-Ouen, especially, and the *bouquinistes* along the Seine are good places to look for old records. **In the classical department**, the choice of interpretations is very generous and un-xenophobic. For all new and mainstream records, *FNAC* usually has the best prices.

Also listed below are a couple of **bookshops** selling sheet music, scores and music literature, and some that sell instruments. Victor-Massé, Douai, Houdon, boulevard Clichy and other streets in the Pigalle area are full of instrument and sound system shops (guitarists will enjoy a look in at 16 rue V-Massé, 9e – afternoons only – where François Guidon

builds jazz guitars for the greats and the gifted amateurs).

Afric' Music, 3 rue des Plantes, 14e (Mº Mouton-Duvernet). Mon–Sat 10am–7pm. A small shop but with an original selection of African, Caribbean and reggae discs.

Blue Moon, 7 rue Pierre-Sarrazin, 6e (Mº Odéon). Mon–Sat 11am–7pm. Exclusive imports from Jamaica and Africa: ska and reggae.

BPM Records, 1 rue Keller, 11e (Mº Bastille). Tues–Sat 1–9pm. Specialists in house, including acid, hip-hop and rap.

Camara, 45 rue Marcadet, 18e (Mº Marcadet-Poissonnière). Daily 10am–7pm. The best selection of West African music on cassette and video in town.

Crocodisc, 40–42 rue des Écoles, 5e (Mº Maubert-Mutualité). Tues–Sat 11am–7pm. Folk, oriental, Afro-Antillais, funk, reggae, soul, country, new and secondhand. Some of the best prices in town.

Crocojazz, 64 rue de la Montagne-Ste-Geneviève, 5e (Mº Maubert-Mutualité). Tues–Sat 11am–1pm & 2–7pm. Jazz, blues and gospel: mainly new imports.

Disc' Inter, 2 rue des Rasselins, 20e (Mº Porte de Montreuil). Mon–Sat 10am–7pm. Wide-ranging stock of Afro-Caribbean music on CD, cassette, video and vinyl.

Le Disque Arabe, 116bis bd de la Chapelle, 18e (Mº Porte-de-la-Chapelle). Mon–Sat 10am–8pm. Good range of Arab music.

Dream Store, 4 place St-Michel, 6e (Mº St-Michel). Tues–Sat 9.30am–7pm. Good discounted prices on blues, jazz, rock, folk and classical.

Édition Bouarfa, 32 rue de la Charbonnière, 18e (Mº Barbès). Daily 9.30am–7.30pm. Large selection of raï; the shop is run by a raï producer.

FNAC Musique, 4 pl de la Bastille, 12e, next to opera house (Mº Bastille). Mon–Sat 10am–8pm, Wed & Fri 10am–10pm; closed Sun. Extremely stylish shop in black, grey and chrome with computerized catalogues, every variety of music, books, and a concert booking agency. Branch at 24 bd des Italiens, 9e, with a greater emphasis on

Shops and Markets

The Cité de la Musique in La Villette has a whole range of shops devoted to all things musical.

Shops and Markets

rock and popular music. The other *FNAC* shops (see above under *Books*) also sell music and hi-fi.

Hamm, 135 rue de Rennes, 6ᵉ (Mᵉ St-Placide). Mon 2–7pm, Tues–Sat 10am–7pm. The biggest general music shop in Paris, selling instruments new and old, sheet music, scores, manuals, librettos etc.

Istanbul Express, 3 rue de Metz, 10ᵉ (Mᵉ Strasbourg-St-Denis). Mon–Sat 10am–7pm. The address for Turkish music.

La Klavé, 6 rue Androuet, 18ᵉ (Mᵉ Abbesses). Daily 2–10pm. The best Cuban music, much of it on vinyl and stocks diminishing fast.

Librairie Musicale de Paris, 68bis rue Réaumur, 3ᵉ (Mᵉ Réaumur-Sébastopol). Mon–Sat 10am–12.45pm & 2–7pm. Huge selection of books, on music and of music: Baroque oratorios to heavy metal.

Maison Sauviat, 124 bd de la Chapelle, 18ᵉ (Mᵉ Barbès). Mon–Sat 10am–7.30pm. Wonderful shop that's been going strong since the 1920s. Now selling African and Arab music.

Parallèles, 47 rue St-Honoré, 1ᵉʳ (Mᵉ Châtelet-Les Halles). The bookshop (see above) also sells records and cheap secondhand CDs.

Paris Musique, 10 bd St-Michel, 6ᵉ (Mᵉ St-Michel). Mon–Fri 10am–8pm, Sat 10am–9pm, Sun 2–8pm. Secondhand, bootlegs and new – jazz, classical and rock.

Rough Trade, 38 rue de Charonne, 11ᵉ (Mᵉ Ledru-Rollin). Mon–Sat 11am–7pm. Indie labels and fanzines – an offshoot of London's Portobello Road store.

Virgin Megastore, 56–60 av des Champs-Élysées, 8ᵉ (Mᵉ Franklin-Roosevelt), and Carrousel du Louvre, under the Louvre, 1ᵉʳ (Mᵉ Palais-Royale/Musée-du-Louvre). Mon–Thurs 10am–midnight, Fri & Sat 10am–1am, Sun noon–midnight. *Virgin* has trumped all Paris music shops. It's the biggest and the trendiest, but it does not have the wax rock heroes of the London store. Concert booking agency.

Sport

Bicloune, 7 rue Froment, 11ᵉ (Mᵉ Bréguet-Sabgin). Tues–Fri 10.30am–

1.30pm & 2–7pm, Sat 10am–1pm & 2–6.30pm. A bike shop with some bizarre models on show. Repairs carried out.

La Boutique Gardien du But, 89ter rue de Charenton, 12ᵉ (Mᵉ Gare-de-Lyon). "The Goalkeeper": a very friendly, young shop specializing in French soccer. Stock includes shirts of every French club.

Le Ciel est à Tout le Monde, 10 rue Gay-Lussac, 5ᵉ (Mᵉ Luxembourg); 7 av Trudaine, 9ᵉ (Mᵉ Anvers). Tues–Sat 10am–7pm; closed Mon in Aug. The best kite shop in Europe also sells frisbees, boomerangs and anything else that flies without a motor. Prices from 120F to 1500F for really serious models. Also, material for making your own.

La Gazelle, 47–49 bd Jean-Jaurès, Boulogne (Mᵉ Boulogne-Jean-Jaurès). Tues–Sat 9am–noon & 2–7pm. Traditional bike enthusiasts' shop: hand-built racers, mountain bikes etc.

La Haute Route, 33 bd Henri-IV, 4ᵉ (Mᵉ Bastille). Mon 2–7pm, Tues–Sat 9.30am–1pm & 2–7pm. Skiing and mountaineering equipment principally: to rent, to buy – new and secondhand.

La Maison du Vélo, 11 rue Fenelon, 10ᵉ (Mᵉ Gare-du-Nord). Tues–Sat 10am–7pm. Classic models, mountain bikes, tourers and racers.

Marathon, 29 rue de Chazelles, 17ᵉ (Mᵉ Monceau). Specialists in running shoes. The shop is owned by an experienced marathon runner.

La Roue d'Or, 7 rue de la Fidelité, 10ᵉ (Mᵉ Gare-de-l'Est). Tues–Sat 9am–6.30pm; closed Aug. Another cycling enthusiast.

Au Vieux Campeur, 48 rue des Écoles, 5ᵉ (Mᵉ Maubert-Mutualité). Mon 2–7pm, Tues–Fri 9.30am–8.30pm, Sat 9.30am–8pm. Maps, guides, climbing, hiking, camping, ski gear, and mountain bikes – and a climbing wall for kids. With its various mushrooming departments the shop now occupies half the *quartier*.

A miscellany

Au Facteur Cheval, 66 rue de Javel, 15ᵉ (Mᵉ Charles-Michels). Tues–Sat 9.30am–

1.30pm & 3–7pm. Small antiques shop with reasonably priced glass and china ware, perfume bottles, knick-knacks and furniture.

Le Chat en Majesté, 1 rue des Prouvaires, 1er (Mº Louvre). All kinds of catty things: things with cats on them, shaped like cats etc.

Cocody, 14 rue Descartes, 5e (Mº Cardinal-Lemoine). Beautiful bags, belts and material from Mali and the Ivory Coast.

Ivan Estivalet, 9 rue Oberkampf, 11e (Mº Filles-du-Calvaire); 77 rue du Cherche-Midi, 6e (Mº Vaneau). A florist who creates bouquets in outlandish holders made of cane, hemp, bamboo and other plant material.

La Maison du Collectionneur, 137 av Émile-Zola, 15e (Mº Émile-Zola). Old books, hats, newspapers of the wartime liberation and assorted junk.

Pentagram, 15 rue Racine, 6e (Mº Cluny). Hand-blown glass pens, pharaonic board games, stationery, PCs for kids.

Pylones, 57 rue St-Louis-en-l'Ile, 4e (Mº Sully-Morland), and many other branches. Daily 10.30am–7.30pm. Playful and silly things: tulip-handled umbrellas, rubber ties and the like.

Travelingue, 20 rue Boulard, 14e (Mº Denfert-Rochereau). Lots of bizarre accessories: ties, earrings, kitchenware and socks.

Thé-Troc, 52 rue J.P.-Timbaud, 11e (Mº Parmentier). Mon–Sat 9am–8pm. Wide selection of teas, plus secondhand records, books, jewellery and assorted junk.

Markets

Several of the markets which we list below are described in the text of Chapters 2 to 11. These, however, are the details – and the highlights. The map on the next page shows the location of them all.

Flea markets (*marchés aux puces*)

Paris has three main flea markets of ancient descent gathered about the old gates of the city. No longer the haunts of the flamboyant gypsies and petty crooks of literary tradition, they are nonetheless good entertainment and if you go early enough you might just find something special. Some of the food markets have spawned secondhand clothes and junk stalls, notably the place d'Aligre in the 12e and the place des Fêtes in the 20e.

Carreau du Temple, between rue Perrée and rue du Petit-Thouars, 3e (Mº Temple). Tues–Fri until noon, Sat & Sun until 1pm. Specializes in plain and practical new clothes.

Porte de Montreuil, 20e (Mº Porte-de-Montreuil). Sat, Sun & Mon 6.30am–1pm. Best of the flea markets for secondhand clothes – cheapest on the Monday when leftovers from the weekend are sold off.

Porte de Vanves, 14e (av Georges-Lafenestre/av Marc-Sangnier) (Mº Porte-de-Vanves). Sat & Sun 7am–6pm. The obvious choice for bric-à-brac searching, with amateurs spreading wares on the pavement as well as the professional dealers. See account on p.140.

St-Ouen/Porte de Clignancourt, 18e (Mº Porte-de-Clignancourt). Sat, Sun & Mon 7.30am–7pm. The biggest and most touristy, with stalls selling clothes, shoes, records, books and junk of all sorts as well as expensive antiques. Trading usually starts well before the official opening hour – as early as 5am.

Flowers and birds

Paris used to have innumerable **flower markets** around the streets, but today just the three listed below remain. Throughout the week, however, there's also the heavy concentration of plant and pet shops along the quai de la Mégisserie between Pont-Neuf and Pont-au-Change.

Place Lépine, Île de la Cité, 1er. Daily 8am–7.30pm. On Sundays flowers give way to birds and pets.

Place de la Madeleine, 8e. Tues–Sun 8am–7.30pm; closed Mon. Flowers and plants.

Place des Ternes, 8e. Tues–Sun 8am–7.30pm; closed Mon. Flowers and plants.

Shops and Markets

For a detailed description of the Puces de *St-Ouen, see p.158.*

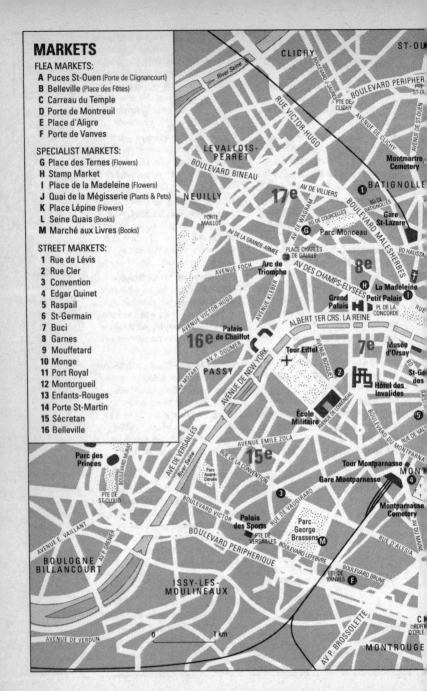

MARKETS

FLEA MARKETS:
- **A** Puces St-Ouen (Porte de Clignancourt)
- **B** Belleville (Place des Fêtes)
- **C** Carreau du Temple
- **D** Porte de Montreuil
- **E** Place d'Aligre
- **F** Porte de Vanves

SPECIALIST MARKETS:
- **G** Place des Ternes (Flowers)
- **H** Stamp Market
- **I** Place de la Madeleine (Flowers)
- **J** Quai de la Mégisserie (Plants & Pets)
- **K** Place Lépine (Flowers)
- **L** Seine Quais (Books)
- **M** Marché aux Livres (Books)

STREET MARKETS:
- **1** Rue de Lévis
- **2** Rue Cler
- **3** Convention
- **4** Edgar Quinet
- **5** Raspail
- **6** St-Germain
- **7** Buci
- **8** Garnes
- **9** Mouffetard
- **10** Monge
- **11** Port Royal
- **12** Montorgueil
- **13** Enfants-Rouges
- **14** Porte St-Martin
- **15** Sécretan
- **16** Belleville

Shops and Markets

Books and stamps

As well as the specialized book markets listed below, you should of course remember the wide array of books and all forms of printed material on sale from the *bouquinistes* who hook their green padlocked boxes onto the riverside *quais* of the Left Bank (see p.107).

Paris' **stamp market** is at the junction of avenues Marigny and Gabriel, on the north side of place Clemenceau in the 8e (Thurs, Sat, Sun & hols 10am–dusk).

Marché aux Cartes Postales Anciennes, Marché St-Germain, 3ter rue Mabillon, 6e (Mº Mabillon). Wed & Thurs 9am–1pm & 4–6.30pm. Old postcards.

Marché du Livre Ancien et d'Occasion, Pavillon Baltard, Parc Georges-Brassens, rue Brancion, 15e (Mº Porte-de-Vanves). Sat & Sun 9am onwards. Secondhand and antiquarian books.

Marché aux Vieux Papiers de St-Mandé, av de Paris (Mº St-Mandé). Wed 10am–6pm. Old books, postcards and prints.

Food markets

The street markets provide one of the capital's more exacting tests of willpower. At the top end of the scale, there are the Satanic arrays in **rue de Lévis** in the 17e and **rue Cler** in the 7e, both of which are more market street than street market, with their stalls mostly metamorphosed into permanent shops. The real street markets include a tempting scattering in **the Left Bank** – in rue de Buci (the most photographed) near St-Germain-des-Prés, rue Mouffetard, place Maubert and place Monge. Bigger ones are at **Montparnasse**, in boulevard Edgar-Quinet, and opposite Val-de-Grâce in boulevard Port-Royal, the biggest in rue de la Convention in the 15e.

For a different feel and more exotic foreign produce, take a look at the Mediterranean/Oriental displays in **boulevard de Belleville and rue d'Aligre**.

Markets usually start between 7am and 8am and tail off around midday. The covered markets have specific opening hours, which are given below along with details of locations and days of operation.

Place d'Aligre, 12e (Mº Ledru-Rollin). Tues–Sat. Until noon.

Belleville, bd de Belleville, 20e (Mº Belleville/Ménilmontant). Tues & Fri.

Buci, rue de Buci and rue de Seine, 6e (Mº Mabillon). Tues–Sun.

Carmes, place Maubert, 5e (Mº Maubert-Mutualité). Tues, Thurs & Sat.

Rue Cler, 7e (Mº École-Militaire). Tues–Sat.

Convention, rue de la Convention, 15e (Mº Convention). Tues, Thurs & Sun.

Edgar-Quinet, bd Edgar-Quinet, 14e (Mº Edgar-Quinet). Wed & Sat.

Enfants-Rouges, 39 rue de Bretagne, 3e (Mº Filles-du-Calvaire). Tues–Sat 8am–1pm & 4–7.30pm, Sun 8am–1pm.

Rue de Lévis, 17e (Mº Villiers). Tues–Sun.

Monge, place Monge, 5e (Mº Monge). Wed, Fri & Sun.

Montorgueil, rue Montorgueil and rue Montmartre, 1er (Mº Châtelet-Les Halles/Sentier). Daily.

Mouffetard, rue Mouffetard, 5e (Mº Censier-Daubenton). Daily.

Porte-St-Martin, rue du Château-d'Eau, 10e (Mº Château-d'Eau). Tues–Sat 8am–1pm & 4–7.30pm, Sun 8am–1pm.

Port-Royal, bd Port-Royal, near Val-de-Grâce, 5e (Mº Porte-Royale). Tues, Thurs & Sat.

Raspail, bd Raspail, between rue du Cherche-Midi and rue de Rennes, 6e (Mº Rennes). Tues & Fri. Organic on Sundays.

Secrétan, av Secrétan/rue Riquet, 19e (Mº Bolivar). Tues–Sat 8am–1pm & 4–7.30pm, Sun 8am–1pm.

Saint-Germain, rue Mabillon, 6e (Mº Mabillon). Tues–Sat 8am–1pm & 4–7.30pm, Sun 8am–1pm.

Tang Frères, 48 av d'Ivry, 13e (Mº Porte d'Ivry). Tues–Sun 9am–7.30pm. Not really a market, but a vast emporium of all things Oriental, where speaking French will not help you discover the nature and uses of what you see before you. In the same yard there is also a Far Eastern flower shop.

Ternes, rue Lemercier, 17e (Mº Ternes). Tues–Sat 8am–1pm & 4–7.30pm, Sun 8am–1pm.

Chapter 18

Music and Nightlife

The strength of the Paris **music scene** is its diversity – a reputation gained mainly from its absorption of immigrant and exile populations. The city has no rivals in Europe for the variety of **world music** to be discovered: West and Central African, Caribbean and Latin American sounds are represented in force both by city-based bands and by club or arena appearances by groups on tour. You can spend any number of nights sampling mixtures of salsa, calypso, reggae and African sounds from Zaire, Congo, Senegal and Nigeria. Algerian raï has come out from the immigrant ghettoes and the French language has been discovered to be a great vehicle for **rap** and **hip-hop** or the ragamuffin combination.

Jazz fans, too, are in for a treat. Paris has long been home to new styles and old-time musicians. The *Caveau de la Huchette* in the Latin Quarter is the no. 1 venue. The *New Morning* club hosts big names from all over the world, and it's not hard to fill the late hours passing from one club to another in St-Germain or Les Halles – assuming your wallet can take it. Standards are high and the line-ups varied, and the ancient cellars housing many of the clubs make for great acoustics and atmosphere.

One variety of home-grown popular music that survives is the tradition of *chansons*, epitomized by Édith Piaf and developed to its greatest heights by Georges Brassens and the Belgian Jacques Brel. This music is undergoing something of a revival since the return of

the 1950s star Juliette Greco to the *Olympia* stage in 1991 brought rapt media attention. Another retrospective experience is **ballroom dancing** at the old music halls or surburban *guinguettes*.

Commercial French popular music is to be avoided. Although most singers – like Patrick Bruel, idol of depressed adolescents – lay claim to the *chansonniers* tradition, few have genuine roots in it, with the notable exception of Patricia Kaas. Vanessa Paradis went so far as to switch to English in order to pursue an international career. One group whose music mixes all kinds of styles – including rock with *chansons* – is **Pigalle**.

Classical music, as you might expect in this neoclassical city, is alive and well and takes up twice the space of "jazz-pop-folk-rock" in the listings magazines. The **Paris Opéra** at the Bastille continues to be plagued by terrible management problems, but still manages to put on interesting productions in between strikes. The **Théâtre Musical de Paris** is considered by some to have far more interesting productions. For **concerts** the choice is enormous. The two main orchestras are the Orchestre de Paris based at the Salle Pleyel, and the Orchestre Nationale. Many concerts are put on in the city's churches – at very reasonable prices – but generally, the need for advance reservations rather than the price is the major inhibiting factor. If you're interested in the **contemporary** scene of Systems composition and the like, check out the state-sponsored experiments of Laurent

Music and Nightlife

Bayle at Beaubourg and Iannis Xenakis out at Issy-Les-Moulineaux.

In the listings in this chapter, **nightlife** recommendations – for **dance clubs and discos** – are to some extent incorporated in those for rock, world music and jazz, with which they merge. Separate sections, however, detail places that are mainly disco, and which cater for a gay or lesbian clientele.

The chapter's final section details all the **big venues**, where major concerts – from heavy metal to opera – are promoted.

Tickets and information

The best place to get **tickets** for concerts, whether rock, jazz, *chansons* or classical, is *FNAC Musique*, 4 pl de la Bastille, 12ᵉ; Mᵒ Bastille (Mon, Tues, Thurs & Sat 10am–8pm, Wed & Fri 10am–10pm) and 24 bd des Italiens, 9ᵉ; Mᵒ Richelieu-Drouot/Quatre Septembre/Chausée d'Antin (Mon–Sat 10am–midnight), at the *FNAC* bookshops (see p.306), or the *Virgin Megastore*, 56–60 av des Champs-Élysées, 8ᵉ; Mᵒ Franklin-Roosevelt; and Carrousel du Louvre, beneath the Louvre, 1ᵉʳ; Mᵒ Palais-Royale/Musée-du-Louvre (Mon–Thurs 10am–midnight, Fri & Sat 10am–1am, Sun 2pm–midnight).

Pariscope, Officiel des Spectacles and *Paris Free Voice* list a fair selection of concerts, clubs etc, and you'll see posters around town (particularly in the Latin Quarter). *Les Inrockuptibles* is the serious magazine with in-depth analysis and interviews on the independent music scene. At *Parallèles*, 47 rue St-Honoré, 1ᵉʳ (Mᵒ Châtelet-les-Halles), you're likely to come across phone numbers for **raves**, if you're interested. For information about African music gigs, good places to go are the record shops *Blue Moon*, 7 rue Pierre-Sarrazin, 6ᵉ; ☎46.34.63.89; Mᵒ Odéon (Mon–Sat 11am–7pm), and *Crocodisc*, 42 rue des Écoles, 5ᵉ; Mᵒ Maubert-Mutualité (Tues–Sat 11am–7pm). The *Le Disque Arabe* shop, 116bis bd de la Chapelle, 18ᵉ; Mᵒ Porte-de-la-Chapelle (Mon–Sat 10am–8pm), is a useful starting point for checking out raï concerts.

World music and rock

The last few years have seen considerable diversification in the Paris clubs and rock venues, which now concentrate more on international sounds, leaving the big Western rock bands to play the major arenas. Almost every club features **Latin and African dance music**, and big names from these worlds in particular **zouk** musicians from the French Caribbean – for whom Paris is a second home – are almost always in town. The divisions between world sounds are mixing more and more, too. Even "ethnically French" Parisians have produced their own

---

Music on TV and Radio

The private TV channel *Canal Plus* broadcasts big European concerts (Michael Jackson, Dire Straits etc) and was responsible for initiating presenter Antoine Decaunes' *Rapido* to bring new popular sounds to a wider audience. *M6* has some late-night music programmes as well as numerous video clips during the day while *Arte*, the new fifth channel, shows contemporary opera productions and documentaries on all types of music.

Of the **local radio stations**, *Radio Nova* (101.5 MHz) plays a good cross-section of what's new from rap to funk; *Radio Beur* (106.7 MHz) and *Radio France-Mahgreb* (99.5MHz) have raï; *Africa Paris* (94 MHz) and *Africa Numero 1* (107.5MHz) have African music; *Radio Latina* (99.0MHz) is the Latin American music station; *Oui* (102.3 MHz) is the all-day rock radio. The national station *Europe I* (104.7 MHz) has some imaginative music programming, and *France Musique* (91.7 and 92.1 MHz) carries classical, contemporary, jazz, opera and anything really big. Under strict new language laws, 40 percent of pop music played by any radio station has to be French, and there is now a dire Parisian radio station playing nothing but French music.

rewarding hybrids, best exemplified in the Pogue-like chaos of Les Négresses Vertes, whose future must now be in doubt following the death in January 1993 of lead singer Helno. One brilliant vocalist to look out for at the moment is Angélique Kidjo, from Benin.

The **listings** overleaf provide good starting points for enjoying the range of what's on offer; the only music they don't properly cover is Algerian **raï**, whose gigs – which sometimes start a couple of days late – are mostly advertised by word of mouth. For up-to-the-minute advice, ask at *Le Disque Arabe* (see opposite) or at cassette stalls in the predominantly North African quarters of Belleville and Ménilmontant.

The only rock'n'roll megastar of France turned 50 in 1993. His birthday, celebrated with solo gigs at the Parc des Princes, was fêted by prime minister Balladur, culture minister Jacques Toubin and Jacques Chirac, mayor of Paris: fortunately **Johnny Haliday** does not represent contemporary French rock. The best "alternative" rock band is **Mano Negra**, whose core members are French-born Spaniards. Their latest album, *Casa Babylon*, has been heavily influenced by their Latin American tours and combines rap, reggae, rock and salsa sounds. Their lyrics are good, though on *Casa Babylon* every track is in Spanish apart from *Santa Maradona*, a French tribute to the Argentinian footballer. Other quality rock musicians include Louis Bertignac and Paul Personne. However, half of all albums bought in France are still recorded by British and American bands.

There are numerous **heavy metal bands** with English names like "Megadeath". Then there's **trashpop**, an amalgam of funk, punk and splashes of bebop, heavy metal and psychedelia. An emerging new trend is French "country" music, known as **Astérix rock**, a bawdy, raucous energetic sound with accordions as the main instruments. Les French Lovers and Les Garçons Bouchers are two of the current bands making it.

French **rap**, much to the disgust of its practitioners, was given subsidies by the last government. The former minister of culture, Jack Lang, decided rap was "the French *commedia dell'arte*", while the rappers decided it would make more sense for Lang to give money to the people living in the rotting suburbs whose plight makes up much of their subject matter. Names to look out for are NTM, IAM and MC Solaar, who moves beyond traditional rap to something a good deal more melodic and musical, with superb words that you need to be pretty fluent to appreciate.

Music venues

Most of the venues listed below are clubs. A few of them will have live music all week, but the majority host bands on just a couple of nights, usually Friday and Saturday, when admission prices are also hiked up. *La Locomotive* and *Le Saint* are your best bets for a not-too-expensive good night out.

Mainly rock

Chapelle des Lombards, 19 rue de Lappe, 11ᵉ; ☎43.57.24.24 (Mᵒ Bastille). See p.325, under *Bals Musettes*.

La Cigale, 120 bd de Rochechouart, 18ᵉ; ☎42.23.15.15 (Mᵒ Pigalle). Music from 8.30pm. *Rita Mitsouko*, punk, indie etc: an eclectic programming policy in an old-fashioned converted theatre, long a fixture on the Pigalle scene.

City Rock Café, 13 rue Berry, 8ᵉ; ☎47.23.07.72 (Mᵒ George V). Daily noon–2am. Live rock'n'roll every night in the cellar below the American café of rock idol memorabilia. Drinks around 60F.

Élysée Montmartre, 72 bd de Rochechouart, 18ᵉ; ☎42.52.25.15 (Mᵒ Anvers). A historic Montmartre nightspot, now dedicated to rock. Inexpensive and fun, it pulls in a young and excitable crowd.

Farenheit, Espace Icare, 31 bd Gambetta, Issy-Les-Molineaux; ☎40.93.44.48 (Mᵒ Corentin-Celton). An energetic, sweaty suburban venue for mainly, but not exclusively, heavy metal bands. Around 50F.

Le Gibus, 18 rue du Faubourg-du-Temple, 11ᵉ; ☎47.00.78.88 (Mᵒ République).

Music and Nightlife

Music and Nightlife

Tues–Sat 11pm–5am; Sat only in Aug. For twenty years English rock bands on their way up have played their first Paris gig at *Gibus*, the Clash and Police among them. Fourteen nights of dross will turn up perhaps one decent band, but it's always hot, loud, energetic, and crowded with young Parisians heavily committed to the rock scene. This is also one of the cheaper clubs, both for admission and drinks.

La Locomotive, 90 bd de Clichy, 18e; ☎42.57.37.37 (Mo Blanche). Concerts start at 1am. Closed Monday. Enormous high-tech nightclub refurbished in the 1980s. Three dance floors: one for Techno; one for rock, heavy metal and concerts; and one for rap and funk. One of the most crowded, popular, and democratic in the city and you're sure of a good time. 60F weekdays, 100F weekends, Sunday 60F for men and free for women. Tues–Thurs 50F; Fri & Sat & Sun 90F.

New Riverside, 7 rue Grégoire-de-Tours, 6e; ☎43.54.46.33 (Mo Odéon). Daily 11pm–dawn. Good, friendly club playing rock and pop music in a sixteenth-century cellar. Breakfast included in admission price at the weekend. Free admission for women, except Fri and Sat; otherwise, Mon–Thurs 70F, Fri, Sat & Sun 100F.

Le Rex Club, 5 bd Poissonnière, 2e; ☎42.36.10.96 (Mo Montmartre). Tues–Sun 11pm–6am; sometimes closed Sun & Mon. Mainly live music – rock, funk, soul, raï, rap (mainly on Tues and Sat from 8pm; rave night, Thurs), charging 50–100F. Disco from 11pm, 60–90F.

Le Saint, 7 rue St-Séverin, 5e; ☎43.25.50.64 (Mo St-Michel). Tues–Sun 11am–dawn. Good value, varied music played in an ancient cellar; popular with students. 50F including one drink Tues–Thurs, 70F weekends.

Mainly Latin and Caribbean

L'Escale, 15 rue Monsieur-le-Prince, 6e; ☎43.25.55.22 (Mo Odéon). 11pm–4am. More Latin American musicians must have passed through here than any other club. The dancing sounds, salsa mostly, are in the basement (disco on Wed), while on the ground floor every variety of

South American music is given an outlet. Drinks 80F.

Mambo Club, 20 rue Cujas, 5e; ☎43.54.89.21 (Mo St-Michel/Odéon). Open 11pm till dawn, Sunday 4pm till dawn for "themed *soirées*"; closed Monday & Tuesday. Afro-Cuban and Antillais music in a seedy dive with people of all ages and nationalities.

La Plantation, 45 rue de Montpensier, 1er; ☎49.27.06.21 (Mo Palais-Royal). 11pm–dawn; closed Mon. In spite of the reputation for welcoming everyone, the doormen are fussy, particularly if you're white. Inside, excellent Cuban, Angolan, Congolese and Antillais music awaits you. 90F for entry and first drink; from 50F for drinks thereafter.

Les Trottoirs de Buenos Aires, 37 rue des Lombards, 1er; ☎40.26.29.32 (Mo Châtelet). Tues–Sun 6pm–4am. Argentinian tango is the only music performed on the stage of "the pavements of Buenos Aires". They say that the reason the tango evolved the sudden head turns was because dancing was banned during one repressive period in Argentinian history, so people danced in secret at home, turning their heads each time they heard a noise at the door. True or not, the range of music built around tango rhythms is completely transporting. Highly recommended. There are different bands almost every night (100F entrance); drinks are from 50F.

Music and Nightlife

Bals musettes and guinguettes.

Balajo, 9 rue de Lappe, 11ᵉ; ☎47.00.07.87 (Mº Bastille). Mon, Fri & Sat 10pm–4.30am. The last and greatest survivor of the old-style dance halls of working-class and slightly louche Paris. The *Balajo* dates from the 1930s and has kept its extravagant contemporary décor, with a balcony for the orchestra above the vast dance floor. The clientele is all sorts now, and all ages, though recently the bouncers have started to show a preference for teenyboppers. The music encompasses everything from mazurka to tango, cha-cha, twist, and the slurpy *chansons* of between the wars. There are disco and modern hits as well, but that's on Monday nights when the kids from across town come and all the popular nostalgia disappears. Admission price is around 30F. Monday, free for women between 11.30pm and 1am.

Chapelle des Lombards, 19 rue de Lappe, 11ᵉ; ☎43.57.24.24 (Mº Bastille). Mon–Sat and the eve of public holidays 8pm–dawn; closed Sun. This erstwhile *bal musette* of the rue de Lappe still plays the occasional waltz and tango, but for the most part the music is salsa, reggae, steel drums, gwo-kâ, zouk, raï and the blues. The doormen are not too friendly and once inside, we've heard bad stories of serious hassle and harassment inside. 100F admission and first drink; 50F upwards for the next drinks.

Chez Gégène, 162bis quai de Polangis, Joinville-le-Pont; ☎48.83.29.43 (*RER* Joinville-Le-Pont). Open mid-March to mid-October: Fri & Sat 9pm–2am, Sun 3–7pm. Just the other side of the Bois de Vincennes, this is a genuine *guinguette* (riverside eating, drinking and dancing venue) established in the 1900s. You don't have to dine to dance (around 70F extra for non-diners). *Le Petit Robinson*, fifty metres along from *Chez Gégène* and a bit more upmarket, is the place where very serious dancers go to show off their immaculate waltzes, foxtrots and tangos. Like its neighbour, it has a huge dance floor, with *rétro* Tuesday to Thursday nights and disco at the weekend. Admission and drink 80F evening, 75F afternoon.

Le Tango, 13 rue Au-Maire, 3ᵉ; ☎42.72.17.78 (Mº Arts-et-Métiers). Fri, Sat & the eve of public holidays only, 11pm–dawn. No vetting here. People wear whatever clothes they happen to be in and dance with abandon to please themselves, not the adjudicators of style. The music is jazzy Latin American: salsa, calypso and reggae. It is, however, a prime pick-up joint, and women are likely to be propositioned in no uncertain terms the moment they've agreed to a dance. Best to go with friends. Admission 60F Sat, 40F Fri. Drinks from 30F; obligatory cloakroom fee.

Nightclubs and discos

Clubs listed below are essentially **discos**, though a few have the odd live group. They come and go at an exhausting rate, the business principle being to take over a place, make a major investment in the décor, and close after two years, well in the black. As a customer, you contribute on a financial level – and in many places your ornamentation potential is equally important. Being sized up by a leather-

Details of afternoon sessions at the Balajo are given on p.288.

Music and Nightlife

clad American bouncer acting as the ultimate arbiter of style and prosperity can be a very demeaning experience. Men generally have a harder time than women. English-speakers are at an advantage, blacks are not. The one place that doesn't discriminate and should be at the top of any disco list is *Le Palace*.

Les Bains, 7 rue du Bourg-l'Abbé, 3e. ☎48.87.01.80. Mº Étienne-Marcel. Midnight–dawn every day (Sun, rock; Mon, 'disturbance of the peace'; Wed, 'disco inferno'). 150F admission, drinks expensive. This is as posey as they come – an old Turkish bathhouse where the *Stones* filmed part of their *Undercover of the Night* video, now redone in the antiperspirant, passionless style pioneered for the *Café Costes*. The music is house, rap and funk, with occasional live (usually dross) bands. It's not a place where a 500-franc note has much life expectancy. The décor features a plunging pool by the dance floor in which the punters are wont to ruin their non-colour-fast designer creations. Whether you can watch this spectacle depends on the bouncers, who have their fixed ideas. If you're turned away, be thankful and head down the road to *Le Tango* (see above).

Bar de la Plage, 12 rue du Colonel-Oudot, 12e. ☎43.45.55.55 (Mº Porte-Dorée). Tues–Sat 11.30pm–dawn. Solarium, deckchairs, fine sand, parasols and cocktails...

La Casbah, 18-20 rue de la Forge-Royale, 11e. ☎43.71.71.89. Mº Bastille). 9pm–5am. Bar upstairs, dancing down. The outstanding feature of this rather fancy and exclusive place is the décor: beautiful and authentic stuff from Morocco – doors, furniture, plasterwork – matched by the *zouave* costumes of the waiters and waitresses.

Discophage, 11 passage du Clos-Bruneau (off 31-33 rue des Écoles), 5e. ☎43.26.31.41 (Mº Maubert-Mutualité). Mon–Sat 9pm–3am, music begins at 10pm; closed Aug. A jam-packed, tiny and under-ventilated space, but all such discomforts are irrelevant for the best Brazilian sounds you can hear in Paris.

El Globo, 8 bd Strasbourg, 10e; ☎42.01.37.33 (Mº Strasbourg-St-Denis). Sat, Sun & public hols 10pm–dawn. Entry 60F plus drink. Currently very popular with Beaux Quartiers rebels, 10e *arrondissement* punks and all sorts. Lots of room to dance to international hits past and present.

Flash Back, 37 rue Grégoire-de-Tours, 6e; ☎43.25.56.70 (Mº Mabillon). 70F entry. 11am–dawn. Closed Monday. Techno and commercial rock in a futuristic decor.

Keur Samba, 79 rue la Béotie, 8e; ☎43.59.03.10 (Mº Franklin-Roosevelt). Until breakfast every day. An expensive and fashionable Arab and African venue, where you need to be very well dressed. Afro-Antillais music. Not cheap.

Le Malibu, 44 rue Tiquetonne, 2e; ☎42.36.62.70 (Mº Étienne-Marcel). 8.30pm–5.30am. Closed Mon & Tues. Around 150F. Black music from all over West Africa and the West Indies in a crowded basement beneath a restaurant. No strict admission policy here: blacks outnumber whites and everyone is under thirty and fairly well off.

Le Moloko, 26 rue Fontaine, 9e; ☎48.74.50.26 (Mº Blanche). 9pm-6am every day. A new, fashionable and successful addition to the night scene, frequented by the young and gorgeous, the trendy and posey, all sorts. Juke box instead of DJs, occasionally live music in the early evening. No admission; drinks from 50F.

Le Palace, 8 rue du Faubourg-Montmartre, 9e; ☎42.46.10.87 (Mº Montmartre). 11pm–dawn. Time was when everyone went to the Palace; it's still packed nightly with revellers, whether they've scraped together their week's savings or are just out to exercise the credit cards, and they all don their best party gear. Some nights it's thematic fancy dress, some nights the music is all African, other times the place is booked for TV dance shows. It's big, the bopping is good, and the clientele are an exuberant spectacle in themselves. Entry 100F Mon–Thurs, 120F weekends.

Le Shéhérazade, 3 rue de Liège, 9e; ☎48.74.41.68 (Mº Liège). Mon–Thurs 11pm–dawn, weekends midnight–dawn.

Popular with the youthful, mixed, dancing crowd. House music, with occasional variant evenings. Exotic décor in a former Russian cabaret; vodka 80–90F a shot. 100F admission plus drink.

Zed Club, 2 rue des Anglais, 5e; ☎43.54.93.78 (Mº Maubert-Mutualité. Wed–Sat 10.30pm–3.30am. *The* rock 'n' roll club. 50F entry Wed, 50F entry plus drink Thurs, 100F entry and drink Fri & Sat.

Lesbian and gay clubs and discos

Lesbian clubs find it hard to be exclusively female, and you may find that none of the varied atmospheres is agreeable. The pleasures of gay men are far better catered for, though AIDS has changed the scene, and the wicked little bars with obscure backrooms around Les Halles have all but ceased to exist. High-tech, well-lit, sense-surround disco beat is the current style.

While the selection of gay male-oriented establishments below only scratches the surface, for gay women our listings more or less cover all that's available. Lesbians, however, are welcome in some of the predominantly male clubs. For a complete rundown, consult *Paris Scene* (Gay Men's Press, £5.99), *Gai-Pied's Guide Gai* or the newspaper *Exit* (see p.47).

Women

La Champmeslé, 4 rue Chabanais, 2e; ☎42.96.85.20 (Mº Opéra). Mon–Sun 6pm–2am. Intimate, relaxed bar with yuppie clientèle. Cabaret on Thurs. Drinks 25–40F.

Chez Moune, 54 rue Pigalle, 18e; ☎45.26.64.64 (Mº Pigalle). 10pm–dawn. In the red-light heart of Paris, this mixed but predominantly women's cabaret and disco may shock or delight feminists. The evening includes a strip tease (by women) without the standard audience for such shows (any man causing the slightest fuss is kicked out). Sunday tea-dance afternoons from 4.30–8pm are strictly women-only.

L'Entracte, 25 bd Poissonnière, 2e; ☎40.26.01.93 (Mº Montmartre). Sun–Fri from 11pm; Sat & Sun 50F entrance from

midnight. Happy hour 11pm–1.30am. Drinks 40F. Diverse music.

Entre Nous, 17 rue Laferrière, 9e; ☎48.78.11.67 (Mº St-Georges). Sat only 11pm–dawn. A small women-only club with an intimate atmosphere and catholic taste in music.

Le New Look tea dance See under "Afternoon Tangos", Chapter 15.

Le New Monocle, 60 bd Edgar-Quinet, 14e; ☎43.20.81.12 (Mº Montparnasse). 11pm–dawn; closed Sun. This women's cabaret has been revitalized since the closing of its rival, *Le Baby Doll*. A small scattering of men is allowed in every evening.

Le Privilège-Kat, 3 cité Bergère, 9e; ☎42.46.50.98 (Mº Rue-Montmartre). Fri & Sat 11.30pm–6am. Entry 90F, drinks from 60F. A venue run by two stylish women. No men.

Mixed

Le Bar Central, 33 rue Vieille-du-Temple, 4e; ☎42.72.16.94 (Mº Hôtel-de-Ville). Daily 4pm–2am. Small, crowded, friendly bar. Mostly men. Drinks 20–60F.

Men

Le BH, 7 rue du Roule, 1er (Mº Châtelet-Les-Halles). 11pm–8am. The downstairs rooms have been knocked into one sizeable and illuminated disco, but this is still one of the cheapest gay discos in the city; exclusively male.

Club 18, 18 rue de Beaujolais, 1er; ☎42.97.52.13 (Mº Bourse). 11pm–dawn; closed Monday. Mainly young gay clientele in this friendly cellar bar with Sunday cabaret. 60F entry Fri & Sat.

La Luna, 28 rue Keller, 11e; ☎40.21.09.91 (Mº Bastille). Wed–Sun 11pm–6am. Weekend entry 50F, drinks from 45F. The latest high-tech rendezvous for the gay Bastille, complete with mirrors to dance to.

Le Manhattan, 8 rue des Anglais, 5e; ☎43.54.98.86 (Mº Maubert-Mutualité). Fri, Sat & Sun 11pm–6am. Admission 48F; drinks from 37F. Men-only club with a good funky disco.

Music and Nightlife

For gay and lesbian contacts and information, see Basics, p.46.

Music and Nightlife

Le Palace tea dance. See under "Afternoon Tangos", Chapter 15.

Le Piano Zinc, 49 rue des Blancs-Manteaux, 4e; ☎ 42.74.32.42 (Mº Rambuteau/Hôtel-de-Ville). 6pm–2am; closed Mon. From 10pm, when the piano-playing starts, this bar becomes a happy riot of songs, music-hall acts, and dance, which may be hard to appreciate if you don't follow French very well. Drinks 36–47F.

Le Queen, 102 av des Champs-Élysées, 8e; ☎ 42.89.31.32 (Mº George-V). 11pm–dawn. Women welcome, except Thurs. Good boppy music. Racy theme nights Mon, Wed & Sun. Admission free weekdays; weekends 80F. Drinks 50F.

Jazz, blues, and chansons

Jazz has long enjoyed an appreciative audience in France, most especially since the end of World War II when the intellectual rigour and agonized musings of bebop struck an immediate chord of sympathy in the existentialist hearts of the *après-guerre*. Charlie Parker, Dizzy Gillespie, Bud Powell, Miles Davis – all were being listened to in the Fifties, when in Britain their names were known only to a tiny coterie of fans.

Gypsy guitarist Django Rheinhardt and his partner, violinist Stéphane Grappelli, whose work represents the distinctive and undisputed French contribution to the jazz canon, had much to do with the music's popularity. But it was also greatly enhanced by the presence of many front-rank black American musicians, for whom Paris was a haven of freedom and culture after the racial prejudice and philistinism of the States. Among them were the soprano sax player Sidney Bechet, who set up in legendary partnership with French clarinetist Claude Luter, and Bud Powell, whose turbulent exile partly inspired the tenor man played by Dexter Gordon (himself a veteran of the *Montana* club) in the film *Round Midnight*.

Jazz is still alive and well in the city, with new venues opening all the time, where you can hear all styles from New Orleans to current experimental. Some

local names to look out for are: saxophonists François Jeanneau, Barney Willen, Didier Malherbe, André Jaume and Steve Lacey; violinist Didier Lockwood; British-born but long Paris-resident guitarist John McLaughlin; pianist Alain Jeanmarie; accordionist Richard Galliano; and bass player Jean-Jacques Avenel. All of them can be found playing small gigs, regardless of the size of their reputations.

Mainly jazz

Le Baiser Salé, 58 rue des Lombards, 1er; ☎ 42.33.37.71 (Mº Châtelet). 8.30pm–4am. Drinks from 60F. A bar downstairs and a small, crowded upstairs room with live music every night from 11pm – usually jazz, rhythm & blues, Latino-rock, reggae or Brazilian.

Le Bilboquet, 13 rue St-Benoît, 6e; ☎ 45.48.81.84 (Mº St-Germain). Mon–Sat 9pm–dawn, closed Sun. A very comfortable bar/restaurant with live jazz every night – local and international stars, like baritone player Gary Smulyan. Food served until 1am. The music starts at 10.45pm. No admission, but pricey drinks, 70F plus. This is the street where Dexter Gordon, Miles Davis, Bud Powell, and others played and hung out in the Fifties.

Les Bouchons, 19 rue des Halles, 1er; ☎ 42.33.28.73 (Mº Châtelet-Les-Halles). Until 2am. This is a restaurant, with live jazz every evening – from traditional to contemporary in a room below the brasserie reminiscent of a gentleman's club. But, surprisingly, no admission charge and reasonably priced cocktails. A good place if you want to sit and talk.

Le Café de la Plage, 59 rue de Charonne, 11e; ☎ 47.00.91.60 (Mº Bastille). Daily 10pm–2am. A smoky, low-ceilinged, arty bar where it is easy to talk to people. Jazz in the basement. During concerts, first drink 100F, thereafter 50F plus.

Caveau de la Huchette, 5 rue de la Huchette, 5e; ☎ 43.26.65.05 (Mº Saint-Michel). Daily 9.30pm till 2am or later. Sun–Thurs 60F (students 55F), Fri & Sat 70F; drinks from 20F. A wonderful slice of old Paris life in this horribly touristified area. Live jazz music to dance to on a floor surrounded by tiers of benches, and a bar decorated with caricatures of the barman drawn on any material to hand.

La Closerie des Lilas, 171 bd Montparnasse, 6e; ☎ 43.54.21.68 (Mº Port-Royal). 10pm–1am. Brilliant piano-playing the nights when Ivan Meyer is on. Having chosen your cocktail (around 60F), you can make your musical requests and sit back in a chair that may well bear the name-plate of Trotsky, Verlaine or André Gide.

Au Duc des Lombards, 42 rue des Lombards, 1er; ☎ 42.36.51.13 (Mº Châtelet-Les-Halles). Until 2am. Drinks from 40F. Small, unpretentious bar with performances every night from 11pm – jazz piano, blues, ballads, fusion.

Théâtre Dunois, 108 rue du Chevaleret, 13e; ☎ 42.33.22.88 (Mº Chevaleret). Daily from 7pm. Concerts Mon–Fri & Sun 8.30–11.30pm. A new location for the *Dunois*, more modern, no stage, and a bigger bar. The musical policy still gives consistent support to free and experimental jazz. One of the few places in Paris to hear impro-vised music, as opposed to free jazz. 70F admission, 50F students.

L'Eustache, 37 rue Berger, 1er; ☎ 40.26.23.20 (Mº Châtelet-Les-Halles). 11am–4am; Thurs, Fri & Sat live jazz 10.30pm–2am. Cheap beer and very good jazz by local musicians in this young and friendly Les Halles café – in

fact, the cheapest good jazz in the capital.

Instants Chavirés, 7 rue Richard-Lenoir, Montreuil; ☎ 42.87.25.91 (Mº Robespierre). Tues–Sat 9pm–1am; concerts at 9.30pm. Avant-garde jazz joint, on the eastern edge of the city, close to the Porte de Montreuil: a place where musicians go to hear each other play. Its reputation has already attracted subsidies from both state and local authorities. Jam sessions Wed at 9pm. Admission 35–80F, depending on the celebrity of the band; drinks from 15F.

Le Latitudes Jazz Club, 7–11 rue St-Benoît, 6e; ☎ 42.60.23.02 (Mº St-Germain-des-Prés). Daily 6pm–2am; live jazz Thurs–Sat 10pm–2am. French and foreign stars play in the swish downstairs bar of the hotel. Around 110F for the first drink, thereafter 15–65F depending on your choice.

Lionel Hampton Bar, Hôtel Méridien, 81 bd Gouvion-St-Cyr, 17e; ☎ 40.68.34.34 (Mº Porte-Maillot). 10pm–2am, closed Sun. First-rate jazz venue, with big-name musicians. Inaugurated by Himself, but otherwise the great man is only an irregu-lar visitor. Drinks from 130F.

Le Montana, 28 rue St-Benoît, 6e; ☎ 45.48.62.15 (Mº St-Germain-des-Prés). Mon–Fri noon–7am, Sat & Sun 6pm–7am; music 10.30pm–2am. Jazz, French songs . . . but not one of the best venues for jazz. Drinks from 110F.

New Morning, 7–9 rue des Petites-Écuries, 10e; ☎ 45.23.51.41 (Mº Château-d'Eau). 9pm–1.30am (concerts start around 10pm). This is the place where the big international names in jazz come to play. It's not all it's cracked up to be, though. The sound is good but the décor, though spacious, is rather cold – and no marks either for the ludicrous drink prices.

Le Petit Journal, 71 bd St-Michel, 5e; ☎ 43.26.28.59 (Mº Luxembourg). Mon–Sat 10pm–2am. A small, smoky bar, long frequented by Left Bank student types, with good, mainly French, traditional and mainstream sounds. First drink 100–150F. Rather middle-aged and tourist-prone. Closed in August.

Music and Nightlife

**Music and
Nightlife**

Le Petit Journal Montparnasse, 13 rue du
Commandant-Mouchotte, 14ᵉ;
☎ 43.21.56.70 (Mº Montparnasse). Mon–
Sat 10pm–2am, closed Sun and July.
Under the *Hôtel Montparnasse*, and sister
establishment to the above, with bigger
visiting names, both French and international. Drinks around 80F.

Le Petit Opportun, 15 rue des
Lavandières-Ste-Opportune, 1ᵉʳ;
☎ 42.36.01.36 (Mº Châtelet-Les-Halles).
Tues–Sat 9pm–3am; closed Sun, Mon
and August. Music from 11pm. It's worth
arriving early to get a seat for the live
music in the dungeon-like cellar where
the acoustics play strange tricks and you
can't always see the musicians. Fairly
eclectic policy and a crowd of genuine
connoisseurs. First drink 120F.

Slow Club, 130 rue de Rivoli, 1ᵉʳ;
☎ 42.33.84.30 (Mº Châtelet/Pont-Neuf).
Tues–Sat 10pm–4am, closed Sun & Mon.
Admission 55F, Fri & Sat 70F. A jazz club
where you can bop the night away to the
sounds of Claude Luter's sextet and visiting New Orleans musicians.

Le Sunset, 60 rue des Lombards, 1ᵉʳ;
☎ 40.26.46.20 (Mº Châtelet-Les-Halles).
Mon–Sat 8pm–3am. Admission 100F with
drink. Restaurant upstairs, jazz club in the
basement, featuring the best musicians –
the likes of Alain Jeanmarie and Turk
Mauro – and frequented by musicians, in
the wee small hours.

Utopia, 1 rue de l'Ouest, 14ᵉ;
☎ 43.22.79.66 (Mº Pernety). 10.30pm–
dawn; closed Sun & Mon. No genius
here, but good French blues singers interspersed with jazz and blues tapes, the
people listening mostly young and
studentish. Drinks from 50F. Generally
very pleasant atmosphere.

Mainly *chansons*

Le Brin de Zinc, 50 rue Montorgueil, 2ᵉ;
☎ 42.21.10.80 (Mº Sentier). Tues–Sat
8pm–2am. A *caveau à vin et à chansons*
where you can drink or dine at 8.30pm,
with a performance of *chansons* to follow
at 10pm Wed–Sat. Prices are reasonable
(*plats du jour* 52F) and there's no extra
charge for the music.

Casino de Paris, 19 rue de Clichy, 9ᵉ;
☎ 49.95.99.99 (Mº Trinité). Tickets from
100F to 200F. This decaying, once plush
casino in one of the seediest streets in
Paris is a venue for all sorts of performances – *chansons*, poetry combined
with flamenco guitar, cabaret. Check the
listings magazines under "*variétés*".

Caveau des Oubliettes, 11 rue St-Julien-
le-Pauvre, 5ᵉ; ☎ 43.54.94.97 (Mº St-
Michel). 9pm–2am; closed Sun. 140F with
drink. French popular music of bygone
times – Piaf and earlier – sung with
exquisite nostalgia in the ancient prisons
of Châtelet.

Le Piston Pélican, 15 rue de Bagnolet,
20ᵉ; ☎ 43.70.23.93 (Mº Alexandre-
Dumas). Wed–Sun 10pm–2am, Tues
7pm–2am. A scruffy bar seeing a revivial
of *café-conc'* – listening to live music for
the price of a coffee, but getting a bit too
popular for its own good.

Classical and contemporary music

Paris is a stimulating environment for **classical music**, both established and contemporary. The former is well represented with
a choice of ten to twenty concerts every
day of the week, with numerous performances taking place in the appropriate
acoustical setting of churches, often for
free or very cheap. **Contemporary and
experimental computer-based** work flourishes too; leading exponents are Paul
Mefano and Pierre Boulez, founder of
Beaubourg's *IRCAM* centre and himself
one of the first pupils of Olivier Messiaen,
the grand old man of modern French
music, who died in 1992.

The city hosts a good number of musical festivals which vary from year to year.
For details, pick up the current year's
festival schedule from the tourist office or
the Hôtel de Ville.

Two periodicals for those with a serious interest in the music scene are the
monthly *Le Mélomane*, published by the
Maison de la Radio, and the trimonthly
Résonance, published by *IRCAM* at the
Centre Beaubourg and specializing in
contemporary music.

Music and Nightlife

Regular concert venues

Tickets for classical concerts are best bought at the box offices, though for big names you may find overnight queues, and a large number of seats are always booked by subscribers. The price range is very reasonable. The listings magazines and daily newspapers will have details of concerts in these venues, in the churches and in the suburbs. Look out for posters as well.

The **Cité de la Musique** project at La Villette (see p.173) promises two major new concert venues. The **Conservatoire**, the national music academy, has already opened its doors on avenue Jean-Jaurès (information and bookings: ☎40.40.46.46/ 40.40.46.47). And next door, a new **auditorium** is scheduled to open in 1995, designed to be adaptable to all kinds of novel configurations of instruments.

These apart, the top **auditoriums** are:

Auditorium des Halles, porte St-Eustache, Forum des Halles, 1er; ☎42.33.00.00 (Mᵒ Châtelet-les-Halles).

Épicerie-Beaubourg, 12 rue du Renard, 4e; ☎42.72.23.41 (Mᵒ Hôtel-de-Ville).

Salle Gaveau, 45 rue de la Boétie; ☎49.53.05.07 (Mᵒ Miromesnil).

Salle Pleyel, 252 rue du Faubourg-St-Honoré, 8e; ☎45.61.06.30 (Mᵒ Ternes). Home of the *Orchestre de Paris*, the Paris symphony orchestra.

Théâtre des Champs-Élysées, 15 av Montaigne, 8e; ☎49.52.50.50 (Mᵒ Alma-Marceau).

Théâtre Musical de Paris, Théâtre du Châtelet, 1 place du Châtelet, 1er; ☎40.28.28.40 (Mᵒ Châtelet).

Opera

Opera would seem to have had its rewards in President Mitterrand's millennial endowments. The **Opéra-Bastille** (see p.101) is his most extravagant legacy to the city. It opened, with all due pomp, in 1989. Its first production – a six-hour performance of Berlioz's *Les Troyens* – cast something of a shadow on the project's proclaimed commitment to popularizing the art. "We are audacious", was the defence of the president, Pierre Bergé, who got his job after a lot of acrimonious political wrangling which included the dismissal of Daniel Barenboim as musical director. This was shortly followed by the dismissal of Nureyev from the same post. Both Jessye Norman and Dietrich Fischer-Dieskau have boycotted the place. Resignations and a severe loss of morale followed the company's accident at the Seville Expo 92, when a chorus singer was killed and many others injured. Meanwhile, Bergé, a self-proclaimed anarchist, lunches regularly with Mitterrand and retains his equally prestigious job running Yves St-Laurent's fashion house. Just to keep the controversy going, the current musical director is a relatively unknown South Korean, Myung Whun Chung, who has seemed more interested in forwarding his

One of the pleasantest places in Paris to listen to soloists, quartets or chamber orchestras is L'Opus Café, a café where you can eat, drink and smoke – see p.258.

Music and Nightlife

recording career, and has recently been barred from entering the building by the management.

Opera in Paris creams off almost two-thirds of the whole annual state budget for music. Potentially the Bastille orchestra is one of the best, and most people agree that the acoustics of the building are marvellous. But the auditorium is so big that beyond about row 15 you need opera glasses or binoculars to see the expressions of the singers. And there is a feeling that productions are too big and stagey (and not the best on offer). To judge the place for yourself: **tickets** (40–520F) can be booked Monday to Saturday 11am to 6pm on ☎44.73.13.00 or at the ticket offices (Mon–Sat 11am–6.30pm within two weeks of the performance). The cheapest seats are only available to personal callers; unfilled seats are sold at discount to students five minutes before the curtain goes up. For programme details phone ☎43.43.96.96.

More big-scale opera productions are staged at the **Théâtre Musical de Paris**, part of the Théâtre du Châtelet (see above). Rather less grand opera is performed at the **Opéra-Comique** (Salle Favard, 5 rue Favart, 2ᵉ. ☎42.86.88.83; Mᵒ Richelieu-Drouot.). Occasional operas and concerts by solo singers are hosted by the **Théâtre des Champs Elysées** (see p.342). Both opera and recitals are also put on at the multipurpose performance halls (see final section, opposite).

Contemporary music

One of the few disadvantages of the high esteem in which the French hold their intellectual and artistic life is that it encourages, at the extremes, a tendency to sterile *intellectualisme*, as the French themselves call it. In the eyes of many music-lovers, and musicians, this has been nowhere more evident than in music, where the avant-garde is split into post-serialist and spectral music factions. Doyen of the former is composer Pierre Boulez; of the latter, it is Paul Mefano, director of the *2E2M* ensemble.

Boulez's experiments for many years received massive public funding in the form of a vast laboratory of acoustics and "digital signal processing" – a complex known as *IRCAM* – housed underneath the Beaubourg arts centre. If you want to find out exactly what all this means, you can go and decide for yourself by playing around, for free, with the tapes in the *IRCAM* lobby (entrance down the stairs by the Stravinsky pool on the south side of Beaubourg). If you're impressed, you might want to attend a performance by Boulez's own orchestra, the *Ensemble Inter-Contemporain* (details from Beaubourg information desk).

But the project has been much criticized for the amount of money spent on what is widely seen as sterile and elitist experimentation – honks and thumps, to the layman. Boulez himself has bowed out, but the project survives, using the *Next* generation of computers, under the more liberal musical leadership of Laurent Bayle. One of his collaborators is the English composer George Benjamin.

Other Paris-based practitioners of contemporary and experimental music include Jean-Claude Eloy, Pascal Dusapin and Luc Ferrarie. Among the younger generation of less sectarian composers, some names to look out for are Nicos Papadimitriou, Thierry Pécourt, François Leclere, Marc Dalbavie, and Georges Aperghis, whose speciality is musical theatre.

The big performance halls

Events at any of the performance spaces listed below will be well advertised on billboards and posters throughout the city. Tickets can be obtained at the halls themselves, though it's easier to get them through agents like *FNAC* or *Virgin Megastore* (see p.322).

Le Bataclan, 50 bd Voltaire, 11ᵉ; ☎48.05.65.23 (Mᵒ Oberkampf). One of the best places for visiting and native rock bands.

Forum des Halles, Niveau 3, Porte Rambuteau, 15 rue de l'Équerre-d'Argent, 1ᵉʳ; ☎42.03.11.11 (Mᵒ Châtelet). Varied functions – theatre, performance art, rock etc, often with foreign touring groups.

Maison des Cultures du Monde, 101 bd Raspail, 6e; ☎45.44.72.30 (Mº Rennes). All the arts from all over the world and undominated for once by the Europeans.

Olympia, 28 bd des Capucines, 9e; ☎47.42.25.49 (Mº Madeleine/Opéra). An old music hall hosting occasional well-known rock groups and large popular concert performers.

Palais des Congrès, place de la Porte-Maillot, 17e; ☎40.48.25.50 (Mº Porte-Maillot). Opera, ballet, orchestral music, trade fairs, and the superstars of US and British rock.

Palais des Glaces, 37 rue du Faubourg-du-Temple, 10e; ☎42.02.27.17 (Mº République). Smallish theatre used for rock, ballet, jazz, and French folk.

Palais Omnisports de Bercy, 8 bd de Bercy, 12e; ☎43.42.01.23 (Mº Bercy). Opera, bicycle racing, Bruce Springsteen, ice hockey, and Citroën launches – the newest multipurpose stadium with seats to give vertigo to the most level-headed, but an excellent space when used in the round.

Palais des Sports, Porte de Versailles, 15e; ☎48.28.40.48 (Mº Porte-de-Versailles). Another vast-scale auditorium, ideal if you want to see your favourite rock star in miniature half a mile away.

Zenith, Parc de la Villette, 211 av Jean-Jaurès, 20e; ☎42.08.60.00/42.40.60.00 (Mº Porte-de-Pantin). Seating for 6,500 people in an inflatable stadium designed exclusively for rock and pop concerts. Head for the concrete column with a descending red aeroplane.

Music and Nightlife

Chapter 19

Film, Theatre and Dance

Movie-goers have a choice from over 350 films showing in Paris in any one week, which puts moving visuals on an equal footing with the still visuals of the art museums and galleries. And they cover every place and period, with new works (with the exception of British movies) arriving here long before they reach London and New York. If your French is good enough to cope with subtitles, go and see a Senegalese, Taiwanese, Brazilian or Finnish film that might never be seen in Britain or the US at all, except perhaps on television in the middle of the night a year or two later.

Theatre, on the other hand, is less accessible to non-natives, especially the *café-théâtres* touted by "knowing" guide-writers. However, there is stimulation in the cult of the director; Paris is home to Peter Brook, Ariane Mnouchkine and other exiles, as well as French talent. Also, transcending language barriers, there are exciting developments in dance, much of it incorporating mime, which, alas, no longer seems to have a separate status.

Tipping

It is common practice in Parisian thea-tres and cinemas for the ushers to expect a small tip from each customer – on the scale of 5F per person – and to ask for the money if it is not imme-diately forthcoming.

As for **sex shows** and **soft porn caba-rets**, with names that conjure up the clas-sic connotations of the sinful city – *Les Folies Bergères* or the *Moulin Rouge* – they thrive and will no doubt continue for as long as Frenchmen's culture excuses anything on the grounds of stereotyped female beauty. See p.161 for a fuller account.

Listings

Listings for all films and stage productions are detailed in *Pariscope*, etc, with brief resumés or reviews. Venues with wheel-chair access will say "*accessible aux handicapés*".

Film

Paris remains one of the few cities in the world in which it's possible to get not only serious entertainment but a **serious film education** from the programmes of regular – never mind the specialist – cinemas.

In a typical week in March 1994, for example, it was possible – not counting new and recent releases of American and other films – to catch retrospective seasons of films by Mike Nicols, Orson Welles, Pedro Almodovar, David Lynch, Peter Greenaway, Roman Polanski, and Serge Gainsbourg, plus seasons of impor-tant westerns and Vietnamese films, and any number of historically significant films such as Orson Welles' *Lady from Shanghai*, Monty Python's *Holy Grail*, Carné's *Hôtel du Nord*, David Lynch's

Dune, James Ivory's *A Room with a View*, Rossellini's *Rome Open City* and *Viaggio in Italia*, Bresson's *Pickpocket*, and Resnais' *Hiroshima Mon Amour*.

Almost all of the huge selection of foreign films will be shown at some cinemas in the original language – *version originale* or *v.o.* in the listings – as opposed to *version française* or *v.f.*, which means it's dubbed into French. *Version anglaise* or *v.a.* means it's the English version of an international co-production.

Among **cinemas which run seasons** of the work of a particular director or actor/actress, such as those outlined above, are the *Action* chain, the *Escurial*, the *Entrepôt* and *Le Studio 28*. In addition, some of the **foreign institutes** in the city have occasional screenings, so if your favourite director is a Hungarian, a Swede or a Yugoslav, for example, check what's on at those countries' cultural centres. These will be listed along with other cinema-clubs and museum screenings

Film, Theatre and Dance

French cinema

The French have treated cinema as an art form, deserving of state subsidy, ever since its origination with the Lumière brothers in 1895. Investment in film production is nearly twice the level as in the UK, and the number of films made annually is three times as great. The medium has as yet never had to bow down to TV, the seat of judgement stays in Cannes, and Paris remains the cinema capital of Europe. The Archives du Film at the Centre National de la Cinématographie in the Palais de Tokyo possess the largest collection of silent and early talkie movies in the world. They have embarked on a fifteen-year, 17-million franc programme to transfer all the pre-1960 stock, whose celluloid nitrate is dissolving, onto acetate. A yearly festival is planned to show selections of these lesser-known films, including turn-of-the-century one-minute shorts featuring new inventions such as the hose-pipe.

While the old is treasured and preserved, the new in French cinema revolves around the Nureyev of moviedom, **Gérard Départieu**. Jean-Paul Rappeneau's 1989 screening of the late nineteenth-century play *Cyrano de Bergerac*, starring Départieu and with rhyming couplets throughout, was the most expensive French film ever made and exceeded all box office expectations in America and Britain. Départieu went on to act in English in the American film *Green Card*, and then to play Columbus in the American-French co-production *1492: Conquest of Paradise*. His latest role is as the collier Maheu in the movie version of *Germinal*, Zola's stirring and evocative novel of life, work, love and politics in a northern French mining community in the late nineteenth century.

The daring brilliance of *Cyrano de Bergerac* was a welcome departure from the style movies of the early 1980s, such as *Diva* and *Subway*, and Départieu has reinvigorated French cinema as an export industry. But there is no current force in French movie-making to touch on the prolific New Wave period of the Sixties, pioneered by **Jean-Luc Godard** and others. Luc Besson, Leos Carax, Agnès Varda, Bernard Tavernier and Patrice Chereau (also well known as a theatre director) are some of the stalwarts, and many foreign directors – notably Kurosawa and Wajda – work or have worked in France, benefiting from public subsidies.

Since *Germinal*, big French films have included the serious two-part period piece *Jeanne la Pucelle* (Joan of Arc) and *Les Visiteurs*, a happy medieval romp. Nostalgia rather than postmodernism seems to be the current mood in French film making. The row over cultural subsidies in the world GATT talks revealed just how threatened France feels by American movie imports.

However, the top box-office hits in Paris tend to be transatlantic imports, and a quick scan down the listings for any week shows a dominance of foreign films. Nonetheless, the city remains the perfect place to see movies, from the latest blockbuster to the least-known works of the earliest directors.

Film, Theatre and Dance

Every year Paris plays host to an **International Festival of Women's Films**, which takes place at the end of March or beginning of April. It's organized by the Maison des Arts in Créteil, a southeastern suburb at the end of the Balard-Créteil métro line.

1994 was the sixteenth year of this festival, which has been very influential in promoting and encouraging works by women, particularly in France. Chinese, Russian, American, Japanese and European films compete for the eight awards, six of which are voted for by the audiences. Programme details are available from mid-March onwards, from the Maison des Arts, place Salvador-Allende, Créteil; ☎ 49.80.38.98 (Mº Créteil-Préfecture), or from the Maison des Femmes, 8 Cité Prost, 11e ; ☎ 43.48.29.91 (Mº Faidherbe-Chaligny).

under "*Séances exceptionnelles*" or "*Ciné-clubs*", and are usually cheaper than ordinary cinemas.

Times and prices

Movie-going is not exclusively an evening occupation: the *séances* (programmes) start between 1 and 3pm at many places, and usually continue through to the early hours.

Cinema tickets rarely need buying in advance, and are cheap by European standards. The average price is 45F; and most cinemas have lower rates on Monday or Wednesday, as well as reductions for students from Monday to Thursday. Some matinée *séances* also have discounts. Two of the biggest chains, *UGC* and *Gaumont*, sell multi-tickets at 150F for 5; two people can use the tickets for the same film.

All Paris' cinemas are non-smoking, and in some cases the ushers are unwaged and so positively *have* to be tipped (see box on previous page).

Cinemas

L'Entrepôt, 7–9 rue Francis-de-Pressensé, 14e (Mº Pernety). One of the best alternative Paris movie houses, which has been keeping ciné-addicts happy for years with its three screens dedicated to the obscure, the subversive and the brilliant, and to showing among those categories many Arab and African films. It also shows videos, satellite and cable TV, has a bookshop selling books and posters on the cinema (Mon–Sat 2–8pm), and a restaurant (noon–midnight daily).

L'Escurial Panorama, 11 bd de Port-Royal, 13e (Mº Gobelins). A cinema that combines plush seats, big screen, and more art than commerce in its screening policy, this is likely to be showing something like *Eraserhead* on the small screen and the latest offering from a big-name director, French, Japanese or American, on the panoramic screen (never dubbed).

Grand Action & Action Écoles, 5 & 23 rue des Écoles, 5e; Mº Cardinal-Lemoine/ Maubert-Mutualité; Action Christine, 4 rue Christine, 6e; Mº Odéon/St-Michel. The Action chain specializes in new prints of ancient classics.

Le Grand Rex, 1 bd Poissonnière, 2e (Mº Bonne-Nouvelle). Just as outrageous as the *Pagode* (see opposite) but in the kitsch line, with a Metropolis-style tower blazing its neon name, 2800 seats and a ceiling of stars and a Spanish city skyline, all as a frame for the largest cinema screen in Europe. It's the good old Thirties public movie-seeing experience, though unfortunately all foreign films are dubbed.

Gaumont Kinopanorama, 60 av de la Motte-Piquet, 15e (Mº La Motte-Picquet). One of the big ones, but since it has fallen into the hands of *Gaumont* you can expect big-draw movies, with all foreign titles dubbed.

Lucernaire Forum, 53 rue Notre-Dame-des-Champs, 6e (Notre-Dame-des-Champs/Vavin). An art complex with three screening rooms, two theatres, an art gallery, bar and restaurant, showing mainly old arty movies.

Max Linder Panorama, 24 bd Poissonnière, 9e (Mº Bonne-Nouvelle).

Opposite *Le Grand Rex*, this always shows films in the original, and has almost as big a screen, state-of-the-art sound, and Art Deco décor.

La Pagode, 57bis rue de Babylone, 7e (Mº François-Xavier). The most beautiful of all the capital's cinemas, originally transplanted from Japan at the turn of the century to be a rich Parisienne's party place. The wall panels of the *Grande Salle* are embroidered in silk; golden dragons and elephants hold up the candelabra; and a battle between Japanese and Chinese warriors rages on the ceiling. If you don't fancy the films being shown you can still come here for tea and cakes (see p.250).

Le Studio des Ursulines, 10 rue des Ursulines, 5e (Mº Censier-Daubenton). This was where *The Blue Angel* had its world première.

Le Studio 28, 10 rue de Tholozé, 18e (Mº Blanche/Abbesses). In its early days, after one of the first showings of Bunuel's *L'Age d'Or*, this was done over by extreme right-wing Catholics who destroyed the screen and the paintings by Dali and Ernst in the foyer. The cinema still hosts avant-garde premières, followed occasionally by discussions with the director, as well as regular festivals.

Utopia, 9 rue Champollion, 5e (Mº Odéon). Another favourite.

Cinémathèques

For the seriously committed film-freak, the best movie venues in Paris are the three *cinémathèques*, in the *Salle Garance* on the top floor of Beaubourg, 4e (Mº Rambuteau; closed Tues) and the *Cinémathèque Française* in the Musée du Cinéma, Palais de Chaillot, corner of avs Président-Wilson and Albert-de-Mun, 16e (Mº Trocadéro) and in the Palais de Tokyo, 13 av du Président-Wilson, 16e (Mº Trocadéro), with screenings every day. These give you a choice of over fifty different films a week, many of which would never be shown commercially, and tickets are only 25F, 15F for students. At the end of 1997 the whole of the Palais de Tokyo will become the Palais des Arts

de l'Image, with four cinemas and everything the dedicated film-goer could want, including festivals of restored films (see box on p.355).

The *Vidéothèque de Paris* in the Forum des Halles (see p.288) is another excellent-value venue for the bizarre or obscure on celluloid or video. Their repertoires are always based around a particular theme with some connection with Paris.

The largest screen

There is one cinematic experience that has to be recommended, however trite and vainglorious the film – and that's the 180-degree projection system called Omnimax, which works with a special camera and a 70mm horizontally progressing – rolling loop – film.

There are fewer than a dozen Omnimax cinemas in existence, of which two are to be found in Paris. One is **La Géode**, the mirrored globe bounced off the **Cité des Sciences** at La Villette, and the other, its offspring, is the new **Dôme-Imax** on the *Colline de l'Automobile* beside the Grande Arche at La Défense.

Unfortunately, Omnimax owners are not the sort to produce brilliant films. What you get is a *Readers' Digest* view of outer space, great cities of the world, monumental landscapes or whatever, on a screen wider than your range of vision into which you feel you might fall at any moment. Low-flying shots, or shots taken from the front of moving trains, bobsleighs, cars and so on are sensational.

There are several screenings a day at both places, but you usually need to book in advance (**La Géode**: 10am–9pm, closed Mon; tickets 55F or 75F/65F for combined ticket with Cité des Sciences; reservations ☎36.68.29.30 and best way to avoid the queues is to go at 9.30am for the first showing; Mº Porte-de-la-Villette/Corentin-Cariou; **Le Dôme-Imax**; daily 12.15–8pm; tickets 55F/45F; information ☎46.92.45.45; Mº/RER line A, Grande-Arche-de-la-Défense). The films are the same for months at a time (listed in *Pariscope*, etc). Don't worry if you don't

Film, Theatre and Dance

For more details of La Villette, see p.200.

Film, Theatre and Dance

understand French – in this instance it's a positive advantage.

One final cinematographic treat, also in the Parc de la Villette, is the **Cinaxe**, which shows high-resolution action film with seats that move in synchronization with the image (part of the Cité des Sciences; Tues–Sun 11am–7pm; 32F/27F; not recommended if you're pregnant or have a weak heart; no admission for under-6s).

Film on Television

At the other end of the scale of screen size, French TV has six channels – three public, *F2*, *Arte* and *F3*; one subscription, *Canal Plus* (with some unencrypted programmes); and two commercial open broadcasts, *TF1* and *M6*.

In addition there are the cable networks, including *France Infos* French news, *CNN*, the *BBC World Service*, *Euronews* with news in the original version from around Europe, *MTV* and *Planète* specializing in documentaries.

Arte, which took over the defunct La Cinq channel in September 1992, is a joint Franco-German cultural venture, very much part of Mitterand and Kohl's European politics. Its high-brow programmes, daily documentaries, *Horizon* from the BBC, art criticism, serious French and German movies, complete operas, and – in its first month – *Monty Python*, are transmitted simultaneously in French and German. Though almost certain to be successful in Germany, where it's a cable channel, *Arte* may find high ratings very difficult to obtain in France, accustomed to La Cinq's popular programming on button five. It will survive for as long as Mitterand, no doubt, and be adored by the Parisian intellectual masses.

Canal Plus is the main **movie channel** (and funder of the French film industry), with repeats of foreign films usually shown at least once in the original language. *F2*'s Friday-night Ciné-Club (around midnight) sometimes shows British and American films in the original, and *F3* has a late Sunday-evening movie slot with the odd undubbed Hollywood classic.

The main French news comes at 8.30pm on *Arte* and *F2*, and at 8.30pm on *Arte*. At 7am on *Canal Plus* (unencrypted) you can watch the American *CBS* evening news.

Drama

Certain directors in France do extraordinary things with the medium of theatre. Classic texts are shuffled into theatrical moments, where spectacular and dazzling sensation takes precedence over speech. Their shows are overwhelming; huge casts, vast sets – sometimes real buildings never before used for theatre – exotic lighting effects, original music scores. A unique experience, even if you haven't understood a word.

Ariane Mnouchkine, whose *Théatre du Soleil* is based at the *Cartoucherie* in Vincennes, is the director par excellence of this form. Her production of *Les Atrides* (*The House of Atreus* in her own translation from Euripides and Aeschylus) stunned and delighted audiences in France, Britain and the United States. It lasted ten hours – relatively short for the *Théatre du Soleil*, some of whose performances have gone on for several days.

Peter Brook, the English director based at the *Bouffes du Nord* theatre, is another great magician of the all-embracing several-day show. Another big name, though often involved in films rather than the theatre, is **Patrice Chereau**. Any show by these three should not be missed, and there are likely to be other weird and wonderful productions by younger directors following their example.

At the same time, bourgeois farces, postwar classics, Shakespeare, Racine and the like, are staged with the same range of talent or lack of it that you'd find in London or New York. What you'll rarely find are the home-grown, socially concerned and realist dramas of the sort that have in the past kept theatre alive in Britain. An Edward Bond or David Edgar play crops up in translation often enough, although, frequently, such adaptations are not very successful because of the enormous differences between the

British and French ways of thinking. The French equivalent, however, hardly exists.

The great generation of French or Francophone dramatists, which included Anouilh, Genet, Camus, Sartre, Adamov, Ionesco, and Cocteau, came to an end with the death of **Samuel Beckett** in 1990 and Ionesco in 1994. Their plays, however, are still frequently performed. The *Huchette* has been playing Ionesco's *La Cantatrice Chauve* every night since October 1952, and Genet's *Les Paravents*, which set off riots on its opening night, can now be included alongside Corneille and Shakespeare in the programme of the *Comédie Française*, the national theatre for the classics.

Perhaps partly as a corollary of this pre-eminence of directors, the general standard of acting is not as high as in Britain. A production is more likely to be sustained by one or two big-name actors, supported by a cast of nonentities. Growing commercial pressures don't help either.

But one of the encouraging things about France and its public authorities is that they take their culture, including the theatre, seriously. Numerous theatres and theatre companies in Paris are subsidized, either wholly or in part, by the government or the Ville de Paris, whose right-wing mayor, Jacques Chirac, even contributes the theatre listings blurb, eulogizing freedom of expression and non-conformism. And the suburbs are not left out, thanks to the ubiquitous **Maisons de Culture**, which were the brainchildren of André Malraux, man of letters, de Gaulle's wartime aide, and, eventually, in the 1960s, his Minister of Culture. Ironically, however, although they were designed to bring culture to the masses, their productions are often among the most "difficult" and intellectually inaccessible.

Another plus is the openness to **foreign influence** and foreign work. There is little xenophobia in Paris theatre; foreign artists are as welcome as they've always been. In any month there might be an Italian, Mexican, German or Brazilian production playing in the original language, or offerings by radical groups from Turkey, Iraq or China, who have no possibilities of a home venue.

The best time of all for theatre-lovers to come to Paris is for the **Festival d'Automne** from October to December (see p.42), an international festival of all the performing arts, which attracts stage directors of the calibre of the American Bob Wilson, who directed the Opéra Bastille's highly successful *Magic Flute*, and Polish director Tadeusz Kantor.

Venues to look out for

Bouffes du Nord, 37bis bd de la Chapelle, 10e; ☎46.07.34.50 (Mº Chapelle). Peter Brook has made this his permanent base in Paris, where he

Film, Theatre and Dance

Buying theatre tickets

The easiest place to get tickets to see a stage performance in Paris, with the possible exception of one of the *FNAC* shops and *Virgin Megastore* (see p.306, p.322), is at one of two ticket kiosks.

These are at the Châtelet-Les-Halles *RER* station (through the turnstiles, alongside *FNAC* Photo-Service and the *bureau de change*; Tues–Fri 12.30–7.30pm, Sat 2–7.30pm) and on place de la Madeleine, 8e (opposite no. 15; Tues–Sat 12.30–8pm, Sun 12.30–4pm). They sell same-day tickets at half price and 16F commission, but queues can be very long.

Booking well in advance is essential for new productions and all shows by the superstar directors. These are sometimes a lot more expensive, quite reasonably so when they are the much-favoured epics, lasting seven hours or even carrying on over several days.

Prices for the theatre vary between 50F and 165F for state theatres, going up to 200–295F for some privately owned ones. There are weekday discounts for students. Most theatres are closed on Monday.

Film,
Theatre and
Dance

produces such events as the nine-hour show of the Indian epic, *Mahabharata*.

Cartoucherie, rte du Champ-de-Manoeuvre, 12e (Mº Château-de-Vincennes). As well as the *Théâtre du Soleil* (see p.338; ☎ 43.74.24.08), the *Cartoucheries* is home to the French-Spanish troupe, *Théâtre de l'Épée de Bois* (☎ 43.08.39.74), the *Théâtre de la Tempête* (☎ 43.28.36.36), the *Atelier du Chaudron* (☎ 43.28.97.04) and the *Théâtre de l'Aquarium* (☎ 43.74.99.61).

Centre Dramatique National, 41 av des Grésillons, Gennevilliers; ☎ 47.93.26.30 (Mº Gabriel-Péri). Several stimulating productions have brought acclaim – and audiences – to this suburban venue in recent years.

Comédie Française (national theatre), 2 rue de Richelieu, 1er. ☎ 40.15.00.15 (Mº Palais-Royal). The national theatre for the classics. However, the trend now seems to be to be cut down on traditional productions, with the exception of Molière and Feydeau, in favour of more contemporary work and modernized versions of the classics.

Maison des Arts de Créteil, place Salvador-Allende, Créteil; ☎ 45.13.19.19 (Mº Créteil-Préfecture). As well as its movie programmes (see above), this also serves as a lively suburban theatre.

Maison de la Culture, 1 bd Lénine, Bobigny; ☎ 48.31.11.45 (Mº Pablo-Picasso). The resident company, *MC93*, astounded theatre critics and theatre-goers in early 1991 by an extraordinarily successful dramatization of *De Rerum Natura – The Nature of Things* – a scientific treatise by the first-century BC Roman poet Lucretius, using the auditorium as stage, considerable amounts of Latin, a boxing match, mime and giant swings.

Odéon Théâtre de l'Europe (national theatre), 1 place Paul-Claudel, 6e; ☎ 44.41.36.36 (Mº Odéon). Contemporary plays, as well as *version originale* productions by well-known foreign companies. During May 1968, this theatre was occupied by students and became an open parliament with the backing of its directors, Jean-Louis Barrault (of Baptiste fame in *Les Enfants du Paradis* and who died in

1994) and Madeleine Renaud, one of the great French stage actresses. Promptly sacked by de Gaulle's Minister for Culture, they formed a new company and moved to the disused Gare d'Orsay until President Giscard's museum plans sent them packing.

Rond-Point Théâtre Renaud-Barrault, 2bis av Franklin-Roosevelt, 18e; ☎ 44.95.98.00 (Mº Franklin-D-Roosevelt). The permanent home of the Renaud-Barrault troupe (see *Odéon* above), where their performances of Beckett are unequalled.

Théâtre des Amandiers, 7 av Pablo-Picasso, Nanterre, 92; ☎ 46.14.70.00 (*RER* Nanterre-Université and theatre bus). Renowned as the suburban base for Jean-Paul Vincent's exciting productions.

Théâtre des Artistic-Athévains, 45bis rue Richard-Lenoir, 11e; ☎ 48.06.36.02 (Mº Voltaire). Small company heavily involved in community and educational theatre.

Théâtre de la Bastille, 79 rue de la Roquette, 11e; ☎ 43.57.42.14 (Mº Bastille). One of the best places for new work and fringe productions.

Théâtre La Bruyère, 5 rue La Bruyère, 9e; ☎ 48.74.76.99 (Mº St-Georges). New French work, as well as English and American.

Théâtre de la Colline (national theatre), 15 rue Malte-Brun, 20e; ☎ 43.66.43.60 (Mº Gambetta.) The director is an Argentinian: Lavelli. Most of the work he puts on is twentieth-century and innovative, and nearly always worth seeing.

Théâtre de la Commune, 2 rue Edouard-Poisson, Aubervilliers; ☎ 48.34.67.67 (Mº Aubervilliers). Suburban theatre with an excellent reputation.

Théâtre de l'Est Parisien, 159 av Gambetta, 20e; ☎ 43.64.80.80 (Mº Gambetta). Well respected for its innovative work.

Théâtre de la Main-d'Or, 15 passage de la Main-d'Or, 11e; ☎ 48.05.67.89 (Mº Bastille). An interesting experimental space, with occasional classics.

Théâtre Marie Stuart, 4 rue Marie Stuart, 2e; ☎ 45.08.17.80 (Mº Étienne-Marcel). Occasional shows in English.

Théâtre National de Chaillot (national theatre), Palais de Chaillot, pl du Trocadéro, 16e; ☎ 47.27.81.15 (Mº Trocadéro). The great Antoine Vitez may be no more, but the mega-spectacles go on. Roger Planchon from Lyon has his Parisian showings here.

Théâtre Silvia-Montfort, parc Georges-Brassens, 106 rue Briançon, 15e; ☎ 45.31.10.96 (Mº Porte-de-Vanves). A pyramidal theatre, playing "classics" such as Anouilh, but also dedicated to staging original works.

Café-Théâtre

Literally a revue, monologue or mini-play performed in a place where you can drink, and sometimes eat, *café-théâtre* is probably less accessible than a Racine tragedy at the *Comédie-Française*. The humour or puerile dirty jokes, word-play, and allusions to current fads, phobias and politicians can leave even a fluent French speaker in the dark.

If you want to give it a try, the main venues are concentrated around the Marais. Tickets average around 80F and it's best to book in advance – the spaces are small – though you have a good chance of getting in on the night during the week.

Blancs-Manteaux, 15 rue des Blancs-Manteaux, 4e; ☎ 48.87.15.84 (Mº Hôtel-de-Ville/Rambuteau). Somewhat cramped venue, beneath a restaurant.

Café de la Gare, 41 rue du Temple, 4e; ☎ 42.78.52.51 (Mº Hôtel-de-Ville/Rambuteau). This may not be operating its turn-of-the-wheel admission price system any more, but it has retained a reputation for novelty.

Point Virgule, 7 rue Ste-Croix-de-la-Bretonnerie, 4e; ☎ 42.78.67.03 (Mº Hôtel-de-Ville/St-Paul). Occasionally interesting, but more often predictable and self-regarding.

Dance and mime

In the 1970s all the dancers left Paris for New York, and only **mime** remained as the great performing art of the French,

thanks to the Lecoq School of Mime and Improvisation, and the famous practitioner **Marcel Marceau**. Since Marceau's demise, no new pure mime artists of his stature have appeared. Lecoq foreign graduates return to their own countries while the French incorporate their skills into dance, comedy routines and improvisation. While this cross-fertilization has given rise to new standards in performing art, it is still a pity that mime by itself is rarely seen (except on the streets, and on Beaubourg's piazza in particular).

The best-known and loved French clown, **Coluche**, died in a motorcycle accident in 1986. Most of his acts were incomprehensible to foreigners, save jests such as starting a campaign for the presidency, for which he posed nude with a feather up his bum. A troupe of mimes and clowns who debunk the serious in literature rather than politics are *La Clown Kompanie*, famous for their Shakespearian tragedies turned into farce. Joëlle Bouvier and Régis Obadia trained both at dance school and at Lecoq's; their company, *L'Esquisse*, combines both disciplines, takes inspiration from paintings, and portrays a dark, hallucinatory world.

The renaissance of French **dance** in the 1980s was not, on the whole, Paris-based. Subsidies have gone to regional companies expressly to decentralize the arts. But all the best contemporary practitioners come to the capital regularly. Names to look out for are Régine Chopinot's troupe from La Rochelle, Jean-Claude Gallotta's from Grenoble, Roland Petit's from Marseille, Dominique Bagouet's from Montpellier, and Joëlle Bouvier and Régis Obadia's from Angers. Creative choreographers based in or around Paris include Maguy Marin, Karine Saporta, François Verret and Jean-François Duroure.

Humour, everyday actions and obsessions, social problems, and the darker shades of life find expression in the myriad current dance forms. A multi-dimensional performing art is created by combinations of movement, mime, ballet, music from the medieval to contemporary

Film, Theatre and Dance

Film, Theatre and Dance

jazz-rock, speech, noise, and theatrical effects. The Gallotta-choreographed film *Rei-Dom* opened up a whole new range of possibilities. Many of the traits of the modern epic theatre are shared with dance, including crossing international frontiers.

Many of the theatres listed above under drama include both mime and dance in their programmes: the *Théâtre de la Bastille* shows works by young dancers and choreographers; Maguy Marin's company is based at the Créteil Maison des Arts and François Verret's at the Maison de la Culture in Bobigny, where a prestigious competition for young choreographers is held in March; and the *Amandiers* in Nanterre hosts major contemporary works.

More experimental venues to keep an eye out for in the listings magazines, in addition to those below, are *L'Espace Kiron*, the *Théâtre Gémier*, and the rehearsal space *Ménagerie de Verre*.

Plenty of space and critical attention are also given to **tap**, **tango**, **folk** and **jazz dancing**, and visiting traditional dance troupes from all over the world. There are also a dozen or so black African companies in Paris, who, predictably, find it hard to compete with Europeans and the fashionable Japanese for venues, as well as several Indian dance troupes, the *Ballet Classique Khmer*, and many more from exiled cultures.

As for **ballet**, the principal stage is at the old *Opéra Garnier*, where the company is directed by Patrick Dupont, who suffered as a dancer under his predecessor's temperamental tantrums and unreliability. This was the late, great Rudolf Nureyev, sacked in 1990 for failing to come up with the promised programme. Patrick Dupont has succeeded in bringing back many of the best French classical dancers, with the exception, however, of the ravishing superstar Sylvie Guillem, currently in London, who is determined to plough her own independent furrow. Paris has also lost Maurice Béjart – wooed back to his home town of Marseille – who used to

run the *Ballet du XXe Siècle*. But ballet fans can still be sure of masterly performances, at the *Opéra*, the *Théâtre des Champs-Elysées* and the *Théâtre Musical de Paris*.

The highlight of the year for dance is the *Festival International de Danse de Paris* in October and November, which involves contemporary, classical and different national traditions. Other festivals combining theatre, dance, mime, classical music and its descendants include the *Festival du Marais* in June, the *Festival "Foire Saint-Germain"* in June and July and the *Festival d'Automne* from mid-September to mid-December.

Venues

Centre Mandapa, 6 rue Wurtz, 13e; ☎ 45.89.01.60 (Mº Glacière). The one theatre dedicated to traditional dances from around the world.

Le Déjazet, 41 bd du Temple, 3e; ☎ 48.87.52.55 (Mº République). Experimental dance productions, with a particular emphasis on mime.

Opéra de Paris-Garnier, place de l'Opéra, 9e; ☎ 47.42.53.71 (Mº Opéra). Now that the Bastille opera house has opened, the former opera is given over exclusively to ballet.

La Piscine, 254 av de la Division-Leclerc, Châtenay-Malabry; ☎ 46.61.14.27 (RER Robinson and bus #194). *Le Campagnol* company of dance and improvisation that featured in Ettore Scola's film *Le Bal* have their own theatre out here in the suburbs.

Théâtre de la Bastille, 76 rue de la Roquette, 11e; ☎ 43.57.42.14 (Mº Bastille). As well as more traditional theatre (see above), there are also dance and mime performances.

Théâtre des Champs-Élysées, 15 av Montaigne, 8e; ☎ 49.52.50.50 (Mº Alma-Marceau). Forever aiming to outdo the Opéra with even grander and more expensive ballet productions.

Théâtre Contemporain de la Danse, 9 rue Geoffroy-l'Asnier, 4e; ☎ 42.74.44.22 (Mº Pont-Marie). Established producer of innovative work.

Théâtre Musical de Paris, place du Châtelet, 4e; ☎ 40.28.28.40 (Mº Châtelet). This theatre, opposite the *Théâtre de la Ville*, remains a major ballet venue. It was here, in 1910, that Diaghilev put on the first season of Russian ballet, assisted by Cocteau, Rodin, Proust and others.

Théâtre de la Ville, 2 place du Châtelet, 4e; ☎ 42.74.22.77 (Mº Châtelet). The height of success for dance productions is to end up here. Karine Saporta's work is regularly played, and the 1994 season, for example, included works by Maguy Marin and Pina Bausch, together with modern theatre classics, comedy and concerts. The review performances at 6 or 6.30pm are excellent value at 65F/55F.

Film, Theatre and Dance

Part 4

Beyond the City

Day Trips from Paris

The region that surrounds Paris – known as the Île de France – and the borders of the neighbouring provinces are studded with large-scale châteaux. In this chapter, we detail a select few of them. Many were royal or noble retreats for hunting and other leisured pursuits; some, such as **Versailles**, were for more serious state show. However, if you have limited time and even the slightest curiosity about church buildings, your first priority should be to make instead for the **cathedral of Chartres** – which is all it is cracked up to be, and more. Also, much closer in, on the edge of the city itself, **St-Denis** has a cathedral second only to Notre-Dame among Paris churches. A visit to it could be combined with an unusual approach to the city: a walk back (the best direction to follow) along the banks of the **St-Denis canal**.

Note that Disneyland Paris has a chapter to itself, starting on p.371.

Whether the various outlying **museums** deserve your attention will depend on your degree of interest in the subjects they represent. Several, however, have authoritative collections: **china** at Sèvres, **French prehistory** at St-Germain-en-Laye, the **history of flying machines** at Le Bourget, and the **Île de France** at Sceaux.

But the most satisfying experience is undoubtedly **Monet's garden** at Giverny, the inspiration for all his waterlily canvases in the Marmottan and Musée d'Orsay.

We've also included a brief foray into the architecture and planning of the suburbs since the 1950s, culminating in the bizarre constructions in the sprawling satellite town of **Marne-la-Vallée**.

The Cathedrals

An excursion to **Chartres** can seem a long way to go from Paris just to see one building; but then you'd have to go a very long way indeed to find any edifice to beat it. The cathedral of **St-Denis**, right on the edge of Paris, predates Chartres and represents the first breakthroughs in Gothic art. It is also the burial place of almost all the French kings.

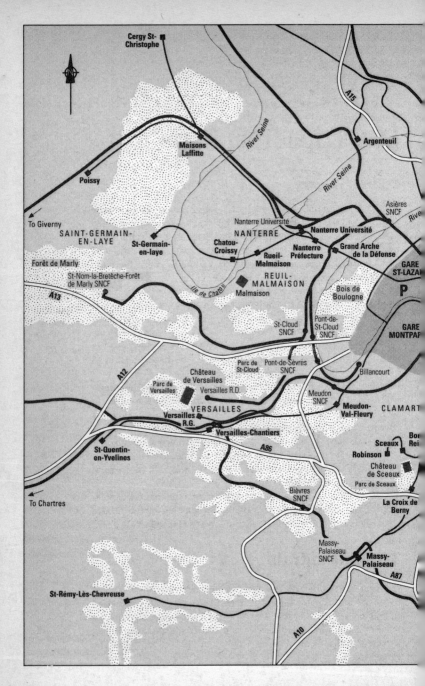

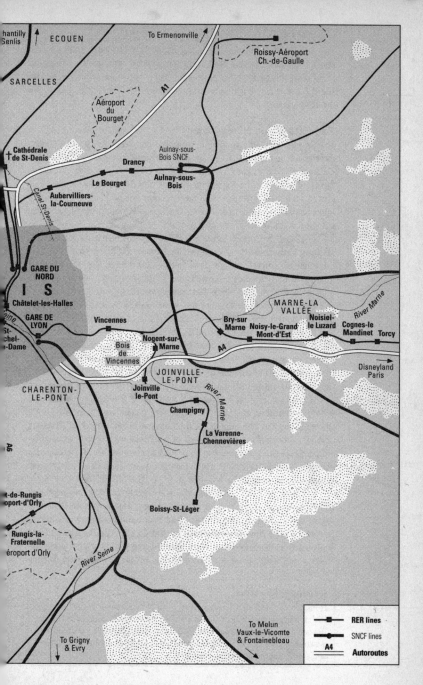

To Ermenonville

Roissy-Aéroport
Ch.-de-Gaulle

ECOUEN

hantilly
Senlis

SARCELLES

A1

Aéroport
du
Bourget

Aulnay-sous-
Bois SNCF

Cathédrale
de St-Denis

Drancy

Le Bourget

Aulnay-sous-
Bois

Aubervilliers-
la-Courneuve

Canal St-Denis

GARE DU
NORD

I S

Châtelet-les-Halles

Vincennes

MARNE-LA-
VALLÉE

River Marne

GARE DE
LYON

Bry-sur
Marne

Noisiel-
le Luzard

Cognes-le
Mandinet

Torcy

ichel-

Bois
de
Vincennes

Nogent-sur-
Marne

Noisy-le-Grand
Mont-d'Est

Dame

A4

JOINVILLE-
LE-PONT

River Marne

Disneyland
Paris

CHARENTON-
LE-PONT

Joinville
le-Pont

Champigny

A6

La Varenne-
Chennevières

-de-Rungis
oport-d'Orly

Rungis-la-
Fraternelle
éroport d'Orly

Boissy-St-Léger

River Seine

To Melun
Vaux-le-Vicomte
& Fontainebleau

To Grigny
& Evry

	RER lines
	SNCF lines
A4	Autoroutes

DAY TRIPS FROM PARIS

Chartres

The small and relatively undistinguished city of Chartres lies 80km southwest of Paris; an hour-long journey by train which brings an immediate reward in the moment as you approach, when you first see the great cathedral standing as if alone on the slight rise above the River Eure.

The Cathédrale Notre-Dame

The mysticism of medieval thought on life, death and deity, expressed in material form by the glass and masonry of **Chartres Cathedral** (daily March–Sept 7.20am–7.20pm; Oct–Feb 7.10am–7pm), should best be experienced on a cloud-free winter's day. The low sun transmits the stained-glass colours to the interior stone, the quiet scattering of people leaves the acoustics unconfused, and the exterior is unmasked for miles around.

The best-preserved medieval cathedral in Europe is, for today's visitors, only flawed by changes in Roman Catholic worship. The immense distance from the door to the altar which, through mists of incense and drawn-out harmonies, emphasized the distance that only priests could mediate between worshippers and worshipped, has been abandoned. The central altar undermines (from a secular point of view) the theatrical dogma of the building and puts cloth and boards where the coloured lights should play.

A less recent change, that of allowing the congregation to use chairs, covers up the labyrinth on the floor of the nave – an original thirteenth-century arrangement and a great rarity, since the authorities at other cathedrals had them pulled up as distracting frivolities. The **Chartres labyrinth** traces a path over 200m long, enclosed within a diameter of 13m, the same size as the rose window above the main doors. The centre used to have a bronze relief of Theseus and the Minotaur and the pattern of the maze was copied from classical texts – the medieval Catholic idea of the path of life to eternity echoing Greek myth. During pilgrimages, when the chairs are removed, you may be lucky enough to see the full pattern.

But any medieval pilgrims who were projected to contemporary Chartres would think the battle of Armaggedon had been lost. For them, the cathedral would seem like an abandoned shrine with its promise of the New Jerusalem shattered. In **the Middle Ages** all the sculptures above the doors were painted and gilded while inside the walls were white-washed. The colours in the clean stained-glass

---

Getting to Chartres

Hourly trains run to Chartres from Paris-Montparnasse (122F return), with a journey time of just under an hour. From the station, avenue J-de-Beauce leads up to place Châtelet. Diagonally opposite, past all the parked coaches, is rue Ste-Même, which meets rue Jean-Moulin. Turn left and you'll find the SI and the cathedral.

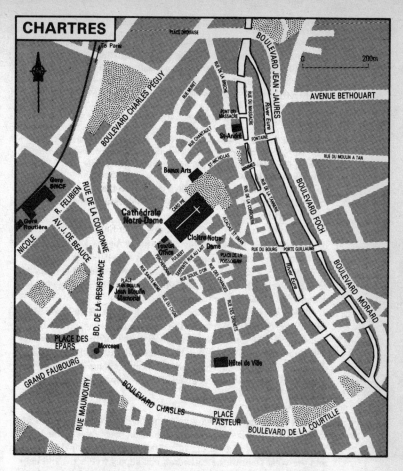

windows would have been so bright they would have glittered from
the outside along with the gold of the crowns and halos of the statuary. Inside, the reflected patterns from the windows on the white
walls would have jewelled the entire building.

It is difficult now to appreciate just how important colour used
to be, when the minerals or plant and animal extracts to make the
different shades cost time, effort, and considerable amounts of
money to procure. Perhaps in a later age, the statues will again be
painted. Demands for whitewash are occasionally made and
ignored. Cleaning the windows does go on, but each one takes years
and costs run into millions.

There remain, however, more than enough wonders to enthral
modern eyes: the geometry of the building, unique in being almost
unaltered since its consecration in the thirteenth century; the details

Cathedral Tours

One of the best ways to appreciate the detail of the Cathédrale Notre-Dame is to join a **guided tour** given by the erudite Englishman Malcolm Miller. This is no ordinary patter, but a labour of love from someone who has studied and written and lectured about Chartres for decades. Mr Miller's performance as the slightly camp, eccentric academic is impeccably done and he knows so much about the cathedral that you can follow several consecutive tours without fear of repetition. His explanation for the endless scope is that the cathedral is a library in which the windows and the statuary are the books. He reveals the storylines (which the illiterate medieval worshipper would have had no trouble reading) with fascinating digressions into the significance, past and present, of symbols, shapes and numbers.

Mr Miller's tours (30F/20F for students) take place daily, except Sundays, from April to January at noon and 2.45pm, starting just inside the West Door.

of the stonework, most notably the western façade which includes the Portail Royal saved from the cathedral's predecessor, destroyed by fire in 1195, the Renaissance choir screen, and the hosts of sculpted figures above each transept door; and the shining circular symmetries of the transept windows.

There are separate admission fees for various of the less public parts of the cathedral. Probably the best value of these, preferable to the crypt and the treasures, is the climb up the **north tower** (crowds permitting; times vary, check in the cathedral; price 20F/12F). There are gardens at the back from where you can contemplate at ease the complexity of stress factors balanced by the flying buttresses.

The Town

Though the cathedral is why you come here, a wander round the town of Chartres has its rewards. The SI on place de la Cathédrale, between an archeological dig of a first-century municipal building and the West Door of the cathedral, can supply free maps and help with rooms if you want to stay.

The **Beaux Arts museum** in the former episcopal palace just north of the cathedral has some beautiful tapestries, a room full of Vlaminck, and Zurbaran's *Sainte Lucie*, as well as good temporary exhibitions (daily except Tues April–Sept 10am–6pm; Oct–March 10am–noon & 2–6pm; 12F/16F). Behind it, rue Chantault leads past old town houses to the River Eure and Pont des Massacres. You can follow this reedy river lined with ancient wash-houses upstream via **rue des Massacres** on the right bank. The cathedral appears from time to time through the trees, and closer at hand, on the left bank is the Romanesque **church of St-André**, now used for art exhibitions, jazz concerts, and so on.

Crossing back over the river at the end of rue de la Tannerie into rue du Bourg brings you back to the **medieval town**. At the top of rue du Bourg there's a turreted staircase attached to a house, and at the eastern end of place de la Poissonerie, a carved salmon decorates an entrance. The **food market** takes place on place Billard and rue des Changes, and there's a **flower market** on place Marceau (Tues, Thurs, & Sat).

Cloître-Notre-Dame along the south side of the cathedral has expensive eating places. Cheaper options include *La Brasserie* on place Marceau, *Le Vesuve* pizzeria on place de l'Hôtel-de-Ville and the *Bar de l'Hôtel-de-Ville* next door. The liveliest place to drink on market days is *Le Brazza* on place Billard.

At the edge of the old town, on the junction of boulevard de la Résistance and rue Jean-Moulin (to the right as you're coming up from the station), stands a memorial to **Jean Moulin**, Prefect of Chartres until he was sacked by the Vichy government in 1942. When the Germans occupied the town in 1940, Moulin refused under torture to sign a document to the effect that black soldiers in the French army were responsible for Nazi atrocities. He later became de Gaulle's number-one man on the ground, co-ordinating the Resistance. He died at the hands of Klaus Barbie in 1943.

St-Denis

St-Denis, just 10km north of the centre of Paris and accessible by métro, nonetheless remains a very distinct community, focused as it has been for centuries around its magnificent cathedral, the **basilica of St-Denis**. Thirty-thousand-strong in 1870, one-hundred-thousand-strong today, its people have seen their town grow into the most heavily industrialized community in France, bastion of the Red suburbs and stronghold of the Communist Party, with nearly all the principal streets bearing some notable left-wing name. Today, however, recession and the advance of the Pacific Rim have taken a heavy toll in closed factories and unemployment.

Although the centre of St-Denis still retains traces of its small town origins, the area immediately abutting the cathedral has been transformed in the last ten years into a fortress-like housing and shopping complex. The **thrice-weekly market**, however (Tues, Fri & Sun), still takes place in the square by the Hôtel de Ville and in the covered *halles* nearby. It is a multi-ethnic affair these days, and the quantity of offal on the butchers' stalls – ears, feet, tails and bladders – shows this is not rich folks' territory.

The Cathedral

Begun by Abbot Suger, friend and adviser to kings, in the first half of the twelfth century, **St-Denis cathedral** (summer daily 10am–7pm; winter closes 5pm; closed Jan 1, May 1, Nov 1, Nov 11 & Dec 25) is generally regarded as the birthplace of the Gothic style in European architecture. Though its west front was the first ever to have a rose window, it is in the choir that you see the clear emergence of the new

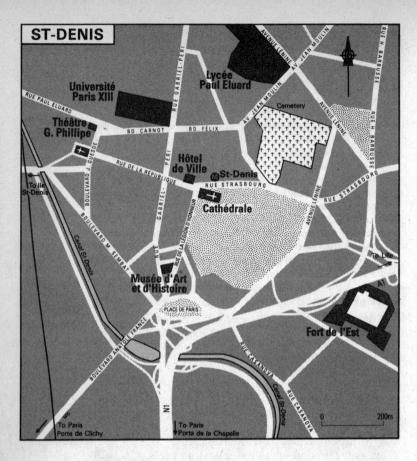

ST-DENIS

Université
Paris XIII

RUE PAUL ELUARD

Théâtre
G. Phillipe

BD CARNOT

Lycée
Paul Eluard

AVENUE LENINE

AV. JEAN MOULIN

RUE GABRIEL-PERI

BD FÉLIX

Cemetery

RUE H. BARBUSSE

AVENUE LENINE

RUE H. BARBUSSE

To Ile
St-Denis

BOULEVARD J. GUESDE

RUE DE LA RÉPUBLIQUE

PERI

Hôtel
de Ville

RUE GABRIEL

St-Denis

RUE STRASBOURG

RUE STRASBOURG

AVENUE LENINE

AV. JEAN MOULIN

Canal St-Denis

BOULEVARD M. SEMBAT

RUE DE LA LEGION D'HONNEUR

Cathédrale

To Lille

Musée d'Art
et d'Histoire

PLACE DE PARIS

Fort de l'Est

A1

BOULEVARD ANATOLE FRANCE

N1

RUE CASANOVA

Canal St-Denis

RUE CASANOVA

0   200m

To Paris
Porte de Clichy

To Paris
Porte de la Chapelle

style: the slimness and lightness that comes with the use of the pointed arch, the ribbed vault and the long shafts of half-column rising from pillar to roof. It is a remarkably well-lit church too, thanks to the clerestory being almost wholly glass – another first for St-Denis – and the transept windows being so big that they occupy their entire end walls.

Once the place where the kings of France were crowned, since 1000 AD the cathedral has been the burial place of all but three. Their very fine **tombs and effigies** are deployed about the transepts and ambulatory (Mon–Fri 10am–6.30pm, Sat & Sun noon–6.30pm; closed during services; 26F/17F/under-17s free). Among the most interesting are the enormous Renaissance memorial to François 1er on the right just beyond the entrance, in the form of a triumphal arch with the royal family perched on top and battle scenes depicted below, and the tombs of Louis XII, Henri II and Catherine de Médicis on the left side of the church. Also on the left, close to the altar steps, Philippe the Bold's is one of the earliest lookalike portrait statues, while to the right of the ambulatory steps you can see the stocky little general, Bertrand du Guesclin, who gave the English a run-around after the death of the Black Prince, and on the level above him, invariably graced by bouquets of flowers from the royalist contingent, the undistinguished statues of Louis XVI and Marie-Antoinette. Around the corner on the far side of the ambulatory is Clovis himself, king of the Franks way back in 500, a canny little German who wiped out Roman Gaul and turned it into France with Paris for a capital.

The SI has an office right opposite.

The Musée d'Art et d'Histoire

Not many minutes' walk away on rue Gabriel-Péri is the **Musée d'Art et d'Histoire de la Ville de St-Denis** (Mon & Wed–Sat 10am–5.30pm, Sun 2–6.30pm; 15F/10F). The quickest route is along rue de la Légion-d'Honneur, then take the third right.

The museum is housed in a former Carmelite convent, rescued from the clutches of the developers and carefully restored. The exhibits on display are not of spectacular interest, though the presentation is excellent. The **local archeology** collection is good and there are some interesting paintings of nineteenth- and twentieth-century industrial landscapes, including the St-Denis canal. The one unique collection is of documents relating to **the Commune**: posters, cartoons, broadsheets, paintings, plus an audiovisual presentation. There is also an exhibition of manuscripts and rare editions of the Communist poet, Paul Eluard, native son of St-Denis.

Canal St-Denis

To get to the canal – at the St-Denis end – you follow rue de la République from the Hôtel de Ville to its end by a church. (To the right at 46 boulevard Jules-Guesde is the birthplace of the poet Paul Eluard.) Go down the left side of the church until you reach the canal bridge. Turn left, and you can walk all the way back to Paris along the towpath, taking something between an hour and a half and two hours. You come out at Porte de la Villette. There are stretches where it looks as if you're probably not supposed to be there. Just pay no attention and keep going.

Not far from the start of the walk, past some peeling villas with lilac and cherry blossom in their unkempt gardens, you come to a cobbled ramp on the left by a now-defunct restaurant, *La Péniche* (*The Barge*). Rue Raspail leads thence to a dusty square where the town council named a side street for IRA hunger-striker Bobby Sands. The whole neighbourhood is calm, poor and forgotten.

Continuing along the canal, you pass patches of greenery, sand and gravel docks, wasteground where larks rise above rusting bedsteads and doorless fridges, lock-keepers' cottages with roses and vegetable gardens, decaying tenements and improvised shacks, derelict factories and huge sheds where trundling gantries load bundles of steel rods on to Belgian barges. Barge traffic is regular and the life appears attractive, for these barges are proper family homes, with a dog at the prow, lace curtains at the window, potted plants, a bike propped against the cabin side, a couple of kids. But the keynote is decay and nothing looks set to last.

The Châteaux

The mansions and palaces around the capital are all very impressive on first sighting, but they can be hard work, if not downright tedious, to tour around – and none more so than **Versailles**.

That said, **Vaux-le-Vicomte's** classical magnificence and **Fontainebleau's** Italianate decoration are easy to appreciate; **Chantilly** has a gorgeous Book of Hours and a bizarre horse connection; and **Malmaison** is interesting for its former occupants. The main satisfaction, however, is in breathing country air in the **gardens, parks and forests** that surround the châteaux, and being able to get back to Paris comfortably in a day. If you get a bout of château mania, there are many more places in addition to those detailed in this section. Some, whose principal function these days is to house museums, are described later in this chapter, while the tourist office in Paris can provide full lists of others.

Versailles

The **Palace of Versailles** is one of the three most visited monuments in France. It was inspired by the young Louis XIV's envy of his finance minister's château at Vaux-le-Vicomte (see below), which he was determined to outdo. He recruited the design team of Vaux-le-Vicomte architect Le Vau, painter Le Brun and gardener Le Nôtre, and ordered something a hundred times the size. Versailles is a monster from every aspect – a mutated building gene allowed to run like a pounding fist for lengths no feet or eyes were made for, its décor a grotesque homage to the self-propaganda of the Sun King.

In the park, a mere two and a half square miles in area, the fountains only gush on selected days. The rest of the time the statues on the empty pools look like gargoyles dismantled from cathedral walls. It's hard to know why so many tourists come out here in preference to all except the most obvious sights of Paris. Yet they do, and the château is always a crush of bodies.

That this is not just a modern judgement could have no better witness than the English poet Alexander Pope. Satirizing the vainglorious and tasteless buildings of his rich contemporaries, he wrote in his *Epistle to the Earl of Burlington* of 1731:

> *Something there is more needful than Expence,*
> *And something previous ev'n to Taste – 'tis Sense:*
> *. . . Without it, proud Versailles, thy glory falls . . .*

The château

May–Sept Tues–Sun 9am–7pm; Oct–April Tues–Sun 9am–5.30pm. Closed hols. 40F adults, 26F 18-25s and over-60s, under-18s free.

Visitors to the château have a choice of itineraries, and whether to be guided or not. Apart from the state apartments of the king and queen and the Galerie des Glaces (the Hall of Mirrors, where the Treaty of Versailles was signed to end World War I), which you can visit on your own, most of the palace can only be viewed in guided groups, and whose times are much more restricted. Long queues are common.

Don't set out to see all the palace in one day – it's not possible. Quite apart from the size, tours of both Mme du Barry's apartments and of the Dauphin and Dauphine's apartments take place at 2pm.

If you want to be sure of **a place on a guided tour**, it is wise to phone ahead (*Bureau d'Action Culturelle* for reservations, ☎30.84.76.18; general information, ☎30.84.74.00). A word of warning, however, about guided tours: first, there are often several going on around you simultaneously in a distracting babel of languages; second, the guides' spiel consists largely of anecdotes about court life with a heavy emphasis on numbers of mistresses and details of the cost, weight and so on of various items of furniture.

The construction of the château began in 1664 and lasted virtually until Louis XIV's death in 1715. It was never meant to be a home; kings were not homely people. Second only to God, and the head of an immensely powerful state, Louis XIV was an institution rather than a private individual. His risings and sittings, comings and goings, were minutely regulated and rigidly encased in ceremony, attendance at which was an honour much sought after by courtiers. Versailles was the headquarters of every arm of the state. More than twenty thousand people – nobles, administrative staff, merchants, soldiers and servants – lived in the palace in a state of unhygienic squalor according to contemporary accounts.

Following Louis XIV's death, the château was abandoned for a few years before being reoccupied by Louis XV in 1722. It remained the residence of the royal family until the Revolution of 1789, when the furniture was sold and the pictures dispatched to the Louvre. Thereafter it fell into ruin and was nearly demolished by Louis-

In 1961, a law was passed requiring the return of all the original furniture in existence to Versailles. The process still continues.

Philippe. In 1871, during the Paris Commune, it became the seat of the nationalist government, and the French parliament continued to meet in Louis XV's opera building until 1879. Restoration only began in earnest between the two world wars.

The park and Grand and Petit Trianons

If you just feel like taking a look and a walk, **the park** (daily 7am–dusk; fountains play May–Sept Sun 3.30–5pm) is free (Sun 20F) and the scenery better the further you go from the palace. There are even informal groups of trees near the lesser outcrops of royal mania: the Italianate **Grand Trianon**, designed by Hardouin-Mansart in 1687 as a "country retreat" for Louis XIV, and the more modest Greek **Petit Trianon**, built by Gabriel in the 1760s (both Tues–Fri 10am–12.30pm & 2–5.30pm; Grand Trianon 20F/13F, Petit Trianon 12F/8F).

More charming and rustic than either of these is **Le hameau de Marie-Antoinette**, a play-village and farm built in 1783 for Louis XVI's queen to indulge the fashionable Rousseau-inspired fantasy of returning to the natural life.

Distances in the park are considerable. If you can't manage them on foot, a *petit train* shuttles between the terrace in front of the château and the Trianons (26F/15F for kids aged 3–12). There are also **bikes for rental** by the Grand Canal, itself a good fifteen minutes' walk across the formal gardens, and boats for rental on the canal (around 55F for 4 people for 1hr).

The Town

Versailles has a wonderfully posh place to take **tea**: the *Hôtel Palais Trianon*, where the final negotiations for the Treaty of Versailles took place in 1919. Near the park entrance at the end of boulevard de la Reine, it offers much better value than the château itself, with trayfuls of *pâtisseries* to the limits of your desire for about 90F. The style of the hotel is very much that of the town in general. The dominant population is aristocratic, with those holding prerevolutionary titles disdainful of those dating merely from Napoléon. On Bastille Day both lots show their colours with black ribbons and ties in mourning for the guillotined monarchy.

Oddly enough, though, Versailles' **markets** offer excellent bargains, both for food (Sun, Tues & Fri 8am–1pm) and for second-hand stuff (Tues, Wed, Fri & Sat noon–7pm). The markets take place in the centre of town in the Marché Notre-Dame.

Vaux-le-Vicomte

April–Oct daily 10am–6pm; Nov–March daily 11am–5pm. Closed Jan. Château, gardens and Musée des Équipages 48F/38F; garden and museum 27F/22F.

Of all the great mansions within reach of a day's outing from Paris, the classical **château of Vaux-le-Vicomte** is the most architecturally harmonious, the most aesthetically pleasing and the most human in

Getting to Vaux-le-Vicomte

By road, Vaux-le-Vicomte is 7km east of Melun, which is itself 46km
southeast of Paris by the A4 autoroute (exit Melun-Sénart) or a little
further by the A6 (exit Melun). **By rail** there are regular services from
Gare de Lyon as far as Melun (40min), but, short of walking, the only
means of covering the last 7km is **by taxi** (80F one way at the time of
writing). There is a taxi rank on the forecourt of the train station, with
telephone numbers to call if there are no taxis waiting. A cheaper way
would be to take a coach tour – check the Paris tourist office (see p.33).

scale. It stands isolated in the countryside amid fields and woods,
meaning that its gardens make a lovely place to picnic.

The château was built between 1656 and 1661 for **Nicolas
Fouquet**, Louis XIV's finance minister, to the designs of three of the
finest French artists of the day. Fouquet, however, had little chance
to enjoy his magnificent residence. On August 17, 1661 he invited
the king and his courtiers to a sumptuous housewarming party.
Three weeks later he was arrested – by d'Artagnan of Musketeer
fame – charged with embezzlement, and clapped into jail for the rest
of his life. Thereupon the design team of Le Vau, Le Brun, and Le
Nôtre were carted off to build the king's own gross and gaudy piece
of oneupmanship, the palace of Versailles.

Stripped of much of its furnishings by the king, the château
remained in the possession of Fouquet's widow until 1705, when it
was sold to the Maréchal de Villars, an adversary of the Duke of
Marlborough in the War of Spanish Succession. In 1764 it was sold
again to the Duc de Choiseul-Praslin, Louis XV's navy minister. His
family kept it until 1875, when, in a state of utter dereliction – the
gardens had vanished completely – it was taken over by Alfred
Sommier, a French industrialist, who made its restoration and refur-
bishment his life's work. It was finally opened to the public in 1968.

The château and gardens
Seen from the entrance the **château** is a rather austere grey pile
built on a stone terrace surrounded by an artificial moat and flanked
by two matching brick courtyards. It is only when you go through to
the south side, where the gardens decline in measured formal
patterns of grass and water, clipped box and yew, fountains and
statuary, that you can look back and appreciate the very
harmonious and very French qualities of the building – the
combination of steep, tall roof and central dome with classical
pediment and pilasters. It is a building which manages to have
charm in spite of its size.

As to the interior, the predominant impression as you wander
through is inevitably of opulence and monumental cost. The main
artistic interest lies in the work of **Le Brun**. He was responsible for
the two fine **tapestries** in the entrance, made in the local workshops

Vaux-Le-Vicomte

set up by Fouquet specifically to adorn his house (and subsequently removed by Louis XIV to become the famous Gobelins works in Paris), as well as numerous **painted ceilings**, notably in Fouquet's bedroom, the Salon des Muses, his *Sleep* in the Cabinet des Jeux, and the so-called King's bedroom, whose décor is the first example of the style that became known as Louis Quatorze. The two oval marble tables in the Salle d'Hercule are the only pieces of furniture never to have left the château.

Other points of interest are the **kitchens**, which have not been altered since construction, and – if you read French – a room displaying **letters** in the hand of Fouquet, Louis XIV and other notables. One, dated November 1794 (ie in mid-Revolution), addresses the incumbent Duc de Choiseul-Praslin as *tu*. "Citizen," it says, "you've got a week to hand over one hundred thousand pounds . . ." and signs off with, "Cheers and brotherhood". You can imagine the shock to the aristocratic system.

The **Musée des Équipages** in the stables comprises a collection of horsedrawn vehicles, including the method of transport used by Charles X fleeing Paris and the Duc de Rohan retreating from Moscow (a Russian model).

Every Saturday evening during May, June and Oct, and July to September Friday and Saturday between 8.30pm and 11pm, the state rooms are illuminated with a thousand candles, as they probably were on the occasion of Fouquet's fateful party (65F entrance). **The fountains and other waterworks** can be seen in action on the second and last Saturdays of each month between April and October, from 3pm until 6pm.

Fontainebleau

Daily except Tues 9.30am–12.30pm & 2–5pm; 31F/20F/under-18s free; Sun 20F. The Petits Appartements can only be seen on guided visits (July–Sept only, Mon & Wed–Fri 10am, 11am, 2.15pm, & 3pm). Gardens open dawn to dusk.

The **château of Fontainebleau**, 70km southeast of Paris, owes its existence to its situation in the middle of a magnificent forest, which made it the perfect base for royal hunting expeditions. Its transformation into a luxurious palace only took place in the sixteenth century on the initiative of François 1er, who imported a colony of Italian artists to carry out the decoration: among them Rosso il Fiorentino

---

Getting to Fontainebleau

Getting to Fontainebleau from Paris is straightforward. By road it is 16km from the A6 autoroute (exit Fontainebleau). **By train**, it is 50 minutes from the Gare de Lyon to Fontainebleau-Avon station, whence bus #A takes you to the château gates in a few minutes. You can rent **bikes** from the *gare SNCF* or *La Petite Reine*, 14 rue de la Paroisse (☎64.22.72.41). For further information, contact the SI at 31 place Napoléon (Mon–Sat 9am–12.30pm & 1.30–7pm, Sun 9am–12.30pm & 1.30–5pm; ☎64.22.25.68).

---

and Niccolò dell'Abate. It continued to enjoy royal favour well into the nineteenth century; Napoléon spent huge amounts of money on it, as did Louis-Philippe. And after World War II, when it was liberated from the Germans by General Patton, it served for a while as Allied military HQ in Europe. The town in the meantime has become the seat of *INSEAD*, a prestigious and élite multilingual business school.

The **buildings**, unpretentious and attractive despite their extent, have none of the architectural unity of a purpose-built residence like Vaux-le-Vicomte. Their distinction is the sumptuous interiors worked by the Italians, notably the celebrated **Galerie François-1er** – which had a seminal influence on the subsequent development of French aristocratic art and design – the Salle de Bal, the Salon Louis XIII, and the Salle du Conseil with its eighteenth-century decoration.

The **gardens** are equally luscious. If you want to escape into the relative wilds, head for the surrounding **Forest of Fontainebleau**, which is full of walking and cycling trails, all marked on Michelin map 196 (*Environs de Paris*). Its rocks are a favourite training ground for Paris-based climbers.

Chantilly

The main association with **Chantilly**, a small town 40km north of Paris, is **horses**. Some 3000 thoroughbreds prance the forest rides of a morning, and two of the season's classiest flat races are held here. The stables in the **château** are given over to a museum dedicated to live horses.

The Château

Daily except Tues March–Oct 10am–6pm; Nov–Feb 10.30am–12.30pm & 2–5pm. Admission 37F/32F, park only 15F.

The Chantilly estate used to belong to two of the most powerful clans in France: first to the Montmorencys, then through marriage to the Condés. The present château was put up in the late nineteenth century. It replaced a palace, destroyed in the Revolution, which had been built for the Grand Condé, who smashed Spanish military power for Louis XIV in 1643. It's an imposing rather than beautiful structure, too heavy for grace, but it stands well, surrounded by water and looking out in a haughty manner over a formal arrangement of pools and pathways designed by the busy Le Nôtre.

The entrance to the château is across a moat past two realistic bronzes of hunting hounds. The visitable parts are all museum

---

Getting to Chantilly

The town of Chantilly is accessible by frequent train from the Gare du Nord (about 30min). You can rent bikes at Chantilly station, but it's an easy walk to the château. Footpaths GR11 and 12 pass through the château **park** and its surrounding **forest**, if you want a peaceful and leisurely way of exploring this bit of country.

(same hours as the château): mainly an enormous collection of paintings and drawings. They are not well displayed and you quickly get visual indigestion from the massed ranks of good, bad and indifferent, deployed as if of equal value. Some highlights, however, are a collection of portraits of sixteenth- and seventeenth-century French monarchs and princes in the Galerie de Logis; interesting Greek and Roman bits in the tower room called the Rotonde de la Minerve; a big series of sepia stained glass illustrating Apuleius' *Golden Ass* in the Galerie de Psyche, together with some very lively portrait drawings; and, in the so-called Santuario, some Raphaels, a Filippino Lippi and forty miniatures from a fifteenth-century *Book of Hours* attributed to the French artist Jean Fouquet.

The museum's single greatest treasure is in the library, the Cabinet des Livres, entered only in the presence of the guide. It is *Les Très Riches Heures du Duc de Berry*, the most celebrated of all Books of Hours. The illuminated pages illustrating the months of the year with representative scenes from contemporary (early 1400s) rural life – like harvesting and ploughing, sheepshearing and pruning – are richly coloured and drawn with a delicate naturalism, as well as being sociologically interesting. Unfortunately, and understandably, only facsimiles are on display, but they give an excellent idea of the original. Sets of postcards, of middling fidelity, are on sale at the entrance. There are thousands of other fine books here as well.

Sleeping Beauty's castle at Disneyland Paris is based on an illustration in the Très Riches Heures; see p.378

The Horse Museum

Daily except Tues May–Aug 10.30am–5.30pm; April, Sept & Oct 10.30am–5.30pm. Closed Nov–March. Admission 45F/35F.

Five minutes' walk along the château drive at Chantilly, the colossal stable block has been transformed into a museum of the horse, the **Musée Vivant du Cheval**. The building was erected at the beginning of the eighteenth century by the incumbent Condé prince, who believed he would be reincarnated as a horse and wished to provide fitting accommodation for 240 of his future relatives.

In the main hall horses of different breeds from around the world are stalled, with a ring for **demonstrations** (May–July & Sept Sun & holidays 3.15pm & 4.45pm; 80F/70F including admission), followed by a series of life-size models illustrating the various activities horses are used for. In the rooms off are collections of paintings, horseshoes, veterinary equipment, bridles and saddles, a mock-up of a blacksmith's, children's horse toys (including a chain-driven number, with handles in its ears, which belonged to Napoléon III), and a fanciful Sicilian cart painted with scenes of Crusader battles.

Malmaison

Wed–Mon 10am–noon & 1.30–4.30/5.30pm. Closed Tues. Guided tours only; combined ticket with Bois-Préau museum 27F/18F.

The relatively small and surprisingly enjoyable **château of Malmaison** is set in the beautiful grounds of the Bois-Préau, about 15km west of central Paris. This was the home of the Empress Josephine. During the 1800–1804 Consulate, Napoléon would drive out at weekends, though by all accounts his presence was hardly guaranteed to make the party go with a bang. Twenty minutes was all the time allowed for meals, and when called upon to sing in party games, the great man always gave a rendition of *Malbrouck s'en va-t'en guerre* (*Malbrouck goes to war*), out of tune. A slightly odd choice, too, when you remember that it was Malbrouck, the Duke of Marlborough, who had given the French armies a couple of drubbings 100 years earlier. According to his secretary, Malmaison was "the only place next to the battlefield where he was truly himself". After their divorce, Josephine stayed on here, occasionally receiving visits from the emperor, until her death in 1814.

Visits today include private and official apartments, in part with original furnishings, as well as Josephine's clothes, china, glass and personal possessions. During the Nazi occupation, the imperial chair in the library was rudely violated by the fat buttocks of Reichsmarschall Goering, dreaming perhaps of promotion or the conquest of Egypt. There are other Napoléonic bits in the **Bois-Préau museum** nearby (daily except Tues 10.30am–1pm & 2–6pm).

On a high bump of ground behind the château, and not easy to get to without a car, is the 1830s fort of **Mont Valérien**. It was once a place of pilgrimage, but the Germans killed four and a half thousand hostages and Resistance people there during the war. It is again a national shrine, though the memorial itself is not much to look at.

Getting to Malmaison

To reach Malmaison, either take the métro to Grande Arche de la Défense, then bus #258 to Malmaison-Château, or, if you don't mind a walk, take the *RER* direct to Rueil-Malmaison and walk from there. In fact you could make a feature of the walk, and follow the GR11 footpath from the Pont de Chatou along the left bank of the Seine and into the château park.

Other Museums

Of the assortment of museums in the general vicinity of Paris, the one with the widest appeal must be the **Musée de l'Île-de-France** at Sceaux, with its delightfully eclectic collection of mementos of the region. But for specialist interest, the **ceramics** at Sèvres, **prehistory** at St-Germain-en-Laye, and **aviation** at Le Bourget are all excellent. Some of the museums, such as those at **Meudon**, also provide a good excuse for wanderings in the countryside.

Musée de l'Air et de l'Espace

Aéroport du Bourget, Le Bourget (15km northeast of Paris). Tues–Sun 10am–5pm; 20F/15F. Take RER line B3/B5 from Gare du Nord to Drancy (not all trains on this line stop here). Follow avenue Francis-de-Pressensé from the station as far as the main road. Turn left and, by a tabac on the left at the first crossroads, get bus #152 to Le Bourget/Musée de l'Air. Alternatively, bus #350 from Gare du Nord, Gare de l'Est, and Porte de la Chapelle, or #152 from Porte de la Villette, will also get you there.

The French were always adventurous, pioneering aviators and the name of Le Bourget is intimately connected with their earliest exploits. Lindbergh landed here after his epic first flight across the Atlantic. From World War I until the development of Orly in the 1950s it was Paris' principal airport.

Today Le Bourget is used only for internal flights (and for international arms fairs), while some of the older buildings have been turned into the museum of flying machines. It consists of five adjacent hangars, the first devoted to **space**, with rockets, satellites, space capsules etc. Some are mock-ups, some the real thing. Among the latter are a Lunar Roving Vehicle, the Apollo XIII command module in which James Lovell and his fellow-astronauts nearly came to grief, the Soyuz craft in which a French astronaut flew, and France's own first successful space rocket. Everything is accompanied by extremely good explanatory panels – though in French only.

The remainder of the exhibition is arranged in chronological order, starting with **Hangar A** (the furthest away from the entrance), which covers the period 1919–39. Several record-breakers here, including the Bréguet XIX, which made the first ever crossing of the South Atlantic in 1927. Also here is the corrugated iron job that featured so long on US postage stamps: a Junkers F13, which the Germans were forbidden to produce after World War I and which was taken over instead by the US mail.

Hangar B shows a big collection of World War II planes, including a V-1 flying bomb and the Nazis' last jet fighter, the largely

At **Drancy**, near the Aéroport du Bourget, the Germans and the French Vichy regime had a transit camp for Jews en route to Auschwitz – this was where the poet Max Jacob, among others, died. A cattle wagon and a stone stele in the courtyard of a council estate commemorate the nearly 100,000 Jews who passed through here, of whom only 1518 returned.

wooden Heinkel 162A. Incredibly, the plans were completed on September 24, 1944, and it flew on December 6. There are photographic displays and some revealing statistics on war damage in France. The destruction included two-thirds of rail wagons, four-fifths of barges, 115 large train stations, 9000 bridges, 80 wharves, and one house in twenty-two (plus one in six partially destroyed).

Hangars C and D cover the years 1945 to the present day, during which the French aviation industry, having lost eighty percent of its capacity in 1945, has recovered to a pre-eminent position in the world. Its high-tech achievement is represented here by the super-sophisticated best-selling Mirage fighters, the first Concorde prototype and the Ariane space-launcher (the two latter parked on the tarmac outside). No warheads on site, as far as we know . . . **Hangar E** has light and sporty aircraft.

Musée des Antiquités Nationales

Château de St-Germain-en-Laye; opposite St-Germain-en-Laye RER station (terminus of line A1). Wed–Sun 9am–5.15pm; 20F/13F/under-18s free.

The unattractively renovated château of St-Germain-en-Laye, 10km west of Malmaison and a total of 25km out of Paris, was one of the main residences of the French court before the construction of Versailles was built. It now houses the extraordinary national archeology museum, which will prove of immense interest to anyone who has been to the prehistoric caves of the Dordogne.

The presentation and lighting make the visit a real pleasure. The extensive Stone Age section includes a mock-up of the **Lascaux caves** and a profile of Abbé Breuil, the priest who made prehistoric art respectable, as well as a beautiful collection of decorative objects, tools and so forth. All ages of prehistory are covered, right on down into historical times with Celts, Romans and Franks: abundant evidence that the French have been a talented arty lot for a very long time. The end piece is a room of **comparative archeology**, with objects from cultures across the globe.

From right outside the château, a **terrace** – Le Nôtre arranging the landscape again – stretches for more than two kilometres above the Seine with a view over the whole of Paris. All behind it is the **forest of St-Germain**, a sizeable expanse of woodland, but criss-crossed by too many roads to be convincing as wilderness.

Musée de l'Île-de-France

Château de Sceaux. Take RER line B4 to Parc de Sceaux (15min from Denfert-Rochereau): turn left on avenue de la Duchesse-du-Maine, right into avenue Rose-de-Launay and right again on avenue Le-Nôtre and you'll find the château gates on your left (5–10min walk). Wed–Sun 10am–6pm; Oct–March closes 5pm; 20F/12F; disabled access.

The **château of Sceaux**, 20km south of Paris, is a nineteenth-century replacement of the original – demolished post-Revolution – which matched the now-restored Le Nôtre grounds of terraces,

water and woods in classical geometry. It houses the newly renovated **Musée de l'Île de France**, which evokes the Paris countryside
of the *ancien régime* with its aristocratic and royal domains; of the
nineteenth century, with its riverside scenes and eating and dancing
places, the *guinguettes*, that inspired so many artists; and documents the twentieth century's new towns and transport systems.
There are models, pictures and diverse objects: a back-pack hot
chocolate dispenser with a choice of two brews, 1940s métro seats,
early bicycles and a series of plates and figurines inspired by the
arrival of the first giraffe in France in the 1830s. The changes since
the days of the tree-house music and dance venue in Robinson are
graphically illustrated – a painting of river laundering at Cergy-
Pontoise is set alongside photos of the new town high-rise – and
though some of the rooms hold little excitement, most people, kids
included, should find enough to make the visit worthwhile.

Temporary exhibitions and a summer festival of classical
chamber music are held in the *Orangerie*, which, along with the
Pavillon de l'Aurore (in the northeast corner of the park), survives
from the original residence. The concerts take place at weekends,
from July to October – details from the museum (☎46.61.06.71) or
from the *Direction des Musées de France* (Palais du Louvre, cours
Visconti, 34 quai du Louvre, Paris 1ᵉʳ; ☎42.60.39.26). In the
summer you can get snacks and drinks in the park.

Musée National de la Céramique

*Place de la République, Sèvres. Daily except Tues 10am–5pm. Admission 17F/11F/
under-18s free. Take the métro to the Pont-de-Sèvres terminus, cross the bridge and
spaghetti junction – the museum is the massive building facing the river bank on your
right.*

A ceramics museum may possibly seem a bit too rarefied an attraction to justify a trip out of Paris, but if you do have the taste, there
is much to be savoured at Sèvres' **Musée National de la Céramique**.
As well as French pottery and china, there's also Islamic, Chinese,
Italian, German, Dutch, and English produce, though the displays
inevitably centre around a comprehensive collection of Sèvres ware,
as the stuff is made right here.

Right by the museum is the **Parc de St-Cloud**, good for fresh air
and visual order, with a geometrical sequence of pools and fountains. You could, if you wanted, take a train from St-Lazare to St-
Cloud and head south through the park to the museum.

Meudon-Val-Fleury

Meudon-Val-Fleury, on the C5/C7 *RER* lines just southwest of the
city, is the easiest accessible patch of Seine countryside. To give a
walk some purpose there is the **Villa des Brillants** at 19 avenue
Auguste-Rodin, off rue de la Belgique (July–Sept Sat & Sun 1.30–
6.30pm; 12F/7F), the house where Rodin spent his last years, with
an annexe containing some of his maquettes, plaster casts and other

bits and bobs. From the station make your way up the east flank of
the valley through the twisty rue des Vignes. You can either go up
rue de la Belgique until you reach avenue Rodin on the left towards
the top, or turn down it to the rail embankment, go through the
tunnel and take the footpath on the right, which brings you out by
the house. It stands in a big picnickable garden, where Rodin
himself is buried, on the very edge of the hill looking down on the
old Renault works in Boulogne-Billancourt.

To the south, on the edge of Meudon's forest, is the **Musée et
Jardin de Sculptures de la Fondation Hans Arp** at 21 rue des
Châtaigniers, Clamart (Fri–Sun 2–6pm; 20F/12F). This was the
home and studio of Dadaists Hans Arp and Sophie Taeuber – both
the house and garden have examples of their work and the house
itself is a curiosity.

Works by Arp, Taeuber, Rodin and others are exhibited at the
Musée d'Art et d'Histoire de Meudon, in what was once Molière's
residence at 11 rue des Pierres (Wed–Sun 2–6pm). There are
mementos of various characters – including Wagner – who stayed or
had some connection with the house.

Giverny

*Giverny, Normandy. Gardens are open all year Tues–Sun 10am–6pm; house April–
Oct only, Tues–Sun 10am–noon & 2–6pm. Closed Mon. Combined admission 36F/25F
students, 15F under-12s; entrance to the gardens alone costs 25F/20F.*

Monet's gardens in Giverny are in a class by themselves. They are
a long way out from Paris (80km), in the direction of Rouen, and
there's no direct transport. If you're planning a future holiday in
Normandy, or if you're visiting in winter, leave them for another
time. But if not, consider making the effort – the rewards are
greater than all the châteaux put together.

Monet lived in Giverny from 1883 till his death in 1926, and the
gardens he laid out leading down from his house towards the river
were considered by most of his friends to be his greatest masterpiece. Each month is reflected in a dominant colour, as are each of
the rooms, hung as he left them with his collection of Japanese
prints. May and June, when the rhododendrons flower round the lily

---

Getting to Giverny

Without a car, the easiest approach to Giverny is by train to Vernon from
Paris-St-Lazare (35min–1hr; hourly). The noon train gets you there in
time to catch the 1.15pm bus, which leaves for Giverny from just outside
the station (6F), returning at 3.15pm and 5.15pm. If you miss it, you'll
have to take a taxi, hitch, rent a bike from the station or walk the remaining 6km. For the latter, cross the river and turn right on the D5; take care
as you enter Giverny to take the left fork, otherwise you'll make a long
detour to reach the garden entrance. In any event, the station always has
an information board detailing whatever transport is available.

pond and the wisteria winds over the Japanese bridge, are the best of all times to visit. But any month, from spring to autumn, is overwhelming in the beauty of this arrangement of living shades and shapes. Although you have to contend with crowds with cameras snapping up images of the waterlilies far removed from Monet's renderings, there's no place like it.

Giverny also now boasts a new museum, the **Musée Americain** at 99 rue Claude-Monet (Tues–Sun 10am–6pm; 30F/20F), which focuses on American painters in France from 1865 to 1915.

New Towns and *Grands Ensembles*

Investigating life in the **suburbs** is hardly a prime holiday occupation but if you are interested in housing and urban development, or the arrogance of architects and nose-length perspectives of planners, then the "Greater Paris" new towns of the 1970s and 1980s, and the 1950s and 1960s vast housing estates known as *Grands Ensembles*, could be instructive.

Wealthy Parisians who have moved out from the Beaux Quartiers have always had their flats or houses (with tennis courts and swimming pools) southwest of the city, in the garden suburbs that now stretch out beyond Versailles. Those forced to move by rising rents, or who have never afforded a Paris flat, live, if they're lucky, in the soulless *Villes Nouvelles*, and if not, in the *Grands Ensembles* that were the quick-fix solution to the housing crisis brought on by the postwar population growth and city slum clearance programmes.

The *Villes Nouvelles* became the mode in the late 1960s when the accumulating problems of high-rise low-income society first started to filter through to architects and planners. Unlike their English equivalents, the Parisian new towns were grafted on to existing towns but conceived as satellites to the capital rather than places in their own right. Streets of tiny detached *pavillons* with old-time residents cower beneath buildings from another world. There's the unsettling reversal that the people are there because of the town, not vice versa. Added to which the town seems to be there only because of the rail and *RER* lines.

Sarcelles, twelve kilometres to the north, is the most notorious of the *Grands Ensembles*. It gave a new word to the French language, "*sarcellitis*", the social disease of delinquency and despair spread by the horizons of interminable, identical, high-rise hutches.

In the 1990s social housing is no longer on the agenda. Instead the planners have, unoriginally, come up with the idea of a "business city" beside the Roissy-Charles-de-Gaulle airport. The site, called **Roissypôle**, is already a major commercial centre and set to attract many more businesses with the new Lille-Lyon *TGV* line, which will eventually link with Britain, Germany, the Netherlands, Belgium and Italy. The combination of air and high-speed train links will bring all of Europe and north Africa within three hours travelling time from Roissy. The idea is to add residential areas and services, but considerable opposition to the plan has yet to be overcome.

La Grande Borne, Evry and Cergy-Pontoise

A few years after Sarcelles' creation, at the end of the 1960s, the architect Émile Aillaud tried a very different approach in the *Grand Ensemble* called **La Grande Borne**. Twenty-five kilometres south of Paris and directly overlooking the Autoroute du Sud, which cuts it off from the town centre and nearest rail connection of Grigny, it was hardly a promising site. But for once a scale was used that didn't belittle the inhabitants and the buildings were shaped by curves instead of corners. The façades are coloured by tiny glass and ceramic tiles, there are inbuilt artworks – landscapes, animals, including two giant sculpted pigeons, and portraits of Rimbaud and Kafka – and the whole ensemble is pedestrians only. Unfortunately the planners failed to integrate any small businesses or community spaces, so La Grande Borne remains a dormitory complex.

To get there by public transport is a bit exhausting: train from the Gare de Lyon, direction Corbeil-Essones, to Grigny-Centre, then bus or walk; but by road it's a quick flit down the A6 from Porte d'Orléans: turn off to the right on the D13 and both the first and second right will take you into the estate.

Having come out this way, you could also take a look at **Evry**, one of the five new towns in the Paris region (Evry-Courcouronnes *SNCF*, two stops on from Grigny). Follow the signs from Evry station to the *centre commercial* and keep going through it till you surface on a walkway that bridges boulevard de l'Europe. This leads you into Evry 1 housing estate, a multi-matt-coloured ensemble resembling a group of ransacked wardrobes and chests-of-drawers. The architects call it pyramidal and blather on about how the buildings and the landscape articulate each other. But it's quite fun, as a monument, even if the "articulating" motifs on the façade overlooking the park are more like fossils than plants.

Cergy-Pontoise, thirty kilometres northwest of Paris (*RER* line A3, Cergy-St-Christophe), has giant clocks decorating its station. Take the left-hand exit and keep going straight up through pedestrianized squares until you see a high white column. Circled by awful mock classical colonnades and mirrored façades, this is the start of an "Axe Majeur" pointing towards La Défense. The 3km vista has yet to have its full complement of architectural fantasies and may not have for a long time given the recession. There are very few cafés and brasseries in Cergy and those there are seem full of arcade machines and bored men.

Marne-la-Vallée

The new town with the most to shock or amuse, or even please, is undoubtedly **Marne-la-Vallée**, where Terry Gilliam's totalitarian fantasy *Brasil* was filmed. It starts ten kilometres east of Paris and hops for twenty kilometres from one new outburst to the next, with odd bits of wood and water in between, until it reaches its apogee, **Disneyland Paris** (see Chapter 21). All the *RER* stops from Bry-sur-Marne to Marne-la-Vallée/Chessy are in Marne-la-Vallée; journeys north or south from the rail line are not so easy.

To sample the architectural styles of Marne-la-Vallée you need only go as far as **Noisy-Le-Grand-Mont-d'Est**. You surface on the *Arcades*, a stony substitute for a town square. And there you have the poetic panorama of a controlled community environment. Bright blue tubing and light blue tiling on split-level walkways and space-less concrete fencing; powder-blue boxes growing plants on buildings beside grey-blue roofs of multi-angled leanings; walls of blue, walls of white, deep blue frames and tinted glass reflecting the water of a chopped-up lake; islands linked by bridges with more blue railings . . .

The two acclaimed architectural pieces in this monolith have only one thing in their favour – neither is blue in any bit. They are both low-cost housing units, gigantic and unmitigatedly horrible. The **Arènes de Picasso** is in the group of buildings to the right of the *RER* line as you look at the lakes from the *Arcades*, about half a kilometre away. It's soon visible as you approach: two enormous circles like loudspeakers facing each other across a space that would do nicely for a Roman stadium. Prepare to feel as if the lions are waiting. At the other end of Noisy-Mont d'Est, facing the capital, is the extraordinary semicircle, arch and half square of **Le Théâtre et Palacio d'Abraxas**, creation of Ricardo Boffil. Ghosts of ancient Greek designs haunt the façades but proportion there is none, whether classical or any other.

Disneyland Paris

C hildren will love Disneyland Paris, 25km west of the capital – there are no two ways about it. What their minders will think of it is another matter. For a start, there has to be the question of whether it's worth the money. Quite why American parents might bring their charges here is hard to fathom: even British parents might well decide that it would be easier, and cheaper, to buy a family package to Florida, where sunshine is assured, where Disney World has better rides (though Disneyland Paris is adding new attractions by the month), and where the conflict between enchanted kingdom and enchanting city does not arise.

In fact, foul north European weather does have its advantages. On an off-season wet and windy weekday (Mon & Thurs are the best) you can probably get round every ride you want.

Before setting out, you should be clear about just what Disneyland Paris is, and what it is not. The physical buzz of shocks, fright and gravitational pulls is not a priority on the Disney agenda. They want you to feel safe and secure, and for a visit to be a thoroughly *wholesome* experience, so the park is short on real fear-thrill rides. Originally there was only *Big Thunder Mountain, Indiana Jones and the Temple of Doom*. Now there's the first 360° loop ever in a Disney park in *Discovery Mountain*, with three loops and corkscrew turns, under construction at the time of writing and due to open in 1995.

Getting to Disneyland Paris

From Paris, take *RER* line A (Châtelet-Les-Halles, Gare de Lyon, Nation) to Marne-la-Vallée/Chessy, the Disneyland Paris stop. The journey takes about 40 minutes, and costs 66F return.

If you're coming straight from the airport, there's a half-hourly **shuttle bus** from Charles de Gaulle, and another every 45 minutes from Orly (75F, no reductions for children). Marne-la-Vallée/Chessy also has its own *TGV* train station, linked to Roissy Charles-de-Gaulle station, and to Lille, Lyon and the Chunnel.

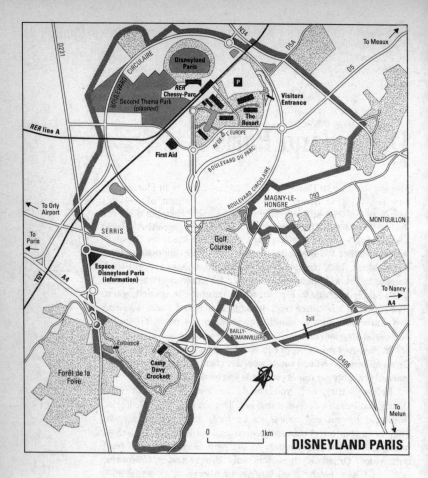

DISNEYLAND PARIS

Disneyland Paris is mainly about film sets, not funfairs or big tops. Which is why it's so wonderful for children, because these sets are "real" – you can go into them and round them and the characters talk to you. All the structures are incredibly detailed, and their shades and textures have been worked out with the precision of a brain surgeon. But if you're not a child, solid three-dimensional buildings masquerading as flimsy film sets and constantly being filmed by swarming hordes of camcorder operators can well fail to fulfil any kind of escapist fantasy.

Besides the **Disneyland Paris Park**, the complex includes **Festival Disney** – the evening entertainments complex – and the Disney hotels. These, unlike the park, are radically different from their US or Japanese counterparts, having been designed especially for Europeans, who, according to Disney executives, invented fairy tales and castles, but have run out of good ideas since.

Michael Eisner, Chair and Chief Executive of *Disney USA*, stated that "Euro Disney introduces a new level of design and innovation to Europe". Paris can take such bombast; it has existed for about 27 times the 69 years that Mr Eisner's company has been in business, and at the end of two millenia of sustained design achievement it remains the most innovative and stylish capital city in Europe.

The Park

The introduction to Disneyland Paris is the same as in Florida, LA, and Tokyo. **Main Street USA** is a mythical vision of a 1900s American town, West Coast with a dash of East Coast, but more the mishmash memories of a thousand and one American movies – without the mud.

Main Street leads to **Central Plaza**, the hub of the standard radial layout. Clockwise from Main Street are **Frontierland**, **Adventureland, Fantasyland** and **Discoveryland**. The **castle**, directly opposite Main Street across Central Plaza, belongs to Fantasyland. A steam train **Railroad** runs round the park with stations at each "land" and at the entrance.

Some Background

For the opening of Euro Disney in April 1992, the Parisian regional transport workers went on strike, electricity pylons supplying the site were blown up, French commentators spoke of a "cultural Chernobyl", contractors claimed they were still owed millions, Disneyland Paris share prices plummeted, and British travel agents refused to sell Disney packages.

Some £2.2 billion had been spent on setting up the park. After nine months, American Disney Inc. had raked in royalty fees (on admissions, food, drink, hotel rooms – everything) and management fees amounting to £40–50 million, while the public shareholders (owning 51 percent) had received no dividend at all. After a disastrous summer in 1993, annual losses of £614 million were announced and share prices again dropped dramatically. Unreliable weather, the greater cost to British visitors because of the fall in the pound, the unwillingness of visitors to spend money inside the park and on hotel rooms, had all brought the park to the brink of bankruptcy. Disney, however, were not going to give up. And with French taxpayers having forked out for the land, the *RER* and rail lines, motorway exits and the like, the French government were not keen to see it go bust. Lengthy negotiations for a £1.5 billion restructuring package carried on into 1994. Then a Saudi prince agreed to buy up to 24 percent of the £700 million worth of new shares being sold. Jobs have gone, hotel prices lowered, the MGM studio plans put on hold. The last major overhaul was the change of name in September 1994 to Disneyland Paris, a ploy calculated to whitewash the past "Euro-dismal" image of the park. Depending on the recovery of the world recession and the unchanging needs of media-driven children, Disneyland Paris will probably survive.

Information and access

You enter the park under Main Street Station. **City Hall** is to the left, where you can get **information** about the day's programming of events and about the hotels and evening's entertainments. For people in **wheelchairs** there's the *Guest Special Services Guide* that details accessibility of the rides. All the loos, phones, shops and restaurants have wheelchair access. Wheelchairs and pushchairs can be rented (30F plus 20F deposit) in the building opposite City Hall (you are allowed to bring in your own).

The **lost property office** is in City Hall. **Lost children** can be found in the Baby Care Centre by the Plaza Gardens Restaurant in the block between Main Street and Discoveryland. **Luggage** can be left in lockers in "Guest Storage" under Main Street Station.

Food and Drink

The former Disney policy of no alcohol has been abandoned – maybe in a desperate attempt to beat their overdraft (see box on previous page). Adults can now sip wine or beer at any of the park's restaurants, at a considerable price, of course. Coke, fruit juices, tea, coffee, chocolate, mineral water, fizzy drinks and alcohol-free cocktails are also readily available, and coffee away from Main Street is reasonably priced, if a bit weak compared to the French café norm. The **food** in Disneyland Paris, however, tastes as if it's been first cooked, then sterilized, then put on your plate. This is certainly not the place to blow precious meal money, so avoid the restaurants on Main Street and go for hamburgerish snacks at the various themed eateries around the park.

Officially, you're not allowed to bring any refreshments into the park, but, if you don't want to spend anything more than the entrance fee, eat a good Parisian breakfast and smuggle in some discreet snacks. Whether Goofy turns nasty if he sees you eating a brand name not on the list of Disney sponsors is anyone's guess.

Admission fees for the park

	Age 12 and over	Age 3–11
1 day	225F	150F
2 days	425F	285F
3 days	565F	375F

These are mid-season prices. 1 day high season costs 250F and 175F. 1 day low season costs 175F and 125F.

The passes, known as passports, can be purchased in advance at the Paris Tourist Office, the *Galeries Lafayette* department store (bd Haussmann, Mº Havre-Caumartin), major stations on the *RER* A line, at all *Virgin* Megastores, *FNAC* shops, and of couse, all Disney shops.

Multiday passes don't have to be used on consecutive days. Your wrist is stamped with invisible ink when you leave the park, allowing you to return.

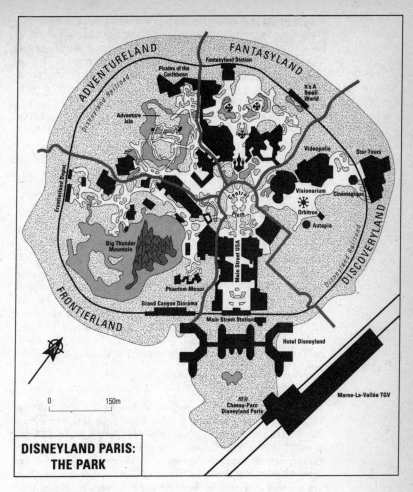

**DISNEYLAND PARIS:
THE PARK**

Smoking is allowed in the park, but not in the queues for the rides. You won't see a cigarette butt anywhere; all litter gets swept up instantaneously.

Main Street USA

On the corner of **Main Street**, *Town Square Photography* rents out still and video cameras (50F and 300F per day), and sells film, lenses, cameras and tripods amid a collection of museum pieces. *Kodak* is one of Disney's main sponsors, and kiosks throughout the park sell film and offer two-hour print developing.

If you succumb at this stage to the idea of takeaway snapshots and the Disneyland Paris home movie, you'll be in serious financial trouble by the end of the day. As a practice run, see if you can get down Main Street without buying one of the following: a balloon, a hat with your name embroidered on it, an ice cream, bag of sweets, silhouette portraits of your kids, the *Wall Street Journal* of 1902, a Disney version of a children's classic in hardback, an evening dress and suit and tie, a Donald Duck costume, a haircut, a model rocket, a genuine vintage car, a tea service and set of crystal glasses, some muffins, a coke, a few cakes, a limited edition Disney lithograph, and a complete set of Disney characters in ceramics, metal, plastic, rubber or wool.

Leaving Main Street is quickest on foot (crowds permitting), although omnibuses, trams, horse-drawn streetcars, fire trucks and police vans are always on hand, plus the Disney *pièce de résistance*, the Railroad, for which **Main Street Station** has the longest queues.

The Railroad

The "attraction" on the circular Railroad is the **Grand Canyon Diorama** between Main Street and Frontierland. You enter a tunnel, and there below you, in all its tiny glory, is a miniature plastic Grand Canyon. While you ruminate on the fact that it is the *size* of the real Grand Canyon that is the source of its fascination, you can look out the window and appreciate how enormous Disneyland Paris is. Once you've been in the park a few hours, however, you may begin to find yourself unable to imagine any fantasy, discovery, adventure or "frontier experience" other than those created by the scenes laid out before you.

The Parades

La Parade Disney happens every day at 3pm. This is not a bad time to go on the most popular rides, but if you have kids they will no doubt force you to press against the barriers for the ultimate Disney event. The best place is on the queuing ramp for *It's a Small World*, right by the gates through which the floats appear. You can even see them over the fence "backstage", but Disney cast members are too well trained to be frowning and smoking a fag before their entrance. From here, the parade progresses, very slowly, to Town Square.

The parade floats represent all the top box-office Disney movies – *Dumbo, Snow White, Cinderella, Pinocchio, The Jungle Book, Peter Pan, Roger Rabbit, Beauty and the Beast,* and *Aladdin.* Everyone waves and smiles, characters on foot shake hands with the kids who've managed to get to the front, and *Sleeping Beauty*'s medieval valets trundle bins and brushes to mop up behind the knights on horseback – a small concession to reality.

The night-time parades that feature in Florida are not a regular event here. They do have **Electrical Parades**, with characters' costumes strung with light bulbs, but not every night. **Firework**

displays happen about twice a week during the summer (and have had to be toned down because of complaints by people living in villages ten miles away). Check with the *Programme des Spectacles* available at City Hall for dates and times.

The Rides

The listings below are a selection of the best and worst rides, or "attractions," as they like to be called. As the guide you get on entry covers the park in a clockwise direction, this does the opposite in the hope that you might be competing with slightly fewer of your fellow *RER* travellers on the first few rides.

For the youngest kids, **Fantasyland** is likely to hold the most thrills. **Adventureland** has the most outlandish sets and two of the best rides – *Pirates of the Caribbean* and *Indiana Jones and the Temple of Doom*. Boat trips in canoes, keelboats and a paddle-steamer are to had in **Frontierland,** where *Big Thunder Mountain* provides a decent roller-coaster ride. The design and technology of **Discoveryland** suggests that no advances have been made since *Star Wars* first came out. It's the most disappointing of the four, unless you're an avid Michael Jackson fan.

Discoveryland

Le Visionarium

A slow build-up to a 360° film (shot with nine cameras and screened with nine projectors), presented by a robotic time-keeper host and his nervous android assistant. The story involves their travelling through time and picking up Jules Verne at the 1900 *exposition universelle* in Paris just as he and H.G. Wells are discussing time travel. They show Jules Verne all the wonders of contemporary life (*TGV*s and Mirages mainly), with bit parts for the likes of Gérard Dépardieu as an airport baggage handler.

The only drawback to the complete surround film is that, not having nine eyes, you have to keep deciding which way to look. An English translation is available on headphones.

Les Mystères du Nautilus

More Jules Verne fetish, with a visit in a miniature Nautilus submarine – Captain Nemo's vessel in "20,000 Leagues Under the Sea" – through an oversize Nautilus. Apart from the giant squid attack on the big Nautilus' porthole window, what's supposed to impress you is the faithfulness of the decor to the original Disney set: the organ is even an exact replica.

Orbitron

The "rockets" on this hideous structure go round and round extremely slowly and go up (at your control) even more laggardly to a daring 30° above the horizontal. Only suitable for small kids and for those who hate more violent rides (whatever the special boarding restrictions say).

Star Tours
Simulated ride in a space craft (with 60 other people all in neat rows) piloted by friendly incompetent C3PO of *Star Wars* fame. The projection of what you're supposed to be careering through is from the film, which is the only thing that makes this superior to space tour simulations elsewhere. When you come off the ride there's an arcade of video games, which only those adept at this kind of entertainment can work out how to use.

Cinémagique
A Michael Jackson movie with impressive animations, deafening sound, and 3-D specs to turn it from film into stage. Not for those with sensitive eyes or ears, nor for those whose sensitivities don't extend to adoring Mr Jackson.

Autopia
Miniature futuristic cars to drive on rails with no possibility of any dodgems stratagems.

Discovery Mountain
A huge new attraction opening in autumn 1995: a roller-coaster-type ride which invites you to experience being thrown from Earth to the Moon....

Fantasyland

Le Château de la Belle au Bois Dormant
Sleeping Beauty was originally *La Belle au Bois*, heroine of a seventeenth-century French tale. Disney is very smug about having based the design of the castle on an illustration in the medieval manuscript *Les Très Riches Heures du Duc de Berri* (see p.362). In the picture, the château is a veritable fortress, grey and forbidding. In the foreground grumpy peasants till the fields. The château here copies the shapes of some of the turrets and the blue of the roof tiles, but that's about it. In fact, it has about the same connection as the originals of *Alice in Wonderland*, *The Jungle Book* and *La Belle au Bois* to the Disney versions.

You might wonder why after a hundred years' enforced slumber, finally rescued by the Prince's kiss, Sleeping Beauty should decide to turn her place of torment into a shopping arcade – but she has. The one thing you can't buy are the tapestries of Disney scenes that adorn the walls; these are genuine one-offs, painstakingly manufactured by the d'Aubusson workshops. Down below, in the dungeon, you'll find one of the better bits of fantasy apparatus: a huge dragon with red eyes that wakes on cue to snap its jaws and flick its tail.

Peter Pan's Flight

Disney must have cursed the appearance of *Hook* in the same year that Disneyland Paris opened. Anyone who has seen Spielberg's movie will have problems returning to the Disney version. But the very young will probably appreciate the jerky ride above Big Ben and the lights of London to Never-Never Land.

Le Pays des Contes de Fées

An unenthralling ride through fairytale scenes: Alice in Wonderland, Pinnochio, etc. Fine for little kids.

Le Carrousel de Lancelot

No complaints about this stately merry-go-round, whose every horse has its own individual medieval equerry in glittering paint.

Blanche-Neige et les Sept Nains

Unlike *Peter Pan*, *Snow White and the Seven Dwarfs* no longer exist as anything but their Disney manifestations. So this ride, through lots of menacing moving trees, swinging doors and cackling witches, is less grating than some of the others.

Mad Hatter's Tea Cups

These look wonderful – great big whirling teacups sliding past each other on a chequered floor – even if the connection with Alice is a little strained. Again, not a whizzy ride, but fun for younger ones.

Dumbo the Flying Elephant

Dumbo and his clones provide yet another safe, slow and low aerial ride.

Alice's Curious Labyrinth

The best things about this maze are the slow-motion fountains spurting jets of water over your head. There are passages that only those under three feet tall can pass through, and enough false turns and exits to make it an irritatingly good labyrinth. As for the Disneyized White Rabbit, Tweedledum and Tweedledee and the Cheshire Cat, think of them as fellow tourists.

It's a Small World

This is a quintessential Disney experience: there's one in every Disneyland, and Walt considered it to be the finest expression of his corporation's philosophy. For a jaded adult, it is certainly one of the most entertaining of all the "attractions". It is quite definitively, and spectacularly, revolting. Your boat rides through a polystyrene and glitter world where animated dolls in national/ethnic/tribal costumes dance beside their most famous landmarks or landscapes, singing the song *It's a small world*. The lyrics and the context make it clear that what unites the human race is the possibility that every child could have its imagination totally fed by Disney products. What a relief that the global telecommunications network trumpeted by *French Telecom*, who sponsor this "attraction", does not in fact reach every corner of the globe.

Adventureland

Le Passage enchanté d'Aladdin
A magic carpet ride – of course, with the film's soundtrack and all the highlights of the film, which rather lose their charm in three dimensions.

Pirates of the Caribbean
Disney are dead proud of this ride, which doesn't exist in the other Disneylands. The animated automatons are the best yet, to the extent that it's hard to be convinced that they're not actors (perhaps they are). The ride consists of an underground ride on water and down waterfalls, past scenes of evil piracy. Baddies in jail try coaxing a dog who has the keys in its mouth, sitting just out of reach. Battles are staged across the water, skeletons slide into the water, parrots squawk, chains rattle and a treasure trove is revealed. Note that queues for this one are horrendous, and once you're inside there's still a very long way to go.

Indiana Jones and the Temple of Doom (Le Temple du Péril)
This is a fast and quite violent roller-coaster with the first 360° loop on a Disney ride. Impressive stone vipers wait for you above the flame torches after you've lined up through tents filled with fossils and the ruined temple. Visually one of the best, though the ride itself doesn't last long.

Working for Disney

No facial hair, daily deodorant, clipped fingernails, unbleached hair, no jewellery of any kind, hair neither short nor long – these are just some of the conditions imposed on the 10,000 people or so who work as "cast members" at Euro Disney. Pay is abysmal, accommodation is neither provided nor subsidized, and turnover, not surprisingly, is very high. The cardinal rule here is to be in character – in sweet, smiley, have-a-good-day persona – all the time.

In the nearby village of Neufmoutiers-en-Brie, a monastery was set up specifically to give a stress-free space to Disney cast members. The priests who work there have described Disney world as "a fortress", "a world of money and imitation", where everything is passive except the shooting gallery.

Another Roman Catholic priest has been a major irritant to Disney (and to his bishop). He joined the CGT (the Communist trade union) and got a job on the Disney railway where he managed to unionize his workmates. CGT members amongst the cleaning staff have staged strikes and caused serious embarrassment during visits by VIPs.

La Cabane des Robinson

The 27m mock Banyan tree at the top of Adventure Isle is one of Disneyland Paris' most obsessively detailed creations, complete with hundreds of thousands of false leaves and blossoms. Not much point, though, unless you're a dedicated Swiss Family Robinson fan.

Adventureland Bazaar

This is a clever bit of shopping mall, disguised as a *souk*, with traditional Arab latticed walls, desert pastel colours, and all sorts of genuine Hollywood details. In the alleyway to the right of the archway (with Adventureland behind you) there's an inset in the wall where a laughing genie appears out of Aladdin's lamp every few minutes.

Frontierland

Big Thunder Mountain

For those who like proper heart-in-the-mouth funfair thrills, this is the only decent ride in Disneyland Paris. It's a roller coaster round the "mining mountain", under the lake to the other island and back again, with wicked twists and turns, splashes and collapsing roofs. The modelling on the upward sections is very effective; there are no Disney characters, and the dogs and goats do very good impressions of ordinary dogs and goats. Also, all the mining bits and pieces are genuine articles, bought up by Disney from museums and old mines in California and Nevada.

Phantom Manor

This starts off very promisingly: a *Psycho*-style house on the outside and Hammer Horror Edwardian mansion within. Holographic ghosts appear before cobweb-covered mirrors and ancestral portraits. But horror is not part of Disney's world; the dead bride story suddenly switches to a Wild West graveyard dance, and any lurking heebie-jeebies are well and truly scuttled. The other problem with Disney doing a Ghost Train ride is that the last thing they want to do is to scare you. So nothing jumps out and screams at you, no deathly hand skims your hair.

Rustler Roundup Shootin' Gallery

The only "attraction" for which there's a fee (10F), because, without some check, people stay for hours and hours when they might otherwise be consuming.

River Rogue Keelboats and Indian Canoes

Northern European weather is a problem here. If it's raining and there's more than a ripple on the lake's surface, the boats don't go out.

Festival Disney and the hotels

When the park gates close, you're not supposed to hop it back to Paris. Oh no. It's Disney **festival** time. *Buffalo Bill's Wild West Show*, *Billy Bob's Country Western Saloon*, *Annette's Diner*, *Rock 'n' Roll America* and the *Champions Sports Bar* await you with live music on summer nights: bluegrass bands, rock 'n' roll and the Top 40 hits. You can eat seafood in a bootleggers' hideout on Key West, or steaks in a Chicago meat-packing warehouse, while the kids pretend to be in *Peter Pan* at the *Never Land Club Children's Theatre*.

When you're nearing exhaustion from so much enchantment, you can return to your themed **hotel** and have a sauna, a jacuzzi or a whirlpool dip, eat and drink some more, purchase more "giftware", play video games and be in bed in time to feel fresh and fit to meet Micky and Minnie again over breakfast. Then out for a round of golf, a work-out, some pony or bike riding or serious team sports. You can skate (in winter), sail (in summer), jog on a special "health circuit", shop some more, mainline more video games, and return to the park for another go at the queues.

In reality, partaking of this end of the resort on top of the park is well beyond most people's budgets. The cheapest hotel room off season is 300F (for 2 adults, 2 children), the Davey Crockett Campsite is 300F for a campsite, 425F for a cabin (again low season), and entertainments such as the Wild West Show (real guns, horses, bulls and bison) is 300F (200F for 3–11-year-olds) for the dinner and show. Accommodation is based on a family of four sharing a room or campsite.

Special packages are available, based on four people sharing a room at the Sequoia Lodge, two-day theme park entrance and breakfast. For details, phone %60.30.60.30 in France, %071/753 2900 in the UK, or %407/IN-DISNEY in the US.

Even if you don't stay, you may be intrigued enough to take a look at the state of **contemporary American architecture**, as patronized by the Disney Corporation. Producing some way-out buildings with big signatures was an important ploy in persuading the French cultural establishment to accept Disneyland Paris. Two hundred internationally renowned architects were invited to compete. Only one, James Stirling, turned down the offer, and only one non-American won a contract. The star of the show is **Frank D. Gehry**, currently the most fashionable architect in the US, and renowned for "deconstructing" buildings (making them look as if a bomb's gone off in them).

A tour of **Festival Disney** and the **six hotels** would be quite an effort on foot. The hotels spread as if they've been given growth hormones, and the whole site is twice that of the park. Fortunately, however, you can get around by hopping in and out of the free bright yellow shuttle buses.

DISNEYLAND PARIS: THE RESORT

Festival Disney

This is the shops, shows, bars and restaurants complex between the
station and the lake. It's Frank Gehry's work, and the bomb here
has carried off the circus top tent, in case you were wondering what
all the wires and zig-zag towers were. There's a huge great red
thing, a shiny white rocket cone thing, some greenhouses, and lots
of slanting roofs and fairy lights.

Disneyland Hotel

Situated over the entrance to the park with wings to either side, the
Disneyland Hotel is in the Main Street *à la Hollywood* style, and is
the most upmarket. Rooms vary from 1600F off season to over
1950F in peak season.

Hotel New York

The architect of the *Hotel New York*, Michael Graves, says things
like "The idea of two dimensions versus three is something that

Disney, in a sense, teaches in a very solemn way." A peculiar statement for anyone, even an architect and one who has spectacularly failed to translate the skyline of New York onto the outline of this hotel. It is a very ugly building, mixing Mickey-ear-shapes with postmodernist triangles, stripes and upright tombs in ochres and greys. Within, the furnishings are pseudo Art Deco with lots of apples – in case you'd failed to recognize New York from outside.

The rooms are 1000F all year round.

Newport Bay Club
This "New England seaside resort circa 1900" spreads like a game of dominoes, with no apparent reason why the wings have turned one way rather than another. Blue and white striped canopies over the balconies fail to give it that cosy guesthouse feel, while the cupola roof resembles a cross between a Kaiser Wilhelm and a Nazi helmet. Robert Stern is the architect. Rooms start at 600F, 850F peak season.

Sequoia Lodge
Prison blocks, minus fence and watchtowers, masquerading as the National Parks of the western United States, by the only non-American architect, Antoine Grumbach. Rooms from 500F to over 750F.

Hotel Cheyenne
Along with *Sante Fe*, *Cheyenne* deals with the scale problem by breaking into small units: the film-set buildings of a Western frontier town, complete with wagons, cowboys, a hanging tree and scarecrows. The architect is again Robert Stern. Rooms from 400F to 650F.

Hotel Santa Fe
Accommodation in the *Hotel Santa Fe* takes the form of smooth, mercifully unadorned, imitation sun-baked mud buildings in various shapes and sizes. Between them are tasteful car wrecks, a cactus in a glass case, irrigation systems, strange geological formations, ancient desert ruins and other products of the distinctly un-Disney imagination of New Mexican architect Antoine Predock. He cites Wim Wender's film *Paris Texas*, the Roman archeological site in Marne-la-Vallée, and UFOs as part of his reference material. But the dominant icon, visible from the autoroute, is a scowling cheroot-chewing Clint Eastwood. This gigantic mural creates the drive-in movie entrance to *Santa Fe*.

This is the cheapest hotel, at 300F low season to 550F.

Davy Crockett Range and camping
The log cabin experience at the Davy Crockett Range costs from 425F–875F for a 4-person cabin (475F–1000F for a 6-person cabin). Camping on the ranch is 300F for the site (for 4 people).

The Contexts

Paris in History

Two thousand years of compressed history – featuring riots and revolutions, shantytowns, palaces, new street plans, sanitation and the Parisian people.

Beginnings

It was **Rome** that put Paris on the map, as it did the rest of western Europe. When Julius Cæsar's armies arrived in 52 BC, they found a Celtic settlement confined to an island in the Seine – the Île de la Cité. It must already have been fairly populous, as it had sent a contingent of eight thousand men to stiffen the Gallic chieftain Vercingétorix's doomed resistance to the invaders.

Under the name of Lutetia, it remained **a Roman colony** for the next three hundred years, prosperous commercially because of its commanding position on the Seine trade route but insignificant politically. The Romans established their administrative centre on the Île de la Cité, and their town on the Left Bank on the slopes of the Montagne Sainte-Geneviève. Though no monuments of their presence remain, except the baths by the Hôtel de Cluny and the amphitheatre in rue Monge, their **street plan**, still visible in the north–south axis of rue St-Martin and rue St-Jacques, determined the future growth of the city.

When Roman rule disintegrated under the impact of **Germanic invasions** around 275 AD, Paris held out until it fell to **Clovis the Frank** in

486. In 511 Clovis' son commissioned the cathedral of St-Étienne, whose foundations can be seen in the *crypte archéologique* under the square in front of Notre-Dame. Clovis' own conversion to Christianity hastened the **Christianization** of the whole country, and under his successors Paris saw the foundation of several rich and influential monasteries, especially on the Left Bank.

With the election of **Hugues Capet**, Comte de Paris, as king in 987, the fate of the city was inextricably identified with that of the **monarchy**. The presence of the kings, however, prevented the development of the middle class, republican institutions that the rich merchants of Flanders and Italy were able to obtain for their cities. The result was recurrent political tension, which led to open **rebellion**, for instance, in 1356, when Étienne Marcel, a wealthy cloth merchant, demanded greater autonomy for the city. Further rebellions, fuelled by the hopeless poverty of the lower classes, led to the king and court abandoning the capital in 1418, not to return for more than a hundred years.

The Right Bank, Latin Quarter, and Louvre

As the city's livelihood depended from the first on its river-borne trade, commercial activity naturally centred round the place where the goods were landed. This was the **place de Grève** on the **Right Bank**, where the Hôtel de Ville now stands. Marshy ground originally, it was gradually drained to accommodate the business quarter. Whence the continuing association of the Right Bank with commerce and banking today.

The **Left Bank**'s intellectual associations are similarly ancient, dating from the growth of schools and student accommodation round the two great **monasteries** of Ste-Geneviève and St-Germain-des-Prés. The first, dedicated to the city's patron saint who had saved it from destruction by Attila's raiders, occupied the site of the present Lycée Henri IV on top of the hill behind the Panthéon. In 1215 a papal licence allowed the formation of what gradually became the renowned **University of Paris**, eventually to be known as **the Sorbonne**, after Robert de Sorbon, founder of a college for poor scholars. It was the fact that Latin was the language of the schools both inside and outside the classroom that gave the district its name of Latin Quarter.

To protect this burgeoning city, Philippe Auguste (king from 1180 to 1223) built the Louvre fortress (remains of which are now on display in the newly excavated Cour Carrée in the Louvre museum) and a wall, which swung south to enclose the Montagne Ste-Geneviève and north and east to encompass the Marais. The administration of the city remained in the hands of the king until 1260, when Saint Louis ceded a measure of responsibility to the leaders of the Paris watermen's guild, whose power was based on their monopoly control of all river traffic and taxes thereon. The city's government, when it has been allowed one, has been conducted ever since from the place de Grève/place de l'Hôtel de Ville.

Civil Wars and Foreign Occupation

From the mid-thirteenth to mid-fourteenth centuries Paris shared the same unhappy fate as the rest of France, embroiled in the long and destructive **Hundred Years War** with the English. Étienne Marcel let the enemy into the city in 1357, the Burgundians did the same in 1422, when the Duke of Bedford set up his government of northern France here. Joan of Arc made an unsuccessful attempt to drive them out in 1429 and was wounded in the process at the Porte St-Honoré. The following year the English king, Henry VI, had the cheek to have himself crowned king of France in Notre-Dame.

It was only when the English were expelled – from Paris in 1437 and from France in 1453 – that the economy had the chance to recover from so many decades of devastation. It received a further boost when **François 1er** decided to re-establish the royal court in Paris in 1528. Work began on reconstructing the Louvre and building the Tuileries palace for Cathérine de Médicis, and on transforming Fontainebleau and other country residences into sumptuous Renaissance palaces.

But before these projects reached completion, war again intervened, this time **civil war** between Catholics and Protestants, in the course of which Paris witnessed one of the worst atrocities ever committed against French Protestants. Some three thousand of them were gathered in Paris for the wedding of Henri III's daughter,

Marguerite, to Henri, the Protestant king of Navarre. On August 25, 1572, St Bartholomew's Day, they were massacred at the instigation of the Catholic Guise family. When, through this marriage, Henri of Navarre became heir to the French throne in 1584, the Guises drove his father-in-law, Henri III, out of Paris. Forced into alliance, the two Henris laid siege to the city. Five years later, Henri III having been assassinated in the meantime, Henri of Navarre entered the city as king **Henri IV**. "Paris is worth a Mass", he is reputed to have said to justify renouncing his Protestantism in order to soothe Catholic susceptibilities.

The Paris he inherited was not a very salubrious place. It was overcrowded. No domestic building had been permitted beyond the limits of Philippe Auguste's twelfth-century walls because of the guilds' resentment of the unfair advantage enjoyed by craftsmen living outside the jurisdiction of the city's tax regulations. The population had doubled to around 400,000, causing an acute housing shortage and a terrible strain on the rudimentary water supply and drainage system. It is said that the first workmen who went to clean out the city's cesspools in 1633 fell dead from the fumes. It took seven months to clean out 6420 cartloads of filth that had been accumulating for two centuries. The overflow ran into the Seine, whence Parisians drew their drinking water.

Planning and Expansion

The first systematic attempts at **planning** were introduced by Henri IV at the beginning of the seventeenth century: regulating street lines and uniformity of façade, and laying out the first geometric squares. The **place des Vosges** dates from this period, as does the **Pont Neuf**, the first of the Paris bridges not to be cluttered with medieval houses. Henri thus inaugurated a tradition of grandiose public building, which was to continue to the Revolution and beyond, that perfectly symbolized the bureaucratic, centralized power of the newly self-confident state concentrated in the person of its absolute monarch.

The process reached its apogee under **Louis XIV**, with the construction of the **boulevards** from the Madeleine to the Bastille, the places Vendôme and Victoire, the Porte St-Martin and St-Denis gateways, the Invalides, Observatoire and the Cour Carrée of the Louvre – not to mention the vast palace at **Versailles**, whither he repaired with the court in 1671. The aristocratic *hôtels* or mansions of the Marais were also erected during this period, to be superseded early in the eighteenth century by the Faubourg St-Germain as the fashionable quarter of the rich and powerful.

The underside of all this bricks and mortar self-aggrandizement was the general neglect of the living conditions of the ordinary citizenry of Paris. The centre of the city remained a densely packed and insanitary warren of medieval lanes and tenements. And it was only in the years immediately preceding the 1789 Revolution that any attempt was made to clean it up. The buildings crowding the bridges were dismantled as late as 1786. Pavements were introduced for the first time and attempts were made to improve the drainage. A further source of pestilential infection was removed with the emptying of the overcrowded cemeteries into the catacombs. One gravedigger alone claimed to have buried more than ninety thousand people in thirty years, stacked "like slices of bacon" in the charnel house of the Innocents, which had been receiving the dead of 22 parishes for 800 years.

In 1786 Paris also received its second from last ring of fortifications, the so-called wall of the Fermiers Généraux, with 57 *barrières* or toll gates (one of which survives in the middle of place Stalingrad), where a tax was levied on all goods entering the city.

The 1789 Revolution

The immediate cause of the revolution of 1789 was a campaign by the privileged classes of the clergy and nobility to protect their status, especially exemption from taxation, against erosion by the royal government. The revolutionary movement, however, was quickly taken over by the middle classes, relatively well off but politically underprivileged. In the initial phases this meant essentially the provincial bourgeoisie. It was they who comprised the majority of the representatives of the **Third Estate**, the "order" that encompassed the whole of French society after the clergy, who formed the First Estate, and the nobility who formed the Second. It was they who took the initiative in setting up the **National Assembly** on June 17, 1789. The majority of them would probably have been content with constitutional reforms that checked monarchical power on the English model. But their power depended largely on their ability to wield the threat of a Parisian popular explosion.

Although the effects of the Revolution were felt all over France and indeed Europe, it was in Paris that the most profound changes took place. Being as it were on the spot, the people of Paris discovered themselves in the Revolution. They formed the revolutionary shock troops, the driving force at the crucial stages of the Revolution. They marched on Versailles and forced the king to return to Paris with them. They stormed and destroyed the Bastille on July 14, 1789. They occupied the Hôtel de Ville, set up an insurrectionary Commune and captured the Tuileries palace on August 10, 1792. They invaded the Convention in May 1793 and secured the arrest of the more conservative Girondin faction of deputies.

Where the bourgeois deputies of the Convention were concerned principally with political reform, the *sans-culottes* – literally, the people without breeches – expressed their demands in economic terms: price controls, regulation of the city's food supplies, and so on. In so doing they foreshadowed the rise of the working class and socialist movements of the nineteenth century. They also established by their practice of taking to the streets and occupying the Hôtel de Ville a tradition of revolutionary action that continued through to the 1871 Commune.

Napoléon – and the Barricades

Apart from some spectacular bloodletting, and yet another occupation of the city by foreign powers in 1814, Napoléon's chief legacy to France was a very centralized, authoritarian and efficient **bureaucracy** that put Paris in firm control of the rest of the country. In Paris itself, he left his share of pompous architecture – in the **Arcs de Triomphe** and **Carrousel**, rue de Rivoli and rue de la Paix, the Madeleine and façade of the Palais-Bourbon, plus a further extension for the Louvre and a revived tradition of court flummery and extravagant living among the well-to-do. For the rest of the nineteenth century after his demise, France was left to fight out the contradictions and unfinished business left behind by the Revolution of 1789. And the arena in which these conflicts were resolved was, literally, the streets of the capital.

On the one hand, there was a tussle between the class that had risen to wealth and power as a direct result of the destruction of the monarchy and the old order, and the survivors of the old order, who sought to make a comeback in the

1820s under the restored monarchy of **Louis XVIII** and **Charles X**. This conflict was finally resolved in favour of the new bourgeoisie. When Charles X refused to accept the result of the 1830 National Assembly elections, Adolphe Thiers – who was to become the veteran conservative politician of the nineteenth century – led the opposition in revolt. Barricades were erected in Paris and there followed three days of bitter street fighting, known as *les trois glorieuses*, in which 1800 people were killed (they are commemorated by the column on place de la Bastille). The outcome was the election of **Louis-Philippe** as constitutional monarch, and the introduction of a few liberalizing reforms, most either cosmetic or serving merely to consolidate the power of the wealthiest stratum of the population. Radical republican and working-class interests remained completely unrepresented.

The other, and more important, major political conflict was the extended struggle between this enfranchised and privileged bourgeoisie and the heirs of the 1789 *sans-culottes*, whose political consciousness had been awakened by the revolution but whose demands remained unsatisfied. These were the people who died on the barricades of July to hoist the bourgeoisie firmly into the saddle.

As their demands continued to go unheeded, so their radicalism increased, exacerbated by deteriorating living and working conditions in the large towns, especially Paris, as the Industrial Revolution got under way. There were, for example, twenty thousand deaths from cholera in Paris in 1832, and in 1848 65 percent of the population were too poor to be liable for tax. Eruptions of discontent invariably occurred in the capital, with insurrections in 1832 and 1834. In the absence of organized parties, opposition centred on newspapers and clandestine or informal political clubs in the tradition of 1789. The most notable – and the only one dedicated to the violent overthrow of the regime – was Auguste Blanqui's *Société Républicaine*.

In the 1840s the publication of the first Socialist works like Louis Blanc's *Organization of Labour* and Proudhon's *What is Property?* gave an additional spur to the impatience of the opposition. When the lid blew off the pot in **1848** and the **Second Republic** was proclaimed in Paris, it looked for a time as if working-class demands might be at least partly met. The provisional government included Louis Blanc and a Parisian

manual worker. But in the face of demands for the control of industry, the setting up of cooperatives and so on, backed by agitation in the streets and the proposed inclusion of men like Blanqui and Barbès in the government, the more conservative Republicans lost their nerve. The nation returned a spanking reactionary majority in the April elections.

Revolution began to appear the only possible defence for the radical left. On June 23, 1848, **working-class Paris** – Poissonnière, Temple, St-Antoine, the Marais, Quartier Latin, Montmartre – rose in revolt. Men, women and children fought side by side against fifty thousand troops. In three days of fighting, nine hundred soldiers were killed. No one knows how many of the *insurgés* – the insurgents – died. Fifteen thousand people were arrested and four thousand sentenced to prison terms.

Despite the shock and devastation of civil war in the streets of the capital, the ruling classes failed to heed the warning in the events of June 1848. Far from redressing the injustices which had provoked them, they proceeded to exacerbate them – by, for example, reducing the representation of what Adolphe Thiers called "the vile multitude". The Republic was brought to an end in a coup d'état by **Louis Napoléon**, who within twelve months had himself crowned Emperor Napoléon III.

Rewards of Colonialism

There followed a period of **foreign acquisitions** on every continent and of **laissez-faire capitalism** at home, both of which greatly increased the economic wealth of France, then lagging far behind Britain in the industrialization stakes. Foreign trade trebled, a huge expansion of the rail network was carried out, investment banks were set up and so forth. The rewards, however, were very unevenly distributed, and the regime relied unashamedly on repressive measures – press censorship, police harassment and the forcible suppression of strikes – to hold the underdogs in check.

The response was entirely predictable. Opposition became steadily more organized and determined. In 1864, under the influence of Karl Marx in London, a French branch of the International was established in Paris and the youthful trade union movement gathered its forces in a federation. In 1869 the far from socialist Gambetta, briefly deputy for Belleville, declared, "Our generation's mission is to complete the French Revolution."

During these nearly twenty years of the Second Empire, while conditions were ripening for the most terrible of all Parisian revolutions, the 1871 Commune, the city itself suffered the greatest ever shock to its system. **Baron Haussmann**, appointed Prefect of the Seine department with responsibility for Paris by Napoléon III, undertook the total transformation of the city. In love with the straight line and grand vista, he drove 85 miles of broad new streets through the cramped quarters of the medieval city, linking the interior and exterior boulevards, and creating north–south, east–west cross-routes. His taste dictated the uniform grey stone façades, mansard roofs and six to seven storeys that are still the architectural hallmark of the Paris street today. In fact, such was the logic of his planning that construction of his projected streets continued long after his death, boulevard Haussmann itself being completed only in 1927.

While it is difficult to imagine how Paris could have survived without some Haussmann-like intervention, the scale of demolitions entailed by such massive redevelopment brought the direst social consequences. The city boundaries were extended to the 1840 fortifications where the *boulevard périphérique* now runs. The prosperous classes moved into the new western *arrondissements*, leaving the decaying older properties to the poor. These were divided and subdivided into ever smaller units as landlords sought to maximize their rents. Sanitation was nonexistent. Water standpipes were available only in the street. Migrant workers from the provinces, sucked into the city to supply the vast labour requirements, crammed into the old villages of Belleville and Ménilmontant. Many, too poor to buy furniture, lived in barely furnished digs or *demi-lits*, where the same bed was shared by several tenants on a shift basis. Cholera and TB were rife. Attempts to impose sanitary regulations were resisted by landlords as covert socialism. Many considered even connection to Haussmann's water mains an unnecessary luxury. Until 1870 refuse was thrown into the streets at night to be collected the following morning. When in 1884 the Prefect of the day required landlords to provide proper containers, they retorted by calling the containers by his name, *poubelle* – and the name has stuck as the French word for "dustbin".

Far from being concerned with Parisians' welfare, Haussmann's scheme was at least in part designed to keep the workers under control. Barracks were located at strategic points like the place du Château-d'Eau, now République, controlling the turbulent eastern districts, and the broad boulevards were intended to facilitate troop movements and artillery fire. A section of the Canal St-Martin north of the Bastille was covered over for the same reason.

The Siege of Paris and the Commune

In September 1870 Napoléon III surrendered to Bismarck at the border town of Sedan, less than two months after France had declared war on the well-prepared and superior forces of the Prussian state. The humiliation was enough for a Republican government to be instantly proclaimed in Paris. The **Prussians** advanced and by September 19 were laying **siege** to the capital. Gambetta was flown out by hot air balloon to rally the provincial troops but the country was defeated and liaison with Paris almost impossible. Further balloon messengers ended up in Norway or the Atlantic; the few attempts at military sorties from Paris turned into yet more blundering failures. Meanwhile, the city's restaurants were forced to change menus to fried dog, roast rat or peculiar delicacies from the zoos. For those without savings, death from disease or starvation became an ever more common fate. At the same time, the peculiar conditions of a city besieged gave a greater freedom to collective discussion and dissent.

The government's half-hearted defence of the city – more afraid of revolution within than of the Prussians – angered Parisians, who clamoured for the creation of a 1789-style Commune. The Prussians meanwhile were demanding a proper government to negotiate with. In January 1871, those in power agreed to hold elections for a new national assembly with the authority to surrender officially to the Prussians. A large monarchist majority, with Thiers at its head, was returned, again demonstrating the isolation from the countryside of the Parisian leftists, among whom many prominent old-timers, veterans of '48 and the empire's jails like Blanqui and Delescluze, were still active.

On March 1, Prussian troops marched down the Champs-Élysées and garrisoned the city for three days while the populace remained behind closed doors in silent protest. On March 18, amid growing resentment from all classes of Parisians, Thiers' attempt to take possession of the National Guard's artillery in Montmartre (see p.154) set the barrel alight. The Commune was proclaimed from the Hôtel de Ville and Paris was promptly subjected to a second siege by Thiers' government, which had fled to Versailles, followed by all the remaining Parisian bourgeoisie.

The **Commune** lasted 72 days – a festival of the oppressed, Lenin called it. Socialist in inspiration, it had no time to implement lasting reforms. Wholly occupied with defence against Thiers' army, it succumbed finally on May 28, 1871, after a week of street-by-street warfare, in which three thousand Parisians died on the barricades and another twenty to twenty-five thousand men, women and children were killed in random revenge shootings by government troops. Thiers could declare with satisfaction – or so he thought – "Socialism is finished for a long time."

Among the non-human casualties were several of the city's landmark buildings, including the Tuileries palace, Hôtel de Ville, Cours des Comptes (where the Musée d'Orsay now stands) and a large chunk of the rue Royale.

The *Belle Époque*

Physical recovery was remarkably quick. Within six or seven years few signs of the fighting remained. Visitors remarked admiringly on the teeming streets, the expensive shops and energetic nightlife. Charles Garnier's Opéra was opened in 1875. Aptly described as the "triumph of moulded pastry", it was a suitable image of the frivolity and materialism of the so-called naughty Eighties and Nineties. In 1889 the **Eiffel Tower** stole the show at the great Exposition. For the 1900 repeat, the *Métropolitain* (métro) – or *Nécropolitain*, as it was dubbed by one wit – was unveiled.

The lasting social consequence of the Commune was the confirmation of the them-and-us divide between bourgeoisie and working class. Any stance other than a revolutionary one after the Commune appeared not only feeble, but also a betrayal of the dead. None of the contradictions had been resolved. The years up to World War I were marked by the increasing organization of the left in response to the unstable but thoroughly conservative governments of the Third Republic. The trade union movement

unified in 1895 to form the **Conféderation Genérale du Travail** (*CGT*), and in 1905 Jean Jaurès and Jules Guesde founded the **Parti Socialiste** (also known as the *SFIO*). On the extreme right, fascism began to make its ugly appearance with Maurras' proto-Brownshirt organization, the *Camelots du Roi*, which inaugurated another French tradition, of violence and thuggery on the far right.

Yet despite – or maybe in some way because of – these tensions and contradictions, Paris provided the supremely inspiring environment for a concentration of **artists and writers** – the so-called **Bohemians**, both French and foreign – such as Western culture has rarely seen. Impressionism, Fauvism and Cubism were all born in Paris in this period, while French poets like Apollinaire, Laforgue, Max Jacob, Blaise Cendrars and André Breton were preparing the way for Surrealism, concrete poetry and symbolism. Film, too, saw its first developments. After World War I, Paris remained the world's art centre, with an injection of foreign blood and a shift of venue from Montmartre to Montparnasse.

In the postwar struggle for recovery the interests of the urban working class were again passed over, with the exception of Clemenceau's eight-hour day legislation in 1919. An attempted general strike in 1920 came to nothing, and workers' strength was again weakened by the irredeemable split in the Socialist Party at the 1920 Congress of Tours. The pro-Lenin majority formed the **French Communist Party**, while the minority faction, under the leadership of Léon Blum, retained the old *SFIO* title.

As **Depression** deepened in the 1930s and Nazi power across the Rhine became more menacing, fascist thuggery and anti-parliamentary activity increased in France, culminating in a pitched battle outside the Chamber of Deputies in February 1934. (Léon Blum was only saved from being lynched by a funeral cortege through the intervention of some building workers who happened to notice what was going on in the street below.) The effect of this fascist activism was to unite the Left, including the Communists, led by the Stalinist Maurice Thorez, in the **Popular Front**. When they won the 1936 elections with a handsome majority in the Chamber, there followed a wave of strikes and factory sit-ins – a spontaneous expression of working-class determination to get their just deserts after a century and a half of frustration. Frightened by the apparently revolutionary situation, the major employers signed the Matignon Agreement with Blum, which provided for wage increases, nationalization of the armaments industry and partial nationalization of the Bank of France, a 40-hour week, paid annual leave and collective bargaining on wages. These reforms were pushed through parliament, but when Blum tried to introduce exchange controls to check the flight of capital the Senate threw the proposal out and he resigned. The Left returned to Opposition, where it remained, with the exception of coalition governments, until 1981. Most of the Popular Front's reforms were promptly undone.

The German Occupation

During the occupation of Paris in World War II, the Germans found some sections of Parisian society, as well as the minions of the Vichy government, only too happy to hobnob with them. For four years the city suffered fascist rule with curfews, German garrisons and a Gestapo HQ. Parisian Jews were forced to wear the star of David and in 1942 were rounded up — by other Frenchmen — and shipped off to Auschwitz (see p.364).

The **Resistance** was very active in the city, gathering people of all political persuasions into its ranks, but with communists and socialists, especially of east European Jewish origin, well to the fore. The job of torturing them when they fell into Nazi hands — often as a result of betrayals — was left to their fellow citizens in the fascist militia. Those who were condemned to death — rather than the concentration camps — were shot against the wall below the old fort of Mont Valérien above St-Cloud.

As Allied forces drew near to the city in 1944, the FFI (armed Resistance units), determined to play their part in driving the Germans out, called their troops onto the streets — some said, in a leftist attempt to seize political power. To their credit, the Paris police also joined in, holding their Île de la Cité HQ for three days against German attacks. Liberation finally came on August 25, 1944.

Postwar Paris — One More Try at Revolution

Postwar Paris has remained no stranger to **political battles** in its streets. Violent demonstrations accompanied the Communist withdrawal from the coalition government in 1947. In the Fifties

the Left took to the streets again in protest against the colonial wars in Indochina and Algeria. And in 1961, in one of the most shameful episodes in modern French history, some two hundred Algerians were killed by the police during a civil rights demonstration.

This **"secret massacre"**, which remained covered by a veil of total official silence until the 1990s, took place during the Algerian war. It began with a peaceful demonstration against a curfew on North Africans imposed by de Gaulle's government in an attempt to inhibit FLN resistance activity in the French capital. Whether the police were acting on higher orders or merely on the authority of their own commanders is not clear. What is clear from hundreds of eyewitness accounts, including some from horrified policemen, is that the police went berserk. They opened fire, clubbed people and threw them in the Seine to drown. Several dozen Algerians were killed in the courtyard of the police HQ on the Île de la Cité. For weeks afterwards, corpses were recovered from the Seine, but the French media remained silent, in part through censorship, in part perhaps unable to comprehend that such events had happened in their own capital. Maurice Papon, the police chief at the time, was subsequently decorated by de Gaulle.

The state attempted censorship again during the events of **May 1968**, though with rather less success. Through this extraordinary month, a radical, libertarian, leftist movement spread from the Paris universities to include, eventually, the occupation of hundreds of factories across the country and a general strike by nine million workers. The old-fashioned and reactionary university structures that had triggered the revolt were reflected in the hierarchical and rigid organizations of many other institutions in French life. The position of women and of youth, of culture and modes of behaviour, were suddenly highlighted in the general dissatisfaction with a society in which big business ran the state.

There was no revolutionary situation on the 1917 model. The vicious battles with the paramilitary CRS police on the streets of Paris shook large sectors of the population — France's silent majority — to the core, as the government cynically exploiting the scenes for TV knew full well. There was no shared economic or political aim in the ranks of the opposition. With the exception of Michel Rocard's small *Parti Socialiste Uni*, the traditional parties were taken completely by surprise and uncertain how to react. The French Communist Party, stuck with its Stalinist traditions, was far from favourably disposed to the adventurism of the students and their numerous Maoist, Trotskyist and anarchist factions or *groupuscules*. Right-wing and "nationalist" demonstrations orchestrated by de Gaulle left public opinion craving stability and peace; and a great many workers were satisfied with a new system for wage agreements. It was not, therefore, surprising that the elections called in June returned the Right to power.

The occupied buildings emptied and the barricades in the Latin Quarter came down. For those who thought they were experiencing The Revolution, the defeat was catastrophic. But French institutions and French society did change, shaken and loosened by the events of May 1968. And most importantly it opened up the debate of a new road to socialism, one in which no old models would give all the answers.

Modern Developments of the City

Until World War II, Paris remained pretty much as Haussmann had left it. Housing conditions showed little sign of improvement. There was even an outbreak of bubonic plague in Clignancourt in 1921. In 1925 a third of the houses still had no sewage connection. Of the seventeen worst blocks of slums designated for clearance, most were still intact in the 1950s, and even today they have some close rivals in parts of Belleville and elsewhere.

Migration to the suburbs continued, with the creation of **shantytowns** to supplement the hopelessly inadequate housing stock. Post-World War II, these became the exclusive territory of **Algerian** and other **North African immigrants**. In 1966 there were 89 of them, housing 40,000 immigrant workers and their families.

Only in the last thirty years have the authorities begun to grapple with the housing problem, though not by expanding possibilities within Paris but by siphoning huge numbers of people into a ring of **satellite towns** encircling the greater Paris region.

In Paris proper this same period has seen the final breaking of the mould of Haussmann's influence. Intervening architectural fashions, like Art Nouveau, Le Corbusier's International style and the Neoclassicism of the 1930s, had little more than localized cosmetic effects. It was devotion to the needs of the motorist – a cause unhesitatingly espoused by Pompidou – and the development of the high-rise tower that finally did the trick, starting with the **Tour Maine-Montparnasse** and **La Défense**, the redevelopment of the 13e, and, in the 1970s, projects like **Beaubourg**, the **Front de Seine**, and **Les Halles**. In recent years, new colossal public buildings in a myriad of conflicting styles have been inaugurated at an ever-more astounding rate. At the same time, the fabric of the city – the streets, the métro and the graffitied walls – have been ignored.

When the Les Halles flower and veg market was dismantled it was not just the nineteenth-century architecture that was mourned. The city's social mix has changed more in twenty-five years than in the previous hundred. Gentrification of the remaining working-class districts is accelerating, and the population has become essentially middle-class and white-collar.

As a sign posted during the redevelopment of Les Halles lamented: "The centre of Paris will be beautiful. Luxury will be king. But we will not be here." And these days it is no longer just the centre of the city. If those "we" do come into Paris at all any more, it is as commuting service workers or weekend shoppers. "Renovation is not for us."

The Political Present

1995 will be marked by the end of François Mitterrand's presidency. He has been the French head of state for fourteen years, presiding over two Socialist and two Gaullist governments. When he won the elections in 1981, he embodied all the hopes of a generation of socialists who had never seen their party in power. The last years of his presidency have seen him becoming ill and aged, with his reputation tarnished and his party's popularity reduced to the point where even its continued existence is in question.

The recession started to take hold during Mitterrand's presidency, official unemployment figures have passed three million, both the president and the Socialist Party have been touched by scandals and become deeply unpopular, while divisions in the Right have opened up. The French public seem to have lost faith in their rulers as a whole, and lost interest in the old political debates. The Maastricht referendum in September 1992 cut across the Right–Left divide, following instead old and unchanged geographical and class divisions.

The European elections of 1994 saw huge numbers of votes going to mavericks opposing the established Left and Right parties: to the charismatic arch-spiv Bernard Tapie and the traditionalist, far right Philippe de Villiers.

The Parties in Power, 1981–95

The **Socialists** began their first five years in power under the prime ministership of **Pierre Mauroy**. In his cabinet were four Communist ministers: an alliance reflected in the government commitments to expanded state control of industry, high taxation for the rich, support for liberation struggles around the world, and a public spending programme to raise the living standards of the least well-off. By 1984, however, the government had done a complete volte-face with **Laurent Fabius** presiding over a cabinet of centrist to conservative "socialist" ministers, clinging desperately to power.

The commitments had come to little. Attempts to bring private education under state control were defeated by mass protests in the streets;

ministers were implicated in cover-ups and corruption; unemployment continued to rise. Any idea of peaceful and pro-ecological intent was dashed, as far as international opinion was concerned, by the French Secret Service's murder of a Greenpeace photographer on the *Rainbow Warrior* in New Zealand.

There were sporadic achievements – in labour laws and women's rights, notably – but no cohesive and consistent socialist line. The Socialists' 1986 election slogan was "Help – the Right is coming back", a bizarrely self-fulfilling tactic which they defended on the grounds of humour. For the unemployed and the low paid, for immigrants and their families, for women wanting the choice of whether to have children, for the young, the old and all those attached to certain civil liberties, the return of the Right was no laughing matter.

Throughout 1987 the chances of Mitterrand's winning the presidential election in 1988 seemed very slim. But **Chirac**'s economic policies of privatization and monetary control failed to deliver the goods. Millions of first-time investors in "popular capitalism" lost all their money on Black Monday. Terrorists planted bombs in Paris and took French hostages in Lebanon. Unemployment steadily rose and Chirac made the fatal mistake of flirting with the extreme right. Several leading politicians of the centre-right, among them Simone Weil, a concentration-camp survivor, denounced Chirac's concessions to Le Pen, and a new alignment of the centre started to emerge. **Mitterrand**, the grand old man of politics, with decades of experience, played off all the groupings of the Right in an all-but-flawless campaign, and won another mandate.

His party, however, did not fare so well in the parliamentary elections soon afterwards. The Socialists failed to achieve an absolute majority and Mitterrand's new prime minister, **Michel Rocard**, went for the centrist coalition, causing friction in the party grassroots for whom the Communists were still the natural partners. The *FN*s lost all their seats – the consequence of an abandonment of proportional representation – but retained their popularity.

Parties and Politicians

ON THE LEFT

PS (Parti Socialist). The Socialist party of President **François Mitterrand**, divided into "Mitterrandists", "Rocardians" who support **Michel Rocard** (prime minister 1988–91); "Jospians", followers of **Lionel Jospin**, who has served in every Socialist government; "Fabiusians" whose man is **Laurent Fabius** (prime minister 1984–86, and ousted by Rocard as party leader in 1993); and the left wingers who favour a new coalition with the Greens, the Communists and the *Mouvement des Radicaux de Gauche (MRG)*. The only possible presidential candidate at the moment is **Jacques Delors** (former president of the European Commission), though **Jack Lang**, the former culture minister and a champagne socialist, might have a go. He was thrown out of parliament for overspending in the 1993 elections, and is now an *MEP* (his campaign was backed by Moët et Chandon, Cartier and Yves St-Laurent). In 1994 the *PS* did well in local and by-elections – even winning a seat in Paris – although they fared very badly in the Europeans.

PCF (Parti Communist Français). **Robert Hue** has finally replaced the veteran Stalinist leader **Georges Marchais** as party leader. Hue has proposed a new broad coalition with progressive Greens, Socialists, community groups, churches etc, which forms a big break from the old line, but has probably come too late to get very far. The *PCF* remains influential with the country's trade unions and also in local government.

ON THE RIGHT

UDF (Union pour la Démocratie Française). Union of centre-right parties usually in alliance with *RPR* (see below), led by aloof, aristo former president **Valéry Giscard d'Estaing** – who has his eye on the April 1995 presidentials.

PR (Parti Républicain). Part of the *UDF* though many members want to form their own independent group. Key figure is **François Léotard**, culture minister under Chirac and defence minister under Balladur, despite charges of corruption brought against him.

RPR (Rassemblement pour la République). Gaullist, conservative party headed by **Jacques Chirac**, mayor of Paris, and prime minister 1986–88; desperate to become president, his main rival is **Edouard Balladur**, prime minister since 1993 and known by his opponents in the media as "Ballamou" (Balla-wimp). The other notable Gaullist is **Philippe de Villier**, anti-Maastricht aristo against abortion, divorce, immigration, state education etc. Ran against his party in the 1994 Euro elections with Jimmy Goldsmith and de Gaulle's grandson on an anti-European union ticket, and won 12 percent of the vote. **Charles Pasqua**, home affairs minister under Chirac and Balladur, is another strong right-winger, and unlike the two prime ministers he has served, he is also anti-Europe.

FN (Front National). Extreme right party led by arch-racist **Jean-Marie Le Pen** and his unspeakable deputy **Bruno Méguet**. *FN députés* in the last parliament they sat in (1986–88, after which the voting system was changed to exclude them) included publishers of Hitler's speeches, Moonies and an octogenarian who as Paris councillor in 1943 voted full powers for Pétain's Vichy regime. The *FN* has 11 *MEPs* but its share of the vote dropped in 1994 local elections.

GREEN PARTIES

GE (Génération Ecologie). One of the two green parties, led by **Brice Lalonde**, who served in the Socialist government of 1988–91 but switched allegiance in 1993 to the Gaullists and failed to win a local countil seat in 1994. The party, like *Les Verts*, did very badly in the Euro elections, losing all its seats.

Les Verts. The other Greens, more "pure" than *GE*. All eight Green European seats were lost in 1994. Unofficial coalitions at the local level take place with left-wing socialists, anti-racists, reforming communists etc. Many Greens now stand independently from *Les Verts* and *GE* (known together as *L'Ecologistes*).

Rocard's ensuing **austerity measures** upset traditional Socialist supporters in the public-service sector, and nurses, civil servants, teachers and the like were quick to take industrial action. Additionally, though Chirac's programmes were halted, they were not reversed.

The 1980s ended with the most absurd blow-out of public funds ever – the **Bicentennial celebrations of the French Revolution**. They symbolized a culture industry spinning mindlessly around the vacuum at the centre of the French vision for the future. And they highlighted the contrast between the unemployed and homeless begging on the streets and the limitless cash available for prestige projects.

In 1991, Mitterrand sacked Michel Rocard and appointed **Edith Cresson** as prime minister. Initially the French were happy to have their first woman prime minister, who promised to wage economic war against the Germans and the Japanese. The Left, including the Communists, were pleased with Cresson's socialist credentials. But she soon began to turn a few heads with her comments about special charters for illegal immigrants; her dismissal of the stock exchange as a waste of time; her description of the Japanese as yellow ants and British males as homosexual; and by attacks on her own ministers. Cresson became the most unpopular prime minister in the history of the Fifth Republic.

Cresson's worst move was to propose a tax on everyone's insurance contributions to pay for compensation to haemophiliacs infected with HIV. The knowing use of infected blood in transfusions in 1985 became one of the biggest scandals of the Socialist regime.

Pierre Bérégovoy succeeded Cresson in 1992. Universally known as *Béré*, and mocked for his bumbling persona, he survived strikes by farmers, dockers, car workers and nurses, the scandals touching the Socialists and the Maastricht referendum. But then a private loan was revealed from one Roger-Patrice Pelat, a friend of Mitterrand's accused of insider dealing. Mitterrand distanced himself from his prime minister, who then shot himself two months after losing the elections, leaving no note of explanation.

The new prime minister, **Eduard Balladur**, a fresh and fatherly face from the Right, started off with great popularity. But a series of U-turns after demonstrations by *Air France* workers, teachers, farmers, fishermen and school pupils, and the state's rescue of the *Crédit Lyonnais* bank after spectacular losses, have wiped away his successes over GATT and keeping the franc strong and inflation down.

His home affairs minister, **Charles Pasqua** (who served in the same post under Chirac), is a highly unpopular right-winger with a strong anti-immigration and anti-immigrant line. In 1992, Pasqua joined forces with another senior Gaullist bully boy, Philippe Séguin, and the extreme *UDF* right-winger Philippe de Villiers to oppose the Maastricht treaty. Opposition to the treaty also

came from the *PCF*, the breakaway socialist Jean-Pierre Chèvenement and the Front National. Clearly, the long-established certainty of the absolute divide between Right and Left loyalties was no longer tenable. The actual voters divided along the lines of the poorer rural areas voting "No" and the rich urbanites voting "Yes". In Paris the "Yes" vote was overwhelming. Disillusionment with the established parties was confirmed in the 1994 Euro elections. The *RPR/UDF* lost votes to the anti-Europeans and for the *PS* it was a total disaster. Rocard had to resign as the party secretary – his attempts to "modernize" the party had failed.

Meanwhile Mitterrand totters on to the end of his presidential term (April 1995), looking less and less like the nation's favourite uncle. Two months after Bérégovoy's suicide, Réné Bousquet, a friend of Mitterrand's thought to have known shady secrets about the president, was murdered. The following year a secret service agent and close advisor and friend, Jacques Attali, had to resign from the European Bank for Reconstruction and Development for suspected filching of the bank's money. In January 1994, the Elysée Palace was caught phone-tapping a journalist from *Le Monde*.

On the twentieth anniversary of President Pompidou's death in April 1994, there was a wave of nostalgia for a time when "things were right and proper". A month later, a leading French businessman was arrested for corruption, and there have since been other corruption scandals touching business people and politicians. Cracks are opening up in the French establishment, the recession is biting and cynicism and nostalgia are the order of the day.

Political Issues

Foreign Policy

Throughout the postwar years, France has maintained an independent and nationalist-orientated **foreign policy**, staying outside NATO and sustaining its own **nuclear arsenal**. For this, there has long been cross-party consensus, and indeed national pride.

The end of the Cold War does not seem to have changed matters. At the end of the 1980s Mitterrand said that France would finally sign the Nuclear Non-Proliferation Treaty, while giving the go-ahead for a new series of hydrogen warhead tests in the South Pacific. He has hosted international disarmament conferences in Paris while promising the French that their status as a nuclear power will not be threatened. Since 1992, the development of new ballistic missiles for the French nuclear submarine fleet has been underway. Increased defence spending of £70 billion was approved by both sides in parliament in 1994. Though Mitterrand has changed his mind on nuclear testing, Balladur is very much in favour.

In 1992 Mitterrand launched, with Chancellor Kohl, the "Eurocorps" of 40,000 troops based in Strasbourg. The two leaders claimed to be putting into practice the Maastricht accord on a joint European defence policy. Its relationship to NATO and the Western European Union is unclear and Britain's dismissive line is that the German half won't fight outside Europe and the French half won't fight inside.

In major conflicts France always tries to play a key role (and as one of the five permanent members of the UN Security Council, it gets a say). But high-profile diplomacy gives way to unprestigious military action, as in the Gulf War when the small French force was under American command. In the eyes of its allies, France puts its own trade interests before those of the West's and fails to share a proper concern with geopolitical issues. But Mitterrand's visit, under gunfire, to Sarajevo in July 1992 was universally applauded. The French were also stronger on South African sanctions than the British government, and unlike the Americans, have admitted that their Indo-China war was a mistake. Mitterrand was the first Western head of state to visit Vietnam after the American's defeat, and has been instrumental in trying to find a solution in Cambodia. On the other hand, the French have been reluctant to commit troops for UN actions in former Yugoslavia. In 1994 a group of intellectuals ran a "Sarajevo" campaign to put Bosnia at the centre of the European debate, and included the philosophers Bernard-Henri Lévy and André Glucksmann, receiving considerable support. But the government's response after the elections, in a cynical move to deflect attention from domestic problems, was to suddenly decide to commit troops to Rwanda, whose previous murderous government they had supported and armed.

Overseas Territories

Southeast Asia apart, the French have decolonized to a lesser extent than any other former powers. They maintain strong links with – and exercise much influence over – most of the former colonies in North and West Africa, as exemplified by their military forays into Chad and Zaire.

With France's remaining **overseas territories**, governments through the last two decades have said a resounding "no" to independence claims. When the Kanaks of **Nouvelle Calédonie** (New Caledonia, an island near New Zealand) rebelled against direct, unelected rule by Paris, Mitterrand responded with "autonomy" measures which kept defence, foreign affairs, law and order, control of the television, and education in the French governor's hands. Eventually, though, after a massacre by French settlers of indigenous tribe members in 1986, the situation proved too sensitive, and a referendum in 1988 committed France to granting independence in ten years' time.

Both the **New Zealand and Australian governments**, however, were warned to desist from their support for the island's independence – to stop meddling in French internal affairs as Paris sees it. Both countries have taken strong stands against the nuclear tests at **Mururoa** and felt the force of French economic muscle as a result. Meanwhile the subjugation of the Polynesian people to French interests, with slum dwellers surviving on subsistence while imported French goods decimate local economies, goes on and will no doubt continue, whether independence comes or not.

France and Europe

As a founder member of the **European Union (EU)**, France sees itself very much at the centre – and very much in control – of developments. The French people were able to debate the **Maastricht treaty** at length, with almost non-stop discussion in the media in the weeks leading up to the referendum. Every voter received a copy of the treaty and the turn-out was very high at seventy percent. French national interests were the key motivating factor, with Mitterrand promising that a "Yes" vote would not affect French sovereignty in any way and the "No" campaigners claiming the contrary. Internal politics were also crucial – voting "yes" to support Mitterrand and the Socialists and vice versa, voting "Yes" to oppose the *Front National* and the *RPR* extreme right-wingers. Perceived economic interests also played their part. What was missing in the debate was the actual concept of a unified Europe – the construction of a new European identity, the democracy of its governing structures, its relationship to eastern Europe and the Third World, its dominant ideology. For the French voter, the referendum was about France, not about Europe. The same was true of the 1994 European elections, when the turnout was much lower. De Villier's anti-Europe votes and Tapie's pro ones were again a reflection of the French political morass, not about a vision for Europe.

The city with the highest "Yes" vote for Maastricht was Strasbourg on the German border. The **French-German axis** has dominated the European Community with France well aware that its own political clout matched with German economic clout makes a powerful partnership. Maintaining the franc's position against the Deutschmark has been a major feature of French economic policy. Mitterrand has been keen for the French to forget the German occupation of France (when he himself for a short time worked for the Vichy government before joining the Resistance). On July 14, 1994, German troops joined the French army parade – at Mitterand's invitation. But a French psychosis still exists about World War II. Only very recently has Mitterrand stopped laying an official wreath on Pétain's grave, politicians are still questioned about their war activities, and war-crimes trials – like that of Paul Touvier, sentenced to life imprisonment – still continue to send tremors through the establishment. The main problem is that France and the French have never confessed to the extent of their collaboration and anti-semitism.

Unlike Chancellor Kohl, Mitterrand has been cautious about recognizing the newly emerging former **Soviet states**, and about the possible entry of east European countries to the EU. In this, he is responding to a deeply protectionist impulse in France. Meat imports from Poland, Hungary and Czechoslovakia were banned after French farmers made their views clear with barricades of manure and burning tyres. New immigration laws turned many long-term residents from eastern Europe into illegal aliens. The close ties France once enjoyed with the countries of the old Soviet bloc have been severely strained. The power of French farmers has also forced France into highly unpopular positions with its trading partners over the last round of GATT talks.

The French stance over the GATT talks and the new strict laws governing the use of English reveal both the traditional Gaullist distrust of the Americans and French nationalism (in the non-fascist sense), along with a sense of insecurity, a need for protective, inward-looking measures.

The Economy

The ambitious left-wing programme of the 1981–84 Socialist government was scuppered by the massive flight of capital, by bureaucracy, and by the opposition of half the country. When **Chirac** subsequently came to power, his **privatization programme** went much further than reversing the preceding Socialists' nationalizations – banks that de Gaulle took into the public sector after 1945 were sold off along with *Dassault*, the aircraft manufacturer, and *Elf-Aquitaine*, the biggest French oil company.

Workers attempting to protect their jobs found themselves being hauled before the law. The shock of Chirac's approach to the unions, which in France are mostly organized along political lines rather than by profession, galvanized the usually irreconcilably divided Communist *CGT*, Socialist *CFDT* and Catholic *FO* unions into finding common cause.

The return of the Socialists put further wholesale privatizations on hold – and brought an amnesty for trade unionists who had been prosecuted – but **Rocard** ruled out renationalization. Public spending was again increased, but not enough to compensate for all the jobs already lost. Rocard's centrist programme provoked a wave of strikes, but lay-offs continued in the mines, shipyards, transport industry and the denationalized industries.

For all this action, **unemployment** never became a key issue in the 1980s. When Chirac came to power in 1986 the official figures stood at 2.4 million. Under Balladur it has reached 3.3 million, 12.2 percent of the workforce. Adding young people palmed off with training schemes and older people forced into early retirement, the real figure is around 4.5 million. The school and university students' protest against reducing the national minimum wage for young people in 1994 brought the issue of unemployment to the top of the agenda.

No-one has any solutions, though Jacques Delors, to his credit, made unemployment a priority issue for the European Union. Public opinion in France has been supportive of the fishermen, farmers, *Air France* workers and students who have gone on strike, rioted or demonstrated. Large sums of money have been promised for better training schemes and retraining opportunities, but the costs of social security are taking their toll on the economy.

In industry, however, partial privatizations (a quarter of *Renault* has gone to *Volvo*; shares in *Total, Elf Aquitaine, Bull* and *Thompson* have been sold) and continuing state subsidies (much to the disgust of British EU commissioners) have allowed the big nationalized firms to weather the recession. Balladur's $13 billion privatization programme is keeping private business happy. The trade balance remains in surplus, the franc has not had to leave the ERM, and the public deficit is still much, much lower than in Britain.

Overall, France has fared well over the last decade, far better than Britain, thanks to keeping rampant monetarism at bay. **Inflation**, down to zero in 1990, has not passed four percent. Interest rates and the budget deficit have been kept low. The standard of living of those in full-time work is much higher than in Britain. French **hospitals** have been offering British NHS patients operations like hip replacements with less than a week's wait. The **education** budget has outstripped defence spending for the first time ever – after successful strikes by *lycée* students in 1990. And, unlike in Britain, no-one has yet suggested taking water, energy, transport and communications out of state control. These are seen as legitimate national assets, whose subsidy is an assertion of French pride. The state and municipal building programme in Paris makes it look as if no-one has heard of the recession. But the people begging on the métro and living on the streets tell a different tale. The crunch is going to come and there will be many more confrontations between the state and the people.

Nuclear Power and the Green Parties

Throughout the 1980s and early 1990s, the environmental movement in France grew from almost total non-existence to having a minister in government and two green political parties that between them were able to take 15 percent of the vote. Brice Lalonde, founder of **Génération Écologie**, was appointed to Rocard's government as environmental minister in 1988, with his post upgraded to cabinet level in 1991. The other, more radical, green party, **Les Verts**, had eight

MEPs. In 1993 the parties overcame their differences and agreed an electoral pact for the parliamentary elections, but Brice Lalonde's flirtation with the Gaullists has caused a new rupture. Several green councillors now stand as independents and in the Euro elections all the seats were lost.

The two parties, and Brice Lalonde's period as minister, have however had a significant impact on green consciousness in France, and been effective in stopping major developments such as the damming of the Loire River and in introducing waste and pollution taxes.

But the bastion of **nuclear power** has yet to be breached. The PWR nuclear power station at Nogent-sur-Marne, on the doorstep of Paris, must be one of the closest nuclear reactors to a major population centre anywhere. The French nuclear industry is the world's second largest, and the biggest in proportion to its energy needs. It's a major exporter, and the question of its safety is hardly ever raised. In 1990, however, it was revealed that two nuclear waste dumps close to Paris, closed in the 1970s, were thirty times above the acceptable radioactivity levels. After initial denials, the Green parties' demands for an independent inquiry were met. In 1991 the *Assemblée Nationale* discussed legislation on high-level nuclear waste disposal. This was the first time any aspect of nuclear energy policy had ever been put before parliament. Plans for the new generation fast-breeder reactor, however, the *Super-Phénix* in central France, proceed apace, and that despite the 1993 accident at the Cadarache nuclear reactor in Provence.

The Immigration Issue

From the mid-1950s to the mid-1970s a labour shortage in the French cities led to massive recruitment campaigns for workers in North Africa, Portugal, Spain, Italy and Greece. People were promised housing, free medical care, trips home and well-paid jobs. When they arrived in France, however, these **immigrants** found themselves paid half of what their French co-workers earned, accommodated in prison-style hostels, and sometimes poorer than they were at home. They had no vote, no automatic permit renewal, were subject to frequent racial abuse and assault and, until 1981, were forbidden to form their own associations.

The Socialist government lifted this ban, gave a ten-year automatic renewal for permits and even promised voting rights. Able to organize for the first time, immigrant workers staged protests at the racist basis of lay-offs in the major industries. The *Front National* responded with the age-old bogey of foreigners taking jobs from the French. The Gaullists joined in with the spectre of falling birth rates (a French obsession since 1945). Both benefited from these declarations in the 1986 elections.

Once in power, Chirac instituted a series of **anti-immigration laws** so extreme that they sparked unprecedented alliances. The Archbishop of Lyon and the head of the Muslim Institute in Paris together condemned their injustice. Human rights groups, churches and trade unions joined immigrants' groups in saying that France was on its way to becoming a police state. In 1992 the International Federation of Human Rights published a highly critical report on racism in the French police force in which they said that France "was not the home of human rights". Natality measures and the position of women immigrants brought French feminists into the battle. *SOS Racisme* was born, an anti-racist organization appealing to young people, in particular to well-educated second- and third-generation immigrants, but it has failed to engage the most disenfranchised, the notorious *banlieue* (suburban) kids, who are seen by the middle classes as natural criminals.

On returning to power, the Socialists played electoral games with the immigration issue, reneged on the vote promise, and failed to tackle the social and economic deprivation of France's immigrant ghettoes. Polls showed over two-thirds of the adult French population to be in favour of deporting legal immigrants for any criminal offence, or for being unemployed for over a year. Le Pen's proposals that immigrants have second-class citizenship, segregated education and separate social security have received massive support.

This rampant racism struck such a chord that politicians of right and left jumped onto the bandwagon. Edith Cresson, while prime minister, said special planes should be chartered to deport illegal immigrants. Kofi Yamgname, the minister for integration and only black member of the Socialist cabinet, suggested that immigrants who maintained traditional habits should go home. On the right, Giscard has used the potent word "invasion" and said that citizenship should be based on blood ties, not on place of birth.

Chirac talked of the "noise and smell" of immigrants, and a *UDF* senator compared the four million immigrants in France to the German occupation. All of which boosted the confidence of Jean-Marie Le Pen and of the current home affairs minister, Charles Pasqua, who has reintroduced random identity checks and clamped down on immigration.

The fate of immigrants and their French descendants has never been so precarious. Fury and frustration at discrimination, assault, abuse and economic deprivation has erupted . into battles on the street. Several young blacks have died at the hands of the police, while the right-wing media have revelled in images of violent Arab youths. Confrontations in the poorest Paris suburbs have become commonplace, but mini-riots are far from being the sole outlet for the grievances of French blacks. Tent cities were erected by homeless Africans in the 13e *arrondissement* and in Vincennes, bringing some public sympathy, but the current government has been very successful in distinguishing the "deserving" from the "undesirable undeserving". Organizations like *SOS Racisme* continue to campaign against discrimination in housing, jobs and the law, and when two Algerian boys were deported during the school pupil's actions in 1994, their release immediately became another popular demand.

New Political Movements

With the Socialist Party firmly positioned towards the centre, and the Communist Party only beginning – rather late in the day, to open itself up to new debates, there has been a vacuum on the Left. Jean-Pierre Chevènment, a pacifist left-wing socialist who resigned as defence minister after the outbreak of the Gulf War, has left the *PS* to form his own grouping, the *Mouvement des Citoyens*, which involves *Les Verts* and some reformers in the Communist Party. But the most interesting potential new development was *Le Mouvement*, a new political grouping initiated by Harlem Désir, the founder of *SOS Racisme*. It aimed to unite Arabs, Africans, Jews, Asians and West Indians in the demand for equal rights and allow joint membership with the Socialist, Green and Communist parties. Unfortunately it has failed to get beyond small local initiatives, and the issues of unemployment, poverty and resisting the neo-fascists have been appropriated by the charismatic and highly suspect Bernard Tapie, whose business affairs will either end him up in jail or in Marseille's town hall as mayor, or even – a very long shot – in the Elysée.

On the Right, well established alliances are under strain, mainly because of Europe. No party of the Left or Right has been immune from scan-dal – mostly of a financial nature. While it hasn't necessarily put the voters off particular individu-als, there is a growing disillusionment and apathy and a sense that the choice now lies with a much more radical Left – or no Left at all – and a much more right-wing Right.

Books

The publishers of the following Paris-themed books are detailed below in the form of British publisher/American publisher, where both exist.

History

Alfred Cobban, *A History of Modern France* (3 vols: 1715–99, 1799–1871 and 1871–1962; Penguin/Viking Penguin). Complete and very readable account of the main political, social and economic strands in French – and inevitably Parisian – history.

Ronald Hamilton, *A Holiday History of France* (UK only: Hogarth Press). Convenient pocket reference book: who's who and what's what.

Norman Hampson, *A Social History of the French Revolution* (Routledge & Kegan Paul/University of Toronto Press). An analysis that concentrates on the personalities involved. Its particular interest lies in the attention it gives to the *sans-culottes*, the ordinary poor of Paris.

Christopher Hibbert, *The French Revolution* (Penguin/Morrow). Good, concise popular history of the period and events.

Lissagaray, *Paris Commune* (UK only: New Park). A highly personal and partisan account of the politics and fighting by a participant. Although Lissagaray himself is reticent about it, history has it that the last solitary Communard on the last barricade – in the rue Ramponneau in Belleville – was in fact himself.

Karl Marx, *Surveys from Exile* (Penguin/Vintage/Random); *On the Paris Commune* (Lawrence & Wishart/Beekman Pubs). *Surveys* includes Marx's speeches and articles at the time of the 1848

Revolution and after, including an analysis, riddled with jokes, of Napoléon III's rise to power. *Paris Commune* – more rousing prose – has a history of the Commune by Engels.

Paul Webster, *Pétain's Crime: The full story of French collaboration in the Holocaust* (UK only: Macmillan). The fascinating and alarming story of the Vichy regime's more than willing collaboration with the German authorities' campaign to implement the final solution in occupied France and the bravery of those, especially the Communist resistance, who attempted to prevent it. A mass of hitherto unpublished evidence.

Theodore Zeldin, *France, 1845–1945* (OUP, 5 paperback volumes). Series of thematic volumes on all matters French – all good reads.

Society & Politics

John Ardagh, *France in the 1980s* (Penguin/Viking Penguin). Comprehensive overview up to 1988, covering food, film, education and holidays as well as politics and education – from a social democrat and journalist position. Good on detail about the urban suburbs (and the shift there from the centre) of Paris.

Roland Barthes, *Mythologies* (Paladin/French & European); *Selected Writings* (UK: Fontana); *A Barthes Reader* (US: Hill & Wang). The first, though dated, is the classic: a brilliant description of how the ideas, prejudices and contradictions of French thought and behaviour manifest themselves, in food, wine, cars, travel guides and other cultural offerings. Barthes' piece on the Eiffel Tower doesn't appear, but it's included in the *Selected Writings*, published in the US as *A Barthes Reader* (ed Susan Sontag).

Simone de Beauvoir, *The Second Sex* (Picador/Vintage/Random). One of the prime texts of western feminism, written in 1949, covering women's inferior status in history, literature, mythology, psychoanalysis, philosophy and everyday life.

Claire Duchen, *Feminism in France: From May '68 to Mitterrand* (Routledge & Kegan Paul/ Routledge Chapman & Hall). Charts the evolution of the women's movement through to the 1980s, setting out to clarify the divergent political stances and the feminist theory which informs the various groups.

Gisèle Halimi, *Milk for the Orange Tree* (UK only: Quartet Books). Born in Tunisia, daughter of an Orthodox Jewish family; ran away to Paris to become a lawyer; defender of women's rights, Algerian *FLN* fighters and all unpopular causes. A gutsy autobiographical story.

D.L. Hanley, A.P. Kerr and **N.H. Waites**, *Contemporary France* (Routledge & Kegan Paul/ Routledge Chapman & Hall). Well-written and academic textbook, if you want to fathom the practicalities of power in France: the constitution, parties, trade unions etc. Includes an excellent opening chapter on the period since the war.

Peter Lennon, *Foreign Correspndents: Paris in the Sixties* (UK only: Picador). Irish journalist Peter Lennon went to Paris in the early 1960s unable to speak a word of French. He became a close friend of Samuel Beckett and was a witness to the May '68 events.

François Maspero, *Roissy Express*, photographs Anaïk Frantz, trans Paul Jones (Verso). A "Travel book" along the *RER* B line from Roissy to St-Rémy-lès-Chevreuse (excluding the Paris stops). Brilliant insights into the life of the Paris suburbs and fascinating digressions into French history and politics. As the blurb on the back says, this is "proof that a month on the *RER* can teach one more about *la France profonde* than a year in Provence".

Theodore Zeldin, *The French* (Collins Harvill/ Vintage/Random). A coffee-table book without the pictures, based on the author's conversations with a wide range of people, about money, sex, phobias, parents and everything else.

Art, Architecture & Photography

Brassai, *Le Paris Secret des Années 30* (Thames & Hudson/Pantheon). Extraordinary photos of the capital's nightlife in the 1930s – brothels, music halls, street cleaners, transvestites and the underworld – each one a work of art and a familiar world (now long since gone) to Brassai and his mate, Henry Miller, who accompanied him on his nocturnal expeditions.

Norma Evenson, *Paris: A Century of Change, 1878–1978* (US only: Yale). A large illustrated volume which makes the development of urban planning and the fabric of Paris an enthralling

subject, mainly because the author's concern is always with people, not panoramas.

John James, *Chartres* (Routledge & Kegan Paul/ Routledge Chapman & Hall; o/p). The story of Chartres Cathedral with insights into the medieval context, the character and attitudes of the masons, the symbolism, and the advanced mathematics of the building's geometry.

Edward Lucie-Smith, *Concise History of French Painting* (UK only: Thames & Hudson). If you're after an art reference book, then this will do as well as any, though there are of course dozens of other books available on particular French artists and art movements.

William Mahder, ed, *Paris Arts: The '80s Renaissance* (France only: Autrement). Illustrated, magazine-style survey of French arts now. The design and photos are reason enough in themselves to look it up. Fortunately, the French edition, *Paris Creation: Une Renaissance*, remains available; the English one now seems to be out of print.

Willy Ronis, *Belleville Ménilmontant* (France only: Arthaud 1989). Misty black and white photographs of people and streets in the two "villages" of eastern Paris in the 1940s and 1950s.

Paris in Literature

British/American

Charles Dickens, *A Tale of Two Cities* (Penguin/ Viking Penguin). Paris and London during the 1789 Revolution and before. The plot's pure Hollywood, but the streets and at least some of the social backdrop are for real.

Robert Ferguson, *Henry Miller* (Hutchinson/ Norton). Very readable biography of the old rogue and his rumbunctious doings, including, of course, his long stint in Paris and affair with Anaïs Nin.

Brion Gysin, *The Last Museum* (Faber & Faber/ Grove Weidenfeld). Setting is the *Hotel Bardo*, the Beat hotel: co-residents Kerouac, Ginsberg and Burroughs. Published posthumously, this is Sixties Paris in its most manic mode.

Ernest Hemingway, *A Moveable Feast* (Panther/ Collier Macmillan). Hemingway's American-in-Paris account of life in the 1930s with Ezra Pound, F. Scott Fitzgerald, Gertrude Stein, etc. Dull, pedestrian stuff, despite the classic best-seller status.

Jack Kerouac, *Satori in Paris* (Quartet/Grove Weidenfeld) . . . and in Brittany, too. Uniquely inconsequential Kerouac experiences.

Herbert Lottman, *Colette: A Life* (Secker/Little). An interesting if somewhat dry account of this enigmatic Parisian writer's life.

Henry Miller, *Tropic of Cancer* (Panther/Random); *Quiet Days in Clichy* (Allison & Busby/Grove Weidenfeld). Again 1930s Paris, though from a more focused angle – sex, essentially. Erratic, wild, self-obsessed writing, but with definite flights of genius.

Anaïs Nin, *The Journals 1931–1974* (7 vols; Quartet/Harcourt Brace Jovanovich). Miller's best Parisian mate. Not fiction, but a detailed literary narrative of French and US artists and fiction-makers from the first half of this century – not least, Nin herself – in Paris and elsewhere. The more famous *Erotica* (Quartet) was also of course written in Paris – for a local connoisseur of pornography.

George Orwell, *Down and Out in Paris and London* (Penguin/Harcourt Brace Jovanovich). Documentary account of breadline living in the 1930s – Orwell at his best.

Paul Rambali, *French Blues* (Minerva/Trafalgar Square). Movies, sex, down-and-outs, politics, fast food, bikers – a cynical, streetwise look at modern urban France.

French (in translation)

Baudelaire's Paris, translated by Laurence Kitchen (UK only: Forest Books). Gloom and doom by Baudelaire, Gérard de Nerval, Verlaine and Jiménez – in bilingual edition.

André Breton, *Nadja* (US only: Grove Weidenfeld). A surrealist evocation of Paris. Fun.

Blaise Cendrars, *To the End of the World* (1956; UK only: Peter Owen). An outrageous bawdy tale of a randy septuagenarian Parisian actress, having an affair with a deserter from the Foreign Legion.

Didier Daeninckx, *Murder in Memoriam*, trans Liz Heron from the French *Meutres pour Mémoire* (UK only: Serpent's Tail). A thriller involving two murders: one of a Frenchman during the massacre of the Algerians in Paris in 1961, the other of his son 20 years later. The investigation by an honest detective lays bare dirty tricks, corruption, racism and the cover-up of the massacre.

Alexandre Dumas, *The Count of Monte Cristo* (World's Classics). One hell of a good yarn, with Paris and Marseilles locations.

Gustave Flaubert, *Sentimental Education* (OUP). A lively, detailed 1869 reconstruction of the life, manners, characters and politics of Parisians in the 1840s, including the 1848 Revolution.

Victor Hugo, *Les Misérables* (Penguin Classics/Viking Penguin). A racy, eminently readable novel by the French equivalent of Dickens, about the Parisian poor and low-life in the first half of the nineteenth century. Book Four contains an account of the barricade fighting during the 1832 insurrection.

Édith Piaf, *My Life* (Peter Owen/Defour). Piaf's dramatic story told pretty much in her words.

François Maspero, *Le Sourire du Chat* (translated as *Cat's Grin*, King Penguin, o/p). Semi-autobiographical novel of the young teenager Luc in Paris during the war with his adored elder brother in the Resistance, his parents taken to concentration camps as Paris is liberated, and everyone else busily collaborating. An intensely moving and revealing account of the war period.

Marcel Proust, *Remembrance of Things Past* (Penguin Classics/Random). Written in and of Paris: absurd but bizarrely addictive.

Jean-Paul Sartre, *Roads to Freedom Trilogy* (Penguin/Vintage Random). Metaphysics and gloom, despite the title.

Georges Simenon, *Maigret at the Crossroads* (Penguin/Viking Penguin), or any other of the Maigret novels. Ostensibly crime thrillers but, of course, Real Literature too. The Montmartre and seedy criminal locations are unbeatable.

Michel Tournier, *The Golden Droplet* (UK only: Methuen Paperback). A magical tale of a Saharan boy coming to Paris where strange adventures, against the backdrop of immigrant life in the slums, overtake him because he never drops his desert oasis view of the world.

Emile Zola, *Nana* (1880; Penguin Classics/Viking Penguin). The rise and fall of a courtesan in the decadent times of the Second Empire. Not bad on sex, but confused on sexual politics. A great story nevertheless, which brings mid-nineteenth-century Paris alive, direct, to present-day senses. Paris is also the setting for Zola's *L'Assommoir* (enguin Classics/Viking Penguin), *L'Argent* (Penguin Classics/Schoenhof) and *Thérèse Raquin* (Penguin Classics/Viking Penguin).

Language

French can be a deceptively familiar language because of the number of words and structures it shares with English. Despite this it's far from easy, though the bare essentials are not difficult to master and can make all the difference. Even just saying "Bonjour Madame/Monsieur" and then gesticulating will usually get you a smile and helpful service.

People working in tourist offices, hotels, and so on almost always speak English and tend to use it when you're struggling to speak French – be grateful, not insulted.

French Pronunciation

One easy rule to remember is that **consonants** at the ends of words are usually silent. *Pas plus tard* (not later) is thus pronounced pa-plu-tarr. But when the following word begins with a vowel, you run the two together: *pas après* (not after) becomes pazapre.

Vowels are the hardest sounds to get right. Roughly:

a	as in hat		*i*	as in machine
e	as in get		*o*	as in hot
é	between get and gate		*o, au*	as in over
è	between get and gut		*ou*	as in food
eu	like the **u** in hurt		*u*	as in a pursed-lip version of **u**se

More awkward are the **combinations** in/im, en/em, an/am, on/om, un/um at the ends of words, or followed by consonants other than n or m. Again, roughly:

in/im	like the **an** in **an**xious	*on/om*	like the **don** in **Don**caster said by
an/am, en/em	like the **don** in **Don**caster		someone with a heavy cold
	when said with a nasal accent	*un/um*	like the **u** in **u**nderstand

Consonants are much as in English, except that: ch is always sh, c is s, h is silent, th is the same as t, ll is like the y in yes, w is v, and r is growled (or rolled).

Learning Materials

Harrap's French Phrase Book (Harrap/Prentice Hall). Good pocket reference – with useful contemporary phrases and a 5000-word dictionary of terms.

Mini French Dictionary (Harrap/Prentice Hall). French–English and English–French, plus a brief grammar and pronunciation guide.

Breakthrough French (Pan; book and two cassettes). Excellent teach-yourself course.

French and English Slang Dictionary (Harrap); ***Dictionary of Modern Colloquial French*** (Routledge). Both volumes are a bit large to carry, but they are the key to all you ever wanted to understand.

A Vous La France; Franc Extra; Franc-Parler (BBC Publications; each has a book and two cassettes). BBC radio courses, running from beginners' to fairly advanced language.

A Brief Guide to Speaking French

Basic Words and Phrases

French nouns are divided into masculine and feminine. This causes difficulties with adjectives, whose endings have to change to suit the gender of the nouns they qualify. If you know some grammar, you will know what to do. If not, stick to the masculine form, which is the simplest – it's what we have done in this glossary.

today	*aujourd'hui*	that one	*celà*
yesterday	*hier*	open	*ouvert*
tomorrow	*demain*	closed	*fermé*
in the morning	*le matin*	big	*grand*
in the afternoon	*l'après-midi*	small	*petit*
in the evening	*le soir*	more	*plus*
now	*maintenant*	less	*moins*
later	*plus tard*	a little	*un peu*
at one o'clock	*à une heure*	a lot	*beaucoup*
at three o'clock	*à trois heures*	cheap	*bon marché*
at ten-thirty	*à dix heures et demie*	expensive	*cher*
at midday	*à midi*	good	*bon*
man	*un homme*	bad	*mauvais*
woman	*une femme*	hot	*chaud*
here	*ici*	cold	*froid*
there	*là*	with	*avec*
this one	*ceci*	without	*sans*

Accommodation

a room for one/two people	*une chambre pour une/deux personnes*	do laundry	*faire la lessive*
a double bed	*un lit double*	sheets	*draps*
a room with a shower	*une chambre avec douche*	blankets	*couvertures*
		quiet	*calme*
a room with a bath	*une chambre avec salle de bain*	noisy	*bruyant*
		hot water	*eau chaude*
For one/two/three nights	*Pour une/deux/trois nuits*	cold water	*eau froide*
		Is breakfast included?	*Est-ce que le petit déjeuner est compris?*
Can I see it?	*Je peux la voir?*	I would like breakfast	*Je voudrais prendre le petit déjeuner*
a room on the courtyard	*une chambre sur la cour*	I don't want breakfast	*Je ne veux pas de petit déjeuner*
a room over the street	*une chambre sur la rue*	Can we camp here?	*On peut camper ici ?*
first floor	*premier étage*	campsite	*un camping/terrain de camping*
second floor	*deuxième étage*	tent	*une tente*
with a view	*avec vue*	tent space	*un emplacement*
key	*clef*	youth hostel	*auberge de jeunesse*
to iron	*repasser*		

Days and Dates

January	*janvier*	October	*octobre*	Saturday	*samedi*
February	*février*	November	*novembre*	August 1	*le premier août*
March	*mars*	December	*décembre*	March 2	*le deux mars*
April	*avril*	Sunday	*dimanche*	July 14	*le quatorze juillet*
May	*mai*	Monday	*lundi*	November 23	*le vingt-trois novembre*
June	*juin*	Tuesday	*mardi*	1995	*dix-neuf-cent-quatre-vingt-quinze*
July	*juillet*	Wednesday	*mercredi*		
August	*août*	Thursday	*jeudi*	1996	*dix-neuf-cent-quatre-vingt-seize*
September	*septembre*	Friday	*vendredi*		

Numbers

1	*un*	11	*onze*	21	*vingt-et-un*	95	*quatre-vingt-quinze*
2	*deux*	12	*douze*	22	*vingt-deux*	100	*cent*
3	*trois*	13	*treize*	30	*trente*	101	*cent-et-un*
4	*quatre*	14	*quatorze*	40	*quarante*	200	*deux cents*
5	*cinq*	15	*quinze*	50	*cinquante*	300	*trois cents*
6	*six*	16	*seize*	60	*soixante*	500	*cinq cents*
7	*sept*	17	*dix-sept*	70	*soixante-dix*	1000	*mille*
8	*huit*	18	*dix-huit*	75	*soixante-quinze*	2000	*deux milles*
9	*neuf*	19	*dix-neuf*	80	*quatre-vingts*	5000	*cinq milles*
10	*dix*	20	*vingt*	90	*quatre-vingt-dix*	1,000,000	*un million*

Talking to People

When addressing people you should always use *Monsieur* for a man, *Madame* for a woman, *Mademoiselle* for a girl. Plain *bonjour* by itself is not enough. This isn't as formal as it seems, and it has its uses when you've forgotten someone's name or want to attract someone's attention.

Excuse me	*Pardon*	please	*s'il vous plaît*
Do you speak English?	*Vous parlez anglais?*	thank you	*merci*
		hello	*bonjour*
How do you say it in French?	*Comment ça se dit en français?*	goodbye	*au revoir*
What's your name?	*Comment vous appelez-vous?*	good morning/ afternoon	*bonjour*
My name is . . .	*Je m'appelle . . .*	good evening	*bonsoir*
I'm English/	*Je suis anglais[e]/*	good night	*bonne nuit*
Irish/Scottish	*irlandais[e]/écossais[e]/*	How are you?	*Comment allez-vous? / Ça va?*
Welsh/American	*gallois[e]/américain[e]/*		
Australian/	*australien[ne]/*	Fine, thanks	*Très bien, merci*
Canadian	*canadien[ne]/*	I don't know	*Je ne sais pas*
a New Zealander	*néo-zélandais[e]*	Let's go	*Allons-y*
yes	*oui*	See you tomorrow	*À demain*
no	*non*	See you soon	*À bientôt*
I understand	*Je comprends*	Sorry	*Pardon, Madame/je m'excuse*
I don't understand	*Je ne comprends pas*		
Can you speak slower?	*S'il vous plaît, parlez moins vite*	Leave me alone (aggressive)	*Fichez-moi la paix!*
OK/agreed	*d'accord*	Please help me	*Aidez-moi, s'il vous plaît*

Questions and Requests

The simplest way of asking a question is to start with *s'il vous plaît* (please), then name the thing you want in an interrogative tone of voice. For example:

Where is there a bakery?	*S'il vous plaît, la boulangerie?*
Which way is it to the Eiffel Tower?	*S'il vous plaît, la route pour la tour Eiffel?*

Similarly with requests:

We'd like a room for two .	*S'il vous plaît, une chambre pour deux.*
Can I have a kilo of oranges?	*S'il vous plaît, un kilo d'oranges?*

Question words

where?	*où?*	when?	*quand?*
how?	*comment?*	why?	*pourquoi?*
how many/how much?	*combien?*	at what time?	*à quelle heure?*
		what is/which is?	*quel est?*

Finding the Way

bus	*autobus, bus, car*	hitchhiking	*autostop*
bus station	*gare routière*	on foot	*à pied*
bus stop	*arrêt*	Where are you going?	*Vous allez où ?*
car	*voiture*	I'm going to . . .	*Je vais à . . .*
train/taxi/ferry	*train/taxi/ferry*	I want to get off	*Je voudrais*
boat	*bâteau*	at . . .	*descendre à . . .*
plane	*avion*	the road to . . .	*la route pour . . .*
railway station	*gare*	near	*près/pas loin*
platform	*quai*	far	*loin*
What time does it leave?	*Il part à quelle heure ?*	left	*à gauche*
		right	*à droite*
What time does it arrive?	*Il arrive à quelle heure ?*	straight on	*tout droit*
		on the other side of	*à l'autre côté de*
a ticket to . . .	*un billet pour . . .*	on the corner of	*à l'angle de*
single ticket	*aller simple*	next to	*à côté de*
return ticket	*aller retour*	behind	*derrière*
validate your ticket	*compostez votre billet*	in front of	*devant*
valid for	*valable pour*	before	*avant*
ticket office	*vente de billets*	after	*après*
how many kilometres?	*combien de kilomètres?*	under	*sous*
		to cross	*traverser*
how many hours?	*combien d'heures?*	bridge	*pont*

Cars

garage	*garage*	put air in the tyres	*gonfler les pneus*
service	*service*	battery	*batterie*
to park the car	*garer la voiture*	the battery is dead	*la batterie est morte*
car park	*un parking*	plugs	*bougies*
no parking	*défense de stationner/ stationnement interdit*	to break down	*tomber en panne*
petrol station	*poste d'essence*	petrol can	*bidon*
petrol	*essence*	insurance	*assurance*
fill it up	*faire le plein*	green card	*carte verte*
oil	*huile*	traffic lights	*feux*
air line	*ligne à air*	red light	*feu rouge*
		green light	*feu vert*

French and Architectural Terms: a Glossary

These are either terms you'll come across in this book, or come up against on signs, maps, etc, while travelling around. For food items see p.228 onwards.

ABBAYE abbey

AMBULATORY covered passage around the outer edge of a choir of a church

APSE semicircular termination at the east end of a church

ASSEMBLÉE NATIONALE the French parliament

ARRONDISSEMENT district of the city

AUBERGE DE JEUNESSE (AJ) youth hostel

BAROQUE High Renaissance period of art and architecture, distinguished by extreme ornateness

BEAUX ARTS fine arts museum (and school)

CAR bus

CAROLINGIAN dynasty (and art, sculpture, etc) founded by Charlemagne, late eighth to early tenth centuries

CFDT Socialist trade union

CGT Communist trade union

CHASSE, CHASSE GARDÉE hunting grounds

CHÂTEAU mansion, country house, or castle

CHÂTEAU FORT castle

CHEMIN path

CHEVET end wall of a church

CIJ (Centre d'Informations Jeunesse) youth information centre

CLASSICAL architectural style incorporating Greek and Roman elements – pillars, domes, colonnades etc – at its height in France in the seventeenth century and revived in the nineteenth century as **NEOCLASSICAL**

CLERESTORY upper storey of a church, incorporating the windows

CODENE French CND

CONSIGNE luggage consignment

COURS combination of main square and main street

COUVENT convent, monastery

DÉFENSE DE . . . It is forbidden to . . .

DÉGUSTATION tasting (wine or food)

DÉPARTEMENT county – more or less

ÉGLISE church

EN PANNE out of order

ENTRÉE entrance

FERMETURE closing period

FLAMBOYANT florid form of Gothic

FN (Front National) fascist party led by Jean-Marie Le Pen

FO Catholic trade union

FRESCO wall painting – durable through application to wet plaster

GALLO-ROMAIN period of Roman occupation of Gaul (first to fourth centuries AD)

GARE station; **ROUTIÈRE** – bus station; **SNCF** – train station

GOBELINS famous tapestry manufacturers, based in Paris; its most renowned period was in the reign of Louis XIV (seventeenth century)

GRANDE RANDONEE (GR) long-distance footpath

HALLES covered market

HLM public housing development

HÔTEL a hotel, but also an aristocratic townhouse or mansion

HÔTEL DE VILLE town hall

JOURS FÉRIÉS public holidays

MAIRIE town hall

MARCHÉ market

MEROVINGIAN dynasty (and art, etc), ruling France and parts of Germany from the sixth to mid-eighth centuries

NARTHEX entrance hall of church

NAVE main body of a church

PCF Communist Party of France

PLACE square

PORTE gateway

PS Socialist party

PTT post office

QUARTIER district of a town

RENAISSANCE art-architectural style developed in fifteenth-century Italy and imported to France in the early sixteenth century by François 1er

RETABLE altarpiece

REZ DE CHAUSSÉE (RC) ground floor

RN (Route Nationale) main road

ROMANESQUE early medieval architecture distinguished by squat, rounded forms and naive sculpture

RPR Gaullist party led by Jacques Chirac

SI (Syndicat d'Initiative) tourist information office; also known as OT, OTSI and MAISON DU TOURISME

SNCF (Société Nationale des Chemins de Fer) French railways

SORTIE exit

STUCCO plaster used to embellish ceilings, etc

TABAC bar or shop selling stamps, cigarettes, etc

TOUR tower

TRANSEPT cross arms of a church

TYMPANUM sculpted panel above a church door

UDF centre-right party headed by Giscard d'Estaing

VAUBAN seventeenth-century military architect – his fortresses still stand all over France

VILLA a mews or a series of small residential streets, built as a unity

VOUSSOIR sculpted rings in arch over church door

ZONE BLEUE restricted parking zone

ZONE PIETONNE pedestrian zone

Index

DIRECT ORDERS IN THE UK

Title	ISBN	Price
Amsterdam	1858280869	£7.99
Andalucia	185828094X	£8.99
Australia	1858280354	£12.99
Barcelona & Catalunya	1858281067	£8.99
Berlin	1858280338	£8.99
Brazil	1858281024	£9.99
Brittany & Normandy	1858280192	£7.99
Bulgaria	1858280478	£8.99
California	1858280907	£9.99
Canada	185828001X	£10.99
Classical Music on CD	185828113X	£12.99
Corsica	1858280893	£8.99
Crete	1858280494	£6.99
Cyprus	185828032X	£8.99
Czech & Slovak Republics	185828029X	£8.99
Egypt	1858280753	£10.99
England	1858280788	£9.99
Europe	185828077X	£14.99
Florida	1858280109	£8.99
France	1858280508	£9.99
Germany	1858280257	£11.99
Greece	1858280206	£9.99
Guatemala & Belize	1858280451	£9.99
Holland, Belgium & Luxembourg	1858280877	£9.99
Hong Kong & Macau	1858280664	£8.99
Hungary	1858280214	£7.99
India	1858281040	£13.99
Ireland	1858280958	£9.99
Italy	1858280311	£12.99
Kenya	1858280435	£9.99
Mediterranean Wildlife	0747100993	£7.95
Malaysia, Singapore & Brunei	1858281032	£9.99
Morocco	1858280400	£9.99
Nepal	185828046X	£8.99
New York	1858280583	£8.99
Nothing Ventured	0747102082	£7.99
Pacific Northwest	1858280923	£9.99
Paris	1858280389	£7.99
Poland	1858280346	£9.99
Portugal	1858280842	£9.99
Prague	185828015X	£7.99
Provence & the Côte d'Azur	1858280230	£8.99
Pyrenees	1858280931	£8.99
St Petersburg	1858280303	£8.99
San Francisco	1858280826	£8.99
Scandinavia	1858280397	£10.99
Scotland	1858280834	£8.99
Sicily	1858280370	£8.99
Spain	1858280818	£9.99
Thailand	1858280168	£8.99
Tunisia	1858280656	£8.99
Turkey	1858280885	£9.99
Tuscany & Umbria	1858280915	£8.99
USA	185828080X	£12.99
Venice	1858280362	£8.99
Wales	1858280966	£8.99
West Africa	1858280141	£12.99
Women Travel	1858280710	£7.99
World Music	1858280176	£14.99
Zimbabwe & Botswana	1858280419	£10.99

Rough Guide Phrasebooks

Czech	1858281482	£3.50
French	185828144X	£3.50
German	1858281466	£3.50
Greek	1858281458	£3.50
Italian	1858281431	£3.50
Spanish	1858281474	£3.50

Rough Guides are available from all good bookstores, but can be obtained directly in the UK* from Penguin by contacting:

Penguin Direct, Penguin Books Ltd, Bath Road, Harmondsworth, West Drayton, Middlesex UB7 0DA; or telephone our credit line on 081-899 4036 (9am–5pm) and ask for Penguin Direct. Visa, Access and Amex accepted. Delivery will normally be within 14 working days. Penguin Direct ordering facilities are only available in the UK.

The availability and published prices quoted are correct at the time of going to press but are subject to alteration without prior notice.

* For USA and international orders, see separate price list

DIRECT ORDERS IN THE USA

Title	ISBN	Price
Able to Travel	1858281105	$19.95
Amsterdam	1858280869	$13.95
Andalucia	185828094X	$14.95
Australia	1858280354	$18.95
Barcelona & Catalunya	1858281067	$13.95
Berlin	1858280338	$13.99
Brazil	1858281024	$15.95
Brittany & Normandy	1858280192	$14.95
Bulgaria	1858280478	$14.99
California	1858280907	$14.95
Canada	185828001X	$14.95
Classical Music on CD	185828113X	$19.95
Corsica	1858280893	$14.95
Crete	1858280494	$14.95
Cyprus	185828032X	$13.99
Czech & Slovak Republics	185828029X	$14.95
Egypt	1858280753	$17.95
England	1858280788	$16.95
Europe	185828077X	$18.95
Florida	1858280109	$14.95
France	1858280508	$16.95
Germany	1858280257	$17.95
Greece	1858280206	$16.95
Guatemala & Belize	1858280451	$14.95
Holland, Belgium & Luxembourg	1858280877	$15.95
Hong Kong & Macau	1858280664	$13.95
Hungary	1858280214	$13.95
India	1858281040	$22.95
Ireland	1858280958	$16.95
Italy	1858280311	$17.95
Kenya	1858280435	$15.95
Malaysia, Singapore & Brunei	1858281032	$16.95
Mediterranean Wildlife	1858280699	$15.95
Morocco	1858280400	$16.95
Nepal	185828046X	$13.95
New York	1858280583	$13.95
Pacific Northwest	1858280923	$14.95
Paris	1858280389	$13.95
Poland	1858280346	$16.95
Portugal	1858280842	$15.95
Prague	185828015X	$14.95
Provence & the Côte d'Azur	1858280230	$14.95
Pyrenees	1858280931	$15.95
St Petersburg	1858280303	$14.95
San Francisco	1858280826	$13.95
Scandinavia	1858280397	$16.99
Scotland	1858280834	$14.95
Sicily	1858280370	$14.99
Spain	1858280818	$16.95
Thailand	1858280168	$15.95
Tunisia	1858280656	$15.95
Turkey	1858280885	$16.95
Tuscany & Umbria	1858280915	$15.95
USA	185828080X	$18.95
Venice	1858280362	$13.99
Wales	1858280966	$14.95
Women Travel	1858280710	$12.95
World Music	1858280176	$19.95
Zimbabwe & Botswana	1858280419	$16.95

Rough Guide Phrasebooks

Czech	1858281482	$5.00
French	185828144X	$5.00
German	1858281466	$5.00
Greek	1858281458	$5.00
Italian	1858281431	$5.00
Spanish	1858281474	$5.00

Rough Guides are available from all good bookstores, but can be obtained directly in the USA and Worldwide (except the UK*) from Penguin:

Charge your order by Master Card or Visa (US$15.00 minimum order): call 1-800-253-6476; or send orders, with complete name, address and zip code, and list price, plus $2.00 shipping and handling per order to: Consumer Sales, Penguin USA, PO Box 999 – Dept #17109, Bergenfield, NJ 07621. No COD. Prepay foreign orders by international money order, a cheque drawn on a US bank, or US currency. No postage stamps are accepted. All orders are subject to stock availability at the time they are processed. Refunds will be made for books not available at that time. Please allow a minimum of four weeks for delivery.

The availability and published prices quoted are correct at the time of going to press but are subject to alteration without prior notice. Titles currently not available outside the UK will be available by July 1995. Call to check.

* For UK orders, see separate price list

You are
A STUDENT

You **travel**
THE WORLD

You **want**
TO SAVE MONEY

Here's
how

The International
Student Identity Card

Available at Student Travel Offices Worldwide.

Entitles you to discounts and special services worldwide.